Lecture Notes in Computer Science   1023

Edited by G. Goos, J. Hartmanis and J. van Leeuwen

Advisory Board: W. Brauer   D. Gries   J. Stoer

Springer
Berlin
Heidelberg
New York
Barcelona
Budapest
Hong Kong
London
Milan
Paris
Santa Clara
Singapore
Tokyo

Kanchana Kanchanasut
Jean-Jacques Lévy (Eds.)

Algorithms, Concurrency and Knowledge

1995 Asian Computing Science Conference
ACSC '95
Pathumthani, Thailand, December 11-13, 1995
Proceedings

Springer

Series Editors

Gerhard Goos, Karlsruhe University, Germany

Juris Hartmanis, Cornell University, NY, USA

Jan van Leeuwen, Utrecht University, The Netherlands

Volume Editors

Kanchana Kanchanasut
Asian Institute of Technology
P.O. Box 2754, 10501 Bangkok, Thailand

Jean-Jacques Lévy
INRIA
BP 105, F-79153 Rocquencourt, Le Chesnay Cedex, France

Cataloging-in-Publication data applied for

Die Deutsche Bibliothek - CIP-Einheitsaufnahme

Algorithms, concurrency and knowledge : proceedings / 1995 Asian Computing Science
Conference, ACSC '95, Pathumthani, Thailand, December 11 - 13, 1995. Kanchana
Kanchanasut ; Jean-Jacques Levy (ed.). - Berlin ; Heidelberg ; New York ; Barcelona ;
Budapest ; Hong Kong ; London ; Milan ; Paris ; Tokoy : Springer, 1995
  (Lecture notes in computer science ; Vol. 1023)
  ISBN 3-540-60688-2
NE: Kanchana Kanchanasut [Hrsg.]; Asian Computing Science Conference <1995,
    Pathumthani>; GT

CR Subject Classification (1991): F.2.2, D.3.1-2, D.2.1, I.2.3, C.2.4, H.2.4

ISBN 3-540-60688-2 Springer-Verlag Berlin Heidelberg New York

Typesetting: Camera-ready by author
SPIN 10512334   06/3142 – 5 4 3 2 1 0   Printed on acid-free paper

Foreword

In recent years, researchers from Asia have begun to participate in many international academic conferences in computer science. However, many of these come from the more economically advanced Asian countries like Japan, Korea, Taiwan, Hong Kong and Singapore, as opposed to India and China, amongst others. In the less developed Asian region, the Asian Institute of Technology has been playing a leading role in bringing together computer scientists from different countries to attend a series of Asian Schools over the past nine years. Many participants at these schools are beginning to establish research activities in their own countries; Thailand, Malaysia, the Philippines, and Indonesia, for example. This conference represents a continuation of this effort, by bringing state-of-the-art papers, as well as invited talks by eminent scientists like Gérard Berry, Philippe Flajolet, Jean-Louis Lassez, and Zohar Manna, within reach of the local community.

Though the scope of AsianCSC'95 seemed to include all of computer science, in order to achieve some semblance of a direction, special attention was paid to the areas of algorithms, knowledge representation, programming and specification languages, verification, concurrency, networking and distributed systems, and databases. The program committee was thus chosen, and appropriately, the submitted papers were consistent with this focus to a remarkable degree.

A total of 102 submissions was received from 26 countries, most of them in electronic form, and 29 of them were eventually accepted. Each paper was reviewed by at least two committee members, or by someone nominated by the member. It was the general impression that there were far more acceptable papers than the 29 we had space and time for.

We are indebted to the excellent group of reviewers who helped us define the conference program, and to the local organizing committee. We also owe special thanks to Jean-Jacques Lévy who with K. Kanchanasut served as the INRIA editorial liaison.

The Conference was organized by the Asian Institute of Technology, the Institut National de Recherche en Informatique et Automatique and the United Nations University International Institute of Software Technology. The Conference organizing committees acknowledge financial support and other substantial assistance provided by the Communication Authority of Thailand, the Thai National Information Technology Committee, Nippon Telegraph and Telephone, Tourism Authority of Thailand and the Thai Airways International.

October 1995

Shigeki Goto, NTT Japan
Joxan Jaffar, IBM USA and NUS, Singapore
Kanchana Kanchanasut, AIT Thailand

Organizing Committee

Dines Bjørner (UNU/IIST, Macau)
Jean-Jacques Lévy (INRIA, France)
Kesav Nori (Tata RDDC, India)
Huynh Ngoc Phien (AIT, Thailand)

Advisory Committee

Kilnam Chon (KAIST, Korea)
Phan Dinh Dieu (Hanoi, Vietnam)
Nguyen Hau Le (Northern Telecom, Canada)
Gérard Huet (INRIA, France)
Haruhisa Ishida (Univ. Tokyo, Japan)
Gilles Kahn (INRIA, France)
Kanchit Malaivongse (NECTEC, Thailand)

Local Organizing Committee

Thit Siriboon (Chulalongkorn Univ., Thailand)(Chairman)
Pensri Charoenchai (AIT, Thailand)
Nongluck Covavisaruch (Chulalongkorn Univ., Thailand)
Olivier Nicole (AIT, Thailand)
Mano Pallawatta (AIT, Thailand)
Proadpran Punyabukkana (Chulalongkorn Univ., Thailand)
Angelo C. Restificar (ABAC, Thailand)

Program Committee

Serge Abiteboul (INRIA, France)
A. Anuchitanukul (Stanford Univ., USA)
S. Auwatanamongkol (NIDA, Thailand)
Philippe Flajolet (INRIA, France)
Chris W. George (UNU/IIST, Macau)
Mordecai J. Golin (HKUST, Hong Kong)
Christian Huitéma (INRIA, France)
Dang Van Hung (UNU/IIST, Macau)
Hsien-Kuei Hwang (Academia Sinica, Taiwan)
P. Jongsatitwatana (Chulalongkorn Univ., Thailand)
K. Karlapalem (HKUST, Hong Kong)
S. Keretho (Kasetsart Univ., Thailand)
Jean-Jacques Lévy (INRIA, France)
Hongjun Lu (NUS, Singapore)
Hoshi Mamoru (Univ. Elec-Comm, Japan)
A. A. Nazief (Univ. of Indonesia, Indonesia)
Akko Oka (NTT, Japan)
Amir Pnueli (Weizmann Inst, Israel)
S. Prasitjutrakul (Chulalongkorn Univ., Thailand)
Xu Qiwen (UNU/IIST, Macau)
R. Sureswaran (USM, Malaysia)
S. Ramesh (IIT Bombay, India)
Louiqa Raschid (Univ. of Maryland, USA)
R. Sadananda (AIT, Thailand)
Masahiko Sato (Tohoku Univ., Japan)
Taisuke Sato (TIT, Japan)
R.K. Shyamasundar (TIFR Bombay, India)
Nguyen Thanh Son (Polytech HCM, Vietnam)
D. Srivastava (ATT Bell Lab, USA)
Peter J. Stuckey (Univ. of Melbourne, Australia)
W. Vacharawittayakul (NIDA, Thailand)
Qi Yulu (AIT, Thailand)

List of Referees

Ishfaq Ahmad, (HKUST, Hong Kong)
Sunil Arya,(HKUST, Hong Kong)
Doung Tuan Anh, (AIT, Thailand)
Decho Batanov, (AIT, Thailand)
Purandar Bhaduri, (TIFR, India)
Phil Bradford, (MPI, Germany)
Alex Brodsky, (George Mason Univ., USA)
Michael Butler, (Abo Akademi, Finland)
Antonio Cau, (Liverpool John Moores Univ., UK)
Bernard Chazelle, (Princeton Univ., USA)
Damien Doligez, (INRIA, France)
Ramesh Hariharan, (MPI, Germany)
Evan Harris, (CITRI, Australia)
Hitoshi Iba, (ETL, Japan)
Masaki Itoh, (NTT, Japan)
Lu Jian, (UNU/IIST, Macau)
Wang Juan, (Univ. of Macau, Macau)
Gilles Kahn, (INRIA, France)
Solange Karsenty, (Hebrew Univ. of Jerusalem, Israel)
Lydia Kavraki, (Stanford Univ., USA)
Ming-Tat Ko, (Inst. of Information Science, Academia Sinica, Taiwan)
Padmanabhan Krishnan, (Univ. of Canterbery, New Zealand)
Zoe Lacroix, (INRIA, France)
Zhiming Liu, (Leicester Univ., UK)
Eric Madelaine, (INRIA, France)
Michael Maher, (IBM T.J.Watson Inst., USA)
Michel Mauny, (INRIA, France)
Alistair Moffat, (Univ. of Melbourne, Australia)
Ekawit Nantajeewarawat, (AIT, Thailand)
Raymond Ng, (Univ. of British Colombia, Canada)
P. K. Pandya, (TIFR, India)
Michel Scholl, (INRIA, France)
Marc Shapiro, (INRIA, France)
Naresh Srikalra, (AIT, Thailand)
Akevute Sujare, (AIT, Thailand)
Francesca Toni, (Imperial College, UK)
Kwok-Kee Wei, (NUS, Singapore)
Han Yan, (Univ. of Hong Kong, Hong Kong)
Roland Yap, (Univ. of Melbourne, Australia)
Toshisugu Yuba, (Univ. Electro-Communication, Tokyo, Japan)
Philip Vines, (RMIT, Australia)
Benjamin Werner, (INRIA, France)
Shmuel Zaks, (Techion Univ., Israel)

Table of Contents

Leapfrogging Samplesort

ELIEZER A. ALBACEA

Institute of Computer Science, University of the Philippines Los Baños
4031 College, Laguna, PHILIPPINES
Email: eaa@ics.uplb.edu.ph

Abstract

In this paper, we present a practical Quicksort-based sorting algorithm that exhibits the following properties: (1) $O(n(\log n)^2)$ worst case; (2) the expected number of comparisons is equal to the information-theoretic lower bound; and (3) the expected number of data interchanges is slightly higher than that of Quicksort. Considering the worst-case complexity, the average-case complexity and the simplicity of the algorithm, we claim that this algorithm is so far the most practical alternative to Quicksort. This is particularly true when one is not willing to take the risk of the worst case occuring when running Quicksort.

Keywords: Samplesort, Quicksort, Leapfrogging Samplesort, sorting, analysis of algorithms.

CR Categories and Subject Descriptors: F.2.2 [Analysis of Algorithms and Problem Complexity]: Nonnumerical Algorithms and Problems - Sorting and Searching.

General Terms: Algorithms, Theory

1. Introduction

Quicksort is one of the most well studied and analyzed sorting algorithm. Because of its simplicity and efficiency, it has been the subject of several improvements. Sedgewick [10], however, commented that few real improvements have been made beyond those suggested by Hoare [6]. One of the many improvements to Quicksort is the *Samplesort* algorithm of Frazer and McKellar [3]. Frazer and McKellar [3] showed that the expected number of comparisons required by Samplesort slowly approaches the information-theoretic lower bound. Hence, for large input sizes Samplesort is faster than Quicksort. Peters and Kritzinger [8] implemented Samplesort and presented empirical evidence supporting the claims of Frazer and McKellar [3]. Apers [2], on the other hand, improved Samplesort by making use of Samplesort itself, instead of Quicksort, to sort the sample and called his improvement *Recursive Samplesort*. The expected number of comparisons of Recursive Samplesort was shown by Apers [2] to be close to the information-theoretic lower bound. However, when the number of data moves is considered, Recursive Samplesort is faster than both Samplesort and Quicksort only with respect to certain linear combinations of number of comparisons and move instructions needed. Unfortunately, not one of these implementations of Samplesort is practical enough to rival the accepted best implementation of Quicksort given in Sedgewick [10]. The implementation of Peters and Kritzinger [8], for example, uses temporary storage locations for storing the sample which eventually are used to store pointers to positions in the array bounded by the sample. The implementation of Apers [2], on the other hand, uses a stack to store pointers to positions in the array which are bounded by the sample. Finally, the main weakness of Quicksort, which is its worst-case complexity being $O(n^2)$, is preserved by the existing implementations of Samplesort.

In this paper, we extend Recursive Samplesort to one where Samplesort itself is used to sort not only the sample but also the subsequences bounded by the sample. We call this new algorithm *Leapfrogging Samplesort* (the use of this name will become clear after we described the algorithm). By using Samplesort itself to sort the subsequences, we produce a Samplesort-based (consequently, Quicksort-based) sorting algorithm that breaks the $O(n^2)$ worst-case complexity barrier. In a succeeding section, we shall show that the worst-case complexity of our new algorithm is $O(n(log\ n)^2)$. Unlike the implementations of Peters and Kritzinger [8] and Apers [1], our algorithm sorts the input without any auxiliary storage for the sample and without additional storage for storing pointers to locations bounded by the sample. To support the claim that this is a practical alternative to Quicksort, we show that the average running time (where running time includes the number of comparisons and the number of data interchanges) of the algorithm is just slighly higher than Quicksort. In fact, the number of comparisons involved in our algorithm is optimal, but the number of data interchanges is slightly higher than that of Quicksort.

2. Description of the Algorithm

The idea behind the algorithm is quite simple. Every stage of the sorting process involves the first $(2s+1)$ elements of the array, where the first s elements is already sorted and the remaining $(s+1)$ elements is to be partitioned and sorted using the sorted s elements as the sample (Figure 1a). The objective of each stage is to produce a sorted $(2s+1)$-element subarray. Let $S\ (S_1, S_2, ..., S_s)$ and U be the sorted sample and the remaining unsorted elements, respectively. Using $v = S_{\lceil s/2 \rceil}$, i.e., the median of S, as pivot element, we partition U. This divides U into two regions, namely: a region consisting of elements less than or equal to v and a region consisting of elements greater than or equal to v (Figure 1b). Then, we move $[S_{\lceil s/2 \rceil} .. S_s\ ]$ to the left of the region containing the elements greater than or equal to v (Figure 1c). After moving half the sample, we note that $S_{\lceil s/2 \rceil}$ is already in its correct position. Moreover, we are left with two subsequences where each subsequence is composed of a sorted sample of size $(\lceil s/2 \rceil - 1)$ and an unsorted part. We can therefore apply the same process as above on both subsequences, i.e., we can partition each subsequence using the median of the sample prefixing the unsorted part. We refer to the above process as the *Leapfrog* procedure. The call to *Leapfrog* stops when the size of the sorted sample prefixing an unsorted part of the region is 0. In which case, the main procedure *LF-Samplesort* (described below) is called. The recursive call to *Leapfrog* also stops when the partition step above produces an unsorted part with no element. In this case, no action is taken since the subsequence, which is composed only of the elements of the sample, is already sorted.

Now, let us consider the main body of the *LF-Samplesort* procedure. Let A be the array to be sorted and is composed of n elements. We can sort A by applying *Leapfrog* repeatedly using $A_1, A_2, ..., A_s$ as the sorted sample to partition the unsorted elements $A_{s+1}, A_{s+2}, ..., A_{2s+1}$, where $s=2^m-1$ and $m = 1, 2, ..., \lceil log\ n \rceil$. At the start, we know that A_1 is already sorted so we use this as a sample to partition the unsorted A_2 to A_3. Then using the sorted A_1 to A_3, we use this as a sample to partition the unsorted A_4 to A_7 and so on. Hence, the name *Leapfrogging Samplesort*. See Figure 2 for an illustration of these steps. We note that at the last stage, we may have a sorted sample of size $2^{\lfloor log\ n \rfloor}-1$ and an unsorted part that may contain less than $2^{\lfloor log\ n \rfloor}$ elements (this happens when n is not exactly equal to 2^m-1, where $m \geq 1$). This, however, should not pose any problem since we can still apply *Leapfrog* even if the size of the unsorted part is shorter than the size of the sample.

The *Leapfrog* procedure (Figure 3) is composed of two stages, namely: the *Partition* and the *Move-Sample* stages. It should be noted that its only difference from Quicksort is the addition of the *Move-Sample* procedure.If we place a copy of the pivot element $v = A[sm]$ in $A[ss]$ and another copy of v in $A[u+1]$ (we, however, restore the old values of $A[ss]$ and $A[u+1]$ after partitioning), then we can implement the Partition stage as in Quicksort. However, we can get the same effect at a lower cost by simply leaving v in its current position and then setting $A[n+1]$ to ∞ (or moving the maximum element in $A[n]$). This should be done before calling *LF-Samplesort*. We adopt this alternative method of partitioning in our implementation in Figure 4. The *Move-Sample* stage, on the other hand, can be implemented by simply swapping the last $\lceil s/2 \rceil$ elements of the region containing elements less than or equal to $S_{\lceil s/2 \rceil}$ with $[S_{\lceil s/2 \rceil} .. S_s]$ but preserving the order of $[S_{\lceil s/2 \rceil} .. S_s]$ (Figure 5). Finally, the implementation of the body of *LF-Samplesort* is straightforward (Figure 6).

Figure 1. One execution of Partition and Move-Sample stages

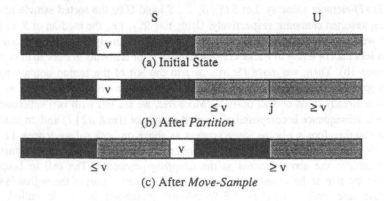

(a) Initial State

(b) After *Partition*

(c) After *Move-Sample*

Figure 2. Initial stages of Samplesort's execution

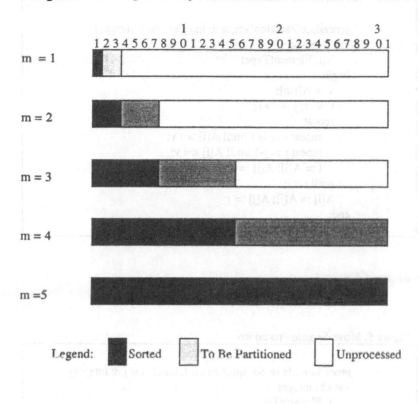

Legend: ■ Sorted ▧ To Be Partitioned □ Unprocessed

Figure 3. Leapfrog Procedure

```
procedure Leapfrog(s1,ss,u: integer);
var j,sm,d: integer;
begin
  if s1 > ss then LF-Samplesort(ss+1,u)  { We run out of sorted sample}
  else
    if u > ss then begin                  { There is at least one }
                                          { element in A[ss+1..u] }

      sm := (s1+ss) div 2;
      Partition(sm,ss,u,j)
      Move-Sample(sm,ss,j,d)
      Leapfrog(s1,sm-1,sm+d-1);
      Leapfrog(sm+d+1,j,u);
      end;
    {else u <= ss, i.e., Unsorted part is empty}
end;
```

Figure 4. Partition Procedure

```
procedure Partition(sm,ss,u: integer; var j: integer)
var i: integer;
    v,t: ElementType;
begin
  v := A[sm];
  i := ss; j := u+1;
  repeat
    repeat i := i+1 until A[i] >= v;
    repeat j := j-1 until A[j] <= v;
    t := A[j]; A[j] := A[i]; A[i] := t;
  until j < i;
  A[i] := A[j]; A[j] := t;
end;
```

Figure 5. Move-Sample Procedure

```
procedure Move-Sample(sm,ss: integer; var j,d: integer)
var i,k: integer;
    t: ElementType;
begin
  if j > ss then begin
    d := j-ss;
    for i := ss downto sm do begin
      k := i+d;
      t := A[i]; A[i] =: A[k]; A[k] := t;
      end;
    end
  else begin
    j := ss; d := 0;
    end;
end;
```

Figure 6. Leapfrogging Samplesort

```
procedure LF-Samplesort(f,l: integer);
var s: integer;
begin
   if l > f then begin
      s := 1;
      while s <= (l-f-s) do begin
         Leapfrog(f,f+s-1,f+2*s);
         s := 2*s + 1;
      end;
      Leapfrog(f,f+s-1,l);
   end
end;
```

3. Worst-Case Complexity

Without loss of generality, we assume that the number of elements to be sorted is $n = 2^m-1$, where $m > 0$. Also, all logarithms in the succeeding analysis are to base 2 and for all recurrences, $C(1) = 0$. The worst case of the algorithm occurs when the elements of the sample are always all greater than or all less than the elements to be sorted. Given n elements to sort, we know that at the last stage the size of the sample is $\lfloor n/2 \rfloor$ and the number of unsorted elements is $\lceil n/2 \rceil$. Similarly, the second to the last stage involves a sample of size $\lfloor \lfloor n/2 \rfloor /2 \rfloor$ and an unsorted part of $\lceil \lfloor n/2 \rfloor /2 \rceil$ elements and so on. Therefore, the worst number of comparisons can be described by the following recurrence relation:

$$C(n) = C(\lfloor n/2 \rfloor) + \lceil n/2 \rceil log (\lfloor n/2 \rfloor + 1) + C(\lceil n/2 \rceil)$$

where $C(\lfloor n/2 \rfloor)$ is the cost of sorting the sample using *LF-Samplesort* itself, $\lceil n/2 \rceil log (\lfloor n/2 \rfloor + 1)$ is the cost of partitioning the $\lceil n/2 \rceil$ elements using the sorted $\lfloor n/2 \rfloor$-element sample, and $C(\lceil n/2 \rceil)$ is the cost of sorting the largest remaining unsorted subsequence. Simplifying the recurrence yields $C(n)=O(n(log\ n)^2)$.

The worst number of data interchanges, on the other hand, occurs only when the elements of the sample are always all greater than the elements of the unsorted part. In such a situation, we move all the elements in the sample everytime the *Move-Sample* part of the algorithm is executed. This leads to the following recurrence relation for the worst number of data interchanges:

$$I(n) = I(\lfloor n/2 \rfloor) + \lfloor n/2 \rfloor + I(\lceil n/2 \rceil)$$

where $I(\lfloor n/2 \rfloor)$, $\lfloor n/2 \rfloor$ and $I(\lceil n/2 \rceil)$ are the number of data interchanges required to sort the sample, to move all the elements of the sample, and to sort the largest remaining unsorted subsequence, respectively. This recurrence relation simplifies to $I(n) = O(n\log n)$.

4. Average-Case Complexity

Without loss of generality, let $n = 2s+1$ be the number of elements in the input, where s is the size of the sample and is equal to $\lfloor n/2 \rfloor$ and $(s+1) = \lceil n/2 \rceil$. In the average-case analysis, we use the probabilistic model. Let $C(n)$ be the expected number of comparisons needed to sort the input. Since *LF-Samplesort* itself is used to sort the sample, sorting the sample, therefore, requires $C(\lfloor n/2 \rfloor)$ number of comparisons. When the size of the sample is $s = 2^k-1$, then the number of comparisons required to partition the unsorted part is $(n-s)\log(s+1)$ (Frazer and McKellar [3]). Hence, the number comparisons needed by our algorithm in order to partition the unsorted part is $\lceil n/2 \rceil \log (\lfloor n/2 \rfloor+1)$. From Lemma 3 of Frazer and McKellar [3], the expected number of comparisons needed to sort the subsequences produced after partitioning is

$$\lceil n/2 \rceil \sum_{j=0}^{m} p(j) E[c(j)]$$

where $m = \lceil n/2 \rceil$, $p(j) = \binom{n-j-1}{s-1} / \binom{n}{s}$ is the probability that the size of the subsequence bounded by the consecutive elements of the sample is j, and $E[C(j)]$ is the expected number of comparisons required to sort a subsequence of size j. Therefore, the average number of comparisons involved in the algorithm is given by:

$$C(n) = C(\lfloor n/2 \rfloor) + \lceil n/2 \rceil \log (\lfloor n/2 \rfloor+1) + \lceil n/2 \rceil \sum_{j=0}^{m} p(j) E[c(j)]$$

In order to simplify this recurrence, however, we note that the partitioning process partitions the set U into $(s+1)$ subsets $U_0, U_1, U_2, ..., U_s$, where

$U_0 = \{x \mid x < S_1\}$,
$U_i = \{S_i < x < S_{i+1}\}$, $1 \le i < s$,
$U_s = \{x \mid S_s < x\}$.

Let u_i be the number of elements in U_i. From Lemma 1 of Frazer and McKellar [3], the expected value of u_i, $E[u_i]$, is 1. With $E[u_i]=1$, the elements in the subsequences are already sorted. This implies that we can take away the third term in the recurrence relation, i.e., the average performance of our algorithm is:

$$C(n) = C(\lfloor n/2 \rfloor) + \lceil n/2 \rceil \log (\lfloor n/2 \rfloor + 1)$$

This simplifies to $C(n) = n \log n + O(n)$.

Next, we consider the expected number of data interchanges involved in the algorithm. To do this, we estimate the expected number of data interchanges involved in the partition stage and the number of data interchanges involved in moving the sample. The sum of the expected number of data interchanges of these two stages is the expected number of data interchanges required by the algorithm.

From Theorem 1 of Apers [2], the average number of data interchanges involved in partitioning a sequence of $\lceil n/2 \rceil$ elements using a sample of size $\lfloor n/2 \rfloor$ elements is given by:

$$((n+1)/4)((\log (n+1)-1)/2 - \sum_{j=1}^{\log n} \frac{1}{2^{j}+1}$$

Again, since the $E[u_i] = 1$, the number of data interchanges involved in partitioning is given by the following recurrence:

$$I_P(n) = I_P(\lfloor n/2 \rfloor) + ((n+1)/4)((\log (n+1)-1)/2 - \sum_{j=1}^{\log n} \frac{1}{2^{j}+1}$$

Simplifying this yields $I_P(n) \approx (n/4) \log n + O(n)$.

The average number of data interchanges involved in moving a sample of size $s=\lfloor n/2 \rfloor$ into the remaining $s+1= \lceil n/2 \rceil$ elements is $\lceil n/2 \rceil \log (s+1) = \lceil \lfloor n/2 \rfloor /2 \rceil \log (\lfloor n/2 \rfloor + 1)$ and the number of data interchanges needed to sort the sample is $I_M(\lfloor n/2 \rfloor)$. Since $E[u_i]=1$, this leads to the following number of data interchanges involved in moving the sample:

$$I_M(n) = I_M(\lfloor n/2 \rfloor) + \lceil \lfloor n/2 \rfloor /2 \rceil \log (\lfloor n/2 \rfloor + 1).$$

Simplifying this, we get $I_M(n) \approx (n/2) \log n + O(n)$.

5. Conclusions

From the average performance results, we note that the average number of comparisons and the number of data interchanges involved in the partition stage of our algorithm is in fact better than the $1.714n \log n - O(n)$ comparisons and the $0.343n \log n - O(n)$ data interchanges required by the best implementation of Quicksort as given in Sedgewick [9]. What degrades the average performance of our algorithm is the amount of data interchanges involved in moving the sample. In fact, the basic LF-Samplesort does not perform better than Heapsort. In Albacea [1], however, several ways of reducing the amount of data interchanges involved in moving the sample were outlined. The results of running some of these improvements are shown in Table 1. In Table 1, QS, HS, FS, BS, SS1, SS3, and SS7 correspond to Quicksort, Heapsort, Frazer and McKellar [2] Samplesort, Basic LF-Samplesort algorithm, improved LF-Samplesort with sample size s used to partition an unsorted set of size $(s+1)$, improved LF-Samplesort with sample size s used to partition an unsorted set of size $3(s+1)$, improved LF-Samplesort with sample size s used to partition an unsorted set of size $7(s+1)$, respectively. The result on Frazer and McKellar [3] Samplesort is based on a practical implementation where techniques employed in *Move-Sample* procedure are used. The column labeled #ofInv indicates the number of inversions in the permutation used (#ofInv=0 means totally sorted and #ofInv=$0.5n^2$ means inversely sorted). Also, the times shown on the table are in seconds.

Table 1. Simulation results for n = 8,000.

#ofInv	QS	HS	FS	BS	SS1	SS3	SS7
0	129.18	2.08	100.78	2.80	1.59	1.92	2.74
$0.0625n^2$	0.71	2.03	0.98	2.14	1.42	1.26	1.31
$0.1250n^2$	0.71	2.03	0.93	2.08	1.37	1.20	1.09
$0.1875n^2$	0.76	2.03	0.93	2.08	1.42	1.26	1.15
$0.2500n^2$	0.82	1.97	0.93	2.19	1.42	1.31	1.04
$0.2500n^2$	0.76	2.03	0.87	2.14	1.42	1.26	1.04
$0.3125n^2$	0.76	2.03	0.87	2.08	1.37	1.26	1.15
$0.3750n^2$	0.76	1.97	0.93	2.08	1.37	1.20	1.09
$0.4375n^2$	0.76	1.97	0.98	2.30	1.42	1.31	1.26
$0.5000n^2$	127.42	1.92	75.24	4.11	2.63	2.63	3.35

6. References

1. Albacea, E.A., Leapfrogging samplesort and its improvements, *ICS-UPLB Technical Report #95-2*, Institute of Computer Science, University of the Philippines Los Baños, 1995.

2. Apers, P.M.G., Recursive samplesort, *BIT* 18 (1978), 125-132.

3. Davidson, C.M., Quicksort revisited, *IEEE Transactions on Software Engineering* 14 (1988), 1480.

4. Frazer, W.D. and McKellar, A.C., Samplesort: A sampling approach to minimal storage tree sorting, *J. ACM* 17 (1970), 496-507.

5. Gonnet, G.H. and Baeza-Yates, R. *Handbook of Algorithms and Data Structures: In Pascal and C (2nd Ed)* (Addison-Wesley, 1991).

6. Hoare, C.A.R., Partition: Algorithm 63; Quicksort: Algorithm 64; and Find: Algorithm 65, *Communications of the ACM* 4 (1961), 321-322.

7. Hoare, C.A.R., Quicksort, *Computer Journal* 5 (1962), 10-15.

8. Knuth, D.E., *The Art of Computer Programming, Vol 3: Sorting and Searching* (Addison-Wesley, Mass., 1973).

9. Peters, J.G., and Kritzinger, P.S., Implementation of samplesort: a minimal storage tree sort, *BIT* 15 (1975), 85-93.

10. Rohrich, A hybrid of Quicksort with $O(n \log n)$ worst-case complexity, *Information Processing Letters* 14 (1982).

11. Sedgewick, R., *Quicksort* (Garland, N.Y., 1978).

12. Sedgewick, R., Implementing Quicksort programs, *Communications of the ACM* 21 (1978), 847-857.

13. Wainwright, A class of sorting algorithms based on Quicksort, *Communications of the ACM* 28 (1985).

Spanning 2-Trees*

Leizhen Cai

Department of Computer Science and Engineering
The Chinese University of Hong Kong
Shatin, New Territories, Hong Kong
E-mail: lcai@cs.cuhk.hk

Abstract. A *k-tree* is defined recursively to be either a *k*-clique or a graph T that contains a vertex v whose neighbourhood in T induces a *k*-clique and whose removal results in a *k*-tree. The existence of a spanning *k*-tree in a communication network is closely related to the reliability of the network, and it is known that the problem of determining whether a graph contains a spanning *k*-tree is NP-complete for any fixed $k \geq 2$. In this paper, several sufficient conditions are given for the existence of spanning 2-trees in a graph. An approximation algorithm is presented for finding a spanning 2-tree with minimum weight in a weighted complete graph. The asymptotic performance ratio of the algorithm is 2 when edge weights satisfy the triangle inequality, and 1.655 when the graph is a complete Euclidean graph on a set of points in the plane. It is also shown that it is NP-complete to determine whether a graph admits a spanning 2-tree that contains a given spanning tree.

Key words: Graph algorithm, spanning *k*-tree, approximation algorithm, NP-completeness

1 Introduction

In this paper, we consider undirected simple graphs and follow terminology and notation in a textbook by Bondy and Murty [2]. The notion of spanning trees plays an important role in graph theory and graph algorithms. It is well known that a graph is connected iff it contains a spanning tree. To obtain efficient algorithms on graphs, one often uses various spanning trees, such as the depth-first search tree and the breadth-first search tree, to explore edges and vertices of a graph to gather useful information about the graph. An excellent exposé on how to utilize various spanning trees to obtain efficient algorithms can be found in a monograph by Tarjan [10].

* This work was partially supported by a Direct Grant for Research from the Chinese University of Hong Kong and an Earmarked Research Grant from the Research Grants Council of Hong Kong.

The concept of trees can be generalized to *k-trees*: a *k-tree* is defined recursively to be either a *k*-clique or a graph T that contains a vertex v whose neighbourhood in T induces a *k*-clique and whose removal results in a *k*-tree. It is clear that a 1-tree is the same as a tree. A *spanning k-tree* $T = (V', E')$ of a graph $G = (V, E)$ is a *k*-tree that satisfies $V' = V$ and $E' \subseteq E$.

As trees are used in constructing minimum cost networks, *k*-trees with $k \geq 2$ can be used to construct reliable networks. In particular, the existence of a spanning 2-tree in a communication network is crucial to the reliability of the network when isolated failures of sites and lines occur; in fact, it guarantees that such failures will not affect the communication among operative sites [7]. The complexity of finding a spanning *k*-tree ($k \geq 2$) in a graph was first studied by Bern [1], where he established the NP-completeness of the problem for any fixed $k \geq 2$. Later, Cai and Maffray [5] strengthened his result by showing that the problem remains NP-complete for degree-bounded graphs, split graphs, and planar graphs (for $k = 2$). They also provided efficient algorithms for finding spanning *k*-trees in interval graphs and split-comparability graphs.

In this paper, we study spanning 2-trees in graphs and weighted graphs. In Section 2, several sufficient conditions are given for the existence of spanning 2-trees in a graph. In Section 3, an approximation algorithm is presented for finding a spanning 2-tree with minimum weight in a weighted complete graph. In Section 4, we prove that it is NP-complete to determine whether a graph admits a spanning 2-tree that contains a given spanning tree. A brief summary and some open problems are given in Section 5.

2   Sufficient conditions

In this section we present several sufficient conditions for the existence of a spanning 2-tree in a graph. First, we fix some definitions and describe some useful properties of 2-trees.

Call a vertex *2-simplicial* if its neighbourhood induces an edge. ¿From the recursive definition of a 2-tree, it is easy to see that a graph T with n vertices is a 2-tree iff there exists an ordering $v_1, \ldots, v_n$ of its vertices such that $v_{n-1}v_n$ is an edge and each v_i, $1 \leq i \leq n - 2$, is a 2-simplicial vertex of the induced subgraph $T[v_{i+1}, \ldots, v_n]$ of T. Such an ordering is called a *2-simplicial elimination scheme* (*2-SES* in short) of T. One should also note that a 2-tree can be constructed from an edge by repeatedly adding a new vertex and making it adjacent to the two ends of an edge in the graph formed so far. In fact, the reverse of a 2-SES gives an ordering of vertices that are added in sequence to form a 2-tree; we refer to the initial edge in constructing such a 2-tree as a *base* of the 2-tree. See Figure 1 for an example of a 2-tree and the related concepts.

An *edge bonding* of two disjoint graphs G and G' is any graph formed from G

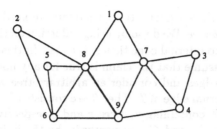

Fig. 1. A 2-tree, where 1,2,3,4,5,6,7,8,9 is a 2-SES. Edge $\{8, 9\}$ is the base with respect to this 2-SES.

and G' by identifying an edge of G with an edge of G'. We summarize some useful properties of a 2-tree in the following theorem, whose proof is straightforward by induction.

Theorem 1. *Let T be a 2-tree with $n \geq 3$ vertices. Then*

1. *T does not contain any chordless cycle of length at least 4;*

2. *T does not contain any 4-clique;*

3. *T is 2-connected;*

4. *Every edge of T is contained in a triangle;*

5. *Every edge of T can be a base.*

6. *An edge bonding of two disjoint 2-trees is a 2-tree;*

7. *T contains exactly $2n - 3$ edges.*

We now present several sufficient conditions for the existence of a spanning 2-tree. These conditions are based on the existence of certain structures in a graph. For a tree T, any non-leaf vertex is an *internal vertex*, and any edge not incident with a leaf is an *internal edge*. We first show a close relation between a tree and a 2-tree.

Lemma 2. *Let T be a nontrivial tree. For each vertex $v \in V(T)$, let T_v be an arbitrary tree on the neighbourhood $N_T(v)$ of v. Then $T \cup (\bigcup_{v \in V(T)} T_v)$ is a 2-tree.*

Proof. Let $I(T)$ be the set of internal vertices of T. It is clear that

$$T \cup \left(\bigcup_{v \in V(T)} T_v \right) = T \cup \left(\bigcup_{v \in I(T)} T_v \right)$$

since for any leaf v, T_v is a trivial tree. Therefore we need only show that $G = T \cup (\bigcup_{v \in I(T)} T_v)$ is a 2-tree. We do so by using induction on the number of internal edges of T. If T has no internal edge then it is a star. In this case, it is easy to see that G is a 2-tree. Assume that the claim is true for any nontrivial tree with less than $i \geq 1$ internal edges and consider an arbitrary tree with i internal edges. Let $e = xy$ be an internal edge of T. Then $T - e$ consists of exactly two connected components X and Y containing vertices x and y respectively. Let $X' = X + e$ and $Y' = Y + e$. Let G_x and G_y, respectively, be the induced subgraphs of G on $V(X')$ and $V(Y')$. Then $I(X') = I(T) \cap V(X)$ and $I(Y') = I(T) \cap V(Y)$, respectively, are the sets of internal vertices of trees X' and Y'. Furthermore,

$$G_x = X' \cup \left(\bigcup_{v \in I(X')} T_v \right)$$

and

$$G_y = Y' \cup \left(\bigcup_{v \in I(Y')} T_v \right).$$

Since e is not an internal edge of either X' or Y', both X' and Y' contain less than i internal edges. Therefore, by the induction hypothesis, both G_x and G_y are 2-trees. Since $G = G_x \cup G_y$ and e is the only edge shared by G_x and G_y, G is an edge bonding of two disjoint 2-trees G_x and G_y. By Theorem 2.1-(6), G is a 2-tree. ∎

The above lemma can be used to deduce the following result which indicates that the existence of a certain spanning tree in a graph guarantees the existence of a spanning 2-tree.

Theorem 3. *Let G be a nontrivial graph. If G contains a spanning tree T where the induced subgraph $G[N_T(v)]$ is connected for every vertex v of T, then G admits a spanning 2-tree that contains T.*

Proof. From the assumption that $G[N_T(v)]$ is connected, we deduce that $G[N_T(v)]$ contains a spanning tree T_v. Then by Lemma 2.2, $T \cup (\bigcup_{v \in V(T)} T_v)$ is a spanning 2-tree of G, which obviously contains T. ∎

Indeed, there are interesting graphs that contain spanning trees satisfying the condition in Theorem 2.3. A *tree 2-spanner* of G is a spanning tree where the distance between the two ends of any edge of G is at most two. It was shown in [3, 4] that a tree 2-spanner in a graph, if it exists, can be found in linear time.

Corollary 4 *Let G be a 2-connected graph that contains tree 2-spanners. Then for every tree 2-spanner T of G, there is a spanning 2-tree of G that contains T.*

Proof. Let v be an arbitrary internal vertex of T, and $G_v = G[N_T(v)]$. In light of Theorem 2.3, it suffices to show that G_v is connected. Suppose that G_v is disconnected. Let H_1 be a connected component of G_v, and $H_2 = G_v - H_1$. For $i = 1, 2$, let

$$V_i = \{x : \; x \in V(G) \text{ and the } (x, v)\text{-path in } T \text{ passes through } H_i\}.$$

Then $V_1 \cap V_2 = \emptyset$ and $V(G) = V_1 \cup V_2 \cup \{v\}$. Since there is no edge of G between H_1 and H_2, for any edge e of G between V_1 and V_2, at least one end of e is outside $H_1 \cup H_2$, implying that the distance in T between the two ends of e is at least three. Therefore no edge of G lies between V_1 and V_2 since T is a 2-spanner. However, this would imply that v is a cut vertex of G, contradicting the 2-connectivity of G. Therefore G_v is connected. ∎

We now give a sufficient condition for the existence of spanning 2-trees in a chordal graph. A graph is *chordal* if it contains no induced chordless cycle of length at least 4. Then every 2-tree is a chordal graph. Notice that it is NP-complete to determine whether a chordal graph contains a spanning 2-tree [5].

Theorem 5. *Let G be a hamiltonian chordal graph. Then for every Hamilton cycle C of G, there is a spanning 2-tree of G that contains C.*

Proof. We use induction on the number of vertices of G. The only hamiltonian chordal graph with at most three vertices is a triangle and the theorem is clearly true in this case. Assume that the theorem is true for all hamiltonian chordal graphs with less than $n \geq 4$ vertices and let G be a hamiltonian chordal graph with n vertices. Without loss of generality, we may assume that $C = v_0 v_1 \ldots v_{n-1} v_0$ is a Hamilton cycle of G. Since G is chordal and $n \geq 4$, there is a chord $v_i v_j$ in G. Let $G_1 = G[\{v_i, v_{i+1}, \ldots, v_j\}]$ and $G_2 = G[\{v_j, v_{j+1}, \ldots, v_i\}]$ (indices are taken module n). Then both G_1 and G_2 are hamiltonian chordal graphs since $C_1 = v_i v_{i+1} \ldots v_j v_i$ and $C_2 = v_j v_{j+1} \ldots v_i v_j$ are Hamilton cycles of G_1 and G_2 respectively. By the induction hypothesis, there is a spanning 2-tree T_1 of G_1 that contains C_1 and a spanning 2-tree T_2 of G_2 that contains C_2. It follows from Theorem 2.1-(6) that $T_1 \cup T_2$ is a spanning 2-tree of G since it is an edge bonding (at edge $v_i v_j$) of two disjoint 2-trees T_1 and T_2. Clearly $T_1 \cup T_2$ contains C, and we have a required spanning 2-tree of G. ∎

To finish this section, we consider plane triangulations. Recall that a *plane triangulation* is a plane graph in which each face is a triangle.

Theorem 6. *Every 4-connected plane triangulation contains a spanning 2-tree.*

Proof. Let G be a 4-connected plane triangulation. Then by a theorem of Tutte [11] that every 4-connected planar graph is hamiltonian, G contains a Hamilton cycle C. Now C together with all edges in the interior of C form a maximal outerplanar graph, which is a 2-tree. In fact C together with all edges in the exterior of C also form a maximal outerplanar graph. ∎

3 Approximating minimum spanning 2-trees

In this section, G is a weighted complete graph. For an edge e of G, $w(e)$ denotes the weight of e; and for a subgraph G' of G, $w(G')$ denotes the weight of G', i.e., the sum of the weights of all edges in G'. Let $MST(G)$ denote the weight of a minimum spanning tree of G, and $MS2T(G)$ denote the weight of a *minimum spanning 2-tree* (a spanning 2-tree with the minimum weight) of G. It is well known that a minimum spanning tree in a weighted graph can be found efficiently [10, 8]. On the other hand, it is NP-hard to find a minimum spanning 2-tree, even for weighted complete graphs [1] and weighted plane triangulations [5]. We now discuss the possibility of finding a spanning 2-tree in a weighted complete graph G whose weight is close to the weight of a minimum spanning 2-tree. First we present an efficient algorithm for constructing a spanning 2-tree in a weighted complete graph G:

> **Algorithm** MSTE(G); {Minimum spanning tree extension method
> for constructing a spanning 2-tree}
> **Input:** a weighted complete graph G;
> **Output:** a spanning 2-tree S;
>
> Find a minimum spanning tree T of G;
> $S := \emptyset$;
> **for each** internal vertex v of T **do**
>   Find a minimum spanning tree T_v of $G[N_T(v)]$;
> $S := S \cup T_v$;
> **end for.**

By Lemma 2.2, it is clear the S is a spanning 2-tree of G. Furthermore, we can implement the algorithm to run in $O(n^3)$ time by using Prim's algorithm [10]. Of course, S is normally not a minimum spanning 2-tree. So what is the weight of S comparing to the weight of a minimum spanning 2-tree of G? For a spanning 2-tree finding algorithm A, let $A(G)$ denote the weight of the spanning 2-tree of G constructed by the algorithm. Then it is easy to find a weighted complete graph G for which the ratio between $MSTE(G)$ and $MS2T(G)$ is arbitrarily large. This is not a coincident as indicated by the following result:

Theorem 7. *If $P \neq NP$ then for any constant $c \geq 1$ there is no polynomial-time approximation algorithm A for the minimum spanning 2-tree problem that guarantees $A(G)/MS2T(G) \leq c$.*

Proof. Suppose, to the contrary, that A is such an approximation algorithm. Then we show that A can be used to solve the spanning 2-tree problem in polynomial time. Given an arbitrary instance G' of the spanning 2-tree problem (without loss of generality, we may assume $n = |V(G')| \geq 3$), we construct a weighted complete graph G on $V(G')$ by assigning weight 1 to every edge in $E(G')$ and weight $c(2n-3)$ for each edge not in $E(G')$. Note that a 2-tree contains $2n - 3$ edges (Theorem 2.1-(7)). It is easy to see that this weight assignment ensures that G' admits a spanning 2-tree iff $MS2T(G) = 2n - 3$, which is equivalent to that G contains a spanning 2-tree of weight $\leq c(2n-3)$. Therefore if the spanning 2-tree S of G constructed by A has weight $\leq c(2n-3)$, we know that $MS2T(G) \leq 2n-3$ and thus G' contains a spanning 2-tree; else G' contains no spanning 2-tree. Since G can be constructed in polynomial time, we would then have a polynomial-time algorithm to determine whether a graph contains a spanning 2-tree, a contradiction to the assumption that $P \neq NP$ since the spanning 2-tree problem is NP-complete. ∎

In spite of the negative result in the above theorem, weighted complete graphs we deal with often possess certain properties. For example, the edge weights may satisfy the *triangle inequality*, i.e., for any three vertices x, y and z, $w(xz) \leq w(xy) + w(yz)$; or the graph may be a complete Euclidean graph on a set of points in the plane. In both cases, we will see that algorithm MSTE performs quite well. To quantify the performance of MSTE, we first relate $MS2T(G)$ to $MST(G)$.

Lemma 8. *For any nontrivial weighted complete graph G,*

$$MS2T(G) \geq \frac{2n-3}{n-1} MST(G).$$

Proof. Let S be a minimum spanning 2-tree of G and e be an edge in S that has the smallest weight. By Theorem 2.1-(5), there is a 2-SES of S with e as its base. Construct a spanning tree T of S as follows: First we put e into T. Then we follow the reverse order of the 2-SES. In forming the 2-tree S, we add a new vertex v and also two new edges incident with v; among these two edges, we put the edge with smaller weight into T.

By the construction of T, we have $w(T) - w(e) \leq w(S - T) = w(S) - w(T)$. Since e has the minimum weight amongst all $2n - 3$ edges in S, we have $w(e) \leq w(S)/(2n-3)$. Therefore

$$MST(G) \leq w(T) \leq \frac{n-1}{2n-3} w(S) = \frac{n-1}{2n-3} MS2T(G). ∎$$

We are now ready to quantify the performance of algorithm MSTE. We first consider weighted complete graphs with triangle inequality on edge weights.

Theorem 9. *If edge weights of a weighted complete graph G satisfy the triangle inequality then*

$$\frac{MSTE(G)}{MS2T(G)} < 2.$$

as the number of vertices of G tends to infinity.

Proof. Let S and T, respectively, be the spanning 2-tree and the minimum spanning tree of G constructed by algorithm MSTE. For each interval vertex v of T, let T_v be the minimum spanning tree of $G[N_T(v)]$ constructed by the algorithm.

We use an algorithm of Farley [7] to construct another spanning 2-tree S' of G and use $w(S')$ to provide an upper bound for $w(S)$. Arbitrarily choose a vertex r of T, and make T into a rooted tree with root r. For any vertex v, let $p(v)$ be its parent and let P_v be a spanning path of $G[N_T(v)]$ that starts with vertex $p(v)$. Let $S' = T \cup (\bigcup_{v \in I(T)} P_v)$. Then, by Lemma 2.2, S' is also a spanning 2-tree of G, and furthermore $w(S) \leq w(S')$ since $w(T_v) \leq w(P_v)$ for every vertex v.

To estimate $w(S')$ we charge $w(P_v)$ to edges of T. There are two types of edges in P_v: parent-child edge and child-child edge. In fact, only one edge in P_v is a parent-child edge. Now for each edge xy in P_v, we have

$$w(xy) \leq w(xv) + w(vy).$$

So we charge the weight of edge xy to the two tree edges xv and vy. Overall, every tree edge will be charged at most three times: once from a parent-child edge, and twice from two child-child edges. Therefore $\sum_{v \in I(T)} w(P_v) < 3w(T)$ and thus $w(S') < 4w(T)$. Combining with Lemma 3.2, we have

$$w(S')/MS2T(G) < 4(n-1)/(2n-3).$$

Since $MSTE(G) = w(S) \leq w(S')$, we deduce $MSTE(G)/MS2T(G) < 2$ as $|V(G)|$ tends to infinity. ∎

Given a set of points in the Euclidean plane, the *complete Euclidean graph* on the set of points is a weighted complete graph G whose vertices correspond to the points and where the weight of an edge is the Euclidean distance between the corresponding points of its ends. In this case, the algorithm has a better performance ratio:

Theorem 10. *For any complete Euclidean graph G,*

$$\frac{MSTE(G)}{MS2T(G)} < \frac{3 + 4\sqrt{3}}{6} \approx 1.655$$

as the number of vertices of G tends to infinity.

Proof. Let S and T, respectively, be the spanning 2-tree and the minimum spanning tree of G constructed by algorithm MSTE. For each internal vertex

v of T, let T_v be the minimum spanning tree of $G[N_T(v)]$ constructed by the algorithm, and let $T_v^* = T[\{v\} \cup N_T(v)]$.

We will use the weight of T to obtain an upper bound of the weight of S. To do so, we first establish a relation between $w(T_v)$ and $w(T_v^*)$. Because T_v^* is a Steiner tree for the set of points corresponding to $N_T(v)$, we have

$$w(T_v) \le \frac{2}{\sqrt{3}} T_v^*$$

by the Steiner ratio [6]. Let $I(T)$ denote the set of internal vertices of T. Then

$$w(S) = w(T) + \sum_{v \in I(T)} w(T_v) \le w(T) + \frac{2}{\sqrt{3}} \sum_{v \in I(T)} w(T_v^*).$$

Since $\sum_{v \in I(T)} w(T_v^*) < 2w(T)$, we have

$$MSTE(G) = w(S) < \frac{4 + \sqrt{3}}{\sqrt{3}} w(T).$$

Combining with Lemma 3.2, we deduce

$$\frac{MSTE(G)}{MS2T(G)} < \frac{3 + 4\sqrt{3}}{6}$$

as $|V(G)|$ tends to infinity. ∎

4   An NP-completeness result

The approximation algorithm in the previous section constructs a light weight spanning 2-tree by extending a minimum spanning tree of a weighted complete graph. It is then natural to ask about the complexity of extending a given spanning tree T into a spanning 2-tree, as well as the complexity of extending T into a spanning 2-tree whose weight is minimum among all spanning 2-trees containing T. We show that the former problem is intractable, which in turn implies that the latter problem is also intractable.

Theorem 11. *Given a graph G and a spanning tree T of G, it is NP-complete to determine whether G possesses a spanning 2-tree that contains T.*

Proof. The problem is clearly in NP since a nondeterministic algorithm need only guess a spanning subgraph S of G and check in polynomial time whether S is a 2-tree containing T.

To establish the NP-completeness we transform 3SAT ([LO2] in [9]) to the problem. Recall that an instance (U, C) of 3SAT consists of a set U of n distinct variables and a collection C of m clauses over U where each clause contains exactly three distinct literals over U. Let (U, C) be an arbitrary instance of 3SAT. We must construct a graph G and a spanning tree T of G such that G admits a spanning 2-tree containing T if and only if C is satisfiable. The following lemma will be useful in the construction.

Lemma 12. *Let e be an arbitrary edge of G, and G' be the graph constructed from G by adding a new vertex $f(e)$ and two edges joining $f(e)$ with the two ends of e. Then any spanning 2-tree of G' contains edge e.*

Proof. Every vertex of a 2-tree with more than two vertices belongs to a triangle, and the only triangle containing vertex $f(e)$ contains edge e. ∎

The above lemma allows us to force an edge e to appear in every spanning 2-tree of G. Hereafter, we will refer to the construction in the lemma as "to force an edge e", and the new vertex $f(e)$ as a *forcing vertex*.

The graph G is constructed as follows (see Figure 2 for an example):

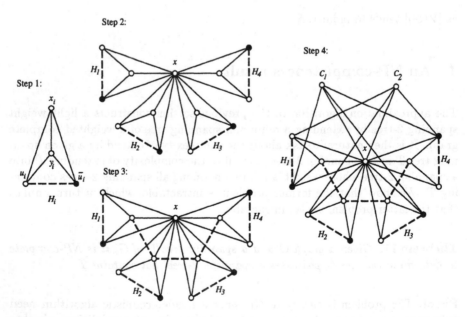

Fig. 2. The construction of the graph G for $(\{u_1, u_2, u_3, u_4\}, \{c_1, c_2\})$, where $c_1 = \{\bar{u}_1, \bar{u}_3, \bar{u}_4\}$ and $c_2 = \{u_1, u_2, \bar{u}_4\}$. Dashed lines indicate forced edges. Forcing vertices are omitted.

1. for each variable $u_i \in U$, $1 \leq i \leq n$, form a 4-clique H_i on four vertices $u_i, \overline{u}_i, x_i$ and y_i, and force edge $u_i\overline{u}_i$;
2. merge all H_i's together into a single graph by identifying all x_i's into a single vertex x;
3. for each i, $1 \leq i < n$, join y_i with y_{i+1} by an edge and force edge y_iy_{i+1}; and
4. for each clause $c_j \in C$, $1 \leq j \leq m$, create a vertex c_j and connect c_j with x and three vertices corresponding to the three literals in c_j.

The spanning tree T of G is specified by edges $xy_i, y_iu_i, y_i\overline{u}_i$ for each H_i, $1 \leq i \leq n$, xc_j for each $c_j \in C$, $1 \leq j \leq m$, and for each forcing vertex an arbitrary edge incident with it (see Figure 3).

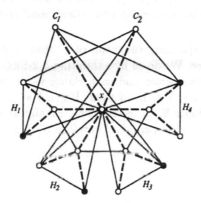

Fig. 3. The spanning tree T (dashed lines) in G. Forcing vertices are omitted.

For each i, $1 \leq i \leq n$, vertices u_i and $\overline{u}_i$ are *literal vertices*, and edges xu_i and $x\overline{u}_i$ are *literal edges*. For each j, $1 \leq j \leq m$, vertex c_j is a *clause vertex*. As we will see shortly, the presence (respectively absence) of a literal edge in a spanning 2-tree of G is used to indicate the truth (respectively false) of its corresponding literal under a truth assignment.

It is clear that both G and T can be constructed in polynomial time. It remains to be shown that C is satisfiable if and only if G has a spanning 2-tree containing T.

Suppose that S is a spanning 2-tree of G containing T. Then S contains exactly one literal edge from each H_i, $1 \leq i \leq n$. To see this, we observe that if both literal edges of H_i were contained in S then S would contain the 4-clique H_i (since all non-literal edges of H_i are either forced or contained in T), and that if neither literal edges were contained in S then either y_i would be a cut vertex of S or S would contain a chordless cycle of length at least four, contradicting S

being a 2-tree. Therefore we can define a truth assignment ξ_S by setting, for each i with $1 \leq i \leq n$, $\xi_S(u_i) = 1$ if the literal edge xu_i belongs to S and $\xi_S(u_i) = 0$ otherwise. For each clause $c_j \in C$, it is easy to see, by the construction of G, that the literal vertex c_j belongs to a triangle of S containing a literal edge of G. By the definition of ξ_S, the corresponding literal of this literal edge is true under ξ_S. Therefore c_j is satisfied by ξ_S, implying that C is satisfied by ξ_S.

Conversely, suppose that C is satisfiable and let ξ be a satisfying truth assignment for C. We construct a subgraph S' of G as follows:

1. put the spanning tree T in S';
2. put in S' all the forced edges and all the edges incident with forcing vertices;
3. for each i, $1 \leq i \leq n$, if $\xi(u_i) = 1$ then put literal edge xu_i in S', else put literal edge $x\overline{u}_i$ in S'; and
4. for each clause vertex c_j, $1 \leq j \leq m$, choose a true literal l in clause c_j and put in S' the edge between c_j and the corresponding literal vertex of l.

Obviously, S' is a spanning subgraph of G that contains T. It remains to verify that S' is a 2-tree. We do so by exhibiting a 2-SEO of S' as follows: First we eliminate each forcing vertex and each clause vertex one by one. After that we consider each H_i, $1 \leq i \leq n$, in turn. If $\xi(u_i) = 1$, we eliminate $\overline{u}_i, u_i$ in sequence; else we eliminate $\overline{u}_i, u_i$ in sequence. Finally we eliminate $y_1, \ldots, y_{n-1}$ in sequence and get an edge $\{x, y_n\}$. Therefore S' is a 2-tree and the proof is completed. ∎

5 Conclusion

In this paper we have considered certain aspects of spanning 2-trees in graphs and weighted graphs. Several sufficient conditions have been provided for the existence of a spanning 2-tree in a graph. An approximation algorithm has been presented for finding a light weight spanning 2-tree in a weighted complete graph. On the other hand, we have shown that the problem of whether a spanning 2-tree is extendible to a spanning 2-tree is NP-complete.

There are several interesting open problems that call for our attention.

1. Although the bound on the weight of a spanning 2-tree of G obtained by algorithm MSTE is almost tight with respect to MST(G), the performance ratio of the algorithm seems not tight. Bern [1] claimed that Farley's algorithm mentioned in the proof of Theorem 3.3 gives asymptotic performance ratio 1.5 for complete Euclidean graphs. Unfortunately, the proof of his claim is false. Can one provide a better bound for the performance ratio of algorithm MSTE?

2. The complexity of the sufficient conditions in Section 2 varies largely. In particular, the conditions in Corollary 2.4 and Theorem 2.6 are polynomial-

time checkable, the complexity of checking the condition in Theorem 2.5 is NP-complete, and the complexity of checking the condition in Theorem 2.3 is unknown. This brings us the second open problem: what is the complexity of finding a spanning tree T of G so that the neighbourhood of each vertex in T is connected in G?

3. The existence of a spanning 2-tree in a plane triangulation seems to be quite intriguing. Does every plane triangulation contain a spanning 2-tree?

References

1. M.W. Bern. *Network design problems: Steiner trees and spanning k-trees.* PhD thesis, University of California, Berkeley, 1987.
2. J.A. Bondy and U.S.R. Murty. *Graph Theory with Applications.* North-Holland, New York, 1976.
3. L. Cai. *Tree Spanners: Spanning Trees that Approximate Distances.* Ph.D. Dissertation, Technical Report 260/92, Department of Computer Science, University of Toronto, 1992.
4. L. Cai and D.G. Corneil. Tree spanners. *SIAM J. of Discrete Math.*, to appear, 1995.
5. L. Cai and F. Maffray. On the spanning k-tree problem. *Disc. Appl. Math.*, 44:139–156, 1993.
6. D.Z. Du and F.K. Hwang. A proof of the Gilbert-Pollak conjecture on the Steiner ratio. *Algorithmica*, 7:121–135, 1992.
7. A.M. Farley. Networks immune to isolated failures. *Networks*, 11:255–268, 1981.
8. H.N. Gabow, Z. Galil, T.H. Spencer, and R.E. Tarjan. Efficient algorithms for finding minimum spanning trees in undirected and directed graphs. *Combinatorica*, 6 (2):109–122, 1986.
9. M.R. Garey and D.S. Johnson. *Computers and Intractability : A Guide to the Theory of NP-completeness.* W.H. Freeman, San Fransisco, 1979.
10. R.E. Tarjan. *Data Structures and Network Algorithms.* SIAM, Philadelphia, 1983.
11. W.T. Tutte. A theorem on planar graphs. *Trans. Amer. Math. Soc.*, 82:99–116, 1956.

Minimal Linear Invariants

Ming-Yang Kao*

Department of Computer Science
Duke University
Durham, NC 27708
U.S.A.

Abstract. To protect sensitive information in a cross tabulated table, it is a common practice to suppress some of the cells. A linear combination of the suppressed cells is called a *linear invariant* if it has a unique feasible value. Because of this uniqueness, the information contained in a linear invariant is not protected. The *minimal* linear invariants are the most basic units of unprotected information. This paper establishes a fundamental correspondence between minimal linear invariants of a table and minimal edge cuts of a graph constructed from the table. As one of several consequences of this correspondence, a linear-time algorithm is obtained to find a set of minimal linear invariants that completely characterize the linear invariant information contained in individual rows and columns.

1 Introduction

Cross tabulated tables are routinely used to organize and exhibit information in a wide variety of documents, including statistical reports. For the purpose of protecting information in a table, it is a common practice to suppress the values of certain sensitive cells. Concerned with the effectiveness of this practice [10], statisticians have been studying two fundamental issues [3], [5], [6], [7], [8], [9], [14], [15], [16], [13]. The *detection* issue is whether an adversary can deduce significant information about the suppressed cells from the published data of a table. The *protection* issue is how a table maker can suppress a small number of cells in addition to the sensitive ones such that the resulting table does not leak significant information.

This paper focuses on the issue of detecting information in a two-dimensional table that publishes three types of data (see [12] for examples): (1) the values of all cells except a set of sensitive ones, which are *suppressed*, (2) an upper bound and a lower bound for each suppressed cell, and (3) all row sums and column sums of the complete set of cells. The suppressed cells may have real or integer values. They may have different bounds, and the bounds may be finite or infinite. The upper bound of a suppressed cell should be strictly greater than its lower bound; otherwise, the value of that cell is immediately known.

* Email address: kao@cs.duke.edu. Supported in part by NSF Grant CCR-9101385.

A *bounded feasible assignment* to a table is an assignment of values to the suppressed cells such that each row or column adds up to its published sum and that the bounds of the suppressed cells are all satisfied. An *invariant cell* is a suppressed cell that has the same value at all bounded feasible assignments. The information contained in an invariant cell is unprotected because its value can be precisely deduced from the published data. Gusfield [11] gave an algorithm that can find all invariant cells of a table in optimal linear time. This algorithm employs a graph theoretic approach that encodes a table into a mixed graph called the *suppressed graph*, where a *mixed* graph is one that may contain both undirected and directed edges.

A linear combination of the suppressed cells of a table is called a *linear invariant* if it has the same value at all bounded feasible assignments (see [12] for examples). An invariant cell is a special case of a linear invariant where its coefficient is 1 and all other suppressed cells have coefficients 0. Kao and Gusfield [12] gave an algorithm for testing whether a linear combination of suppressed cells of a table is a linear invariant. It runs in optimal linear time and has an efficient parallel implementation. To achieve these computational complexities, the algorithm relies on a fundamental relationship between the classic Z_2 vector spaces generated by directed and undirected cycles in the suppressed graph of a table.

The main contribution of this paper is a general tool, called the *Minimal Decomposition Theorem*, for protecting and detecting information in a table. The theorem describes how to decompose a linear invariant into *minimal linear invariants*, which can be regarded as the most basic units of unprotected information in a table. This paper shows that the minimal linear invariants correspond to the minimal edge cuts of the suppressed graph, where a (*minimal*) *edge cut* of a graph is a (minimal) set of edges whose removal disconnects a connected component of the graph. Through this correspondence, a further relationship is established between linear invariants of a table and edge cuts of its suppressed graph. As a consequence of this decomposition theorem, an algorithm is obtained for finding a set of minimal linear invariants that completely characterize the linear invariant information contained in individual rows and columns. Since these minimal linear invariants include all invariant cells, this algorithm substantially generalizes the invariant cell detection algorithm of Gusfield [11]. Moreover, this algorithm is very simple and runs in optimal linear time.

Section 2 reviews useful previous results. Section 3 characterizes minimal linear invariants. Section 4 gives the decomposition theorem. Section 5 uses this theorem to design the linear-time algorithm that finds all the minimal linear invariants for individual rows and column.

2 Previous Results

Throughout this paper, let $\mathcal{T}$ be a table. The *suppressed graph* $\mathcal{H}$ of $\mathcal{T}$ is the bipartite mixed graph constructed below (see Figure 1 for an example). For each row (resp., column) of $\mathcal{T}$, there is a unique vertex in $\mathcal{H}$. This vertex is called a *row* (resp., *column*) vertex. Let $E_{i,j}$ be the cell at row i and column j. For each

row column index	a	b	c	row sum
1	☐0	☐9	1	10
2	☐9	☐9	☐0	18
3	6	☐0	☐5	11
column sum	15	18	6	

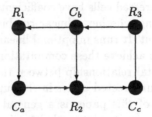

In the above 3 × 3 table, the number in each cell is the value of that cell. A cell with a box is a suppressed cell. The lower and upper bounds of the suppressed cells are 0 and 9. The graph below the table is the suppressed graph of the table. Vertex R_p corresponds to row p, and vertex C_q to column q.

Fig. 1. A Table and Its Suppressed Graph.

suppressed cell $E_{i,j}$ of $\mathcal{T}$, there is a unique edge e in $\mathcal{H}$ between the vertices of row i and column j. If the value of $E_{i,j}$ is strictly between its bounds, then e is undirected. Otherwise, if the value is equal to the lower (resp., upper) bound, then e is directed towards to its column (resp., row) endpoint.

A *traversable* cycle or path in a mixed graph is one that can be traversed along the directions of its edges. A *direction-blind* cycle or path is one that can be traversed if the directions of its edges are disregarded; the word direction-blind is often omitted for brevity. A mixed graph is called *strongly connected* if for each pair of vertices, there is some traversable cycle containing the pair. A *strongly connected component* is a maximal subgraph that is strongly connected.

Theorem 1 ([11]). *A suppressed cell of $\mathcal{T}$ is not an invariant cell if and only if its corresponding edge in $\mathcal{H}$ is in an edge-simple traversable cycle.*

The *mod 2 sum* of two edge sets of $\mathcal{H}$ is the set of edges that appear in exactly one of the two given sets [2]. Let $CS(\mathcal{H})$ be the Z_2 vector space that consists of the mod 2 sums of edge-simple direction-blind cycles in $\mathcal{H}$. Because $\mathcal{H}$ is bipartite, the edges of an edge-simple cycle of $\mathcal{H}$ can be alternately labeled with $+1$ and -1. Such a labeling is called a *direction-blind labeling*. Since every vector of $CS(\mathcal{H})$ can be decomposed into an edge-disjoint set of edge-simple cycles of $\mathcal{H}$, this labeling process can be extended to every vector of $CS(\mathcal{H})$ by direction-blindly labeling each cycle in a decomposition of that vector. Furthermore, a *direction-blindly labeled* basis of $CS(\mathcal{H})$ is one where each vector is direction-blindly labeled.

A direction-blindly labeled vector of $CS(\mathcal{H})$ is regarded as an assignment to the suppressed cells of T. If the corresponding edge of a suppressed cell is in the given vector of $CS(\mathcal{H})$, then the value assigned to that cell is the label of the corresponding edge; otherwise, the value is 0.

Throughout this paper, let $\mathcal{H}_1, \cdots, \mathcal{H}_k$ be the strongly connected components of $\mathcal{H}$, and let Ω_i be a direction-blindly labeled basis of $CS(\mathcal{H}_i)$.

Theorem 2 ([12]). *A linear combination F of the suppressed cells in T is a linear invariant if and only if $F(\gamma) = 0$ for all $\gamma \in \cup_{i=1}^{k} \Omega_i$.*

3 Minimal Linear Invariants

The *effective area* of a linear invariant F of T, denoted by $EA(F)$, is the set of suppressed cells in the nonzero terms of F. The set $EA(F)$ is also regarded as an edge set of $\mathcal{H}$. A *nonzero linear invariant* is one with at least one nonzero term. A nonzero linear invariant F of T is a *minimal* linear invariant if T has no nonzero linear invariant whose effective area is a proper subset of $EA(F)$. Note that every invariant cell forms a minimal linear invariant. Also, a minimal linear invariant is unique with respect to its effective area, i.e., for all minimal linear invariants F and F', if $EA(F) = EA(F')$, then $F' = c \cdot F$ for some c.

Lemma 3. *If $\mathcal{H}$ is strongly connected and F is a nonzero linear invariant of T, then $EA(F)$ is an edge cut of $\mathcal{H}$.*

Proof. For the sake of contradiction, assume that $\mathcal{H} - EA(F)$ is connected. Let $e \in EA(F)$. Let P be a vertex-simple path in $\mathcal{H} - EA(F)$ between the endpoints of e. Let C be the direction-blindly labeled edge-simple cycle formed by P and e with e labeled by $+1$. Because P and $EA(F)$ share no edge, $F(C) = 1$ and by Theorem 2 F cannot be an invariant.

In light of this lemma, it is natural to investigate the relationship between minimal linear invariants of T and minimal edge cuts of $\mathcal{H}$.

3.1 Technical Lemmas

This section develops lemmas to allow later discussion to focus on the case where $\mathcal{H}$ is strongly connected. Let T_i be the table constructed from T by deleting the rows and columns corresponding to the vertices not in $\mathcal{H}_i$. All (un)suppressed cells in the remaining rows and columns remain (un)suppressed with their values and bounds unchanged. Note that the suppressed graph of T_i is $\mathcal{H}_i$.

Lemma 4. *Let F be a linear combination of the suppressed cells of T. Let $F_i = \sum_x c_x \cdot x$, where x is over all edges in $\mathcal{H}_i$ and c_x is the coefficient of x in F. The following statement are equivalent: (1) F is a linear invariant of T. (2) Each F_i is a linear invariant of T_i. (3) Each F_i is a linear invariant of T.*

Proof. This lemma follows from Theorem 2 and the fact that $F_i(\alpha) = F(\alpha)$ for all $\alpha \in \Omega_i$ and $F_i(\beta) = 0$ for all $\beta \in \Omega_j$ with $j \neq i$.

Lemma 5. *A linear invariant F of T is minimal if and only if either $EA(F)$ consists of an edge not in any $\mathcal{H}_i$, or $EA(F)$ is contained in some $\mathcal{H}_i$ and F is a minimal linear invariant of T_i.*

Proof. The proof follows from Lemma 4 and Theorem 1.

Fact 6 *An edge set Y of $\mathcal{H}_i$ is a minimal edge cut if and only if $\mathcal{H}_i - Y$ has exactly two connected components $\mathcal{H}'$ and $\mathcal{H}''$, and each edge of Y is between $\mathcal{H}'$ and $\mathcal{H}''$.*

Lemma 7. *Let $Y = \{e_1, \cdots, e_k\}$ be a minimal edge cut of $\mathcal{H}_i$. Let $\mathcal{H}'$ and $\mathcal{H}''$ be the two connected components of $\mathcal{H}_i - Y$. Let $\Omega = \{C_2, \cdots, C_k\}$ be a set of direction-blindly labeled edge-simple cycles in $\mathcal{H}_i$ such that each C_j and Y share exactly e_1 and e_j. Then a linear combination F of the suppressed cells in Y is a linear invariant of T_i if and only if $F(C_j) = 0$ for all C_j.*

Proof. Let Ω' and Ω'' be direction-blindly labeled bases of $CS(\mathcal{H}')$ and $CS(\mathcal{H}'')$, respectively. Because F contains no suppressed cells that appear in the vectors of $\Omega' \cup \Omega''$, $F(\gamma) = 0$ for all $\gamma \in \Omega' \cup \Omega''$. Thus, by Theorem 2, it suffices to show that $\Omega' \cup \Omega'' \cup \Omega$ is a basis of $CS(\mathcal{H}_i)$ as follows.

    Part 1: $\Omega' \cup \Omega'' \cup \Omega$ is linearly independent. Let $\Omega' = \{A_1, \cdots, A_p\}$. Let $\Omega'' = \{B_1, \cdots, B_q\}$. The goal is show that if $\alpha = \sum_{j=1}^p a_j \cdot A_j + \sum_{j=1}^q b_j \cdot B_j + \sum_{j=2}^k c_j \cdot C_j = 0$, then the coefficients a_j, b_j, c_j are all 0. Because e_j only appears in the term C_j of α, the coefficients c_j are all 0, and $\alpha = \sum_{j=1}^p a_j \cdot A_j + \sum_{j=1}^q b_j \cdot B_j$. Next, because $\mathcal{H}'$ and $\mathcal{H}''$ are disjoint, $CS(\mathcal{H}') \cap CS(\mathcal{H}'') = \{0\}$. Thus, $\sum_{j=1}^p a_j \cdot A_j = 0 = \sum_{j=1}^q b_j \cdot B_j$. Then, because Ω' and Ω'' are bases of $CS(\Omega')$ and $CS(\Omega'')$, the coefficients a_j and b_j are all 0.

    Part 2: $\Omega' \cup \Omega'' \cup \Omega$ generates all $\beta \in CS(\mathcal{H}_i)$. Let X be the set of edges in β. Let $V = (X \cap Y) - \{e_1\}$. Let $\delta = \beta + \sum_{e_j \in V} C_j$. The goal is to show that β is a linear combination of $\Omega' \cup \Omega'' \cup \Omega$. It suffices to show that δ is a linear combination of $\Omega' \cup \Omega''$. For each j with $2 \leq j \leq k$, e_j either does not appear in any terms of $\beta + \sum_{e_h \in V} C_h$, or appears exactly once in β and once in C_j. In either case, the coefficient of e_j in δ is 0. Furthermore, because e_1 is between $\mathcal{H}'$ and $\mathcal{H}''$, no cycle of $\mathcal{H}_i$ can contain e_1 without containing some e_j with $j \geq 2$. Thus, e_1 is also cancelled in δ. Now that δ contains no edge from Y, $\delta = \delta' + \delta''$ for some $\delta' \in CS(\mathcal{H}')$ and $\delta'' \in CS(\mathcal{H}'')$. Then, because Ω' and Ω'' are bases of $CS(\Omega')$ and $CS(\Omega'')$, δ is a linear combination of $\Omega' \cup \Omega''$.

3.2 Characterizations of Minimal Linear Invariants

An edge set of $\mathcal{H}$ is a *basic set* if it either consists of an edge not in any $\mathcal{H}_i$ or is a minimal edge cut of some $\mathcal{H}_i$.

Theorem 8 (minimal linear invariants versus basic sets).
For each basic set Y of $\mathcal{H}$, T has a minimal linear invariant F with $EA(F) = Y$. Moreover, a linear invariant F of T is minimal if and only if $EA(F)$ is a basic set of $\mathcal{H}$.

Proof. By Lemma 5, this proof focuses on the case where $\mathcal{H}$ is strongly connected. To construct F for the first statement, let $Y = \{e_1, \cdots, e_k\}$. By Fact 6, $\mathcal{H} - Y$ has exactly two connected components $\mathcal{H}'$ and $\mathcal{H}''$. Also, each e_j has one end $s_j \in \mathcal{H}'$ and the other end $t_j \in \mathcal{H}''$. For each index j such that $2 \leq j \leq k$, let Q_j be a vertex-simple path in $\mathcal{H}''$ between t_1 and t_j. Let P_j be a vertex-simple path in $\mathcal{H}'$ between s_1 and s_j. Let n_j be the number of edges in P_j. Let $n_1 = 0$. Let $F = \sum_{j=1}^{k} (-1)^{n_j} \cdot e_j$. To show that F is a minimal linear invariant, let $\Omega = \{C_2, \cdots, C_k\}$ where C_j is the direction-blindly labeled edge-simple cycle formed by e_1, P_j, e_j, Q_j with e_1 labeled by $+1$. Note that the label of e_j in C_j is $(-1)^{n_j+1}$. Because C_j and Y share exactly e_1 and e_j, $F(C_j) = (-1)^0 \cdot 1 + (-1)^{n_j} \cdot (-1)^{n_j+1} = 0$. By Lemma 7 F is a linear invariant of T with $EA(F) = Y$. Because Y is a minimal edge cut of $\mathcal{H}$, by Lemma 3, F must be a minimal linear invariant of T.

To prove the direction $\rightarrow$ of the second statement by contradiction, assume that $EA(F)$ is not a minimal edge cut of $\mathcal{H}$. Because by Lemma 3 $EA(F)$ is an edge cut of $\mathcal{H}$, some minimal edge cut Y' of $\mathcal{H}$ is a proper subset of $EA(F)$. By the first statement there is a linear invariant F'' with $EA(F'') = Y'$, contradicting the minimality of F. To prove the direction $\Leftarrow$ by contradiction, assume that F is not a minimal linear invariant of T. Then there is a nonzero linear invariant F' such that $EA(F')$ is a proper subset of $EA(F)$. By Lemma 3, $EA(F')$ is an edge cut of $\mathcal{H}$, contradicting the minimality of $EA(F)$.

Assume that Y is a minimal edge cut of $\mathcal{H}$. Let $\mathcal{H}'$ be as stated in Fact 6. Y is called a *bipartite* minimal edge cut if the endpoints of Y in $\mathcal{H}'$ are all row vertices or all column vertices. A *bipartite* basic set of $\mathcal{H}$ is one that either consists of an edge not in any $\mathcal{H}_i$ or is a bipartite minimal edge cut of some $\mathcal{H}_i$.

A *unitary* linear invariant is one whose coefficients are $+1$, 0, or -1. A *sum* linear invariant is one whose coefficients are $+1$ or 0.

Theorem 9 (the coefficients of minimal linear invariants).
Every minimal linear invariant of T is a multiple of a unitary linear invariant. Moreover, a minimal linear invariant F of T is a multiple of a sum linear invariant if and only if $EA(F)$ is a bipartite basic set of $\mathcal{H}$.

Proof. By Lemma 5, the proof may focus on the case where $\mathcal{H}$ is strongly connected. The first statement follows from the fact that the F in the proof of the first statement of Theorem 8 is unitary. To prove the second statement, let

$\{e_1, \cdots, e_k\} = EA(F)$. Without loss of generality, assume $F = \sum_{j=1}^{k} (-1)^{n_j} \cdot e_j$ as in the proof of the first statement of Theorem 8. The following three statements are equivalent: (1) F is a sum linear invariant. (2) For all j, n_j is even. (3) $EA(F)$ is a bipartite cut edge of $\mathcal{H}$.

4 Decomposition of Linear Invariants

This section discusses how to simultaneously decompose a linear invariant into minimal ones and its effective area into minimal edge cuts and invariant cells. The Minimal Decomposition Theorem is in §4.2.

4.1 A Technical Lemma

Lemma 10. *If a nonzero linear invariant F of T is not minimal, then T has a unitary minimal linear invariant F' such that $EA(F')$ is a proper subset of $EA(F)$ and for each $d \in EA(F')$, the coefficients of d in F and F' are either both positive or both negative.*

By Theorem 1, Lemma 4 and Theorem 9, the proof of this lemma may focus on the case that $\mathcal{H}$ is strongly connected. Some definitions are in order. For each edge $d \in \mathcal{H}$, let $\sigma(d) = +1$, 0, or -1 if the coefficient of d in F is positive, zero, or negative, respectively. Without loss of generality, assume that there is an edge $e \in EA(F)$ with $\sigma(e) = 1$. Let x and y be the endpoints of e corresponding to a row and a column, respectively. An *unbalanced* path is an edge-simple path $z_1, \cdots, z_k$ in $\mathcal{H}$ with $z_1 = x$ such that for each row (resp., column) z_i with $1 \le i \le k - 1$, the edge d between z_i and z_{i+1} satisfies $\sigma(d) = 0$ or -1 (resp., $\sigma(d) = 0$ or $+1$).

By Theorem 8, to construct F', it suffices to find a suitable minimal edge cut Y of $\mathcal{H}$ with $Y \subset EA(F)$. Let U be a maximal connected vertex subset of $\mathcal{H}$ such that $x \in U$, $y \notin U$, and for each $z \in U$ incident with U^c (the set of vertices not in U), U contains an unbalanced path from x to z. (If a vertex in U is not incident with U^c, it may not be reachable from x via unbalanced paths.) Let Y be the set of edges in $\mathcal{H}$ between U and U^c.

Claim 1 *U exists and Y is a minimal edge cut of $\mathcal{H}$.*

Proof. The existence of U follows from the fact that $\{x\}$ has the required properties of U. Next, because $x \in U$ and $y \notin U$, Y is an edge cut of $\mathcal{H}$. To prove its minimality by contradiction, by Fact 6, assume that $\mathcal{H} - Y$ has at least three connected components U, W_1, W_2 with $y \in W_1$. Because the edges of Y are between U and U^c, the graph $\mathcal{H}$ has no edge between W_1 and W_2 but has at least one edge between U and W_2. Thus, $U \cup W_2$ has the required properties of U, contradicting the maximality of U.

Claim 2 *For each row (resp., column) vertex $z \in U$, $\sigma(d) = +1$ (resp., -1) for all edges d between z and U^c.*

Proof. By symmetry, only the row case is proved here. To prove it by contradiction, let d be an edge in $\mathcal{H}$ between z and a column vertex $w \in U^c$ with $\sigma(d) = 0$ or -1. By Step 1, U contains an unbalanced path P from x to z. By the value of $\sigma(d)$, the path Q formed by P and d is an unbalanced path. If $w \neq y$, then the set $\{w\} \cup U$ has the required properties of U, contradicting the maximality of U. Otherwise, $w = y$. Let C be the direction-blindly labeled cycle formed by Q and e with e labeled $+1$. Together with its edge labels from C, the path Q is considered an assignment to the suppressed cells of T in the same way C is. Then, $F(C) = c + F(Q)$, where c is the coefficient of e in F. Because $\mathcal{H}$ is a bipartite graph and Q is an unbalanced path, for each edge d' in Q, if d' is labeled $+1$ (resp., -1) in C, then $\sigma(d') \geq 0$ (resp., ≤ 0). Thus, $F(Q) \geq 0$ and $F(C) \geq c > 0$. By Lemma 7, F is not a linear invariant, reaching a contradiction.

The next claim finishes the proof of Lemma 10.

Claim 3 $F' = \sum_{d \in Y} \sigma(d) \cdot d$ *satisfies Lemma 10.*

Proof. To prove that F' is a linear invariant, let $d_1, \cdots, d_h$ be the edges in Y with $e = d_1$. For each d_i with $2 \leq i \leq h$, let v_i and w_i be the endpoints of d_i in U and U^c, respectively. Let P_i be an edge-simple path in U between x and v_i. Let Q_i be an edge-simple path in U^c between y and w_i. Let C_i be the direction-blindly labeled cycle formed by d_1, P_i, d_i, Q_i with d_1 labeled $+1$. To evaluate $F(C_i)$, assume by symmetry that v_i is a row vertex. Then, because $\mathcal{H}$ is a bipartite graph, d_i is labeled -1 in C_i. By Claim 2, the coefficient of d_i in F' is $+1$. Because $EA(F'')$ and C_i share only d_1 and d_i, $F''(C_i) = 1 \cdot 1 + 1 \cdot (-1) = 0$. Thus, by Lemma 7, F' is a linear invariant of T. Next by Claim 2, $EA(F') = Y$. By Claim 1 and Theorem 8 F' is a minimal unitary linear invariant. Because F is not minimal, $EA(F')$ is a proper subset of $EA(F)$. The sign property of the coefficients of F' follows from the definition of $\sigma(d)$.

4.2 Decomposition Theorems

Theorem 11 (the Minimal Decomposition Theorem).
For each nonzero linear invariant F, T has unitary minimal linear invariants $F_1, \cdots, F_k$ with the properties below:

1. *$F = \sum_{i=1}^{k} c_i \cdot F_i$ for some $c_i > 0$.*
2. *$EA(F) = \cup_{i=1}^{k} EA(F_i)$.*
3. *For each F_i and each $e \in EA(F_i)$, the coefficients of e in F and F_i are either both positive or both negative.*

If F is unitary, then $F_1, \cdots, F_i$ have two additional properties:

4. *$F = \sum_{i=1}^{k} F_i$.*
5. *$EA(F_1), \cdots, EA(F_k)$ are pairwise disjoint.*

Proof. By means of recursive decomposition, it suffices to show that if F is not minimal, there are two linear invariants F_1, F' with the first five properties below and that if F is unitary, F_1 and F' also have the other three properties.

1. F_1 is unitary and minimal. F' is nonzero.
2. $F = c_1 \cdot F_1 + F'$ for some $c_1 > 0$.
3. $EA(F_1)$ and $EA(F')$ are proper subsets of $EA(F)$.
4. $EA(F) = EA(F_1) \cup EA(F')$.
5. For each $e \in EA(F_1)$ (resp., $EA(F')$), the coefficients of e in F and F_1 (resp., F') are either both positive or both negative.
6. F' is unitary.
7. $F = F_1 + F'$.
8. $EA(F_1) \cap EA(F') = \emptyset$.

F_1, F' and c_1 are constructed as follows. Let F_1 be a unitary minimal linear invariant of T that satisfies Lemma 10. Let $d_1, \cdots, d_k$ be the edges in $EA(F_1)$. Let $a_1, \cdots, a_k$ be their coefficients in F. Let $b_1, \cdots, b_k$ be those in F_1. Without loss of generality, assume that $\frac{a_1}{b_1} = \min\{\frac{a_1}{b_1}, \cdots, \frac{a_k}{b_k}\}$. Let $c_1 = \frac{a_1}{b_1}$ and $F' = F - c_1 \cdot F_1$. The eight desired properties follow from Lemma 10 and can be easily verified.

Theorem 12 (graphic structures of linear invariants).
For each linear invariant F of T, $EA(F)$ is a union of basic sets of $\mathcal{H}$. For each union Y of basic sets of $\mathcal{H}$, there is a linear invariant F of T with $EA(F) = Y$.

Proof. The first statement follows from Theorems 11 and 8. To prove the second statement, let $Y = Y_1 \cup \cdots \cup Y_k \cup \{d_1, \cdots, d_h\}$, where $Y_1, \cdots, Y_k$ are distinct minimal edge cuts of strongly connected components of $\mathcal{H}$ and $d_1, \cdots, d_h$ are distinct edges not in the strongly connected components of $\mathcal{H}$. By Theorem 1, each d_j is an invariant cell. By Theorem 8, for each Y_i, there is a minimal linear invariant F_i with $EA(F_i) = Y_i$. Let $F = \sum_{i=1}^{k} 2^i \cdot F_i + \sum_{j=1}^{h} d_j$. Then, F is a linear invariant. $EA(F) = Y$ because the coefficients of the right hand side of F are assigned in such a way that no edges in Y are cancelled.

A *positive* linear invariant is one with at least one nonzero term whose coefficients are all nonnegative.

Corollary 13 (decomposition of positive linear invariants).

1. *For every positive linear invariant F of T, there exist sum minimal linear invariants $F_1, \cdots, F_k$ of T such that $F = \sum_{i=1}^{k} c_i \cdot F_i$ for some $c_i > 0$ and $EA(F) = \cup_{i=1}^{k} EA(F_i)$.*
2. *For every positive linear invariant F of T, $EA(F)$ is a union of bipartite basic sets of $\mathcal{H}$. For each nonempty union Y of bipartite basic sets of $\mathcal{H}$, there is a positive linear invariant F of T with $EA(F) = Y$.*

Proof. Statement 1 is a corollary of Theorem 11. The proof of Statement 2 is similar to that of Theorem 12.

Corollary 14 (decompositions of unitary and sum linear invariants).

1. *For every nonzero unitary (resp., sum) linear invariant F of $\mathcal{T}$, $\mathcal{T}$ has unitary (resp., sum) minimal linear invariants $F_1, \cdots, F_k$ such that $F = \sum_{i=1}^{k} F_i$ and $EA(F_1), \cdots, EA(F_k)$ form a partition of $EA(F)$.*
2. *For every unitary (resp., sum) linear invariant F of $\mathcal{T}$, $EA(F)$ is a disjoint union of basic (resp., bipartite basic) sets of $\mathcal{H}$. For each disjoint union Y of basic (resp., bipartite basic) sets of $\mathcal{H}$, there is a unitary (resp., sum) linear invariant F of $\mathcal{T}$ with $EA(F) = Y$.*

Proof. Similar to the proof of Corollary 13.

5 Detection of Row and Column Linear Invariants

A *row* (resp., *column*) linear invariant on a row (resp., column) is one whose variables in the nonzero terms are suppressed cells in that row (resp., column). The discussion below focuses on row linear invariants. A discussion for column linear invariants can be obtained by symmetry. Let R be a row of $\mathcal{T}$. An edge set of $\mathcal{H}$ is *centered at R* if its edges are all adjacent with R. Note that a linear invariant F of $\mathcal{T}$ is a row linear invariant on R if and only if $EA(F)$ is centered at R.

Fact 15 *Every centered basic set is bipartite. Moreover, an edge set of $\mathcal{H}$ centered at R is a basic set if and only if it consists of either an edge not in any $\mathcal{H}_i$ or all the edges incident with R in a biconnected component of some $\mathcal{H}_i$. Consequently, if two basic sets of $\mathcal{H}$ centered at R are distinct, then they are disjoint.*

Corollary 16 (characterizations of row linear invariants).

1. *For each basic set Y of $\mathcal{H}$ centered at R, there is a row minimal linear invariant F of $\mathcal{T}$ on R with $EA(F) = Y$. A row linear invariant F of $\mathcal{T}$ on R is minimal if and only if $EA(F)$ is a basic set of $\mathcal{H}$ centered at R.*
2. *Every row minimal linear invariant is a multiple of a sum linear invariant.*
3. *For each nonzero row linear invariant F of $\mathcal{T}$ on R, there exist sum minimal linear invariants $F_1, \cdots, F_k$ of $\mathcal{T}$ on R such that F is a linear combination of $F_1, \cdots, F_k$ and $EA(F_1), \cdots, EA(F_k)$ form a partition of $EA(F)$.*
4. *For each row linear invariant F of $\mathcal{T}$ on R, $EA(F)$ is a disjoint union of basic sets of $\mathcal{H}$ centered at R. For each union Y of basic sets of $\mathcal{H}$ centered at R, there is a sum linear invariant F of $\mathcal{T}$ on R with $EA(F) = Y$.*

Proof. This corollary follows from Fact 15 and Theorems 8, 9, 11 and 12.

Corollary 16 has important algorithmic implications for the problem of detecting linear invariants. It shows that the row and column linear invariants have very regular decompositions and that the row and column minimal linear invariants provide all explicit knowledge about the row and column linear invariants. Also, by Fact 15, the number of row and column minimal linear invariants of $\mathcal{T}$ is linear in the size of $\mathcal{H}$. (In contrast, there may be an exponential number of general minimal linear invariants.)

33

Theorem 17. *Given $\mathcal{H}$, the row and column minimal linear invariants of T can be found in linear time in the size of $\mathcal{H}$, i.e., the total number of suppressed cells, rows and columns in T.*

Proof. By Corollary 16 and Fact 15, the desired invariants can be found with linear-time algorithms for strong connectivity and biconnectivity [1], [4].

Acknowledgements

The author wishes to thank Dan Gusfield for his help and encouragement.

References

1. A. V. Aho, J. E. Hopcroft, and J. D. Ullman. *The Design and Analysis of Computer Algorithms.* Addison-Wesley, Reading, MA, 1974.
2. C. Berge. *Graphs.* North-Holland, New York, NY, second revised edition, 1985.
3. G. J. Brackstone, L. Chapman, and G. Sande. Protecting the confidentiality of individual statistical records in Canada. In *Proceedings of the Conference of the European Statisticians 31st Plenary Session, Geneva,* 1983.
4. T. H. Cormen, C. L. Leiserson, and R. L. Rivest. *Introduction to Algorithms.* MIT Press, Cambridge, MA, 1991.
5. L. H. Cox. Disclosure analysis and cell suppression. In *Proceedings of the American Statistical Association, Social Statistics Section,* pages 380–382, 1975.
6. L. H. Cox. Suppression methodology in statistics disclosure. In *Proceedings of the American Statistical Association, Social Statistics Section,* pages 750–755, 1977.
7. L. H. Cox. Automated statistical disclosure control. In *Proceedings of the American Statistical Association, Survey Research Method Section,* pages 177–182, 1978.
8. L. H. Cox. Suppression methodology and statistical disclosure control. *Journal of the American Statistical Association, Theory and Method Section,* 75:377–385, 1980.
9. L. H. Cox and G. Sande. Techniques for preserving statistical confidentiality. In *Proceedings of the 42nd Session of the International Statistical Institute.* the International Association of Survey Statisticians, 1979.
10. D. Denning. *Cryptography and Data Security.* Addison-Wesley, Reading, MA, 1982.
11. D. Gusfield. A graph theoretic approach to statistical data security. *SIAM Journal on Computing,* 17:552–571, 1988.
12. M. Y. Kao and D. Gusfield. Efficient detection and protection of information in cross tabulated tables I: Linear invariant test. *SIAM Journal on Discrete Mathematics,* 6(3):460–476, 1993.
13. G. Sande. Towards automated disclosure analysis for establishment based statistics. Technical report, Statistics Canada, 1977.
14. G. Sande. A theorem concerning elementary aggregations in simple tables. Technical report, Statistics Canada, 1978.
15. G. Sande. Automated cell suppression to preserve confidentiality of business statistics. *Statistical Journal of the United Nations,* 2:33–41, 1984.
16. G. Sande. Confidentiality and polyhedra, an analysis of suppressed entries on cross tabulations. Technical report, Statistics Canada, unknown date.

Parallel Maximal Matching on Minimal Vertex Series Parallel Digraphs

Luca Baffi and Rossella Petreschi

Department of Computer Science, University "La Sapienza"
Via Salaria 113 - 00198 Rome, Italy

Abstract. In this paper is presented a parallel algorithm to find a maximal matching on a minimal vertex series parallel dag. The algorithm requires $O(m)$ processors and runs in $O(\log n)$ parallel time on a PRAM-EREW model of computation. This algorithm improves of a factor $\log^2 n$ the parallel time of the general algorithm when it is specified to this class of graphs. Also the number of processors decreases from $O(n + m)$ to $O(m)$.

1 Introduction

It is well known that, on a sequential model of computation, the problem of finding a maximum or a maximal matching for general graphs can be solved in polynomial time. Polynomialty of the former problem is obtained via Edmonds algorithm or any of its descendants , while polinomialty of the latter is essentially trivial by the greedy algorithm [18].

The situation is quite different when one moves to a parallel setting. It is not at all clear how efficiently parallelize Edmonds algorithm, in fact the outstanding open question regarding matching in parallel is whether or not maximum matching belongs to NC. Nowadays the known NC algorithms for maximum matching use randomization and tools from linear algebra. Deterministic algorithms for this problem are or simply not polylog time or polylog algorithms specified to some particular classes of graphs [14, 19].

Also the simpler maximal matching problem is not easy in a parallel model of computation, even if it is shown to be in NC. The best known algorithm is due to Israeli and Shiloach and works in $O(\log^3 n)$ time on the CRCW PRAM with $O(n+m)$ processors [14, 19]. At th best of our knowledge, there is only a sketched result of Datta and Sen [5] that reaches the same cost on the weakest PRAM model of computation, the EREW model. Moreover, in 1993 Luby developed an algorithm that works on a EREW PRAM in $O(\log^5 n)$ time using $O(n + m)$ processors. This algorithm has a cost greater than the previouses algorithms, but it is important for the new techniques presented which allow to remove randomness from randomized NC algorithms, without a blowup in the number of processors [11].

In this paper we present a parallel algorithm which uses $O(m)$ processors on a EREW PRAM model of computation and requires $O(\log n)$ time to find a maximal matching on a minimal vertex series-parallel dag. This class of digraphs was introduced in 1977 as a model of a particular problem of scheduling [10, 12] and it is strictly correlated with the class of edge series-parallel multidigraphs, introduced in 1965 by Duffin [6] as a mathematical model of electrical networks.

Even if for the edge series parallel multidigraphs it exists an NC maximum matching parallel algorithm [9] nothing it is possible to say about maximum matching on MVSP dags.

2 Basic definitions

Throughout this paper we follow the standard graph terminology of [2] and [13].

Definition 1 [16]. A minimal vertex series parallel dag, MVSP, is defined recursively as follows:

1- The dag having a single vertex and no edges is MVSP.

2- If $G_1 = (V_1, E_1)$ and $G_2 = (V_2, E_2)$ are two MVSP dags, so are the dags constructed by each of the following operations:

(a) Parallel composition: $G_p = (V_1 \cup V_2, E_1 \cup E_2)$

(b) Series composition: $G_s = (V_1 \cup V_2, E_1 \cup E_2 \cup (T_1 \times S_2))$, where T_1 is the set of sinks of G_1 and S_2 is the set of sources of G_2. (See Fig. 1.)

A dag is transitive if for any two vertices v and w such that there is a path from v to w, either $v = w$ or (v, w) is an edge. The transitive closure G_c of a dag G is a dag such that (v, w) is an edge of G_c if and only if there is a path in G from v to w. An edge (v, w) in a dag is redundant if there is a path from v to w which avoids (v, w). A dag with no redundant edges is minimal. The transitive reduction of a dag G is the unique minimal dag having the same transitive closure as G.

Definition 2 [16]. A dag is vertex series parallel, VSP, if and only if its transitive reduction is MVSP.

Definition 3 [16]. An edge series parallel multidigraph, ESP, is defined recursively as follows:

1- A digraph consisting of two vertices joined by a single edge is ESP.

2- If G_1 and G_2 are ESP multidigraphs, so are the multidigraphs constructed by each of the following operations:

(a) Two-terminal parallel composition: Identify the source of G_1 with the source of G_2 and the sink of G_1 with the sink of G_2.

(b) Two-terminal series composition: Identify the sink of G_1 with the source of G_2 (See Fig. 2).

Remark. We highlight that an ESP is a weakly connected acyclic multidigraph with a single source and a single sink.

Definition 4 [8]. The line digraph of a digraph G is the digraph $L(G)$ having a vertex $f(e)$ for each edge e of G and an edge $(f(e_1), f(e_2))$ for each pair of edges e_1, e_2 in G of the form $e_1 = (u, v)$ and $e_2 = (v, w)$.

The following theorem strictly ties the classes of graphs introduced in Def.1 and in Def.2.

Theorem 1 ([16]). *An acyclic multidigraph with a single source and a single sink is ESP if and only if its line digraph is a MVSP dag.*

The multidigraph in Fig. 2 is the line digraph of the dag in Fig. 1.

Definition 5. The reduce graph $R(G) = (V, E_1)$ of a given multidigraph $G = (V, E)$ is the graph obtained from G substituting each multiedge with the corresponding edge.

Definition 6. Given a digraph G, an unimodal spanning tree T is a spanning tree such that the subgraph induced by the set of the edges in $G \setminus T$ is a forest of trees when it is considered with the opposite orientation.

In the following, we'll call the set of the edges in $G \setminus T$ back-edges. It is to notice that an unimodal spanning tree is a tree in which no pair of back-edges share a start-point.

Definition 7. Given a graph $G(V, E)$ an edge matching , EM, is a subset of $E \times E$ such that:
  - each $\epsilon_i \in EM$ is a pair $(x, y), (y, t)$ with $(x, y), (y, t) \in E$;
  - doesn't exist any edge in E that belongs to two different elements in EM.

Remark. An edge matching of a graph $G(V, E)$ is the vertex matching of the line digraph $L(G)$.

Definition 8 [8, 16]. A given digraph $G(V, E)$ is complete bipartite composite, CBC, if the edges are partitionable in classes B_i such that:
  - each subgraph induced by a B_i is complete bipartite;
  - it exists a unique class $B_h(v)$ containing all the edges $(v, x) \in E$, for each $v \in V$ with $d^+(v) > 0$;
  - it exists a unique class $B_t(v)$ containing all the edges $(x, v) \in E$, for each $v \in V$ with $d^-(v) > 0$.

Theorem 2 ([16]). *A minimal vertex series parallel digraph is complete bipartite composite.*

In Fig. 3 the complete bipartite components of a MVSP digraph are in evidence.

Theorem 3 ([8]). *Given an MVSP dag G, there exists an unique ESP multidigraph G_1 such that $L(G_1) = G$.*

3 The algorithm

In this section we present a parallel algorithm to find a maximal matching of a MVSP dag. It works on a EREW PRAM model of computation and has a cost $O(m \log n)$, where n and m are the number of vertices and edges in the dag, respectively. In order to make clear the exposition, we first sketch our algorithm and then we present a detailed description of it.

3.1 High-level view of the algorithm

The input of the algorithm is a MVSP dag $G = (V, E)$ represented by a list of edges and with the vertices identified by integer values. The algorithm is organised in the following four phases:

a) Construction of $GESP = (V', E')$, the ESP multidigraph such that $L(GESP) = G$.
 a1) Locate $\{B_1, B_2, ..., B_k\}$ the complete bipartite components of the MVSP dag (i.e. the vertices of $GESP$);
 a2) Compute $GESP$, known $\{B_1, B_2, ..., B_k\}$.

b) Determination of T, an unimodal spanning multitree for $GESP$.
 b1) Computation of $R(GESP)$, the reduce graph of the multigraph $GESP$;
 b2) Computation of $R(T)$, an unimodal spanning tree for $R(GESP)$;
 b3) T is derived from $R(T)$.

c) Computation of MEM, a maximal edge matching on $GESP$. MEM is the union of the maximal edge matching computed on the following sets, in the order:
 c1) all the pair , (e_i, e_j) , of adjacent edges such that e_i is a tree-edge and e_j is a back-edge, respect to T.
 c2) all the remained tree-edges;
 c3) all the remained back-edges;
 c4) all the remained edges.

d) Derivation from MEM of a maximal vertex matching for G.

3.2 The algorithm in detail

a) Construction of $GESP = (V', E')$: the ESP multidigraph such that $L(GESP) = G$

Definition 9. Given a vertex $v \in V$, let us define $m_{in}(v)$ and $m_{out}(v)$ as $m_{in}(v) = \min\{x \in V \mid (x, v) \in E\}$ and $m_{out}(v) = \min\{x \in V \mid (v, x) \in E\}$. We call minimum the edge (x, y) such that $m_{out}(x) = y$ and $m_{in}(y) = x$.

Remark. The set of the minimum edges corresponds, one by one, to the set of complete bipartite components. Moreover to identify each component it is sufficient to consider only one of the end-points of the minimum edge. In the following, we will speak about the source point. (in Fig. 1, the bold edges are the minimal edges)

To complete step a1), we need to know for each vertex and for each edge the component they belong to. From definition 8, it is sufficient to compute $B_h(v)$ and $B_t(v)$ for each v and from definition 9, we derive $B_h(v) = m_{in}(m_{out}(v))$ and $B_t(v) = m_{in}(v)$.

Now we have to execute the last part of phase a), the computation of $GESP = (V', E')$. Our construction is the same of that in the proof of theorem 3 (see [8]).

Let $V' = \{B_\alpha, B_1, B_2, ..., B_k, B_\omega\}$, where $B_1, B_2, ..., B_k$, are the bipartite complete components of G, while B_α and B_ω are two added vertices working as source and sink in $GESP$, respectively. For each vertex $v \in V$, we insert an edge, (B_i, B_j), in $GESP$ according to the following rules:
- if v is an isolated vertex, the edge is (B_α, B_ω);
- if v is a source, but not a sink, the edge is $(B_\alpha, B_h(v))$;
- if v is a sink, but not a source, the edge is $(B_t(v), B_\omega)$;
- if v is neither a sink nor a source, the edge is $(Bt(v), Bh(v))$.

b) Determination of T , an unimodal spanning multitree for $GESP$

Definition 10. Given two edges in E', (u, v) and (r, s), we say that (u, v) precedes (r, s) if $(u < r) \vee (u = r \wedge v < s)$.

Let us order the edges in GESP according to the definition 10. Two edges with the same start-points will be adjacent in the sorted list. Therefore, in order to reduce the multigraph $GESP$ in a graph $R(GESP)$, it is sufficient to insert in $R(GESP)$ each edge of the ordered list different from its predecessor. Obviously, the first edge in the list is in $R(GESP)$. Let us classify the edges of $R(GESP)$ according to the in- and out-degree in the following way:
- (u, v) is an open-edge, if $d^+(u) > 1$ and $d^-(v) = 1$;
- (u, v) is a close-edge, if $d^+(u) = 1$ and $d^-(v) > 1$;
- (u, v) is a jump-edge, if $d^+(u) > 1$ and $d^-(v) > 1$;
- (u, v) is a link-edge, if $d^+(u) = 1$ and $d^-(v) = 1$.

The building of the unimodal spanning tree of $R(GESP)$ passes through the construction of a general spanning tree. This is obtained first deleting all the jump-edges and then, for each vertex v, eliminating all the close-edges entering v, except one. The fact that this subgraph is a spanning tree derives from the following considerations:
- For each vertex of the subgraph there is exactly one edge entering it according to the choose of the edges to delete.
- The subgraph is acyclic, because $R(GESP)$ is acyclic.
- The subgraph is weakly connected: this is the more tricky property to prove and it is based on the following theorem:

Theorem 3 *Let $G = (V, E)$ be an ESP digraph, and (u, v) an edge of G. (u, v) is a jump-edge of G if and only if it is in parallel with a subgraph ESP $G^* \subseteq G$.*

Proof. The necessity is trivial. For the sufficiency, let us suppose (u, v) serially composed with an ESP subgraph $G^* \subseteq G$. Then either $d^+(u) = 1$ or $d^-(v) = 1$ in G, contradicting the hypothesis that (u, v) is a jump-edge. □

¿From the theorem follows that deleting a jump edge doesn't change the weakly connectivity of the digraph, because the parallel connection guarantees the existence of another path from u to v.

Now to complete step b2), we have to transform the spanning tree just derived in an unimodal one, i.e. we have to change each back-edge of a group with the same start-point (except one, at most!) with some tree-edge. It is to notice that this back-edges are, for construction, jump-edges.

The procedure "unimodal" is the following:
- compute $l(v)$: the level of the vertex v on the tree; for each vertex v, let us consider all the jump-edges (u, v) and let u' be the vertex at the minimum level between all the start-points u;
- change (u', v) with the tree-edge with end-point v.

Finally to obtain T from $R(T)$ we have only to consider that all the edges in $GESP$ maintain in T the characteristic to be tree-edges or back-edges.

In Fig. 4 is represented the generation of the unimodal spanning multitree T.

c) Computation of MEM: a maximal edge matching on $GESP$

Definition 11. A star graph is a directed acyclic multigraph, $G(V, E)$, in which it is possible to identify a point $c \in V$, neither sink nor source, that is either start-point or end-point of each edge in E (see Fig. 7). A star graph with only one source is called star bunch (see Fig. 8); If it has also only one sink it is called falling star (see Fig. 9). In the following, we call in-edges and out-edges the edges entering or leaving the centre of the stars, respectively.

Definition 12. A directed acyclic multigraph G is said star composite if its edges are partitionable in classes such that every subgraph induced by one of these classes is a star. G is said isolated star composite if each pair of stars in it is vertex disjoint.

Previously, we announced that this phase has to compute a maximal edge matching on four different sets of edges. Actually we notice that all the graphs induced by these sets of edges are star composite graphs, therefore phase c) is restricted to compute a MEM on star graphs.

For each of the four sets we may derive, in the order, the following star composite graphs:
- for each vertex v who has at least one entering tree-edge and at least one leaving back- edge, the subgraph induced by all the tree-edges entering in v and all the back-edges leaving v is a falling star.

- for each vertex v belonging to an odd level in T, the subgraph induced by all the in- and out-edges of v is a star bunch. The same thing is true for each vertex v belonging to an even level in T.

- for each vertex v belonging to an odd level in $E' \setminus T$, the subgraph induced by all the in- and out-edges of v is a star bunch. The same thing is true for each vertex v belonging to an even level in $E' \setminus T$.

- the subgraph induced by all the remained edges is an isolated star composite graph in which the in-edges are back-edges and the out-edges are tree-edges.

To compute MEM for each star, it is sufficient to number both the in- and the out-edges in increasing order and then matching the edges with the same number. In Fig. 6 is pointed out the computation of MEM.

d) Derivation, from MEM, of a maximal vertex matching for G. It follows from theorem 1 and definition 7.

4 Correctness and complexity of the algorithm

In this section we prove that the algorithm derives correctly a maximal matching for a MVSP dag and then we calculate its cost analysing the implementation of the single steps.

We start by showing that each phase works correctly. For phase a) this is guaranteed by the existence and unicity of $GESP$ [Th.3]. In order to prove the correctness of phase b), it remains to show that the "unimodal" procedure generates an unimodal spanning tree for $R(GESP)$.

Theorem 4 *The "unimodal" procedure generates an unimodal spanning tree.*

Proof. First of all we have to prove that considering only jump-edges it isn't a restrictive choice. This derives from the fact that the back-edges are either close-edges or jump-edges and therefore if $d^+(v) > 1$, all the back-edges leaving v must be jump-edges.

Now we have to prove that at the end of "unimodal" procedure there is only one back- edge leaving each vertex. This implies to prove that:

- each tree-edge changed in the procedure is a close-edge;

- for each vertex u there is almost one jump-edge leaving u that is not selected in the procedure.

Let (u, v) be a tree-edge. The first point follows from the fact that $dg^-(v) > 1$ and that (u, v) can not be, for construction, a jump-edge.

Now we have to prove the last point. Let $G^* \subseteq GESP$ be the minimal subgraph ESP that contains all the jump-edges leaving u. Obviously u is the source of G^*, let v be the sink. We prove that almost the jump-edge (u, v), if it exists, can not be selected. In fact let (u, w) be another not selected jump-edge of G^* and let (u', w) be a jump-edge with $level(u') < level(u)$. But (u', w) cannot belong both to G^* (because u is the source) and to $G \setminus G^*$ because the operations of composition act only on terminals. $\square$

The following theorem guarantees the correctness of the phase c) of the algorithm:

Theorem 5 *MEM, the edge matching on GESP generated in phase c) of the algorithm, is a maximal edge matching.*

Proof. MEM is an edge matching by construction. To prove that this matching is maximal, it is sufficient to show that at the end of phase c) there isn't any pair of adjacent edges in *GESP*. This derives from the fact that in the last step of phase c) the subgraph induced by all the edges not yet in the matching is an isolated star composite graph with all the in-edges of type back and all the out-edges of type tree. □

Now we are ready to state the following theorem:

Theorem 6 *The algorithm of the previous section 3 correctly generates a maximal matching for a MVSP dags.*

Proof. It follows from the previous theorems and considerations, being correctness of the phase d) trivial. □

Theorem 7 *The algorithm presented in section 3 finds a maximal matching of a MVSP dag on a EREW-PRAM with $O(m)$ processors in order $O(\log n)$ time.*

Proof. The outline of the computation of the cost of the algorithm will be given according to the four phases detailed in the previous section. We start from the analysis of the cost of the two steps in phase a).

The cost of the computation of the CBC components is due to the sum of the following three operations:

- For each $v \in V$, the computation of the values $m_{in}(v)$ ($m_{out}(v)$) is done through a lexicographic order of the edges respect to the end-point (start-point). In the ordered sequence of the edges, we select the start-point (end-point) of the first edge with end-point i (out-point i), for all $i = 1..n$. With m processors, the sort requires $O(\log n)$ time [4], while the selection needs constant time, therefore the cost of this operation is $O(m \log n)$.

- Each edge $(v, w) \in E$ needs to know if it is minimum or not. From the definition 9, we derive that this analysis requires constant time on a CREW-PRAM with m processors, therefore in our model of computation will need $O(\log n)$ time.

- The last operation concerns the computation of $B_h(v)$ and $B_t(v)$ that is obviously constant on a CREW-PRAM, with m processors. The time required for the computation of *GESP* known $\{B_1, B_2, ..., B_k\}$ is constant on our model of computation.

In the phase b), the only operation different from those of phase a) is the computation of the vertices' level. This may be done with the Euler tour technique in $O(\log n)$ time (see [1]) on an EREW-PRAM with n processors. Then also the whole cost of the phase b) is not greater than $O(m \log n)$.

In phase c), in order to number both the in- and the out-edges in increasing order and then matching the edges for each star, we may work in the following way:

- first of all we order all the in- (out-) edges in lexicographic order respect the end-points (start-point);

- then we locate all the different sets of edges characterised with the same end-point (start- point);

- at this moment, on each set of edges, we number the edges by prefix sums technique and we associate the in-edges and out-edges, of each star, with the same number.

Prefix sum can be done in $O(\log n)$ time on our model of computation [3], therefore the whole phase c) has a cost not greater than $O(m \log n)$.

Finally the phase d) is obviously constant. □

5   Conclusions and open problems

In this paper we present a new algorithm to find a maximal matching on a MVSP dags. This algorithm improves of a factor $\log^2 n$ the general algorithm when it is specified to this class of graphs. Also the number of processors decreases from $O(n + m)$ to $O(m)$. But, in spite of it, this algorithm isn't optimum because its cost is $O(m \log n)$ against $O(m)$ time complexity of the serial algorithm. To see if this lower bounds will be reached remains an open problem.

Another problem, that seems to the authors much more complex than the previous one, is to find an algorithm for maximal matching on a VSP graph. In fact it is impossible to extend the algorithm of this paper to the class of VSP, because the subgraph induced by all the redundant edges may be an arbitrary graph.

Finally, at the best of our knowledge, it doesn't exist any NC maximum matching algorithm for MVSP or VSP digraphs.

References

1. S.Baase, Introduction to parallel connectivity, list ranking and Euler tour tecniques, (see [15]), (1993), pp. 61-114.
2. C. Berge, Graphs and Hypergraphs, North-Holland (1970).
3. G.E.Blelloch, Prefix sums and their applications , (see [15]), (1993), pp.35-60.
4. R.Cole, Parallel merge sort , (see [15]), (1993), pp. 453-494.
5. A. K. Datta, R. K. Sen, An efficient Parallel Algorithm for Maximal Matching, INCS 634, (1993), pp. 813-814.
6. R. J. Duffin, Topology of series-parallel networks, J. Mathematical Analysis and Applications 10, (1965), pp. 303-318.
7. Gimbel, J.W.Kennedy and L.V.Quintas, Quo vadis, graph theory?, Elsevier Science Publishers,N.Y. (1993).
8. F. Harary and R. Norman, Some properties of line-digraphs, Rendiconti del Circolo Matematico Palermo, Vol 9, 1960, pp. 149-163.

43

9. X. He and Y.Yesha, Binary tree algebraic computation and parallel algorithms for simple graphs, Journal of Agorithms , Vol 9, 1988, pp. 92-113.
10. E. L. Lawler, Sequencing jobs to minimize total weighted completion time subject to precedence constraints, Annals of Discrete Math., Vol 2, (1978), pp. 75-90.
11. M. Luby, Removing randomness in parallel computation without a processor penalty, Journal of Computer and System Sciences, Vol 47(2), (1993), pp. 250-286.
12. C. L. Monma, and J.B. Sidney, A general algorithm for optimal job sequencing with series-parallel constraints, Math. of Operations Research, Vol 4, (1977), 215-224.
13. C.H. Papadimitrou and K. Steiglitz, Combinatorial optimization: algorithm and complexity, Prentice Hall, Inc. Englewood Cliffs, New Jersey 1982.
14. M.D.Plummer, Matching and vertex packing: how "hard" are they?, (see [7]), (1993), pp. 275-312.
15. J. H. Reif, Synthesis of parallel algorithms, Morgan Kaufmann Publishers, San Mateo, California (1993).
16. J. Valdes, R.E. Tarjan and E.L. Lawler, The recognition of series parallel digraphs, SIAM Journal of Computation , Vol 11, no 2 , 1982, pp. 298-313
17. J. Van Leeuwen, Handbook of Theorical Computer Science,Vol A: Algorithms and Complexity, Elsevier Science Publishers , Amsterdam (1990).
18. J. Van Leeuwen, Graph algorithms, (see [17]), (1990), pp.527-631.
19. V.V.Vazirani, Parallel graph matching, (see [15]), (1993), pp.783-811.

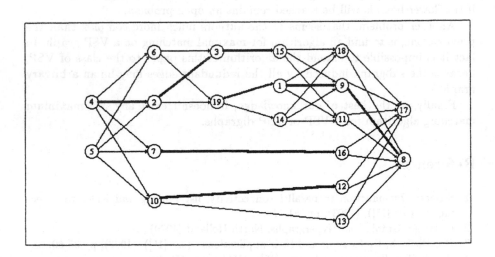

Fig. 1. An MVSP digraph.

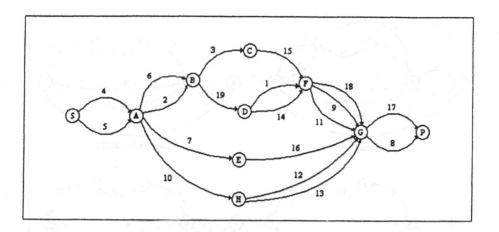

Fig. 2. An ESP multidigraph.

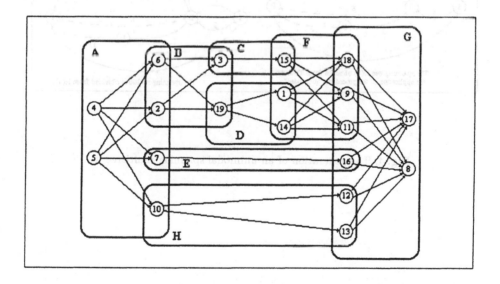

Fig. 3. The complete bipartite components of an MVSP dag.

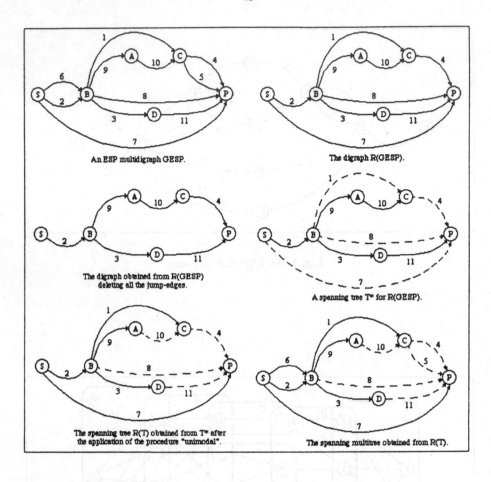

An ESP multidigraph GESP.

The digraph R(GESP).

The digraph obtained from R(GESP) deleting all the jump-edges.

A spanning tree T* for R(GESP).

The spanning tree R(T) obtained from T* after the application of the procedure "unimodal".

The spanning multitree obtained from R(T).

Fig. 4. The generation of an unimodal spanning multitree T.

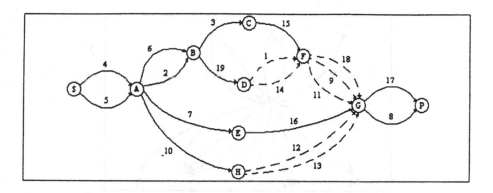

Fig. 5. An ESP multidigraph and its unimodal spanning multitree T.

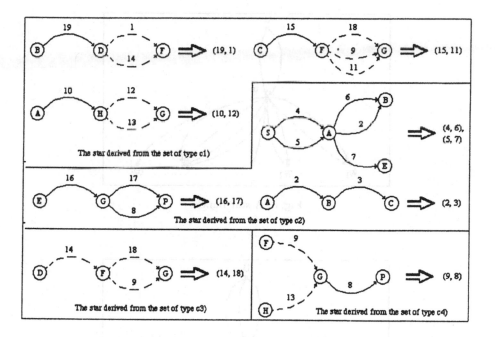

Fig. 6. The computation of MEM.

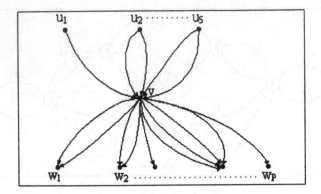

Fig. 7. A star.

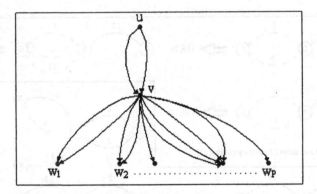

Fig. 8. A star bunch.

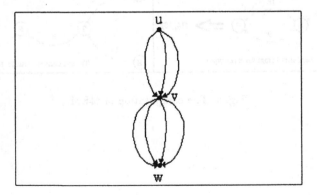

Fig. 9. A falling star.

Efficient Equality-Testing and Updating of Sets

Tak Wah Lam   Ka Hing Lee

Department of Computer Science
University of Hong Kong
Pokfulam Road, Hong Kong
Email: {twlam, khlee}@csd.hku.hk

Abstract. This paper is concerned with data structures and algorithms for managing an arbitrary number of sets such that we can dynamically update each individual set and test whether any two sets are equal. Previous schemes can support set equality-testing in constant time and an update operation (i.e. insert or delete an element) in time $O(\log^2 m)$ [7, 5] or $O(\log m \log^* m)$ [2], where m is the number of insert operations performed. Note that m is an upper bound of n, the total size of the sets, but maybe a loose one. When we have performed a lot of delete operations, having few elements left in the sets, it is natural to expect the operations to be performed faster. Yet existing schemes are not favored when n is much smaller than m. It is desirable to have a scheme whose performance is in terms of n instead of m.

This paper presents a new scheme which is more dynamic in nature and supports each insert or delete operation in $O(\log n)$ time, while maintaining the constant time complexity of set equality-testing.

1 Introduction

Many well-known data structures such as AVL trees can represent a set such that we can insert, delete, or query the membership of an element efficiently. However, if there is a collection of sets and we also want to perform equality-testing of sets, these data structures become inadequate. This paper addresses the problem of representing sets to support any sequence of the following operations efficiently.

- Create()—create a new set and return a unique set identifier;

- Insert(i, x), Delete(i, x)—insert the key x into (or delete the key x from) the set with identifier i;

- Member(i, x)—return true if the set with identifier i contains the key x, and false otherwise;

- Equal(i, j)—return true if the sets with identifiers i and j contain the same set of keys, and false otherwise.

As with previous work, we assume keys are chosen from an ordered universe. The time complexity of each operation is measured in terms of m, the number of insert operations performed starting from an empty configuration, or even better, n, the total size of the sets when the operation is performed.

Suppose we represent each set individually by an AVL tree. Membership query can be performed in $O(\log n)$ worst-case time, but set equality-testing may require linear time. In the following our primary concern is about the representation of the relationship between the sets rather than individual sets. We focus on the update and equality-testing operations.

The first non-trivial solution to the problem was given by Sassa and Goto [4] in the 70s. Their solution can perform equality-testing in $O(1)$ time, but it requires $O(n)$ time for the insert or delete operations. A few years later, several researchers succeeded in making use of randomization to improve the linear time complexity. Wegman and Carter [6] devised a randomized solution based on hashing—every operation can be done in $O(1)$ time, but set equality-testing may fail with small probability. Pugh and Tietelbaum [3] showed another randomized scheme which never errs. It supports equality-testing in $O(1)$ time and each insert or delete operation in $O(\log n)$ *expected* time.

Deterministic solutions that can support all operations in polylogarithmic time was not known until the 90s. Yellin [7] was the first to devise a deterministic scheme that supports equality-testing in $O(1)$ time and each insert or delete operation in $O(\log^2 m)$ worst-case time, where m is the number of insert operations that have been performed starting from an empty configuration. Sundar and Tarjan [5] gave another deterministic scheme requiring $O(\log m)$ *amortized* time per operation but still $O(\log^2 m)$ time in the worst case. Recently, Lam and Lee [2] have improved Yellin's scheme to support each insert or delete operation in $O(\log m \log^* m)$ time, while maintaining the constant time complexity of set equality-testing. Note that the total size of the sets (i.e. n) is not reflected in the performance of these recent schemes [7, 5, 2]. In other words, even if there are very few elements left in the sets after we have performed a large number of insert and delete operations, these schemes cannot guarantee a better performance.

In regard to the space complexity, the data structures in [7, 5] are more space efficient and require only $O(m \log m)$ space, while the solution in [2] needs $O(m^2 \log m)$ space.

In this paper we devise a new scheme which supports equality-testing in $O(1)$ time and each insert or delete operation in $O(\log n)$ worst-case time. Our scheme is more dynamic in nature and can take advantage of a decrease in the total size of the sets after a number of delete operations.

Our scheme is based on the work in [7, 2]. In particular, we note that partition trees, the main data structure used in [7], have a simple and more efficient implementation if the maximum number of sets is fixed in advance [2]. But in reality the maximum number of sets is not fixed and such a "static" partition tree will soon be found inadequate as more and more sets are created. A natural way to remedy this situation would be to rebuild a new partition tree periodically so that it adapts to the current content of the sets. This is of course not acceptable as the rebuilding process would require linear time. The most innovative idea in this paper is that a new partition tree can be constructed incrementally while we process a sequence of operations. Our scheme guarantees that the time complexity of each operation is not affected by the incremental construction of the partition tree. (We will highlight the implementation of "static" partition trees in Section 3 and will give the details of the incremental construction technique in Section 4.)

The space complexity of our scheme is $O(n^2 \log n)$. The incremental reconstruction technique mentioned above can also be applied to the original implementation of partition trees [7], producing a solution using $O(n \log n)$ space and $O(\log^2 n)$ time for each update operation.

2   Preliminaries

Initially, we do not have any set. After processing some set creation and update operations, we may have some empty sets kept in our data structures. Interestingly, if we allow a lot of empty sets to exist, the value of n (i.e. the total size of the sets) may be much smaller than the number of sets and the value of n fails to capture the actual size of the problem. To avoid such anomaly, we assume sets are always non-empty and n is always an upper bound of the number of sets. Such assumption is enforced as follows. Whenever a new set is created, we assume there is an extra insert operation to put a dummy key into the set and the size of the set becomes one. Thus a set creation operation will be treated as an update operation. Note that adding a dummy key to every set does not affect the result of set equality-testing.

We will often make use of an algorithmic trick to "conceptually" initialize all entries in an array to a certain value in constant time [1]. See Appendix I for details.

3   Static implementation of partition trees

In this section we first review the basic definition of a data structure called partition trees [7]. Then we consider the special case in which the maximum number of sets is fixed in advance. We give a simple implementation of partition trees such that it can support each insert or delete operation in $O(\log m)$ time and set equality-testing $O(1)$ time, where m is the number of insert operations performed. Such implementation has been discussed in [2].

Consider a sequence of operations in which there are m insert operations, involving k sets $S_1, S_2, \cdots, S_k$ and l distinct keys $x_1, x_2, \cdots, x_l$. Let S and X denote respectively the sets $\{S_1, S_2, \cdots, S_k\}$ and $\{x_1, x_2, \cdots, x_l\}$. A partition tree T for S is an almost complete binary tree in which every node stores a different partition of S. T has l leaves, each at a depth of either $\lceil \log l \rceil$ or $\lceil \log l \rceil + 1$ from the root, corresponding to a distinct key in X. At a node α of T, S is partitioned into at most k classes as follows:

Let $L(\alpha)$ denote the set of keys associated with the leaves of the subtree of T rooted at α. For any sets $S_i, S_j \in S$, they are put in the same class w.r.t. α if and only if they contain the same set of keys over $L(\alpha)$ (i.e. $S_i \cap L(\alpha) = S_j \cap L(\alpha)$).

Note that sets having empty intersection with $L(\alpha)$ are all put in the same class. This class, though may be empty, is always labeled by 0. Other classes are labeled by integers chosen from $\{1, 2, \cdots, k\}$. A class labeled by an integer r is referred to as α_r. Figure 1 shows an example.

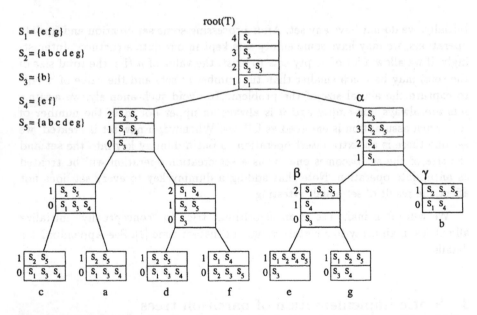

Fig. 1. A partition tree with $X = \{a, b, c, d, e, f, g\}$. At each node, S is partitioned into several classes. Note that the way S is partitioned at a node is related to that at its children, e.g. $\alpha_1 = \beta_2 \cap \gamma_0$, $\alpha_2 = \beta_1 \cap \gamma_0$, $\alpha_3 = \beta_2 \cap \gamma_1$, $\alpha_4 = \beta_0 \cap \gamma_1$.

For any internal node α of T, let $Left(\alpha)$ and $Right(\alpha)$ be the left and right child of α, respectively. Any sets S_i and S_j are in the same class w.r.t. α if and only if S_i and S_j are in the same class w.r.t. both $Left(\alpha)$ and $Right(\alpha)$. In other words, if the children of α have two classes $Left(\alpha)_p$ and $Right(\alpha)_q$ such that $Left(\alpha)_p \cap Right(\alpha)_q$ is non-empty, there must exist a class α_r at α such that $\alpha_r = Left(\alpha)_p \cap Right(\alpha)_q$.

In the rest of this section, we assume the maximum number of sets is fixed in advance to be a constant d. We show how to implement the partition tree such that the operations Insert(i, x) and Delete(i, x) can be performed in time $O(\log l)$ (i.e. $O(\log m)$).

3.1 Data Structures and Algorithms

Suppose the number of sets is fixed in advance to be at most d. Every node α of T is associated with two arrays $Class_\alpha[1..d]$ and $Count_\alpha[1..d]$. Recall that k ($\leq d$) is the number of sets created so far. For any $1 \leq i \leq k$, $Class_\alpha[i] = r$ if S_i belongs to the class α_r. For any non-empty class α_r, $Count_\alpha[r]$ stores the number of sets in α_r. Other entries in these two arrays contain the value zero.

An internal node α has additional data structures. $Intersect_\alpha[0..d, 0..d]$ is a table storing the relationship between the classes of α and the classes of its children. For any indices $p, q \leq k$, $Intersect_\alpha[p, q] = r$ if either $p = q = r = 0$, or α_r is a non-empty class at α such that $\alpha_r = Left(\alpha)_p \cap Right(\alpha)_q$; otherwise, $Intersect_\alpha[p, q]$ is said to be undefined. Note that at most $k + 1$ entries in $Intersect_\alpha$ are well defined. Also, we need some data structures to facilitate the recycling of labels of empty classes: $Largest\_Class_\alpha$ is an integer variable storing the largest class label that have ever been used to label a non-empty class and $Stack_\alpha$ is a stack keeping track of labels of empty classes that are in the range $[1, Largest\_Class_\alpha]$. Whenever we form a new class at α, we try to get a class label from $Stack_\alpha$ before we use the label $Largest\_Class_\alpha + 1$. Assigning class labels in this manner guarantees that the largest class label is always bounded by the current number of sets.

Let $Root(T)$ denote the root of T. It is obvious that two sets S_i and S_j are equal if and only if $Class_{Root(T)}[i] = Class_{Root(T)}[j]$. Thus, equality-testing can be done in constant time. To create a new set, we simply use $k+1$ as the next set identifier. Note that the new set is empty and at each node α of T, $Class[k + 1]$ stores correctly the default value zero. Then we proceed with the extra insert operation to add a dummy key into this set.

Next, we illustrate how to update the partition tree due to an insert operation. For simplicity, we only consider the case that does not involve a new key. The details of handling the general case can be found in [2].

Consider the operation Insert(i, x) where $1 \leq i \leq k$ and $x \in X$. Let α be the leaf node of T containing x. For any node γ of T, if $L(\gamma)$ does not contain x, the partitioning of sets at γ remains the same after Insert(i, x) is processed. Thus, only those nodes on the path from α to the root of T are to be updated. Below, we show that such nodes can be updated efficiently in a bottom-up manner.

Basis: The leaf node α has at most two non-empty classes: α_0 contains the sets in which x is absent and α_1 contains the others. Insert(i,x) causes the set S_i to move from α_0 to α_1.

Inductive Step: Suppose we have just updated a node β on the path from α to $Root(T)$ and, in particular, have moved S_i from a class β_p to another class β_q. Let γ and β' be respectively the parent and sibling of β. See the right figure. Without loss of generality, we assume that β is the left child of γ. At this point, let $r = Class_\gamma[i]$ and let $t = Class_{\beta'}[i]$. That is, just before Insert(i,x) is executed, S_i was in the classes γ_r and β'_t. As mentioned earlier, S_i should remain in the class β'_t. Yet, w.r.t. γ, S_i should move from γ_r to another class γ_s such that $\gamma_s = \beta_q \cap \beta'_t$.

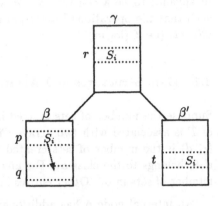

The destination class γ_s can be determined easily as follows: If $Intersect_\gamma[q,t]$ is not undefined (i.e. β_q and β'_t had some sets in common before Insert(i,x) is executed), we let $s = Intersect_\gamma[q,t]$. Otherwise, we let $s \geq 1$ be a label of an empty class of γ. Obviously, the updating of γ due to Insert(i,x) takes constant time. Since the height of T is $\lceil \log l \rceil + 1$, Insert(i,x) costs $O(\log l)$ time. Delete(i,x) can be processed in a similar fashion using $O(\log l)$ time. Note that when a key x no longer belongs to any set, it still remains in the partition tree.

4 Dynamic adaptation of partition trees

Suppose we have built a partition tree T in which the data structures *Class*, *Count*, and *Intersect* are implemented by fixed-size arrays of dimension d. At any time, as long as no more than d sets have been created, the partition tree can support an insert or delete operation in $O(\log l)$ time and set equality-testing in $O(1)$ time, where l is the current number of leaves in the partition tree. However, after a sequence of insert and delete operations, it is possible that some of the keys that are stored in the leaves of T no longer belong to any set and, at the worst, the total size of the sets (i.e. n) is much smaller than l. In other words, T cannot guarantee $O(\log n)$-time performance for an update operation. If we simply restructure or rebuild the partition tree every time a key is found to be redundant, it takes at least linear time.

Moreover, we do not want to impose an upper bound on the number of sets. When the current number of sets is approaching d, we need another partition tree with "bigger" arrays at each node in order to make room for the new sets. If we rebuild the partition tree when the $(d+1)$-th set is created or the first time a key is inserted into the $(d+1)$-th set, it also requires at least linear time.

In the rest of this section, we show a scheme in which the partition tree can evolve gradually according to the sequence of operations. We attempt to maintain two partition trees T_0 and T_1 at the same time. Intuitively, T_0 is used for processing the coming operations over a certain period. We ensure that within that period, T_0 will not have too many redundant leaves (i.e. $l = \Theta(n)$) and it will have room to accommodate new sets. Using T_0, set equality-testing can be done in $O(1)$ time and each insert or delete operation $O(\log n)$ time. At the end of the period, T_0 may, however, have deteriorated so much that it can no longer guarantee the required performance. Fortunately, T_1, which is actually built starting from scratch during the period, is in a much better shape now and can be used to serve the coming operations over the next period. In other words, T_1 will take over the role of T_0 in the next period, during which another T_1 is built.

The most non-trivial part of our scheme is about the way of spreading the construction of T_1 over a sequence of operations, while maintaining the time complexity of an update or equality-testing operation same as before.

Before proceeding further, we define two more notations. (a) A partition tree T is said to be of dimension d if the data structures in every node of T are of dimension d (i.e. each node α is allocated with arrays $Class_\alpha[1..d]$, $Count_\alpha[1..d]$, and $Intersect_\alpha[0..d, 0..d]$). (b) T is also said to be of width l if it has l leaves.

4.1 Building a new partition tree periodically

At a particular time t, let S denote the current collection of sets and let n_0 be their total size (recall that every set is non-empty and the number of sets in S cannot exceed n_0). Suppose that we have built a partition tree T_0 for S, whose dimension is at least $\frac{3}{2}n_0$ and width at most $3n_0$.

Let R denote any sequence of coming operations, containing $\frac{1}{2}n_0$ update operations. We are going to use T_0 to serve R. Moreover, while we operate on T_0, we can build another partition tree T_1 such that the redundant keys found in T_0 at time t are all removed and the dimension of T_1 is adjusted in accordance with the total size of the sets at time t.

First of all, we observe that T_0 suffices to serve every operation of R efficiently.

Claim: Using T_0, we can execute an insert or delete operation of R in $O(\log n)$ time and set equality-testing in $O(1)$ time, where n is the total size of the sets when the operation is executed.

Proof: As R contains $\frac{1}{2}n_0$ update operations, at most $\frac{1}{2}n_0$ sets can be created. In the course of processing R, we need to represent at most $n_0 + \frac{1}{2}n_0$ ($= \frac{3}{2}n_0$) sets. As the dimension of T_0 is at least $\frac{3}{2}n_0$, it has no problem to accommodate all these sets.

R contains at most $\frac{1}{2}n_0$ insert operations; at most $\frac{1}{2}n_0$ new keys are inserted into T. The width of T_0 is always upper bounded by $3n_0 + \frac{1}{2}n_0$. Using the algorithm described in Section 3, we can execute each insert or delete operation in $O(\log n_0)$ time and each set equality-testing $O(1)$ time.

It remains to show that $\log n_0 = \Theta(\log n)$. At any time during the processing of R, the total size of the sets (i.e. n) cannot increase or decrease by more than $\frac{1}{2}n_0$; thus, we have

$$\frac{1}{2}n_0 \leq n \leq \frac{3}{2}n_0$$

and $\log n_0 = \Theta(\log n)$. $\square$

Let S' denote the collection of sets after we have applied the update operations of R to S; let n_1 denote the total size of the sets in S'. As explained earlier, we have $\frac{1}{2}n_0 \leq n_1 \leq \frac{3}{2}n_0$.

Below, we show that while R is processed, we can gradually build another partition tree T_1 for S' of dimension at least $\frac{3}{2}n_1$ and width at most $3n_1$. More precisely, the construction of T_1 is divided into $\frac{1}{2}n_0$ phases, each requires $O(\log n_0)$ time. One phase of the construction is carried out immediately after an update operation of R has been performed on T_0. In other words, when all update operations of R have been performed, the construction of T_1 is complete.

We call the first $\frac{1}{4}n_0$ phases Stage 1 and the remaining phases Stage 2. Stage 1 aims at building a partition tree T_1 of dimension $\frac{9}{4}n_0$ and width at most n_0 to represent S, while in Stage 2, we apply the update operations of R to T_1 so that T_1 eventually becomes a partition tree for S'.

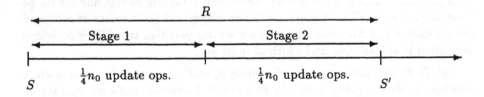

Before giving the details of constructing T_1, we need to introduce two extra data structures. A queue Q is set to empty when we start to process the operations of R. Every time an update operation has been processed using T_0, we store the operation in Q. Also, we assume that before we start to process the operations of R, an AVL tree has been built for each set of S, representing the keys of that set. Let G denote the collection of these AVL trees. G will remain intact during Stage 1, but will get updated during Stage 2 so that it will represent S' by the end of Stage 2.

Stage 1: We start with an empty partition tree T_1 of dimension $\frac{9}{4}n_0$. In each of the $\frac{1}{4}n_0$ phases, we pick four keys from some AVL trees of G and use the algorithms of Section 3 to update T_1 as if these four keys are inserted into the corresponding sets. Recall that the AVL trees in G are not altered in Stage 1 and they store a total of exactly n_0 keys. At the end of Stage 1, all keys in G should have been inserted into T_1, which becomes a partition tree for S of dimension $\frac{9}{4}n_0$ and width at most n_0.

Stage 2: In each of the $\frac{1}{4}n_0$ phases, we remove two update operations from Q and update T_1 in respect of these two operations. Also, we update the corresponding AVL trees in G. New AVL trees may be created in G. (Note that just before the current phase starts, we have processed an update operation of R using T_0 and have inserted a new entry into Q.) At the end of Stage 2, Q should be empty and we should have updated T_1 with all update operations of R. T_1 is now a partition tree for S' of dimension $\frac{9}{4}n_0$ and width at most $n_0 + \frac{1}{2}n_0$. Since $\frac{1}{2}n_0 \leq n_1 \leq \frac{3}{2}n_0$, the dimension of T_1 is at least $\frac{3}{2}n_1$ and the width of T_1 is at most $3n_1$.

In summary, for each update operation of R, it takes $O(\log n)$ time to serve the operation using T_0 as well as to execute a phase of constructing T_1. A set equality-testing does not induce any work on T_1 and can be done in $O(1)$ time.

4.2 The evolution of partition trees

The technique developed in Section 4.1 can be used repeatedly to adapt the partition tree to handle any sequence of operations in which the maximum number of sets is not known in advance.

Let n_0 be any fixed constant. Without loss of generality, assume that we start off with a collection of sets, S, whose total size is n_0. (We use a brute force method to handle the case where the total size is less than n_0.) We first construct a partition tree T_0 for S, of dimension $\frac{3}{2}n_0$ and width at most n_0. This construction requires constant time only.

Conceptually, the first period comprises all coming operations up to the $(\frac{1}{2}n_0)$-th update operation. During this period, we use T_0 to perform each operation in the required time bound, and we build another partition tree T_1 as described in Section 4.1. Let S' be the collection of sets after we have performed all operations in the first period; let n_1 denote the total size of the sets in S'. Note that T_1 is built to represent S', its dimension is at least $\frac{3}{2}n_1$ and width at most $3n_1$.

At the end of the first period, T_0 is no longer useful and can be discarded. T_1 now takes over the role of T_0 to serve the operations in the second period, which spans over the next $\frac{1}{2}n_1$ update operations. Again, during the period we build another partition tree T_1. It is easy to see that as long as we keep on building and discarding partition trees, every update operation requires $O(\log n)$ time and set equality-testing $O(1)$ time.

Space complexity: At any time t there are two partition trees T_0 and T_1 kept in the memory. We are going to show that they only occupy $O(n^2 \log n)$ space, where n is the total size of the sets at time t. Consider the period that covers t; let n_0 be the total size of the sets at the beginning of this period. As mentioned before, $\frac{1}{2}n_0 \leq n \leq \frac{3}{2}n_0$.

We first analyze the space requirement of T_1 at time t. Let d $(= \frac{9}{4}n_0)$ be the dimension of T_1. At each node of T_1, the space required by the data structures *Class* and *Count* is $O(d)$. Since at most $\frac{3}{2}n_0$ keys have been inserted into T_1, the number of nodes in T_1 is $O(n_0)$. Summing over all nodes, the data structures *Class* and *Count* occupy $O(dn_0)$ (i.e. $O(n_0^2)$) space. For the data structure *Intersect* of each internal node, we implement it as an array of arrays instead of a 2-dimensional array in order to reduce the space requirement. When a node α is first created, *Intersect$_\alpha$* is represented by a single array of dimension d storing null pointers. The i-th entry in this array may later store a pointer to another array of dimension d representing the i-th row of *Intersect$_\alpha$*. Note that we will not allocate the array for the i-th row of *Intersect$_\alpha$* until we access *Intersect$_\alpha[i,j]$* for some j. With respect to the algorithms in Section 3, in the course of performing an update operation on T_1, we may need to allocate $O(d)$ space for the data structure *Intersect* of each node on the path from a leaf to the root. The height of T_1 is $O(\log n_0)$ and the total space allocated for the data structures *Intersect* due to an update operation is $O(d \log n_0)$. At time t we have applied at most $\frac{3}{2}n_0$ update operations to T_1. The total space allocated for the data structures *Intersect* is $O(dn_0 \log n_0)$. The space occupied by T_1 is $O(n_0^2 \log n_0)$, i.e. $O(n^2 \log n)$.

It is easy to prove by induction that T_0, at the beginning of the period covering t, also occupies $O(n_0^2 \log n_0)$ space. Since then, we have performed at most $\frac{1}{2}n_0$ update operations on T_0. Thus T_0 also uses $O(n^2 \log n)$ space.

References

[1] A.V. Aho, J.E. Hopcroft, and J.D. Ullman, *The Design and Analysis of Computer Algorithms*, Ex 2.12, 71.

[2] T.W. Lam and K.H. Lee, On Set Equality-Testing, *Proceedings of the 2nd Italian Conference on Algorithms and Complexity*, 1994, 179-191.

[3] W. Pugh and T. Teitelbaum, Incremental Computation via Function Caching, *Proceedings of the Sixteenth ACM Symposium on Principles of Programming Languages*, 1989, 315-328.

[4] M. Sassa and E. Goto, A Hashing Method for Set Operations, *Information Processing Letters*, 5, 1976, 265-279.

[5] R. Sundar and R.E. Tarjan, Unique Binary Search Tree Representations and Equality Testing of Sets and Sequences, *Proceedings of the Twenty-second Annual ACM Symposium on Theory of Computing*, 1990, 18-25.

[6] M.N. Wegman and J.L. Carter, New Hash Functions and Their Use in Authentication and Set Equality, *Journal of Computer and System Sciences*, 22, 1981, 265-279.

[7] D.M. Yellin, Representing Sets with Constant Time Equality Testing, *Journal of Algorithms*, 13, 1992, 353-373; a preliminary version appeared in the *Proceedings of the First Annual ACM-SIAM Symposium on Algorithms*, 1990, 64-73.

Appendix I: Constant time initialization of an array

Given an array B of size s, setting every entry of B to a certain initial value costs $O(s)$ time. However, using the following trick [1], we can avoid such initialization and can still ensure that each entry of B gets the same initial value (say, zero) the first time it is accessed. The time required to access an entry of B subsequently is always a constant.

Allocate two extra arrays A_1 and A_2 both of size same as B. Let Top be a counter of the number of distinct indices that have been used to access B. We maintain the invariant that an entry $B[i]$ has ever been accessed if and only if $A_1[i] \le Top$ and $A_2[A_1[i]] = i$. Thus, we can always verify in constant time whether the content in any entry $B[i]$ is garbage. The first time an entry $B[i]$ is accessed (i.e., $A_1[i] > Top$ or $A_2[A_1[i]] \ne i$), we treat $B[i]$ as if it contains the default initial value and we execute the following steps: $Top \leftarrow Top + 1$; $A_1[i] \leftarrow Top$; $A_2[Top] \leftarrow i$.

Binary Space Partitions for Sets of Hyperrectangles

Viet Hai Nguyen, Peter Widmayer

Swiss Federal Institute of Technology (ETH) Zürich,
ETH Zentrum, CH–8092 Zürich, Switzerland

Abstract. In this paper we prove the existence of binary space partitions (BSPs) with linear size for sets of axis-parallel boxes in three dimensional space under certain conditions that are often satisfied in practical situations. In particular, we give an $O(n \log n)$ time algorithm to construct a BSP tree with linear size for a set S of axis-parallel boxes where the ratio between the lengths of the longest and the shortest edges of boxes in S is bounded by a constant. The BSP tree constructed is balanced if S has a constant profile.

In view of the lower bound of $\Omega(n^{3/2})$ for the size of BSPs for set of n line segments (or boxes) in $\mathbb{R}^3$, this is the first class of high dimensional objects that are found, for which linear size BSPs exist. We generalize the results for sets of hyperrectangles in dimension greater than three and extend our method also for a useful class of d-dimensional fat objects. All the algorithms for constructing linear size binary space partitions presented in this paper are simple enough to be favorable for implementations.

1 Introduction

The divide-and-conquer paradigm is one of the earliest yet powerful problem-solving techniques in computer science. For geometric problems, where the input is a set of objects in the space, a variation of the technique, often used to design efficient algorithms, involves a recursive partitioning of the object space into several subspaces by means of a set of planes, until finally subspaces containing only a trivial number of objects are obtained. Binary space partition is one such scheme where the object space is divided by a cutting hyperplane into two subspaces, which can then be divided recursively, until all objects are separated. The solutions for the problem in each subspace then can be obtained by some straightforward method and be merged to form a global solution for the original problem. Since each divide step may split some of the objects into two parts, the number of objects in the final subdivision can be larger than the number of input objects, and hence the recursive partitioning strategy above may lead to an inefficient algorithm. Therefore, a proper splitting strategy leading to a space partition with the minimum number of object fragments plays an important role.

In this paper, we consider the problem of constructing a small size binary space partition (BSP). In particular, we will consider the conditions to ensure the existence of a linear size BSP tree for a set of n d-dimensional axis-parallel hyperrectangles. The reason why we consider hyperrectangles in $\mathbb{R}^d$ or boxes in $\mathbb{R}^3$ is simple. In computer graphics or geographic information systems (GIS), when visualizing or displaying 3-d scenes, to avoid unnecessary details, geometric objects are not directly stored in the primary structure. Instead, their bounding boxes are stored in the primary structure and accessed first to get a pointer to the detailed description of each object stored at the lower level.

Here is a brief history of the problem of computing binary space partitions. Binary space partition is probably first introduced by Schumaker et al., ([16], see also [17]), but only received attention in computer graphics and computational geometry when it was further developed by Fuchs et al. [8]. Note that quadtree, octree, grid file structures [15, 12] are very closely related to binary space partition trees. Binary space partition trees have been intensively used in computer graphics for many applications: visible-surface determination (for real-time applications such as flight simulation and computer animation) [8, 7], illumination and shading computation [18, 7], representation of polyhedra and manipulation of boolean operations on polyhedra [19, 10], etc. (Foley et al. [7] contains a detailed discussion and many references on applications of BSP trees in computer graphics). Recently, binary space partitions also found applications in spatial databases [21, 15].

In two dimensional space, Paterson and Yao gave the first $O(n \log n)$ time deterministic and randomized algorithms to construct an $O(n \log n)$ size balanced BSP for a set of n (arbitrary) line segments [13]. For a set of axis-parallel line segments, they presented an elegant algorithm to construct an $O(n)$ size BSP [14]. This algorithm was later improved by d'Amore and Franciosa [2], resulting in the same asymptotical bounds on the running time and the size of the constructed BSPs, but with a slightly better constant for the combinatorial bound on the size of the BSPs.

The existence of linear size BSPs for a more general class of objects in the plane was also proved by de Berg et al. [5]. They have given efficient algorithms to construct linear size BSPs for sets of fat objects and for sets of line segments with bounded length ratios, i.e. the ratio between the lengths of the longest and shortest segments is bounded by a constant. Their result on linear size BSP for sets of fat objects is based on a lemma about the fatness property obtained by van der Stappen et al. [20]. Although this is an interesting result from a theoretical point of view, their algorithm, with running time of $O(n \log n \log \log n)$, employs a rather complicated transformation and a segment arrangement construction which may not be useful for practical implementations. They also state the importance for further study of objects with certain realistic properties in three dimensional space.

In higher dimensions, Paterson and Yao have also proved that for any set of $(d-1)$ simplices in $\mathbb{R}^d$ there is a BSP of size $O(n^{d-1})$. In the case of axis-parallel line segments, this upper bound is proved to be $O(n^{d/(d-1)})$. In particular, in three dimensional space, they have given examples (which they credited to Eppstein and Thurston) showing that there is a lower bound which matches their upper bound, namely $\Omega(n^2)$ for the general case, and $\Omega(n^{3/2})$ for the case of axis-parallel line segments, 2-dimensional rectangles or boxes [13, ?]. In dimension greater than three, no good lower bounds for the size of BSPs are known.

However, the lower bound examples given in [13, ?] are rather artificial. Hence, from a practical point of view, it is necessary to find efficient solutions for a more realistic class of objects in three or higher dimension. An important question is: which class of geometric objects admits a small, at best a linear size BSP ? An efficient solution for this problem will be very useful in practice.

Driving towards this direction, de Berg et al. [4] consider a restricted instance of the problem and proved that for any set of cubes in $\mathbb{R}^3$ there is a BSP of size $O(n \log^2 n)$, which can be constructed in $O(n \log^3 n)$ time. This is the only result we know of in this direction.

There are several ways to generalize this result. The first is to generalize the results for hypercubes in $\mathbb{R}^d$. The second is to consider a set S of bounded-length-ratio boxes in $\mathbb{R}^3$ where *bounded length ratio* means the ratio between the lengths of the longest and the shortest x_i-edges of boxes in S is bounded by a constant.

In this paper we shall prove a stronger result:

- there is always a balanced BSP tree with linear size for a set of axis-parallel hyperrectangles in $\mathbb{R}^d$, provided that the profile factor of the scene k^* is a constant.
- there is always a BSP tree with linear size for a set of axis-parallel hyperrectangles with bounded length ratios in $\mathbb{R}^d$. This BSP tree can be constructed in $O(n \log n)$ time.
- for a useful class of fat objects, which we call k-*bounding overlap* fat objects, our method can be extended to construct a linear size BSP within the same time bound of $O(n \log n)$.

The general idea is to subdivide the set of hyperrectangles into voxels by a number of $O(n)$ cuts without increasing asymptotically the number of sub-hyperrectangles (fragments generated). The first step in the subdivision process stops when the configuration of hyperrectangles in each voxel satisfies the *bounded profile* condition, i.e. the profile factor of the voxel is small enough to be considered as a constant. The second step is a straightforward application of a partition procedure for each voxel.

The above results can obviously be stated for the corresponding three dimensional case. For a set S of n axis-parallel boxes with bounded length ratios, we can always construct in $O(n \log n)$ time a linear size BSP tree for S

In view of the lower bound of $\Omega(n^{3/2})$ for the size of BSPs for set of n line segments (or boxes) in $\mathbb{R}^3$ this is the first class of objects that are found, for which a linear size BSP exists. We believe that the class of geometric objects we consider here is also a practically relevant class of objects. In addition, all the algorithms for constructing linear size binary space partitions presented in this paper are simple, yet efficient. They can be implemented without using any complicated data structures or transformations.

The paper is organized as follows. After introducing some necessary definitions in Section 2, we present an algorithm for constructing a linear size BSP for a set of axis-parallel line segments in the plane, to motivate solutions in higher dimensions. Main results on constructing linear size BSPs for boxes and hyperrectangles in $\mathbb{R}^d$ are obtained in Sections 4 and 5. In Section 6, these results are extended for sets of fat objects in $\mathbb{R}^d$. In the last section, we give some conclusions.

2 Preliminaries

A d-dimensional *binary space partition* is a recursive partition of d-dimensional Euclidean space $\mathbb{R}^d$ by means of a set of hyperplanes. Given a set S of n (hyper)rectangles in $\mathbb{R}^d$, a binary space partition (henceforth BSP) of S is obtained by recursively dividing S into two subsets S^- and S^+ by means of a hyperplane H. If the cutting hyperplane crosses a rectangle, this is cut into two rectangles. The subdivision stops when each subset contains only one rectangle. The binary tree structure, naturally generated from the subdivision procedure, is called a *BSP tree*. The *size* of a BSP is the number of rectangles generated during the subdivision. The *height* of a BSP tree is the length of a longest path from its root to a leaf. A BSP tree is called *balanced* if its height is $O(\log n)$.

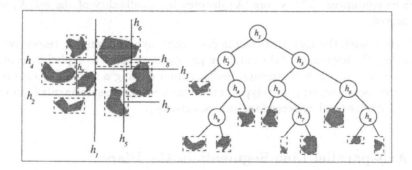

Fig. 1. a BSP and its tree structure

Let C be a hyperplane orthogonal to the x_j-axis (which can be regarded as some degenerate axis-parallel hyperrectangle) separating $\mathbb{R}^d$ into two closed half-spaces. Any hyperrectangle R whose interior is intersected by C is split into two non-overlapping[1] parts corresponding to the respective sides of C. More precisely, for any $c \in (a_j, b_j)$, the hyperplane $\{x_j = c\}$ splits the hyperrectangle $R = [a_1, b_1] \times \ldots \times [a_d, b_d]$ into two parts:

$$R_{low} := [a_1, b_1] \times \ldots \times [a_j, c] \times \ldots \times [a_d, b_d]$$

and

$$R_{high} := [a_1, b_1] \times \ldots \times [c, b_j] \times \ldots \times [a_d, b_d]$$

So, any hyperplane C induces a nontrivial partition of S in the sense that some hyperrectangles may lie entirely on one side of the hyperplane while others may intersect it. Let $C^<$ and $C^>$ denote the sets of hyperrectangles lying entirely in the lower and the upper of the two halfspaces generated by the cut C, respectively, and let $C^=$ denote the set of hyperrectangles whose relative interior is intersected by C. The *profile* k_i^* of a set S of objects w.r.t. dimension i is the maximal number of objects intersected by a cut orthogonal to the x_i axis. The profile $k^*(S)$ of S is the minimum of all $k_i^*(S)$, i.e.

$$k^*(S) = \min\{k_1^*(S), \ldots k_d^*(S)\}$$

The edge $[a_i, b_i]$ of a hyperrectangle R is sometimes called an x_i-edge. A set S of non-overlapping axis-parallel hyperrectangles in $\mathbb{R}^d$ is said to be r-*bounded* if $r = \max_{1 \leq i \leq d} r_i$ and the ratio between the lengths of the longest and shortest x_i-edges of hyperrectangles in S is bounded by a constant r_i, for $1 \leq i \leq d$.

A *best balanced cut* of a set of hyperrectangles is defined to be a cut that minimizes the maximal number of hyperrectangles on either side of the cutting hyperplane after the split. In [11] it was proved that a best balanced cut for a set of hyperrectangles can be computed in optimal $O(dn)$ time and space. A tight bound of $\Theta(n \log n)$ for computing a nontrivial *minimum intersection* cut C which minimizes $|C^=|$, where $|X|$ denotes the cardinality of the set X, was also proved.

In the sequel, the segments (rectangles, boxes, hyperrectangles, respectively) in S before the beginning of the partition process are refered to explicitly as *original segments*; two new fragments resulting from cutting a segment (rectangle, box, hyperrectangle, respectively) s are sometimes called *subsegments* (subrectangles, subboxes, subhyperrectangles, respectively).

3 Axis-parallel Line Segments in the Plane

Given a set S of non-intersecting axis parallel line segments in the plane, we consider the problem of constructing efficiently a linear size BSP for S. This is a basic problem, since in many typical situations, configurations of objects in three

---

[1] i.e. their interiors have no point in common

or higher dimension can be projected onto a plane and an efficient algorithm working for the planar case can be applied. We present now a modified version of the planar orthogonal partition algorithm and its analysis, slightly improving the result of [2]: a) Either we can avoid splitting some segments (i.e. we generate a smaller number of subsegments) or our BSP is more balanced; b) The space usage of our BSP construction algorithm is cut down by a factor of $O(\log \log n)$. We attempt to expose the nature of the algorithm, in order to generalize it later. The idea of the algorithm is to alternate the cutting directions in each region of the subdivision, in order to avoid cutting a segment too many times. During the partition we maintain two invariants:

(I_1) If a region R of the subdivision contains more than one line segment, then it has at least a free edge, where a *free edge* is an edge that does not intersect the interior of a segment orthogonally;

(I_2) When cutting a region R, only original segments are cut.

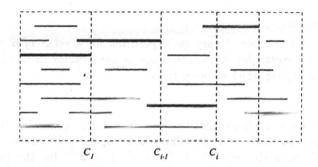

Fig. 2. Illustrations for the Planar Orthogonal Partition Algorithm

For each non-empty set of line segments bounded by a box R, the *Planar Orthogonal Partition Algorithm* works as follows. W.l.o.g. assume the region R has its right edge free (otherwise we can rotate R). If R has two opposite edges free, then the balanced cut algorithm [11] can be applied. We process from the left to the right, and always make a vertical cut. The first cut C_1 is placed at the right end point of the longest horizontal segment touching the left edge of R. The next cut C_{i+1} is placed at the right end point of the horizontal segment H reaching furthest to the right among the set of all horizontal segments intersected (or touched on the left) by the last cut C_i. We will stop making the cut C_{i+1} if there were no vertical segments on the right of C_i.

It is easy to see that

(i) each region R_i between two cuts C_i and C_{i+1} (or between the left edge of R and C_1) can be divided into two sub-regions, each with a free edge by cutting along one of the segments intersecting two opposite sides of R_i, i.e. intersecting one and touching the other side of R_i (this segment could also touch both opposite sides of R_i). The algorithm then can be applied recursively for these two sub-regions of each R_i. The last region on the right inherits the free edge of R.

(ii) during the recursive partitioning process, no original segment will be cut more than one time by any cut C_i.

It follows immediately from the second invariant (I_2) that no original segment is cut more than one time, therefore the size of the generated BSP is at most $2n$.

Using the *priority search tree* of Edelsbrunner and McCreight [6, 9] and the *filtering search* technique of Chazelle [1], the algorithm can be implemented to construct a linear size BSP for S in $O(n \log n)$ time and using $O((n \log n)/ \log \log n)$ storage space. It can be adapted for constructing a BSP with size at most $4n$ for a set of rectangles in the plane within the same time and space bounds.

Theorem 1. *A linear size binary space partition for a set S of n axis-parallel non-overlapping rectangles in the plane can be constructed in $O(n \log n)$ time, using $O((n \log n)/ \log \log n)$ memory space.*

What can we learn from this algorithm in order to generalize it for sets of hyperrectangles in three or higher dimensional space ? Of course we can not expect a BSP with size $o(n^{d/(d-1)})$ (or $o(n^{3/2})$ in $\mathbb{R}^3$) for the general class of axis-parallel hyperrectangles. Assume that the rectangles of S satisfy the *bounded length ratio* condition, i.e. the ratio between the lengths of the largest and smallest x_i-side of rectangles in S is bounded by a constant r. Then the recursivity of the planar orthogonal partition algorithm can be removed. This suggests an idea for the following orthogonal partition algorithm in $\mathbb{R}^d$:

(P_1) Subdivide S into *voxels*, i.e. cells of the subdivision, by (at most) $(d - 1)$ rounds of cuts. In each round of cuts, only a linear number of sub-hyperrectangles is generated. After this step, each voxel has a constant profile, thus contains only a constant number of hyperrectangles;

(P_2) Partition each voxel by a straightforward procedure, which we call the *Voxel Partition Procedure*, presented in Section 4.1.

In fact, step P_1 stops to subdivide a voxel (or slab) as soon as the voxel has at least one "thin" profile. In the next section we will study more details of the algorithm and its analysis.

4   Axis-parallel Boxes in $\mathbb{R}^3$

4.1   Sets of Boxes with Small Profile in $\mathbb{R}^3$

Consider a set S of n axis-parallel non-intersecting boxes with profile k^* in three dimensional space. W.l.o.g assume the horizontal direction is the direction of the x_i-axis, and the profile of S is $k^* = k_i^*$. The existence of a linear size BSP can be seen by observing that, if we cut the set S along $2n - 2$ sides of the boxes in S (except the leftmost and the rightmost), orthogonal to the x_i-axis, these cuts will define $O(n)$ vertical slabs $R_1, R_2, ...$, each containing no more than k^* (fragments of) boxes. The number of fragments generated from $O(n)$ cuts is $O(k^*n)$. Now consider the projection of any of these subsets in a slab R_j on a plane orthogonal to x_i. This gives us an instance of the BSP problem for rectangles in $\mathbb{R}^2$, for which we can apply the Planar Orthogonal Partition Algorithm of Section 3 to obtain a BSP of size $O(k^*)$ for each subset of rectangles.

Note that instead of cutting along *all* boxes' sides, we can recursively apply the balanced cut in dimension i (i.e. using plane orthogonal to the x_i-axis), until all regions contain no endpoint in this dimension. Since in the last stage we apply the Planar Orthogonal Partition Algorithm for a set of constant number ($k^* = O(1)$) of rectangles, the BSP tree is still balanced. More precisely, the BSP obtained is k^*-*balanced* and has size of $O(k^*n)$. This allows us to conclude

Lemma 2. *There is always a linear size, balanced BSP tree for a set of n boxes in $\mathbb{R}^3$, provided that the profile factor k^* is a constant value. This BSP tree can be constructed in $O(n \log n)$ time.*

In the following we will call the above orthogonal partition algorithm in $\mathbb{R}^3$ the *Voxel Partition Procedure*.

4.2   Sets of Boxes with Bounded Length Ratios in $\mathbb{R}^3$

Let S now be a set of r-bounded boxes in three dimensional space, i.e. the ratio between the lengths of the longest and shortest x_i-edges of boxes in S is bounded by a constant value r_i and $r = \max\{r_1, r_2, r_3\}$. Let F be the bounding box of all boxes in S. The *Orthogonal Partition Algorithm* for S in $\mathbb{R}^3$ consists of the following two stages. In the first stage, we shall do two rounds of cuts to subdivide F into voxels with constant profile. In each round of cuts, we maintain the invariant that each box is cut only once and in each region between two consecutive cuts, there is at least one long box which intersects two opposite sides of that region. In the second stage, we apply the Voxel Partition Procedure to each voxel separated in the first stage.

The details of the first stage is as follows. Choose a dimension i for the first round of cuts. Assume now that x_i is the horizontal orientation. We cut F

vertically into vertical slabs by using planes $H_0, H_1, H_2, \ldots$ orthogonal to x_i from left to right as follows. Let H_0 - the dummy cut - be the left side of F. Now, a cut H_j is defined recursively based on the set $H_{j-1}^=$ of boxes cut by H_{j-1} on the left. Among all boxes in $H_{j-1}^=$ choose the one with its right side reaching furthest from H_{j-1} to the right w.r.t. x_i. H_j is the plane of the right side of this box. By proceeding this way until reaching the right side of the bounding box F we can guarantee our invariant. That is, in each round of cuts, each box is cut only once, and in each region between two cuts, there is one long box touching the opposite sides of the region. Choose a second dimension and repeat the same process for the set of (sub-) boxes in each vertical slab. The number of boxes generated after these two rounds of cuts is $O(n)$. We have a set of voxels, each of which has the property that at least two out of three pairs of parallel planes incident with its opposite sides are intersected, each by at least a sub-box (these two sub-boxes need not both be contained in the same voxel).

The applicability of the Voxel Partition Procedure in the second stage is assured by the following Lemma:

Lemma 3. *If in a voxel ν there are two boxes intersecting two different pairs of opposite sides then ν has profile $O(r^2)$.*

Proof: At least two opposite faces of ν have their edge lengths correspondingly equal to the side lengths of the two boxes intersecting opposite sides of ν. A cut parallel with these two faces can not intersect more than $O(r^2)$ rectangles in ν. $\square$

Note that instead of cutting the set S as above we can also apply the balanced cut algorithm to S until the condition of Lemma 3 is satisfied. As soon as a separated voxel or slab ν is found having a profile factor $k^*(\nu)$ not exceeding a pre-defined constant value, we can apply the Voxel Partition Procedure presented in the previous section for ν. If the vertices of the boxes are presorted in each dimension, the profile k_i^* for each cell of the subdivision can be computed in time linear in the number of vertices contained in the cell. Now we can make our conclusion in the following theorem.

Theorem 4. *Let S be a set of non-overlapping axis-parallel boxes in $\mathbb{R}^3$, such that the ratio between the lengths of the longest and shortest x_i-edges of boxes in S is bounded by a constant. Then there is a binary space partition for S of size $O(n)$, which can be computed in $O(n \log n)$ time, using $O((n \log n)/\log \log n)$ space.*

Proof: Note that in the first stage of the algorithm, the invariant remains true in each round of cuts. After this stage, each box is cut at most twice. Each voxel satisfies the condition of Lemma 3 and then can be subdivided using the Voxel Partition Procedure of section 4.1. The bound on the size of the constructed BSP immediately follows from Lemma 2.

The algorithm can be implemented to run in $O(n \log n)$ time as follows. We need data structures which support the following operations.

> *Intersect*(H): returns some box intersected by a plane H orthogonal to the x_i-axis.
>
> *NextRight*(H, x_i): returns some box on the right of a plane H orthogonal to the x_i-axis.
>
> *MaxRight*(H, x_i): returns the rightmost (maximal or minimal, depending on the orientation of F w.r.t. x_i) x_i-coordinate of boxes intersected by a plane H orthogonal to the x_i-axis.

The set S of input boxes is represented by six doubly-linked lists A_i, B_i, $1 \leq i \leq 3$. Each list A_i (or B_i) stores the set of vertices a_i's (or b_i's) of boxes in S, sorted in increasing order of the x_i-axis. Each member of a list A_i or B_i has also cross pointers refering to corresponding coordinates of the same box. The six lists can be constructed in $O(n \log n)$ time. The time cost for the second stage is already proved in Lemma 2. We analyze the time cost of the first stage of the algorithm, which consists of $d - 1$ rounds of cuts.

A balanced cut can be done in linear time and requires no presorting. But each call to *Intersect* then may cost also linear time in the worst case. However, it can be shown that the depth of cutting is $O(\log n)$, so each vertex of a box can be charged $O(\log n)$ for the cost of all calls to *Intersect* and for building the new vertex sets whenever a balanced cut is done. Note also that at most $O(n)$ balanced cuts can be made and as long as we can make a balanced cut, no sorting is needed. Therefore the cost of making all balanced cuts in a round of cuts is $O(n \log n)$.

On the other hand, to determine all the cuts H_j's orthogonal to the x_i-axis in a round i, it suffices to step through the pair of lists A_i and B_i. Calls to *Intersect*, *NextRight*, *MaxRight* altogether in a round of cuts can be charged by one pass through the two lists. The construction of the six sublists A_i' and B_i', $1 \leq i \leq 3$, for the recursion of the algorithm on each slab between the two cuts requires more careful treatment. The two sublists A_i' and B_i' can be constructed as a by-product of the one-pass walk through the two lists A_i and

B_i. The construction of the new sublists A'_i and B'_i and all updates made to the two lists A_i and B_i in one round i of cuts is charged to the number of subboxes generated, i.e. $O(n)$. For the other four sublists A'_k, B'_k, $k \neq i$, we need to sort the vertices a_k, b_k pointed to by the cross pointers stored in the corresponding vertices a_i, b_i of the same box. The construction of each pair of sublists A'_k, B'_k requires $O(m \log m)$ time for sorting the new sublists, where m is the number of subboxes in the slab between the two cuts. Each vertex a_k or b_k can be charged at most $O(\log n)$ for each round i of cuts. All updates to A_k, B_k in a round are also done in total $O(n)$ time as with A_i and B_i. During one round of cuts, each box is split only once. Since the number of rounds of cuts is 2, each subbox generated in the first stage is charged at most $O(\log n)$, therefore the total time spent to construct all the sorted lists for recursion in the first stage is bounded by $O(n \log n)$. Since this part of the algorithm requires only $O(n)$ storage, the space bound follows from Theorem 1. □

5   Hyperrectangles in Higher Dimensional Space

Let S now be a set of r-bounded hyperrectangles in $\mathbb{R}^d$, i.e. the ratio between the lengths of the longest and shortest x_i-edges of hyperrectangles in S is bounded by a constant r_i and $r = \max_{1 \le i \le d} r_i$. Let F be the hyperrectangle bounding volume of S. The general idea of our *Orthogonal Partition Algorithm in $\mathbb{R}^d$* can be outlined as follows.

- The first stage of the subdivision proceeds exactly as in the three dimensional case with $(d-1)$ rounds of cuts in the first stage. In each round of cuts, we maintain the invariant that each hyperrectangle is cut only once, and in each space slab between two consecutive cuts, there is at least one long hyperrectangle which intersects two opposite sides of that slab.
- In the second stage, we apply a procedure which is similar to the Voxel Partition Procedure for each voxel separated in the first stage.

For the correctness of the second stage of our algorithm in $\mathbb{R}^d$, a generalized version of Lemma 3 is straightforward:

Lemma 5. *If in a voxel ν there are $(d-1)$ hyperrectangles intersecting $(d-1)$ different pairs of opposite sides then ν has profile $O(r^{d-1})$.*

Proof: Similar to the proof of Lemma 3. □

Theorem 6. *Let S be a set of non-overlapping axis-parallel hyperrectangles in $\mathbb{R}^d$, such that the ratio between the lengths of the longest and shortest x_i-edges of hyperrectangles in S is bounded by a constant value r_i. Then there is a binary space partition for S of size $O((d-1)r^{d-1}n)$, where $r = \max_{1 \leq i \leq d} r_i$, which can be constructed in $O(dn \log n)$ time.*

Proof: By induction in dimension d. □

6 Fat Objects in $\mathbb{R}^d$

We now consider a more general class of geometric objects, namely the class of fat objects, where a set of *fat objects* is any set of convex objects with their bounding hyperrectangles satisfying the bounded length ratio condition[2].

Let S now be a set of non-intersecting fat objects in $\mathbb{R}^d$ and S' be the set of their corresponding bounding hyperrectangles. With the definition of the profile factor k^*, it is likely that all the results obtained in the previous sections for hyperrectangles can be easily generalized for sets of fat objects. Unfortunately, although fat objects in S do not intersect, their bounding hyperrectangles in S' may intersect. But in many practical situations, the objects' density can be low, such that their bounding hyperrectangles do not intersect heavily. Let k be the maximum number of hyperrectangles that intersect in a common point; we call the set of hyperrectangles k-overlapping. In the case of fat objects with constant overlapping of bounding hyperrectangles, the results of the previous section on hyperrectangles with bounded length ratios in $\mathbb{R}^d$ can be applied. The subsequent lemmas follow directly.

Lemma 7. *There is always a linear size, balanced BSP tree for a set of n (possibly overlapping) hyperrectangles in $\mathbb{R}^d$, provided that the profile factor k^* is a constant value. This BSP tree can be constructed in $O(dn \log n)$ time.*

Lemma 8. *Let S be a set of r-bounded, k-overlapping hyperrectangles in $\mathbb{R}^d$. If in a voxel ν (separated after the first stage of the Orthogonal Partition Algorithm in $\mathbb{R}^d$) there are $(d-1)$ hyperrectangles intersecting $(d-1)$ different pairs of opposite sides, then ν has profile $O(kr^{d-1})$.*

This leads us to the following conclusion:

Theorem 9. *Let S be a set of n non-intersecting fat objects in $\mathbb{R}^d$ such that the maximal overlapping of their bounding hyperrectangles is bounded by a constant. Then there is always a linear size BSP for S; such a BSP can be constructed in $O(dn \log n)$ time.*

---

[2] Note that this concept of fatness is different from that defined by van der Stappen et al [20]. The two definitions do not subsume each other.

7 Conclusions

In contrast with the lower bound of $\Omega(n^{3/2})$ for the size of BSPs for a set of n line segments (or boxes) in $\mathbb{R}^3$, we have proven the existence of a linear size BSP for a useful class of geometric objects in $\mathbb{R}^3$. This is the first class of three-dimensional objects for which linear size BSPs have been shown to exist[3]. Our algorithms to construct linear size BSPs can be considered as a generalization of the planar orthogonal partion algorithms in [14, ?]. The results are generalized also for dimensions greater than three and extended for a useful class of d-dimensional fat objects. All the algorithms for constructing linear size binary space partitions presented in this paper are simple, yet efficient. They can be implemented to run in $O(n \log n)$ time, without using any complicated data structures or transformations.

References

1. B. Chazelle. Filtering search: a new approach to query-answering. *SIAM J. Comput.*, 15:703–724, 1986.
2. F. d'Amore and P. G. Franciosa. On the optimal binary plane partition for sets of isothetic rectangles. *Inform. Process. Lett.*, 44:255–259, 1992.
3. M. de Berg. Linear size binary space partitions for fat objects. To appear, Dept. of Computer Science, Utrecht University, the Netherlands, 1995. (accepted for Euro. Symp. on Algorithms, ESA'95).
4. M. de Berg and M. de Groot. Binary space partitions for sets of cubes. In *Abstracts 10th European Workshop Comput. Geom. (CG'94)*, pages 84–88, 1994.
5. M. de Berg, M. de Groot, and M. Overmars. New results on binary space partitions in the plane. In *Proc. 4th Scand. Workshop Algorithm Theory*, volume 824 of *Lecture Notes in Computer Science*, pages 61–72, 1994.
6. H. Edelsbrunner. *Algorithms in Combinatorial Geometry*, volume 10 of *EATCS Monographs on Theoretical Computer Science*. Springer-Verlag, Heidelberg, West Germany, 1987.
7. J. D. Foley, A. van Dam, S. K. Feiner, J. F. Hughes, and Phillips. *Introduction to Computer Graphics*. Addison-Wesley, Reading, MA, 1993.
8. H. Fuchs, Z. M. Kedem, and B. Naylor. On visible surface generation by a priori tree structures. *Comput. Graph.*, 14(3):124–133, 1980.
9. E. M. McCreight. Priority search trees. *SIAM J. Comput.*, 14:257–276, 1985.
10. B. Naylor, J. A. Amatodes, and W. Thibault. Merging BSP trees yields polyhedral set operations. *Comput. Graph.*, 24(4):115–124, August 1990.
11. V. H. Nguyen, T. Roos, and P. Widmayer. Balanced cuts of a set of hyperrectangles. In *Proc. 5th Canad. Conf. Comput. Geom.*, pages 121–126, Waterloo, Canada, 1993.
12. J. Nievergelt, H. Hinterberger, and K. C. Sevcik. The Grid File: An Adaptable, Symmetric Multikey File Structure. *ACM Trans. on Database Systems*, 9:38–71, 1984.

---

[3] When completing this paper, we heard that de Berg [3] has just announced a new method which generates in $O(n \log^2 n)$ time also a linear size BSP for a set of objects with their bounding boxes satisfying the so-called *bounding-box-fitness* condition

13. M. S. Paterson and F. F. Yao. Efficient binary space partitions for hidden-surface removal and solid modeling. *Discrete Comput. Geom.*, 5:485–503, 1990.

14. M. S. Paterson and F. F. Yao. Optimal binary space partitions for orthogonal objects. *J. Algorithms*, 13:99–113, 1992.

15. H. Samet. *Applications of Spatial Data Structures: Computer Graphics, Image Processing, and GIS*. Addison-Wesley, 1990.

16. R. A. Schumaker, R. Brand, M. Gilliland, and W. Sharp. Study for applying computer-generated images to visual simulation. Report AFHRL-TR-69-14, U.S. Air Force Human Resources Lab., 1969. cited in [8].

17. I. E. Sutherland, R. F. Sproull, and R. A. Schumaker. A characterization of ten hidden surface algorithms. *ACM Comput. Surv.*, 6:1–55, 1974. cited in [8].

18. S. Teller and P. Hanrahan. Global visibility algorithms for illumination computations. In *Proc. SIGGRAPH '93*, pages 239–246, 1993.

19. W. C. Thibault and B. F. Naylor. Set operations on polyhedra using binary space partitioning trees. In *Proc. SIGGRAPH'87*, pages 153–162, 1987.

20. A. F. van der Stappen, D. Halperin, and M. H. Overmars. The complexity of the free space for a robot moving amidst fat obstacles. *Comput. Geom. Theory and Appl.*, 3:353–373, 1993.

21. P. van Oosterom. A modified binary space partition for geographic information systems. *Int. J. GIS*, 4(2):133–146, 1990.

Transformation of Orthogonal Term Rewriting Systems

Sugwoo Byun[1], Richard Kennaway[2], and Ronan Sleep[2]

[1] Computer Technology Division, ETRI,
161 Kajong-Dong, Yusong-Gu, Taejon 305-350, Korea
swbyun@rose.etri.re.kr
[2] School of Information Systems, University of East Anglia,
Norwich NR4 7TJ, United Kingdom
jrk@sys.uea.ac.uk and mrs@sys.uea.ac.uk

Abstract. Orthogonal term rewriting systems (OTRSs) provide a well-known description of functional languages and their implementation. This paper describes some ways of transforming such systems into systems having simpler left-hand sides, the goal being to transform them into "flat" OTRSs, which have a particularly simple form. A class of systems, the *transformable* OTRSs, is defined which allow such a transformation. This class lies between the strongly sequential constructor systems and the strongly sequential systems.

1 Introduction

There is a well-developed theory of orthogonal term rewriting systems *OTRSs* [HL91] [Klo80] [DJ90] [Klo92]. Such systems are well-known as a description of computation in functional languages. The task of pattern-matching in such systems can be rather complex, as demonstrated by [HL91]. One method of simplifying this task is to transform OTRSs into OTRSs whose rules have simpler left-hand sides. In this paper, we define several such transformations, which together transform many OTRSs into a particularly simple form, the so-called *flat* systems. The class of systems which these transformations can "flatten", the *transformable* systems, lies strictly between the class of strongly sequential constructor systems and the class of strongly sequential systems.

Huet and Lévy developed a foundational theory of pattern-matching semantics known as *strong sequentiality* [HL91], where pattern-matching sequences of strong sequential systems are described as *matching dags*. In this paper, we define *separation trees* for *constructor systems*, the idea of which is borrowed from Böhm separability in the λ-calculus. Each pattern-matching sequence in *strongly sequential constructor systems* is described as a separation tree. Intuitively the condition of transformation is that a transformed system should preserve a pattern-matching sequence of the original system. Given a TRS R with a separation tree U and a transformation function T, a relation between R and $T(R)$ can be represented by a relation between U and subtrees of U.

Kennaway has introduced some transformation functions in [Ken90]. Here, we define the *generic transformation* which generalizes Kennaway's transformation functions. Whereas those functions are defined for constructor systems, we would like to consider a TRS which can be transformed into a strongly sequential constructor system. It is difficult for us to show every strongly seqential system as well as orthogonal TRSs can be transformed. We show *transformable systems*, a subclass of strongly sequential systems, can be transformed. The correctness condition is strengthened. Given a system and its transformation, we show that not only a transformed system simulates the original system (forward simulation) but the original system also simulates the transformed system (backward simulation). This means the existence of a bisimulation between two systems.

Transformation techniques based on strong sequentiality are applied to the the implementation of functional programming languages [Mar94] and a term graph rewriting language Dactl [Ken90]. Unless it is mentioned, TRSs mean orthogonal TRSs in this paper.

2 Preliminaries

A TRS over signature Σ is a pair $(Ter(\Sigma), R)$ consisting of the set $Ter(\Sigma)$ of terms over the signature Σ and a set of rewrite rules $R \subseteq Ter(\Sigma) \times Ter(\Sigma)$. The signature Σ consists of:

- a countably infinite set Var of variables denoted as $x, y, z, \ldots$,
- a non-empty set of function symbols denoted as capital characters $F, G, \ldots$, each equipped with arity (a natural number). Function symbols with arity 0 are called *constants*.

The set $Ter(\Sigma)$ of terms over a signature Σ is defined inductively:

- variables $x, y, z, \ldots \in Ter(\Sigma)$,
- If F is an n-ary function symbol and $t_1, \ldots, t_n \in Ter(\Sigma)$, then $F(t_1, ..., t_n) \in Ter(\Sigma)$.

The set R of rewrite rules contains pairs (l, r) of terms in $Ter(\Sigma)$, written as $l \to r$, such that

- the left-hand side (or LHS) l is not a variable,
- every variable occurring in the right-hand side (or RHS) r also occurs in l.

If the principal function symbol of l is F, then $l \to r$ is called a *rule for F*, or an *F-rule*. $s \equiv t$ indicates the identity of two terms s and t. The set $O(t)$ of *occurrences* (or *positions*) of a term $t \in Ter(\Sigma)$ is defined by induction on the structure of t as follows: $O(t) = \{\lambda\}$ if t is a variable, and $O(t) = \{\lambda\} \cup \{i \cdot u | 1 \le i \le n$ and $u \in O(t_i)\}$, if t is of the form $F(t_1, \ldots, t_n)$. If $u \in O(t)$ then the *subterm* $t|u$ at a position u is defined as follows: $t|\lambda = t$ and $F(t_1, \ldots, t_n)|i \cdot u = t_i|u$. A subterm s of a term t is *proper* if $s \ne t|\lambda$. The *depth* of a subterm of t at position u is the length of u. Similarly *levels* of a term are defined. Given a term t, $level(t) = 0$ if t is a variable, and $level(F) = 1$ and $level(F(t_1, \ldots, t_n)) = 1 +$ the maximum of $level(t_1), \ldots, level(t_n)$ if $t \equiv F(t_1, \ldots, t_n)$.

Contexts are terms in $Ter(\Sigma \cup \{\Box\})$, in which the special constant $\Box$, denoting an empty place, occurs exactly once. Contexts are denoted by $C[]$ and the result of substituting a term t in place of $\square$ is $C[t] \in Ter(\Sigma)$. $s[v := t]$ means the substitution of a term t for the occurrence v in a term s.

A *substitution* is a map $\sigma : Var \rightarrow Ter(\Sigma)$ satisfying the equation $\sigma(F(t_1, \ldots, t_n)) = F(\sigma(t_1), \ldots, \sigma(t_n))$. The result l^σ of the application of the substitution σ to the term l is an *instance* of l. A *redex* (reducible expression) is an instance of a LHS of a rewrite rule. A reduction step $s \rightarrow t$ is a pair of terms of the form $C[l^\sigma] \rightarrow C[r^\sigma]$, where $l \rightarrow r$ is a rewrite rule in R. $\rightarrow^*$ denotes the reflexive transitive closure of $\rightarrow$.

A *normal form* is a term containing no redexes. A term t *has a normal form* n if t is reducible to n and n is a normal form.

The function symbol at λ of a term t is called the *principal function symbol* of t. Principal function symbols of LHSs of R are called *operators* and other function symbols *constructors*. A term t is an *operator term* (resp. a *constructor term*) if the leftmost symbol of t is an operator (resp. a constructor).

Let R be a TRS. A rewrite rule $l \rightarrow r$ is *left-linear* if no variable occurs twice or more in l. R is *non-overlapping* if for any two LHSs s and t, any position u in t, and any substitution σ and $\tau : Var \rightarrow Ter(\Sigma)$ it holds that if $(t|u)^\sigma = s^\tau$ then either $t|u$ is a variable or t and s are LHSs of the same rewrite rule and $u = \lambda$ (i.e. non-variable parts of different rewrite rules do not overlap and non-variable parts of the same rewrite rule overlap only entirely). R is *orthogonal* if its rules are left-linear and non-overlapping. Orthogonal systems are called *constructor systems* if the LHSs of rules do not include a proper operator term.

3 Strongly Sequential Systems

A redex in a term t is *needed* if it must be contracted in order to get to the normal form of t, and the *call-by-need* computation means that no redex is ever reduced unless it is needed. Neededness is not decidable in orthogonal TRSs, hence Huet & Lévy proposed a decidable approximation known as *strong sequentiality* [HL91]. However, strongly sequential systems are still too complicated to be used practically, and several simpler versions are proposed.

Definition 1. Let R be an orthogonal TRS and Ω be a new constant symbol. The set Ter_Ω of Ω-*terms* consists of signature $(\Sigma \cup \{\Omega\})$.

1. On $Ter_\Omega(R)$ we define a partial order $\leq$ by:
   - $\Omega \leq t$ for all $t \in Ter_\Omega(R)$.
   - $F(t_1, \ldots, t_n) \leq F(s_1, \ldots, s_n)$ if $t_i \leq s_i$ for $i = 1, \ldots, n$. We write $t < s$ if $t \not\equiv s$ and $t \leq s$.
2. $s, t \in Ter_\Omega$ are said to be *compatible* (notation $s \uparrow t$) if there exists a term $p \in Ter_\Sigma$ such that $s \leq p$ and $t \leq p$. Otherwise, s and t are *incompatible* (notation $s \# t$).
3. Let $S \subseteq Ter_\Omega$ and $t \in Ter_\Omega$. Then $t \geq S$ (respectively, $t \uparrow S$) if there exists some $p \in S$ such that $t \geq p$ (respectively, $t \uparrow p$); otherwise $t \not\geq S$ (respectively, $t \# S$).
4. l_Ω denotes the Ω-term obtained from a term t by replacing each variable in t with Ω. The *redex schemata* of a TRS R is $Lhs = \{l_\Omega | l \rightarrow r \in R\}$.

5. *ω-reduction*, written as $\to_\omega$ is defined on Ter_Ω as

$$C[t] \to_\omega C[\Omega] \quad \text{if } t \uparrow Lhs \text{ and } t \not\equiv \Omega.$$

A redex w.r.t. $\to_\omega$ is an *ω-redex*.

Ω means 'unknown' or 'bottom'. Ordering relation $s \leq t$ is read "s is weaker than t" or "t is stronger than s".

Definition 2. Let R be a TRS and s and t Ω-terms of $Ter_\Omega(R)$.

1. A predicate P is *monotonic* when it is considered as a function mapping from an Ω-term to truth-values ordered by $ff < tt$ such that
   $$\text{if } s \leq t, \text{ then } P(s) < P(t).$$
2. A monotonic predicate P is *sequential at a term t* if:
   $$(\neg P(t) \wedge \exists s > t.\, P(s)) \implies \exists u.\, (t|u \equiv \Omega \wedge \forall s \geq t.\, P(s) \implies s|u \not\equiv \Omega).$$
   An occurrence u as above is an *index* of P in t. P is sequential if it is sequential at every term which is in normal form (by the original rules of the system, not ω-reduction). $I_p(t)$ is the set of indexes of P in t.
3. $s \to' t$ if and only if $t \equiv s[u := q]$ for some redex occurrence u at s and an arbitrary term q. A predicate nf' of *strong normal form* is defined w.r.t. the reduction $\to'$ such that $nf'(s) = tt$ if $s \to'^* t$ for some t in normal form.
4. An orthogonal system R is *strongly sequential* if nf' is a sequential predicate.

Strongly sequential systems are sequential, but not vice versa. Let $\Omega(t)$ be the result of substituting Ω for every outermost redex t. A *strongly needed redex* of t is a redex at an occurrence in $I_{nf'}(\Omega(t))$.

Proposition 3. *[HL91] Indexes of strongly sequential systems are decomposable but not transitive.*

Definition 4. 1. Let $t \in Ter_\Omega(R)$ such that $\omega(t) = \Omega$ and $u \in I_{nf'}(s), v_1, \ldots, v_n \in I_{nf'}(t)$. If $u \cdot v_i \in I_{nf'}(s[u := t])$ for every $s \in Ter_\Omega$ and $u \in I_{nf'}(s)$, then v_i is a *transitive index*.
2. A TRS R is called *index-transitive* if each $t \in Ter_\Omega(R)$ such that $\omega(t) = \Omega$ has a transitive index.

Index-transitive at Definition 4 is the same as *transitive* at [TSvEP93].

Proposition 5. *[TSvEP93] If a TRS R is index-transitive, then R is strongly sequential.*

Definition 6. 1. Let $q, t \subseteq Ter_\Omega$. An occurrence u at t such that $t|u \equiv \Omega$ is said to be a *direction for q* if $t[u := error] \# q$.
2. Let $Lhs^* = \{p | \Omega < p$ and p is a subterm of l for some $l \in Lhs\}$. A *transitive direction* is defined as a direction for Lhs^*.

Definition 7. A *simple ω-redex* is a closed ω-redex s such that $\Omega < s$, no proper subterm of s is an ω-redex, and s is not a redex.

Proposition 8. *Let s be a simple ω-redex. An occurrence v is a transitive index of s if and only if v is a transitive direction of s.*

Proof. By [Byu94].   □

Theorem 9. *[TSvEP93] Let R be a TRS. R is index-transitive if and only if every simple ω-redex $t \in \{p | \Omega < p < r$ for some $r \in Lhs \}$ has a transitive direction.*

Strongly sequential constructor systems are orthogonal constructor systems which are strongly sequential. Strongly sequential constructor systems are index-transitive [KM91].

Often operators at proper subterms in the LHSs of rules make the system intricate while constructor systems are more manageable. We concern systems which can be transformed into strongly sequential constructor systems.

Definition 10. A *simple ω-term* is a closed ω-term s such that s is an operator term, $s \uparrow Lhs^*$, no proper subterm of s is an ω-redex, and s is not a redex.

Definition 11. A TRS R is *transformable* if every simple ω-term has a transitive direction.

Obviously transformable systems are strongly sequential, but not vice versa. For example, cosider LHSs : $F(G(x, S(0)), B), F(A, G(x, S(y))), G(1, 1)$. A system with these rules are strongly sequential, but it is not transformable as a simple ω-term $G(\Omega, S(\Omega))$ has no transitive direction.

4 Separable Systems

4.1 Separation trees

Every term of the λ-calculus has a Böhm tree, which is considered to be the 'value' of a term [Bar84]. The concept has been extended to orthogonal TRSs [AKK+94], in which there are several candidates for a notion of "undefined" term on which to base the definition of Böhm trees. Common to these is the minimal condition that the proper subterms of left-hand sides should be meaningful. Based on this notion, we construct *separation trees*, which adapt to term rewrite systems the "Böhm-out" construction of λ-calculus.

Definition 12. $\mathcal{P}_F$ is the set of tuples obtained by removing the principal function symbol F from the LHSs of F-rules.

1. An occurrence u is *useful* for $\mathcal{P}_F$ if $\forall p \in \mathcal{P}_F, u \in O(p)$ and $p|u$ is not a variable. (For convenience, occurrences of $\mathcal{P}_F$ will be those of LHSs of the F-rules. So, every occurrence of $\mathcal{P}_F$ is not λ.)
2. A *separation tree* U for a set $\mathcal{P}_F$ is a tree, whose nodes are labelled by occurrences, such that
   - the root u_0 is a useful occurrence of $\mathcal{P}_F$,
   - subtrees are separation trees of $\mathcal{P}_{F_i}$, for $1 \le i \le n$, which do not re-use previous useful occurrences again, where $\mathcal{P}_F$ is partitioned into equivalence classes modulo the symbols at u_0 such that $\mathcal{P}_F = \mathcal{P}_{F_1} \cup \ldots \cup \mathcal{P}_{F_n}$.

3. A separation tree U is *complete* if, in the result of recursive partition of $\mathcal{P}_F$, the corresponding partitioned set for every leaf of U is a singleton; otherwise it is *partial*.

4. $\mathcal{P}_F$ is *distinct* if $\mathcal{P}_F$ has a complete separation tree. The F-rules are *separable* if $\mathcal{P}_F$ are distinct.

5. A constructor system is *separable* if every set of rewrite rules for an operator is separable.

Example 1.

(i) Rules-1

$F(x, A, B, C) \rightarrow 1$
$F(B, x, A, C) \rightarrow 2$
$F(A, B, x, C) \rightarrow 3$

(ii) Rules-2

$F(x, A, B, C) \rightarrow 1$
$F(B, x, A, C) \rightarrow 2$
$F(A, B, x, D) \rightarrow 3$

(iii) Rules-3

$F(x, A, B, C, S(D)) \rightarrow 1$
$F(B, x, A, C, S(D)) \rightarrow 2$
$F(A, B, x, C, S(E)) \rightarrow 3$

The occurrence 4 is useful at (i). Because every symbol at 4 is the same, no partition is made, and then there is no other useful occurrence. Hence, (i) is not separable. (ii) and (iii) are separable.

The following shows that the selection order of useful occurrences is irrelevant to the success of constructing a separation tree.

Proposition 13. *Let the F-rules be separable and have more than one useful occurrences. Then choosing any one of them arbitrarily leads to a separation tree.*

Proof. By [Byu94]. □

4.2 Transformable separation trees

Definition 14. A *transformable separation tree* U is a separation tree such that wherever there is a path from the root of U containing nodes labelled by u and v, and $u < v$, then the node labelled by v is deeper than the node labelled by u.

Lemma 15. *Every separable system has a transformable separation tree.*

Proof. Let u be a useful occurrence whose depth is not 2. Then, by the structure of terms, there exists another useful occurrence v such that $v < u$ and the depth of v is 2. By Proposition 13, there is a separation tree whose root is v. □

Lemma 16. *Suppose that the F-rules are in a constructor system. The F-rules are strongly sequential if and only if the F-rules are separable.*

Proof. Here, we present only a proof sketch. A detail proof is in [Byu94]. Strongly sequential constructor systems are index-transitive, and then by Theorem 9 every simple ω-redex of the F-rules has a transitive direction. By Lemma 15 every separable system has a transformable separation tree. Then, the proof can be given by showing "every simple ω-redex of the F-rules has a transitive direction if and only if there is a complete transformable separation tree for the F-rules".

Consider a partitioning procedure to construct a complete transformable separation tree U. U is increasing as the partition proceeds. Then, we claim that *there exists an equivalence class P partitioned by U and P has a useful occurrence u $\Leftrightarrow$ there exists a corresponding simple ω-redex s such that*

$$u \text{ is a } TD \text{ of } s \text{ such that } s|u \equiv \Omega, \text{ and } s|v \not\equiv \Omega \Leftrightarrow v \in U,$$

where Ω means a subterm which has not been used previously for partitioning. We prove the above claim by using induction on the size of U. $\quad\Box$

Theorem 17. *Let a system R be a constructor system. R is a strongly sequential if and only if R is separable.*

5 Transformation

5.1 Generic transformation

In the implementation of pattern-matching, pattern-matching for some function symbols should be performed in advance of others. This notion should be preserved in transformation.

Definition 18. Let the F-rules be separable, O_u the set of some useful occurrences of $\mathcal{P}_F$, $O_n = \{u | u$ is an every occurrence of $l \in \mathcal{P}_F$ such that u is not useful for $\mathcal{P}_F\}$, and $O_B = \{u | u$ is a disjoint-minimal occurrence in $O_n \cup O_u\}$. B's are subterms at O_B and A's are subterms other than B's in $\mathcal{P}_F$. Given the F-rules and O_u, O_B is decidable and the *generic transformation* is applied to every F-rule as follows;

$$F(B_{11}, \ldots, B_{1n}, A_{11}, \ldots, A_{1m}) \rightarrow R_1$$
$$\vdots \qquad\qquad\qquad \vdots$$
$$F(B_{k1}, \ldots, B_{kn}, A_{k1}, \ldots, A_{km}) \rightarrow R_k$$

is transformed into

$$F(x_1, \ldots, x_n, A_{11}, \ldots, A_{1m}) \rightarrow F_1(x_1, \ldots, x_n, y_1, \ldots, y_h)$$
$$\vdots \qquad\qquad\qquad \vdots$$
$$F(x_1, \ldots, x_n, A_{p1}, \ldots, A_{pm}) \rightarrow F_p(x_1, \ldots, x_n, y_1, \ldots, y_r)$$
$$F_1(B_{11}, \ldots, B_{1n}, y_1, \ldots, y_h) \rightarrow R_1$$
$$\vdots \qquad\qquad\qquad \vdots$$
$$F_i^1(B_{i1}, \ldots, B_{in}, y_1, \ldots, y_q) \rightarrow R_i$$
$$\vdots \qquad\qquad\qquad \vdots$$
$$F_i^j(B_{(i+j)1}, \ldots, B_{(i+j)n}, y_1, \ldots, y_q) \rightarrow R_{i+j}$$
$$\vdots \qquad\qquad\qquad \vdots$$
$$F_p(B_{p1}, \ldots, B_{pn}, y_1, \ldots, y_r) \rightarrow R_k$$

which satisfies the following conditions. (For convenience sake, the above rules describe the case that all B's are subterms at the level 2.)

1. If all symbols B's are variables in an F-rule, it remains unchanged. Otherwise, B's in the F-rules are replaced by new variables (not already occurring in the system being transformed) x's, the RHSs in the transformed F-rules consist of new operators and include no function symbols but all variables appearing in the LHS at arguments, where y's are variables occurring in A's. At this time, the replacement is made simultaneously for all B's. New rules with new operators $F_1, \ldots, F_p$ for $p \leq k$ are introduced.

2. Define $\simeq$ *equivalence relation* between two terms l and l' as follows:
$$l \simeq l' \Leftrightarrow l \text{ and } l' \text{ differ only the names of their variables.}$$
The rewrite rules are partitioned, based on the equivalence classes of their transformed LHSs (i.e. the equivalence classes modulo symbols A's), and every such equivalence class is replaced by a single rule (every rewrite rule belongs to one of partitioned equivalence classes). In 1, if no equivalence class with two or more rules is created, then $p = k$; otherwise $p < k$ and, for an equivalence class with $j \geq 2$ rules in the original F-rules, there are corresponding j F_i-rules.

3. Let $\mathcal{F}_i \subseteq R$ be an equivalence class created in the generic transformation and F_i-rules its corresponding new rules in the transformed system. For every $v \in O_B$ and every pair of LHSs l_1 and l_2 of $\mathcal{F}_i$, there is a corresponding occurrence u and a pair of LHSs l_1' and l_2' of the F_i-rules such that u is at the level 2, $l_1|v \simeq l_1'|u$ and $l_2|v \simeq l_2'|u$.

In Definition 18, all function symbols appearing in the LHSs of the original system appear in the LHSs of a transformed system. All RHSs of the original F-rules never change and appear as RHSs in the transformed system. On the other hand, O_n is decidable. Hence, given the F-rules and O_u, O_B is decidable. The set O_A of occurrences of A's are useful and decidable such that $O_A = O_U - O_u$ for the set O_U of all useful occurrences of $\mathcal{P}_F$.

Example 2. Suppose the following F-rules are given.

$$F(C(z, A), B, E) \rightarrow 1$$
$$F(C(B, z), A, E) \rightarrow 2$$
$$F(C(A, B), z, D) \rightarrow 3$$

Given $O_u = \{3\}$ and $O_u = \phi$, the rules are transformed as (i) and (ii), respectively. It is easy to see $O_n = \{1 \cdot 1, 1 \cdot 2, 2\}$. In (i), $O_B = \{1 \cdot 1, 1 \cdot 2, 2, 3\}$, and substitution of O_B creates a equivalence class with three rules, hence they are replaced with a single rule, and three new rules are created. In (ii), $O_B = \{1 \cdot 1, 1 \cdot 2, 2\}$, and substitution of O_B creates a equivalence class with two rules, hence they are replaced with a single rule, and two new rules are created.

(i)
$$F(C(x_1, x_2), x_3, x_4) \rightarrow F_1(x_1, x_2, x_3, x_4)$$
$$F_1(z, A, B, E) \rightarrow 1$$
$$F_1(B, z, A, E) \rightarrow 2$$
$$F_1(A, B, z, D) \rightarrow 3$$

(ii)
$$F(C(x_1, x_2), x_3, E) \rightarrow F_1(x_1, x_2, x_3)$$
$$F(C(x_1, x_2), x_3, D) \rightarrow F_2(x_1, x_2, x_3)$$
$$F_1(z, A, B) \rightarrow 1$$
$$F_1(B, z, A) \rightarrow 2$$
$$F_2(A, B, z) \rightarrow 3$$

The generic transformation can be described by transformable separation trees. Suppose a transformable separation tree U in a form of Fig. 1, where U_A consists of O_A in Definition 18. After the generic transformation, the pattern-matching sequence for U_A is performed in the transformed F-rules and the pattern-matching sequence for U_i's ($1 \leq i \leq p$) in the new rules. By Definition 18.3, when some subterms in the patterns of an equivalence class created by the generic transformation are moved to patterns of new rules, their 'structure' is preserved in the new rules. It is not difficult to see that, for every U_i, there is a corresponding separable trees V_i in the corresponding new rules so that there is a one-to-one corresponding mapping between U_i's and V_i's. By Proposition 13, we don't have to care what the specific structures of U_i's and V_i's are.

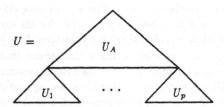

Fig. 1. Transformable separation tree

Lemma 19. *A set of rewrite rules is separable if and only if its transformed rules satisfying the generic transformation are separable.*

5.2 Transformation functions

In this subsection, we demonstrate how transformable systems are transformed. Three transformation functions $Co, T2$, and ES are introduced. The application of Co (resp. $T2$ and ES) to a transformable system R is written as $Co(R)$ (resp. $T2(R)$ and $ES(R)$).

Definition 20. Let R be a separable system whose patterns are not deeper than the level 2 and $F(t_1, \ldots, t_n)$ be a LHS. We say that F *pattern-matches at the ith place* if t_i is not a variable. If there is a useful occurrence i for the F-rules, then i is an *always-matched* place of F. If there is no function symbol at i for all F-rules, then i is a *never-matched* place of F. Otherwise, i is a *sometimes-matched* place of F. A separable system is *flat* if every LHS has level no more than 2 and there exist no sometimes-matched patterns.

Operator terms in patterns In Example 3.(i), proper subterms $G(x, S(0))$ and $G(x, E)$ in LHSs have an operator G. The LHSs of these rules are transformed into terms in constructor form by adding new rules, whose corresponding LHSs are $G(x, S(0))$ and $G(x, E)$ and RHSs consists of new function symbols C_1 and C_2 and variables occurring at LHSs, and by replacing subterms of $G(x, S(0))$ and $G(x, E)$

in the original rules by RHSs of the new rules, which transforms the LHSs of the F-rules into $F(C_1(x), B)$ and $F(C_2(x), C)$.

In Example 3.(ii), an operator G is nested in the pattern. By one application of Co, a new rule $G(G(A)) \rightarrow C_1$ is created, which still has an operator G in the pattern. Another application of Co transforms them into a constructor system.

In Example 3.(iii), two proper subterms $G(1, x)$ and $G(1, y)$ of LHSs are $\simeq$ equivalent, $G(1, x) \simeq G(1, y)$. Such $\simeq$ equivalent operator terms are replaced by a same constructor term $C_1(x)$, and only one new rule whose LHS is $G(1, x)$ is introduced.

Example 3.

(i)

$F(G(x, S(0)), B) \rightarrow 1$
$F(G(x, E), C) \rightarrow 2$
$G(D, D) \rightarrow 3$
is transformed into
$F(C_1(x), B) \rightarrow 1$
$F(C_2(x), C) \rightarrow 2$
$G(x, S(0)) \rightarrow C_1(x)$
$G(x, E) \rightarrow C_2(x)$
$G(D, D) \rightarrow 3$

(ii)

$F(G(G(A))) \rightarrow 1$
$G(B) \rightarrow 2$
is transformed into
$F(C_1) \rightarrow 1$
$G(C_2) \rightarrow C_1$
$G(A) \rightarrow C_2$
$G(B) \rightarrow 2$
$G(A, B) \rightarrow 3$

(iii)

$F(G(1, x), A) \rightarrow 1$
$F(B, G(1, y)) \rightarrow 2$
$G(A, B) \rightarrow 3$
is transformed into
$F(C_1(x), A) \rightarrow 1$
$F(B, C_1(x)) \rightarrow 2$
$G(1, x) \rightarrow C_1(x)$

Algorithm 21. *(Co)*
Let s be an outermost proper operator term in LHSs. Then, replace s by a new term $C(x_1, \ldots, x_n)$, where C is a new constructor and the x_i's are variables occurring in s, and make a new rule $s \rightarrow C(x_1, \ldots, x_n)$. If there exists another proper operator term s' in LHSs such that $s \simeq s'$, then s' is also replaced by $C(x_1, \ldots, x_n)$. Repeat this procedure until there exist no operators at proper subterms in the patterns. □

Co is not an instance of the generic transformation of Definition 18.

Patterns at deeper than level 2 The transformation function $T2$ has already been introduced as *Transformation-1* at [Ken90]. $T2$ eliminates sometimes-matched patterns as well as patterns whose level is greater than 2. Then, repeating $T2$ transforms a strongly sequential constructor system into a flat system.

In the Example 4.(i), the first rule has the pattern 0 at level 3, and the second rule has the symbol S at the level 3 and 0 at 4, and there are sometimes-matched pattern at occurrences *1* and *2*. The algorithm 'trims' the LHSs to level 2, by replacing deeper subterms and sometimes-matched patterns by new variables. Then, two new LHSs, $H(y, x, S(z))$ and $H(x, y, S(x))$, are obtained. Since $H(y, x, S(z)) \simeq H(x, y, S(z))$, these two rules are replaced by a single rule $H(x, y, S(z)) \rightarrow H_1(x, y, z)$ where H_1 is a new function symbol. This rule does the pattern-matching common to the first and the second rule, down to level 2 for always-matched patterns. By adding two rules, $H_1(C, y, 0) \rightarrow 1$ and $H_1(x, C, S(0)) \rightarrow 2$ the rest of pattern matching is done. The second rules has the pattern 0 at level 3. The algorithm is applied again to the second rule, the Example 4.(i) is obtained.

Example 4.

(i)

$H(C, x, S(0)) \to 1$

$H(x, C, S(S(0))) \to 2$

is transformed into

$H(x, y, S(z)) \to H_1(x, y, z)$

$H_1(C, y, 0) \to 1$

$H_1(x, C, S(w)) \to H_2(w)$

$H_2(0) \to 2$

(ii)

$F(G(G(A))) \to 1$

$G(B) \to 2$

is transformed into

$F(G(x)) \to F_1(x)$

$F_1(G(A)) \to 1$

$G(B) \to 2$

The algorithm of $T2$ can be defined simply by using the Definition 18; define the set O_u of useful occurrences whose levels are greater than 2.

Sometimes-matched patterns A transformation function ES has already been introduced as the *Transformation-2* at [Ken90]. In Example 5.(i), the occurrence *1* of the F-rules is sometimes-matched. Subterms of Nil and $Cons(x, y)$ are replaced by fresh variables, and rules of a new function symbol F_1 are added. In this replacement, an equivalent class is created. The second and third rule of Example 5.(i) become equivalent, so they are replaced by a single rule: $F(x_1, Cons(x, y)) \to F_1(x_1, x, y)$.

Rules in Example 5.(ii) are not strongly sequential. The G_1-rules are introduced by ES, and then they cannot be simplified further.

Example 5.

(i)

$F(x, Nil) \to 1$

$F(Nil, Cons(x, y)) \to 2$

$F(Cons(x, y), Cons(x, y)) \to 3$

are transformed into

$F(x, Nil) \to 1$

$F(x_1, Cons(x, y)) \to F_1(x_1, x, y)$

$F_1(Nil, x, y) \to 2$

$F_1(Cons(x, y), z) \to 3$

(ii)

$G(x, A, B, C) \to 1$

$G(B, x, A, C) \to 2$

$G(A, B, x, C) \to 3$

transformed into

$G(x, y, z, C) \to G_1(x, y, z)$

$G_1(x, A, B) \to 1$

$G_1(B, y, A) \to 2$

$G_1(A, B, x) \to 3$

The algorithm of ES is simply obtained by defining $O_u = \phi$ in the Definition 18.

5.3 Transformation of transformable systems

Lemma 22. *If R is transformable, then $Co(R)$ is a strongly sequential constructor system.*

Proof. Immediate from Definition 11. □

Theorem 23. *If R is transformable, then both $T2(Co(R))$ and $ES(Co(R))$ are flat.*

Proof. By Lemma 22 $Co(R)$ is strongly sequential (or separable). $T2$ and ES satisfy the generic transformation. Then, by Lemma 19 $T2(Co(R))$ and $ES(Co(R))$ are separable with whose LHSs have levels no more than 2. □

6 Correctness

In this section, transformation means the transformation of transformable systems by $Co, T2$, or ES.

6.1 Adequate simulation

Fact 24. *Let τ_1 be one of transformation functions $Co, T2$, and ES, and suppose a transformable system R is transformed into a system R'; i.e. $\tau_1 : R \to R'$. Then the following facts are observable.*

1. *R' consists of all signature of R and some new function symbols; $Ter(R') \supsetneq Ter(R)$.*
2. *The reduction steps of R' are finer than R. For every one step reduction of R, there is at least one or more corresponding reduction steps in R': $s \to_R t \implies \tau_1(s) \to_{R'}^* \tau_1(t)$.*
3. *All normal forms of R are not normal form in R'. Hence, normal forms of R and R' are not the same.*
   - *In Example 3.(ii), $G(A)$ is normal form in R but not in R'.*
   - *In Example 4.(i), $H(C, 0, S(A))$ is normal form in R but not in R'.*
4. *If a term s has normal form in R, s has normal form in R'; the notion of normalizing is preserved.*

Definition 25. A *reduction graph* of a term s is rooted directed graph labeled as follows.

- Each node is labeled with a term.
- For each arc, the term labeling its source is reducible in one step to the term labeling its target.
- The root of the graph is labeled with s, and all nodes are accessible from the root.

Fig. 2.(i) shows that a reduction of R is implemented by multiple 'finer' reduction steps of R'. Fig. 2.(ii) means the same simulation of Fig. 2.(i) but it says one more thing that every 'finer' reduction step of R' is a part of implementation of a 'coarser' reduction step of R. If a transformation statisfies Fig. 2.(i) and Fig. 2.(ii), then R and R' *bisimulate*.

In the simulation that, for a reduction $s \to_R t$, there are multiple-step reductions $\tau_1(s) \to_{R'}^* \tau_1(t)$ in R', the last reduction step to reach to $\tau_1(t)$ is called an *external step*, and all other reduction steps starting from $\tau_1(s)$ are called *internal steps*. Terms of R' reached by internal steps are called *internal terms*. Terms of R' which are not internal are called *original terms*, which are the same as the terms of R. Note that there is a one-to-one correspondence between external steps of R' and reduction steps of R.

Fact 26. *Suppose the system R is transformed into the system R'. Let $R'' \subseteq R'$ be a set of rules whose RHSs are newly created by transformation. Then, we can see that the newly created RHSs has only one function symbol at the root, and all its*

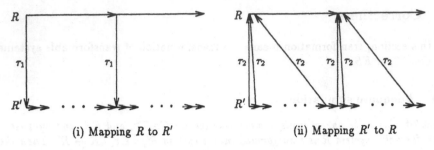

(i) Mapping R to R' (ii) Mapping R' to R

Fig. 2. Bisimulation(R, R', τ_1, τ_2)

arguments are variables and linear if they exists. Consider a set S of rewrite rules obtained by swapping the LHSs and the RHSs in R''. Then, S has the following properties.

- *S is strongly normalizing; in T2 and ES, the principal function symbols of LHSs of S do not appear at RHSs, and, in Co, they appear at RHSs but not recursively.*
- *S is orthogonal.*
- *A term t is normal form in S if and only if $t \in Ter(R)$.*
- *Given an internal term of R', S returns a corresponding original term. Given an original term, S returns it.*

We define a function rev : $Ter(R') \to Ter(R)$ as the the set S of rewrite rules.

Definition 27. Suppose a system R is transformed into a system R' by a transformation function $\tau_1 : R \to R'$ and its reverse mapping is $\tau_2 : R' \to R$.

1. The mapping τ_1 is an *adequate forward* mapping if:
   - $\tau_1(s) \equiv s$ for every $s \in Ter(R)$.
   - If $s \in Ter(R)$ has a normal form R, then $\tau_1(s)$ has normal form in R'.
   - For every reduction $s \to_R t$, there exist reductions $\tau_1(s) \to_{R'}^* \tau_1(t)$.
2. The mapping τ_2 is an *adequate backward* mapping if:
   - $\tau_2 = rev$ (which is surjective).
   - If $s \in Ter(R')$ is normal form, $\tau_2(s)$ is normal form in R.
   - For $s, t \in R'$, if $s \to_{R'}^* t$, there exist reductions $\tau_2(s) \to_R^* \tau_2(t)$.
3. Suppose the above 1 and 2 hold. Transformation (R, R', τ_1, τ_2) is *adequate bisimulation* if:
   - $\tau_1(\tau_2(t))$ is convertible to t and $\tau_2(\tau_1(s)) \equiv s$ for all $t \in Ter(R')$ and for all $s \in Ter(R)$.
   - $\tau_2(t) \to_R s \Leftrightarrow t \to_{R'}^* \tau_1(s)$ for $s \in Ter(R)$ and $t \in Ter(R')$.

Fact 24 and Fact 26 support the following simulation properties.

Lemma 28. *(Soundness of simulation). Suppose a system R is transformed into a system R' by one of transformation functions $Co, T2$, and ES. Then, there exists an adequate forward mapping $\tau_1 : R \to R'$.*

Lemma 29. *(Completeness of simulation) Suppose a system R is transformed into a system R' by one of $Co, T2$, and ES. Then, there is an adequate backward mapping $\tau_2 : R' \to R$.*

Theorem 30. *Suppose a transformable system T is transformed into a flat system F by $Co, T2$, and ES. Then, the transformation (T, F, τ_1, τ_2) is an adequate bisimulation.*

Proof. Suppose that T is transformed into F by one-step transformation. Then, by Lemma 28 and Lemma 29, there are adequate forward and backward mappings, and then it is immediate that the transformation is an adequate bisimulation. In case of multi-step transformations, given two adequate forward mappings $\tau_1^1 : R_1 \to R_2$ and $\tau_1^2 : R_2 \to R_3$, it is obvious to see $\tau_1^2 \cdot \tau_1^1$ is also an adequate forward mapping. Similarly the composition of two adequate backward mappings is an adequate backward mapping, since they are surjective. Then, it is immediate that the composition of multi-step adequate bisimulations is also an adequate bisimulation. □

References

[AGM92] S. Abramsky, D. Gabbay, and T. Maibaum, editors. *Handbook of Logic in Computer Science*, volume II. Oxford University Press, 1992.

[AKK+94] Z. Ariola, J.R. Kennaway, J.W. Klop, M.R. Sleep, and F.J. de Vries. Syntactic definitions of undefined: On defining the undefined. In *Theoretical Aspect of Computer Software*, Springer-Verlag, Lecture Notes in Computer Science 789, pages 543–554, 1994.

[Bar84] H.P. Barendregt. *The Lambda Calculus, its Syntax and Semantics*. North-Holland, second edition, 1984.

[Byu94] S. Byun. *The Simulation of Term Rewriting Systems by the Lambda Calculus*. PhD thesis, Univeristy of East Anglia, 1994.

[DJ90] N. Dershowitz and J.-P. Jouannaud. Rewrite systems. In van Leeuwen [vL90], chapter 15.

[HL79] G. Huet and J.-J. Lévy. Call-by-need computations in non-ambiguous systems. Technical Report 359, INRIA, 1979.

[HL91] G. Huet and J.-J. Lévy. Computations in orthogonal rewrite systems I and II. In Lassez and Plotkin [LP91], pages 394–443. (Originally appeared as [HL79].).

[Ken90] J.R. Kennaway. Implementing term rewriting languages in Dactl. *Theoretical Computer Science*, 72:225–249, 1990.

[Klo80] J.W. Klop. *Combinatory Reduction Systems*, volume 127 of *Mathematical Centre Tracts*. CWI, Amsterdam, 1980. PhD Thesis.

[Klo92] J.W. Klop. Term rewriting systems. In Abramsky et al. [AGM92], pages 1–116.

[KM91] J.W. Klop and A. Middeldorp. Sequentiality in orthogonal term rewriting systems. *Journal of Symbolic Computation*, 12:161–195, 1991.

[LP91] J.-L. Lassez and G.D. Plotkin, editors. *Computational Logic: Essay in Honor of Alan Robinson*. MIT Press, 1991.

[Mar94] L. Maranget. Two techniques for compiling lazy pattern matching. Technical Report 2385, INRIA, 1994.

[SPvE93] M.R. Sleep, M.J. Plasmeijer, and M.C.J.D. van Eekelen, editors. *Term Graph Rewriting Theory and Practice*. John Wiley & Sons, 1993.

[TSvEP93] Y. Toyama, S. Smetsers, M.C.J.D. van Eekelen, and M. J. Plasmeijer. The functional strategy and transitive term rewriting systems. In Sleep et al. [SPvE93], pages 61–75.

[vL90]　J. van Leeuwen, editor. *Handbook of Theoretical Computer Science*, volume B: Formal Method and Semantics. North-Holland, Amsterdam, 1990.

An Automaton-Driven Frame Disposal Algorithm and its Proof of Correctness

M Satpathy, A Sanyal and G Venkatesh
email:{mrs,as,gv}@cse.iitb.ernet.in

Department of Computer Science and Engineering,
Indian Institute of Technology, Bombay-400076, India

Abstract. Activation records or frames of function calls, in a functional programming implementation, are either maintained in a stack or in heap. A frame is usually treated alive till the function returns, though long before that its requirement may have been over.

In this paper, we define the concept of disposing a frame at *earliest point in time* and do dispose a frame as soon as we are sure that it will no longer be required. To do this we first construct a finite automaton from the program text and use this automaton to guide the frame disposal. We also prove that the disposal strategy is correct.

The advantages are many. It reduces the size of *root-set* from which the garbage collector starts *pointer-chasing* to scan the live data. It also delays the occurrences of garbage collection and in the process may improve upon the number of such occurrences in a program execution.

Keywords: Functional Programming, Garbage Collection and Static Analysis.

1 Introduction

In an implementation of a functional language, the activation record or the frame of a function could either be kept in stack or in heap. The default strategy, in both the cases, is that a frame is considered alive till the execution of the associated function is complete. But in many cases, somewhere during the evaluation of its body, the function might cease to refer to its frame for the evaluation of its remaining part. In our discussion, the implementation strategy is *call-by-need* or *lazy*. So the natural choice is to keep frames in heap though it is possible to maintain many of them in stack [4]. If a frame is known to be obsolete, it can immediately be returned to the memory-allocator, or, the later could be informed that the frame is no more live. Disposing a frame as early as possible, and not waiting till the function returns, has the following advantages.

– Minimizing space leakage : Garbage collectors collect the whole of live data by traversing pointers from a *root-set* which comprises of the machine registers and the runtime stack. But there can be cases when a function frame is reachable from the root-set, but it is obsolete in the sense of our earlier description. Traversing from such obsolete frames to collect live data will in

turn declare some garbage as genuine data. This problem is otherwise known as *space leakage* [8]. Providing the garbage collector with the information that some frames are obsolete, helps in reducing the amount of space leakage.
- Reducing burden on the garbage collector: If frames are in heap, they are to be collected by a garbage collector. Disposing them as early as possible may prevent the heap area from getting filled up too often, thereby avoiding garbage collection in some cases. Moreover, the frame space that gets collected do not have to undergo the expensive operations usually used to detect garbage objects at run time.

The organization of the paper is as follows. Section 2 defines the concept of frame disposal at near-earliest point in time and describes how frames could be disposed under this strategy with information from the runtime call-tree. Section 3 describes the algorithm to construct an automaton from a given program and how it can be used for disposal. Section 4 describes how to specialize the automaton for efficiency. Section 5 contains the correctness proof. Section 6 extends the near-earliest strategy to the earliest strategy. The final section concludes the paper.

2   Disposal of frames in near-earliest time

When a function body gets executed according to some evaluation order, at some point in between, all information, necessary for the computation of function result, may have already been available. Then at this point in evaluation, the frame can be disposed of without violating the safety criteria. This could better be seen from some examples.

Example 1:   Let   F x y = 1 + (x + y) in   F 1 2.

We assume right-to-left order of evaluation of the arguments to a strict primitive. Evaluation starts by a call to F, whose frame contains the bindings of x and y to 1 and 2 respectively. y will be evaluated first, followed by the evaluation of x. As soon as the evaluation of x is complete, observe that the frame is no longer required and hence could be disposed of.

Example 2:   Let   F x y = 1 + (x + y);   G   z = 2 * z
              in   F (G 2) 3.

Evaluation starts with a call to F, with x bound to (G 2) and y bound to 3. Figure 1(a) shows how the evaluation proceeds. y is evaluated first. Then for the evaluation of x, a call to G is made with its only argument z bound to 2. Now we are in the body of G and for the evaluation of z we have just to get its value from G's frame. After getting this value observe that it is not just that the frame of G is no longer required but so is the frame of F. So at this point in evaluation, both the frames of G and F could be disposed of.

Example 3: Let   F x = H 1 + (2 * G x)
                  G z = z + 1; H p = p - 1
              in   F 2.

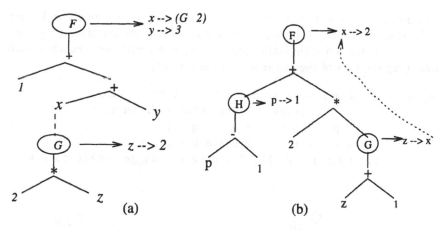

Fig. 1.

In Figure 1(b), see that as soon as the evaluation of z, in the body of function G, is complete, both the frames of G and F could be disposed of. Later when H will be called, evaluation of argument p in its body will dispose its frame. In all these examples a frame was getting disposed as soon as its requirement was over.

Whenever a frame gets disposed as soon as its requirement is over, we say that the frame is getting disposed under *earliest disposal scheme* (EDS). For the purposes of presentation, we shall first discuss a slightly different disposal strategy. In example 3 (figure 1(b)), as soon as evaluation of z is complete, we discard the frame of G but not that of F. We wait till the frame of H gets disposed which in turn disposes F's frame. The modified strategy could be defined as follows:

A frame will be disposed either by the last argument occurrence in its body or by the last function call in its body – whichever occurs later. Now onwards, whenever a frame disposal sticks to this definition, we say that it is getting disposed under *near-earliest disposal scheme* (NEDS).

The points in function bodies which can activate frame disposal (disposal of one or more frames) are termed *release points*. There can be more than one release point in a function body (refer figure 1(b)).

2.1 Runtime call-tree and garbage collection

The way NEDS works could be best described by considering a variant of the runtime call-tree (RTCT) for a particular run of a program. The RTCT, that we intend to describe, of an example program has been shown in figure 2(a). An edge in a RTCT is either labeled with a function name to signify a call to the function, or it is labeled with cond/then/else to signify a control branch. A node in RTCT represents an expression evaluation and it may have a label which could either be *if* or a strict primitive operator. A node with label *if* has two branches – one containing the part of the call-tree for the condition branch and the other containing the part of the call-tree for either the then or the else branch. A node labeled with a strict primitive operator will have branches, each representing the part of the call-tree for an argument.

```
Example 4: Let F m n = if (Minus n 2) <= 0 then   G(n)
                          else   F1 P(n) Q(m) + F2 (m-1) n
            G p    = p + 1; P q   = q - 2
            Q r    = r - 1; Minus a b = a - b
         in  F0 3 4.   /* F0,F1 and F2 are tagged calls to F */
```

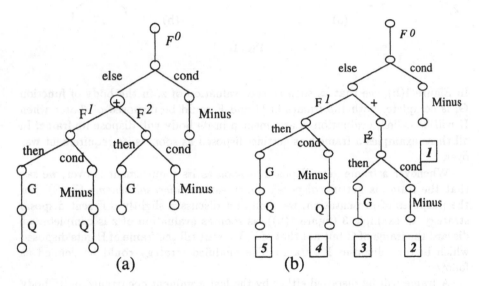

(a)   (b)

Fig. 2.

Under right-to-left order of evaluation, if a function call is the left child of a binary primitive node then whenever it disposes its own frame, it can also dispose its parent frame. A call to the right child cannot do so (under NEDS). To make this evaluation order explicit, we do some minor transformation on the RTCT. The transformation is done at all nodes with primitive operators as labels. The transformed call tree of figure 2(a) has been shown in figure 2(b). A node, labeled with a primitive operator (+ in the figure) is converted to an edge with the the same primitive operator as the label. This edge separates the right branch from the original node.

Now the rules for disposing frames, in the RTCT under NEDS, could be formalized as follows:
– Any function can dispose its immediate parent function frame
– Any function can dispose its ancestor frame provided only a *then* or an *else* edge separates the ancestor and the descendant.

A function frame could be disposed of by the last argument or by the last function call in its body and whichever occurs later. So in the RTCT, leaf-level nodes are the places where disposal will be initiated. A leaf-level call, after disposing its frame, sees if it can dispose its parent. The parent, if gets disposed, will judge its position w.r.t. its own parent and then can think of disposing the later. Like this climbing up in the tree and simultaneous disposal continues till either we reach root of the tree, or an edge labeled with a strict primitive, or an edge labeled with *cond*.

If we reach the root, then disposal is complete. Otherwise we shall have to jump to another leaf-level node. The disposal has stopped at this point since we have encountered an edge, labeled either with a primitive operator or *cond*. We define such an edge as a *blocking edge*. A blocking edge always contains information which leaf-level call to jump next, to continue with the disposal.

Let us explain the whole scenario w.r.t. the transformed call-tree of figure 2(b). There are five leaf-level nodes in the tree. When evaluation order is taken into account, it is not hard to see that the leaf-level node, marked 1, will receive control first. Function *Minus* will get disposed and we will reach the blocking edge *cond*. Then node, marked 2, will receive control next. Again frame of *Minus* will get disposed and we will reach a blocking edge. The node, marked 3, will receive control next which will dispose both, the frame of G and the frame of F^2. Like this it continues till we reach the root.

The conclusion is that, given a RTCT, we can exactly know when and how to dispose all the frames, under NEDS, in a consistent manner. We now intend to mimic the whole process by constructing an automaton from the program text.

2.2 A motivating example

$$M\ [] \ \rightarrow\ []$$
$$M\ x\ :\ xs\ \rightarrow\ S(x)\ :\ (M\ xs)$$

where, S is the successor function and : is the *cons* operator in lists. Assume the *cons* operator is strict in the sense that the *cons-cell* is created only after its arguments are evaluated. Moreover assume that this evaluation order is left-to-right. Figure 3 depicts the RTCT of a particular run of this program. After evaluating function S, the cons operator calls M. In the figure, when execution is at point B, it means that it has encountered the last call to M. At this point, all the frames of M, in the path from R to B, are no longer required and as per NEDS could be disposed. Observe that the cons cells shown in the same path are yet to be created. So if necessary, the space just returned to the memory allocator could be given back for the creation of cons cells. So if a garbage collection was occurring earlier at point B – since no space was available to accommodate the cons cells – it may not occur now.

3 Automaton construction

We will make the following assumptions about the functional program.

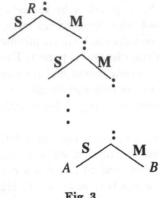

Fig. 3.

- The underlying language is of first order. The evaluation strategy is *lazy*.
- The programs are already in *lambda-lifted* form [6].
- All the recursive call occurrences in the program are distinctly tagged.

3.1 The construction algorithm

At any point of time during the construction, we will have a partial automaton
(PA). A PA is a FSM. We call it partial because the construction is incomplete
and therefore the automaton may not have a final state. Moreover, each state of
the automaton is labeled with a set of pairs. Each pair consists of an expression
drawn from Exp and a binding from $Var \times Exp$. Var is the set of variables
in the program. We use the notation PA(CS) to denote a PA with CS as the
current state.

The automaton construction proceeds as follows. We start with a PA consisting of an initial state which is labeled with the main expression and the empty
binding. A driver routine repeatedly checks whether there is a state and an attached expression-binding pair, such that the state has not been expanded with
respect to the pair. In such a case the driver calls a function *Expand* to do the
expansion.
New states are actually created by the function Expand whose type is
$Expand :: PA \to Exp \to B \to PA$
Here PA is the set of partial automata and B is the set of bindings. The function
Expand is to be inductively defined over the structure of expressions.
$Expand[\![PA(CS)]\!] \, c_{exp} \, \emptyset \, = \,$ Make CS a final state in PA.
where, c_{exp} is any expression involving constants only. A constant expression
evaluation neither creates frames nor it is dependent on any other frame.
$Expand[\![PA(CS)]\!] \, x \, B[x \to e] \, = \,$ Make CS a final state and let PA' be the
resultant automaton ; $Arg\_Expand[\![PA'(CS)]\!] \, e \, \emptyset$
A binding is always closed. Description of Arg_Expand will follow later.
$Expand[\![PA(CS)]\!] \, (* \, c_{exp} \, e) \, B \, = \, Expand[\![PA(CS)]\!] e \, B$

A constant sub-expression has no contribution to creation of frames.

$Expand[\![PA(CS)]\!] \ (* \ e \ c_{exp}) \ B \ = \ Expand[\![PA(CS)]\!]e \ B$

$Expand[\![PA(CS)]\!] \ (* \ e_1 \ e_2) \ B \ = \ $ Extend PA as shown in the figure

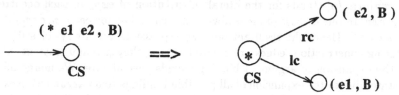

lc and rc stand for the left and right children of the primitive.

$Expand[\![PA(CS)]\!] \ (if \ e_1 \ then \ e_2 \ else \ e_3) \ B = \ $ Extend PA as in the figure

$Expand[\![PA(CS)]\!] \ (F \ e_1 \dots e_n) \ B \ = \ /*F \ a_1 \dots a_n = E$ is the definition*/

```
if ((F is non-recursive) OR
    (F is recursive but not yet occurred in path from initial
     state to CS)) then extend PA as shown:
```

(F e1 ... en , B)
$\Longrightarrow$
(E , [a1->e1,...,an->en]#B)

CS   CS   F

```
else
    if (F is recursive but has already occurred in path from
        initial state to CS) then extend PA as shown:
    where, S_F is the state at which F was expanded in the path.
```

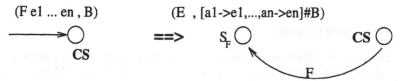

In the schema described, # stands for the composition of bindings and it is defined as follows.

$$B_1 \# B_2 \ = \ \{(x, exp \# B_2) \mid (x, exp) \in B_1\}, \text{ where}$$

$$exp \# B_2 = \text{for each variable } y \in exp, \text{ find the pair } (y, exp_y) \in B_2$$
$$exp \leftarrow exp[exp_y/y]$$
$$\text{endfor}$$

Here $exp[exp_y/y]$ stands for the literal substitution of exp_y in each occurrence of y in exp. In our discussion, it is always the case that for each $(y, exp_y) \in B_2$, exp_y is closed. Hence the resultant binding expressions are always closed.

During construction, edges are created only if they are non-existent. Moreover, the expansion of argument bindings needs special care. We merge all the final states due to the expansion of all possible bindings to an argument. Next we merge the final state of the argument (where argument evaluation starts) with the already merged final states due to possible bindings. The merging strategy not only optimizes the traversal over the automaton (will be discussed later), but it has an important consequence so far as the termination of the automaton is concerned. In a function definition, F x y = . . . (F (x-1) E (y)) . . ., the possible bindings to y is given by $\{G(1), E(G(1))), E(E(G(1))), ...\}$, assuming an initial binding of $G(1)$ to y. In the automaton we need a finite representation for this. By merging the final states we have, for the various possible bindings of y, the convenient representation as shown in figure 4(b).

The function Arg-Expand handles the business of expanding an expression at an argument position in the PA.

Arg-Expand $[PA(CS)]$ e $\emptyset$ = Expand $[PA(CS)]e$ $\emptyset$;
        Merge all the final states that got generated with CS
        and return the resulting partial automaton.

We will now take an example program and use the schema described to construct the corresponding automaton (refer figure 5(a)).

Example 6: F m n = if (Minus n 2) $\leq$ 0 then G^0 T(m) 1
              else F^1 Q(n) P(m) + F^2 (m$-$1) Q(n)
      G a b = if (a=0) then $X_1(1) + X_2(a)$
            else G^1 $(a-1)$ b ; Minus x y = x$-$y
      P,Q,X_1,X_2,T (i) = i$-$1 /*different names for the same function*/
      main: F^0 10 10.

In order to take care of evaluation order of strict primitives, we apply the transformation shown in figure 4(a). The automaton for the example program that we have shown in figure 5(a) has undergone through this transformation.

3.2 Termination issues

The algorithm described works fine excepting that it may not terminate. The source of non-termination is due to recursive edges. Recursive edges are those edges in the automaton which are due to recursive calls and for which, instead of creating a new state, we put a backward edge in the *Expand* scheme. A recursive edge always adds a new expression-binding pair at its target state. The added pair, after due expansion, will in turn add another pair via the same recursive

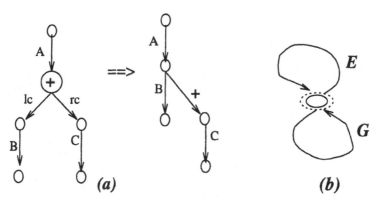

Fig. 4.

edge. So the driver routine will always find a pair for expansion and will not terminate.

But it is always the case that only a finite number of pairs that reach the target of a recursive edge do some useful work in the sense that either they will add new edge(s) to the automaton or they will change a non-final state to a final state. The rest are redundant. To ensure termination, the algorithm should reject such redundant pairs.

Let us call the target of a recursive edge as a *recursive state*. We build at a recursive state a simplified FSM for each argument of a recursive function. The pairs that reach this state modify them incrementally. We call each of them as a state automaton (SA). The structure of a SA for an argument can at most reach a finite structure and then it represents an abstract representation of all possible runtime bindings to the argument. [9].

Theorem 1. *The main automaton algorithm terminates.*

Proof: We add a new pair due to a recursive edge only if the new pair can modify any of the SAs at the target state. But each such SA can at most attain a finite structure. It implies that the number of times a SA can be modified (starting from an initial SA) is also finite. Hence the construction process will be able to add only a finite number of pairs at a recursive state.   □.

4   Specialization of the automaton

As described earlier, frame disposal is done in a bottom-up manner in a RTCT. That is why, for disposal purposes, we shall have to move in reverse order along the edges in the automaton.

A final state in our automaton refers to some point in evaluation, where frame disposal should be triggered. We term such states as *release states*(RS). A possible frame disposal strategy could be like this. As calls are made, we maintain entries for each call in a stack, called the *garbage collection stack* (GCS).

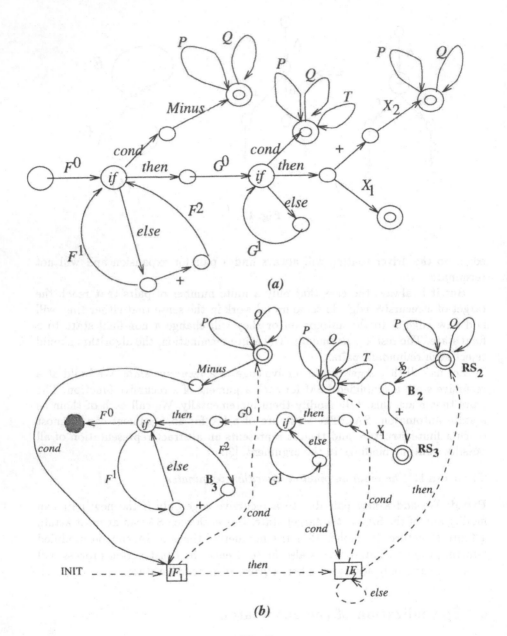

Fig. 5.

Simultaneously we will make traversal, starting from the initial state, on the automation. This we will term as *forward traversal*. A forward traversal terminates with a RS and then a release instruction will initiate frame disposal. A frame, corresponding to the call on the GCS top, will be disposed if there exists a transition from the RS with same function name. This transition on the automaton has to be done in reverse direction. Frame disposal now continues till the GCS top matches with any transition from the current state and stops when the matching fails. We term this traversal during disposal as *backward traversal*.

The forward traversal on the automation is really not necessary. By relying on evaluation order information, and which branch of an if-expression is taken, we can uniquely identify a RS, where control should be, when execution is at a leaf-level node in RTCT. We will now make some modification to the automaton to simulate the forward traversal cheaply.

Let us subscript all if-nodes in the automaton distinctly and address the corresponding *cond/then/else* edges with the same subscripts. Define the sequence of subscripted cond/then/else edges, that we encounter in a loop-free path, from the initial state to a RS, as the path identifier(PI) of the RS. A PI is represented by the set $\{c_{i_1}^1, c_{i_2}^2, \ldots c_{i_k}^k\}$, where $c^i \in \{cond, then, else\}$ and $i_1, \ldots, i_k$ are the subscripts of the corresponding *ifs*. Several RSs can have the same path identifier. Because of our assumption about evaluation order, we can exactly know, given a path identifier, to which RS control will go first, and how control will move from one RS to another within it.

To simplify forward traversal, we create and add a new state IF_j for each node if_j in the automaton, which figure in any of the PIs. The former state will be called as the *if-image* state of the later. The if-image states will be connected in a manner similar to the connectivities of the original if-nodes in the automaton (see figure 5(b)). The intention is – when a forward traversal is in progress, transitions will be done only on the if-image states and when traversal terminates, the last if-image state will make a transition to reach the desired RS.

We will not describe the specialization algorithm here. Figure 5(b) shows the specialized automaton for the one in figure 5(a). In the figure dotted-lines are the edges on which transitions are done in a forward traversal. In a backward traversal, transitions are done on edges with solid lines. When a backward traversal terminates a transition is done on a blocking edge. Such edges have been shown in bold lines.

Let in the figure, control is at RS_2 and a release instruction occur. Then after necessary disposal, control will block at B_2. Since execution will take the left-branch of $+$, RS_3 will be the next RS. So from B_2, there is a transition to RS_3 on blocking edge $+$. When the next release instruction occurs, let backward traversal carries control to finally get blocked at B_3. Then execution will take the left branch of the $+$ operator there and in the process will pass through the if-node there. So from state B_3 there is a transition to IF_1, on the blocked edge $+$. Other edges in the figure can similarly be explained.

4.1 Automaton driven frame disposal

The specialized automaton (see figure 5(b)) is now ready for frame disposal. The procedure is as follows. Whenever a function call is made, an entry for it is pushed to GCS. An entry for a function call in the GCS is identified by the function name and it also stores the frame address. Whenever a frame is no longer required, things will be so engineered that in the program code, we will hit upon an instruction called *RELEASE* and in the automaton, at the same time, we will be at an appropriate RS. The semantics of a release instruction is:

RELEASE: If current state (CS) is not a RS do nothing.
        while GCS *top* matches with any function name,say F, from CS
           Dispose the frame at GCS top and *pop* GCS
           CS ← TRANSIT (CS, F)
        endwhile
        let b be the blocking edge coming out of CS
           TRANSIT(CS,b)

4.2 Non-determinism in the automaton

For garbage collection to proceed smoothly, one requirement is that the automaton should be deterministic. To break the non-determinism we take note of adjacency conditions in the automaton and generate code accordingly. For instance, sometimes we may have to rename various occurrences of the same function call.

5 Proof of correctness

We will prove the correctness of our disposal scheme w.r.t. the strategy we have described in relation to the RTCT. Consider our old automaton, i.e., the one before going through the *specialization phase*. Frame disposal under NEDS, involves a combination of forward and backward traversals. For correctness purposes we will prove that this scheme is semantically equivalent to the scheme in relation to the RTCT. GCS normally stores entries for each function call. Now let us also push entries for blocking edges and if's branches, i.e., whenever the right operand to a primitive operator is evaluated, we push the primitive operator to GCS; and whenever an if-branch is taken, we push the corresponding cond/then/else label. During backward traversals we will ignore all such additional entries.

Theorem 2. *When execution reaches a leaf-level node in RTCT, then the control in the automaton will be at a* release *state.*

Proof Sketch : As execution reaches a leaf-level node, GCS then stores the current execution path, starting from the root of RTCT to the leaf-level node. GCS entries, from bottom to top, can now be thought of as a string. If such a string is accepted by the automaton, we are done. This can be proved by induction on the length of the prefixes of the string that GCS represents (i.e. for a prefix of any length, there exists a valid transition path in the automaton) [9]. □.

Our algorithm instead of doing forward traversal, makes some alternative transitions on the automaton to simulate it. The alternative transition is correct since it relies on evaluation order information and takes note of which if-branch is taken.

Theorem 3. *The frames that get disposed during a backward traversal are indeed disposed under NEDS.*

Proof: When execution is at a leaf-level node in RTCT, GCS by then stores the complete trace of the execution path. Then a release instruction is issued to start a backward traversal which refers to GCS each time for disposing a frame. So the way we dispose a frame and which frames are the candidates are disposal are exactly same as they are in relation to the RTCT. The only thing we have to show is that after disposing the desired sequence of frames, nothing else should be disposed. This is ensured by generating code such that after the disposal of the desired sequence of frames, matching of the frame at GCS top with the transition from the current state fails. □

For correctness, another safety issue has to be taken care of. Release instructions, which immediately follow a forward traversal, induce backward traversals and such instructions are the only ones which should dispose frames. Other redundant release instructions should not have any impact on frame disposal.

Consider the following example.

let $Q(a) = a + 1; P(b) = b;$
in $Q(1) + P(P(2)).$

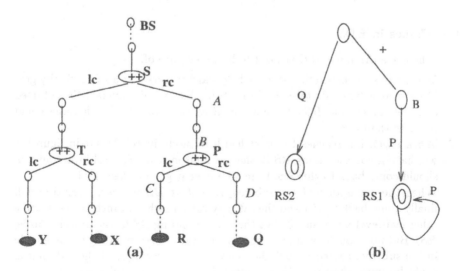

Fig. 6.

In figure 6(b), when control is at $RS1$, a RELEASE instruction will dispose both the frames of P and then control will move to state B. But execution is still at $RS1$ (at corresponding position in the current execution path) and when it comes to state B, it will encounter another RELEASE instruction due to the interior call to P. This will be so since both the calls to P do share the same code. The present RELEASE instruction is clearly redundant. When the automaton is specialized there will be a transition from B to $RS2$ on the blocking edge $+$. So when the redundant release instruction comes, control will be at $RS2$. And now no disposal should occur. To prevent this, we take into account the adjacency conditions in the program and ensure that at this point, the above instruction will never find a match on the GCS top.

6 Back to earliest-time disposal

Let the definition of a function B be of the form
$$B(x) = C(1) + D(x).$$
Observe that, the last use of the frame of B gets over with the evaluation of the right operand of $+$. In figure 6, the node with label $++$ signifies this fact. Similar things can also be said about nodes S and T. So under EDS, when D's frame gets disposed, B's frame can also be dispossed along with it. Disposal of B will lead to the disposal of A and since the left-child of node S is independent of its parent frame, at this point A can also dispose its parent frame. Disposal in this manner continues till control gets blocked at some state, say BS. But thread of execution is still at Q from where it will come back to P to take the path from P to R. Execution will never take the path from P to S till the evaluation of the left branch of P is not over. So under EDS, control in the automaton has deviated from the path of execution which never happens in case of NEDS.

6.1 Issues in EDS

Now there are three issues that need to be taken care of.

1. When a release instruction starts a backward traversal at a RS, it finally gets blocked at a blocked state (In figure 6(b), backward traversal that started at Q gets blocked at BS). In an automaton, the number of such states could be more than one.

2. When execution reaches the next leaf-level node in RTCT (R in figure) it will have a corresponding RS in the automaton. Now control in automaton should come back to this RS, from wherever it got blocked in (1).

3. When the evaluation of the subtree, rooted at BS is over, execution will finally come back to BS and then it may take another branch to reach some other leaf-level node, say Z. Let the corresponding RS in the automaton be RS_z. But now control will be lying at some state, corresponding to some node in the subtree, rooted at BS. The number of such nodes in the automaton could be more than one. Now control, from there, should come to RS_z so that the next backward traversal will be in order.

The problem can be solved if we remember the branches which are encountered in a backward traversal path and which execution will pick up one by one for subsequent evaluation. So all ++-nodes that we encounter in a backward traversal path should be stored in a queue. Each backward traversal path will have its own queue. Such queues will be referred to in a LIFO manner. So what is needed is to maintain this stack of queues at runtime. Alternatively we can annotate all ++-nodes (each ++ occurrence in the program) and generate code accordingly to simulate such a stack of queue behavior [9].

7 Conclusion

In this paper, we have discussed a frame disposal algorithm that disposes frames as soon as their use is over. The disposal is guided by a finite automaton that is constructed from programs in a first order language. We have shown that the disposal strategy is safe and correct.

If we construct an automaton for a large program its structure may be quite complex. Then we can create a set of automata instead of making one so that each one remains simple enough and they will interact among themselves to do necessary disposal [9].

References

1. Appel A. W., Garbage Collection *in Topics in Advanced Language Implementation (Ed. Peter Lee)*, The MIT Press, 1991.
2. Chase D. R., *Garbage Collection and other Optimizations*, Ph. D. thesis, Dept. of Computer Science, University of Houston, Texas, 1987.
3. Fairbrain J. & Wray C., TIM: A simple lazy abstract machine to execute supercombinators, Proc. of *Conference on Functional Programming and Computer Architecture*, LNCS 274, Springer Verlag, 1987.
4. Goldberg B. & Young G. P., Higher Order Escape Analysis: Optimizing Stack Allocation in Functional Programming Implementations, European Symposium on Programming (ESOP-90), LNCS 432, Springer Verlag, 1990.
5. Inoue K., Seki H. & Yagi H., Analysis of Functional Programs to Detect Run-Time Garbage Cells, ACM TOPLAS, October 1988.
6. Johnsson T., Lambda-lifting – transforming programs to recursive equations, Proc. of the *Conference on Functional Programming and Computer Architecture*, Nancy, LNCS 201, Springer Verlag, 1985
7. Lieberman H., Hewitt C., A real-time garbage collector based on the lifetimes of objects, Communication of the ACM, 23(6):419-429, 1983.
8. Peyton Jones S.L.P., *The Implementation of Functional Programming Languages*, Printice Hall, 1987.
9. Satpathy M., Issues in Implementation of Functional Programming Languages, Ph. D. Thesis, Dept. of Computer Science and Engg., I.I.T. Bombay (In Preparation).

Labeled λ-Calculus and a Generalised Notion of Strictness (An Extended Abstract)

Milind Gandhe and G. Venkatesh and Amitabha Sanyal

Department of Computer Science and Engineering
Indian Institute of Technology
Bombay 400 076

Abstract. The problem of analyzing functional programs requires us to identify subterms of a given term with certain properties. In this paper, we introduce a variant of λ-calculus called labeled λ-calculus to help us build a theory of positional analysis. Labeled λ-calculus uses sets of labels as a means of naming subterms and keeping track of them. We then define a stronger form of strictness called need and show how labeled λ-calculus can be used to compute need. We extend the notion of the need to subterms and use labeled λ-calculus to identify needed subterms. We also use this notion to qualify a function's need for its argument – to identify how much of the argument to a function is needed to evaluate an application to head normal form.

1 Introduction

In recent years, there has been considerable interest in analysis of functional programs (for a good survey, see [1]). An analysis problem typically requires identification of subexpressions of a given program expression that satisfy a given property. Analysis helps in optimizing or debugging the programs by replacing or modifying the identified subterms. A well-studied analysis problem is the problem of strictness [10, 4, 6]. If a function can be shown to be strict, then calls to that function can be made using the cheaper "call-by-value" strategy rather that the usual "call-by-name" strategy without any change in the meaning of the program. Other examples of analysis problems include *slicing* and *profiling*. The slicing problem is to identify subterms in the functional program that could contribute to a specified error. The problem of profiling to attribute the use of resources such as space and time to subterms.

While a lot of work has been done on analysis of functional programs, a theoretical basis for such "positional analysis" is made difficult by the fact that computation in λ-calculus, *viz* β-reduction actually changes the programs. This is unlike imperative programs, where the program remains the same and only the state is affected by the execution of the program. Thus, during the execution of a functional program, entire subterms may get deleted and new subterms that did not exist in the original program may get created. To solve the analysis problem, we need to correlate a single β-step in the modified program to subterms in the original programs.

In this paper, we introduce an enriched form of λ-calculus called *labeled λ-calculus*. Labeled λ-calculus uses *labels* as a means of naming subterms and keeping track of them. This idea of marking subterms of a λ-term was first proposed by Levy [8]. Levy used to prove a completeness result for a reduction strategy called *inward-out* reduction. Our approach is slightly different from Levy's, in that we permit sets of labels instead of sequences and are basically interested in the sets that would annotate the spine after reduction. Labeled λ-calculus was also used by Hyland [7] to restrict the amount of resources available to a redex. We present the theory of labeled λ-calculus in Section 2.

In Section 3, we study the problem of analyzing strictness and show how labeled λ-calculus can be used for this problem. A function f is said to be strict if $f \perp = \perp$. This was intended to formalize the notion of *need* – a function is strict in its argument if it "needs" its argument. However, there are functions such as $\lambda x.\perp$, which do not need its argument and yet are strict. We show how this stronger problem of need can also be solved using labeled λ-calculus. We then extend the notion of need to cover subterms of a given term. This generalizes the definition of a needed redex [9]. The notion of a needed sub-term finds application in many analysis problems such as strictness and slicing. In this paper, we discuss one such application – we use labeled λ-calculus to qualify a function's need for its arguments. Thus we given a function f and a Λ_l term M, we can identify what subterms of M are needed to evaluate the application $f M$ to head normal form.

2 Labeled λ-Calculus

The notational conventions used here are those of [2]. We let $x, y, z, \ldots$ range over the set Var of variables. In addition, we assume a set L of labels and let $l_0, l_1, l_2, \ldots$ range over subsets of L. We let $M, N, \ldots$ range over the terms Λ_l of labeled λ-calculus.

Definition 1 A Λ_l Term. M is a term belonging to Λ_l iff M is generated by the following rules:

1. x is a Λ_l term.
2. If M is a Λ_l term, then so is $\lambda x.M$.
3. If M and N are Λ_l terms, then so is MN.
4. If M is a Λ_l term and $l \subseteq L$, then $l : M$ is a Λ_l term.
5. Nothing else is a Λ_l term.

$FV(M)$ denotes the set of free variables of M. Following the variable convention of [2, Convention 2.1.13], we assume that all bound variables occuring in a given mathematical context are chosen to be different from the free variables. This assumption makes the following definition simpler.

Definition 2 Substitution. The result of substituting N for x in M (notation $M[x := N]$) is defined as follows:

$$x[x := N] \equiv N$$

$$y[x := N] \equiv y, \qquad x \not\equiv y$$
$$(\lambda y.M_1)[x := N] \equiv \lambda x.(M_1[x := N])$$
$$(M_1 M_2)[x := N] \equiv (M_1[x := N])(M_2[x := N])$$
$$(l : M_1)[x := N] \equiv l : (M_1[x := N])$$

We now present the basic computation rule for the labeled λ-calculus, *viz* the β reduction rule.

Definition 3 β-**reduction.** Any Λ_l term of the form $(\lambda x.M)N$ or $(l : \lambda x.M)N$ is called a *beta redex* and can be reduced using the following rules:

$$(\lambda x.M)N \Rightarrow M[x := N]$$

$$(l : \lambda x.M)N \Rightarrow l : M[x := N]$$

This may result several labels "piling" up at a given Λ_l expression, as can be seen in the following example.

Example 1. Consider the Λ_l term $l_0 : ((l_1 : \lambda x.l_2 : x)(l_3 : \underline{2}))$. A single application of the β-rule gives us the following:

$$l_0 : ((l_1 : \lambda x.l_2 : x)(l_3 : \underline{2})) \Rightarrow l_0 : l_1 : l_2 : l_3 : \underline{2}$$

In order to simplify such terms, we provide another reduction rule – the ϵ-rule.

Definition 4 ϵ-**Reduction.** Any Λ_l term of the form $l_0 : l_1 : M$ is called an ϵ-*redex* and can be reduced using the following rule:

$$l_0 : l_1 : M \Rightarrow (l_0 \cup l_1) : M$$

We say that a Λ_l term is in *normal form* if it has no β- or ϵ-redex. We will use Ω to denote any Λ_l term that does not have a normal form. Thus, we could use Ω to denote the term $(\lambda x.xx)(\lambda x.xx)$.

We now state (without proof) the following important lemma:

Lemma 5 Diamond Lemma. *Let* $\Rightarrow$ *stand for a single* β *or* ϵ *reduction, and* $\Rightarrow *$ *stand for a sequence of such reductions. Then the following holds:*

$$\forall M, M_1, M_2, [M \Rightarrow M_1 \wedge M \Rightarrow M_2 \supset \exists M_3[M_1 \Rightarrow *M_3 \wedge M_2 \Rightarrow *M_3]]$$

The Church-Rosser theorem for labeled λ-calculus is a natural consequence of this lemma:

Theorem 6 Church-Rosser. *Labeled* λ-*calculus is Church-Rosser.*

$$\forall M, M_1, M_2, [M \Rightarrow *M_1 \wedge M \Rightarrow *M_2 \supset \exists M_3[M_1 \Rightarrow *M_3 \wedge M_2 \Rightarrow *M_3]]$$

We now define a function ρ that associates a Λ_l term with the "underlying" unlabeled λ-term.

Definition 7 Label Stripping Function. Define the label stripping function ρ as follows:

$$\rho(x) = x$$
$$\rho(\lambda x.M) = \lambda x.\rho(M)$$
$$\rho(MN) = ((\rho M)(\rho N))$$
$$\rho(l : M) = \rho(M)$$

This function allows to show various results correlating labeled λ-calculus with standard λ-calculus. Thus, the following lemma shows that $\beta\epsilon$-reduction is a conservative extension of the underlying β-reduction.

Lemma 8. *Let M, N be Λ_l terms such that $M \Rightarrow N$. Further, let $\rightarrow$ denote β-reduction in standard λ-calculus. Then, the following holds:*

$$\rho(M) \equiv \rho(N) \vee \rho(M) \rightarrow \rho(N)$$

Proof. By induction on the structure of M.

We extended the notion of *solvability* [2, Definition 2.2.10] to labeled λ-calculus.

Definition 9. A Λ_l term M is said to be solvable if the following holds

$$\exists n \exists M_1 \ldots \exists M_n.M \; M_1 \ldots M_n \Rightarrow *N \wedge (\rho N) = \lambda x.x$$

Then the following lemma follows from Lemma 8.

Lemma 10. *Let M is Λ_l term. M solvable iff ρM is solvable.*

Let us now try to relate standard λ-terms with Λ_l terms. We would like to define a labeling function $\phi : \Lambda \rightarrow \Lambda_l$ such that $\rho(\phi M) = M$. In other words, we are looking for the right inverse of the label stripping function. Clearly such an inverse would not be unique.

Definition 11 Initial Labeling. A labeling function ϕ is said to be initial if

1. Whenever it labels a term M to $l : M$, the set l is singleton.
2. The labeling is distinct – whenever it labels a term M to $l : M$, labels from the set l are not used in labeling any of the subterms of M.

To solve the problem of strictness, we need the concept of the spine. Intuitively the spine of a Λ_l term is the information that we can obtain from a term without performing any reductions on it.

Definition 12 Spine. The spine of a Λ_l term M is a Λ_l term $\Sigma(M)$ defined recursively as follows:

$$\Sigma(x) = x$$
$$\Sigma(\lambda x.M) = \lambda x.\Sigma(M)$$
$$\Sigma(M \; N) = (\Sigma(M)) \; \Omega$$
$$\Sigma(l : M) = l : (\Sigma(M))$$

When we will address the issue of need, we will need to collect the labels of the subterms on the spine together. For this, we define the following function σ which computes the *spine set* of a term.

Definition 13 Spine Set. The *spine set* σM of a labeled term M is defined as follows:

$$\sigma x = \emptyset$$
$$\sigma \lambda x.M = \sigma M$$
$$\sigma(M\ N) = \sigma M$$
$$\sigma(l : M) = l \cup (\sigma M)$$

Then the following lemma is obvious.

Lemma 14. β_ϵ-*reduction monotonically increases the spine set. That is,*

$$M \Rightarrow {*}N \quad \supset \quad (\sigma M) \subset (\sigma N)$$

3 The Notion of Need

We now have enough machinery to address of the issue of strictness analysis using the labeled λ-calculus. Recall that a function f is said to be strict if $f\bot = \bot$. This definition was intended to capture the notion that a function "needs" its argument. The intuition behind such a definition was that if a function which needed its argument was given an argument with no normal form, then head reduction sequence for the application would try to reduce the argument to a normal form and would thus be infinite. Hence the application itself would not have an normal form. However, this ignores the fact that the head reduction sequence could be infinite because of the function itself. Consider the $M \equiv \lambda$-term $\lambda f((\lambda x.xx)(\lambda x.xx))$. $M\ N$ does not have a normal form for any λ-term N. Hence M is strict. However, we can see that the argument of the term is never needed or reduced. To remedy this, we propose the following stronger notion:

Definition 15 Need. A function f is said to *need* its argument if

1. f is strict ie. $f\bot = \bot$.
2. f is solvable ie $\exists N.f\ N \rightarrow \lambda x.x$

We can now give a general characterization of functions that need their arguments.

Lemma 16. *A term M needs its argument iff it has a head normal form of the form $\lambda x_1 \ldots \lambda x_n.x_1\ M_1 \ldots M_m$.*

We now state without proof a useful property about the need of functions.

Lemma 17. *Need is transitive. Let f_1 and f_2 be two functions. f_1 and f_2 need their arguments iff $f_1 \circ f_2$ needs its argument.*

3.1 Needed Subterms

So far we have only spoken about when a function may need its argument. However, we would like to talk about needed subterms as well. We now extend the notion of need to subterms. We write $N \ll M$ to mean N is a subterm of M. Recall from [2] that any term M can be expressed in terms of a subterm N written as $C[N]$, where $C[\ ]$ is a *context*.

Definition 18 Needed Subterm. Let N be a subterm of M, ie $M = C[N]$. N is said to be a *needed* subterm if the function $\lambda z.C[z]$ needs its argument, where $z \notin FV(C[\ ])$.

The concept of needed subterms has been studied earlier in the restricted case of those subterms which are redexes [9]. A redex N in a term M is said to be needed if some residual of the redex is reduced on every terminating reduction sequence originating from M. If a residual of the redex is reduced on the head reduction sequence, then the redex is needed. We now compare our notion of need with that defined in [9].

Lemma 19. *f needs its argument iff the redex $(\lambda x.M)N$ is a needed redex in the application $P = f((\lambda x.M)N)$.*

Proof. We present only an outline of the proof. Suppose f needs its argument. Let us examine the head reduction sequence starting from P. Since f is solvable, f has a head normal form. Since the head reduction sequence will choose the outermost leftmost redex first, it will first reduce f to a head normal form, say $\lambda x_1 \ldots \lambda x_n.y\, Q_1 \ldots Q_m$. By Lemma 10, this term is needs its argument x_1 only if $x_1 \equiv y$. Thus it is easy to see that after a single reduction step, the redex in the argument would become the head redex and get reduced. The reverse implication is easier to prove and the proof is omitted here.

The following properties hold for needed subterms .

Lemma 20. *Let $M_2 \ll M_1 \ll M$. Further, let M_2 be needed in M_1 and M_1 be needed in M. Then M_2 is needed in M.*

Proof. By Lemma 17.

Lemma 21. *Let $M_1 \ll M$. If M_1 is needed in M, then $\forall M_2 \ll M$, $M_1 \ll M_2 \supset M_2$ is needed in M.*

Lemma 22. *Every term on the spine is needed.*

Proof. By Lemma 16.

We are now in a position to state our main result.

Theorem 23. *Let M be an Λ_l term with an initial labeling. Further, let $l : N$ be a subterm of M. N is needed in M iff*

$$\exists N_1.M \Rightarrow * N_1 \wedge l \subseteq \sigma N_1$$

where the reduction sequence from M to N_1 uses head redexes only.

109

Proof. Suppose $l : N$ is a needed subterm. Since $l : N$ is a subterm of M, we can write M as $C[l : N]$. Let $f \equiv \lambda z.C[z]$. M can then be expressed as $f\, l : N$. Since $l : N$ is a needed subterm, f needs its argument. By Lemma 16, f must have the form $\lambda x_1 \ldots \lambda x_n.x_1\ M_1 \ldots M_m$. Hence $f\, l : N$ reduces to $N' \equiv \lambda x_2 \ldots \lambda x_n.(l : N)\ M_1 \ldots M_m$. Now it is easy to see that $l \subseteq \sigma N'$. The reverse implication is easier and is omitted here.

3.2 Qualifying Need

Labeled λ-calculus allows us to answer a question that is often of interest to programmers who use a lazy language – what part of an argument M of a function f is needed to evaluate the application $f\ M$ to a given extent. Here, we address a restricted version of that question *viz.* what part of the term M is needed to evaluate the application $f\ M$ to head normal form.

Lemma 24. *Let M have a head normal form. Further let $M = C[N]$. Then $C[\Omega]$ has a head normal iff N is not needed in M.*

Proof. Suppose $C[\Omega]$ has a head normal form. Then the context function $\lambda z.C[z]$ is not strict and hence does not need its argument.Therefore, N is not a needed subterm of M.

On the other hand, suppose N is not a needed subterm of M. Then the function $g \equiv \lambda z.C[z]$ does not need its argument. This means that g is either not solvable or not strict. However, since M is solvable, so is g. Hence g is not strict. Therefore $g\ \Omega \not\equiv \Omega$ and thus $C[\Omega]$ has a normal form.

As a result of this lemma, we can now state a corollary which will let us say "how much" of an argument a function needs.

Corollary 25. *Let N be a subterm of M ie $M = C[N]$. Further, let f be a function that needs its argument and that $f\ M$ has a head normal form. Then the application $f(C[\Omega])$ has a head normal form iff N is not a needed subterm of $f\ M$.*

Note that in the above corollary, N needed not be a needed subterm in M. Consider the following example:

Example 2. Let f be the function $\lambda g.g(\lambda x\lambda y.x)$. Further, let M be the term $\lambda h.h\ \underline{1}\ \underline{2}$. Neither $\underline{1}$ nor $\underline{2}$ is a needed subterm in M. However, it is easy to see that $\underline{1}$ is needed in $f\ M$ but $\underline{2}$ is not. Thus $f\ (\lambda h.h\ \Omega\ \underline{2})$ does not have a head normal form. On the other hand, $f\ (\lambda h.h\ \underline{1}\ \Omega)$ has the normal form $\underline{1}$.

4 Conclusions

We have presented a new variant of λ-calculus called labeled λ calculus and shown how it can be used to address the issue of need. Using this formalism, we are also in a position to qualify a function's need for its argument. We feel that labeled λ-calculus is a good starting point for a theory of analysis of functional programs. We propose to use labeled λ-calculus for various analyses of functional programs such as slicing and profiling.

References

1. Samson Abramsky and Chris Hankin, editors. *Abstract Interpretation of Declaration Languages*, Chicester, Great Britain, 1987. Ellis Horwood.
2. H. P. Barendregt. *The Lambda Calculus : Its Syntax and Semantics*. North Holland, 1984.
3. C. Bohm, editor. *Lambda Calculus and Computer Science*, volume 37 of *Lecture Notes in Computer Science*, Berlin, 1975. Springer Verlag. Proceedings of the Symposium held in Rome.
4. Geoffrey L. Burn, Chris Hankin, and Samson Abramsky. The theory and practice of strictness analysis for higher order functions. *Science of Computer Programming*, 7:249–278, 1986.
5. J.R. Hindley and J.P. Seldin, editors. *To H. B. Curry : Essays on Combinatory Logic, Lambda Calculus and Formalism*, New York and London, 1980. Academic Press.
6. J. Hughes. Strictness detection in non-flat domains. In *Programs as Data Objects*, volume 217 of *Lecture Notes in Computer Science*, pages 42–62, New York, 1986. Springer Verlag.
7. J.M.E. Hyland. A syntactic characterisation of the equality in some models of the λ calculus. *Journal of the London Mathematical Society*, 12(2):361–370, 1976.
8. J.-J. Levy. An algebraic interpretation of the $\lambda\beta k$ calculus and a labelled λ-calculus. In Bohm [3]. Proceedings of the Symposium held in Rome.
9. J.-J. Levy. Optimal reductions in the lambda calculus. In Hindley and Seldin [5], pages 159–192.
10. Alan Mycroft. The theory and practice of transforming call-by-need into call-by-value. In *Procs. of an International Symposium on Programming*, volume 83 of *Lecture Notes in Computer Science*, pages 269–281, New York, 1980. Springer Verlag.

Preemption Primitives in Reactive Languages *
(*A Preliminary Report*)

Sophie Pinchinat**, Éric Rutten**, R.K. Shyamasundar***

Abstract. In this paper, we study preemption primitives in reactive languages such as ESTEREL and SIGNAL (and its extension SIGNAL*GTi*) in a common framework. This enables us to compare behavioural/structural *expressive* powers of different languages and gives an insight into the complementarity of different control and data-flow abstractions in the reactive languages. Such a study also provides a basis on which a basic set of preemption primitives can be incorporated in reactive languages from the point of view of expressive completeness.

1 Introduction

A wide spectrum of operators for concurrency, synchronization and communication has been developed in [Mil 89, Sim 85]. These works have concentrated on arriving at notions of expressiveness and completeness starting from a basic set of combinators. A notion of completeness has been derived for the synchronous family in [Sim 85] in the sense that any operator which can be defined by rules of action which obey certain natural conditions can also be defined directly in terms of the basic combinators of the calculi such as Meije [Sim 85] and SCCS [Mil 89].

In the context of reactive programming, Gerard Berry has applied with success the Meije calculus for the design and verification of ESTEREL. One of the principal operators that plays a significant role in some form or the other is the process preemption operator – which is the process of controlling the life of a process. Berry [Ber 93] has argued the need and importance of *process preemption* for the specification of reactive systems and has elucidated such primitives available in the synchronous programming language ESTEREL. In this paper, we discuss various forms of primitives for process preemption that have been in use in various process calculi [Hoa 85, Mil 89] and various reactive languages such as ESTEREL and SIGNAL and study how the various forms can be derived essentially from the basic preemption primitives and other basic process calculi combinators. The main motivation for the study has been to:

---

* Work supported by IFCPAR (Indo-French Center for the Promotion of Advanced Research), New Delhi.

** EP-ATR Group, IRISA, Campus de Beaulieu, F-35042, Rennes, France, e-mail: {pinchina, rutten}@irisa.fr

*** Computer Science Group, Tata Institute of Fundamental Research, BOMBAY 400 005, India, e-mail: shyam@tcs.tifr.res.in

- show how the seemingly different preemption operators can be obtained by a set of basic preemption primitives and compositional operators (or combinators) along with recursive definitions.
- provide a formal basis as to why reactive languages following imperative or data flow style are in fact equivalent and show how the different abstractions are suitable with different styles.
- lead to the understanding of the issues of expressiveness and completeness.

In the sequel, we study preemptive structures of ESTEREL, and those of SIGNAL and its extension with preemptive structures SIGNAL GTi^4 in the framework of a synchronous calculus and provide an answer to some of the questions raised above. These are preliminary results of a larger study, which is being attempted at in providing a unified framework for reactive languages and providing a precise comparison of the different sets of primitives available, and the relations among them [PRS 95].

The rest of the paper is organized as follows: Section 2 briefly introduces the basic operators of MEIJE and other derived operators which will be used in the sequel, and we derive a spectrum of preemption primitives (such as interrupts, suspend, when etc.) that are available in various reactive languages in the MEIJE calculus. In Section 3, we consider the different preemption mechanisms of ESTERELfollowed by a description of preemption mechanisms of SIGNAL and SIGNAL GTi in section 4. Section 5 discusses the expressive power of operators, and makes comparisons between the different approaches of the languages.

2 Operators of the Process Calculus

In this section, we briefly introduce the MEIJE operators and other operators that are commonly used in an algebraic setting. We follow the usual conventions of [Mil 89, Sim 85]. First, we briefly discuss the MEIJE calculus and discuss several process calculi operators. We will discuss further how the various preemptive suspension operators that exist in synchronous languages such as ESTEREL and SIGNAL can be obtained from such primitives and make a relative comparison of the various operators. With this background, we show how the various preemptive and suspension operators can be derived from each other.

2.1 MEIJE Calculus and Other Compositional Operators

MEIJE actions consist of a free commutative group $G = (A, \cdot, \tau, \bar{\ })$. The infinite set $A = \{a, b, c, ..., \tau\}$ is a set of *actions* with a special symbolœ τ, denoting the neutral element of G. Elements of G, called *events*, written α, β are products of positive (e.g. a, b) and negative (e.g. $\bar{a}, \bar{b}$) actions with $a \cdot \bar{a} = \tau$ for all $a \in A$. For example, an action a can be an act of communication along a channel c carrying

---

[4] GTi stands for *Gestion de Tâches et d'intervalles*, the french for *Tasks and intervals Management*.

a message of value v; it is then written in a more structured fashion like $c(v)$, as used in Section 4.

We say an event α is in *reduced form* if there are no occurrences of a and $\bar{a}$ together in α, for some $a \in \mathcal{A}$. In other words, we can get a reduced form of α by equating every pair of the form $a \cdot \bar{a}$ by the identity denoted τ. Note that, $\alpha \cdot a \cdot \bar{a} = \alpha$ (as it is a commutative structure, the other combinations follow). We shall write $\hat{\alpha}$ the reduced form of α - note that it is unique up to commutativity. Events can be seen as multisets; therefore, we shall use classical notations like $\in, \cap, \backslash$, etc... For example, $a \in b \cdot a \cdot a$, and $\bar{b} \cdot a \cdot a \cap a \cdot \bar{b} = a \cdot \bar{b}$, as well as $a \cdot a \cdot \bar{b} \backslash a \cdot \bar{b} \cdot c = a$. Intuitively, actions can be thought of as emissions or receptions of signals; τ classically denotes the silent action. The events describe the signal-environment in which the system reacts. Operator '$\cdot$' is used for instantaneous product of actions (simultaneity).

$$\text{(a)} \quad \alpha \xrightarrow{\alpha, \mathcal{E}} \text{nothing} \qquad \text{(b)} \quad P \xrightarrow{\alpha, \mathcal{E}} P' \tag{1}$$

$$\frac{P \xrightarrow{\alpha, \mathcal{E}} P'}{P \| Q \xrightarrow{\alpha, \mathcal{E}} P' \| Q} \quad \frac{Q \xrightarrow{\beta, \mathcal{E}} Q'}{P \| Q \xrightarrow{\beta, \mathcal{E}} P \| Q'} \quad \frac{P \xrightarrow{\alpha, \mathcal{E}} P' \quad Q \xrightarrow{\beta, \mathcal{E}} Q'}{P \| Q \xrightarrow{\alpha \cdot \beta, \mathcal{E}} P' \| Q'} \tag{2}$$

$$\text{(a)} \quad \alpha : P \xrightarrow{\alpha, \mathcal{E}} P \quad \text{(b)} \quad \frac{P \xrightarrow{\alpha, \mathcal{E}} P' \quad s \notin \alpha}{P \backslash s \xrightarrow{\alpha, \mathcal{E}} P' \backslash s} \quad \text{(c)} \quad \frac{P \xrightarrow{\alpha, \mathcal{E}} P'}{s * P \xrightarrow{s \cdot \alpha, \mathcal{E}} s * P'} \tag{3}$$

Processes, or reactive systems, are built up from elementary processes and process combinators. An elementary process is either nothing, the process doing nothing, or an event α of $\mathcal{A}$. An elementary process α has only a one-step behavior: it produces α and becomes the process nothing, as in (1.a). More generally, a process P performs an action α in the context of a signal environment $\mathcal{E}$, then becomes a process P', as written in (1.b). The environment $\mathcal{E}$ has the same meaning as in ESTEREL [Ber 93, BRS 93]: it is the set of all the signals produced at that instant by the whole program of which P is part. This set gives the global information about the presence and the absence of signals; this is needed when the choice of the transition to take involves conditions on the absence of signals. In particular, $\alpha \subseteq \mathcal{E}$. The environment is denoted by the second component ($\mathcal{E}$) of the labels in the transition rules.

The most important combinators are *Prefixing* (:), *Parallel composition* ($\|$), *Ticking* (*) and *Restriction* (\). Their definitions are given in Equations (1,2,3). It may be pointed out that '$\cdot$' should not be confused with the prefixing operator of CCS [Mil 89]. In this paper, for prefixing, we shall use ':' as in SCCS [Mil 89] and MEIJE[Sim 85]. Prefixing, parallel composition and restriction are interpreted classically. The *ticking* is an operator that allows to synchronize on each behavioral step of an agent, without prejudging on the nature of its behaviour. Operationally it $s * P$ can be interpreted as: all the actions of P are linked to action s.

Regarding parallel composition, two more specific combinators can be defined: the *Synchronous product*, written $\times$ (as in SCCS), where the two involved processes must move together, and the *Interleaving composition*, written $|$, where only one process moves at a time. Their formal definition is given in Equation (4). It follows that: $P \times \text{nothing} \equiv \text{nothing} \equiv \text{nothing} \times P$ and: $P \,|\, \text{nothing} \equiv P \equiv \text{nothing} \,|\, P$.

$$
\text{(a)} \quad \frac{P \xrightarrow{\alpha, \mathcal{E}} P' \quad Q \xrightarrow{\beta, \mathcal{E}} Q'}{P \times Q \xrightarrow{\alpha \cdot \beta, \mathcal{E}} P' \times Q'} \qquad \text{(b)} \quad \frac{P \xrightarrow{\alpha, \mathcal{E}} P'}{P|Q \xrightarrow{\alpha, \mathcal{E}} P'|Q} \qquad \text{(c)} \quad \frac{Q \xrightarrow{\alpha, \mathcal{E}} Q'}{P|Q \xrightarrow{\alpha, \mathcal{E}} P|Q'} \qquad (4)
$$

An interesting relationship between $\times$ and the *ticking* can be expressed is given by (cf. [Sim 85]): $P \times Q \equiv (\alpha * P || \overline{\alpha} * Q) \backslash \alpha$.

Definition *(Derivative)*: Whenever $P \xrightarrow{\alpha, \mathcal{E}} P'$, we call the pair (α, P') an *immediate derivative* of P; α is referred to as an *action* of P, and we call P' an α-derivative of P. Further, whenever $P \xrightarrow{\alpha_1, \mathcal{E}} \cdots \xrightarrow{\alpha_n, \mathcal{E}} P'$, we refer $(\alpha_1 \cdots \alpha_2, P')$ a derivative of P.

Definition *(Sorts)*: Let $L \subseteq \mathcal{A}$ be a set of actions of process P where $\mathcal{A}$ is the set of actions and all its derivatives lie in $L \cup \{\tau\}$, then we say that P has sort L or L is the sort of P. In the following $Sort(P)$ denotes the sort of process P.

Here we describe the *sequencing* operator, written *seq*, which involves an event and a process. An expression of the form $a : P$, a being in the set of actions, could be interpreted as "perform action a before behaving like process P". The expression P *seq* Q denotes that Q is to be performed after P terminates. Thus, the usual sequencing operator has to account for termination. This can be achieved as in Milner's abstraction, by introducing the convention that termination is signalled through a communication. Thus, in this context, once Q gets a *communication*, a signal, that P has finished, it can start. This convention is formalized below:

Let us introduce the convention that processes may indicate their termination by a distinguished symbol $\overline{done}$ and the processes follow the conventions given below:

All process expressions using *sequencing* can be translated to the version using prefixing and the convention of indicating termination through the distinct signal $\overline{done}$. This in turn calls for the following definitions of [Mil 89]: P is terminating if, for any *derivative* P' of P, we have

1. $P' \xrightarrow{done}$ is impossible

2. If $P' \xrightarrow{\overline{done}}$, then $P' \equiv \overline{done} : \text{nothing}$.

In other words, **done** is a fictitious symbol and no process emits a **done**. However, each process on termination emits the signal $\overline{\text{done}}$. Now the sequencing operator is defined by: $P \; seq \; Q \triangleq (P[b/\textbf{done}] \parallel b : Q) \backslash b$ where b is a new name of action (in order to make sure that $b \notin sort(P)$) and the notation $P[x/y]$ denotes the substitution of x for y in P. In the above equation, $\overline{\text{done}}$ gets renamed to $\overline{b}$ and thus, matches with the prefix b of the second component. The renaming allows us to hide "completion or termination" of local components. Thus, sequencing can be achieved through the parallel composition ($\parallel$), restriction and the above mentioned termination convention. Let us define the useful *repeat* operator based on sequencing by: $repeat(P) \triangleq P \; seq \; repeat(P)$.

2.2 Interrupt Operator

In this section, we discuss the basic preemptive operator *interrupt* of [Hoa 85] and show how it provides the basis of the definitions of the preemptive operators. The *interrupt* operator is written $\triangledown$. $P \triangledown Q$ (reads P *interrrupted by* Q) behaves like P until Q does anything at all, and thereafter behaves like Q. The definition of $\triangledown$ is given in Equation (5), from which we have that: $P \triangledown nothing \equiv P$ and $nothing \triangledown P \equiv nothing$.

$$\frac{P \xrightarrow{\alpha, \mathcal{E}} P'}{P \triangledown Q \xrightarrow{\alpha, \mathcal{E}} P' \triangledown Q} \qquad \frac{Q \xrightarrow{\beta, \mathcal{E}} Q'}{P \triangledown Q \xrightarrow{\beta, \mathcal{E}} Q'} \tag{5}$$

Note that, the conditions not being exclusive, the transitions are nondeterministic. Hence, it could be interpreted as: P *may stop as soon as Q starts*. In other words, there is no guarantee that P would always stop as soon as Q starts. Now let us enforce determinism in the above rules with a side condition such that P would stop making transitions as soon as Q starts.
Definition: Let $beg(Q)$ denote the set of events that can *trigger* process Q. That is, for Q to start it is necessary to have at least one signal from $beg(Q)$, e.g. for any process Q and any action r, $beg(r : Q) = \{r\}$.

Without loss of generality, we assume that $sort(P) \cap beg(Q) = \emptyset$. The deterministic version of $\triangledown$ is given in Equation (6). Note that condition $\mathcal{E} \cap beg(Q) \neq \emptyset$ of rule (6) is redundant since condition $Q \xrightarrow{\beta, \mathcal{E}} Q'$ ensures it.

$$\frac{P \xrightarrow{\alpha, \mathcal{E}} P' \quad \mathcal{E} \cap beg(Q) = \emptyset}{P \triangledown Q \xrightarrow{\alpha, \mathcal{E}} P' \triangledown Q} \qquad \frac{Q \xrightarrow{\beta, \mathcal{E}} Q' \quad \mathcal{E} \cap beg(Q) \neq \emptyset}{P \triangledown Q \xrightarrow{\beta} Q'} \tag{6}$$

We can derive another variant of interruption, so-called *reset* operator. In the variants of this class, usually called "reset" or "restart", a process is reset to its initial state whenever a given reset-signal, r, is present. Such an operator is obtained by the process expression: $reset(P, r) \triangleq P \triangledown (r : reset(P, r))$ That is, $reset(P)$ behaves like P, except that on r it starts all over again.

3 Preemption in ESTEREL

3.1 Strong preemption

The basic preemption construct of ESTEREL is: | do P watching immediate r |
The interpretation is: The statement P is executed normally up to proper termination or up to *the current or future occurrence* of signal r, which is referred to as the guard. If P terminates strictly before r occurs, so does the whole watching-statement; in such a case the guard has no action. Otherwise, the occurrence of r provokes immediate preemption of the body P and the whole watching statement terminates immediately.

The basic behaviour of: do P watching immediate r is described by the process expression: $P \triangledown r$. One of the important features of ESTEREL is that transitions take place deterministically. That is, whenever there is more than one possibility, the semantics chooses only one of them in a predictable fashion. For instance consider the following statement:

```
do   do P watching immediate r1   watching immediate r2
```

The expression $(P \triangledown r1) \triangledown r2$ corresponds to the above fragment of ESTEREL. We can get the transitions for these operators by taking into account the guard expressions of ESTEREL into the rules (6).

Now, we could consider the general watching-construct of ESTEREL which takes the form: do P watching immediate r timeout Q end, which has the same interpretation as given earlier except that the occurrence of r provokes Q and the watching-statement terminates with the termination of Q; the other case of normal termination remains the same as earlier. It is expressible as: $P \triangledown (R \times Q)$ where $R \triangleq r : repeat(\tau)$. Note that like in ESTEREL, an occurrence of signal r can be produced by the environment and not only by Q. In order to ensure termination, instead of blocking, the expression above can be improved as: $P \triangledown [((R \triangledown b) \times Q[b/done]) \backslash b]$ where b is a new name and $R \triangleq r : repeat(\tau)$.

It may be observed that the above rules also ensure priority for the outermost guard. For example in the following statement, when both $r1$ and $r2$ are available, only transition by $r2$ is possible:

```
do   do P watching immediate r1 timeout Q1 end
watching immediate r2 timeout Q2 end
```

3.2 Weak Preemption

In ESTEREL the trap-statement provides the weak-preemption operator which permits *last wills* to be performed before preemption. In fact, the trap-statement provides the exception handling feature in a concurrent environment for ES-TEREL. For example, in the statement $\boxed{\text{trap } T \text{ in } P \text{ end}}$, the body P is run normally until it executes an "exit T" statement. On the execution of the "exit T" (which will be raised at some point of control in P), P is preempted and the whole trap statement terminates with the components concurrent with "exit T" in P performing for the last time – often referred to as the *last wills* of P. In fact, T corresponds to an exception and it can be handled through the handlers specified in the appropriate scope.

It can be easily seen that the trap-construct is state-based and is based on the control-flow. For studying/adapting such a construct in data-flow languages such as SIGNAL we will first adapt the construct to the signal-environment. Consider a new operator wtrap described below. The process P wtrap Q is similar to $P \bigtriangledown Q$ except that when Q is enabled, P can make its last transition. It follows from (7) that P wtrap nothing $\equiv P$ and nothing wtrap $P \equiv$ nothing.

$$\frac{P \xrightarrow{\alpha,\mathcal{E}} P' \quad \mathcal{E} \cap beg(Q) = \emptyset}{P\text{wtrap } Q \xrightarrow{\alpha,\mathcal{E}} P'\text{wtrap } Q} \qquad \frac{P \xrightarrow{\alpha,\mathcal{E}} P' \quad Q \xrightarrow{\beta,\mathcal{E}} Q' \quad \mathcal{E} \cap beg(Q) \neq \emptyset}{P\text{wtrap } Q \xrightarrow{\alpha \cdot \beta,\mathcal{E}} Q'} \tag{7}$$

We can express the behaviour of the operator wtrap in terms of the interrupt and the other compositional operators. The definition is given as follows:

$$P \text{ wtrap } Q \triangleq [\ \bar{a} * P \ || \ [\ R_P \ || \ (R_Q \times Q)\ ]\ \backslash b\ ]\ \backslash a$$

where a and b are new names, $R_P \triangleq ((repeat(a)\bigtriangledown b)$ and $R_Q \triangleq (a \cdot \bar{b}) : repeat(\tau)$. The above expression can be interpreted as follows: process R_P makes process P evolve as long as it performs a's, by use of the ticking operation. When process Q starts, it enforces R_Q to start as well, which in turn forces R_P to perform its b, therefore interrupting production of the a's. As the starting of R_Q contains an a, process P can make a last move at the same time as the first move of Q, as we expect for the wtrap operator.

It can be easily seen that the basic trap construct trap T in P end can be achieved by the expression P wtrap T assuming "T" to be arriving from the signal-environment. Thus, P continues till T is seen in the environment (it could come from P as well) or it terminates and becomes nothing; once "T" is observed, "P" terminates after completing the reaction at that instant. Now, we can define the equations of inference for P wtrap Q as given in Equations (7).

We can generalize the trap-construct with the handlers by essentially using the *seq* operator with the second operand of wtrap. For example, the statement trap T in P handler H end can be abstracted by $(P \text{ wtrap } (T \text{ } seq \text{ } H))$.

In the construct trap T_1 in trap T_2 in P end end the outermost trap T_1 has priority; in a similar way in the expression $((P \text{ wtrap } T_2) \text{ wtrap } T_1)$ the outermost "trap" T_1 has the priority.

3.3   Suspension Operator

Consider the **suspend** operator of ESTEREL. This is a recent addition to ES-
TEREL. The operator is similar[5] to the **when** operator of LUSTRE or the **when**
operator of SIGNAL. Note that even though the operator **when** have essentially the
same meaning in languages SIGNAL and LUSTRE, the underlying semantics could
differ due to the underlying definitions of the clocks. Operationally, a **when** r is
interpreted as: a can make a transition only in the presence of signal r.

The dual of operator **when** is the **suspend** defined in ESTEREL. Operationally,
$\boxed{P \text{ suspend } r}$ is interpreted as: P can make a transition only when the signal
r is not there in the environment. The important difference between the **when**
and the **suspend** is that the latter calls for the notion of *absence of signals*. The
rules for **suspend** are given in Equations (8,9).

$$\frac{P \xrightarrow{\alpha,\mathcal{E}} P' \quad \overline{\text{done}} \notin \alpha \quad r \notin \mathcal{E}}{P\text{suspend } r \xrightarrow{\alpha,\mathcal{E}} P'\text{suspend } r} \tag{8}$$

(a) $\dfrac{P \xrightarrow{\alpha,\mathcal{E}} P' \quad \overline{\text{done}} \in \alpha \quad r \notin \mathcal{E}}{P\text{suspend } r \xrightarrow{\alpha,\mathcal{E}} \text{nothing}}$ (b) $\dfrac{r \in \alpha}{P\text{suspend } r \xrightarrow{\tau,\mathcal{E}} P\text{suspend } r}$ (9)

The above rules bring out some subtle points:

1. **nothing suspend** r is not the same as **nothing**[6].
2. The side condition of rule (8) makes sure that P can make a transition only
   when r is not there in the input environment
3. The side conditions in rules (8) and (9a) ensure that whenever r is there, P
   does not make a transition.
4. As rules (9a) and (9b) are making use of the presence of signals, it is easy to
   see that absence of signal (like in $r \notin \mathcal{E}$) is ensured relatively to the presence
   of some signal (referred to as **tick** in ESTEREL).

Note: In the rules for the watching-statement (6): we have stipulated side conditions that ensure a priority for the outermost guard. However, it is not necessary
to do the same thing for the suspend-statement, as this statement stops from
doing transitions. For instance, $(P \text{ suspend } r_1) \text{ suspend } r_2$ will be suspended on
either r_1 or r_2.

---

[5] Note that, in an imperative language, one has to account for termination of a statement unlike the case of data flow languages.

[6] Note that **nothing** is relevant in the context of imperative terminating programs.

3.4 Immediate and Delayed Operators

In the previous sections, we have discussed various preemption operators in the context of a synchronous algebraic calculus. As argued in [Ber 93], for an effective use of the *preemption feature*, it is necessary that it be used freely without any restriction. Further, for an effective use of preemption, it is necessary to work in the context of a time-dependent model. The model that allows *multi-form notions of time* without resorting to a physical clock is the *perfect synchrony or the zero delay paradigm* [Ber 93] where time is defined externally to programs by the flow of inputs, and the internal bookkeeping in the program is done in zero-delay with respect to all external time units. It is only those instructions that are explicitly written to keep track of the flow of events that can take time. Thus, at a global level, we can refer to actions that take place at the *nth instant* where *instant* corresponds to the reaction to the inputs at that point of time.

The introduction of the notion of instants enables us to specify:

- reactions at the current instant (or immediate operators).
- reactions at the future instants (or delayed operators).

For this purpose, the definitions would require the complete signal environment to check for the presence or absence of signals. In fact, such a structure has been used already while defining interrupt-operator and watching-constructs. With this modification, let us see the effect of using the *delayed* or *immediate* operators on the following operators which appear in one form or the other in the synchronous languages:

1. Strong Preemption: Here, both delayed and immediate preemptions are possible:
   (a) *Immediate strong preemption* corresponds to abortion of the program at the earliest instant, including the current instant, at which the *guard*[7] is present.
   (b) *Delayed strong preemption* corresponds to abortion of the program at the earliest instant, not including the current instant, at which the *guard* is present.
2. Weak Preemption: Here, we can arrive at *immediate* and *delayed* variants assuming that the preemption takes effect through the signal environment. However, it is control-point based as in the case of *traps* of ESTEREL, then we can have only the *immediate* operator.
3. Suspension: Here, again the *immediate* and *delayed* operators are possible with the interpretation given above.
   Berry [Ber 93] has shown how many of the delayed and immediate operators can be derived starting from weak abort and suspension.

---

[7] That is, the signal on which the statement is to be preempted.

4 Preemption in SIGNAL: SIGNALGT*i*

The synchronized data-flow language SIGNAL is declarative, and more specifically equational [BLGJ 91]. Specifications are made in the form of a system of equations on the values and synchronizations of involved signals. Special signals are called **event**, and always have the boolean value **true**: they are characterized only by their presence. The behaviour amounts to solving the same system of equation for every instant of the execution. Delays on signals introduce the notion of state, in the form of the memorization of the previous value. In this sense a SIGNAL process P has an internal state (the valuation of its delayed signals) and makes transitions between these states upon the occurrence of signals. Schematically, the system of equations defines the new values of the output signals and state variables, depending upon the input signals and current value of the state variables. The kernel of SIGNAL features primitive processes on signals: functions on the values of synchronous signals (e.g. boolean functions), delays on signals: $e\$$ init v_0 (giving the previous of e value, initialized at v_0), selection of occurrences of a signal e according to the value of boolean condition b: e when b (intersection of the presences of signal e and signal b at true), merge of two signals: e_1 default e_2 (union of the presences of e_1 and e_2; it is made deterministic by the priority given to e_1 in case of simultaneous presence). The synchronous composition of processes noted "|" constrains signals featured in the composed processes to agree regarding their presence and value (see [BLGJ 91] for a complete presentation).

Regarding the previous sections, comments may be done when we consider data-flow programs. First of all, it is worthwhile noting that termination issues make no sense in SIGNAL since programs do not terminate. However, one could introduce a kind of "termination" for data-flow programs by emitting a special signal as we artificially made it with the $\overline{\text{done}}$ signal in Section 2.1. Second in the case of the SIGNAL language, the *ticking* operator could be treated as the clock of a process P or could be treated as the synchronizer for P from an external observation. Finally, for the preemptive operators, nothing$\triangledown P$ = nothing does not play any role, but both $\triangledown$ and **reset** operators preserve non-termination.

Preemption in SIGNAL has been defined in a language extension called SIGNAL*GTi* [RLG 94]. It consists in associating processes with a time interval upon which they are active, and outside of which they are suspended, or preempted. Time intervals can be opened and closed, and then opened again; hence upon re-entering the time interval a process is re-started, either in its current state (suspension) or completely anew, from its initial state (preemption).

4.1 Time intervals

A time interval is a kind of signal with two possible values, or states: **inside** and **outside**. It is initially in a state I0 given by its declaration.

A time interval I moves from state **outside** to state **inside** upon the occurrence of an event b and from state **inside** to state **outside** upon the occurrence of an event e. Such a time interval will be constructed by: $\boxed{\text{I :=]}b\text{, e] init I0}}$

Across transitions and rewritings, the current state of an interval will be encoded in its concrete form as follows: an interval $]b, e]$ in state inside (resp. outside) is written $|b, e]$ (resp. $]b, e|$) The $|$ interval bound means that this bound was the last one met. The transitions of I are described by the following rules:

$$\frac{b \in \mathcal{E}}{\text{I} :=]b, e| \text{ init IO} \xrightarrow{I(outside), \mathcal{E}} \text{I} := |b, e] \text{ init IO}} \quad (10)$$

$$\frac{e \in \mathcal{E}}{\text{I} := |b, e] \text{ init IO} \xrightarrow{I(inside), \mathcal{E}} \text{I} :=]b, e| \text{ init IO}} \quad (11)$$

$$\frac{b \notin \mathcal{E}}{\text{I} :=]b, e| \text{ init IO} \xrightarrow{I(outside), \mathcal{E}} \text{I} :=]b, e| \text{ init IO}} \quad (12)$$

$$\frac{e \notin \mathcal{E}}{\text{I} := |b, e] \text{ init IO} \xrightarrow{I(inside), \mathcal{E}} \text{I} := |b, e] \text{ init IO}} \quad (13)$$

As shown by the above rules, time intervals are *left-open/right-closed*: the new state is enforced only *after* the instant where a bound occurs.

4.2 Suspendable tasks

A *task* is a process built up from a process P and an activity time interval I. Suspension of a task consists in conditioning its activity P upon the "presence" of interval I, while preserving its internal state when suspended otherwise. This suspendable task is written: $\boxed{P \text{ on } I}$. The process is active inside the interval: it behaves as P. Outside the interval, it is inhibited: its clock is cut. When re-entering the interval, it re-starts from its current state.

$$\frac{P \xrightarrow{\alpha, \mathcal{E}} P' \quad \text{I} \xrightarrow{I(inside), \mathcal{E}} \text{I}'}{P \text{ on } I \xrightarrow{\alpha \cdot I(inside), \mathcal{E}} P' \text{ on } I'} \quad (14)$$

$$\frac{\text{I} \xrightarrow{I(outside), \mathcal{E}} \text{I}'}{P \text{ on } I \xrightarrow{I(outside), \mathcal{E}} P \text{ on } I'} \quad (15)$$

In terms of the algebraic operators, suspension on intervals can be derived using the *repeat* and wtrap operators:

$$P \text{ on }]b, e] \stackrel{\triangle}{=} (\, (a * P) \parallel repeat(b : (repeat(\bar{a}) \text{ wtrap } e)) \,) \backslash a$$

where the local signal a has a new name and is used to constrain the activity of P (using $*$) from after b to the occurrence of e (inclusively, hence the use of **wtrap**). Indeed, the behaviour of an interval is given by the expression $repeat(b : (repeat(\bar{a}) \text{ wtrap } e))$. During suspension (between e and b), the current state of the process is kept in the $a * P$ sub-expression.

4.3 Preemptible tasks

In preemption, noted $\boxed{P \text{ each } I}$ the preempted process is re-started (if ever) from its starting point, i.e. form the initial state of its state variables in the case of data-flow processes. The difference between suspension and preemption concerns the opening of the interval; rules are similar to those for on-tasks, but have to be more detailed on the opening of the interval.

$$\frac{P \xrightarrow{\alpha, \mathcal{E}} P' \quad I \xrightarrow{I(inside), \mathcal{E}} I'}{P \text{ each } I \xrightarrow{\alpha \cdot I(inside), \mathcal{E}} P' \text{ each } I'} \tag{16}$$

$$\frac{I \xrightarrow{I(outside), \mathcal{E}} I' \quad b \notin \mathcal{E}}{P \text{ each } I \xrightarrow{I(outside), \mathcal{E}} P \text{ each } I'} \tag{17}$$

When opening the interval, the process of the interruptible task must be re-started from its initial state. Therefore it is reset:

$$\frac{b \in \mathcal{E}}{P \text{ each }]b,e| \xrightarrow{b \cdot \alpha, \mathcal{E}} reinit(P) \text{ each } |b,e]} \tag{18}$$

The function $reinit(P)$ is defined structurally so as to propagate the reset down to the state variables, i.e. in our case to the delays on signals; their stored value in the delay is reset to their initial value without causing an occurrence to be present (we do not detail it here due to space limitation, see [PRS 95]).

In terms of the algebra operators, interruption on intervals is described by:

$$P \text{ each }]b,e] \triangleq b : (P \text{ wtrap } e) \ seq \ (P \text{ each }]b,e])$$

where after an occurrence of b, P is executed until e (inclusively) occurs, then stops, and later might go in sequence into itself recursively.

4.4 Strong, weak, immediate and delayed preemption

With regard to the classification of preemption structures in concurrency by G. Berry [Ber 93], we can say briefly that:

- suspension and abortion are handled respectively by **on** and by **each**.
- delayed preemption is the default case; immediate preemption can be obtained by defining an event subtraction: $e_1 - e_2 \triangleq (\text{when not } e_2 \text{ default } e_1)$. Then, immediate versions i-on and i-each of the task constructors **on** and **each** respectively can be defined by: P i-on $]b,e] \triangleq P$ **on** $](b-e),e]$ and P i-each $]b,e] \triangleq P$ **each** $](b-e),e]$.

– weak preemption is the default case here; strong preemption would involve defining another kind of intervals, instead of the *right-closed* interval: a *right-open* interval $]b,e[$. In that case the event e causing the task to stop must be forbidden to originate in the process, in order to avoid a problem of causality (the process causing its own inhibition within an instant).

5 Expressiveness and Completeness

In this section, we show how preemption and suspension operators can be *derived* from each other along with the other compositional operators. That is, given a program using one class of operators, we show how we can obtain an equivalent program using other operators.

First, let us see whether the **suspend** operator can be realized in terms of the **interrupt** and other compositional operators. We can see that **suspend** can indeed be realized by the parallel composition ($\|$) and the interrupt operator (∇) defined earlier by: $(\ P[b/done]\backslash r)\ \|\ (repeat(\overline{r})\,\nabla\,\overline{b}\ )\backslash b\ =\ P$ **suspend** r where termination of P is carried by b, and causes termination of the *repeat* statement; but this happens only in the absence of r. Note that $P\backslash r$ cannot react for r and thus, the requirement that P**suspend** r does not react when r is present is satisfied.

We can express "**interrupt**" in terms of "**suspend**" as follows assuming $sort(P)\ =\ \{x_1,\cdots,x_n\}$: $P\,\nabla\,r\ \equiv\ (P$ **suspend** $r)\times Q$ where Q is given by $Q\ =\ (x_1+x_2+\cdots+x_n)Q+r$. The equivalence follows from the axioms and the equations for synchronous product. It may be noted that the derivation of "**interrupt**" from "**suspend**" requires the choice operator "$+$" which can be deribed in MEIJE.

This also explains why the various synchronous languages appear to be equally expressive. Of course, some abstractions are expressible more naturally in one paradigm than in others. Further, we get some differences with reference to ease of writing and expressing in ESTEREL and SIGNAL due to the underlying notion of data flow and the fact that programs don't terminate.

Remarks: It must be noted that we have exploited the signalling of completion through a special signal $\overline{done}$. This is not really new and need not have to be construed as enforcing another communication; in fact, it is not uncommon to define transition systems using labels reflecting the termination of constructs (see for example, transition systems of ESTEREL). In the above, we have shown how the various operators can mutually be simulated. It may be observed that we need to know the structure of the program for the translation. In fact, this must be evident from the derivation of "interrupt" from "suspend" and other operators. Now, the question is: Is it possible to compare the power of **suspend** and **preemption** operators at a semantic level. That is, we will be comparing the expressive powers of the two at only a behavioural level. In fact, such a study has been done in [PRS 94]. We state below the main theorems from [PRS 94].

The study in [PRS 94] is based on the notion of ESTEREL contexts. Such contexts represent "derived constructs" of the language. We shall assume a countably infinite supply of "statement" variables, and allow ESTEREL programs to be built up using variables also in place of program statements. A "program" with free variables will be called an ESTEREL *context*. Such contexts represent composite operators constructible in ESTEREL. We shall use C, D, E to denote contexts, and X, Y, Z to denote statement variables. In particular, a context C with X, Y, Z as its only free variables will be denoted by $C(X, Y, Z)$. When X, Y and Z are instantiated with concrete ESTEREL statements, say p, q and r, the resulting ESTEREL program is denoted by $C(p, q, r)$. We shall sometimes parameterize a context with, say, a signal variable S (or a value variable V), writing it as C_S (respectively, C_V). Such a parameterized context represents the class of contexts obtained by instantiating the parameter(s) to a value of the appropriate type. For instance, C_s (respectively, C_5) may represent a context in which S (respectively, V) has been instantiated to the signal s (respectively, the value 5).

Consider the subset of ESTEREL statements obtained using all the preemption operators but without using the suspension operators immediate suspend and delayed suspend. Then we can prove the following theorems:

Theorem 1: The behaviour of ESTEREL programs with preemption operators only is properly contained in the behaviour of ESTEREL programs with preemption and suspension operators.

Theorem 2: The behaviour of ESTEREL programs with suspension operators only is properly contained in the behaviour of ESTEREL programs with preemption and suspension operators.

Further work in the direction of the completeness notions and axiomatization ESTEREL are in progress.

6 Conclusion and Perspectives

We proposed a description of the preemption primitives of the reactive languages ESTEREL and SIGNAL in the framework of operators of a process calculus derived from MEIJE and SCCS. Using operators like synchronous product, sequencing and interrupt, we could describe the behavior of strong and weak preemption, and suspension in ESTEREL, and suspension and preemption of processes associated with time intervals in SIGNAL GTi, a tasking extension of SIGNAL. We have also shown that suspension and preemption could be shown to be derivable from each other. In fact, the result may not be very surprising since MEIJE is complete. However, the study brings out clearly the structure of the various preemptive operators in a single setting and provides comparisons from the point of view of expressive completeness and behavioral completeness. We also examined completeness with reference to the behavioral notion and showed that suspension and preemption are incompatible under such a behavioral notion. It would be nice to show how under such notions one can get a completeness result *à la* MEIJE. That is, to arrive at a subset of operators of suspension and preemption that are complete (under some usual conditions) such that whatever can be derived using the rules of action and reduction can also be directly defined using the chosen subset of operators.

We hope to study the features of the language 2Z [Vul 94] in this framework as it has interesting features for resetting the flow. For getting a complete picture, it would be interesting to include other languages such as LUSTRE, STATECHARTS, ELECTRE, ARGOS, ATP, ... [Hal 93] in this framework – perhaps, in the context of the clock/causal analysis of the underlying languages. Furthermore, it would be interesting and challenging to extend the study to unifying frameworks of synchrony and asynchrony as done in CRP [BRS 93]. There is a similarity between the tasks in ESTEREL, which are at the base of CRP, and those in SIGNAL*GTi*: they are a way of making reference to actions lasting on a non-instantaneous duration. A way of treating external or global nondeterminism is given in [SR 94] where a translation from CSP to ESTEREL is presented, as well as results about the inclusion of CSP behaviors in ESTEREL's. Also, another interesting perspective lies in the area of hybrid systems [GNRR 93], as shown in an earlier paper [Shy 93].

References

[BLGJ 91] A. Benveniste, P. Le Guernic, C. Jacquemot. *Synchronous programming with events and relations: the* SIGNAL *language and its semantics.* Science of Computer Programming, 16, pp. 103–149, 1991.

[BRS 93] G. Berry, S. Ramesh, and R.K. Shyamasundar, *Communicating Reactive Processes*, 20th ACM POPL, South Carolina, Jan 1993, pp. 85-99.

[Ber 93] G. Berry, *Preemption in Concurrent Systems*, Proc. FSTTCS 93, LNCS, 761, pp.72-93, Springer-Verlag, Berlin.

[GNRR 93] R.L. Grossman et al., *Hybrid Systems*, LNCS, 736, Springer-Verlag, 1993.

[Hal 93] N. Halbwachs. *Synchronous programming of reactive systems.* Kluwer, 1993.

[Hoa 85] C.A.R. Hoare, *Communicating Sequential Processes*, Prentice-Hall Int., 1985.

[Mil 89] R. Milner, *Communication and Concurrency*, Prentice-Hall Int., 1989.

[PRS 94] P.K. Pandya, Y.S. Ramakrishna, and R.K. Shyamasundar, *A Compositional Semantics of Esterel in Durational Calculus*, 2nd AMAST Workshop on Real-Time Systems: Models and Proofs, Bordeaux, France, June 1995.

[PRS 95] S. Pinchinat, E. Rutten, R.K. Shyamasundar. *Preemption Primitives in Reactive Languages.* INRIA Research Report, 1995. *(in preparation)*

[RLG 94] E. Rutten, P. Le Guernic. Sequencing data flow tasks in SIGNAL. Proc. *ACM SIGPLAN Workshop on Language, Compiler and Tool Support for Real-Time Systems*, Orlando, Florida, June 21, 1994.

[Shy 93] R.K. Shyamasundar, *Specification of Hybrid Systems in CRP*, Proc. of AMAST 93, Workshops in Computing Series from Springer-Verlag, Edited by M. Nivat, C. Rattray, T. Rus and G. Scollo, pp. 227-238, December 1993.

[SR 94] R.K. Shyamasundar, S. Ramesh, *Languages for Reactive Specifications: Synchrony vs. Asynchrony*, Proc. FT-RT-FTS 94, LNCS, 863, pp. 621–640, Springer-Verlag, Berlin.

[Sim 85] R. de Simone, *Higher-Level Synchronizing Devices in MEIJE-SCCS*, Theoretical Computer Science, 37, pp. 245 267, 1985

[Vul 94] J.E. Vuillemin, *On Circuits and Numbers*, IEEE Transactions on Computers, 43, August 1994, pp. 868-879.

Multi-Action Process Algebra

Wojciech Frączak

Université de Paris-Sud, LRI, Bât. 490,
F-91405 Orsay Cedex, France

Abstract. In this paper we propose a new process algebra based upon only three combinators: *prefixing, composition,* and *restriction,* but whose events (visible aspects of an evolution step) are structured as finite bags of *actions.* These structured events, called *multi-actions,* represent simultaneous execution of their actions and allow to handle the "simultaneity dependence" on events. This approach gives rise to a non trivial notion of *communication channels,* which parameterize composition and restriction operations. Multi-actions allow to avoid the "choice" as a primitive operation without loss of expressiveness of the algebra, which in turn ensures that all the defined equivalences are congruences.

Introduction

Process algebras, e.g. CCS [Mil80, Mil89], MEIJE [AB84], SCCS [Mil83], TCSP [BIIR84, Old86], or PBC [BDH92], can be seen as specification languages for describing communicating system behaviors, called *processes,* which consist of discrete *actions.* Actually, a process defines relations between its *events* (occurrences of actions), usually *causal dependence, concurrency,* or *conflict.* In this work we consider a new kind of dependence between events, called *simultaneity.* Two events are in the "dependence of simultaneity" when neither of them can occur without the other. This relation leads us to enlarge the notion of event and to consider it as a set of actions occurring simultaneously, and no more as an occurrence of a single action. Such an event will be called *multi-action.*

We propose a new process algebra, allowing to handle the simultaneity dependence, which we call Multi-Action Process Algebra (MAPA). The syntax of MAPA includes only three operators: *prefixing, composition,* and *restriction.* The main features of MAPA are the following. The first one is that a process is prefixed by a finite bag of actions instead of a single action. The second one is that the composition of two processes is accompanied by an explicit specification of communication restrictions, formalized by the notion of *channels.*

A channel is characterized by the type and the number of actions able to be carried by it simultaneously. Two processes connected by a channel can only communicate via multi-actions allowed by the channel. We define operations on channels which, for example, allow to reverse the direction of a channel or to group two channels into a single one.

An operational semantics of MAPA is proposed in standard manner via "derivation rules" (à la Plotkin). In the case of MAPA, where "choice" as a primitive operation does not exist, it is possible to consider different (but somehow equivalent) sets of derivation rules, each such set defining a slightly different operational semantics. We analyze a few such semantics and we choose the "most operational" one.

Apart from standard equivalences, like *process graph isomorphism* ($\equiv$), *strong equivalence* ($\simeq$), and *weak equivalence* ($\approx$) on processes, we propose *semantic equivalence* ($\sim$), which in case of MAPA can be seen as a new characterization of *failure equivalence* [BHR84]. The absence of choice as a primitive operator ensures that all the defined equivalences are congruences. We prove the following strict inclusions of the equivalences: $\equiv \subset \simeq \subset \approx \subset \sim$, and we demonstrate that, w.r.t. $\approx$ (and thus also w.r.t. $\sim$), all analyzed operational semantics are equivalent.

At the end we show that MAPA has the "completely general expressive power" w.r.t. at least two of the three criteria proposed by Vaandrager in [Vaa92].

The technical proofs are not included in this version of the paper because of the lack of space.

1 Communication primitives

In this section we describe the "communication primitives", i.e. the primitives which will be used by *agents* defined by our process algebra in order to interact. We start from a very intuitive and simple idea proposed by Milner for CCS [Mil80]. In his approach, *agents* can communicate by means of "links". An agent disposes of two primitive complementary actions for a link : sending (writing) on the link and receiving (reading) on the link. All the communications by links are supposed to be *synchronous* (i.e. neither a single sending nor a single receiving can occur without its inverse) and *binary* (only one receiving of one sending is allowed). In what follows, we will assume a nonempty set of *atomic actions*, L, together with bijection $^- : L \mapsto L$, called *conjugation*, which verifies $\bar{\bar{a}} = a$, for each $a \in L$. By $\bar{\bar{a}}$ we mean double application of the bijection on a, i.e. $\bar{\bar{a}}$ actually denotes $^-(^-(a))$.

Multi-actions. Atomic actions are allowed to be grouped into 'bags' called *multi-actions*. More precisely, a multi-action is a finite bag[1] (multi-set) of atomic actions. The set of all multi-actions over L will be denoted by $\mu_f(L)$. The first intuition behind a multi-action is that it represents a simultaneous execution of several actions (its components), like in [BDH92] or [BB93], but it slightly differs from the intuitive meaning of actions from MEIJE [AB84] or SCCS [Mil83], where a simultaneous execution of two actions always leads to their synchronization.

Let $\{c, b, a\}$ and $\{\bar{a}, \bar{b}\}$ be two multi-actions which represent a simultaneous execution of atomic actions c, b, a, and a simultaneous execution of $\bar{a}$, $\bar{b}$, respectively. Intuitively, a simultaneous execution of these two multi-actions can be seen from outside as:

---

[1] See Appendix for definitions and notations relative to bags (multi-sets).

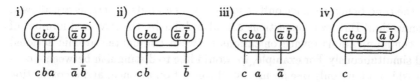

i) multi-action $\{c, b, a, \bar{a}, \bar{b}\}$, if the two multi-actions do not communicate;

ii) $\{c, b, \bar{b}\}$, if the two multi-actions synchronize on $a \leftrightarrow \bar{a}$, and thus a and $\bar{a}$ become invisible;

iii) $\{c, a, \bar{a}\}$, if the two multi-actions synchronize on $b \leftrightarrow \bar{b}$; or

iv) $\{c\}$, if the two multi-actions synchronize on $a \leftrightarrow \bar{a}$ and $b \leftrightarrow \bar{b}$.

The conjugation on atomic actions is extended to multi-actions $m \in \mu_f(L)$ by:

$$\forall a \in L \;\; \overline{m}(a) \stackrel{\text{def}}{=} m(\bar{a}) .$$

Remark that the conjugation on multi-actions still verifies $\overline{\overline{m}} = m$.

A synchronization of two complementary atomic actions always yields an invisible action (in CCS denoted by τ) which synchronizes with no other action. It means that agents able to execute a single atomic action at once do not allow multi-party synchronizations (synchronizations of more than two agents). In contrast, the multi-action approach, which allows agents to execute simultaneously a few atomic actions, obviously allows multi-party synchronization.

The "synchronization schema" between multi-actions can be formalized in the following way[2]:

"$n_1 + m$" can synchronize with "$n_2 + \overline{m}$", yielding "$n_1 + n_2$".

Two important consequences of such a formalization of synchronization between multi-actions are that the simultaneity and synchronization cannot be distinguished by observation (when $m = \emptyset$), and that a synchronization of two multi-actions yields a set of resulting multi-actions.

Communication channels. Consider the construct $P \parallel_{(A,B)} Q$, where P, Q are processes and (A, B) is a pair of sets of actions which describes connections between P and Q. The first set A contains the actions allowed from the left hand side of the connection (P's side), and the second set B contains the actions allowed from the right hand side of the connection (Q's side). Obviously, $P \parallel_{(A,B)} Q$ is equivalent to $Q \parallel_{(B,A)} P$, but not to $Q \parallel_{(A,B)} P$, due to a possible asymmetry of the connection. In general, the sets A and B can be incoherent, in the sense that there is an action a in A, but the inverse action, $\bar{a}$, which could synchronize with a, is not in B. Thus, we will assume that each connection (A, B) is compatible, in the sense that if an action a is in A, then the inverse action $\bar{a}$ is in B, and vice versa. Given a set A from a connection description (A, B), we can easily recalculate the set B by $B = \overline{A} \stackrel{\text{def}}{=} \{\bar{a} \mid a \in A\}$. Thus, we can represent a connection by a single set of actions, A.

---

[2] '+' denotes the multi-set sum (see Appendix).

For the time being, we have only discussed which kinds of actions are allowed by a connection. But two connections can also differ by the maximal number of atomic communications (synchronizations between conjugated atomic actions) allowed simultaneously. For example, we would like to distinguish between a connection which allows only one atomic synchronization at once, and a connection which allows two or more atomic synchronizations simultaneously.

If we always keep the initial intuition for atomic actions (as sending and receiving of signals), a connection between two communicating objects (*communication channel*) can be seen as a bunch of wires, each one able to carry some kind of signals. Let us take, for example, a communication channel composed of three wires: two unidirectional, oriented in the same direction, wires able to carry a signal whose sending (receiving) is represented by action a ($\overline{a}$, respectively), and one bidirectional wire able to carry a signal of actions c and $\overline{c}$. This can be illustrated by the following figure:

$$
\begin{array}{lcr}
a & \rule{6cm}{0.4pt} & \overline{a} \\
a & \rule{6cm}{0.4pt} & \overline{a} \\
c/\overline{c} & \rule{6cm}{0.4pt} & c/\overline{c}
\end{array}
$$

What we are really interested in is to know which multi-actions can be transmitted by the channel. The left end of the channel just depicted allows the following multi-actions to be transmitted: $\emptyset$, $\{a\}$, $\{c\}$, $\{\overline{c}\}$, $\{a,a\}$, $\{a,c\}$, $\{a,\overline{c}\}$, $\{a,a,c\}$, or $\{a,a,\overline{c}\}$. The right end obviously allows the conjugations of these multi-actions, i.e.: $\emptyset$, $\{\overline{a}\}$, $\{\overline{c}\}$, $\{c\}$, $\{\overline{a},\overline{a}\}$, $\{\overline{a},\overline{c}\}$, $\{\overline{a},c\}$, $\{\overline{a},\overline{a},\overline{c}\}$, or $\{\overline{a},\overline{a},c\}$.

Definition 1. A *channel*, ch, over atomic actions L, is a set of multi-actions (i.e. $ch \subseteq \mu_f(L)$) which fulfills:

1. $\emptyset \in ch$,   (where $\emptyset$ stands for an empty multi-action)
2. $\forall m, n \in \mu_f(L)$ $m \in ch, n \subseteq m \Rightarrow n \in ch$.   ([3])

The set of all channels over L will be denoted by $\mathcal{CH}(L)$ (or simply $\mathcal{CH}$).

The two properties of a channel go perfectly well with our intuition: 1. each channel can carry "nothing", represented by an empty multi-action; 2. if a channel can carry a multi-action m, then it can carry any part of m.

We extend conjugation on any set $\mathcal{L} \subseteq \mu_f(L)$ of multi-actions by: $\overline{\mathcal{L}} \stackrel{\text{def}}{=} \{\overline{m} \mid m \in \mathcal{L}\}$, and we define "sum" ($+$) of two sets of multi-actions by: $\mathcal{L}_1 + \mathcal{L}_2 \stackrel{\text{def}}{=} \{m + n \mid m \in \mathcal{L}_1, n \in \mathcal{L}_2\}$.

Proposition 2. *Channels are closed by union ($\cup$), intersection ($\cap$), sum ($+$), and conjugation ($^-$), i.e.:*

$$ch, ch' \in \mathcal{CH} \Rightarrow ch \cup ch', ch \cap ch', ch + ch', \overline{ch} \in \mathcal{CH} .$$

These four operations have very strong intuitive meaning. Union of two channels ($ch \cup ch'$) represents the minimal channel able carry all what ch or ch' can carry.

---

[3] See Appendix for the definition of bag inclusion ($\subseteq$).

Intersection of two channels ($ch \cap ch'$) represents the channel which carry only what ch and ch' can carry. Sum of two channels ($ch + ch'$) puts side by side the two channels, i.e. the resulting channel carries all what the two channels may carry simultaneously. Channel conjugation ($\overline{ch}$) reverses the direction of the channel.

2 Multi-action process algebra

In this section we sketch the syntax of our Multi-Action Process Algebra, constructed over (parameterized by) a set, L, of atomic actions. We define the language $\mathcal{P}$ of MAPA process terms by:

$$\mathbf{P} ::= \mathbf{m}; \mathbf{P} \mid \mathbf{P}\,\mathbf{ch}\,\mathbf{P} \mid \mathbf{P}{:}\mathbf{ch} \mid \mathbf{g}$$

where:

- $\mathbf{m}$ is a nonempty multi-action, i.e. $\mathbf{m} \in \mu_f(L) \setminus \{\emptyset\}$,
- $\mathbf{ch}$ is a channel, i.e. $\mathbf{ch} \in \mathcal{CH}(L)$,
- $\mathbf{g}$ is an *agent identifier* from an infinite countable set *"Agents"*,
- for each agent identifier $\mathbf{g}$, there exists a unique defining equation $\mathbf{g} \doteq \mathbf{P}$.

The intuitive meaning of the syntactic constructs for process terms is very similar to that proposed by Milner for CCS. The term of the shape ($\mathbf{m}; \mathbf{P}$) represents a process able to perform a multi-action $\mathbf{m}$, and after that behaves like $\mathbf{P}$. The term ($\mathbf{P}\,\mathbf{ch}\,\mathbf{Q}$) describes a process which behaves like two processes $\mathbf{P}$ and $\mathbf{Q}$ running in parallel and communicating via an oriented channel $\mathbf{ch}$.

$$\mathbf{P}\,\mathbf{ch}\,\mathbf{Q} \; : \quad \boxed{P} \!\!-\!\! \underset{ch}{\longrightarrow} \!\!\boxed{Q}$$

The construct ($\mathbf{P}{:}\mathbf{ch}$) is called *restriction* (or *interfacing*). The process ($\mathbf{P}{:}\mathbf{ch}$) behaves like $\mathbf{P}$ but its communication capabilities are limited to the channel $\mathbf{ch}$, i.e. only the multi-actions of $\mathbf{P}$ allowed by channel $\mathbf{ch}$ will be able to be seen from outside.

$$\mathbf{P}{:}\mathbf{ch} \; : \quad \boxed{P \; | ch} \!\!\longrightarrow$$

Using *agent identifier* $\mathbf{g}$, one can build processes with infinite behaviors. We suppose that almost all agents are defined by the *trivial* equation $\mathbf{g} \doteq \mathbf{g}$, but some finite number of agents which are defined by a non trivial process term, i.e. when the right hand side of the defining equation is different from the agent identifier (left hand side of the equation).

Note that we have neither "choice" operation nor "relabeling" as primitive operations.

2.1 Operational semantics

The operational semantics of our language $\mathcal{P}$ will be given in terms of *labeled transition systems*.

Definition 3. A *labeled transition system* is a triple $(St, Lab, \rightarrow)$, where St and Lab are two sets of *states* and *labels*, respectively, and $\rightarrow \subseteq St \times Lab \times St$ is a set of transitions. A transition (s, α, s') is usually denoted by $s \xrightarrow{\alpha} s'$.

The operational semantics of the language $\mathcal{P}$ is the labeled transition system $(\mathcal{P}, \mu_f(L), \rightarrow)$, denoted by $sem(\mathcal{P})$, where states are all elements of $\mathcal{P}$ (i.e. process terms), labels are multi-actions, and transitions are defined by the following set $\mathcal{R}$ of rules ([4]):

Inaction $\quad \mathbf{m;P} \xrightarrow{\emptyset} \mathbf{m;P}$ $\qquad\qquad$ Prefix $\;\mathbf{m;P} \xrightarrow{m} \mathbf{P}$

Restriction $\quad \dfrac{\mathbf{P} \xrightarrow{m} \mathbf{P'}}{\mathbf{P:ch} \xrightarrow{m} \mathbf{P':ch}}$ if $m \in \mathrm{ch}$ $\qquad$ Call $\quad \mathbf{g} \xrightarrow{\emptyset} \mathbf{P}$ if $\mathbf{g} \doteq \mathbf{P}$

Composition $\quad \dfrac{\mathbf{P} \xrightarrow{n_1+m} \mathbf{P'} \quad \mathbf{Q} \xrightarrow{n_2+\overline{m}} \mathbf{Q'}}{\mathbf{P} \; \mathbf{ch} \; \mathbf{Q} \xrightarrow{n_1+n_2} \mathbf{P'} \; \mathbf{ch} \; \mathbf{Q'}}$ if $m \in \mathrm{ch}$

where m, n_1, n_2 are multi-actions and $\emptyset$ is the empty multi-action.

A transition $P \xrightarrow{m} Q$ says that an agent described by process term P is able to evolve into a new agent represented by term Q, performing multi-action m, or, equivalently, P is able to evolve into Q if multi-action $\overline{m}$ occurs in its environment. One should not confuse an empty multi-action $\emptyset$ with an invisible step, e.g. τ from CCS. An empty multi-action means no (visible) action, so it may, but does not have to, hide an invisible internal move of an agent.

The rules presented above are slightly different from those proposed by Milner for CCS or SCCS. We have a new rule, Inaction rule, which says that an agent of the shape $\mathbf{m;P}$ can remain non active. Inaction rule actually makes any agent able to "perform" an empty multi-action, i.e.:

Proposition 4. $\forall \mathbf{P} \in \mathcal{P} \; \exists \mathbf{Q} \in \mathcal{P} \; \mathbf{P} \xrightarrow{\emptyset} \mathbf{Q}$.

Also Call rule may seem surprising if one confuses "invisible step" with an empty multi-action.

In Section 4 we will discuss different (but in some sense equivalent) sets of "derivation rules" for MAPA:

$\mathcal{R}_0 = \{\mathrm{Inaction, Prefix, Composition, Restriction, Call}\}$; (i.e. $\mathcal{R}_0 = \mathcal{R}$)
$\mathcal{R}_1 = \{\mathrm{Inaction\text{-}bis, Prefix, Composition, Restriction, Call}\}$;
$\mathcal{R}_2 = \{\mathrm{CompLeft, CompRight, Prefix, Composition, Restriction, Call}\}$;
$\mathcal{R}_3 = \{\mathrm{Inaction\text{-}bis, Prefix, Composition, Restriction, Call\text{-}bis}\}$;
$\mathcal{R}_4 = \{\mathrm{CompLeft, CompRight, Prefix, Composition, Restriction, Call\text{-}bis}\}$;

---

[4] More formally, $\rightarrow$ is the smallest subset of $\mathcal{P} \times \mu_f(L) \times \mathcal{P}$, which verifies the rules.

where alternative rules are defined as follows:

Inaction-bis $\quad P \xrightarrow{\emptyset} P$

CompLeft $\quad \dfrac{P \xrightarrow{m} P'}{P \text{ ch } Q \xrightarrow{m} P' \text{ ch } Q}$

Call-bis $\quad \dfrac{P \xrightarrow{m} Q}{g \xrightarrow{m} Q} \text{ if } g \doteq P$

CompRight $\quad \dfrac{Q \xrightarrow{m} Q'}{P \text{ ch } Q \xrightarrow{m} P \text{ ch } Q'}$

We can easily imagine five different operational semantics, $sem_i(\mathcal{P})$, whose transition relations are generated by the corresponding set of rules, $\mathcal{R}_i$, for each $i \in \{0, 1, 2, 3, 4\}$.

Notation conventions. In order to avoid too many parentheses, a multi-action will be denoted as a simple word, e.g. "$a a \bar{c}$" for $\{a, a, \bar{c}\}$, or "am" for $\{a\} + m$, where m denotes a multi-action.

The square brackets on a set of multi-actions, $\mathcal{L} \subseteq \mu_f(L)$, will be interpreted as the following "channel completion": $[\mathcal{L}] \stackrel{\text{def}}{=} \{n \in \mu_f(L) \mid \exists m \in \mathcal{L} \; n \subseteq m\} \cup \{\emptyset\}$. By "[ ]" we will denote the minimal channel, i.e. $\{\emptyset\}$. Finite channels will be denoted as lists of their maximal (w.r.t. $\subseteq$) elements between square brackets, e.g. "$[aa, b]$" for $\{\{a, a\}, \{a\}, \{b\}, \emptyset\}$. For infinite channels we will use μ_f notation: $\mu_f(A)$, where $A \subseteq L$, will denote the set of all multi-actions constructed over actions from A; e.g. $\mu_f(L)$ stands for the set of all multi-actions, and $\mu_f(\{a, b\})$, usually abbreviated to $\mu_f(ab)$, stands for the set of all multi-actions constructed over actions a and b. Proposition 2 allows us to compose such channels through union ($\cup$), intersection ($\cap$), sum ($+$), and conjugation ($^-$) operations.

By "stop" we will describe an agent with the trivial definition: $\text{stop} \doteq \text{stop}$.

Example. Suppose that we want to model an agent "Clock" with the following behavior. The agent waits for a signal c and then it sends one signal s. After that, it waits for the second c, and after that, it sends two signals s simultaneously (i.e. it performs the multi-action ss), and so on, i.e. after the n-th c signal, Clock performs the multi-action s^n:

$$c \rightarrow s \rightarrow c \rightarrow ss \rightarrow c \rightarrow sss \rightarrow c \rightarrow ssss \rightarrow c \cdots .$$

In order to implement the agent "Clock" in MAPA, we first define the following five agents T, E, E_F, O, O_F:

$$T \doteq c; e; T \quad E \doteq \bar{e}so; E \quad E_F \doteq \bar{e}s; (E \; [o] \; (O_F : \mu_f(s) + [\bar{o}]))$$
$$O \doteq \bar{o}se; O \quad O_F \doteq \bar{o}s; (O \; [e] \; (E_F : \mu_f(s) + [\bar{e}]))$$

Now, Clock can be defined as: $(T \; [e] \; E_F) : [c] \cup \mu_f(s)$. The initial derivation of Clock is sketched below (developed redexes are underlined and $\emptyset$ loops are signaled by $(*)$ on the process term number):

$$(\underline{T} \ [e] \ \underline{E_F}) : [c] \cup \mu_f(s) \xrightarrow{\emptyset} \qquad\qquad\qquad : 1$$

$$(\underline{c}; e; T \ [e] \ \bar{e}s; (E \ [o] \ (O_F : \mu_f(s) + [\bar{o}]))) : [c] \cup \mu_f(s) \xrightarrow{c} \qquad : 2^*$$

$$(\underline{e}; T \ [e] \ \bar{e}s; (E \ [o] \ (O_F : \mu_f(s) + [\bar{o}]))) : [c] \cup \mu_f(s) \xrightarrow{s} \qquad : 3^*$$

$$(\underline{T} \ [e] \ (\underline{E} \ [o] \ (\underline{O_F} : \mu_f(s) + [\bar{o}]))) : [c] \cup \mu_f(s) \xrightarrow{\emptyset} \qquad : 4$$

$$(\underline{c}; e; T \ [e] \ (\bar{e}so; E \ [o] \ ((\bar{o}s; (O \ [e] \ (E_F : \mu_f(s) + [\bar{e}]))) : \mu_f(s) + [\bar{o}]))) : [c] \cup \mu_f(s) \xrightarrow{c} \qquad : 5^*$$

$$(\underline{e}; T \ [e] \ (\underline{\bar{e}so}; E \ [o] \ ((\bar{o}s; (O \ [e] \ (E_F : \mu_f(s) + [\bar{e}]))) : \mu_f(s) + [\bar{o}]))) : [c] \cup \mu_f(s) \xrightarrow{ss} \qquad : 6^*$$

$$(T \ [e] \ (E \ [o] \ (((O \ [e] \ (E_F : \mu_f(s) + [\bar{e}]))) : \mu_f(s) + [\bar{o}]))) : [c] \cup \mu_f(s) \xrightarrow{\emptyset} \cdots \qquad : 7$$

What graphically yields:

If we abstract empty multi-actions, we obtain exactly what we want.

2.2 Sort

A *sort* of a process, according to Milner [Mil89], is a set of *actions* containing all the *actions* which can be performed by the process. In our case, *"actions"* mean multi-actions. The sort of a process can be very useful in a static (syntactic) analysis of the process and can be explored during an implementation, distribution, etc.

Clearly, every process term has a minimal sort (denoted by $sort(P)$): it is the set of all transition labels of its *process graph* (see Def. 6). In general, the minimal sort of a process term P cannot be calculated (because of the non-decidability of the problem, cf. [Mil89]), however it is possible to estimate a sort of a process term via a syntactic analysis. Following Milner, we introduce the notion of *syntactic sort* $\mathcal{L} \subseteq \mu_f(L)$, of a process term P, denoted by $P :: \mathcal{L}$ and defined by the following rules:

1. $P :: \mu_f(L)$
2. $P :: \mathcal{L}_1 \wedge \mathcal{L}_1 \subseteq \mathcal{L}_2 \Rightarrow P :: \mathcal{L}_2$
3. $P :: \mathcal{L}_1 \wedge P :: \mathcal{L}_2 \Rightarrow P :: (\mathcal{L}_1 \cap \mathcal{L}_2)$
4. $P :: \mathcal{L} \Rightarrow m; P :: (\mathcal{L} \cup \{m\})$
5. $P :: \mathcal{L}_1, Q :: \mathcal{L}_2 \Rightarrow P \ ch \ Q :: \{n_1 + n_2 \mid \exists m \in ch \ \ n_1 + m \in \mathcal{L}_1 \wedge n_2 + \overline{m} \in \mathcal{L}_2\}$
6. $P :: \mathcal{L} \Rightarrow P : ch :: (\mathcal{L} \cap ch)$
7. $\left(\left\{ \begin{array}{c} g_1 :: \mathcal{L}_1 \cup [\,] \\ \cdots \\ g_n :: \mathcal{L}_n \cup [\,] \end{array} \right\} \Rightarrow \left\{ \begin{array}{c} G_1 :: \mathcal{L}_1 \\ \cdots \\ G_n :: \mathcal{L}_n \end{array} \right\} \right) \Rightarrow \left\{ \begin{array}{c} g_1 :: \mathcal{L}_1 \\ \cdots \\ g_n :: \mathcal{L}_n \end{array} \right\}, \text{ where: } \begin{array}{c} g_1 \doteq G_1, \\ \cdots \\ g_n \doteq G_n. \end{array}$

The first three rules describe the general assumptions. The next three rules correspond to the three constructs of our language: *prefixing, composition,* and *restriction.* The last rule allows to calculate sorts of recursive agents.

Proposition 5.
If, using rules given above, we prove $P :: \mathcal{L}$ then, $\mathcal{L}$ is indeed a sort of P.

3   Equivalence relations

In this section we recall and adapt for MAPA some basic notions of *process semantics*.

Definition 6. A *process graph* is a 4-uple $(St, Lab, \rightarrow, s)$, where $(St, Lab, \rightarrow)$ is a labeled transition system, and $s \in St$ is an *initial state*. Moreover, we require that all states of St be accessible from s, i.e. $\forall x \in St\ (s, x) \in \overset{*}{\rightarrow}$, where $\overset{*}{\rightarrow}$ denotes the reflexive–transitive closure of $\{(x, y) \in St \times St \mid \exists \alpha\ x \overset{\alpha}{\rightarrow} y\}$.

Let $TS = (St, Lab, \rightarrow)$ be a labeled transition system. For each state $x \in St$, we associate a process graph $graph(x)$ defined as $graph(x) \overset{\text{def}}{=} (St_x, Lab, \rightarrow_x, x)$, where $St_x \overset{\text{def}}{=} \{y \in St \mid x \overset{*}{\rightarrow} y\}$, and where $\rightarrow_x$ is transition relation $(\rightarrow)$ restricted for states St_x. Intuitively, $graph(x)$ describes the part of transition system TS accessible from the state x.

Proposition 7. *For each process term $P \in \mathcal{P}$, the associated process graph $graph(P)$, obtained from transition system $sem(\mathcal{P})$, is finitely branching* [5].

Process graph isomorphism. Two process graphs, $G_1 = (St_1, Lab, \rightarrow_1, s_1)$ and $G_2 = (St_2, Lab, \rightarrow_2, s_2)$, are *isomorphic* iff there exists a bijection $\varphi : St_1 \mapsto St_2$ such that: $\varphi(s_1) = s_2$ and $p \overset{\alpha}{\rightarrow}_1 q \Leftrightarrow \varphi(p) \overset{\alpha}{\rightarrow}_2 \varphi(q)$. In other words, two process graphs are isomorphic iff they differ only in the identity of their nodes.

Definition 8. Let **P** and **Q** be two MAPA process terms. $\mathbf{P} \equiv \mathbf{Q}$ iff the process graphs $graph(\mathbf{P})$, $graph(\mathbf{Q})$ are isomorphic.

Proposition 9. *For all $P, Q, R \in \mathcal{P}$ and for all $ch, ch' \in CH$, we have:*

1. $\equiv$ is a congruence in MAPA.
2. $P \equiv P\ ch\ \underline{\text{stop}}$.
3. $P\ ch\ Q \equiv Q\ \overline{ch}\ P$.
4. $sort(P) \subseteq ch \Rightarrow P \equiv P : ch$.
5. $(P : ch) : ch' \equiv P : ch \cap ch'$.
6. $ch + ch \subseteq ch \Rightarrow (P\ ch\ Q)\ ch\ R \equiv P\ ch\ (Q\ ch\ R)$.

Strong equivalence. Let $TS = (St, Lab, \rightarrow)$ be a labeled transition system. A *strong simulation* in TS is a binary relation on states, $S \subseteq St \times St$, such that:

$$\forall_{p,q,p' \in St}\ \forall_{\alpha \in Lab}\ (p, q) \in S \wedge p \overset{\alpha}{\rightarrow} p' \Rightarrow \exists_{q' \in St}\ q \overset{\alpha}{\rightarrow} q' \wedge (p', q') \in S \ .$$

If S is also symmetric, then it is called a *strong bisimulation*.

It is well known that the largest strong bisimulation $\simeq$ exists: it is the union of all strong bisimulations. $\simeq$ is symmetric, reflexive, and transitive, i.e. it is an equivalence relation on states of the transition system.

---

[5] A process graph $(St, Lab, \rightarrow, s)$ is *finitely branching* if and only if $\forall x \in St$ the set $\{(\alpha, y) \in Lab \times St \mid x \overset{\alpha}{\rightarrow} y\}$ is finite, i.e. in each state there are only finitely many possible ways to proceed.

Definition 10.
Two MAPA process terms **P**, **Q** are *strongly equivalent* iff $\mathbf{P} \simeq \mathbf{Q}$ in $sem(\mathcal{P})$.

Weak equivalence. Let $TS = (St, \mu_f(L), \rightarrow)$ be a labeled (by multi-actions over L) transition system. We define:

1. $\leadsto \overset{\text{def}}{=} \{(p,q) \in St \times St \mid p \overset{\emptyset}{\rightarrow} q\}$, and $\overset{*}{\leadsto}$, as its reflexive–transitive closure.
2. $\Longrightarrow \overset{\text{def}}{=} \left\{(p,m,q) \in St \times \mu_f(L) \times St \mid \exists_{p',q' \in St} \ p \overset{*}{\leadsto} p' \wedge p' \overset{m}{\rightarrow} q' \wedge q' \overset{*}{\leadsto} q\right\}.$

The binary relation $\overset{*}{\leadsto}$ expresses the possibility of silent (i.e. via empty multi-actions) evolution of process.

Let $TS = (St, \mu_f(L), \rightarrow)$ be a labeled (by multi-actions) transition system. A *weak simulation* in TS is a binary relation on states, $S \in St \times St$, such that:

$$\forall_{p,q,p' \in St} \ \forall_{m \in \mu_f(L)} \ (p,q) \in S \wedge p \overset{m}{\rightarrow} p' \ \Rightarrow \ \exists_{q' \in St} \ q \overset{m}{\Longrightarrow} q' \wedge (p',q') \in S \ .$$

It is well known that the largest weak bisimulation ($\approx$) exists: it is the union of all weak bisimulations, i.e. $\approx \overset{\text{def}}{=} \bigcup\{B \mid B \text{ is a weak bisimulation}\}$. This bisimulation, $\approx$, is a symmetric, reflexive, transitive binary relation, i.e. it is an equivalence relation on states.

Definition 11.
Two MAPA process terms **P**, **Q** are *weakly equivalent* iff $\mathbf{P} \approx \mathbf{Q}$ in $sem(\mathcal{P})$.

Proposition 12.

1. $\equiv \subset \simeq$.
2. $\mathbf{P} \simeq \mathbf{stop} \Leftrightarrow sort(\mathbf{P}) = [\,]$.
3. $\mathbf{P} : [\,] \simeq \mathbf{stop}$.
4. $\simeq \subset \approx$.
5. $\mathbf{g} \doteq \mathbf{G} \Rightarrow \mathbf{g} \approx \mathbf{G}$.
6. $\simeq$ and $\approx$ are congruences in MAPA.

3.1 Semantic equivalence

MAPA is a language intended to describe behaviors of "communicating objects", so we are looking for a semantics which only distinguishes between processes which differ in their external behavior. We propose a characterization of identity in external behavior of processes using the notion of "context".

A *context* C is a process term with some holes in it. More formally:

- an agent identifier 'g' is a context,
- $\{\,\}$ is a context (called *hole*),
- if C, C' are contexts, m is a multi-action, and ch is a channel, then $(m;C)$, $(C:ch)$, and $(C \, ch \, C')$ are contexts.

If C is a context and $P \in \mathcal{P}$ is a process term, then $C\{P\}$ denotes the result of placing P in the holes of C; i.e. replacing each hole $\{\ \}$ by P; it can be checked that $C\{P\}$ is a process term. For example, if $C = m; (\{\ \}\ ch\ \{\ \})$ and P is a process term, then $C\{P\}$ denotes $m; (P\ ch\ P)$.

Definition 13. Two MAPA process terms **P**, **Q** are *equivalent*, denoted **P** $\sim$ **Q**, iff for each context C, the process $C\{\mathbf{P}\}$ can silently derive into a process of empty sort iff $C\{\mathbf{Q}\}$ can do so, i.e. :

$$\exists P'\left(C\{\mathbf{P}\} \overset{*}{\leadsto} P' \wedge sort(P') = [\,]\right) \quad \Leftrightarrow \quad \exists Q'\left(C\{\mathbf{Q}\} \overset{*}{\leadsto} Q' \wedge sort(Q') = [\,]\right).$$

This definition can be successfully applied in order to prove that two processes are non equivalent, but if one wants to prove two processes to be equivalent, then clearly the definition cannot be directly used. Thus, the following proposition can be very useful because it says that we inherit all proof methods valid for all previous equivalences.

Proposition 14. $\approx\ \subset\ \sim$.

It turns out that, in the context of MAPA, this characterization of equivalence coincides with the well known *failure equivalence* $\approx_F$, as e.g. defined in [BHR84].

4   Alternative operational semantics for MAPA

In Section 2.1 we have already mentioned that alternative formulations (definitions) of the operational semantics of MAPA can be done by choosing one of the four sets of rules $\mathcal{R}_1$, $\mathcal{R}_2$, $\mathcal{R}_3$, or $\mathcal{R}_4$, instead of the set $\mathcal{R}_0$ ($= \mathcal{R}$). Now, we will prove that all five formulations are equivalent w.r.t. weak equivalence, and we will motivate our choice for $\mathcal{R}_0$ as the "most operational" formulation.

In order to formally compare the five operational semantics, we define the new transition system TS as the disjoint union of the five transition systems, each generated by the corresponding set of rules. More formally, if $sem_i(\mathcal{P}) = (\mathcal{P}, \mu_f(L), \rightarrow_i)$ are labeled transition systems generated by the corresponding set of rules, $\mathcal{R}_i$ (with $i \in \{0, 1, 2, 3, 4\}$), as defined in Section 2.1, then :

- $TS \overset{\text{def}}{=} (\mathcal{P} \times \{0, 1, 2, 3, 4\}, \mu_f(L), \rightarrow)$, where:

$$\forall_{P,Q \in \mathcal{P}}\ \forall_{m \in \mu_f(L)}\ \forall_{i,j \in \{0,1,2,3,4\}}\ \langle P, i\rangle \overset{m}{\rightarrow} \langle Q, j\rangle \overset{\text{def}}{\iff} i = j \wedge P \overset{m}{\rightarrow}_i Q .$$

Theorem 15. $\langle P, i\rangle \approx \langle P, j\rangle$ in TS, for any $P \in \mathcal{P}$ and any $i, j \in \{0, 1, 2, 3, 4\}$.

The question remains why we have chosen $\mathcal{R}_0$ rather then another set of derivation rules. We may first remark that if rule Call-bis takes part in the derivation rules, then Proposition 7 does not hold. Take e.g. the following agent definition "$g \doteq g\ [\ ]\ c; g$". It is not difficult to see that $graph(\langle g, i\rangle)$ is infinitely branching for any $\mathcal{R}_i$ with Call-bis rule, i.e. for $\mathcal{R}_3$ and $\mathcal{R}_4$. This is the reason for which we have removed these formulations.

Another criterion for comparing operational semantics is the size of generated process graphs w.r.t. to number of states and transitions.

Proposition 16. *Let $\to_i$, for $i \in \{0,1,2\}$, denote transitions of $sem_i(\mathcal{P})$ and $\overset{*}{\to}_i$ be the reflexive-transitive closure of $\{(P,Q) \in \mathcal{P} \times \mathcal{P} \mid \exists \alpha\ P\overset{\alpha}{\to}_i Q\}$. Thus, we have:*

1. *$\to_0\ \subset\ \to_1$ and $\overset{*}{\to}_0\ \subset\ \overset{*}{\to}_1$*
2. *$\to_2\ \not\subset\ \to_0$ and $\to_0\ \not\subset\ \to_2$, but $\overset{*}{\to}_0\ \subset\ \overset{*}{\to}_2$*

The semantics $sem_0(\mathcal{P})$ $(= sem(\mathcal{P}))$ makes that for any process term $P \in \mathcal{P}$, the associated process graph $graph(P)$ is always finitely branching (which is not the case for $sem_3(\mathcal{P})$ and $sem_4(\mathcal{P})$) and minimal by inclusion of states w.r.t. $sem_1(\mathcal{P})$ and $sem_2(\mathcal{P})$.

5 Expressive power of MAPA

In [Vaa92] three different criteria in which a process algebra can have "completely general expressive power" are proposed:

1. *Each Turing Machine can be simulated in lock step.*
2. *Each "effective"* [6] *process graph can be specified up to some notion of behavioral equivalence.*
3. *Each operation in a "natural" class of operations is realizable in terms of the operations in the language up to some notion of behavioral equivalence.*

In this section we discuss how *renaming* and *choice* operations can be implemented in MAPA. Then we formulate our main result which says that any "recursively enumerable process graph" can be specified in MAPA up to *weak equivalence* ($\approx$). It means that MAPA has "completely general expressive power" w.r.t. 1 and 2. The point 3 remains open and strongly depends on the meaning of "natural".

Renaming. Let P be a process such that $sort(P) \subseteq [ab]$, i.e. the process communicates by actions a and b, possibly simultaneously. This can be depicted by the following figure, in which the process P communicates via two independent channels $[a]$ and $[b]$ (because $[a] + [b] = [ab]$): $\left(P\right)\!\!\begin{smallmatrix}a\\b\end{smallmatrix}$

In order to rename an action of process P, for example a to c, we can envisage the following configuration: $\left(\!\!\left(P\right)\!\!\overset{a}{\underset{b}{}}\!\!\overset{\bar{a}}{}\!\!\left(g\right)\!\!\overset{c}{}\!\!\right)$

where agent **g** has the following defining equation ($\mathbf{g} \doteq \bar{a}c; \mathbf{g}$). In MAPA syntax we denote that by $((P\,[a]\,\mathbf{g}) : [cb])$.

---

[6] In what follows we will use the name "recursively enumerable" instead of "effective", in order to avoid inconsistency with Vaandrager's terminology, in which a state of an "effective process graph" has a recursive (not recursively enumerable) set of outgoing transitions (c.f. [Vaa92]).

Even if in general a renaming of atomic actions of an arbitrary process is not obvious, we can remark that if the sort of a process is known, we are able to make much more than a simple atomic action renaming, e.g. duplications, multi-way synchronizations, or other nontrivial operations on actions of the process.

Choice. Let $t = ((\overline{c}; \mathtt{stop}\ [\overline{c}]\ (c; P\ []\ c; Q)):ch)$ be a process term. Suppose that the channel ch carries neither c nor $\overline{c}$ (i.e. $\{c\}, \{\overline{c}\} \notin ch$). In this case the process can only perform an empty multi-action from one of two possible synchronizations, becoming either $((\mathtt{stop}\ [\overline{c}]\ (P\ []\ c; Q)):ch)$, equivalent by $\equiv$ to $(P:ch)$, or $((\mathtt{stop}\ [\overline{c}]\ (c; P\ []\ Q)):ch)$, equivalent by $\equiv$ to $(Q:ch)$.

If moreover $sort(P) \subseteq ch$ and $sort(Q) \subseteq ch$, then process t is in fact a nondeterministic choice between P and Q, because in this case $(P:ch) \equiv P$ and $(Q:ch) \equiv Q$.

Multi-actions allow us to slightly modify the process t in order to make the choice "deterministic", i.e. it is the environment which decides which subprocess, P or Q, will be chosen. Let us take, e.g. $t' = ((\overline{c}; \mathtt{stop}\ [\overline{c}]\ (ca; P\ []\ cb; Q)):ch)$ with $\{a\}, \{b\} \in ch$. The process t' intuitively describes a "guarded" choice between P and Q. The environment can choose P or Q by asking it via the action a for P and b for Q.

Remark that the parallel composition by an empty channel [ ], which fulfills $\overline{[\,]} = [\,]$ and $[\,] + [\,] \subseteq [\,]$, is commutative by Proposition 9(3) and associative by Proposition 9(6). It allows us to write $P\ [\,]\ Q\ [\,]\ R$, or more generally $[\,]_{i \in I}\ P_i$, where I is a finite nonempty indexing set, without ambiguity. Let $\{m_i; P_i \mid i \in I\}$ be a finite nonempty set of process terms such that $\{k\}, \{\overline{k}\} \notin [sort(m_i; P_i)]$ for each $i \in I$, for an atomic action $k \in L$. We define a "macro" $\sum\{m_i; P_i \mid i \in I\}$ as $((\ [\,]_{i \in I}\ km_i; P_i\ )\ [k]\ \overline{k}; \mathtt{stop}\ ) : \mu_f(L \setminus \{k, \overline{k}\})$.

The macro is in fact a general implementation of guarded choice operation, so much important in other process algebras. In order to convince ourselves that the macro really implement a guarded choice operator, let us suppose such a n-ary choice operator $\square_n$ with the standard derivation rules:

$$\frac{P_i \overset{m}{\longrightarrow} Q}{\square_n(P_1, .., P_i, .., P_n) \overset{m}{\longrightarrow} Q} \qquad \frac{P_i \overset{\emptyset}{\longrightarrow} Q}{\square_n(P_1, .., P_i, .., P_n) \overset{\emptyset}{\longrightarrow} \square_n(P_1, .., Q, .., P_n)}$$

for each $i \in \{1, \ldots, n\}$ and $m \neq \emptyset$.

Theorem 17. *In* MAPA *enriched by a choice operation* $\square_n$, *we have:*

$$\square_n(m_1; P_1, \ldots, m_n; P_n) \simeq \sum\{m_1; P_1, \ldots, m_n; P_n\}$$

for any multi-actions m_i *and process terms* P_i, *with* $i \in \{1, \ldots, n\}$.

5.1 Recursively enumerable process graphs

Expressive power of process algebras in describing process graphs has been already analyzed, e.g. by Vaandrager in [Vaa92], where he proves that one cannot hope to find a general process algebra with "effective" SOS semantics, able to describe any, even recursive, process graph w.r.t. strong bisimulation. On the other hand almost all of the usual process algebras (e.g. CCS, TCSP, SCCS, ACP [BW90], PA [Vaa92]) are powerful enough to describe any "effective" process graph w.r.t. the weak bisimulation.

Definition 18. A process graph $(St, Lab, \rightarrow, s)$ is *recursively enumerable* if there exists a Turing Machine which for each state $p \in St$ (considered as entry) computes (enumerates) all outgoing transitions, i.e. the set $\{(\alpha, q) \mid p \xrightarrow{\alpha} q\}$.

The following theorem says that our very simple (with only three combinators) process algebra is powerful enough to describe any "recursively enumerable process graph" modulo weak equivalence $\approx$.

Theorem 19.
Any recursively enumerable process graph $(St, \mu_f(L_f), \rightarrow, s)$ with L_f finite, can be described (modulo $\approx$) by a MAPA process term.

We considered here the process graphs whose transitions are labeled by multi-actions over a finite set L_f. Remark that we always stay with infinite domain of transition labels even though L_f is finite. Thus, we can suppose without loss of generality that each element of L_f is coded by a single tape character in the appropriate Turing Machine representation, and that a multi-action (finite bag over L_f) is coded as a word over such characters.

6 Conclusion

In this paper we have proposed a new process algebra called MAPA. The main features of MAPA are that a single step of a process evolution is a *multi-action* which represents a simultaneous execution of several actions, and that a parallel composition of two processes is accompanied by an explicit specification of communication channels between them. This channel specification says what kind of communications can be performed between the two processes.

Acknowledgments. I would like to thank Jean Fanchon for fruitful discussions and Raymond Devillers for careful reading of this text and helpful comments.

References

[AB84]   D. Austry and G. Boudol. Algèbre de processus et synchronisation. *Theoretical Computer Science*, 30:91–131, 1984.

[BB93]   J.C.M. Baeten and J.A. Bergstra. Non interleaving process algebra. In *CONCUR'93*, volume 715 of *LNCS*, pages 308–323. Springer Verlag, 1993.

[BDH92]   E. Best, R. Devillers, and J. Hall. The Box Calculus: a new causal algebra with multi-label communication. In *Advances in Petri Nets 1992*, volume 609 of *LNCS*, pages 21–69. Springer Verlag, 1992.

[BHR84]   S.D. Brookes, C.A.R. Hoare, and A.W. Roscoe. A theory of communicating sequential processes. *Journal of ACM*, 31(3):560–599, July 1984.

[BW90]   J.C.M. Baeten and W.P. Weijland. *Process Algebra*. Tracts in Theoretical Computer Science. Cambrige University Press, 1990.

[Mil80]   R. Milner. A Calculus of Communicating Systems. volume 92 of *LNCS*. Springer Verlag, 1980.

[Mil83]   R. Milner. Calculi for synchrony and asynchrony. *Theoretical Computer Science*, 25:267–310, 1983.

[Mil89]   R. Milner. *Communication and Concurrency*. Prentice Hall, 1989.

[Old86]   E.-R. Olderog. TCSP: Theory of communicating sequential processes. In *Petri Nets: Applications and Relationships to Other Models of Concurrency*, volume 255 of *LNCS*. Springer Verlag, September 1986.

[Vaa92]   F.W. Vaandrager. Expressiveness results for process algebras. In *Semantics: Foundations and Applications*, volume 666 of *LNCS*, pages 609–638. Springer Verlag, 1992.

Appendix

Given a set Q, a *bag* (multi-set) over Q is an application from Q to natural numbers. A bag m is *finite* if for almost all elements $x \in Q$, $m(x)$ yields 0, but some finite subset of Q. The usual set enumeration notation can be used. For instance, $\{a, a, b\}$ denotes a bag m with $m(a) = 2$, $m(b) = 1$, and $m(x) = 0$ for $x \in Q \setminus \{a, b\}$. The empty bag will be denoted by $\emptyset$ (or $\{\}$). We define the following operations on bags:

$$+ \ : \ (m + n)(x) \stackrel{\text{def}}{=} m(x) + n(x)$$

$$\cup \ : \ (m \cup n)(x) \stackrel{\text{def}}{=} \max(m(x), n(x))$$

$$\cap \ : \ (m \cap n)(x) \stackrel{\text{def}}{=} \min(m(x), n(x))$$

$$\setminus \ : \ (m \setminus n)(x) \stackrel{\text{def}}{=} \max(m(x) - n(x), 0)$$

We also use the inclusion relation over bags:

$$\subseteq \ : \ m \subseteq n \ \text{ iff } \ \forall_{x \in Q} \ m(x) \leq n(x).$$

Any ordinary subset of a set Q can be seen as a bag over Q. For that reason we use the same notation for sets and bags, considering the formers as bags. Obviously, by notation $\{x \in Q \mid \dots\}$ we always denotes a subset of Q.

Complexity as a Basis for Comparing Semantic Models of Concurrency

Alan Mycroft[1], Pierpaolo Degano[2] and Corrado Priami[2]

[1] Computer Laboratory, Cambridge University,
New Museums Site, Pembroke Street, Cambridge CB2 3QG, United Kingdom
`Alan.Mycroft@cl.cam.ac.uk`
[2] Dipartimento di Informatica, Università di Pisa
Corso Italia 40, I-56100 Pisa, Italy
`{degano,priami}@di.unipi.it`

Abstract. We investigate some aspects of interexpressiveness of languages and their (denotational) semantic models by viewing semantic functions from a complexity-theory viewpoint. We classify semantic functions as *polynomial* or *finite* if a language term of size n produces a meta-language object respectively polynomially bounded in n or finite. Languages involving concurrency manifest most interest which we associate to the fact that their semantic models in general lack λ-style abstraction. The paper provides a quantifiable reason why labelled event structures form a more reasonable model for the choice and concurrency operators of CCS than do synchronisation trees. Similarly we show the representation of conflict by places within (at least occurrence forms of) Petri-nets is exponentially larger than the relational representation within corresponding event structures. An application is a criterion for selection of semantic models for real-world algorithmic purposes; for example, 'model checking' algorithms which use an exponentially larger semantic representation of programs are unlikely to be efficient.

1 Introduction

The idea of a denotational semantics has several components. Firstly we have an *(object)-language* whose (freely constructed) terms are to be given meaning. We also have a *semantic function* which homomorphically maps object terms into terms of a *meta-language*. Finally, and importantly, we have an equivalence relation on meta-language terms specifying when they are equal. For the typed λ-calculus with constants as a meta-language this is typically $\alpha\beta\eta\delta$-equality. Here we view object- and meta-language terms as *data-structures with a given representation*—two different representations for meta-language terms would count as two separate semantic models (see section 2.2 for more discussion). Also note our emphasis on the separateness of translation into meta-language terms and their equality—this is done in order to study the size of meta-language terms which obviously, in general, is not preserved by replacing a term with an equal one.

For classical programming languages (Pascal for example) the use of typed λ-calculus as a meta-language for their denotational semantics à la Scott is widespread and undisputed. One debates the meaning of a given programming language feature (e.g. parameter passing mechanism) *within* the meta-language. By contrast, there is a plethora of models for concurrent systems and it seems at times that each feature requires a new meta-language to describe it (witness *inter alia* the various forms of event structures).

In spite of the huge amount of theoretical work on semantics for concurrent systems, there is a lack of studies to show how practically useful concepts and theories are. Unfortunately, the choice among different approaches is quite often based on a matter of taste, rather than on comparable and measurable grounds. This is a major drawback because it allows the proliferation of proposals without a measure of their relative merits. This paper amounts to one proposal for this measure.

1.1 Languages

We will consider several languages and models in this paper. Following the definition style of process algebras, our general language $\mathcal{L}$ has *ports* ranged over by α, *co-ports* ranged over by $\overline{\alpha}$ (the sets of ports and co-ports yield the set of *actions*), *(process) names* ranged over by P to yield behaviours *Beh*, ranged over by b:

$$b ::= nil \mid \alpha.b \mid \overline{\alpha}.b \mid \tau.b \mid b + b' \mid b \mid b' \mid b; b' \mid b[\phi] \mid b\backslash\alpha \mid P \mid nonrec\,P.b \mid rec\,P.b.$$

The *nil* operator denotes a process that can perform no action; $\alpha.b$ ($\overline{\alpha}.b$ or $\tau.b$) is a process that fires α ($\overline{\alpha}$ or τ) and then behaves like b; $b + b'$ is a process that non-deterministically behaves like b or like b'; $b \mid b'$ is a process that can perform independently both b and b'; $b; b'$ is a process that performs b and when b stops, b' is executed; ϕ is a relabelling function preserving τ and $\overline{\cdot}$, *rec* allows recursive process definitions and *nonrec* allows simple non-recursive definitions— see below. In the sequel, we assume processes guarded and closed. In examples, we will abbreviate processes like $\alpha.nil$ to α. Sublanguages of $\mathcal{L}$ will be denoted $\mathcal{L}[op_1, \ldots, op_n]$, these always include process names P (if *rec* or *nonrec* present), ϕ and *nil*. For example, $\mathcal{L}[\alpha, \overline{\alpha}, +, \mid, \phi, \backslash, rec]$ coincides with the CCS [19], and $\mathcal{L}[\alpha, +, rec]$ refers to the sublanguage given by

$$b ::= nil \mid \alpha.b \mid b + b' \mid P \mid rec\,P.b$$

which is very close to the idea of classical regular expressions. The above precision (for example separating *rec* and *nonrec*) is important because we argue about complexity results which alter greatly with changes to semantic power. However, in examples, we will feel free to use Milner's original notation of

$$P_1 \Leftarrow b_1$$
$$\ldots$$
$$P_n \Leftarrow b_n$$
$$in\ b_0$$

instead of *rec* and *nonrec*.

Languages (which are later defined to be free algebras) have a simple notion of *size*, for example the number of constructors.

1.2 Semantic models

Here we take a semantic model to be a meta-language (possibly including infinite terms, see below) together with an equivalence relation stating when two terms are equivalent (for example the λ-calculus equality includes β-equivalence). Our semantic models will be taken to include (besides the typed λ-calculus with constants and recursive type definitions) *labelled transition systems* [17]. These are triples $TS = \langle T, A, \rightarrow \rangle$ where T denotes the states of the transition system, i.e. programs ranged over by $t, t', t_1, \ldots$, A is the labelling alphabet ranged over by $\alpha, \beta, \ldots$ and $\rightarrow \subseteq T \times A \times T$ is the transition relation labelled on A. The transition relation specifies the possible changes of states when a program is run. We will write $t \xrightarrow{\alpha} t'$ for $(t, \alpha, t') \in \rightarrow$. Roughly, a transition system is a graph whose nodes are programs and whose arcs are labelled by actions.

Note that any sub-language of $\mathcal{L}$ which does not contain the *rec* operator generates acyclic labelled transition systems under the natural semantic functions. We will use the name *synchronisation DAG* to refer this special kind of transition systems.

Another special case of transition systems are *trees*. They are generated under the assumption that any transition leads to a new node (possibly a copy of one already existing). This is the intuitive idea of unfolding of transition systems. We will write trees as summations with *NIL* for the empty tree. Given a term t, the tree of t is $[\![t]\!] = \sum_{i \in I} \alpha_i.[\![t_i]\!]$ for any $t \xrightarrow{\alpha_i} t_i$ in the transition system of t. Examples of trees used to represent the behaviour of processes are *synchronisation trees* [19], *acceptance trees* [16], *causal trees* [9], *proved trees* [10].

A variant of transition systems are the *compact transition systems* [11]. They are transition systems smaller than the classical ones that still preserve causal relation (but also independency and conflict) between events due to their richer labelling of transitions. Indeed, they are a compact representation of proved transition systems [4] whose transitions are labelled by encodings of their proofs. These compact representations are obtained by exploiting independency and conflict relations between the transitions exiting from the same node. In particular, only one transition (in absence of autoconcurrency) is kept among the mutually concurrent ones.

Also the so-called *algebras of transitions* [12] yield transition graphs. A unique name is associated to each transition (its proof) and composition operators are defined on them according to the constructs of the language which form the algebra of states. As the synchronisation mechanism is completely free (as the treatment of restriction) special transitions labelled *error* must be introduced (e.g. for the (non-existent) synchronisation between α and β in $\alpha \mid \beta$). This implies that more transitions than necessary have to be generated and then, observing the labelling, have to be erased. Moreover, as the name of the transitions is recorded in the states, there is also an explosion in the number of nodes of the graph with respect to classical approaches.

The next model we consider is Petri nets [22]. A *place-transition net* is a quadruple $N = \langle S, T, F, M_0 \rangle$ consisting of two disjoint sets S and T of places and transitions, of a flow multiset relation $F \subseteq S \times T \cup T \times S$ and of the initial marking $M_0 : S \to \mathbb{N}$ ($\mathbb{N}$ being the set of natural numbers). Note that the flow relation F can be interpreted also as a function weight $W : S \times T \cup T \times S \to \mathbb{N}$.

The dynamic behaviour of nets is defined by the *token game*. A transition $t \in T$ is enabled under a marking M if $\forall s \in S, M(s) \geq W(s,t)$. The occurrence of an enabled transition t produces a new marking M' defined by $\forall s \in S, M'(s) = M(s) - W(s,t) + W(t,s)$. A marking M is called *reachable* if there exists a sequence of transitions that starts from M_0 and leads to M. Also, M is said to be safe if $\forall s \in S, M(s) \leq 1$. A place-transition net is said *safe* if all reachable markings are safe.

In order to characterise runs of nets without abstracting from causal relations between events, *nonsequential processes* were defined [14, 2]. We now introduce the notion of pre- and post-sets. Given an element $x \in S \cup T$, the *pre-set* of x is ${}^\bullet x = \{y \in S \cup T | W(y,x) \neq 0\}$ and the *post-set* of x is $x^\bullet = \{y \in S \cup T | W(x,y) \neq 0\}$. Then, a *process* of a net N is a quadruple $\Pi = \langle B, E, F, p \rangle$ such that $\langle B, E, F \rangle$ is a net with no initial marking, $\langle B \cup E, F \rangle$ is an acyclic graph and $\forall b \in B, |{}^\bullet b| \leq 1$ and $|b^\bullet| \leq 1$. Moreover, $p : B \cup E \to S \cup T$ is a function that maps elements of B to elements of S, elements of E to elements of T and initial places of Π (those with ${}^\bullet b = \emptyset$) to places s such that $M_0(s) \geq 1$. Also, $\forall e \in E, \forall s \in S, W(s, p(e)) = |p^{-1}(s) \cap {}^\bullet e|$ and $W(p(e), s) = |p^{-1}(s) \cap e^\bullet|$. Nielsen, Plotkin and Winskel [21] introduced *occurrence nets* which generalise processes by summarising all the processes of a net as a single net. This is done in by removing the restriction $|b^\bullet| \leq 1$ while preserving reachability by forbidding self-conflict.

We now consider *event structures* [21, 25]. Event structures consist of a set of labelled events together with relations of causality, independence and conflict between them. Indeed it is useful to think of such event structures as having the occurrence net notion of condition, B above, replaced by its abstraction (these relations). Events model the occurrence of actions and are labelled with the action that they represent. Note that an event is quite different from a transition and from a state of the transition system. Indeed, many transitions may represent the same event (e.g. the two α transitions in the event structure originated by the term $\alpha \mid \beta$ represent the same event). More formally, a (prime) event structure is a triple $ES = \langle E, \leq, \# \rangle$ consisting of a set E of events that are partially ordered by $\leq$, the causal dependency relation, and a binary, symmetric, irreflexive relation $\# \subseteq E \times E$, the conflict relation which satisfies $\{e' | e' \leq e\}$ is finite and $e \# e' \leq e'' \Rightarrow e \# e''$ for all $e, e', e'' \in E$. Two events, say e and e', are concurrent or independent (written $e \smile e'$) iff they are neither in conflict nor in the causally related.

A *configuration* of an event structure is a subset $x \subseteq E$ which is *conflict-free* ($\forall e, e' \in x, \neg(e \# e')$) and *downward-closed* ($\forall e \in x, e' \in E, e' \leq e \Rightarrow e' \in x$). The computations of a process are the paths in the partial ordered set of the configurations, ordered by inclusion.

The inheritance property of conflict relation in prime event structures implies that if two events are in conflict, then all causal successors of one event are in conflict with all causal successors of the other event. As a consequence, each event is enabled by a unique set of events and this leads in general to duplication of events (and iteratively to asymptotically greater size) . Consider, e.g., the prime event structure associated to the term $(\alpha + \beta); \gamma$. The event γ is duplicated as it can be enabled by two different events.

In order to avoid duplication of events, *flow event structures* have been introduced [3]. A flow event structure is a triple $FES = \langle E, \prec, \# \rangle$ consisting of a denumerable set E of events, a binary, irreflexive relation $\prec \subseteq E \times E$, the flow relation, and a binary, symmetric relation $\# \subseteq E \times E$, the conflict relation. Configurations are defined through *proving sequences*. A proving sequence is a sequence of distinct events $e_1, \ldots, e_n$ such that $\{e_1, \ldots, e_n\}$ is conflict-free and $\forall e_i, e, e \prec e_i \Rightarrow \exists j < i : e_j \prec e_i$ and $(e = e_j$ or $e \# e_j)$. Then, a subset of events $x \subseteq E$ is a configuration if there is a proving sequence $e_1, \ldots, e_n$ such that $x = \{e_1, \ldots, e_n\}$. Note that flow event structures may generate self-conflicting events that will never appear in any configuration.

An alternative to flow event structure for avoiding the unique enabling property of prime event structure are *stable event structures* [25]. In these structures the causality or flow relation is substituted by an explicit enabling relation. Thus, a stable event structure is a triple $SES = \langle E, \vdash, \# \rangle$ where E is a set of events, $\# \subseteq E \times E$ is an irreflexive, symmetric relation, the conflict relation, and $\vdash \subseteq 2^E \times E$ is the enabling relation satisfying consistency ($F \vdash e \Rightarrow F \cup \{e\}$ is conflict free) and stability ($F \vdash e$ and $G \vdash e \Rightarrow F \cup G$ is not conflict-free or $F = G$). Note that the stability condition ensures that the causal relation between events is unambiguous. A proving sequence is a sequence of distinct events $e_1, \ldots, e_n$ such that $\{e_1, \ldots, e_n\}$ is conflict-free and $\forall i, \exists F \subseteq \{e_1, \ldots, e_{i-1}\} : F \vdash e_i$. Finally, a subset of the events $x \subseteq E$ is a configuration if there exists a proving sequence $e_1, \ldots, e_n$ such that $x = \{e_1, \ldots, e_n\}$.

The last class of event structures which we consider is that of *bundle event structures* [18]. Here, the flow, causal or enabling relation is replaced by a bundle set $X \mapsto e$. It represents the set of causal condition for an event e. In order to satisfy stability, all events in X must be pairwise in conflict. Formally, a bundle event structure is a triple $BES = \langle E, \mapsto, \# \rangle$ where E is a set of events, $\# \subseteq E \times E$ is an irreflexive, symmetric relation, the conflict relation, and $\mapsto \subseteq 2^E \times E$ is the bundle set satisfying $X \mapsto e \Rightarrow \forall e, e' \in X : (e \neq e' \Rightarrow e \# e')$. A proving sequence is a sequence of distinct events $e_1, \ldots, e_n$ such that $\{e_1, \ldots, e_n\}$ is conflict-free and $X \mapsto e_i \Rightarrow \{e_1, \ldots, e_{i-1}\} \cap X \neq \emptyset$. Finally, a subset of events $x \subseteq E$ is a configuration if there exists a proving sequence $e_1, \ldots, e_n$ such that $x = \{e_1, \ldots, e_n\}$.

As a last remark, note that all the above classes of event structure may be equipped with a function which labels the events with the actions that they represent.

Note that all the mentioned models may be viewed as algebras (possibly containing infinite terms). Thus, in order to generalise our approach to the complexity of semantic models, we assume that the meta-language into which we map the object-language is an algebra.

Although we rarely spell this out explicitly, it is necessary to regard a meta-language more intensionally than usual and to include its representation as a data-structure. Thus we treat changing the representation of a meta-language as changing the meta-language. Such fine discrimination is necessary to avoid specious claims that *all* semantic functions are linear in size *via* the claim in that they all have a linear size representation of a given object-language term, *viz* itself—see section 2.2.

1.3 Denotational semantics

We wish to cast our net wide in order to include many interpretation[3] mechanisms (including simple translation) as semantic formalisms. We accordingly define a *denotational semantics* to be a 4-tuple $(S, M, \mathcal{E}_{i \in I}, \equiv)$ where

- S, the *object-language*, is a free algebra, possibly many-sorted.[4] Sorts of S are referred to as *syntactic categories*. Identity, $=$, is the usual syntactic identity on free algebras.
- M, the *meta-language*, is an algebra. Typically it is less well-structured that S, for example we might wish to consider S being Pascal and M being a set of flowcharts. We allow M to contain infinite terms in the style common in algebraic semantics [15]. Various CCS programs require infinite event structures or Petri-nets to represent them. It is convenient to require that the operators of M partition into free constructors which generate the algebra and unfree operators which are required to provide maps from free parts to free parts (compare the idea of constructors and user-defined functions in languages like ML). We see examples of this below (interpretation of *fix* or *par* for synchronisation trees). Identity, $=$, is the usual algebraic equality of terms. This is syntactic identity for the case of a free algebra but also takes into account equations defining any unfree constructors.
- $\mathcal{E}_{i \in I} : S \to M$ is an indexed family of *semantic functions*. These are required to be defined by (mutual) primitive recursion. Typically there is one (or more) semantic function for each syntactic category.[5]

---

[3] In the sense of logic, not an SECD-style interpreter.

[4] It is possible to extend this to allow it (as for the meta-language M) to be a continuous free algebra. The complexity behaviour of limits is defined to be that of their approximants. This allows one to study the inate expressiveness of classes of event structures, Petri-nets and the like by giving mutual translations. This version of the paper does not study such issues.

[5] It is convenient to allow the notion of *environment* to be handled by this scheme too. Often a semantic function (e.g. for a functional language) would be defined with a type such as

$$\mathcal{E}[\cdot] : Expr \to (Var \to Val) \to Val$$

where the various $\to$ have differing meanings which require complicated explanation when our meta-language is first order and so lacks a full exponentiation type. This would also make the primitive recursivity and complexity more clumsy to define. However, any possible environment is conveniently handled here by treating it as an

$-$ $\equiv$ is an equivalence relation on $\mathcal{M}$. It is commonly generated by a reduction relation but here we are merely interested in equivalence. We require $m = m' \Rightarrow m \equiv m'$

Although the object- and meta-languages are seen as being (first-order) algebras we can choose to understand various terms as *binding constructs*—this is common for object languages, but the presence of the equivalence relation, $\equiv$, on $\mathcal{M}$ allows natural encoding of the binding rules (e.g. α- and β-equivalence) there too. Such a treatment would normally be considered lacking the necessary abstract elegance. However, we will justify it by our interest in implementation feasibility and complexity.

To clarify the requirements on $\mathcal{M}$ above, suppose it is a meta-language with an operator *fix x.e*. It is possible to regard this operator *either* as a free constructor with equivalence caught by $\equiv$, so that $fix\,x.e \equiv e[fix\,x.e/x] \neq fix\,x.e$; *or* as a unfree operator so that $e[fix\,x.e/x] = fix\,x.e$. The former treatment is common in object languages and the λ-calculus as a meta-language whilst the latter is common in event structure or Petri-nets as semantic meta-language for CCS. These treatments, of course, have very different complexity behaviour.

1.4 Correspondence to operational semantics

Often an object language, $\mathcal{S}$ comes complete with a operational semantics and we wish to ensure the denotational semantics is consistent. For the purposes here, we only require the equivalence relation $\approx$ which holds when two programs $s, s' \in \mathcal{S}$ are operationally indistinguishable (actually in all contexts $C[\,]$). For concurrency purposes, $\approx$ is typically one of the forms of bisimulation (strong, weak, interleaving, step, pomset, causality, history-preserving, locality *etc.*).

Denotational semantics $(\mathcal{S}, \mathcal{M}, \mathcal{E}_{i \in I}, \equiv)$ is *consistent* with $\approx$ (or $\approx$-*respecting*) if for all $s, s' \in \mathcal{S}$ we have

$$\mathcal{E}[s] \equiv \mathcal{E}[s'] \Rightarrow (\forall contexts\; C[\,])(C[s] \approx C[s']).$$

It is *computationally adequate* if

$$\mathcal{E}[s] \equiv \mathcal{E}[s'] \Leftarrow (\forall contexts\; C[\,])(C[s] \approx C[s'])$$

and *fully abstract* if both hold.

---

index to $\mathcal{E}$. Hence we can write (continuing the functional programming example)

$$\mathcal{E}_\rho[\,\cdot\,] : Expr \to Val$$
$$\mathcal{E}_\rho[x] = \rho(x)$$
$$\mathcal{E}_\rho[\lambda x.e] = lam(\lambda v.\mathcal{E}_{\rho[v/x]}[e])$$
$$\mathcal{E}_\rho[e\,e'] = app\langle \mathcal{E}_\rho[e], \mathcal{E}_\rho[e']\rangle$$

Primitive recursivity bans the use of such an index as the main argument to $\mathcal{E}$.

1.5 Examples

1. Take S to be that subset of Pascal generated by the syntactic categories *Cmd* and *Exp* with their usual BNF definition. $\mathcal{M}$ is the usual typed (with recursive types) λ-calculus with $\mathcal{E}_{Cmd}[\![\cdot]\!]$ and $\mathcal{E}_{Exp}[\![\cdot]\!]$ defined in the usual manner. Equivalence is $\alpha\beta\eta\delta$-equivalence (we need δ-rules for the fixpoint-taking constants as an absolute minimum).

2. Take S to be the language $\mathcal{L}[\alpha, +, |\,]$ with syntactic category *Beh* given by $Beh \ni b ::= nil \mid \alpha.b \mid b + b' \mid b \mid b'$ with port names α (we also use β in the example below) but no port co-names. $\mathcal{M}$ can be synchronisation trees, ranged over by t, u. The semantic function is interesting—the prefixing and $+$ operators directly encode as tree-forming operators (i.e. the free constructors $\cdot$ and $\uplus$) whereas the $|$ operator is represented by a non-free operator given by the expansion theorem (this language does not require consideration of port and co-port synchronisation):

$$[\![nil]\!] = \sum_{\emptyset} \alpha \cdot [\![t]\!] = NIL$$
$$[\![\alpha.b]\!] = \alpha \cdot [\![b]\!]$$
$$[\![b + b']\!] = \sum_{i \in I} \alpha_i \cdot [\![t_i]\!] \uplus \sum_{i \in J} \alpha_i \cdot [\![t_i]\!] = \sum_{i \in I \cup J} \alpha_i \cdot [\![t_i]\!]$$
$$\text{where } [\![b]\!] = \sum_{i \in I} \alpha_i \cdot [\![t_i]\!] \text{ and } [\![b']\!] = \sum_{i \in J} \alpha_i \cdot [\![t_i]\!]$$
$$[\![b \mid b']\!] = par([\![b]\!], [\![b']\!])$$
$$\text{where } par(t, u) = \sum_{i \in I} \alpha_i \cdot par(t_i, u) \uplus \sum_{j \in J} \beta_j \cdot par(t, u_j)$$
$$\text{with } \sum_{i \in I} \alpha_i \cdot t_i = t \text{ and } \sum_{j \in J} \beta_j \cdot u_j = u$$

Equivalence $\equiv$ is induced by the strong bisimulation on synchronisation trees (i.e., tree isomorphism with additional axioms like absorption $t \uplus t \equiv t$ and $t \uplus NIL \equiv t$).

3. Take S to be regular expressions. Two alternatives for $\mathcal{M}$ are sets of strings and finite state automata. The corresponding semantic functions are given by the usual constructions in undergraduate texts. However, the focus we wish to make is that the mapping to FSA's has finitary images and is surjective but has a (relatively) complex equivalence which nevertheless is suitable for algorithms; whereas the mapping to sets of strings has infinitary images but with identity as equivalence between semantic images.

To further bring out the discussion of interpreted *versus* free constructors consider the operator *par* above. As defined *par* is an unfree operator which maps the program $\alpha_1.nil|\ldots|\alpha_n.nil$ onto an exponentially bigger synchronisation tree. On the other hand, treating *par* as a free constructor gives a linear-sized semantic function, but with various identities like that of $par(\alpha \cdot NIL, \beta \cdot NIL)$ and $\alpha \cdot \beta \cdot NIL \uplus \beta \cdot \alpha \cdot NIL$ left to be specified in $\equiv$.

1.6 Observation

What we saw above is that there is a spectrum of semantic models and associated semantic functions and equivalences for a given language, S—even when its ostensible semantics is externally prescribed, for example by a relation $\approx$ on object terms. Denotational semantics respecting $\approx$ can range from (essentially) S with identity as the semantic function and a complicated equivalence $\approx$ to (essentially) the term model given by $S/\approx$, the induced map to equivalence classes as semantic function and identity as the equivalence relation.

Note that good (in the sense of being useful for proofs) semantic models are typically neither of the extremes discussed above—consider the λ-calculus for imperative languages. When it comes to implementation, further considerations of representation efficiency come to the fore and we consider these in the next section.

The subject of abstract interpretation (see e.g. [8]) typically studies models which are not $\approx$-respecting but which have the property of being finitely computable.

2 Complexity of a semantic model

Given a language S and a semantics $(S, \mathcal{M}, \mathcal{E}, \equiv)$ we say the semantics is *finite* if every term of S has a finite image in $\mathcal{M}$. We say the semantics is *polynomial* (or indeed any other complexity class) if every term of size n in S has an image in $\mathcal{M}$ which is of at most polynomial size in n. We say it is *infinite* if any (finite) term has an image of infinite size (e.g. due to expansion of $recP.\alpha.P$ as an infinite Petri-net process). Note that these definitions do not include the size of $\equiv$. For example, taking $S = \mathcal{M}$ and the identity as a semantic function gives a linear semantics.

Given an object language S, we say that a *semantic model* $\mathcal{M}$ is polynomial (or again any other complexity class) if there exists a polynomial semantic function. To avoid the trivial $O(n)$ semantic function which maps every source term onto itself as meta-language term, this definition is only useful when we have prescribed inequalities to preserve (from axioms or from an operational equivalence $\approx$ as discussed above).

When we restrict attention to semantics which respect strong interleaving bisimulation we find that event structures [21] are quadratic for $\mathcal{L}[\alpha, +, |]$, but exponential for $\mathcal{L}[\alpha, \overline{\alpha}, +, |]$. However, flow event structures [3] are polynomial for $\mathcal{L}[\alpha, \overline{\alpha}, +, |]$ just as stable event structures [25] and bundle event structures [18] are, even if with a lower degree. Synchronisation trees also with richer labelling (e.g., causal trees [9] and the like) are exponential for $\mathcal{L}[\alpha, |]$ and infinite for $\mathcal{L}[\alpha, rec]$. Transition systems (even if with independence relations like in [26, 1, 23]) are exponential for $\mathcal{L}[\alpha, |]$, but linear for $\mathcal{L}[\alpha, rec]$. They become infinite for $\mathcal{L}[\alpha, |, rec]$. Causal and locational [5] transitions systems are exponential also for $\mathcal{L}[\alpha, rec]$. This happens because the states are incresed at each unfolding with a reference to the activating transitions or to those occurred in the same site, respectively.

If one is interested in truly concurrent equivalences, the above models have the same complexity as for the interleaving semantics, while compact transition systems [11] are linear for $\mathcal{L}[\alpha, +, |]$ and polynomial for $\mathcal{L}[\alpha, \overline{\alpha}, +, |]$ (without autoconcurrency).

As a final remark, languages allowing value or name passing such as π-calculus [20] or higher order languages like $CHOCS$ [24] have exponential or infinite representations depending on the size of data domains.

These results are summarized in the table reported in the Conclusions.

2.1 Cartesian closedness implies linear complexity

The following result can justify why typed λ-calculus suffices for a great many applications, including classical programming languages. Christiansen and Jones [6] use this technique to simplify the semantic description language in the CERES compiler generator which uses a form of λ-calculus.

Suppose we have a semantic function $\mathcal{E}[\![\cdot]\!]$ for a syntactic category in a programming language. Suppose that the meta-language is (rather abusing the term) *cartesian-closed*, i.e. there are notions of abstraction, application, pairing and projection. Its homomorphic (primitive recursive) nature means that we can write the semantics of an operator, binary $+$ say, as

$$\mathcal{E}[\![e_1 + e_2]\!] = \ldots \mathcal{E}[\![e_1]\!] \ldots \mathcal{E}[\![e_1]\!] \ldots \mathcal{E}[\![e_2]\!] \ldots$$

which can be transformed into

$$\mathcal{E}[\![e_1 + e_2]\!] = (\lambda m_1.\lambda m_2. \ldots m_1 \ldots m_1 \ldots m_2 \ldots) \, (\mathcal{E}[\![e_1]\!]) \, (\mathcal{E}[\![e_2]\!]).$$

Note that the former function produces an asymptotically exponentially larger meta-language meaning than the latter which is always linear.

Similarly, suppose we have two or more mutually recursive semantic functions for a given syntactic category. This time pairing comes to our rescue, and functions such as

$$\mathcal{E}[\![e_1 + e_2]\!] = \ldots \mathcal{E}[\![e_1]\!] \ldots \mathcal{F}[\![e_1]\!] \ldots \mathcal{E}[\![e_2]\!] \ldots$$
$$\mathcal{F}[\![e_1 + e_2]\!] = \ldots \mathcal{F}[\![e_1]\!] \ldots \mathcal{E}[\![e_2]\!] \ldots \mathcal{F}[\![e_2]\!] \ldots$$

can be transformed into

$$\mathcal{G}[\![e_1 + e_2]\!] = \left(\begin{array}{c} \ldots \pi_1 \mathcal{G}[\![e_1]\!] \ldots \pi_2 \mathcal{G}[\![e_1]\!] \ldots \pi_1 \mathcal{G}[\![e_2]\!] \ldots, \\ \ldots \pi_2 \mathcal{G}[\![e_1]\!] \ldots \pi_1 \mathcal{G}[\![e_2]\!] \ldots \pi_2 \mathcal{G}[\![e_2]\!] \ldots \end{array} \right)$$

where $(\cdot, \cdot)$ represents pairing and π_i the projection functions. The latter function can then be transformed to linear form (each recursive call occurring at most once) by the technique above. Notional references to $\mathcal{E}$ are replaced by $\pi_1 \mathcal{G}$ and to $\mathcal{F}$ by $\pi_2 \mathcal{G}$.

2.2 Nature of complexity

We argued, by considering (e.g.) the CCS term $\alpha_1.nil | \ldots | \alpha_n.nil$, that, in general, a given CCS term requires an exponentially larger synchronisation tree to express its behaviour.[6] This is sensible from the semantic viewpoint—non-determinism only clumsily represents concurrency. Indeed, if one is interested in "true concurrency", one can build a tree with only a branch representing all the ones differing only in the order in which concurrent transitions are fired (see, e.g., [11, 7, 13]) thus avoiding the exponential size due to state explosion. However, we must be wary of the delicacy of this argument in complexity terms since the resulting tree seen as a data-structure can merely be claimed to be inefficiently represented. (Compare the correct, but unhelpful, argument that binary search is $O(n)$ instead of $O(\log n)$ in total operations if one is required to use linear linked-lists as the data-structure!) In structural complexity terms, all our semantic functions have linear complexity since there is always a linear size representation of the semantics of an object-language term, *viz* the object-language term itself.

We justify our finer distinction by arguing it is reasonable to treat semantics models as specified by their representation as a given data-structure. Thus in general, synchronisation trees are exponentially less powerful than synchronisation DAG's—consider the synchronisation tree and DAG specified by the $CCS[\alpha, +, nonrec]$ program P_n where

$$P_0 \Leftarrow nil$$
$$P_1 \Leftarrow \alpha_1.P_0 + \beta_1.P_0$$
$$\cdots$$
$$P_n \Leftarrow \alpha_n.P_{n-1} + \beta_n.P_{n-1}.$$

¿From a structural complexity viewpoint these are trivially the same but the tree has 2^n arcs and the DAG $2n$ arcs.

Another important aspect we must take into account is the complexity of deducing a computation of a process (simulation) from its semantic representation. Indeed, a transition system may have an exponential size (if interleaving properties are of interest and thus the compact form is not applicable), but the simulation algorithm is linear. Therefore, if we want an estimate of how good a model is for driving the choice of representations for practical purposes, we cannot abstract from dynamic aspects like simulation. A possibility is to associate with each semantic model the higher complexity between the one of the representation and the one of the simulation.

3 Event structures and Petri nets

Interestingly, acyclic Petri-net models fail to be as expressive as event structures for some languages due to possible exponentially bigger representation of conflict (*via* places instead of a relation): consider the language $\mathcal{L}[\alpha, +, |]$, and in particular terms of the form $(\alpha_1.nil \mid \beta_1.nil) + \cdots + (\alpha_n.nil \mid \beta_n.nil)$. This gives an event structure $(E, \leq, \#)$ with $2n$ events E, equality for the causality

---

[6] The best has $n!$ branches. Even using an arbitrary labelled transition system requires 2^n arcs.

relation $\leq$ (i.e. size n) and conflict relation of size $n(n-2)$ relating each event α_i (or β_i) to every event in $E\backslash\{\alpha_i,\beta_i\}$. This is of polynomial size, and it turns out that every term in $\mathcal{L}[\alpha,+,|\,]$ can be so represented. The smallest bisimilar Petri-net for the above term is exponential. It has 2^n places and $2n$ transitions (corresponding to the above events) and 2^n places. Geometrically, visualise an n-dimensional hypercube with a transition at the centre of every hyperface (dimension $n-1$ hyperplane) and place at every vertex (dimension 0-hyperplane) with an arc leading from every place (at vertex v) to every transition whose hyperface has v in its boundary. Thus each transition has 2^{n-1} pre-places (i.e. half of all places).

Of course, simple event structures are far from perfect in a complexity sense; for example the language $\mathcal{L}[\alpha,+,nonrec]$ has linear complexity with acyclic Petri-nets (or synchronisation DAG's) but exponential complexity for event structures (or synchronisation trees). This time the program P_n where

$$P_0 \Leftarrow nil$$
$$P_1 \Leftarrow \alpha_1.P_0 + \beta_1.P_0$$
$$\dots$$
$$P_n \Leftarrow \alpha_n.P_{n-1} + \beta_n.P_{n-1}$$

provides a critique of event structures which was resolved by Boudol's flow event structures.

Again, although the net and event structure constructions corresponding to CCS operators are well-known, looking at this issue from a complexity viewpoint forces one to contemplate the above consequences which appear not to be well-known.

These observations can be retrospectively seen as providing the motivation for the search for more implementation-apt models for CCS such as extensions to elementary event structures.

4   No free lunches

It should be clear from the earlier discussions that low complexity and full abstractness are mutually antagonistic. Indeed, if a language has Turing power (for example full CCS) then its operational equivalence $\approx$ is undecidable. Now, this means that any fully abstract semantics (with equality as meta-language equivalence) must be infinite in the sense of translating some finite term to an infinite one.

On the other hand, it *is* worth studying the complexity results for sub-languages because of the light such results cast on expressiveness of object- and meta-language constructs.

The key to effective implementation of proof systems appears to be to choose a semantic model which answers quickly many of the questions which are likely to be posed, but is willing to admit defeat.

5 Conclusions

We have presented the notion of complexity of a semantic function or semantic model which seems important for helping give quantitative classifications of semantic models. We have shown how these can be written in a form which always yields linear complexity for cartesian-closed semantic models.

To conclude, here is a table showing the complexity of several natural (in the sense of preserving as much structure as possible) semantic functions between the various semantic models discussed above:

Object-Language	meta-language: ON	SNP	ES	xES	TS	xTS	CTS	T
ON	$O(n)$	$O(n^2)$						
SNP	$O(n)$	$O(n)$						
$\mathcal{L}[\alpha,+]$	$O(n)$	$O(n)$	$O(n)$	$O(n)$	$O(n)$	$O(n)$	$O(n)$	$O(n)$
$\mathcal{L}[\alpha,+,|]$	$O(2^n)$	$O(2^n)$	$O(n^2)$	$O(n^2)$	$O(2^n)$	$O(2^n)$	$O(n)$	$O(2^n)$
$\mathcal{L}[\alpha,+,;]$	$O(2^n)$	$O(2^n)$	$O(2^n)$	$O(n^2)$	P	$O(2^n)$	P	$O(2^n)$
$\mathcal{L}[\alpha,+,nonrec]$	$O(2^n)$	$O(2^n)$	$O(2^n)$	P	P	P	P	$O(2^n)$
$\mathcal{L}[\alpha,\overline{\alpha},+,|]$	$O(2^n)$	$O(2^n)$	$O(2^n)$	P	$O(2^n)$	$O(2^n)$	P†	$O(2^n)$
$\mathcal{L}[\alpha,\overline{\alpha},+,|,\backslash]$	$O(2^n)$	$O(2^n)$	$O(2^n)$	P	$O(2^n)$	$O(2^n)$	$O(2^n)$	$O(2^n)$
$\mathcal{L}[\alpha,rec]$	∞	∞	∞	∞	$O(n)$	∞	$O(n)$	∞
$\mathcal{L}[\alpha,|,rec]$	∞	∞	∞	∞	∞	∞	∞	∞

† = only in the absence of autoconcurrency.
Complexity classes: P (polynomial), ∞ (infinite).
Abbreviations: ON (occurrence net), SNP (set of net processes); ES (event structures as above), xES (flow, stable or bundle event structures); TS (transition systems with or without independence); xTS (causal or locational transition systems); CTS (compact transition systems); T (various kind of trees).

Note that an embedding (e.g. of synchronisation trees into event structures) leads to $O(n)$ complexity.

Acknowledgments

We are grateful to the EU ESPRIT BRA grant 8130 "LOMAPS" for financial support. The second author benefitted from support from LIX (Laboratoire d'Informatique, Ecole Polytechnique) whilst on sabbatical leave there.

References

1. M.A. Bednarczyk. *Categories of Asynchronous Transition Systems.* PhD thesis, University of Sussex, 1988.
2. E. Best and R. Devillers. Sequential and concurrent behaviour in Petri net theory. *Theoretical Computer Science*, 55(1):87–136, 1987.

3. G. Boudol. Flow event structures and flow nets. sémantique du parallelisme, i. guessarian (ed.), lncs 469, 1990. In I. Guessarian, editor, *Semantics of systems of concurrent processes, Proc. 18ème école de printemps d' informatique théorique, LNCS 469*. Springer Verlag, 1990.

4. G. Boudol and I. Castellani. A non-interleaving semantics for CCS based on proved transitions. *Foundamenta Informaticae*, XI(4):433–452, 1988.

5. G. Boudol, I. Castellani, M. Hennessy, and A. Kiehn. A theory of processes with localities. *Theoretical Computer Science*, 114, 1993.

6. H. Christiansen and N.D. Jones. Control-flow treatment in a simple semantics-directed compiler generator. In D. Björner, editor, *IFIP WG 2.2:Formal description of programming concepts II*. North-Holland, 1983.

7. M. Clegg and A. Valmari. Reduced labelled transition systems save verification effort. In *Proceedings of CONCUR'91, LNCS 527*. Springer-Verlag, 1991.

8. P. Cousot and R. Cousot. Abstract interpretation frameworks. *Journal of Logic and Computation*, pages 511 – 547, 1992.

9. Ph. Darondeau and P. Degano. Causal trees. In *Proceedings of ICALP'89, LNCS 372*, pages 234–248. Springer-Verlag, 1989.

10. P. Degano and C. Priami. Proved trees. In *Proceedings of ICALP'92, LNCS 623*, pages 629–640. Springer-Verlag, 1992.

11. P. Degano and C. Priami. A compact representation of finite-state processes. Technical Report LOMAPSDIPISA2, LOMAPS Project, 1993. Submitted for publication.

12. G. Ferrari, R. Gorrireri, and U. Montanari. An extended expansion theorem. In *Proceedings of TAPSOFT'91, LNCS 431*, pages 162–176. Springer-Verlag, 1991.

13. P. Godefroid and P. Wolper. Using partial orders for the efficient verification of deadlock freedom and safety properties. In *Proceedings of CAV'91, LNCS 575*, pages 332–342. Springer-Verlag, 1991.

14. U. Goltz and W. Reisig. The non-sequential behaviour of petri nets. *Information and Computation*, 57:125–147, 1983.

15. I. Guessarian. Algebraic semantics. In *LNCS 99*. Springer Verlag, 1981.

16. M. Hennessy. *Algebraic Theory of Processes*. MIT Press, 1988.

17. R.M. Keller. Formal verification of parallel programs. *Communications of the ACM*, 19:371–384, 1976.

18. R. Langerak. *Transformations and semantics for LOTOS*. PhD thesis, Twente University, 1992.

19. R. Milner. *Communication and Concurrency*. Prentice-Hall International, London, 1989.

20. R. Milner, J. Parrow, and D. Walker. A calculus of mobile processes (I and II). *Information and Computation*, 100(1):1–77, 1992.

21. M. Nielsen, G. Plotkin, and G. Winskel. Petri nets, event structures and domains. *Theoretical Computer Science*, pages 85–108, 1981.

22. W. Reisig. Petri nets: An introduction. In *EATCS Monographs*. Springer-Verlag, 1985.

23. A. Stark. Concurrent transition systems. *Theoretical Computer Science*, pages 221–269, 1989.

24. B. Thomsen. *Calculi for Higher Order Communicating Systems*. PhD thesis, Imperial College - University of London, 1990.

25. G. Winskel. Event structures for CCS and related languages. In *Proceedings of ICALP'82, LNCS 140*, pages 561–576. Springer-Verlag, 1982.

26. G. Winskel and M. Nielsen. Models for concurrency. Technical Report DAIMI-PB-429, Computer Science Dept., Aarhus University, 1992. To appear in Handbook of Logic in Computer Science.

Combinatory Formulations of Concurrent Languages

N.Raja and R.K.Shyamasundar

Computer Science Group,
Tata Institute of Fundamental Research,
Bombay 400 005, INDIA
e-mail: {raja,shyam}@tifrvax.tifr.res.in

Abstract. We design a system with six *Basic Combinators*, and prove that it is powerful enough to embed the full asynchronous π-calculus, including replication. Our theory for constructing *Combinatory Versions* of concurrent languages is based on a method, used by Quine and Bernays, for the general elimination of variables in linguistic formalisms. Our *Combinators* are designed to eliminate the requirement of *names* that are bound by an *input prefix*. They also eliminate the need for *input prefix*, *output prefix*, and the accompanying mechanism of *substitution*. We define a notion of *bisimulation* for the *combinatory* version, and show that the *combinatory* version preserves the semantics of the original calculus. One of the distinctive features of this approach is that it can be used to rework many more process algebras in order to derive their equivalent *Combinatory Versions*.

1 Introduction

The discipline of *combinatory logic* [28, ?] began in the study of foundations of mathematics, to overcome the drawbacks of *substitution* in mathematical logic [27]. Subsequently, computer science gave impetus to research on *combinators*. The study of *combinators* has led to deep insights in the theory of sequential programming, and has also had a great influence in the implementation of functional programming languages.

In the field of concurrency there has been very little research in the pursuit of combinators. A major reason for this could be the fact that there was little common meeting ground among the various models of concurrency, in the kind of *primitives* they employed. In the initial period of research on foundational models of concurrency [12, ?], little attention was paid to the communication of data between processes. Value passing was modeled in an indirect way, by encoding data values in the names of ports and then by using infinite disjunctions of pure synchronization. The next generation of process algebras started focusing on the exchange of values. In the last decade many new process algebras which employ similar mechanisms for communication of data have been designed [21, 20, 5, 29]. Influenced by Milner's ideas [18], in these process algebras, communication consists in sending and receiving a value synchronously through a shared port.

Consider the following parallel ("|") composition in the π-calculus [21]:

$$x(y).P \mid \overline{x}z.Q \mapsto P\{y \leftarrow z\} \mid Q$$

In the above expression $x(y).P$ and $\overline{x}z.Q$ are processes which communicate through the common port x. The process $\overline{x}z.Q$ sends the value z on port x, and then activates Q. The process $x(y).P$ receives the value z on port x, *substitutes* z for y in P, and then triggers P. The expression $x(y)$ is called an *input prefix*, which indicates that the name x binds the name y. So, once again we encounter the horrid mechanism of *substitution*, with its attendant paraphernalia of binding mechanisms and bound entities.

At first sight, the problem of eliminating substitution in the process algebras appears to be simple. In the π-calculus, the values we substitute are always *names*, rather than *processes* (vice versa for certain other process algebras like CHOCS [29]). So, eliminating bound names seems to be easy. However, in comparison with the λ-calculus [2], the problem of ridding *substitution* is much more difficult in the setting of concurrent processes. Let us look at some of the reasons for these difficulties. The process calculi for concurrency are syntactically very different from the λ-calculus. Most such calculi do not possess the <operator><operand> kind of applicative structure found in the λ-calculus. Hence, *the flow of information is not just confined to syntactically adjacent terms*. The λ-calculus is a single sorted theory (everything is a term), but most *concurrent calculi are inherently two sorted*, the two sorts being *processes* and *channels*. There is only one 'abstractor' (λ) in the λ-calculus, while *there are infinitely many 'abstractors'* (infinitely many names) in the process algebras. There is only one other 'operation' in the λ-calculus (namely application), while *in the process algebras there is a rich set of other 'operations'* (for example, "|", "+", "ν", and "!" in the π-calculus). Further, there is a plethora of process algebras (which handle *value passing*), each of them as useful and powerful as the other.

The aim of this paper is to design a system of *combinators*, which completely eliminates the need for substitution in process algebras. The *combinators* should explicitly handle all the operational details of the flow of data across processes, without relying on a meta-level operation such as substitution. Such a combinatory reformulation of any process algebra, would not only provide an alternative semantics in terms of *combinators*, but would also prove to be a valuable tool in the implementation of the process algebra.

In this paper, we shall work in the setting of the asynchronous π-calculus with replication. The *combinators* we design, arise from a technique that was formulated independently by Bernays [3] and Quine [24] for the general elimination of variables in linguistic formalisms. We design a system of six *Basic Combinators*, and prove that it is powerful enough to embed the asynchronous π-calculus (including process replication). We define a notion of bisimulation for the combinatory version, and show that the combinatory version preserves the semantics of the original calculus. Further, the same approach can be used to rework many other process algebras [21, 19, 20, 29, 5] in order to derive their combinatory formulations.

2 Background

2.1 Quine's technique in logic

As mentioned earlier, the combinators that we design arise from a technique that was formulated independently by Bernays [3] and Quine [23, 24]. However there are slight differences in the methods proposed by each of them. In this section, we give a brief introduction to the method advocated by Quine.

Consider a theory, over a universe comprising a, b, c; with variables x, y, $z \ldots$ ranging over these elements; with a primitive predicate P defined over the above universe; and a quantifier A, which binds variables in predicates. The problem is to eliminate variables and quantifiers from every formula of the theory. Now consider a formula in this theory, say, $Ax \, Pxyxz$. In order to rid the quantifier A, and the bound variable x, from this formula, we start adding combinators to the theory. The first combinator we add is 'inv' (*Minor Inversion*). This combinator can operate iteratively on the predicate P alone, to yield new predicates which are in turn defined over the original universe only. This property will be the hallmark of all combinators that we shall introduce further on. We define, for any predicate Q over the universe mentioned above, $Q \, x_1 \ldots x_n \, x_{n-1}$. equivalent, $Ax \, (inv \, P) \, x \, y \, z \, x$. Similarly, we introduce two more combinators, '*Inv*' (*Major Inversion*), and '*Ref*' (*Reflection*), defined as follows: $(Inv \, Q) \, x_1 \ldots x_{n-1} \, x_n$ if and only if $Q \, x_n \, x_1 \ldots x_{n-1}$; and, $(Ref \, Q) \, x_1 \ldots x_n$ if and only if $Q \, x_1 \ldots x_n \, x_n$. Now we transform, the formula $Ax \, (inv \, P) \, x \, y \, z \, x$ to the equivalent formula, $Ax \, (Ref \, Inv \, inv \, P) \, y \, z \, x$. After this we introduce the combinator '*Der*' (*Derelativization*), with the definition, $(Der \, Q) \, x_1 \ldots x_{n-1}$ if and only if $Ax_n \, Q \, x_1 \ldots x_{n-1} \, x_n$, where x_n is a new variable. With the use of '*Der*', we achieve the final step of the transformation as $(Der \, Ref \, Inv \, inv \, P) \, y \, z$, which has neither a quantifier, nor a bound variable.

The above is technique is extended to the setting of higher-order languages such as the λ-calculus in [26].

2.2 A Brief Review of the Asynchronous π-Calculus

The presentation in this section closely follows that of [6, 20]. For more details, the reader is referred to those papers. API [6] is a model of concurrent computation that supports process mobility by naming and passing channels. It consciously forbids the transmission of processes as messages.

API is a two sorted theory consisting of *names* (*channels*) and *processes* (*agents*).

Definition 1. *Names* $(x, y, z, \ldots \in \mathcal{N})$, *have no structure.*, *while Processes,* $(P, Q, \ldots \in \mathcal{P})$ *possess a well defined structure :*

$$P ::= 0 \mid \overline{x}y \mid x(y).P \mid (P|Q) \mid !P \mid (\nu x)P$$

The term 0 represents an inactive process, which cannot perform any action. We shall omit the trailing ".0" from process terms. The construct $x(y)$ (called an input prefix) represents an atomic action, where *name* x binds *name* y. The term $x(y).P$ waits for a *name* to be transmitted along the channel x, and substitutes the received *name* for all free occurrences of y in P, and then triggers P. The construct $\overline{x}y$, also representing an atomic action, outputs a the *name* y along x, but does not bind y.

The form $P|Q$ means that P and Q are concurrently active, are independent, and can also communicate. The operator "!" is called replication, and $!P$ means $P|P|\ldots$; as many copies as you wish. Finally, $(\nu x)P$ restricts the use of *name* x to P. Apart from input prefix, "ν" is another mechanism for binding names within a process term in API. The operator "ν" may also be thought of as creating new channels.

We define the operational semantics of API using a chemical abstract machine CHAM [4] since, the CHAM formulation greatly simplifies the reduction rules for systems dealing with concurrently active entities [19].

Definition 2. The molecules are defined as:

1. Any process term P of the calculus is a molecule;
2. Any solution $S = \{m_1, \ldots, m_k\}$ is a molecule;
3. If m is a molecule and x is a name, then $(\nu x)m$ is a molecule.

The specific transformation rules of the CHAM for API are as follows:

Definition 3 (Transformation Rules For API).

Reaction $(x(y).P)$, $\overline{x}z \mapsto P[y \leftarrow z]$
Parallel $(P|Q) \rightleftharpoons P, Q$
Replication $!P \rightleftharpoons P, !P$
Scoping Membrane $(\nu x)P \rightleftharpoons (\nu x)\{|P|\}$
Scope Migration $(((\nu x)P)|Q) \rightleftharpoons (\nu x)(P|Q)$ (x not free in Q)
Name Conversion $(\nu x)P \rightleftharpoons (\nu y)P[x \leftarrow y]$ (y not free in P)
Scope Extinction $(\nu x)P \rightleftharpoons P$ (x not free in P)
Scope Exchange $(\nu x)(\nu y)P \rightleftharpoons (\nu y)(\nu x)P$

Definition 4 (Reduction Relation for API). We say that:

1. Q and R are *structurally congruent* whenever $Q \stackrel{*}{\rightleftharpoons} R$;
2. The term Q reduces to R, in notation $Q \longrightarrow R$, whenever $Q \stackrel{*}{\rightleftharpoons} Q'$, $Q' \mapsto R'$, and $R' \stackrel{*}{\rightleftharpoons} R$.

Note that there is no reduction allowed underneath prefix or replication. Following [22, ?], we define a notion of bisimulation and congruence for API.

Definition 5. A process Q occurs *unguarded* in P if it has some occurrence in P which is not under a prefix.

Definition 6. A process P can perform an *observable action*, written $P \downarrow$, if for some pair of names x, y, either the input prefix $x(y).Q$ or the output construct $\overline{x}y$ occurs unguarded in P with x unrestricted.

Definition 7 (Barbed Bisimulation for API**).** A relation R over processes is a *barbed simulation* if $P \, R \, Q$ implies:

1. If $P \longrightarrow P'$ then $Q \longrightarrow Q'$ and $P' \, R \, Q'$;
2. $P \downarrow$ implies $Q \downarrow$.

The Relation R is a *barbed bisimulation* if R and R^{-1} are *barbed simulations*. Two processes P and Q are *barbed-bisimilar*, if $P \, R \, Q$ for some *barbed bisimulation* R.

Definition 8. A *process context* $C[\,]$ is a process term with a single hole, such that placing a process in the hole yields a well-formed process.

Definition 9 (Barbed Congruence for API**).** Two processes P and Q are said to be *barbed-congruent*, written $P \sim Q$, if for each process context $C[\,]$, it holds that $C[P]$ is barbed-bisimilar to $C[Q]$.

3 Combinatory Version of the Asynchronous π-Calculus

In this section, we introduce a combinatory formulation for the asynchronous π-calculus, through a series of illustrative examples. Section 3.1 shows how the *Basic Combinators* and *Transformation Rules* arise when we try to analyse input prefix away. In Section 3.2 we demonstrate that the same combinators suffice to handle more complex situations. We shall use the acronyms API and CAPI to refer to the asynchronous π-calculus and its combinatory version respectively.

3.1 A Gentle Initiation

API has two distinct sorts of entities: *names (channels)* and *processes (agents)*; there is more distinct sort called *Combinators* in CAPI. *Names* in API are atomic entities devoid of any structure. In API there are two forms of atomic *actions* that a process can perform – sending or receiving a *name*. *Processes* cannot be sent or received. All these facts continue to hold in CAPI.

Combinator "S": We introduce the *Basic Combinator "S"* to represent the action of sending (This is not the **S** of classical combinatory logic). Before the send action can take place, the knowledge of two names is required – on *which* name to send and *what* name to send. The API process $\overline{x}z$ is represented in CAPI as the process – Sxz – which means, on the channel x send the name z. The combinator S needs to be supplied with two names as arguments in order to construct a process term from it. Subsequently we will need the ability to determine the *number of names* that a given combinator needs before it can be turned into a process. So we define a function called 'Valency' to represent this information. Thus, Valency $(S) = 2$.

Combinator "R": The other basic action in API is that of receiving an name. The API process $x(y)$ means, "receive some *name* – call it y – on channel x."

Here the name y is said to be bound by x. In other words y is being used as a dummy *name*, which will get replaced by the actual *name* that is received along x. We introduce the next *Basic Combinator "R"* to represent the action of receiving. In analogy with S, the combinator R needs two arguments before it can represent a process, i.e. Valency(R) = 2. Let us supply the arguments one at a time. So Rx means *receive* on the channel x. Next let us examine how to interpret Rxy. Since bound names have no place in the combinatory version, an expression like Rxy where y is free would take on the following meaning – on the channel x, the *name y was received*. While we want to specify future actions in our calculus, we seem to be able only to report history. However the *"Deg"* combinator described below saves us from this predicament.

Combinator "Deg": We now introduce the third *Basic Combinator "Deg"* with Valency(Deg) = −1. The negative Valency makes it apparent that Deg cannot directly operate on *names*. Instead Deg operates on the combinator R to give a new combinator ($DegR$) which in turn is capable of operating on *names*. We extend the definition of the Valency function to include sequences of *Basic Combinators* in its domain. For example, Valency(($DegR$)) = Valency(Deg) + Valency(R) = −1 + 2 = 1. Thus the expression ($DegR\ x$) now represents a process which may receive any name whatsoever on the channel x. We shall see in the following subsection that after it receives the name y, the process ($DegR\ x$) gets transformed to Rxy which is a historical record of a receive action that has already taken place. We hasten to add that though we give a meaning to the Combinator ($DegR$), we shall never assign a meaning to the combinator ($RDeg$), thus ensuring well-foundedness in the interpretation of the combinators. Further, note that the domain of the newly constructed ($DegR$) is no different from that of R; both work on *names* only.

Transformations "Reaction" and "Cleanup":

REACTION: $(Deg\ C)\ yx\ ,\ S\ xz \mapsto C\ yxz$

where C is any string of *Combinators*, and y is any string of *names*.

CLEANUP $R\ x_1x_2 \rightharpoonup$

Let us compose ($DegR\ x$) in parallel with Sxz and observe the result.

$$(DegR\ x)\ |\ Sxz \rightleftharpoons (DegR\ x), Sxz \quad \text{(Parallel)}$$

$$(DegR\ x), Sxz \mapsto R\ xz \quad \text{(Reaction)}$$

$$R\ xz \rightharpoonup \quad \text{(Cleanup)}$$

The *Reaction* rule captures the act of communication. The molecule ($Deg\ R\ x$) can accept a message on x, while the molecule Sxz can send the message z on x. Hence, *Reaction* occurs. The *Reaction* rule does not involve bound names or binding mechanisms or any *substitution*. The *Cleanup* rule, eliminates the *Precipitate Rxy*, as it cannot perform any more actions.

Discussion: The above example may be dismissed as a trivial case, wherein we could get away without using bound variables because we never needed to refer to them anyway. Before we go on to consider more complicated instances, there are certain features of the Combinatory Version that we wish to point out. First, we chose to introduce a new combinator Deg instead of redefining Valency$(R) = 1$, because the new combinator Deg helps us to uniformly tackle similar situations which will crop up later. Secondly, observe that the structure of the process terms we have considered so far have the form: <Sequence of Combinators><String of Names>. The combinators and the names that constitute a process term are clearly separated as distinct strings. Third, Valency(<Sequence of Combinators>) = Length (<String of Names>) where the Valency of a sequence of Combinators is the sum of the Valencies of the individual Combinators that constitute the sequence. For example in the process term $(Deg\ R\ x)$, Valency$(Deg\ R) =$ Valency(Deg) + Valency$(R) = -1 + 2 = 1 = |x|$.

Transformation "p-Bonding":

P-BONDING: $(C_1\ \mathbf{x}\ |\ C_2\ \mathbf{y}) \rightleftharpoons (C_1|C_2)\ \mathbf{xy}$

where $Valency(C_1) = |\mathbf{x}|$, and $Valency(C_2) = |\mathbf{y}|$

Consider the API composition $\bar{x}z\ |\ u(y)$, which in CAPI is $Sxz\ |\ (DegRu)$. *Reaction* cannot occur because the channels used for sending and receiving are different in the two processes. However, the two process terms may evolve reversibly as:

$$Sxz\ |\ (DegR\ u) \rightleftharpoons (S|(DegR))\ xzu \qquad (p-\text{Bonding})$$

to form a 'molecular bond'. The Valency information is required when the process molecules have to split the 'molecular bond', so as to take part in future reactions. At the time of splitting the molecular bond the combined argument string of names has to be split at the appropriate place.

$$(S|(DegR))\ xzu \rightleftharpoons Sxz\ |\ (DegR\ u)$$

where Valency $(S) = 2 = |xz|$ and Valency$(DegR) = -1 + 2 = |u|$. The p-*Bonding* is not a superfluous rule that we can do away with. It will turn out to be crucial when we want to encode API terms which have nested parallelism in their structure. We shall consider such cases in a later section.

Discussion: In the λ-calculus there is only one 'abstractor' namely λ. The symbol 'λ' by itself has no meaning. On the other hand in API there are infinitely many 'abstractors' since each of the infinitely many names can be used as an abstraction operator. Thus even after eliminating a bound *name*, the identity of the corresponding 'abstractor' should be retrievable. The best way to retain such information is to encode it in the structure of the term itself. Therefore we shall make sure that immediately after the elimination of a bound *name* from a process term, the last element in the string of names is the 'abstractor' corresponding to the bound *name* that has been eliminated. In other words, this requires that the 'abstractor' figures as the penultimate element in the string of names, just before the final step of eliminating a bound *name* from a process term.

Combinator "Ref": Consider the API process $x(y).\overline{y}y$. Here the dummy name y seems to be unavoidable, since the specification of future actions seems to be affected crucially by the name which will be received. However, let us pretend that y is not a bound name, but instead, it is a free name that has already been received on the channel x. Then the situation prevailing in such a case can be represented in CAPI as Rxy, Syy where Rxy is a record of a past action. We now introduce the *"History"* Transformation Rule which *precipitates* records of past actions.

HISTORY: $(R\ C)\ x_1x_2x_3\ldots x_n\ \rightarrow\ R\ x_1x_2,\ C\ x_3\ldots x_n$

Note that we can obtain $(Rxy,\ Syy)$ from $(RS\ xyyy)$ by the *History* transformation rule. Now we introduce the fourth *Basic Combinator "Ref"* with Valency$(Ref) = -1$, and the *"Reflection"* Transformation Rule:

REFLECTION: $(Ref\ C)\ x_1\ldots x_n\ \rightarrow\ C\ x_1\ldots x_nx_n$

we helps in getting the required CAPI term $(DegRefRefRS\ x)$, with the 'abstractor' x in the appropriate position.

Combinators "Inv" and "inv": The *Basic Combinators, "Inv"* and *"inv"*, follow the *"Major Inversion"* and *"Minor Inversion"* transformation rules respectively. Between themselves, they can permute any element of the argument string to an arbitrary position in the string.

3.2 Representing More Complex Terms

Processes with "Par(|)": In order to encode the API term $u(x).(\overline{x}v\ |\ \overline{x}w)$, we begin by encoding the sub-term containing "|". This we immediately obtain as $Sxv\ |\ Sxw$. At this stage the *"p-Bonding"* transformation rule is essential to derive.

$$(S|S)xvxw\ \rightleftharpoons\ Sxv\ |\ Sxw \quad (\text{p} - \text{Bonding})$$

We then proceed as in earlier examples and eliminate the bound name x to obtain the final encoding as:

$$(Deg\ Ref\ Ref\ Inv\ Inv\ inv\ Inv\ inv\ R\ (S\ |\ S)\ vwu)$$

¿From the above encoding we notice that process constructors of API may occur along with the basic combinators in CAPI. But, the separation between *combinators* and *names* still persists. We extend the Valency function to include the process constructors in its domain by defining Valency(|) = 0.

Input Prefix versus Restriction: There exist two distinct mechanisms for binding names in API: input prefix and restriction (denoted by "ν") [21, ?]. The binding of names due to an input prefix is similar to the binding of variables by 'λ' in the λ-calculus. During an interaction, the bound name y acts as a placeholder for any name which is received on the channel x. The received name, can be any name whatsoever. It may even already occur free in P. Further, the replacement is obtained explicitly from another process term within the calculus itself. Our combinators are concerned with this receiving and substitution mechanism.

The restriction mechanism combines two distinct roles in one operator. Firstly, it hides all interactions on the restricted name within a process, thus preventing external processes from interfering on communications on that name. In effect, it declares a local name y, for use exclusively within a process, similar to the '*let-in*' construct in programming languages. Secondly, the restriction operator also ensures that the restricted name is distinct from all external names too [21, ?]. This follows from the fact that API allows local names to be communicated to external processes. Thus the operator "ν" may be thought of as mechanism which creates globally unique channel names. In this role, the closest analog, of "ν" can be found in the *Actor model* of computation [11], which requires a purely local mechanism which generates globally unique *Actor* addresses. Further, since such globally unique names are not received from other process terms within the calculus, there is no accompanying mechanism of *dynamic* substitution.

Retaining "restricted" names: In this subsection and the next, we illustrate the translation of API process terms containing the restriction operator. In this subsection, we do not eliminate names bound by the "ν" operator, i.e. we retain the implicit capability of the "ν" operator, to generate globally unique names in situ. Consider the API term $(\nu x)(\overline{x}y \mid x(u).\overline{u}v)$. We start by encoding $\overline{x}y \mid x(u).\overline{u}v$ to get $(S \mid (Deg\ Ref\ Inv\ Inv\ Inv\ R\ S\ ))xyvx$. The next step in the encoding process is obtained by the ν-*Bonding* Transformation Rule:

$$(\nu - \text{Bonding}) \quad (\nu\ x)(C_1\ \mathbf{x} \mid C_2\ \mathbf{y}) \rightleftharpoons (\nu\ (C_1|C_2))\ \mathbf{x}\mathbf{x}\mathbf{y}$$

which finally yields $(\nu\ (S \mid (Deg\ Ref\ Inv\ Inv\ Inv\ R\ S))\ xxyvx)$. We also extend the definition of Valency to define Valency$(\nu) = 1$.

Eliminating "restricted" names: In this subsection we do not require the implicit capability of 'ν' to generate globally unique names. Instead we introduce a globally accessible parametric process $U(z)$, which captures the meta-level capability of generating unique channel names, and internalizes it as a process term within the calculus itself. We regard the symbol 'ν' as a special, globally accessible channel, over which $U(z)$ transmits globally unique names. Any other process may use the channel 'ν' only for receiving globally unique names. $U(z) = \overline{\nu}z.U(z')$, and it evolves as $\overline{\nu}z.\overline{\nu}z'.\overline{\nu}z'' \ldots$. It is composed in parallel with the entire system of processes. To encode the API term $(\nu x)(x(u)|\overline{x}y)$, we first rewrite it as $\nu(x).(x(u)|\overline{x}y)$. Note the change in notation, (νx) has been changed to $\nu(x)$. The transformed notation clearly indicates that the binding due to the restriction operator can be regarded similar to the binding caused by an input prefix, under the conditions formulated above. Thus, an additional reduction step has been introduced. The transformed term, $\nu(x).(x(u)|\overline{x}y)$, is simply an API process term with multiple input prefixes, and its CAPI translation is $(Deg\ Ref\ Inv\ Inv\ Inv\ R\ ((DegR)\mid S)\ y\nu)$. The results of this subsection are not included in the formal definition of API that we present later in this paper.

Processes with Dynamic Replication: The efficacy of our combinators becomes apparent when we demonstrate that they can encode infinite behavior too. No additional Combinators are required in order to get the combinatory representation of API processes with the "!" operator. Consider the API process $!x(u).\bar{u}v$. Begin by encoding $x(u).\bar{u}v$ to get $(Deg\ Ref\ Inv\ Inv\ Inv\ R\ S\ vx)$. The CAPI translation of $!x(u).\bar{u}v$ follows as $!(Deg\ Ref\ Inv\ Inv\ Inv\ R\ S\ vx)$. We extend the definition of Valency by defining Valency$(!) = 0$.

4 Formal Definition of the Combinatory Calculus

Definition 10. The set of *Basic Combinators* is defined to be:
$BasicCombinators = \{S, R, Deg, Ref, Inv, inv\}$

Definition 11. The set of *Combinators*, denoted by **C**, consists of all finite strings of the elements of the set of *Basic Combinators*, $\mathbf{C} = BasicCombinators^*$.

Definition 12. The set $\mathbf{CAP} = \{S, R, Deg, Ref, Inv, inv, \mid, \nu, !\}^*$.

We shall use $C, C_1, C_2, \ldots$ to range over **CAP**.

Definition 13 (Valency Function). The function *Valency*: $\mathbf{CAP} \to \mathbf{Z}$ is given by:

1. $Valency(\Lambda) = 0$ (where Λ denotes an empty string);
2. $Valency(S) = Valency(R) = 2$;
3. $Valency(Deg) = Valency(Ref) = -1$;
4. $Valency(Inv) = Valency(inv) = 0$;
5. $Valency(\nu) = 1$;
6. $Valency(\mid) = Valency(!) = 0$;
7. $Valency(C_1 C_2) = Valency(C_1) + Valency(C_2)$.

Definition 14. *Names* $(x, y, z, u, v, w \ldots \in \mathcal{N})$, have no structure, while the set of *Processes* is given by the following grammar:

$$P ::= C\ \mathbf{x} \mid (P \mid P) \mid\ !P \mid (\nu x)P$$

where $\mathbf{x}$ is any string of *names*, and $Valency(C) = |\mathbf{x}|\ (\equiv Length(\mathbf{x}))$.

Once again, we define the operational semantics of CAPI using a CHAM [4]. Section 2.2 presents a CHAM for API. The REACTION rule given in the Section 2.2 gets replaced by a new rule of the same name, as given below. Further, there are a few additional rules which specify the transition rules for the atoms. All the other rules remain the same, so we do not repeat them in this section.

Definition 15 (Transformation Rules for CAPI).

REACTION $Deg\ C\ \mathbf{y}x$, $S\ xz \mapsto C\ \mathbf{y}xz$

MAJOR INVERSION $Inv\ C\ x_1 \ldots x_{n-1}x_n \rightharpoonup C\ x_n x_1 \ldots x_{n-1}$

MINOR INVERSION $inv\ C\ x_1 \ldots x_{n-2}x_{n-1}x_n \rightharpoonup C\ x_1 \ldots x_{n-2}x_n x_{n-1}$

REFLECTION $Ref\ C\ x_1 \ldots x_n \rightharpoonup C\ x_1 \ldots x_n x_n$

HISTORY $R\ C\ x_1 x_2 x_3 \ldots x_n \rightharpoonup R\ x_1 x_2,\ C\ x_3 \ldots x_n$

CLEANUP $R\ x_1 x_2 \rightharpoonup$

P-BONDING $(C_1\ \mathbf{x}\ |\ C_2\ \mathbf{y}) \rightleftharpoons (C_1\ |\ C_2)\ \mathbf{xy}$

  where $Valency(C_1) = |\mathbf{x}|$, and $Valency(C_2) = |\mathbf{y}|$

ν-BONDING $(\nu\ x)(C_1\ \mathbf{x}\ |\ C_2\ \mathbf{y}) \rightleftharpoons (\nu\ (C_1\ |\ C_2))\ x\mathbf{xy}$

With the above rules on hand, we can now define $\hookrightarrow$: CAPI $\rightarrow$ CAPI as:

Definition 16 (Reduction relation for CAPI). We say that:

1. Q and R are *structurally equivalent* whenever $Q \overset{*}{\rightleftharpoons} R$;
2. The term Q reduces to R, in notation $Q \hookrightarrow R$, whenever $Q \overset{*}{\rightleftharpoons} Q'$, $Q' \mapsto R'$, and $R' \overset{*}{\rightleftharpoons} R$.

Following [22, ?], we define the notions of observable actions, barbed bisimulation, and barbed congruence for CAPI.

Definition 17. A process P can perform an *observable action*, written $P \downarrow$, if:

1. P (or a P-BOND subcomponent of P) is structurally congruent to some process term $C_p\ \mathbf{z}\mathbf{p}$, where the leading basic combinator of C_p is Deg, and the trailing name of $\mathbf{z}\mathbf{p}$ is some x, such that there is no ν-BOND subcomponent of the form $(\nu\ x)$ in P; or,
2. P (or a P-BOND subcomponent of P) is structurally congruent to some process term $S\ xy$, where for some pair of names x, y, the name x does not occur in a ν-BOND subcomponent of the form $(\nu\ x)$ in P.

Definition 18 (Barbed Bisimulation for CAPI). A relation R_c over processes is a *barbed simulation* if $P\ R_c\ Q$ implies:

1. If $P \hookrightarrow P'$ then $Q \hookrightarrow Q'$ and $P'\ R_c\ Q'$;
2. $P \downarrow$ implies $Q \downarrow$.

The relation R_c is a *barbed bisimulation* if R_c and R_c^{-1} are *barbed simulations*. Two processes P and Q are *barbed-bisimilar*, if $P\ R_c\ Q$ for some *barbed bisimulation* R_c.

Definition 19. A *process context* $C[\ ]$ is a process term with a single hole, such that placing a process in the hole yields a well-formed process.

Definition 20 (Barbed Congruence for CAPI). Two processes P and Q are *barbed-congruent*, written $P \sim_c Q$, if for each process context $C[\ ]$, it holds that $C[P]$ is barbed-bisimilar to $C[Q]$.

5 Embedding API into CAPI

In this section, we shall present a scheme which will help to translate any given API process term, to an equivalent CAPI process term. The translation of process terms which have an input prefix is quite involved. However once we succeed on that account, the translation of the rest of the syntactical forms of API process terms shall follow in a straightforward manner, by induction over the structure of process terms.

We first present a series of lemmas which codify certain properties of the combinators. The following lemmas essentially express the fact that the combinators, Inv and inv, are there to permute the names which are supplied to a combinatory expression, and between them they can express any permutation.

Lemma 21. *Given any* CAPI *process term* $C\ z_1 \ldots z_j \ldots z_n$, *where* $1 \leq j \leq n$, $\exists C_0 \in \{Inv\}^*$ *such that*

$$C_0\ C\ z_j z_{j+1} \ldots z_{n-1} z_n z_1 \ldots z_{j-1} \rightleftharpoons C\ z_1 \ldots z_j \ldots z_n$$

Lemma 22. *Given any* CAPI *process term* $C\ z_1 \ldots z_j \ldots z_n$, *where* $1 \leq j \leq n$, $\exists C_0 \in \{Inv, inv\}^*$ *such that*

$$C_0\ C\ z_j z_1 \ldots z_{j-1} z_{j+1} \ldots z_n \rightleftharpoons C\ z_1 \ldots z_j \ldots z_n$$

Lemma 23. *Given any* CAPI *process term* $C\ z_1 \ldots z_j \ldots z_n$, *where* $1 < j \leq n$, $\exists C_0 \in \{Inv, inv\}^*$ *such that*

$$C_0\ C\ z_1 z_j z_2 \ldots z_{j-1} z_{j+1} \ldots z_n \rightleftharpoons C\ z_1 \ldots z_j \ldots z_n$$

Lemma 24. *Given any* CAPI *process term* $C\ z_1 \ldots z_i \ldots z_j \ldots z_n$, *where* $1 \leq i < j \leq n$, $\exists C_0 \in \{Inv, inv\}^*$ *such that*

$$C_0\ C\ z_1 \ldots z_i z_j z_{i+1} \ldots z_{j-1} z_{j+1} \ldots z_n \rightleftharpoons C\ z_1 \ldots z_i \ldots z_j \ldots z_n$$

Hence, we can now allow ourselves a derived combinator corresponding to any permutation.

The following theorem essentially says that, if you can arbitrarily permute a list of names, then it is easy to permute all occurrences of the bound name to the end of the list, and then combine them using the combinator Ref. After permuting the binding name to the second-last position, the combinator Deg can be applied to eliminate the bound name.

Theorem 25. *Consider an* API *process term of the form* $x(y).P$. *Let the combinatory translation of* P *be* $C_p\ \mathbf{z_p}$ *where* $Valency(C_p) = |\mathbf{z_p}|$. *Then, the translation of* $x(y).P$ *corresponds to* $(Deg\ C''C'R\ C_p\ \mathbf{z}\ x)$ *where,* $C'' \in \{Ref\}^*$, *and* $C' \in \{Inv, inv\}^*$, *and* $\mathbf{z}$ *does not contain any occurrences of* y.

Proof. Follows from Lemmas 21, 22, 23, and 24. □

Definition 26 (Transformation from API to CAPI). Let P and Q denote API process terms. Let $[P]$ and $[Q]$ denote their translations in CAPI respectively. The general rules for translating P to $[P]$ are:

- $[0] = \Lambda$. (where Λ denotes an empty string);
- $[\overline{x}y] = S\ xy$;
- $[x(y)] = (\text{Deg } R\ x)$. (This step is a special case of the following one, and is included only for clarity);
- If $[P] = C_p\ z\mathbf{p}$ then $[x(y).P] = (\text{Deg } C''C'R\ C_p\ z\ x)$ where $C'' \in \{Ref\}^*$, and $C' \in \{Inv, inv\}^*$, and z does not contain any occurrences of y. (This step follows from Theorem 25);
- If $[P] = C_p\ z\mathbf{p}$ and $[Q] = C_q\ z\mathbf{q}$ then $[P \mid Q] = (C_p \mid C_q)\ z\mathbf{p}z\mathbf{q}$;
- If $[P] = C_p\ z\mathbf{p}$ then $[!P] = (!\ C_p\ z\mathbf{p})$;
- If $[P] = C_p\ z\mathbf{p}$ then $[(\nu x)P] = ((\nu\ C_p)\ xz\mathbf{p})$

The next theorem shows that the combinatory version preserves the semantics of the original calculus.

Theorem 27 (Semantic Correspondence). *Given any two process terms P, Q in API, and the corresponding translated process terms $[P]$, $[Q]$ in CAPI, then:*

1. *If there exists a bisimulation R in API such that $P\ R\ Q$, then there exists a bisimulation relation R_c in CAPI such that $[P]\ R_c\ [Q]$.*
2. *If P and Q are barbed-congruent in API ($P \sim Q$), then $[P]$ and $[Q]$ are barbed-congruent in CAPI ($[P] \sim_c [Q]$).*

Proof. By induction on the structure of process terms. □

6 Related Work

6.1 Sequential Systems

The discipline of *combinators* in sequential programming has become a classic in our times. Following Schönfinkel [28] and Curry [10], there have been various related proposals to tame substitution in different contexts [1, 7, 9, 15]. These combinators are well suited to work in calculi which have a term structure similar to the λ-calculus. However, they lead to an undesirable blow up in the expressive power of those calculi which do not inherently possess self-application. The combinators of Bernays [3] and Quine [23], were initially proposed to encode systems which do not employ self-application. This technique preserves the expressive power of the underlying system. The work reported in [26] extends it to include self-application, by encoding the λ-calculus.

6.2 Concurrent Systems

Though, there has been a phenomenal amount of work on combinators for sequential systems, there has not been much in the concurrency domain. The work in [8] comes close to providing a system of combinators. It models CCS [18] with value passing, using explicit routing information between processes. However, unlike our work, it does not deal with processes which have a dynamic interconnection topology. While the technique of our paper can be extended to capture CCS with value passing, in a straightforward manner, the method of [8] does not generalize to cover process calculi which deal with dynamic interconnection topologies between processes.

The two papers [13, ?], construct a combinatory version of a variant of API. They show that the concurrent composition of a small subset of fixed form API processes can represent all API terms. The systems propounded in these papers are geared to work only in the setting of a particular calculus, and cannot be easily modified to suit other calculi as well. However the framework of these papers is completely different from the one in this paper. Precisely due to this reason, the two approaches to *combinators for concurrency* offer complementary insights into the structure of concurrent calculi. Their technique clarifies the synchronization behavior of API processes; while our proposal of combinatory representation sheds more light on the distribution mechanism of the received value, and gives a technique that can be applied to almost any concurrent calculi.

7 Conclusion and Future Directions

Inspired by an unexplored technique of Quine in logic, we devised combinatory formulations in the setting of concurrent systems. We provided an alternative semantics for the asynchronous π-calculus in terms of combinators, by eliminating the need for bound names and the meta-level operation of substitution from the calculus. The combinators explicitly handle all the operational factors that arise in the communication of values between processes, while preserving the semantics of the original calculus. The same set of combinators are amenable to alterations to suit other process algebras as well. Our future research goals include, proving more refined algebraic equivalences, developing type theoretic foundations, and exploring the relation of these combinators with *Interaction Nets* [16] and *Action Structures* [17]. The whole area of concurrent combinators is in a stage of infancy. Further research in this area will elucidate the structure of concurrent systems, and will give valuable insights about the semantic structure of concurrency by providing various representability results. It should have a lasting impact on the theory of concurrency, and also on the implementation of concurrent systems.

Acknowledgements

Our thanks to Prof. Kohei Honda for his comments on an earlier version of this paper. Thanks go to Ms. Margaret D'Souza for typesetting this paper.

References

1. Abadi, M., Cardelli, L., Curien,P.L., Levy, J.J.: Explicit Substitutions, Proc. 17th ACM Annual Symposium on Principles of Programming Languages, (1990) 31-46.
2. Barendregt, H.: Lambda Calculus, Studies in Logic, **103**, North-Holland (1981).
3. Bernays, P.: Über eine natürliche Erweiterung des Relationenkalkuls, in A. Heyting, ed. Constructivity in Mathematics, North-Holland (1959).
4. Berry, G., Boudol, G.: Chemical Abstract Machine, TCS **96** (1992) 217-248.
5. Boudol, G.: Towards a lambda-calculus for concurrent and communicating systems, Proc. TAPSOFT'89, LNCS **351** (1989) 149-161.
6. Boudol, G.: Asynchrony and the π-calculus, Research Report 1702, INRIA (1991).
7. De Bruijn, N.: Lambda-Calculus Notation with Nameless Dummies, A Tool for Automatic Formula Manipulation, Indeg. Mat. **34** (1972) 381-392.
8. Cleaveland, R., Yankelevich, D.: An Operational Framework for Value-Passing Processes, Proc. ACM Annual Symp. of Prog. Lang., (1994) 326-338.
9. Curien, P.-L.: Categorical Combinators, Sequential Algorithms and Functional Programming, Pitman (1986).
10. Curry, H.B., Feys, R.: Combinatory Logic, Vol. 1, North Holland (1958).
11. Hewitt, C., Bishop, P., Sterger, R.: A Universal Modulator Actor Formalism for Artificial Intelligence, Proc. IJCAI (1973) 235-245.
12. Hoare, C.: Communicating Sequential Processes, Prentice-Hall (1985).
13. Honda, K., Yoshida, N.: Combinatory Representation of Mobile Processes, Proc. ACM Annual Symposium of Programming Languages, ACM (1994) 348-360.
14. Honda, K., Yoshida, N.: Replication in Concurrent Combinators, Proc. TACS'94, LNCS **789** (1994) 786-805.
15. Kennaway, R., Sleep, R.: Director Strings as Combinators, TOPLAS, **10**, 4 (1988).
16. Lafont, Y.: Interaction Nets, POPL'90, ACM (1990) 95-108.
17. Milner, R.: Action Structures, Research Report LFCS-92-249, Edinburgh (1992).
18. Milner, R.: Communication and Concurrency, Prentice Hall (1989).
19. Milner, R.: Functions as processes, Research Report 1154, INRIA (1990).
20. Milner, R.: The polyadic π-calculus: a tutorial, Marktoberdorf (1991).
21. Milner, R., Parrow, J., Walker, D.: A calculus of mobile processes (Parts I and II), Information and Computation **100** (1992) 1-77.
22. Milner, R., Sangiorgi, D.: Barbed Bisimulation, ICALP'92, LNCS **623** (1992).
23. Quine, W.V.: Eliminating variables without applying functions to functions, Journal of Symbolic Logic **24**, 4 (1959) 324-325.
24. Quine, W.V.: Variables Explained Away, Proc. American Philosophical Society, April 1960.
25. Raja, N., Shyamasundar, R.K.: The Next 700 Combinatory Representations of Mobile Processes, TIFR Research Report, Bombay (1994).
26. Raja, N., Shyamasundar, R.K.: The Quine-Bernays Combinatory Calculus, Int. Journal of Foundations of Comp. Sci., (to appear).
27. Russell, B., Whitehead, A.N.: Principia Mathematica, Vols. 1,2,3, CUP (1912).
28. Schönfinkel, M.: Über die Bausteine der mathematischen Logik, Math. Annalen **92** (1924) 305-316. English trans. with an introduction by W. V. Quine in J. van Heijenoort, ed., From Frege to Gödel, Harvard Univ. Press (1967) 355-366.
29. Thomsen, B.: Calculi for higher-order communicating systems, Ph.D. thesis, Imperial College (1990).

Constraints for Free in Concurrent Computation

Joachim Niehren   Martin Müller

Programming Systems Lab
German Research Center for Artificial Intelligence (DFKI)
Stuhlsatzenhausweg 3, 66123 Saarbrücken, Germany
{niehren,mmueller}@dfki.uni-sb.de

Abstract. We investigate concurrency as unifying computational paradigm which integrates functional, constraint, and object-oriented programming. We propose the ρ-calculus as a uniform foundation of concurrent computation and formally relate it to other models: The ρ-calculus with equational constraints provides for logic variables and is bisimilar to the γ-calculus. The ρ-calculus without constraints is a proper subset of the π-calculus. We prove its Turing completeness by embedding the eager λ-calculus in continuation passing style. The ρ-calculus over an arbitrary constraint system is an extension of the standard cc-model with procedural abstraction.

1 Introduction

Concurrent computation allows the unification of many programming paradigms. This observation underlies Milner's π-calculus [14, 13], Saraswat's concurrent constraint (cc) model [21], and Smolka's γ-calculus [23]. It is also central to the actor model by Hewitt and Agha [1]. Concurrency is the key to the programming language Oz [24] which integrates functional [16], object-oriented [7] and constraint programming [9, 15].

In this paper we start to relate several computational calculi. An overview is given in the picture below. We formulate the relations by comparison with the

ρ-calculus [19], a concurrent calculus with first-order constraints, higher-order procedural abstraction, and indeterminism via cells. Any constraint system determines an instance of the ρ-calculus. The ρ-calculus serves as a foundation of the concurrent constraint language Oz [24], is part of its language definition [25] and a basis for its implementation [11].

We prove bisimilarity of the γ-calculus [23] and the calculus $\rho(x{=}y)$: The γ-calculus has been designed to model concurrent objects, while $\rho(x{=}y)$ instantiates the ρ-calculus with equational constraints to provide for logic variables. Our bisimulation allows to consider the ρ-calculus as an extension of the γ-calculus with constraints. To obtain this result, we simplified the original ρ-calculus [19]: Now, constraints actually "come for free" in ρ, in contrast to previous extensions of γ with constraints [22, 23, 19, 25].

The ρ-calculus over the trivial constraint system $\rho(\emptyset)$ is a proper subset of the asynchronous polyadic π-calculus [12, 3, 8]. This result is immediate from the identification of procedural abstractions with replicated input agents. Once-only input agents are not available in $\rho(\emptyset)$. Surprisingly, $\rho(\emptyset)$ is still Turing complete: Higher-orderness allows us to embed the eager λ-calculus. A continuation passing style [20] avoids logic variables which have been employed in an earlier embedding of the eager λ-calculus into γ [23, 16].[1] We prove the adequacy of our embedding based on a simulation and uniform confluence [16].[2]

The ρ-calculus is syntactically compositional: Constraints, applications, conditionals, and cells can be freely combined by composition, declaration, and abstraction. The reduction relation of ρ is defined up to a structural congruence, as familiar from recent presentations of π [13, 3, 8] and γ [23]. The central novelty in the version presented here is the distinction of logical conjunction ($\dot{\wedge}$) on constraints from composition ($\wedge$). In the standard cc-model [21, 5, 6], these distinctions hold implicitly due to a monolithic constraint store. In a compositional syntax, the separation of conjunction and composition is central since it yields simple normal forms.

On reduction, applications, cells, or conditionals interact with an arbitrary constraint in their environment, but only one of them. For instance, the conditional if $x=y$ then E else F fi is irreducible in the context of $x=1 \wedge y=1$, since none of $x=1$ or $y=1$ entails or disentails $x=y$, but reducible in the context of $x=1 \dot{\wedge} y=1$ since $x=1 \dot{\wedge} y=1 \models x=y$. Constraints must be combined explicitly by reduction:

$$\phi_1 \wedge \phi_2 \;\rightarrow\; \phi_1 \dot{\wedge} \phi_2$$

This combination rule is the essential difference of the ρ-calculus in this paper to its predecessor [19]. It plays the role of elimination in γ where no conjunction is apparent:

$$\exists x \exists y (x=y \wedge E) \;\rightarrow\; \exists y E[y/x]$$

The separation of conjunction and composition leads to a transparently distributed constraint store. From this point of view, combination can be interpreted as unification which may or may not involve a network transfer.

Related Work: Most surprisingly, the lazy λ-calculus can be embedded into $\rho(\emptyset)$ with call-by-need complexity (see [17]). Alternatively, the call-by-need λ-calculus [2] could be directly embedded into $\rho(\emptyset)$. Both results are stronger than the analogous results for π [4], since both embeddings map into a uniformly confluent subset of $\rho(\emptyset)$ and π. Furthermore, Milner's embedding of the lazy λ-calculus into π [13] does not capture call-by-need complexity, and Smolka's

---

[1] We owe the idea to personal communication with Gert Smolka and Martin Odersky.
[2] Indeterminism via cells cannot arise in $\rho(\emptyset)$ and is not needed for functional computation.

call-by-need embedding of the lazy λ-calculus into γ [23] has been given without a correctness proof.

The relationship between the ρ-calculus and the standard cc model [21] is rather simple: The standard cc model can be obtained by dropping higher-order abstractions from ρ and replacing cells with indeterministic sums. A formal proof of this statement would have to deal with distinct notions of constraint systems.

Plan of the paper: In the Sections 2 and 3 we review γ and introduce ρ. Section 4 shows the coincidence of γ and $\rho(x{=}y)$. Section 5 is devoted to the discussion of uniformly confluent subcalculi of γ and ρ. In Section 6, we embed the eager λ-calculus into $\rho(\emptyset)$ and relate the latter with π.

2 The γ-Calculus

Our presentation of γ mainly follows [23] except that we omit names. The omission of names is argued below. We assume an infinite set of *variables* ranged over by x, y, z, u, v, and w. Sequences of variables are denoted by $\bar{x}$, $\bar{y}$, ... The set of elements of a sequences $\bar{x}$ is written as $\mathcal{V}(\bar{x})$. The γ-calculus is specified by *expressions*, a *structural congruence*, and a *reduction* relation. The *expressions* E, F and G are defined by the following abstract syntax:

$$E, F, G ::= x{:}\bar{y}/E \mid x\,\bar{y} \mid E \wedge F \mid \exists x\,E \mid x{=}y \mid$$
$$\text{if } x{=}y \text{ then } E \text{ else } F \text{ fi} \mid x{:}y \mid \top$$

An *abstraction* $x{:}\bar{y}/E$ has a reference x, *formal arguments* $\bar{y}$ and *body* E. An *application* $x\,\bar{y}$ "calls" the abstraction x with *actual arguments* $\bar{y}$. *Composition* $E \wedge F$ puts the expressions E and F in parallel. *Declaration* $\exists x\,E$ introduces a new local variable x with scope E. *Equations* $x{=}y$ provide for logic variables. Note that conjunction ($\wedge$) of equations is *not* apparent in γ. A *conditional* if $x{=}y$ then E else F fi consists of *guard* $x{=}y$ and *branches* E and F. A *cell expression* $x{:}y$ states that a cell referred to by x currently holds the content y. The *null expression* $\top$ is an expression which does nothing, but is useful for defining prenex normal forms.

Bound variables are introduced as formal arguments of abstractions and by declaration. Variables that are not bound are called *free*. $\mathcal{FV}(E)$ and $\mathcal{BV}(E)$ denote the sets of free respectively bound variables in E.

The *structural congruence* $\equiv$ is the least congruence on expressions satisfying the axioms in Figure 1. It provides for the usual properties of bound variables, composition, and declaration. The *reduction* $\rightarrow$ is the least binary relation on expressions satisfying the axioms and rules in Figure 2. We use a generalised replacement operator $[\bar{z}/\bar{y}]$ for simultaneous substitution. Its application implicitly requires that $\bar{z}$ and $\bar{y}$ have equal length and that $\bar{y}$ be linear; i.e., that all elements of $\bar{y}$ be pairwise distinct.

Application *(A)* executes procedure calls by passing actual parameters for formal ones. The side condition can always be met by α-renaming. Elimination

(α)	capture free renaming of bound variables
(ACI)	$\wedge$ is associative and commutative and satisfies $E \wedge \top \equiv E$.
$(Exch)$	$\exists x \exists y\, E \;\equiv\; \exists y \exists x\, E$
$(Scope)$	$\exists x\, E \wedge F \;\equiv\; \exists x (E \wedge F) \qquad$ if $x \notin \mathcal{FV}(F)$

Fig. 1. Structural Congruence of the γ-Calculus

(A)	$x{:}\bar{y}/E \wedge x\,\bar{z} \;\to\; x{:}\bar{y}/E \wedge E[\bar{z}/\bar{y}] \quad$ if $\mathcal{V}(\bar{z}) \cap B\mathcal{V}(E) = \emptyset$
(E)	$\exists x \exists y (x{=}y \wedge E) \;\to\; \exists y\, E[y/x] \quad$ if $x \neq y$ and $y \notin B\mathcal{V}(E)$
$(Cell)$	$x{:}\,y \wedge x\,u\,v \;\to\; x{:}u \wedge v{=}y$
$(Then)$	if $x{=}x$ then E else F fi $\;\to\; E$

$$\frac{E \to F}{\exists x\, E \to \exists x\, F} \qquad \frac{E \to F}{E \wedge G \to F \wedge G} \qquad \frac{E_1 \equiv E_2 \quad E_2 \to F_2 \quad F_2 \equiv F_1}{E_1 \to F_1}$$

Fig. 2. Reduction of the γ-calculus

(E) executes equations and may trigger all the other rules. Since elimination requires both variables to be declared, equations are symmetric: By (α) we get $\exists x \exists y (x{=}y \wedge E) \to \exists x\, E[x/y]$, if $x \neq y$ and $x \notin B\mathcal{V}(E)$. When a cell expression $x{:}\,y$ and an application $x\,u\,v$ meet, the value y held by x is replaced by u and v is bound to y $(Cell)$. A conditional reduces on equality of variables $(Then)$. Without names or more expressive constraints than equations, an $(Else)$-rule cannot be formulated. We shall discuss several versions of $(Else)$-rules in the sequel.

Elimination and Application. The simplest example is to apply the identity relation $id{:}\,Id \equiv id{:}x\,y/y{=}x$. Here we apply id to itself and the result to u.

$$\begin{aligned} &\exists id(id{:}\,Id \wedge \exists z (id\,id\,z \wedge z\,u\,out)) \;\equiv\; \exists id \exists z (id{:}\,Id \wedge id\,id\,z \wedge z\,u\,out) \\ &\to_A \exists id \exists z (id{:}\,Id \wedge z{=}id \wedge z\,u\,out) \;\equiv\; \exists id \exists z (z{=}id \wedge id{:}\,Id \wedge z\,u\,out) \\ &\to_E \exists id (id{:}\,Id \wedge id\,u\,out) \to_A \exists id (id{:}\,Id \wedge out = u) \end{aligned}$$

As done in this example, we shall freely annotate reduction arrows $\to_R$ with the name of the applied axiom R.

Cells. Cells introduce concurrently mutable state into γ by providing a persistent reference to a changeable value (i.e., a location). The indeterminism of cell reduction is needed to express concurrent objects [23]. Cells destroy confluence For example, consider the reduction of $E \equiv x{:}\,y \wedge x\,u_1\,v_1 \wedge x\,u_2\,v_2$:

$$\begin{aligned} x{:}\,u_2 \wedge x\,u_1\,v_1 \wedge v_2{=}y \;_{Cell}\!\!\leftarrow\; &E\; \to_{Cell}\; x{:}\,u_1 \wedge v_1{=}y \wedge x\,u_2\,v_2 \\ x{:}\,u_1 \wedge v_1{=}u_1 \wedge v_2{=}y \;_{Cell}\!\!\leftarrow\; &\to_{Cell}\; x{:}\,u_2 \wedge v_1{=}y \wedge v_2{=}u_1 \end{aligned}$$

New Names. Compared to the original γ-calculus [23], our presentation lacks the dynamic creation of new and possibly private names. There, names provide a unique identity to all procedures and cells. The same mechanism conveniently provides a unique reference to concurrent objects. Names can also be used as primitive data structures with a built-in equality and for data encapsulation.

We can add the expressiveness of names orthogonally without affecting any of our results. It is not necessary to provide names with a scope of their own as in [23], but it suffices to let them inherit the scope of the variables. We introduce a new expression n_x and add the additional reduction axiom:

$$(Else) \qquad n_x \wedge n_y \wedge \text{if } x{=}y \text{ then } E \text{ else } F \text{ fi} \;\rightarrow\; n_x \wedge n_y \wedge F \; .$$

An expression $n_y \wedge n_y$ would be considered inconsistent since it violates the uniqueness assumption of names. This situation may arise dynamically:

$$\exists x \exists y (x{=}y \wedge n_x \wedge n_y) \rightarrow_E \exists y (n_y \wedge n_y \wedge E[y/x])$$

Inconsistencies destroy confluence by making if $y{=}y$ then E' else F' fi reducible via both *(Then)* and *(Else)*.

3   The ρ-Calculus

The ρ-calculus extends γ with constraints. Let Σ be a first-order signature declaring function and relation symbols with their respective arities. A *theory* is a set of closed first-order formulae (with equality) over Σ. A *constraint system* over Σ consists of a *theory* Δ and a set of first-order formulae called *constraints*. Constraints are ranged over by ϕ and ψ. We assume the theory Δ to be *consistent*, i.e. Δ to have a model. The set of constraints must be closed under *replacement* $\phi[y/x]$: for every constraint ϕ the formulae obtained from ϕ by replacing y for x is again a constraint.

We do not require constraints to be closed under *conjunction* (written as $\phi \wedge \psi$) nor *existential quantification* (denoted by $\exists x\, \phi$). The formula $\top$ stands for logical *truth*. If Φ_1 and Φ_2 are first-order formulae over Σ, then we write $\Phi_1 \models_\Delta \Phi_2$ iff $\Phi_1 \rightarrow \Phi_2$ is valid in all models of Δ. We write $\Phi_1 \models\models_\Delta \Phi_2$ iff $\Phi_1 \models_\Delta \Phi_2$ and $\Phi_2 \models_\Delta \Phi_1$. If Δ is empty, then we omit the subscript Δ and simply write $\Phi_1 \models \Phi_2$ and $\Phi_2 \models\models \Phi_1$.

The definition of ρ is parameterised by a constraint system. The expressions of ρ are those of γ, but with equations replaced by constraints of the underlying constraint system. The calculus $\rho(x{=}y)$ instantiates ρ with *equational constraints* over the empty theory:

$$\phi, \psi ::= x{=}y \mid \top \mid \phi \wedge \psi$$

The calculus $\rho(\emptyset)$ instantiates ρ with the trivial constraint system, which is empty up to $\top$. The structural congruence of ρ extends that of γ by the following axiom:

$$(Equ) \qquad \phi \equiv \psi \qquad \text{if } \phi \models\models_\Delta \psi \text{ and } \mathcal{FV}(\phi) = \mathcal{FV}(\psi)^3$$

Note that we distinguish existential quantification $\dot{\exists}x\,\phi$ from declaration $\exists x\,\phi$ and conjunction $\phi \wedge \psi$ from composition $\phi \wedge \psi$ and that structural congruence preserves this distinction. This is an important technical simplification over [19, 22, 25]. Reduction of ρ is defined by the axioms in Figure 3. As in γ, reduction is allowed in all position but in bodies of abstractions and branches of conditionals.

$(A\rho)$	$\phi \wedge x{:}\bar{y}/E \wedge x'\,\bar{z} \;\rightarrow\; \phi \wedge x{:}\bar{y}/E \wedge E[\bar{z}/\bar{y}]$	if $\phi \models_\Delta x{=}x'$, and $\mathcal{V}(\bar{z}) \cap \mathcal{BV}(E) = \emptyset$
$(C\rho)$	$\phi_1 \wedge \phi_2 \;\rightarrow\; \psi$	if $\phi_1 \wedge \phi_2 \models\!\!\!\models_\Delta \psi$
$(Cell\rho)$	$\phi \wedge x{:}\,y \wedge x'\,u\,v \;\rightarrow\; \phi \wedge x{:}\,u \wedge v{=}y$	if $\phi \models_\Delta x{=}x'$
$(Then\rho)$	$\phi \wedge$ if ψ then E else F fi $\;\rightarrow\; \phi \wedge E$	if $\phi \models_\Delta \psi$
$(Else\rho)$	$\phi \wedge$ if ψ then E else F fi $\;\rightarrow\; \phi \wedge F$	if $\phi \models_\Delta \neg\psi$

Fig. 3. Axioms of Reduction of the ρ-Calculus

The axioms $(A\rho)$, $(Cell\rho)$, and $(Then\rho)$ are triggered by a single constraint of the context if it is sufficiently strong. Combination of constraints $(C\rho)$ makes more information available in a single constraint. Compared to γ, $(C\rho)$ replaces the elimination rule. By $(Else\rho)$, a conditional may reduce to its else branch if its guard is inconsistent with a constraint of the context. We continue with some examples illustrating computation in ρ.

Combining Constraints. To make a conditional reducible in a given context, an application of rule $(C\rho)$ may be necessary. For example, consider:

$$E_1 \;\equiv\; \exists y(\; x{=}1 \wedge y{=}1 \wedge \text{if } x{=}y \text{ then } F_1 \text{ else } F_2 \text{ fi }\,)$$

The conditional is irreducible because neither $x{=}1 \models x{=}y$, nor $y{=}1 \models x{=}y$ hold. However, E_1 reduces to E_2 by an application of $(C\rho)$:

$$E_2 \;\equiv\; \exists y(\; (x{=}1 \wedge y{=}1) \wedge \text{if } x{=}y \text{ then } F_1 \text{ else } F_2 \text{ fi }\,)$$

Now, $x{=}1 \wedge y{=}1 \models x{=}y$ holds, such that the conditional can reduce to F_1.

Higher-Order Programming. The following example illustrates the higher-order nature of ρ. Consider a constraint system providing equations and integers with addition. Its signature Σ should contain the constants $\dots, -1, 0, 1, \dots$ and the binary function symbol $+$. We allow sugared notation $x\,\bar{n}$ for $\exists \bar{y}(x\,\bar{y} \wedge \bar{y}{=}\bar{n})$, where the $\bar{n}$ are integer symbols. Let us define three abstractions:

$$applytwice{:}f\,x\,y/\exists z(f\,x\,z \wedge f\,z\,y) \qquad 2times{:}x\,y/\;y{=}x+x$$
$$4times{:}x\,y/\;applytwice\;2times\;x\,y$$

---

[3] Due to the side condition, structural congruence preserves closedness of expressions.

In the context of these abstractions, the expression $4times\,3\,u$ reduces as follows:

$$4times\,3\,u \;\to_{A\rho}\; applytwice\;2times\;3\,u \;\to_{A\rho}\; \exists z\,(2times\,3\,z \wedge 2times\,z\,u)$$
$$\to_{A\rho}\; \exists z\,(z{=}3+3 \wedge 2times\,z\,u) \;\equiv\; \exists z\,(z{=}6 \wedge 2times\,z\,u)$$
$$\to_{A\rho}\; \exists z\,(z{=}6 \wedge u{=}z+z) \;\to_{C\rho}\; \exists z\,(z{=}6 \wedge u{=}z+z)$$
$$\equiv\; \exists z\,(z{=}6 \wedge u{=}12)$$

The remaining declaration for z and the local binding $z{=}6$ could be dropped by an appropriate garbage collection rule (see also Example 2 in Section 6.).

New Names. The modelling of names as sketched for γ falls short in really mixing names and constraints. For example, the reduction step $n_x \wedge n_y \wedge$ if $f(x){=}f(y)$ then E else F fi $\to F$ is not justified by either of the conditional rules. Mixing names and constraints is important when constraints are used to model data structures holding higher-order data, in particular if they need to be compared for equality [24]. In this case, a closer integration of names and the constraint system is required. An elegant option is to extend the syntax by a declaration construct for names, and to axiomatically require all names to be distinct and different from all elements in the universe of Δ [19, 23].

An alternative approach would take n_x as a constraint for x in a new linear constraint system N, and require N to contain at least the axiom $\forall x \forall y (n_x \wedge n_y \leftrightarrow x \neq y)$. N is linear since $n_x \wedge n_x$ must not be equivalent to n_x. In addition, the entailment relation used in rules $(A\rho)$, $(Then\rho)$, (Equ), etc. must be defined in terms of both first-order entailment and the linear entailment of N. We do not pursue this topic further, since names do not affect our results.

4 Relating the γ-Calculus and the ρ-Calculus

We show that γ can be identified with $\rho(x{=}y)$, when restricted to closed expressions. This statement holds with respect to termination and complexity, measured by the number of application steps.

We need some general notations about computational calculi such as γ, $\rho(x{=}y)$, π [13], or the eager λ-calculus, and lazy λ-calculus. Our notion of a calculus generalises abstract rewrite systems [10]: A *calculus* is a triple $(P, \equiv, \to)$ where P is a set, $\equiv$ an equivalence relation and $\to$ and a binary relation on P. We require a calculus to satisfy $(\equiv \circ \to \circ \equiv) \subseteq \to$, where $\circ$ stands for relational composition. The elements of P are called *expressions*, $\equiv$ *congruence* and $\to$ *reduction*. The least transitive relation containing $\to$ and $\equiv$ is denoted with $\to^*$.

A *derivation* of an expression E is a finite or infinite sequence of expressions $(E_i)_{i=0}^n$ or $(E_i)_{i=0}^\infty$ with $E_i \to E_{i+1}$ for all possible indices i and $E \equiv E_0$. A *computation* of E is a maximal derivation: That is, either an infinite derivation or a finite one whose last element is irreducible with respect to $\to$. Let R be a binary relation on expressions. The *number of R-steps* in a derivation $(E_i)_i$ is the number of indices i such that $(E_i, E_{i+1}) \in R$.

Theorem 1. *For every computation of a closed expression E in γ there exists a computation of $\dot{\top} \wedge E$ in $\rho(x{=}y)$ with the same number of application steps, and vice versa.*

Before we sketch the proof, let us make some additional comments: For every expression in γ and ρ, reduction without application terminates. Reduction with axioms other than (A) or $(A\rho)$ decreases the number of constraints, applications or conditionals. Hence, Theorem 1 implies that termination of E in γ coincides with termination $\dot{\top} \wedge E$ in ρ. However, not all derivations of E need to have the same termination behaviour, due to cells which explicitly introduce indeterminism.[4]

The proof idea is to define a bisimulation similarly to [13] which establishes a bijection between computations of E in γ and $\dot{\top} \wedge E$ in $\rho(x{=}y)$. Our definition of an appropriate bisimulation is based on *normal forms*. These are α-standardised *prenex normal forms (PNFs)*. A PNF D is defined by the following grammar:

$$
\begin{aligned}
B &::= x{:}\bar{y}/D \mid x\,\bar{y} \mid \text{if } \phi \text{ then } D_1 \text{ else } D_2 \text{ fi} \mid x{:}y \mid \phi \quad &\text{molecules} \\
C &::= \top \mid B \mid C \wedge C \quad &\text{chemical solutions} \\
D &::= C \mid \exists x\,D \quad &\text{PNFs}
\end{aligned}
$$

We say that D is a *normal form* of E if D is a normal form and $E \equiv D$.

Proposition 2. *Every expression E has some normalform D.*

Proof. Simple. By Axiom (α) any expression may be α-standardised, such that declarations can freely be moved outside via *(Scope)*.

Reduction can be decomposed into reduction on normal forms followed by normalisation, i.e., transformation of the result into normal form again. Following the notation in [16], we define $\equiv_2$ as smallest congruence satisfying the axioms (ACI) and $(Exch)$. Furthermore, we need a collection of relations for reduction on normal forms, each of which is specified by a single axiom:

$$
\exists \bar{u}(x{:}\bar{y}/D \wedge x\,\bar{z} \wedge C) \xrightarrow{\;}_{A_t} \exists \bar{u}(x{:}\bar{y}/D \wedge D[\bar{z}/\bar{y}] \wedge C)
$$

$$
\exists \bar{u}\exists x\,(x{=}y \wedge C) \xrightarrow{\;}_{E_t} \exists \bar{u}C[y/x] \qquad \text{if } y \in \mathcal{V}(\bar{u})
$$

$$
\exists \bar{u}(x{:}y \wedge x\,u\,v \wedge C) \xrightarrow{\;}_{Cell_t} \exists \bar{u}(x{:}u \wedge v{=}y \wedge C)
$$

$$
\exists \bar{u}(\text{if } x{=}x \text{ then } D_1 \text{ else } D_2 \text{ fi} \wedge C) \xrightarrow{\;}_{Then_t} \exists \bar{u}(D_1 \wedge C)
$$

$$
\exists \bar{u}(\phi \wedge x{:}\bar{y}/D \wedge x'\,\bar{z} \wedge C) \xrightarrow{\;}_{Ap_t} \exists \bar{u}(\phi \wedge x{:}\bar{y}/D \wedge D[\bar{z}/\bar{y}] \wedge C) \quad \text{if } \phi \models_\Delta x{=}x'
$$

$$
\exists \bar{u}(\phi_1 \wedge \phi_2 \wedge C) \xrightarrow{\;}_{Cp_t} \exists \bar{u}(\psi \wedge C) \qquad\qquad \text{if } \phi_1 \wedge \phi_2 \models\!\models_\Delta \psi
$$

$$
\exists \bar{u}(\phi \wedge x{:}y \wedge x'\,u\,v \wedge C) \xrightarrow{\;}_{Cell\rho_t} \exists \bar{u}(\phi \wedge x{:}u \wedge v{=}y \wedge C) \quad \text{if } \phi \models_\Delta x{=}x'
$$

$$
\exists \bar{u}(\phi \wedge \text{if } \psi \text{ then } D_1 \text{ else } D_2 \text{ fi} \wedge C) \xrightarrow{\;}_{Then\rho_t} \exists \bar{u}(\phi \wedge D_1 \wedge C) \quad \text{if } \phi \models_\Delta \psi
$$

$$
\exists \bar{u}(\phi \wedge \text{if } \psi \text{ then } D_1 \text{ else } D_2 \text{ fi} \wedge C) \xrightarrow{\;}_{Else\rho_t} \exists \bar{u}(\phi \wedge D_2 \wedge C) \quad \text{if } \phi \models_\Delta \neg\psi
$$

---

[4] Other expressions should *not* incur indeterminism, or at least allow to detect indeterministic usage as a programming error (cf. admissibility in Section 5).

Proposition 3. *Let D be a normal form, E an expression, and R one of the axioms of reduction in γ or ρ. If $D \to_R E$ then $D \ (\equiv_2 \circ \xrightarrow{-}_{R_t} \circ \equiv) E$.*

Proof. Hard technical work. A complete proof in the case of γ can be found in [16]. It adapts immediately to ρ. The most difficult part is the comparison of congruent normal forms. There we need that the congruences of γ and ρ are both rather simple and similar to each other. More complex congruences can be handled but they incur undue technical problems [19].

Definition 4 Bisimulation. A *bisimulation* for the embedding $E \mapsto \dot{\top} \wedge E$ is a relation S between closed expressions of γ and $\rho(x=y)$ satisfying the conditions:

B1. If E is a closed γ-expression, then $(E, \dot{\top} \wedge E) \in S$.

B2. If $(E, F) \in S$, R an axiom of $\{A, Cell, Then\}$, and $E \to_R E'$, then there exists F' such that $F \to_C^* \circ \to_{R\rho} F'$ and $(E', F') \in S$.

B3. If $(E, F) \in S$ and $E \to_E E'$, then exists F' with $F \to_{C\rho}^* F'$ and $(E', F') \in S$.

B4. If $(E, F) \in S$, R an axiom of $\{A, Cell, Then\}$ and $F \to_{R\rho} F'$, then there exists E' such that $E \to_E^* \circ \to_R E'$ and $(E', F') \in S$.

B5. If $(E, F) \in S$ and $F \to_{C\rho} F'$, then exists E' with $E \to_E^* E'$ and $(E, F') \in S$.

B6. If $(E, F) \in S$, then F is irreducible with respect to $\to_{Else\rho}$.

Definition 5. We define S^γ to be the set of all pairs (E, F) of closed γ and $\rho(x=y)$ expressions which allow the following representation: There exists variables $\bar{x}\bar{y}$, natural numbers n, m, and k, equations $\phi_1 \ldots \phi_n$, equational constraints $\psi_1 \ldots \psi_m$, molecules $E_1 \ldots E_k, F_1 \ldots F_k$ neither of which is a constraint, and a substitution $\theta : \mathcal{V}(\bar{y}) \to \mathcal{V}(\bar{x})$ such that the following conditions hold:

$S^\gamma 1$. $\exists \bar{x}(\phi_1 \wedge \ldots \wedge \phi_n \wedge E_1 \wedge \ldots \wedge E_k)$ is a normal form of E.

$S^\gamma 2$. $\exists \bar{y} \exists \bar{x}(\psi_1 \wedge \ldots \wedge \psi_m \wedge F_1 \wedge \ldots \wedge F_k)$ is a normal form of F and $m \geq 1$.

$S^\gamma 3$. $\psi_1 \wedge \ldots \wedge \psi_m \models \theta$, where θ is considered as $\bigwedge\{z = \theta(z) \mid z \in \mathcal{V}(\bar{y})\}$.

$S^\gamma 4$. $E_i = F_i \theta$ for all $i, 1 \leq i \leq k$,

$S^\gamma 5$. $\phi_1 \wedge \ldots \wedge \phi_n \dashv\vdash \exists \bar{y}(\psi_1 \wedge \ldots \wedge \psi_m)$.

Lemma 6. S^γ *is a bisimulation for the embedding $E \mapsto \dot{\top} \wedge E$.*

Proof. The conditions of a bisimulation can be checked one by one. Condition B1 is a consequence of Proposition 2 which ensures the existence of a normal form for E. A normal form for $\dot{\top} \wedge E$ can be easily constructed from that of E.

We exemplarily prove one of the other cases, say $B3$ (all other cases are similar). Assume $(E, F) \in S^\gamma$ with the properties described in Definition 5 and E' such that $E \to_E E'$. Since $\exists \bar{x}(\phi_1 \wedge \ldots \wedge \phi_n \wedge E_1 \wedge \ldots \wedge E_k)$ is a normal form of

E, Proposition 3 applies. We can assume w.l.o.g. that ϕ_1 has been eliminated. Hence, there exist distinct u, v and $\overline{x'}$ with $\phi_1 \equiv u=v$, $\overline{x} = \overline{x'}u$, $v \in \mathcal{V}(\overline{x'})$, and:

$$E' \equiv \exists \overline{x'}(\phi_2[v/u] \wedge \ldots \wedge \phi_n[v/u] \wedge E_1[v/u] \wedge \ldots \wedge E_k[v/u]) .$$

We define $F' \equiv \exists \overline{y}u \exists \overline{z}v(\psi_1 \wedge \ldots \wedge \psi_m \wedge F_1 \wedge \ldots \wedge F_k)$. Obviously, $F \to^*_{C\rho} F'$, such that it is sufficient to prove $(E', F') \in S^\gamma$. Clearly, E' and F' have normal forms as required in $S^\gamma 1$. and $S^\gamma 2$. We define a substitution $\theta' : \mathcal{V}(\overline{y}u) \to \mathcal{V}(\overline{x'})$ by $\theta' = [v/u] \circ \theta$ (first θ then $[v/u]$). For short, we write $\psi = \psi_1 \wedge \ldots \wedge \psi_m$.

$S^\gamma 3$. Assumptions $\psi \models \theta$ and $\exists \overline{y}\psi \;\dashv\vdash\; \bigwedge_{i=1}^n \phi_i$ imply $\psi \models \phi_1 \wedge \theta \;\dashv\vdash\; u=v \wedge \theta \;\dashv\vdash\; \theta'$.

$S^\gamma 4$. $E_i[v/u] = (F_i\theta)[v/u] = F_i([v/u] \circ \theta) = F_i\theta'$ for $1 \le i \le k$.

$S^\gamma 5$. $(\bigwedge_{i=2}^n \phi_i)[v/u] \;\dashv\vdash\; \exists u(u=v \wedge \bigwedge_{i=2}^n \phi_i) \;\dashv\vdash\; \exists u(\bigwedge_{i=1}^n \phi_i) \;\dashv\vdash\; \exists \overline{y}u\psi$

Proof of Theorem 1. The theorem follows from the existence of a bisimulation (Lemma 6). If $(E_i)_{i=0}^n$ is a finite derivation of E and $(E, F) \in S^\gamma$, then we can inductively construct a derivation $(F_i)_{i=0}^n$ with $(E_n, F_n) \in S^\gamma$ such that both sequences have the same number of application steps. We even get the same result for reduction with cells and conditionals. If $(E_i)_{i=0}^n$ is maximal, then $(F_i)_{i=0}^n$ must be maximal. Otherwise, we could contradict maximality of $(E_i)_{i=0}^n$ by applying our bisimulation the other way around. □

5 Uniformly Concurrent Subcalculi

Functional programming is a special form of concurrent programming [17]. Result, termination, and complexity of functional programs are independent of the execution order. For eager functional programming this is reflected by the eager λ-calculus, and for lazy functional programming by the call-by-need λ-calculus [2]. Concurrent computation satisfying the above three independence properties is called *uniformly concurrent* in [16]. We consider complexity and uniformity, since these notions allow for simple adequacy proofs of calculi embeddings.

A major advantage of γ is the existence of a uniformly concurrent subcalculus which can be easily distinguished. This subcalculus is called δ and has been introduced and investigated in [16]. By Theorem 1, we can carry over most properties from γ to $\rho(x=y)$ and conversely. Termination and complexity in terms of application steps correspond exactly. But our bisimulation is *not* strong enough for carrying over confluence or relating the numbers of elimination and combination steps. In this section, we show how to distinguish a uniform and confluent part of ρ over an arbitrary constraint system. This can be done in analogy to the extraction of δ out of γ.

We need some general properties of computational calculi. All proofs are feasible with standard methods and can be found in [16]. A calculus $(P, \equiv, \to)$ is called *uniformly confluent*, if it satisfies the following condition:

$$(\leftarrow \circ \to) \;\subseteq\; (\equiv \,\cup\, (\to \circ \leftarrow))$$

A uniformly confluent calculus is confluent and uniform with respect to termination and complexity: all computations of the same expression have the same length.

Uniform confluence is a compositional property. If $(P, \equiv, \rightarrow_1)$ and $(P, \equiv, \rightarrow_2)$ are two calculi with commuting reductions, i.e. $({}_1\!\leftarrow \circ \rightarrow_2) \subseteq (\rightarrow_1 \circ {}_2\!\leftarrow)$, then the union $(P, \equiv, \rightarrow_1 \cup \rightarrow_2)$ is uniformly confluent.

We now restrict ρ to a uniformly concurrent calculus. We call an expression E *inconsistent*, if E contains a constraint equivalent to $\perp$ or a subexpression as:

$$\phi \wedge x{:}\bar{y}/E \wedge x'{:}\bar{z}/F \qquad \text{such that } \phi \models_\Delta x{=}x'.$$

E is called *consistent* iff it is not inconsistent. We call an expression E *admissible*, if all expressions F with $E \rightarrow^* F$ are consistent. It is clear that admissility is an undecidable property. But we can characterise admissible subsets by type systems [16]. An appropriate type system for eager functional programming is given in Section 6.

Theorem 7. *The restriction of ρ to admissible expressions without cells is uniformly confluent.*

Proof. It is sufficient to establish the uniform confluence for all relations $\rightarrow_{R\rho}$ where R is in $\{A, C, Then, Else\}$, such as their pairwise commutation. These problems can be reduced to a collection of critical pairs of normal forms.

We exemplify the proof of the uniform confluence of $\rightarrow_{C\rho}$. If $F_1 \, _{C\rho}\!\leftarrow E \rightarrow_{C\rho} F_2$ then we can apply Proposition 3. This yields normal forms E_1 and E_2 of E with $F_1 \, _{C\rho_t}\!\overset{\leftarrow}{=} E_1 \equiv_2 E_2 \overset{\rightarrow}{=}_{C\rho_t} F_2$. By definition of $\overset{\rightarrow}{=}_{C\rho_t}$ there are $\bar{u}$, ϕ_1, ϕ_2, ψ_1, ψ_2, C_1, and C_2 such that:

$$E_1 \equiv_2 \exists \bar{u}(\phi_1 \wedge \psi_1 \wedge C_1) \overset{\rightarrow}{=}_{C\rho_t} \exists \bar{u}(\phi_1 \wedge \psi_1 \wedge C_1) \equiv F_1$$
$$E_2 \equiv_2 \exists \bar{u}(\phi_2 \wedge \psi_2 \wedge C_2) \overset{\rightarrow}{=}_{C\rho_t} \exists \bar{u}(\phi_2 \wedge \psi_2 \wedge C_2) \equiv F_2$$

Lets first treat the case $\phi_1 = \phi_2$. If furthermore $\psi_1 = \psi_2$, then $F_1 \equiv F_2$. If $\psi_1 \neq \psi_2$ then there exists C' such that $C_1 \equiv_2 \psi_2 \wedge C'$ and $C_2 \equiv_2 \psi_1 \wedge C'$. Hence:

$$F_1 \rightarrow_{C\rho} \exists \bar{u}(\phi_1 \wedge \psi_1 \wedge \psi_2 \wedge C') \, _{C\rho}\!\leftarrow F_2$$

Case $\phi_1 \neq \phi_2$ and $\psi_1 = \psi_2$ is symmetric and case $\phi_1 \neq \phi_2$ and $\psi_1 \neq \psi_2$ is similar.

6 The Eager λ-Calculus, ρ-Calculus, and π-Calculus

The ρ-calculus over the trivial constraint system $\rho(\emptyset)$ is Turing complete. We prove this statement by embedding the eager λ-calculus such that termination and complexity are preserved. This embedding employs a continuation passing style (CPS) [20]. An even simpler embedding can be found in [17]. Both embeddings lift into π, since $\rho(\emptyset)$ can be embedded into the asynchronous, polyadic

π-calculus [12, 3, 8]. It suffices to observe the close syntactic similarity of both calculi:

$$P, Q ::= P|Q \quad | \ (\nu x)\, P \mid \overline{x}\langle \overline{y} \rangle \mid \ !\,x(\overline{y})\,.\,P \mid 0$$
$$E, F ::= E \wedge F \mid \ \exists x\, E \quad | \quad x\,\overline{y} \quad | \quad x{:}\overline{y}/E \quad | \top \mid \dot{\top}$$

Application in $\rho(\emptyset)$ corresponds to communication and replication in π. Cells can be ommitted, since $(C\rho)$ is not applicable in $\rho(\emptyset)$ as it refers to equations.

The expressions of the *eager λ-calculus* λ_e are defined by the abstract syntax:

$$V ::= \lambda x.M \qquad\qquad M, N ::= x \mid V \mid MN$$

A variable x is bound in $\lambda x.M$, and there is no other variable binder. Free and bound variables of an expression M ($\mathcal{FV}(M)$ and $\mathcal{BV}(M)$, resp.) are defined as usual. The congruence $\equiv$ of λ_e identifies λ-expressions up to α-renaming. Its reduction $\to_{\beta_e}$ is defined as follows:

$$(\lambda x.M)\, V \ \to_{\beta_e} \ M[V/x] \qquad \text{if } \mathcal{FV}(V) \cap \mathcal{BV}(M) = \emptyset$$

$$\frac{M \to_{\beta_e} M'}{MN \to_{\beta_e} M'N} \qquad \frac{N \to_{\beta_e} N'}{MN \to_{\beta_e} MN'} \qquad \frac{M \equiv M' \quad M' \to_{\beta_e} N' \quad N' \equiv N}{M \to_{\beta_e} N}$$

In Figure 4, we define our CPS-embedding introducing formulae $u(M)$ as abbreviation for $\rho(\emptyset)$-expressions. These reads as: "u is the continuation applied to the eventual result of evaluating M".

$$
\begin{array}{lll}
u(x) & \equiv u\,x & \\[4pt]
u(\lambda x.M) & \equiv \exists y\,(u\,y \wedge y{:}x\,v/v(M)) & uy \text{ linear} \\[4pt]
u(MN) & \equiv \exists v\,\exists w\,(v(M) \wedge w(N) \wedge v{:}y/w{:}z/y\,z\,u) & uvw \text{ linear}
\end{array}
$$

Fig. 4. CPS Embedding

Example 1. We show the reduction of the expression $u(II)$, where $I \equiv \lambda x.x$ is the λ-identity. For brevity, we allow some notation for anonymous ρ-abstractions: For instance, we write $Id = x\,v/v\,x$ for the anonymous CPS-identity and $y{:}Id$ for the CPS-identity named by y, i.e. for the ρ-expression $y{:}x\,v/v\,x$.

We shall additionally use the anonymous abstractions $V = y/w{:}W$ and $W = z/y\,z\,u$. Then we have the following computation in the context of $\dot{\top}$:

$$
\begin{array}{rl}
u(II) \equiv & \exists v\exists w\,(\exists y(\boxed{u\,y} \wedge y{:}Id) \wedge w(I) \wedge v{:}y/w{:}z/y\,z\,u) \\[4pt]
\to_{A\rho} & \exists y\exists w\,(y{:}Id \wedge w(I) \wedge w{:}z/y\,z\,u) \wedge \exists v\,(v{:}V) \\[4pt]
\equiv & \exists y\exists w\,(y{:}Id \wedge \exists z(\boxed{w\,z} \wedge z{:}Id) \wedge w{:}z/y\,z\,u) \wedge \exists v\,(v{:}V) \\[4pt]
\to_{A\rho} & \exists y\exists z\,(y{:}Id \wedge z{:}Id \wedge \boxed{y\,z\,u}) \wedge \exists v\exists w(v{:}V \wedge w{:}W) \\[4pt]
\to_{A\rho} & \exists z\,(u\,z \wedge z{:}Id) \wedge \exists v\exists w\exists y(v{:}V \wedge w{:}W \wedge y{:}Id) \\[4pt]
\equiv & u(I) \wedge \exists v\exists w\exists y(v{:}V \wedge w{:}W \wedge y{:}Id)
\end{array}
$$

Theorem 8. *Eager reduction of a closed λ-expression M terminates if and only if reduction of $\dot{\top} \wedge u(M)$ terminates in $\rho(\emptyset)$. The number of β_e steps in computations of M equals 3 times the number of $(A\rho)$ steps in those of $\dot{\top} \wedge u(M)$.*

The proof is based on a simulation plus uniformity instead of a bisimulation. Given a computation of M in λ_e, we construct a corresponding computation of $\dot{\top} \wedge u(M)$ in $\rho(\emptyset)$ using a simulation. The converse follows from uniformity, since all computations of an admissible ρ-expression have the same termination and complexity behaviour.

In the rest of this section we prove Theorem 8 in two steps: First, we define a appropriate notion of simulation for an embedding $M \mapsto \dot{\top} \wedge u(M)$ and show the existence of such a simulation. Second, we prove admissibility of embedded expressions $\dot{\top} \wedge u(M)$. This is sufficient for combining the proof as sketched above, because we can apply Theorem 7.

Note that the bisimulation technique of Section 4 is not powerful enough for proving Theorem 8, since our CPS-embedding does not establish a bijection between computations in the λ_e and $\rho(\emptyset)$. For instance, the expression $I(II)$ has a unique computation in λ_e, while $\dot{\top} \wedge u(I(II))$ has two distinct computations.

To get rid of the context $\dot{\top}$, we reason in the part of γ bisimilar to $\rho(\emptyset)$, i.e. we use the slightly simpler axiom (A) instead of $(A\rho)$.

Definition 9 Simulation. A *simulation* for an embedding $M \mapsto u(M)$ is a relation $S_u^{\lambda_e}$ between closed λ-expressions and γ-expressions satisfying:

$S_u^{\lambda_e}1$. If M is closed, then $(M, u(M)) \in S_u^{\lambda_e}$.

$S_u^{\lambda_e}2$. If $M \to_{\beta_e} M'$ and $(M, E) \in S_u^{\lambda_e}$, then there exists E' such that $E \to_A^3 E'$ and $(M', E') \in S_u^{\lambda_e}$, where $\to_A^3 \,=\, \to_A \circ \to_A \circ \to_A$.

$S_u^{\lambda_e}3$. If M is irreducible in λ_e and $(M, E) \in S_u^{\lambda_e}$, then E is irreducible in $\to_A$.

Proposition 10. *For all u there is a simulation for the embedding $M \mapsto u(M)$.*

We omit a detailed proof. Instead, we illustrate the exact correspondence between computations of M and those of $u(M)$ by an example. A precise formalisation of this correspondence would yield the simulation. Such a description can be based on explicit substitutions for λ_e [13] and contexts for γ [16].

Example 2. We consider $Copy = \lambda x.x\,x$ and reduce $Copy(I\,I)$. To compare reductions in γ and λ_e, we need to cope with the fact that β_e may copy or annul abstractions. These effects are hidden by our meta notation which makes substitutions explicit.

$$
\begin{aligned}
Copy(I\,I) &\to_{\beta_e} (Copy\,v_1)\,[I/u_1][I/v_1] \\
&\to_{\beta_e} (v_1\,v_1)\,[Copy/u_2][I/u_1][I/v_1] \\
&\to_{\beta_e} v_1\,[Copy/u_2][I/u_1][I/v_1]
\end{aligned}
$$

In γ, contexts play the rôle of explicit substitutions in λ_e. A *context* is an expression with a hole $\bullet$ which acts as a placeholder: Replacement of an expression E or context T_2 for the hole in a context T_1 is denoted by $T_1[E]$ or $T_1[T_2]$.

In order to get rid of unary (continuation) abstractions introduced by $u(MN)$, we extend reduction with garbage collection (G):

$$\exists \bar{y}(\bar{x}:\bar{V}) \rightarrow_G \top \quad \text{if } \mathcal{V}(\bar{x}) \subseteq \mathcal{V}(\bar{y})$$

As proved in [16], the number of application steps in computations is independent of garbage collection. To ease reading, we use the notation $\langle vwu \rangle$ instead of $v{:}y/w{:}z/y\,z\,u$. The eager computation above corresponds to the computation:

$$
\begin{aligned}
u(Copy\,(I\,I)) \rightarrow_A^3 \circ \rightarrow_G\ & T_1[u(Copy\,v_1)] \\
& T_1 = \exists u_1 \exists v_1 (\bullet \wedge u_1{:}I \wedge v_1{:}I) \\
\rightarrow_A^3 \circ \rightarrow_G\ & T_1[T_2[u(v_1\,v_1)]] \\
& T_2 = \exists u_2 (\bullet \wedge u_2{:}Copy) \\
\rightarrow_A^3 \circ \rightarrow_G\ & T_1[T_2[u(v_1)]]
\end{aligned}
$$

We verify the first reduction sequence in detail: Observe that $u(Copy\,(I\,I))$ equals $\exists u_0 \exists v_0 (u_0(Copy) \wedge v_0(I\,I) \wedge \langle u_0 v_0 u \rangle)$. We reduce the subexpression $v_0(I\,I)$:

$$
\begin{aligned}
v_0(I\,I) \equiv\ & \exists u_1' \exists v_1' (u_1'(Id) \wedge v_1'(Id) \wedge \langle u_1' v_1' v_0 \rangle) \\
\rightarrow_A^2\ & \exists u_1 (\exists v_1 (u_1{:}Id \wedge v_1{:}Id \wedge u_1\,v_1\,v_0) \wedge \exists u_1' \exists v_1' (\langle u_1' v_1' v_0 \rangle \wedge v_1{:}z/u_1\,z\,v_0)) \\
\rightarrow_A\ & \exists u_1 (\exists v_1 (u_1{:}Id \wedge v_1{:}Id \wedge v_0(v_1)) \wedge \exists u_1' \exists v_1' (\langle u_1' v_1' v_0 \rangle \wedge v_1{:}z/u_1\,z\,v_0)) \\
\rightarrow_G\ & \exists u_1 \exists v_1 (u_1{:}Id \wedge v_1{:}Id \wedge v_0(v_1)) \\
\equiv\ & T_1[v_0(v_1)]
\end{aligned}
$$

We now obtain the expected derivation:

$$
\begin{aligned}
u(Copy\,(I\,I)) \quad \equiv\quad & \exists u_0 \exists v_0 (u_0(Copy) \wedge v_0(I\,I) \wedge \langle u_0 v_0 u \rangle) \\
\rightarrow_A^3 \circ \rightarrow_G\quad & \exists u_0 \exists v_0 (u_0(Copy) \wedge T_1[v_0(v_1)] \wedge \langle u_0 v_0 u \rangle) \\
\equiv\quad & T_1[\exists u_0 \exists v_0 (u_0(Copy) \wedge v_0(v_1) \wedge \langle u_0 v_0 u \rangle)] \\
\equiv\quad & T_1[u(Copy\,v_1)]
\end{aligned}
$$

Proposition 11. *Every expression $u(M)$ is admissible.*

The proof of this proposition can be done with a linear type system excluding multiple assignment statically. It can be found the in report version of this paper [18].

Proof of Theorem 8. Let $(M_i)_{i=0}^n$ be a computation in λ_e such that M_0 is closed. By Proposition 10 there exists a simulation $S_u^{\lambda_\bullet}$ for $M \mapsto u(M)$. The properties $S_u^{\lambda_\bullet}1$ and $S_u^{\lambda_\bullet}2$ allow the construction of a derivation

$$u(M_0) \rightarrow_A^3 E_1 \rightarrow_A^3 \cdots \rightarrow_A^3 E_n$$

such that $(M_n, E_n) \in S_u^{\lambda_\bullet}$. Since M_n is irreducible, $S^{\lambda_\bullet}3$ implies that E_n is irreducible. Lemma 6 establishes the following computation in $\rho(\emptyset)$:

$$\top \wedge u(M_0) \rightarrow_{A\rho}^3 \top \wedge E_1 \rightarrow_{A\rho}^3 \cdots \rightarrow_{A\rho}^3 \top \wedge E_n$$

We use that combination $\rightarrow_{C\rho}$ is not applicable to expressions containing one constraint only.

A similar construction applies to infinite computations $(M_i)_{i=0}^{\infty}$. Let us consider the converse statements. Suppose d is a computation of $u(M)$ and d' an arbitrary computation of M. As shown above there exists a computation d'' of $u(M)$ 3 times longer than d'. The expression $u(M)$ is admissible (Proposition 11) such that we can apply Theorem 7. This yields that the lengths of d'' and d coincide, and that the length of d is 3 times the length of d'. □

7 Conclusion

We have simplified the ρ-calculus, a syntactically compositional cc-model with procedural abstraction. This allowed us to relate various models for concurrent computation in a single formal framework: The ρ-calculus with equational constraints and the γ-calculus are proved bisimilar. We have embedded the eager λ calculus into ρ without constraints, which is a proper subset of the π-calculus. We have extracted a uniformly concurrent kernel in ρ over an arbitrary constraint system. In particular, this distinguishes a uniformly concurrent part of π which is Turing complete.

Acknowledgments. Motivated by Martin Odersky, the CPS style embedding of the eager λ-calculus grew out of discussions with Gert Smolka. The research reported in this paper has been supported by the Bundesminister für Forschung und Technologie (FTZ-ITW-9105), the Esprit Project ACCLAIM (PE 7195), the Esprit Working Group CCL (EP 6028), and the DFG-Graduiertenkolleg Kognition at the Universität des Saarlandes for the second author.

References

1. Gul Agha. *ACTORS: A Model of Concurrent Computation in Distributed Systems.* The MIT Press, Cambridge, MA, 1986.
2. Z. M. Ariola, M. Felleisen, J. Maraist, M. Odersky, and P. Wadler. A call-by-need lambda calculus. In *Proc. POPL*, pp. 233–246. ACM Press, 1995.
3. G. Boudol. Asynchrony and the π-calculus (note). Rapport de Recherche 1702, INRIA, Sophia Antipolis, France, May 1992.
4. S. Brook and G. Ostheimer. Process semantics of graph reduction. In *Proc. CONCUR*, pp. 238–252, August 1995.
5. F. S. de Boer and C. Palamidessi. A process algebra of concurrent constraint programming. In Krzysztof Apt, ed., *Proc. JICSLP*, pp. 463–477, Cambridge, Massachusetts, 1992. The MIT Press.
6. M. Falaschi, M. Gabbrielli, and C. Palamidessi. Compositional analysis for concurrent constraint programming. In *Proc. LICS*, pp. 210–220. IEEE Computer Society Press, June 1993.

7. M. Henz, G. Smolka, and J. Würtz. Object-Oriented Concurrent Constraint Programming in Oz. In V. Saraswat and P. Van Hentenryck, eds., *Principles and Practice of Constraint Programming*, chapter 2, pp. 27–48. The MIT Press, Cambridge, MA, Cambridge, MA, 1995.

8. K. Honda and N. Yoshida. On Reduction-Based Semantics. In R. K. Shyamasundar, ed., *Proc. FST-TCS*, Bombay, India, December 1993.

9. Sverker Janson. *AKL - A Multiparadigm Programming Language*. PhD thesis, SICS Swedish Institute of Computer Science, SICS Box 1263, S-164 28 Kista, Sweden, 1994. SICS Dissertation Series 14.

10. J. W. Klop. Term Rewriting Systems. In S. Abramsky, D. M. Gabbay, and T. S. M. Maibaum, eds., *Handbook of Logic in Computer Science*, volume 2, chapter 2, pp. 2–116. Oxford University Press, 1992.

11. M. Mehl, R. Scheidhauer, and C. Schulte. An Abstract Machine for Oz. In *Proc. PLILP*, LNCS. Utrecht, NL, 9/20–22/95. Springer, Berlin, Germany. To appear.

12. R. Milner. The polyadic π-calculus: A tutorial. In F. L. Bauer, W. Brauer, and H. Schwichtenberg, eds., *Proc. 1991 Marktoberndorf Summer School on Logic and Algebra of Specification*. NATO ASI Series, Springer, Berlin, Germany, 1993.

13. R. Milner. Functions as Processes. *Mathematical Structures in Computer Science*, 2(2):119–141, 1992.

14. R. Milner, J. Parrow, and D. Walker. A Calculus of Mobile Processes, I and II. *Information and Computation*, 100(1):1–40 and 41–77, September 1992.

15. T. Müller, Konstantin Popow, C. Schulte, and J. Würtz. Constraint programming in Oz. DFKI Oz documentation series, DFKI Saarbrücken, Germany, 1994. Documentation and System: http://ps-www.dfki.uni-sb.de.

16. J. Niehren. *Funktionale Berechnung in einem uniform nebenläufigen Kalkül mit logischen Variablen*. Doctoral Dissertation. Universität des Saarlandes, Technische Fakultät, 66041 Saarbrücken, Germany, December 1994. In German.

17. J. Niehren. Functional computation as concurrent computation, 1995. Submitted, http://ps-www.dfki.uni-sb.de/~niehren.

18. Joachim Niehren and Martin Müller. Constraints for Free in Concurrent Computation. Research Report, German Research Center for Artificial Intelligence (DFKI), Stuhlsatzenhausweg 3, D-66123 Saarbrücken, Germany, September 1995.

19. J. Niehren and G. Smolka. A confluent relational calculus for higher-order programming with constraints. In J.-P. Jouannaud, ed., *Proc. CCL*, LNCS 845, pp. 89–104, Germany, 1994.

20. G. D. Plotkin. Call-by-name, Call-by-value and the λ-Calculus. *Theoretical Computer Science*, 1:125–159, 1975.

21. V. A. Saraswat, M. Rinard, and P. Panangaden. Semantic foundations of concurrent constraint programming. In *Proc. POPL*, pp. 333–352. ACM Press, 1991.

22. G. Smolka. A Calculus for Higher-Order Concurrent Constraint Programming with Deep Guards. Research Report RR-94-03, DFKI, Saarbrücken, Germany, 1994.

23. G. Smolka. A Foundation for Concurrent Constraint Programming. In J.-P. Jouannaud, ed., *Proc. CCL*, LNCS 845, pp. 50–72, Germany, 1994.

24. G. Smolka. An Oz primer. DFKI Oz documentation series, DFKI, Saarbrücken, Germany, 1995. Documentation and System: http://ps-www.dfki.uni-sb.de.

25. G. Smolka. The Definition of Kernel Oz. In Andreas Podelski, ed., *Constraints: Basics and Trends*, LNCS 910, pp. 251–292. Springer, Berlin, Germany, 1995.

Formalizing Inductive Proofs of
Message Recovery in Distributed Systems

Pankaj Jalote

Department of Computer Science and Engineering
Indian Institute of Technology
Kanpur - 208016; India

Abstract

If a process fails in a distributed systems, for proper recovery, the messages sent to the process need to be recovered. We present sufficient conditions for recovering the messages for a distributed application. For a general purpose recovery technique these also become necessary conditions. ¿From the conditions it is clear that requiring messages to be recovered in the same order as they were received by a process before failure is a stricter requirement than necessary.

1 Introduction

Distributed systems potentially can be more fault tolerant than single-node systems. For providing fault tolerance against node failures in a distributed system, work has addressed maintaining a consistent system state, ensuring the atomicity of actions, making data objects resilient, making processes resilient, etc. The various fault tolerant services and methods for supporting them are described in [4].

One of the desired fault tolerant services is making processes resilient to node failures (of fail stop nature [8]). If a process does not communicate, then a simple checkpoint and rollback approach would suffice. However, this checkpoint and rollback scheme has to be augmented if the processes communicate with each other, by recovering the messages for the failed process.

Various approaches and systems have been proposed for recovering messages [1, 2, 5, 6, 7, 9, 10, 11, 12]. In [9], a timestamp based scheme is presented to order and recover messages in a broadcast environment. The system in [1] recovers messages for client/server interaction. The scheme proposed in [7] is a centralized scheme and requires a special processor for recovering messages. Optimistic method for recovery is proposed in [10, 11, 6, 12], in which messages are logged asynchronously on a stable storage, and the backup process for the receiver recovers the messages during recovery. Other processes may also have to roll back to ensure consistency. In [2], messages are recovered by requiring that when a process sends a message to a receiver process, it also sends that message to the backup for the receiver and to its own backup. These three messages are sent atomically to the three different destinations.

In this paper we focus on the conditions that need to be satisfied for message recovery. Most of these works aim to recover the messages lost due to failure in exact same order as before the failure. That is, the message recovery condition is that the recovered messages are received in the same order as the original order. We develop sufficient conditions for message recovery for a distributed application, and show that the "same order as before" requirement is overly strict. For a general system where the message recovery can be applied for any application, the developed conditions are also necessary.

2   System Model

Consider a distributed application with a fixed set of processes that may execute on different nodes. Each process is assumed to be deterministic, so that given the same inputs, the process will execute the same sequence of instructions. Processes communicate exclusively through asynchronous message passing. A process sends a message to another process P_i by executing $send(P_i, msg)$, and receives a message by executing $receive(msg)$. Logical channels are assumed to exist between processes that communicate. These channels are used for sending and receiving messages between processes.

For each process P_i, a queue $msgQ_i$ is maintained by the node on which the process executes. A message for P_i, arriving on one of the channels incident on P_i is appended to the queue $msgQ_i$ (we assume that infinite memory is available for a $msgQ_i$). When P_i executes a receive, it receives the first message in $msgQ_i$. If there is no message in $msgQ_i$, then execution of receive is delayed until a message arrives. The behavior of a process can be sensitive to the order in which it receives the messages.

A process and the messages it receives in this system can be viewed in another manner. Suppose P_i has n channels incident upon it. The source process for each channel sends P_i a sequence of messages. These messages, obtained from different channels, are "merged" together into a single sequence and added to $msgQ_i$, from where P_i actually consumes the messages. How the messages are merged depends on the properties of the underlying communication network. We make no specific assumptions about the nature of the communication network, and so represent the merging of the sequences as a function, which is different for different networks.

We define a function *merge* which takes as input sequences of messages and produces a *set* of sequences.

$$merge : seq \times seq.... \times seq \rightarrow set\ of\ seq$$

That is, if $s_1, ..., s_n$ are the sequence of messages sent on the channels to P_i, then $merge(s_1, ..., s_n)$ is a set of sequences, and the sequence of messages that get added to $msgQ_i$ is a member of this set. We will represent the set of sequences *merge* produces as *merged-seq-set*. The relationship of a sequence in *merge-seq-set* depends on the merge function, which in turn depends on the nature of the communication network. For example, if the channels can loose and reorder messages, then any sequence S whose set of messages is a subset of the messages in $s_1, s_2, ..., s_n$, will be in *merged-seq-set*. Similarly, if the channels do not loose messages and preserve the order also, then any sequence S which contains the same messages as in $s_1, s_2, ..., s_n$, and preserves the ordering of each sequence s_i will be in *merged-seq-set*.

For a sequence of messages sent to P_i along different channels, which of the sequences in *merged-seq-set* get added to $msgQ_i$ is not in the control of the application designer. That is, the choice is non-deterministic and cannot be predetermined. Any sequence in *merged-seq-set* can get added to $msgQ_i$ and hence should be acceptable to the application program.

We consider state of a process as the state of all the variables of the process along with its program counter. A global state of the distributed system comprises of the state of each of the processes, the states of the message queue for each of the processes, and the states of the channels between processes. The initial state of a distributed system is the state in which each process is in its initial state and each of the message queues and channels are empty.

An *execution* of the distributed system is a sequence of states. The state transitions occur by the execution of some action by a process. The actions of different processes interleave non-deterministically, and even for the same initial state of the system, many different executions of the system are possible. The set of all such executions characterize the behavior of the distributed system.

We call an execution failure-free if no process fails during the execution. A system state S is a *consistent state* if S occurs in some failure-free execution.

When a process P_i fails, we assume that $msgQ_i$ is lost. Only checkpointed information survives the failure. We also assume that the messages destined for P_i in channels at the time of failure are discarded by the communication network. The basic approach of checkpoint and rollback recovery technique is to restart a failed process using a previously checkpointed state. We assume that if the failed process resends any messages during recovery, the message is discarded as a duplicate (this can be done easily by the use of sequence numbers). We also assume that only the failed process rolls back.

3   Message Recovery Conditions

If a process fails, the system state may not be consistent. If a failure of a process occurs, we would like a system to perform recovery activities that will transform the system state to a consistent state. In other words, we want the messages to be recovered in a manner such that if the failed process restarts from a previous checkpoint, the system state reaches a consistent state in a finite time.

As a result of a process failure, in addition to losing messages in the message queue and channels, effects due to messages the process received since its last checkpoint are also lost. Hence, such messages must also be recovered. In recovery from the failure of a process P_i, therefore the messages of interest are messages P_i has received since its last checkpoint, the messages in $msgQ_i$ at the time of the failure, and the messages in the channels at the time of failure. We assume that at the time of failure, the channels are empty and that all the messages in the channels were added to the message queue before failure. As the messages in $msgQ_i$ are also lost during failure, this assumption preserves the generality and is only for convenience.

3.1 Sufficient Conditions

Suppose a process P_i fails at time F, and restarts from a previously saved checkpoint taken at time C. Consider the case where P_i sends messages between C and F. That is, the internal state of P_i between C and F may have been "seen" by other processes. Since the messages produced by P_i during recovery are discarded as duplicates, for reaching a consistent state the message content of the messages produced during recovery must exactly be the same as before failure. Otherwise, the system will reach a state in which P_i sent some value but some other value is actually received and used by the recipient process. This will be an inconsistent state unless the network is such that it allows changing of the message contents (such a network will be of little use).

Let M_1 be the messages received by P_i after time C but before executing its last send prior to failure at time F. Let M_1' be the sequence in which these messages are recovered on restart. Assume also that all later messages, if lost, are recovered after recovery of messages in M_1, and are recovered properly.

Lemma 1. If $M_1 = M_1'$, then the system reaches a consistent state.
Proof. The state after roll back may not be consistent since some other processes has received a message sent by P_i, but P_i is at C where it has not executed the corresponding send command. If $M_1' = M_1$, then after restart P_i will execute the same sequence of instructions as before and send commands between C and F will produce the same messages. By hypothesis, these messages will be discarded. After P_i reaches F, the system is in a state where all the send commands of P_i for which corresponding messages exist in the message queues of other processes have been executed and there are no extraneous messages in the system. This is a consistent state.
□

If $M_1' \neq M_1$, then on restart P_i may execute a different sequence of instructions and the messages sent after restart can, in general, be different from the messages sent originally by P_i. As discussed above, this can take the system to a state that is not consistent.

Now let us consider the case where P_i does not send any messages between C and F. Let M_2 be the concatenation of the sequence of messages that P_i had received between times C and F, and the value of $msgQ_i$ at time F. M_2 is the sequence of messages which would have been consumed by P_i after C, if no failure occurred. M_2 is a member of *merged-seq-set* of messages sent by different processes to P_i, and contains the set of messages that need to be recovered. Suppose that a sequence of messages M_2', is recovered, that is, during recovery M_2 is added to $msgQ_i$ in the order M_2'

Lemma 2. If P_i sent no messages between C and F and if $M_2' \in$ *merged-seq-set* to which M_2 belongs, then the system state after recovery is consistent.

Proof. Since P_i has sent no messages between times C and F, no other process has any knowledge of the state of P_i. So, the situation after roll back and message recovery is equivalent to P_i not having executed the receives between C and F. As during normal execution any sequence in *merged-seq-set* may get added to $msgQ_i$, and $M_2' \in$ *merged-seq-set*, the state is a consistent state.
□

With lemmas 1 and 2 we can see that the requirements for message recovery are different, depending on whether or not the failed process sent a message between times C and F. That is, the requirements for message recovery before and after the last message sent between C and F are different. The last message sent by P_i between C and F forms a dividing line. Let the sequence of messages received by P_i between C and F be $M = M_1; M_2$ (the ";" is the concatenation operator), where M_1 is the sequence of messages received by P_i before the last message sent by it between C and F, and M_2 is the sequence of messages received for P_i after that (which includes the ones it consumed and the ones in $msgQ_i$). Either M_1 or M_2 or both may be null. Together, M_1 and M_2 include all messages that must be recovered. We have the following message recovery condition.

Message Recovery Condition. Let M be the messages to be recovered. Consider $M = M_1; M_2$, where M_1 and M_2 are as discussed above. Let M' be the sequence of messages that are recovered during recovery, and $M' = M_1'; M_2'$. The message recovery should be such that

1. $M_1 = M_1'$, and
2. $M_2' \in$ *merged-seq-set* to which M_2 belongs.

And now we have the following theorem.

Theorem 1: If the message recovery condition is satisfied, the system will reach a valid state.

Proof. Follows from Lemmas 1 and 2.
□

Clearly, the conditions of the theorem are satisfied if $M' = M$. This, however, is stricter than necessary and can be difficult to satisfy. For example, ordering of old messages sent can be established by checkpoints or by message logging, but recovering the last messages sent to a process in a fixed order can be particularly difficult, due to the possibility of failure between establishing a checkpoint and sending or receiving of a message. To overcome this may require multiple messages to be sent atomically, as in [2], a centralized controller as in [7], other processes to roll back as in [10], etc. Simple retransmissions cannot be employed if a fixed order of receiving the messages by different processes is needed.

For these reason, the flexibility offered by clause 2 of the message recovery condition is useful. On restart, a process can receive some messages - those received after executing the last send - in an order in which it *could have received* them in the original execution, which may be a different order from the one in which the messages were actually received. Due to this, retransmission can be employed to recover these messages.

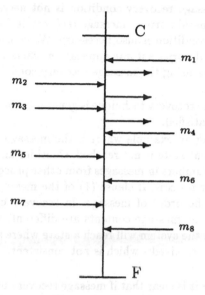

Fig. 1. An Example

As an example, consider the process P and its message exchanges as shown in Figure 1. P receives messages from two channels (on on left and the other on right). In this example, P fails at F and restarts from C. The last message sent by P before F is before receiving m_5. By the message recovery condition, during recovery m_1, m_2, m_3, and m_4 must be received in the same order as before, i.e. in the sequence $m_1; m_2; m_3; m_4$. However, m_5, m_6, m_7, and m_8 can be recovered in any order in $merge(m5; m_7, m_6; m_8)$ for the communication network on which the system is executing. For example, if the network is such that channels do not loose messages but can reorder them (i.e. messages can arrive in any order on a channel), then the *merge-seq-set* will consist of all possible orderings of these four messages (a total of 16). Hence, these messages can be recovered during recovery in any order. The order may clearly be different from $m_5; m_6; m_7; m_8$ - the order in which these messages were received before failure.

3.2 Necessary Conditions

Theorem 1 states that the message recovery condition is sufficient for an application. For a specific application these sufficient conditions may be stronger than needed and weaker conditions may suffice. For example, in a file server which does not keep any state information, the order of requests is not significant. Consequently, the clause (1) of the message recovery condition is stricter than needed. In this application, even the messages received before the last message sent by the server process can be recovered in any order provided the order of requests on the same file is preserved.

So, clearly the message recovery condition is not necessary for all applications. However, if a general purpose message recovery technique is needed, then the message recovery condition is also necessary. We consider a message recovery technique as *general purpose* if *any* application reaches a consistent state by recovering the messages using the message recovery condition.

Theorem 1. A message recovery technique is general purpose only if the message recovery condition is satisfied.

Proof. By constructing an example where if the message recovery condition is not satisfied, a consistent state is not reached. Consider an application in which a process gets unique numbers in messages from other processes, and sends these numbers to some other process. If clause (1) of the message recovery condition is not satisfied, then the order of messages in recovery can be different from the original order. As the message contents are different, but the messages are discarded as duplicate, the system will reach a state where some message is sent, but another message is received - which is not consistent.
□

¿From this theorem it is clear that if message recovery utilities are to be built that can be used by any application to support process resiliency, then the message recovery condition must be satisfied. However, if message recovery is to be supported for a particular application, then the message recovery condition may even be stricter than needed and weaker conditions can be employed, depending on the semantics of the application.

4 Conclusion

In this paper, we have developed conditions for proper message recovery in systems with asynchronous message passing. We have shown that for a distributed application, for recovering the messages of a process, the last message sent by the process forms the dividing line. The recovery condition for the messages received before sending the last message is different than the messages received after it - The messages received before sending the last message should be recovered in the same order, while the messages received after can be recovered in any order in which they could have been received. It is clear that the requirement of recovering all the lost messages in the exact original order, as is done in many existing systems, is overly strict. The main advantage of the flexibility offered by the message recovery technique is that retransmissions can be used to recover the last messages, which are hardest to recover (particularly if the "same order" requirement is to be supported).

Though for a particular application, the message recovery condition is a sufficient condition, if a general purpose message recovery is needed then these conditions are also necessary. For specific applications the conditions may even be weaker than the message recovery condition.

The message recovery condition for a particular type of network (which does not loose or reorder messages) are given in [3]. In [3] these are then used to support process resiliency and a protocol is given to mask the failure of processes in a distributed system. The protocol demonstrates how without any special hardware, and with low overhead, the flexibility of message recovery condition can be exploited and retransmissions used to support process resiliency.

References

1. J. F. Bartlett, "A NonStop kernel", *Proc. of 7th ACM Symp. on Operating Systems Principles*, 1981, pp. 22-29.
2. A. Borg, J. Baumbach and S. Glazer, "A message system supporting fault tolerance", *9th ACM Symp. on Op. Sys. Principles, Op. Sys. Review*, Vol. 17:5, Oct 1983, pp. 90-99.
3. P. Jalote, "Fault tolerant processes", *Distributed Computing*, Vol 3, pp. 187-195, 1989.
4. P. Jalote, "Fault Tolerance in Distributed Systems", *PTR Prentice Hall*, Englewood Cliffs, NJ, 1994.
5. D. B. Johnson and W. Zwaenepoel, "Sender-based message logging", *Digest of Papers: The 17th Int. Fault Tolerant Computing Symposium*, July 1987, Pittsburgh, pp. 14-19.
6. D. B. Johnson and W. Zwaenepoel, "Recovery in distributed systems using optimistic message logging and checkpointing", *Journal of Algorithms*, Vol 11, pp. 462-491, 1990.
7. M. L. Powell and D. L. Presotto, "PUBLISHING: a reliable broadcast communication mechanism", *9th ACM Symp. on Op. Sys. Principles, Op. Sys. Review*, Vol. 17:5, Oct. 1983, pp. 100-109.
8. R. D. Schlichting and F. B. Schneider, "Fail-stop processors: an approach to designing fault-tolerant computing systems", *ACM Tran. on Comput. Systems*, Vol. 1, no. 3, Aug. 1983, pp. 222-238.
9. F. B. Schneider, "Synchronization in distributed programs", *ACM Tran. on Prog. Languages and Systems*, Vol. 4, no. 2, April 1982, pp. 179-195.
10. R. E. Strom and S. Yemini, "Optimistic recovery: an asynchronous approach to fault-tolerance in distributed systems", *Digest of Papers: The 14th Int. Fault Tolerant Computing Symposium*, 1984, Florida, pp. 374-379.
11. R. E. Strom and S. Yemini, "Optimistic recovery in distributed systems", *ACM Tran. on Comput. Sys.*, Vol. 3, no. 3, pp. 204-226, 1985.
12. Y. M. Want and W. K. Fuchs, "Optimistic message logging for independent checkpointing in a message passing system", *Proc. 11th Symp. on Reliable Dist. Sys.*, 1992, pp. 147-154.

Detecting Distributed Termination in the Presence of Node Failure

Xinfeng Ye[1] and John Keane[2]

[1] Dept of Computer Science, University of Auckland, New Zealand
[2] Dept of Computation, UMIST, Manchester, UK

Abstract. Distributed termination detection concerns detecting the termination of a distributed computation spread across a set of processing nodes. Many solutions have been proposed. However, most solutions have not addressed the problem of the failure of the processing node. In this paper, a termination detection scheme which tolerates node failure is proposed. It is both symmetric and distributed. The scheme can be applied to any kind of connection topology. It uses the FIFO property of a single transmission line to cope with system wide non-FIFO message transmission. Some of the information concerning termination detection is backed up for fault tolerant purposes. The "backing up" does not require the synchronisation of the processing nodes, and it does not interfere with the normal computation. Therefore, the overhead to achieve fault tolerance has been minimised. The scheme is derived using the invariant technique.

1 Introduction

A distributed computation is carried out by a set of processing nodes (PN). The nodes are connected by a network, and they communicate with each other by passing messages. The messages are called *basic messages*. A node is either *active* or *idle*. A node which is performing computation is active. Only active nodes can send messages. An active node becomes idle when it finishes its computation. An idle node becomes active when the computation on the node is activated or reactivated. Computation on an idle node can only be (re)activated when the node receives a basic message. The distributed computation is considered to have *terminated* if all nodes are idle and there are no basic messages in the network. Termination detection is superimposed on the distributed computation. Since Dijkstra's and Francez's papers on termination detection [2, 3], many solutions have been proposed [1, 4, 5, 6, 8]. Apart from [6], most of the solutions have not addressed the problem of node failure.

In this paper a termination detection scheme which tolerates node failure is proposed. The scheme is symmetric and distributed. That is, each node executes the same algorithm and the termination can be detected by any node. The scheme takes into account the problem of non-FIFO message transmission. It can be applied to any kind of connection topology.

In the scheme, some of the information is backed up for fault tolerant purposes. In contrast to previous solutions [1, 5, 6], the scheme neither uses message counting to cope with system-wide non-FIFO message transmission nor relies on some special nodes to co-ordinate the detection. Instead, each node collects the information by itself. Hence, the information collected by different nodes is not related. As a result, the nodes do not need to synchronise with each other to back up the information. Also, the backing up of the information on a node only occurs when the node is not performing computation. Hence, the overhead to achieve fault tolerance has been minimised.

The scheme is derived using the *invariant technique*, as in [1, 2, 8]. The technique is based on the simultaneous construction of the rules that govern the scheme and of an invariant that captures the state of the system. In this technique, if the rules keep the invariant valid, then the correctness of the scheme is guaranteed.

2 The Model

The PNs are connected by *channels*. A channel is a direct link (i.e. a transmission line) between two PNs. Each channel is bi-directional, and has the FIFO property. Communication between the PNs is asynchronous. It is *not* assumed that there is a channel between each pair of PNs. However, there exists at least one route[3] between any two PNs. This means that a message sent from PN i to j may pass several PNs before it reaches PN j. If there is more than one route between two PNs, message transmission between the two PNs does not have the FIFO property (since messages can be transmitted on different routes).

The PNs are fail-stop processors. The information on the failed PNs is lost. For simplicity, in this paper, it is assumed that a failed PN can recover from its failure. The scheme can easily be adapted to permanent node failure. This is explained in section 6. The channels do not lose or alter any information. Techniques for constructing this kind of channel can be found in [7].

3 Principles of the Scheme

The principles of the scheme are:

- when a node becomes idle, it sends probes to all other nodes to test whether they have finished their computation,

---

[3] A route consists of one or several channels.

- only idle nodes can acknowledge the receipt of the probes,
- the termination of computation is declared when an idle node has received the acknowledgements for the receipt of all probes sent out by it.

An idle node is re-activated when it receives a basic message. Thus, an idle node can become active again after it has acknowledged the receipt of a probe sent by another node. However, the rules in the scheme will guarantee that a node does not receive all the acknowledgments for its probes if there are either active nodes or basic messages in the system. Thus, termination will not be declared.

4 Terminology and Notation

In the scheme, probes are used to collect information. A probe is a tuple, i.e. *(creator, sequence-number, weight)*. *creator* is the identifier of the node which creates the probe. *sequence-number* is assigned to the probe when it is created. Each probe carries some weight, which is recorded in *weight*. The weight of a probe p is denoted as *p[weight]*.

A probe may split into several probes. *Split* is defined as: if a probe, say p, splits into n probes, i.e. $p_1,...,p_n$, then

1. The *creator* and *sequence-number* of p_i *(1 ≤ i ≤ n)* are the same as the ones of p.
2. $p_i[weight] = \frac{p[weight]}{n}$, i.e. $p[weight] = \sum_{i=1}^{n} p_i[weight]$ □

A *family* is a set of probes created by a node. It is defined as:

1. A probe created by an idle node, say A, belongs to *family(A)*.
2. If a probe i belongs to a family, say *family(A)*, then the probes which are obtained from the splitting of i also belong to *family(A)*.
3. The *creator* of the probes in *family(A)* is node A. □

Probes in a family may carry different sequence numbers[4]. The probes which carry the largest sequence number in a family are called the *living generation* of the family. The probes belonging to the living generation of a family are *living relations* of each other. In a family the probes whose sequence numbers are less than the sequence number of a probe, say p, are the *ancestors* of p.

On each node, four values are kept[5]:

1. *weight$_A$* is a fixed value on node A. It is the weight assigned to a probe when the probe is created by A.

---

[4] The assigning of a sequence number to a probe is explained later.
[5] In the following discussion, the subscript of a symbol is the identifier of a node.

2. $return\text{-}weight_A$ records the sum of the weight of the probes which are the living generation of $family(A)$ and have been returned to node A. The initial value of $return\text{-}weight_A$ is 0.

3. $s\text{-}number_A$ records the number of probes which have been created by node A. The value of $s\text{-}number_A$ is assigned as the sequence number of a probe.

4. $neighbours(A)$ is a set of nodes. Each of these nodes is connected with A by a channel. $|neighbours(A)|$ represents the number of nodes in $neighbours(A)$.

The following notation is used in the description of the invariant:

- *creators* denotes the set of the nodes which create probes. This set includes all nodes in the system. The nodes in the set are called *creators*.
- *not-returned(A)* is a set of probes. These probes are the living generation of *family(A)*, and they have not been returned to node A.
- *visited(A)* is a set of nodes. These nodes have been reached by the probes belonging to the living generation of *family(A)*.
- *c-visited(A)* is a set of channels. The set includes all channels which connect the nodes in *visited(A)*. A channel, say c, in *c-visited(A)* is *empty* if there are no basic messages in c.
- *a-creators* is a subset of *creators*. Each creator, say A, in the set satisfies the following condition: a probe belonging to the living generation of *family(A)* has either (a) encountered an active node or a basic message, or (b) been lost in a node failure.

5 Derivation of the Scheme

The scheme is derived using the invariant technique. The state of the system concerning termination detection is captured by an invariant. The scheme will be constructed in a number of steps. Each step consists of an extension of the state space of the system and the introduction of further rules to keep the invariant valid.

5.1 Basic Rules

The following two rules allow the probes to reach all nodes in the system.
$\mathbf{R_0}$:

1. When an active node, say A, becomes idle, it creates a probe, say p. p carries a weight such that $p[weight] = weight_A$.

2. p is split into $n + 1$ probes, i.e. $p_1,...,p_{n+1}$ where $n = |neighbours(A)|$. One of the probes, say p_j, resides on A, and the other probes are sent to the nodes in $neighbours(A)$ respectively.

3. Node A waits for the living relations of p_j being sent back. $\qquad\qquad\square$

R_1: Assume that an idle node, say B, receives a probe p in a family, say $family(A)$, from its neighbour, say C. If it is the first time B receives a probe belonging to the living generation of $family(A)^6$, then the following operations are carried out:

1. p is split into $n + 1$ probes, where $n = |neighbours(B)|$. One of the probes, say p_j, resides on B, and the other probes are sent to the nodes in $neighbours(B)$.
2. B waits for the *living relations* of p_j from the nodes in $neighbours(B) - \{C\}$. When such a probe, say p_i, is received the following is applied:
   $p_j[weight] := p_j[weight] + p_i[weight]$,
   and, subsequently, p_i is discarded.
3. When B has received a living relation of p_j from each node in $neighbours(B) - \{C\}$, p_j is sent to A. □

An idle node acknowledges the receipt of a probe, say p, by sending a probe to the creator of p. From $R_1(3)$, node B does not send a probe to A until B has received a probe belonging to the living generation of $family(A)$ from each node in $neighbours(B)$. However, this does not cause deadlock, since, according to $R_0(2)$ and $R_1(1)$, a node always sends probes to all its neighbours. Thus, if no probes are lost, all nodes will receive probes from their neighbours. That is, no nodes will wait for some probes forever.

According to the system model, there are at least one route between two nodes. Therefore, the following property can be easily derived from $R_0(2)$ and $R_1(1)$.

Property 1: The probes in any family can reach all nodes in the system. □

According to the definition of "split" and $R_1(2)$, the sum of the weight carried by the probes is always equal to *weight*. Thus, the following can be obtained:

Property 2: If no probes are lost, the following holds for all families:
$\forall A : creators.weight_A = \sum_{j \in not-returned(A)} j[weight] + return\text{-}weight_A$ □

According to **Property 2**, for a creator, say A, if $weight_A = return\text{-}weight_A$ holds, all probes in $family(A)$ have been returned to node A.

From $R_0(2)$ and R_1, a node, say B, only sends one probe belonging to the living generation of a family, say $family(A)$, to each of the nodes in $neighbours(B)$. Thus, no probes will be passed in the system forever. Also, R_0 and R_1 are deadlock free. Hence, according to $R_1(3)$, the following holds:

Property 3: In the absence of failure and active nodes, the probes in any family are returned to their creators eventually. □

---

[6] The case where B has already received a probe in the living generation of A is covered in $R_1(2)$.

5.2 Deriving the Rules

The rules derived in this section have two purposes:

1. If the conditions which indicate that the computation has not terminated hold (i.e. there are active nodes or basic messages), some probes are discarded. As a result, the termination will not be declared.
2. No probes will be lost if the condition which indicates the termination of the computation holds. As a result, termination will be declared.

Probes are used to collect the status information from the system. However, a probe can be created by an idle node when the computation on other nodes has not terminated. Thus, the following factors can complicate the task of determining the system state:

a. Active nodes,
b. Basic messages in the network,
c. Idle nodes being reactivated,
d. Reactivated nodes becoming idle again,
e. Node failure.

The following discussion starts with the system state which is free from the above factors. Then, the system state is expanded to include an extra factor at each step.

Step 1 Firstly, the problem is solved in the absence of active nodes, basic messages and node failure. Also, no nodes have been reactivated during the computation.

Since there are no basic messages, no nodes can be reactivated. Thus, from $R_0(1)$, only one probe is created by each node. This means that all probes are the living generations. In the absence of failure, no probes are lost. Hence, the invariant can be obtained according to **Property 2**:

I_0: $\exists A$: creators.
    $(weight_A = \sum_{j \in not-returned(A)} j[weight] + return-weight_A$
    $\wedge \ \forall B$:visited$(A).B$ is idle
    $\wedge \ \forall c$:c-visited$(A).c$ is empty$)$

According to R_0, when a node becomes idle, it initiates the termination detection algorithm by creating a probe. Therefore, the scheme is started when the first probe in the system is created. The probe is split and sent to the neighbours of its creator and the creator itself[7]. Hence, a newly created probe is

---

[7] According to $R_0(2)$, after the probe is split up, one of the probes will reside on the creator. This probe can be treated as being sent to the creator itself.

a probe which has not been returned to its creator. That is, the probe is in *not-returned(A)*, where A is the creator of the new probe. Thus, I_0 is true initially, i.e. when the first probe in the system is created.

Since all nodes are idle and there are no messages in the network, "$\forall B:visited(A).B$ *is idle* $\land$ $\forall c:c\text{-}visited(A)$. *c is empty*" holds while the probes are passed. In the absence of failure, no probes are lost. Hence, according to **Property 2**, $weight_A = \sum_{j \in not\text{-}returned(A)} j[weight] + return\text{-}weight_A$ holds all the time.

From **Property 3**, all probes will be returned to their creators. This means that "*weight = return-weight*" will hold on a node, say A. According to **Property 1**, the probes in *family(A)* must have visited all nodes in the system. That is, *visited(A)* includes all nodes in the system. It has been shown that I_0 is kept valid all the time. Thus, according to "$\forall B:visited(A).B$ *is idle* $\land$ $\forall c:c\text{-}visited(A).c$ *is empty*" in I_0, all nodes are idle and there are no messages in the network. Hence, the termination of the computation can be declared. Thus, "*weight = return-weight*" is the termination condition.

Property 4: When a node, say A, discovers that $weight_A = returned\text{-}weight_A$, A can declare the termination of the computation. □

Step 2 The system state is expanded to include the case that some nodes are active.

The probes are sent from idle nodes to the neighbouring nodes ($R_0(2)$ and $R_1(1)$). I_0 can be falsified when a probe arrives at an active node. This is because "$\forall B : visited(A)$. B *is idle*" becomes invalid. In order to cope with the problem, a weaker invariant $I_0 \lor I_1$ is adopted.

The equation in I_0 leads to the establishment of the termination condition, i.e. *weight = return-weight*. Therefore, the equation should not hold for the families whose members have encountered an active node. This is because the active node indicates that the computation has not terminated. Hence, I_1 is as follow:

$$I_1: \forall A:a\text{-}creators.\, weight_A > \sum_{j \in not\text{-}returned(A)} j[weight] + return\text{-}weight_A$$

The following rule is chosen to prevent falsifying $I_0 \lor I_1$:

R_2: When an active node receives a probe, the probe is discarded. □

Each probe carries some weight, and the value of *weight* for a node is fixed. Therefore, according to **Property 2**, if a probe in a family is discarded, then the probe in that family will satisfy the inequality in I_1. As a result, $I_0 \lor I_1$ holds.

Step 3 The system state is expanded to allow basic messages to exist in the network.

I_0 is falsified if (a) a probe in *family(A)* is sent to an idle node, say B, and (b) there are basic messages in the channels between B and the other nodes in *visited(A)*. This is because "$\forall c$:*c-visited(A).c is empty*" does not hold. Hence, $I_0 \vee I_1$ can be falsified. As a result, a weaker invariant $I_0 \vee I_1 \vee I_2$ is adopted.

I_2: $\exists A$:*creators*.
$\quad (weight_A = \sum_{j \in not-returned(A)} j[weight] + return\text{-}weight_A$
$\quad \wedge \forall B$:*visited(A).B is idle*
$\quad \wedge \exists c$:*c-visited(A).c is not empty)*

If the probes in *family(A)* satisfies I_2, the basic messages in *c-visited(A)* must be detected. This is because the invariant can still become invalid when the idle nodes are reactivated by the basic messages. In order to detect the basic messages, the following rule is needed.

R_3: When a basic message reaches a node, say A, all probes on A are discarded, and *return-weight$_A$* is set to 0[8]. □

R_0, R_1 and R_3 allow the basic messages which have not been discovered by the probes that satisfy I_2 to be detected. Now it is explained how these messages are detected. Without loss of generality, it can be assumed in Figure 1 that:

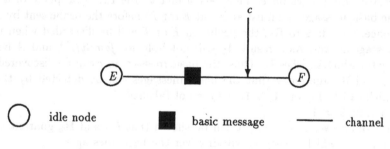

idle node   basic message   —— channel

Figure - 1

1. E and F are idle nodes,
2. Originally the probes in *family(A)* satisfy I_0, and $E \in visited(A) \wedge F \notin visited(A)$,

---

[8] As there is not a channel between every pair of nodes, a basic message may reach its destination by passing through other nodes. When a node receives a basic message, all probes on the node are discarded and the *return-weight* of the node is set to 0 even if the node is not the final destination of the basic message.

3. F receives a probe in *family(A)*; and, as a result, the probes in *family(A)* satisfy I_2[9] and $F \in visited(A)$,
4. E and F are connected by channel c, i.e. $F \in neighbours(E)$ and $E \in neighbours(F)$,
5. The basic message which makes the probes in *family(A)* satisfy I_2 is in c.

According to assumption (2), $F \neq A$ holds. Therefore, there are two cases to consider in terms of the identity of E.

Case 1: $E \neq A$

According to assumption (2), when E receives a probe in *family(A)*, F has not received a probe in *family(A)*. Thus, according to $R_1(1)$, E must have not received a probe in *family(A)* from F. From $R_1(3)$, E will not send a probe in *family(A)* to A until it has received the probes in *family(A)* from all the nodes in *neighbours(E)*. Hence, a probe in *family(A)* must be residing on E.

According to assumption (3), the probes in *family(A)* satisfy I_2 once F receives a probe in *family(A)*. Thus, F must hold a probe in *family(A)* when the probes in *family(A)* satisfy I_2.

The basic messages in c must reach c through either E or F. The basic message must pass through E (or F) before the probe in *family(A)* reaches E (or F). Otherwise, according to R_3, the probe on E (or F) will be discarded when E (or F) receives a basic message; and, as a result, the probes in *family(A)* must satisfy I_1. However, this contradicts assumption (2) and (3).

According to the above discussion, the probe on E (or F) arrives at E (or F) after the basic message in c has passed through E (or F). From $R_1(1)$, E and F send probes to each other through c. Thus, the probes must reach c after the basic message. From $R_1(3)$, the probes on E and F will not leave until E and F have received the probes on c. Thus, according to the FIFO property of a channel, the basic message in c must arrive at E (or F) before the probe sent by F (or E). Hence, according to R_3, the probe on E or F will be discarded when the basic message arrives. As a result, I_2 will not hold for *family(A)*, and A becomes a creator which satisfies I_1. Thus, the basic message in c can be discovered. Hence, R_1 and R_3 guarantee that the basic messages can be detected by the probes which satisfy I_2, and $I_0 \vee I_1 \vee I_2$ is not falsified.

Case 2: $E = A$

In a similar way to case 1, it can be shown that R_0 and R_3 guarantee that all the probes which satisfy I_2 will discover the basic messages.

According to $R_0(2)$, a probe resides on the creator of the probe. This is equivalent to send the probe to the creator of the probe. Since the sending and the receiving of the probe occur on the same processor, they can be treated as occurring at the same instant. Thus, *return-weight* $\neq 0$ holds on each idle node when the node creates a probe. From R_3, *return-weight* is set to 0 when a node receives a basic message. Thus, I_2 will be falsified; and the probes of A will satisfy I_1.

---

[9] Here, the basic messages being considered are the ones which have not been discovered by the probes that satisfy I_2. Therefore, only the probes which satisfy I_2 are considered.

From the above analysis it can be seen that R_0, R_1 and R_3 ensure that the invariant $I_0 \vee I_1 \vee I_2$ cannot be falsified.

Step 4 The system state is expanded to allow the nodes being reactivated.

If a node which has been reached by a probe in a family, say *family(A)*, is reactivated, then I_0 can be falsified because *"∀B:visited(A).B is idle"* becomes false. As a consequence, $I_0 \vee I_1 \vee I_2$ can be falsified.

A basic message must go through a channel to reach a node. The channel must either be in *c-visited(A)* or not in *c-visited(A)*. In the discussion at step 3 it has been shown that a basic message in a channel which is in *c-visited(A)* can be discovered. As a consequence, $I_0 \vee I_1 \vee I_2$ is not falsified. Therefore, only the case that the basic message reaches a node in *visited(A)* through a channel which is not in *c-visited(A)* needs to be considered.

In fact R_0, R_1 and R_3 keep the invariant valid in this case. This is shown in Figure 2. It can be assumed that:

1. B is a node in *visited(A)*,
2. D is a node which has not been reached by a probe in *family(A)*,
3. c is the channel connecting B and D, i.e. c is not in *c-visited(A)*,
4. A basic message arrives at B along c.

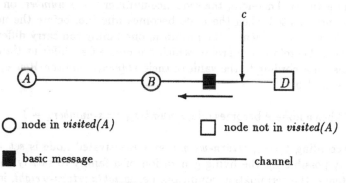

O node in *visited(A)*   □ node not in *visited(A)*

■ basic message   —————— channel

Figure - 2

According to assumption (2) and $R_1(1)$, D has not sent out any probes in *family(A)*. Thus, B has not received a probe in *family(A)* on channel c. From assumption (1), $R_1(1)$ and $R_1(3)$, a probe in *family(A)* is on B. Thus, according to R_3, the probe on B is discarded when the basic message arrives. As a result, A becomes a creator which satisfies I_1. Hence, $I_0 \vee I_1 \vee I_2$ cannot be falsified.

Step 5 The system state is expanded to include the case that a node becomes idle again after it has been reactivated.

Since a node creates a probe when the node becomes idle, the invariant can be falsified. This is because (a) the weight of the new probe is *weight*, and (b) the probes created by the node before the node was reactivated may still be in the system. Thus, the expressions concerning weight in I_0, I_1, and I_2 can be violated. This is shown in Figure 3. Figure 3(a) shows that two probes in *family(A)* reside on two idle nodes, B and C. Figure 3(b) shows that A becomes idle again after it is reactivated. p_3 is created when A becomes idle. Therefore, according to $R_0(1)$, $p_3[weight] = weight_A$. If p_1 and p_2 are still in the system, "$weight_A < p_1[weight] + p_2[weight] + p_3[weight] + return\text{-}weight_A$" holds. Hence, $I_0 \vee I_1 \vee I_2$ can be falsified.

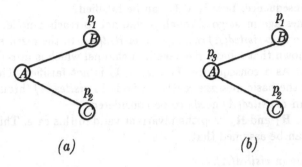

$$(a) \qquad\qquad\qquad (b)$$

Figure - 3

The solution to the problem is to distinguish the probes which are created at different times. Therefore, the sequence-number, i.e. *s-number*, on a node needs to be incremented when the node becomes idle (i.e. before the node creates a probe). As a consequence, the probes in one family can carry different sequence numbers. Therefore, the probes which are created at different times can be distinguished according to the value of their *sequence-number*. Hence, the following rule is needed.

R_4: When a node A becomes idle, $s\text{-}number_A := s\text{-}number_A + 1$. $\square$

According to R_3, *return-weight* on a reactivated node is set to 0. Thus, it is only possible for the living generation of a family to satisfy the equation in I_0. Hence, the termination condition, i.e. *weight=return-weight*, is still valid as long as the testing of the condition is based on the probes which are the living generation. The probes which are not the living generation can be discarded, and the counting based on them is ignored. Hence, the following rule is needed.

R_5: An idle node discards all the ancestors of the probes received by the node[10]. $\square$

---

[10] In practice, if a node is not the creator of a probe, then it is not possible for the node to know whether a received probe belongs to the living generation. Since the probes in the living generation of a family always carry the greatest sequence number in that family, R_5 guarantees that the probes belonging to the living generation will not be discarded.

Step 6 The system state is expanded to allow failure to occur in a system.

A failed node loses the value of *return-weight* and all probes residing on it. Hence, the equation in I_0 and I_2 may not hold[11] for some families. Therefore, I_0 and I_2 can be falsified. If all nodes are idle and there are no basic messages in the network when the failure occurs, the falsification of I_0 means that I_0 can never be satisfied. This is because (a) the equation in I_0 can only be satisfied when a probe is created, and (b) a probe can only be created when an active node becomes idle. If I_0 cannot be satisfied, then the termination condition can never hold[12].

Since an active node does not hold any probes (R_2 and R_3), only the failure of an idle node can cause problems. The following rule makes I_0 satisfiable after a failure:

R_6: When an idle node recovers from a failure, it creates a new probe.　　　□

When a node A fails, the value of *s-number$_A$* is lost. If an arbitrary value is assigned to *s-number$_A$* after the failure, it is possible that the value has been used before the failure. If (a) some probes in *family(A)* created before the failure are still in the system, and (b) the sequence numbers of these probes are equal to the value assigned to *s-number$_A$*, then the expressions concerning weight in I_0, I_1 and I_2 can be violated[13].

The problem is solved by using a variable *base-number* on each node. *base-number* is backed up in the stable storage, and thus not lost in the event of failure. The initial value of *s-number* on each node is based on the value of *base-number*. A fixed value *interval* is given, so that *s-number* can vary between *[base-number..base-number + interval)*. After a failure, *base-number* is restored according to its backup in the stable store. Subsequently, *base-number* is increased by *interval*, and the new value of *base-number* is sent to the stable store. Thus, after the failure, *s-number* varies between *[(base-number + interval)..(base-number + 2 × interval))* (where the value of *base-number* is the one before it is updated). Hence, *s-number* does not overlap with any value which has existed before the failure[14]. The following rule handles *base-number* and *s-number*:

---

[11] Since *weight* is a fixed value, the loss of a probe does not affect the validity of the inequalities in I_1.

[12] At step 3, it has been shown that any creator which satisfies I_2 will satisfy I_1. Hence, only the equation in I_0 leads to the establishment of the termination condition.

[13] The problem is caused by the creation of a new probe, as in Figure-3.

[14] Consider: assume that *base-number*=100 and *interval*=50. In this case, *s-number* can vary between 100 and 149. It can be seen that the backup of *base-number* is equal to 100. If a failure occurs, *base-number* is restored to 100; and subsequently, *base-number* is increased by *interval*. That is, the new value of *base-number* is 150. Hence, after the failure, *s-number* can vary between 150 and 199.

R₇: When an idle node A recovers from its failure, $base\text{-}number_A$ is restored from its backup. Then the following is applied:

$base\text{-}number_A := base\text{-}number_A + interval_A$,

$s\text{-}number_A := base\text{-}number_A$,

and, the new value of $base\text{-}number_A$ is backed up in the stable storage. □

When **R₄** is applied, $s\text{-}number$ may equal $base\text{-}number + interval$. In this case, the following is applied.

R₈: On a node A, when $s\text{-}number_A$ equals $base\text{-}number_A + interval_A$,

$base\text{-}number_A := base\text{-}number_A + interval_A$,

and the new value of $base\text{-}number_A$ is backed up in the stable storage. □

When **R₇** or **R₈** is applied, a probe can only be created after $base\text{-}number$ has been backed up. This is because, if a failure occurs before the backing up is completed, the previously backed up value of $base\text{-}number$ will be used after the failure. Hence, if a probe is created before the completion of the backing up, then the sequence number of the probe can overlap with the sequence number used after the failure. If the probe has been split and sent to other nodes before the failure, then the expressions concerning weight in I_0, I_1 and I_2 will not hold after the failure. That is, the invariant can be falsified.

6 Discussion

In this paper, the equation in I_0 leads to the establishment of the termination condition. I_0 can be satisfied when a probe is created, i.e. when a node becomes idle. Hence, I_0 can be satisfied when the computation terminates. Thus, the termination can be detected eventually. I_1 and I_2 ensure that the termination condition does not hold when there is an active node or a basic message. Hence, no false termination can be declared.

At most $m + k$ probes can be created in the system (where m is the number of the basic messages and k is the number of times that failure occurs in the system). This is because (a) a node becomes active when it receives a basic message, and (b) a probe is created when an active node becomes idle. That is, m basic messages can activate the nodes m times; and, at most m probes are created when the active nodes become idle. Also, according to **R₆**, a probe is created when an idle node recovers from a failure. That is, at most k probes are created if the failure occurs k times.

According to **R₀** and **R₁** the probes will be split and sent to each node in the system through the channels. Therefore, the message complexity of the scheme is $O(em + ek)$ where e is the number of channels in the system. This complexity is the worst case complexity. This is because it has been assumed that a node does not receive any basic message after it is activated. That is, each basic message activates an idle node. However, as Mattern pointed out in [5], it is very unlikely that a node does not receive any basic message while it is active. Therefore, in practice, the message complexity of the scheme should be lower than $O(em + ek)$.

In this paper it has been assumed that a node can recover from its failure. The scheme can easily adapt to permanent node failure if the nodes connected to the failed node can detect the failure. When a node fails permanently, it is equivalent to removing the node from the system. This can be achieved by removing the failed node from the *neighbours* set of the nodes connected to the failed node. As a result the failed node is excluded from the system, and no probes will be sent to the failed node. Only R_6 of the scheme needs to be modified. The modified rule guarantees that I_0 is satisfiable after a failure:

R_6': If a node A fails permanently, all the nodes in *neighbours(A)* remove A from their *neighbours* sets. If all the nodes in *neighbours(A)* are idle, one of the nodes creates a new probe. □

7 Conclusions

The scheme in this paper uses the FIFO property of a single transmission line to cope with system wide non-FIFO message transmission. The rules in the scheme have the effects of flushing the network. Hence, when the termination condition holds, there are no messages in the network.

Unlike the solution in [3] where a pre-defined node is used to detect termination, the scheme in this paper is distributed and symmetric. Unlike the solutions in [4, 5, 6] where nodes exchange information, in this paper a node uses the information which it has collected to test the termination condition. Therefore, the information collected by different nodes is not related. Hence, the backing up of the information concerning fault tolerance, i.e. *base-number*, can be carried out on each node independently. That is, synchronisation among the nodes is not needed when *base-number* is backed up. Hence, it is easier to make the scheme in this paper resilient to node failure. Also, due to the lack of synchronisation among the nodes, the scheme seems to be more efficient.

The backing up of *base-number* only occurs when a node is idle. Hence, it does not interfere with normal computation. Since only one value needs to be backed up for each node, the overhead of backing up is low.

The scheme can be applied to any connection topology. The size of the probes is small and fixed. That is, the size does not depend on the number of the nodes in the system. The message complexity of the scheme in the worst case is $O(em + ek)$. This is comparable with, or better than, some schemes which do not consider node failure, e.g. [5].

Acknowledgments

The work described in this paper is supported in part by Auckland University under grant A18/XXXXX/62090/F3414040 and by UK SERC under grant Gr/J48979.

References

1. P. Blanc, Distributed Termination Detection when Messages Arrive out of Sequence, in Parallel Processing, eds. M. Cosnard, M.H. Barton and M. Vanneschi (North-Holland, 1988) 347-360.
2. E.W. Dijkstra, W.H.J. Feijen and A.J.M. van Gasteren, Derivation of a Distributed Termination Detection Algorithm for Distributed Computations, Information Processing Letters 16(5) (1983) 217-219.
3. N. Francez, Distributed Termination, ACM TOPLAS 2(1) (1980) 42-55.
4. S. Huang, A fully distributed termination detection scheme, Information Processing Letters 29(1) (1988) 13-18.
5. F. Mattern, Asynchronous Distributed Termination - Parallel and Symmetric Solutions with Echo Algorithms, Algorithmica 5 (1990) 325-340.
6. Y. Min, Fault-tolerant termination detection algorithms for distributed system, Proceedings of Third International Conference For Young Computer Scientists, (1993) 191-192
7. M. Morganti, Reliable Communications, in Resilience Computing Systems, eds. T. Anderson (Collins, 1985).
8. R.W. Topor, Termination Detection for Distributed Computation, Information Processing Letters 18(1) (1984) 33-36.

An Extended Gradient Model for NUMA Multiprocessor Systems*

Feixiong Liu, Thomas Peikenkamp and Werner Damm

FB Informatik, Oldenburg Universität, 26111 Oldenburg, Germany

Abstract. In this paper, we present the design and implementation of an effective and scalable dynamic load balancing system for Non-Uniform Memory Access (NUMA) multiprocessors where load balancing is a key issue to achieve adequate efficiency. The proposed load balancing algorithm extends the well-known gradient model to enhance its applicability in a wide range of multiprocessor systems and to improve the overall system performance. A comparative performance study between the two models based on the preliminary simulation results is also reported in the paper.

Keywords: Load balancing, Multiprocessing, Gradient Model.

1 Introduction

It has been widely recognized that load balancing in a scalable multiprocessor system is an essential issue to achieve high performance. A typical distributed shared memory or message passing multiprocessor is a homogeneous parallel system which consists of a set of processing elements (PE) interconnected by a communication network. When parallel programs run on such a system, it is likely to happen that some processors are idle or lightly loaded while others are heavily loaded. It is therefore desirable to balance work load among processors while keeping the communication overhead at minimum.

In general load balancing can be statically or dynamically performed. Static load balancing [13][3] takes place during program compilation and loading. It relies on the initial load distribution determined through a static estimation on the execution and communication costs of parallel tasks. It usually incurs no overhead for load balancing itself. Unfortunately, static load balancing cannot always lead to a well balanced load distribution at run time. Especially when the execution times of parallel tasks vary heavily and dynamic task creations are performed. A dynamic load balancing mechanism, on the other hand, attempts to equalize/balance the work load through dynamic process migrations according to the load situations of individual processing nodes. Dynamic load balancing requires run-time support and can incur overheads due to extra communications for exchanging load information among processors and migrating tasks. There exist many load balancing schemes, most of these schemes have been designed for

---

* This work has been partially supported by the German Science Foundation (DFG)

distributed computing systems and multi-tasking environments. A classification and review of the existing load balancing methods can be found in [1] [4] [10].

This paper concentrates on the design and implementation of a dynamic load balancing model which is based on the extension of the well-known gradient model [6]. It is the kernel part of the task scheduling unit for a non-uniform access multiprocessor system which consists of homogeneous computing nodes interconnected by a communication network. Each computing node is composed of a multithreaded CPU, local memory, cache and units for memory management and network communication. The cache system employs a week cache coherence protocol. The local memories of all computing nodes form a global addressable memory space. Like the gradient model, our load balancing system has the potential to provide a scalable implementation. It migrates tasks according to a pressure gradient which is dynamically established by exchanging local load information among neighbouring processors. It extends the gradient model in three major aspects. First, by using a ticketing technique it overcomes the problem of out-of-date information in a fast load changing environment (which is usually the case for multiprocessors) and avoid the overflow effect. Second, by propagating the identifier of the processor demanding tasks, it allows a fast direct transfer of tasks between any two nodes in the systems if an indirect interconnection network such as the Monarch network in [12] is in use. Third, by introducing the possibility of overriding the thresholds in emergency load situations, it improves the average processor utilization rate. More importantly it allows the task scheduling unit (embedding the extended gradient model) to approximate the BUSD [2] task scheduling strategy. The preliminary simulation results confirms a significant improvement of the overall performance by the above extensions, along the extra functionality enhancement for dynamic granularity control which will be discussed in a separate paper.

The reminder of this paper is organized as follows. In section 2 an overview of the basic concepts and principle of the gradient model is given. Section 3 identifies the necessary extensions to the gradient model in order to achieve an effective load balancing system for NUMA multiprocessors. Section 4 presents the extended gradient model which incorporates the main extensions described in section 3. Section 5 reports our preliminary simulation results to evaluate the performance of the extended gradient model. Section 6 discusses the related research work. And finally the conclusion and future work are given in section 7.

2 An Overview of the Gradient Model

The gradient model proposed by Lin and Keller [6] is a localized and distributed load balancing mechanism with a logical interconnection network. In this logical interconnection structure each processor interacts only with a small, predefined subsets of processors in the machine. These processors are referred to as neighbours of that processor. Thus the load balancing information is exchanged

---

[2] The BUSD task scheduling strategy which stands for Breadth-first Until Situation, then Depth-first has been considered an ideal task breakdown strategy [8]

among neighbouring processors. Every processor can have one of the three load conditions: lightly loaded, moderately loaded, or heavily loaded. If a processor is lightly loaded, it wishes to have more load given to it. If it is heavily loaded, it wishes to get rid of some of its current load. If neither of the two conditions holds, then it is moderately loaded.

The gradient model is a receiver-initiated load balancing method which requires the lightly loaded processors to dynamically initiate load balancing requests. The heavily loaded processors respond to requests by migrating unevaluated tasks toward lightly loaded processors. The requests and migrated tasks are indirectly relayed through a system-wide gradient surface GS = { p_1, p_2, ..., p_n }, where p_i is termed propagated pressure of processor P_i. The propagated pressure of each processor is calculated locally by the processor according to its own load condition and the previously exchanged load information from its neighbouring processors:

$$p_i = \min \{ L_i, 1 + \min \{p_j\} \}$$

where $\{p_j\}$ is the set of propagated pressures of neighbouring nodes, namely at distance of one hop from node i. L_i is the local pressure: 0 if the node is lightly loaded, infinity otherwise. In other words the propagated pressure of a processor represents the logical distance (number of intermediate nodes plus 1) to the nearest lightly loaded processor in the system. According to the surface gradient excessive tasks from a heavily loaded processor are routed to the neighbour of the least propagated pressure , and this neighbour then relays the tasks to its own neighbour which has the least propagated pressure. This task migration procedure continues until either the tasks arrive at the lightly loaded node or some other tasks reach the lightly loaded node and the node becomes non-lightly loaded. Then the gradient surface is re-shaped and the tasks are redirected towards the new nearest lightly loaded processor. Note that the load balancing actions stop when one of the following conditions is satisfied: 1) none of the processors is lightly loaded, i.e. the system is saturated, or 2) none of the processors is heavily loaded.

The gradient surface plays three important roles. First, it is a network-wide indication of all the lightly processors in the system. Second, it relays implicit requests for work load. Third, it serves as a minimum distance routing pointer for task migrations.

3 Basic Extensions

The scalability of the gradient model makes it an attractive approach in developing load balancing systems for scalable multiprocessor systems. A recent comparative study of several load balancing approaches [7] concluded that the gradient scheme has significant advantages over alternative approaches. However based on the recent evaluation results of the gradient model and the feasibility studies in adapting the gradient model in the task scheduling unit of our NUMA multiprocessor, several major areas of the existing gradient model should be extended or improved in order to achieve an effective load balancing mechanism.

Alleviating the problem of out-of-date information

The gradient model uses the calculated propagated pressure to approximate the proximity function. This approximation makes the gradient model to suffer a serious drawback as reported in [11] [9]: out-of-date information. Recall that load information in gradient model is propagated from lightly loaded nodes to heavily loaded nodes through intermediate ones. In the worst-case it has to make "d" hops from a source processor to a destination one, where "d" is the maximum distance between any pair of nodes in the system. Thus the requests from lightly loaded processors demanding more work load may have become out-of-date when they reach heavily loaded processors. In other words, a request for load from a lightly loaded processor may have been fulfilled and a new propagated pressure is formed. However, some heavily loaded processors may be still emitting tasks according to the old propagated pressure. Thus the out-of-date information of the gradient model can result in a lot of unnecessary task movements. In particular, if there are only a few lightly loaded nodes in the system, more than one over-loaded processor may emit tasks towards the same lightly-loaded processors. This "overflow" effect may also lead to many tasks "moving around" in the system and result in a degraded processing network utilization. This problem of out-of-date information can be very severe in a fast load changing environment. Our solution to this problem is to reduce the role of propagated pressure from "decisive" to "advisory". This means that the propagated pressure is not used by a heavily loaded processor to decide if to emit a task. Instead, it is used to guide the relay of tickets representing the real demands from lightly loaded processors to heavily loaded ones. Thus a lightly loaded processor sends out an explicit request as ticket for work load. A heavily loaded processor can migrate a task to the lightly loaded node only when it receives the ticket.

Overriding load thresholds

The thresholds of the local task queues which are used to decide local load states in the gradient model play an important part in the stability of load balancing actions. However, it is in general very difficult to set optimal thresholds for a wide range of parallel programs exhibiting different characteristics and degrees of parallelism. As stated in the section 2, the gradient model only allows heavily-loaded processors to export tasks to the lightly loaded ones. While this can increase the stability of the system, it does restrict the flexibility for load balancing on some extreme load conditions in the system. For example, it can lead to the situation that some nodes are working with a moderate load but some nodes are completely idle waiting hungrily for tasks. Moreover an ideal task breakdown should maximize the run-time task granularity while maintaining balanced load. For a divide-and-conquer program, it means expanding and traversing parallel tree breadth-first by spawning tasks until all processors are busy, and then expanding the tree depth-first within the task on each processor. This strategy is referred to as BUSD in [8]. Obviously, the BUSD task breakdown strategy is difficult to be achieved on this model. In order to increase the flexibility of handling extreme load situations and facilitate the implementation of BUSD (possibly other task scheduling strategies), the model should be extented to allow the possibility of overriding thresholds. This can be done by introducing a special kind of ticket: emergency ticket. When a processor is idle, it sends out an emergency ticket. Any non-lightly loaded processor, when receiving such a ticket, should immediately dispatch a task to the idle processor if there is no heavily loaded processor in the system.

Allowing direct task transfer

In the gradient model, tasks migrated from heavily-loaded processors have to be routed step by step through several (possibly many) intermediate nodes (hops) to lightly-loaded ones. An important optimization is to allow a direct transfer of tasks between any pair of nodes. This is particularly useful when the model is implemented in multiprocessors with indirect interconnection structure, because there exists a physical path between any pair of nodes in such systems. This optimization requires that the identity of a lightly loaded processor is propagated together with gradient information. Interestingly the processor ID of a lightly loaded processor can be carried by its tickets demanding for tasks. With this extension, the task transfer time can be significantly reduced.

4 The Extended Gradient Model

A dynamic load balancing scheme may be receiver-initiated or sender-initiated. In a receiver-initiated scheme it is up to an under-loaded processor to send requests to an over-loaded one, while in the sender-initiated scheme it is the responsibility of over-loaded processors to find an under-loaded one to transfer load to. Our extended gradient model is a receiver-initiated load balancing scheme, in which an idle or lightly loaded processor initiates a load request in terms of a ticket bearing the processor identifier. This request is relayed though an established gradient surface until it reachs a heavily loaded processor. When a heavily loaded processor receives a ticket, it migrates a task to the requesting processor. In the following we will describe our model in four aspects: transfer policy, location policy, information policy, and selection policy which have been referred to, in [10], as four basic components of a typical dynamic load balancing system.

Transfer Policy

The transfer policy determines whether a node is in a suitable state to participate in a task transfer, as sender or a receiver. Like many other load balancing methods, our model uses a load threshold policy. Two main thresholds T_{light} and T_{heavy} are used as in the gradient model. Besides, the model introduces an extra threshold T_{emerg} which indicates that the node is idle. Typically, for a processor with conventional CPU it is set to 1 while for the one with multi-threaded CPU it is set to the number of hardware contexts the CPU supports. These three thresholds, together with the local load index determines the local load state. The local load index of a processor is measured by the number of tasks in the (lazy) task queue (stack). The choice of this simple load index at this stage is justified by the high correlation of this parameter with the processor utilization rate, and by the simple and fast way to calculate it. If the load index falls below T_{emerg}, the processor is *idle*. When the load index is between T_{emerg} and T_{light}, it is *lightly loaded*, while the load index between T_{light} and T_{heavy}, it is *moderately loaded*, and finally if the load index exceeds the threshold T_{heavy}, it is said to be *heavily loaded*. Figure 1 depicts the transition diagram for these four states.

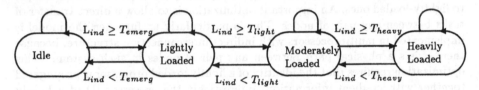

Fig. 1. State transition diagram of processor load

Note that the variation of the state transition frequency can be adjusted by the change of the load thresholds. The implications of local load states on load balancing actions are described as follows:

- Idle: this is an emergency load situation when the processor does not have any local task to compute. In order to get some work as soon as possible, it sends out an emergent request. Any processor, after receiving the request, should send the requesting processor a task if it is at least moderately loaded.
- Lightly loaded: this case means that the processor even does not have enough work to share with an idle processor because it has the risk to rapidly become idle itself. Moreover it still has some capacity to absorb tasks from heavily loaded processors to keep balanced load. Therefore it sends out normal request for work. Only a heavily loaded processor receiving this normal request will migrate a task to it.
- Moderately loaded: this is the state that a processor does not need neither to export tasks nor to input tasks in the normal load situation. When all processors in the system are working in this state, the system load is in an optimal and balanced way. However if it receives an emergency request, it should be allowed to migrate a task to the requesting processor. Note that the possibility of allowing the moderately loaded processors to migrate out tasks is strictly restricted to the situation that there exist idle processors in the

system but no heavily loaded processors, and it enables the idle processors to get some work even no processor in the system is heavily loaded.

– Heavily loaded: this load state indicates that a processor has too much work load, and wishes to migrate some of its work load to other processors.

To summarize, an idle or lightly processor is in a state to participate in a task transfer as a receiver, while a heavily loaded processor as a sender. A moderately loaded processor can be the sender of a task whose receiver is an idle processor.

The requests sent out by idle or lightly loaded processors are represented by tickets. The normal request for load is represented as a normal ticket, while the emergent request for load as an emergency ticket. Both types of tickets must carry the processor identifier.

Location Policy

After the transfer policy determines that a processor is a sender or receiver, the location policy is responsible for finding a suitable tranfer partner for the node. In our model, any heavily loaded processor can be the potential transfer partner of an idle or lightly loaded processor and any moderately loaded processor has the potential to become the transfer partner of an idle processor in the case that no heavily loaded processor exists in the system. However, only the processor which has got a ticket from a processor is allowed to be the real transfer partner of that processor. Now the main problem is how a ticket from an idle or lightly loaded processor can quickly reach a potential sender in a distributed environment. A natural solution is to relay the ticket to the potential sender which is nearest to the receiver (which issues the ticket). Thus as in the gradient model a gradient surface has to be established to facilitate the relay of load requests. However, the gradient surface is a system-wide indication of heavily loaded processors, instead of lightly loaded processors. Accordingly the proximity (using the terminology from the gradient model) w_i of a processor i is the minimum distance between the processor and a heavily loaded processor in the system. Thus the proximity of a heavily loaded processor is zero. The proximity of its immediately neighbouring processors is one as they are one hop away from the heavily loaded processor. The proximity of the neighbour's neighbor is two, and so on.

The gradient surface of the system is the collection of proximities of all processors, $[w_1, w_2, ..., w_n]$. Figure 2 illustrates the gradient surface of a multiprocessor with 16 processors interconnected to a 4 x 4 rectangular logical configuration. The gradient surface and the proximity distribution are shown in the figure at the load situation when the processor P_5 and P_7 are heavily loaded processors.

For the same reason as in the gradient model, our model uses the propagated pressure to approximate the proximity function. Correspondingly the propagated pressure p_i of a processor is defined as the function of local pressure and the propagated pressures of its neighbours, namely:

$$p_i = \min \{p_l, 1 + \min(\{p_j\})\}$$

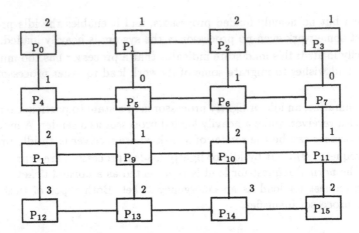

Fig. 2. A gradient surface with its proximity distribution

where p_l is zero if the processor i is heavily loaded, infinity otherwise, and $\{p_j\}$ is the set of propagated pressures of all neighbours of processor i.

The propagated pressure surface[3] of the system is a collection of propagated pressures of all processors, $[p_1, p_2, ..., p_n]$.

It is not difficult to see that the propagated pressure surface can serve as a minimum distance routing pointer for the relay of tickets from idle or lightly loaded nodes to heavily loaded ones. For the distribution of normal tickets, a non-heavily loaded processor, when receiving such a ticket, relays the ticket to one of its neighbours which has the smallest propagated pressure. If the propagated pressures of all of its neighbours are infinity, indicating there is no heavily loaded processor in the system, it then holds the ticket until the propagated pressures of its neighbours change. Here a possible optimization might be that an idle processor will not relay a received normal ticket until it becomes non-idle. This would reflect the higher priority of emergent task requests. Obviously a heavily loaded processor, after receiving a ticket, must migrate a task to the requesting processor. The distribution of an emergency ticket is similar to that of a normal one, with a small exception. That is, when a moderately loaded processor receives an emergency ticket, it must migrate a task to the idle processor which issues the ticket if the propagated pressures of all its neighbouring processors are infinity.

Information Policy

The information policy decides when information about the states of other nodes in the system is to be collected, from where it is collected, and what information is collected. The information policy in our model is a distributed one, and

---

[3] The pressure surface is sometimes also referred to as the gradient surface since it is an approximation of the actual gradient surface

relatively simple: a processor needs only to collect the propagated pressures of its neighbours, and it has to recompute its own propagated pressure only either when its local load state changes from heavily loaded to moderately loaded or vice versa, or when the propagated pressure from one of its neighbour changes. If the newly computed pressure is different from the old one, the processor then has to broadcast the newly computed pressure to all of its neighbours.

Selection Policy

Now the only remaining question is what task should be selected to be transferred if a processor has been decided to be a transfer partner of an idle or lightly loaded processor. This is the responsibility of the selection policy. Many existing load balancing systems choose to transfer one of the newly created tasks that caused the node to become a sender. Our model adopts a quite different approach: the oldest-first task selection strategy. When a processor becomes a sender, it selects the oldest available parallel task to be migrated. If the parallel computation is represented as a program tree, this means that the available fork point which is nearest to the root of the tree is chosen. Note that the oldest fork point usually represents the largest available-subtree and hence a task of maximal run-time granularity.

The implementation of this strategy can be very simple by using a two-end task stack[4]. The local processor accesses one end (the head) of the stack, and remote processors access (indirectly through load balancing unit) the other end (the tail). At the head of the task stack, the local processor, when encountering a fork point, pushes in new tasks into the stack, and pops out a task for execution if its current task is finished. At the tail of the task stack, the load balancing unit pops out a task for transfer if the processor becomes a sender, and pushes in tasks which are migrated from remote processors. Figure 3 shows a scenario that a subtree (starting from task T0) of a parallel binary tree is executed by a processor with its current execution thread reaching the subtask T5, and the corresponding structure of the Janus stack. From the figure, it is not difficult to see that any previously inputed tasks, e.g. Tr, will be migrated out earlier than local tasks if the processor becomes a sender. Moreover, older local tasks are migrated out earlier than younger ones, e.g. in the order T2, T4, and then T6. It is worthwhile to point out that T6, T4 and T2 can be easily coalesced to form a single thread if they are all executed in the local processor, because T4 is the continuation of T6, and T2 is that of T4.

This simple strategy has several important advantages: first, it can maintain good locality because local tasks are executed before the tasks migrated from other processors; second, it allows the tasks selected to be transferred to have a bigger granularity; and finally, it supports the dynamic task inlining according to the system load situation. The dynamic task inlining allows several small grained tasks to be coalesced to form a bigger grained task in order to reduce the overheads for task creations and task communications. A detailed discussion

---

[4] A two-end stack is sometimes referred to as Janus stack

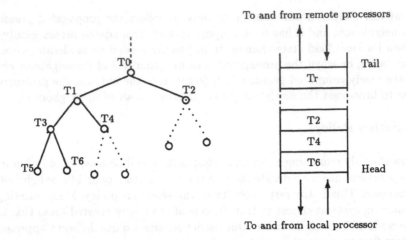

Fig. 3. A scenario of subtree being executed and the corresponding task queue

of the loaded based task inlining mechanism will be discussed in a separate paper.

Of course, there exist many sophisticated task selection strategies. The tasks chosen to be exported from a processor can also be guided by the information generated from a compiler-time analysis such as granularity analysis. Different strategies of choosing tasks to be exported intend to explore the following main properties:

- The tasks chosen to be exported should have reasonablely big granularity so that it is worthwhile to incur the transfer head.
- The tasks chosen to be exported should have as little interactions with other tasks so that synchronizations and communications are minimized between the two processors.

Further investigation is yet to be performed in this area, but it is out of scope of this paper.

5 Simulation and preliminary results

Trace-driven simulation is a popular technique used to evaluate multiprocessor design [5]. In order to perform a comparative study between the proposed load balancing model and the gradient model, we have developed a trace-driven simulator for each model.

Each simulator consists of two parts: Trace generation part and trace simulation part. The trace generation is functional simulation that executes the parallel programs and generates traces for the simluation of load balancing behaviours. The trace simulation is architectural simulation which takes into account of all the *relevant* archetectural details such as network topology, load balancing unit etc. Both simulators share the same trace generation part. This trace generator is build up on top of an extended OR-parallel Warrent Abstract Machine (WAM) simulator that we have designed to evaluate the parallel implemetation of functional and logic languages on the target multiprocessor architecture. Note that the OR-parallel execution of a logic program usually involves dynamic creations of many OR-parallel processes, which is very suitable for load balancing simulation. Besides, there is no direct synchronization and communication between OR-parallel processes, which can lead to a simpler simulation.

The trace simulation parts of the two simulators differ only in the load balancing unit. As a mattter of fact we have simplified the architecture designs in oder to focus on the simulation of the load balancing units. For example, the CPU is simply modelled as a two-end task stack. Since the interaction between load balancing and locality and granularity will be intensively studied in our future reseach, we neglect, at this stage, the design of multithreading, cache and its coherency protocol. In both simulators a logical rectangular configuation of processors is assumed. In the simulation, a typical cost ratio between a local and global memory reference is set to 1/10.

The parallel programs used in the simulations are directly taken from [2]. They exhibit different degrees of parallelism. For example, the BIN10, QUAD6 can generate many parallel tasks, while PERMUTE3, PERMUTE4 have poor parallelism, and LIST, SALESMAN in between. Using some typical inputs, they generate 512, 512, 15, 49, 183 and 211 parallel tasks respectively.

The reason for choosing a couple of programs with very poor parallelism is that the execution of a program with a limit number of parallel tasks will lead the system easily to reach the emergency load situation. Note that it is not unusual in real applications to have programs with small number of parallel tasks and whose execution times vary greatly. The gradient model usually have a very poor performace for this kind of programs. It must be pointed that due to the limited parallelism, the system speed up is very low. However it does not affect our evaluation because we are more interested in relative speedups under variation of a particular parameter than in absolute speedups.

The simulation results have shown a significant performance improvement of the extended gradient model over the gradient model for all the programs with different degrees of parallelism (see the figure 4).

This is due to the imporvement of average processor utilisation rate. In particular the performace gain is espcially obvious when the threholds are inproperly set or the application programs have very limited paralleism. Typically in the begining of a program execution some processors remain idle while some processors are building up their backlogged load because they are not allowed to export tasks before they reach heavily loaded states. This results in a very poor processor utilisation rate. The situation becomes even worse when the thresholds T_{heavy} is set unproportionally higher. In the final phase, some nodes already finish their work and then remain idle while some nodes are still active. Note that emergency load situation may also occur very often in the middle phase of program execution. In principle, as long as there are at least as many processes as

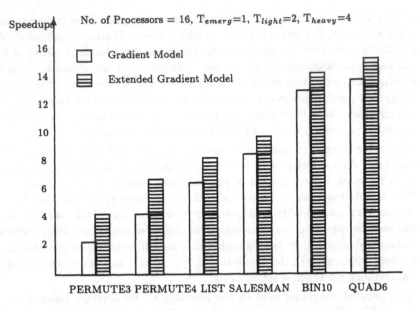

Fig. 4. The speedups of differet progrms on a 16-node multiprocessor

nodes in the system, the load can be redistributed by the load balancing system. From the figure 4, one can also see that the the performance improvement using the extended gradient model is particluarly obvious when application programs lack of parallelism.

Figure 5 and Figure 6 show the speedup curves for the multiprocessor scaling up from 1 node upto 16 nodes. The thresholds are set to 1-2-4 as in figure 4. Here we choose to use two programs with low and high degree parallelism respectively. In both figures, the performance gap between our extended gradient model and the gradient model becomes larger when the system scales up.

The siumlations have also shown some problems of the extended model. In particular, the number of global memory references has increased significantly using this model due to the efforts for keeping more balanced load distribution. This has offsetted lot of performance gain for the extended model. We hope that with the support of caching and multithreading techniques, the extra overheads due to the increased global memory references (communications) will be greatly reduced, and thus the performance gain of the extended model will be even more obvious.

6 Related Work

The work reported in this paper is related to three major works which are reported in [6], [9], and [8] respectively.

The gradient model developed by Lin and Keller has been demonstrated by analytical and simulation studies to be very suitable for large scale and dis-

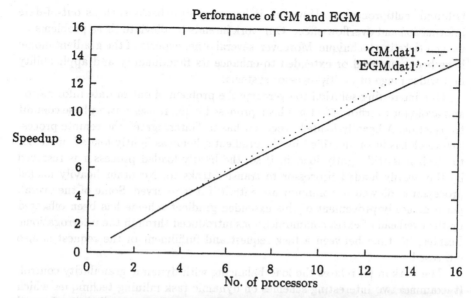

Fig. 5. The speedups of the system with gradient model and extended gradient model respectively for the program QUAD6

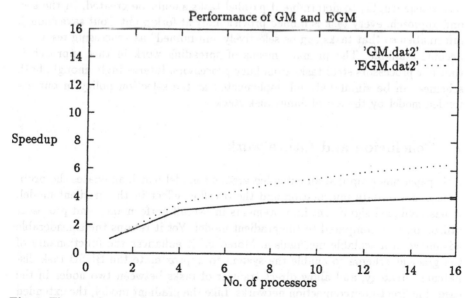

Fig. 6. The speedups of the system with gradient model and extended gradient model respectively for the program PERMUTE4

tributed multiprocessors. However, it has some drawbacks such as out-of-date information and overflow effect. Our work intends to alleviate these problems by using a ticketing technique. Moreover, several other aspects of the gradient model have been improved or extended to enhance its functionality and applicability in a wider range of multiprocessor systems.

One interesting solution to overcome the problem of out-of-date information and avoid the overflow effect has been proposed in [9]. It uses a two-phase commit transaction. A heavily-loaded processor has to "interrogate" the remote processor which has been identified by the gradient scheme as lightly loaded processor to see if it is still lightly loaded. If so, the lightly loaded processor is reserved by the heavily loaded processor to transfer tasks to. No other heavily loaded processor is allowed to communicate with it if it is reserved. Some of the overall performance improvement of this extended gradient scheme has been offsetted by the overhead of extra communications introduced through the interrogations. Besides, the time between a task request and fulfillment of the request is also increased.

The work in [8] relates the load balancing with dynamic granularity control. It examines two interesting schemes on dynamic task inlining techniques which are used to increase run-time granularity. The first scheme is called "load-based inlining", the second is "lazy task creation". In the first approach, parallel tasks are either created or inlined when fork points are encountered according to the load situation of the system. A load threshold T is used, in together with the task queue length, to determine if parallel tasks should be created. In the second approach, every task is inlined provisionally at fork points, but save enough information so that tasks can be selectively "un-inlined" as processing resources become available. The primary means of spreading work in this approach is that idle processors steal tasks from busy processors. Interestingly enough, both schemes can be simulated and implemented as the selection policy in our extended model by the aid of Janus task stack.

7 Conclusion and future work

This paper has proposed an extended gradient model which alleviates the problems of out-of-date information and the overflow effect in the gradient model. It has produced significant improvements in overall performance and processor utilization rate compared to the gradient model. Yet it retains the considerable advantage of a scalable mechanism. Moreover, it enhances the functionality of the gradient scheme to enable the system to approximate the BUSD task dispatching strategy, and allow direct transfer of tasks between two nodes in the case of indirect interconnection networks. Like the gradient model, the extended model migrates tasks according to a pressure gradient which is established by exchanging local load information between neighbouring processors. However the pressure gradient in the extended model is based on the heavily loaded processors instead of lightly-loaded processors as in the gradient model. This facilitates the propagation of tickets which carry the ID of an idle or lightly loaded processors. A heavily loaded processor can migrate a task to an idle or lightly loaded processor only when it receives a ticket from it. The simple and novel task selection policy can maintain good locality and large granularity of tasks. Moreover it facilitates dynamic task inlining strategies.

As an important future work, an intensive evaluation of the extended gradient model using a wider class of benchmarks will be performed. In particular, the interactions between load balancing, task locality and task granularity are to be investigated in the systems which employ caching techniques to reduce memory latency, and multithreading technique to hide latency. Another important work is to embed the lazy task creation technique in the model to form an effective task scheduling and load balancing system.

References

1. I. Ahmad and A. Ghafoor, *Semi-distributed load balancing for massively parallel multicomputer systems*, IEEE trans. Software Eng. 17(10) (Oct. 1991) 987-1004.

2. K.A.M. Ali and M. Wang, *An investigation of an OR-parallel model for Horn clause programs*, SICS research report, Sept, 1986.

3. M.J. Berger adn S. Bokhari, *A partitioning strategy for non-uniform problems on multiprocessors*, IEEE Trans. Computer, C-36, 5 (1987), 570-580.

4. T. Casavant and J.G. Kuhl, *A taxonomy of scheduling in general-purpose distributing systems*, IEEE Trans. Software Eng., 14(2) (Feb. 1988) 141-154.

5. R. Jain, *The art of computer systems performance analysis*, John Wiley and Sons, 1991.

6. F. Lin and R. Keller, *The gradient model load balancing method*, IEEE Trans. Software Eng., 13(1), (January 1987), 32-38.

7. R. Lulin, B. Monien and F. Ramme, *Load balancing in large networks: a comparative study*, 3rd IEEE Symp. on Parallel and Distributed Processing, Dallas 1991, 329-336.

8. E. Mohr, D. A. Kranz and R. H. Halstead, *Lazy Task Creation, A technique for Increasing the Granularity of Parallel Programs*, IEEE Transactions on Parallel and distributed systems, 1990.

9. F.J. Muniz and E.J. Zaluska, *Parallel Load-balancing: An extension to the gradient model*, Parallel Computing, No. 21, Jan, 1995.

10. N. G. Shivaratri, P. Krueger, and M. Singhal, *Load distributing for locally distributed systems*, IEEE Computer, December, 1992.

11. S. Nishimura and T.L. Kunii, *A decentralized dynamic scheduling scheme for transputer networks*, in T.L. Kunii and D, Nay, eds., Proc. 3rd Transputer/OCCAM int. conf., May, 1990, Tokyo, Japan.

12. R.D. Rettberg, W.R. Crowther, R.P. Carvey and R.S. Tomlinson, *The monarch parallel processor hardware design*, IEEE computer, April, 1990, 18-30.

13. V. Sarkar and J. Hennesey, *Compile-time partitioning and scheduling of parallel programs*, Proc. SIGPLAN'86 symp. compiler construction, 21(7), 1986, 17-26.

Efficient Parallel Permutation-Based Range-Join Algorithms on Mesh-Connected Computers

Shao Dong Chen   Hong Shen   Rodney Topor

School of Computing and Information Technology
Griffith University
Nathan, Queensland 4111, AUSTRALIA
Email: {schen,hong,rwt}@cit.gu.edu.au

Abstract. This paper proposes three efficient parallel algorithms for computing the range-join of two relations on two-dimensional $n \times m$ mesh-connected computers, where n and m are the numbers of the rows and columns respectively. After sorting all subsets of both relations, all proposed algorithms permute all sorted subsets of one relation to each processor in the computers, where they are joined with the subset of the other relation at that processor by using a sequential sort-merge range-join algorithm. The *Min-Storage-Shifting* and *Min-Movement-Shifting* algorithms permute the data on a mesh alternatively in the row and column directions, and *Hamiltonian-cycle* algorithm permutes the data along a Hamiltonian cycle of the mesh. The analysis shows that the Hamiltonian-cycle algorithm requires fewer local join operations but more data movements than other two algorithms and that the Min-Movement-Shifting algorithm requires fewer local join operations and data movements but more storage than the Min-Storage-Shifting algorithm.

Keywords: Relational Databases; Parallel Query Optimization; Range-join; Parallel Algorithms; Analytic Cost Models; Mesh-connected Multiple Computers.

1   Introduction

This paper presents and analyzes three new efficient parallel algorithms on two-dimensional mesh-connected computers for computing the range-join operations, which are the generalization of the conventional equi-join and band-join operations [5]. For two given constants e_1 and e_2 with $0 \leq e_1 \leq e_2$, the *range-join* of two relations R and S on attribute A from R and B from S, denoted by $R \bowtie_{e_1}^{e_2} S$, is the relation T obtained by concatenating all tuples r in R and s in S such that $e_1 \leq |r.A - s.B| \leq e_2$ [10]. Range-join operation is an important operation in relational database systems and appears frequently in practice, especially in the queries requiring joins over continuous real world domains such as time and distance. Moreover, since range-join operation is the generalization of the conventional equi-join and band-join operations, the range-join algorithms can be used to compute equi-join and band-join operations directly without any loss of efficiency.

As the join condition of range-joins involves range comparisons rather than equalities, hash-based join algorithms are unsuitable for range-join operations [5]. In contrast, permutation-based join algorithms, which are the parallel versions of sequential nested-loop join algorithms, have been shown to be effective for computing range-joins on hypercube computers [10]. In general, with the assumption that each relation is distributed evenly across all processors initially, permutation-based algorithms sort all subsets of both relations R and S, then permute each subset of S to every processor in turn, where it is joined with the local subset of R at that processor. The local range-join operation in each processor for two sorted subsets is implemented by a sequential sort-merge algorithm SSMRJ.

Obviously, the major problem for developing permutation-based range-join algorithms on a mesh-connected computer is how to permute data efficiently. In this paper, we develop two permutation methods which result in three different algorithms: *Min-Storage-Shifting* and *Min-Movement-Shifting* join algorithms which permute data in the row and column directions alternatively, and *Hamiltonian-cycle* join algorithm which permutes data along a Hamiltonian cycle of the mesh. We analyze and compare these algorithms in terms of running time and storage requirement. The Hamiltonian-cycle algorithm requires less storage and local join operations but more data movements than the other two algorithms; the Min-Movement-Shifting algorithm requires less local join operations and data movements but more storage than the Min-Storage-Shifting algorithm.

The remainder of this paper is organized as follows. In Section 2, we introduce the mesh computers and describe the permutation-based join algorithms in general. Our sequential sort-merge algorithm SSMRJ is presented and analyzed briefly in Section 3. The three mesh parallel range-join algorithms, which use this sequential algorithm in each individual processor, are presented and analyzed in Sections 4, 5 and 6 respectively. Section 7 concludes the paper by comparing the performance of these three parallel algorithms.

2 Preliminaries

A mesh-connected computer ("mesh" for short) is an SIMD parallel computer with mn processors, each having its own local memory and disk, without shared memory or disk. These processors are connected in an $n \times m$ two-dimensional grid. The processor in row i and column j is denoted by $P_{i,j}$, where $1 \leq i \leq n$ and $1 \leq j \leq m$. Each processor can transfer data from its local memory to one of its neighbors' local memory; concurrent data movements are allowed only when they are all in the same direction. There is no wraparound edge between the boundary processors and hence it presents more challenge tasks for designing algorithms on meshes than on toruses which have such wraparound edges.

Due to its flexibility and cost efficiency, the mesh is an important parallel computer system which supports many parallel algorithms [9] and has been used for many applications like image processing [6]. The current commercially available mesh-connected parallel computer is Intel Paragon XP/S [7]. For parallel database design, the share-nothing architecture is known to be more scalable to support very large databases than other architectures [4, 11]. The mesh is an important computer system characterized by the share-nothing architecture and has gained a considerable interest for parallel database design in the recent years [1, 8].

In a mesh, data are accessed and transferred in blocks and the number of blocks needed to store R and S are denoted by B_R and B_S respectively. We assume that both R and S are initially distributed evenly across all processors: As there are mn processors in the mesh, each processor contains one subset of R with B_R/mn blocks and one subset of S with B_S/mn blocks on its disk. (If this is not the case, we can apply the data smoothing technique [3] to balance the size of the subsets in the processors.)

Assume that data are accessed and transferred in blocks. Let T_{read} be the time required to read one block of data from disk to local memory, T_{write} the time to write one block of data to disk from local memory, T_{comm} the time to transfer one block of data from the local memory of one processor to that of its its neighbor, and $T_{compare}$ the time to compare two values of join attributes in memory. Permutation-based join algorithms consist of the following two phases:

1. Every processor simultaneously reads its subset of relation R, sorts it sequentially on the join attribute, and then applies the same process to relation S.
2. Every processor simultaneously computes the local range-join for its two local subsets of R and S, and then repeatedly reads the current subset of S from its neighbor and performs a local range-join operation on this arriving subset, until all subsets of S have visited each processor exactly once.

Phase 1 is a preprocessing step which makes the local range-join operations more efficient. The cost for this local sorting in each processor is much cheaper than any global sorting which must involve inter-processor communication. In addition, for range-joins, it is very difficult and inefficient by using global sorting to partition the relations into processors for computing the range-join individually in each processor.

Let $R_{i,j}$ and $S_{i,j}$ denote the subsets of R and S in processor $P_{i,j}$ respectively. Phase 1 can be implemented by the following statements:

for all processors $P_{i,j}$ **do in parallel**
    Read $R_{i,j}$ from disk to memory & sort it using a sequential sort algorithm;
    Read $S_{i,j}$ from disk to memory & sort it using a sequential sort algorithm;

whose running time is

$$T_{read} \cdot \frac{B_R + B_S}{mn} + T_{compare} \times \left(\frac{|R|}{mn} \log \frac{|R|}{mn} + \frac{|S|}{mn} \log \frac{|S|}{mn} \right).$$

In Phase 2, the local range-join operation for one sorted subset of R and one sorted subset of S is realized by a sequential sort-merge range-join algorithm presented and analyzed in the next section.

3 Sequential Sort-Merge Range Join

This section presents and analyzes an efficient sequential sort-merge algorithm which realizes the local range-join operation for two sorted subsets of both relations in a single processor. This local range-join algorithm is mainly based on standard sort-merge equi-join algorithm [12] with additional phases backwards to inspect previously considered tuples. The result tuples are stored in the local disk of each processor as they are produced, one block at a time

In a processor, its two subsets of relations R and S are denoted by R' and S', each having $|R'|$ and $|S'|$ tuples, and their i-th tuples are denoted by r_i and s_i. Tuples r_j of R' and s_i of S' are said to be *match* if either $r_j.A + e_1 \leq s_i.B \leq r_j.A + e_2$ (*the first condition domain*) or $r_j.A - e_2 \leq s_i.B \leq r_j.A - e_1$ (*the second condition domain*), where $1 \leq j \leq |R'|$ and $1 \leq i \leq |S'|$.

In our range-join algorithm, we search the matching tuples in R' for each tuple in S' in turn, starting from s_1 with the lowest join attribute value, until we meet one tuple s_t such that $s_t.B > r_{|R'|}.A + e_2$. Obviously, if the smallest join attribute value in one relation is greater than the largest join attribute value in the other relation plus c_2, no matching tuple can be found and hence the algorithm terminates. Two variables c_1 and c_2 for R' are used during the search, and initially they are 1.

For each s_i, we search the matching tuples in two condition domains in turn, each with an additional phase of backward inspection to the previous found matching tuples for s_{i-1}. The current c_1 and c_2 keep the indices of the last found matching tuples for s_{i-1} in the first and second condition domains respectively.

In the first condition domain, we search first toward r_1 (backwards) starting at r_{c_1}, then toward $r_{|R'|}$ (forwards), each continuing until either a non-matching tuple is found or the corresponding end point is met. We then update c_1 to the index of the last found matching tuple for s_i in the first condition domain. In the second condition domain, we search first toward r_{c_1} (forwards) starting at $r_{max\{c_1,c_2\}}$, then toward $r_{|R'|}$ (backwards), in the same way as in the first condition domain. We then update c_2 to the index of the last found matching tuple for s_i in the second condition domain. During each of backward-search in both condition domains, we inspect the tuples linearly since all matching tuples for s_i in one condition domain must be in consecutive positions. During each of forward-search, we use a binary-search to locate the first matching tuple and then inspect the following tuples linearly, so that we can avoid inspecting any non-matching tuples between the first matching tuple and the search starting points (c_1 or c_2).

Each matching tuple r_j is concatenated with s_i as soon as it is found. The result tuples, denoted by $r_j \circ s_i$ for $1 \leq j \leq |R'|$ and $1 \leq i \leq |S'|$, are stored in the local disk, as they are produced one block at a time. The algorithm is given as procedure *SSMRJ* (Sequential Sort Merge Range Join), where the searching processes in two condition domains are realized by a sub-procedure *RTJ* (Relation Tuple Join) as below:

procedure SSMRJ (R', S', e_1, e_2)
{Compute $R' \bowtie_{e_1}^{e_2} S'$ and write the result to disk.}

  procedure RTJ $(R', s_i, e_1, e_2, b, c)$
  {Given that c is the index of the last tuple r_j in R' satisfying
  $r_j.A + e_1 \leq s_{i-1}.B \leq r_j.A + e_2$ for s_{i-1}, for all r_j in R' within range $[b, |R'|]$
  such that $r_j.A + e_1 \leq s_i.B \leq r_j.A + e_2$, write $r_j \circ s_i$ to disk, and update c
  to the index of the last such tuple r_j.}
  begin {RTJ}
  1: {Search backwards starting from cursor c}
    $j := c$;
    while $(r_j.A + e_2 \geq s_i.B \geq r_j.A + e_1)$ **and** $(j \geq b)$ **do**
      Write $(r_j \circ s_i)$;
      $j := j - 1$;
  2: {Locate forward-search starting point j}
    if $(c < b)$ **then**
      {Assign j to the index of first matching tuple located by binary-search
      within range $[b, |R'|]$}
      $j := $ binary-search (R', s_i, b, e_2);
    else if $(j < c)$ **then**
      {Assign j to $c + 1$ if find any matching tuples found before c}
      $j := c + 1$;
    else
      {Assign j to the index of first matching tuple located by binary-search
      within range $[c + 1, |R'|]$}
      $j := $ binary-search $(R', s_i, c + 1, e_2)$;
  3: {Search forwards starting from j}
    while $(s_i.B \geq r_j.A + e_1)$ **and** $(j \leq |R'|)$ **do**
      Write $(r_j \circ s_i)$;
      $j := j + 1$;
  4: {Point c to the last matching tuple}
    $c := j - 1$
  end; {RTJ}

begin {SSMRJ}
  if $(s_1.B \leq r_{|R'|}.A + e_2)$ **and** $(r_1.A \leq s_{|S'|}.B + e_2)$ **then**
    $i := 1$; $c_1 := 1$; $c_2 := 1$;
    while $(s_i.B \leq r_{|R'|}.A + e_2)$ **and** $(i \leq n)$ **do**
      RTJ $(R', s_i, e_1, e_2, 1, c_1)$;
      RTJ $(R', s_i, -e_2, -e_1, c_1 + 1, c_2)$;

$$i := i + 1$$
end {SSMRJ}

Let l_r and l_s be the number of bytes needed by one tuple of R' and S' respectively, and hence the tuple in the resulting relation $R' \bowtie_{e_1}^{e_2} S'$, being the concatenation of two operand tuples, takes about $l_r + l_s$ bytes. Let l be the number of bytes in one block. The running time of the above procedure depends on how many matching tuples in R' found in backward-search and forward-search, and how many tuples need to be inspected for locating the first matching tuple in forward-search. For each s_i, let $\beta_i' \cdot |R'|$ and $\beta_i'' \cdot |R'|$ be the number of matching tuples found in backward- and forward-search, $\beta_i''' \cdot |R'|$ the number of tuples inspected for locating the first matching tuple in forward-search. Then the running time $T_{ssmrj}(|R'|, |S'|)$ of procedure SSMRJ is

$$2T_{compare} + T_{compare} \cdot |R'| \cdot \sum_{i=1}^{|S'|} (\beta_i' + \beta_i'' + \beta_i''') + T_{write} \cdot \frac{l_r + l_s}{l} \cdot |R'| \cdot \sum_{i=1}^{|S'|} (\beta_i' + \beta_i''),$$

where $0 \leq \beta_i' + \beta_i'' + \beta_i''' \leq 1$. The first term is the cost of checking whether S' and R' may have any matching tuples or not, the next one is the cost of finding the matching tuples in R' for every s_i, and the last term is the output I/O cost.

Note that, the above procedure SSMRJ for computing range-joins converges to the standard sort-merge join algorithm for computing equi-joins when $e_1 = e_2 = 0$.

Now the remaining problem is how to efficiently permute the subsets of S to all processors. Three new parallel algorithms have been developed to solve this problem on a mesh computer efficiently, and we are going to present and analyze them in the following three sections respectively.

4 Min-Storage-Shifting Parallel Join

We first start with a simple algorithm for permuting the subsets of S on a linear array with p processors. Let R_i and S_i denote the subset of relations R and S stored in processor P_i for $1 \leq i \leq p$. Initially, both R_i and S_i are in memory.

In the shifting algorithm for linear arrays, every processor performs a local join on its initial subsets R_i and S_i, then permutes all subsets of S in *rightward-shift* and *leftward-shift* phases in turn, each having $p - 1$ iterations. Before rightward-shift, P_i store S_i to S_i^o, and restores it after rightward- and leftward-shift.

During the j-th iteration of rightward-shift, P_i reads the subset of S from its left neighbor P_{i-1}, and then performs a local range-join on the new arriving subset of S, where $1 \leq j \leq p - 1$ and $j + 1 \leq i \leq p$. The leftward-shift phase is same as the rightward-shift phase except that the subsets of S are transferred in the reversed direction. The formal description of the shifting algorithm is given in the following procedure *LAP* (Linear Array Permute):

procedure LAP $(S_1, \ldots, S_p)$
{Permute S on linear arrays with p processors to compute the range-join
$\bigcup_{j=1}^{p}(S_j \bowtie_{e_1}^{e_2} R_i)$ in P_i for $1 \le i \le p$.}
begin
  1: **for** $i := 1$ **to** p **do in parallel**
      SSMRJ (R_i, S_i, e_1, e_2); {Compute $S_i \bowtie_{e_1}^{e_2} R_i$}
  2: **for** $i := 1$ **to** p **do in parallel**
      $S_i^o := S_i$; {Store S_i in S_i^o}
  3: **for** $j := 1$ **to** $p - 1$ **do**
      for $i := j + 1$ **to** p **do in parallel**
        {Move S_{i-1} 1-step right and join with R_i}
        3.1: $S_i := S_{i-1}$;
        3.2: SSMRJ (R_i, S_i, e_1, e_2);
  4: **for** $i := 1$ **to** p **do in parallel**
      $S_i := S_i^o$; {Restore S_i from S_i^o }
  5: **for** $j := p - 1$ **downto** 1 **do**
      for $i := j$ **downto** 1 **do in parallel**
        {Move S_{i+1} 1-step left and join with R_i}
        5.1: $S_i := S_{i+1}$;
        5.2: SSMRJ (R_i, S_i, e_1, e_2);
  6: **for** $i := 1$ **to** p **do in parallel**
      $S_i := S_i^o$ {Restore S_i from S_i^o again}
end

The above procedure consists of $2p - 2$ parallel movements, each requiring $T_{comm} \cdot B_S/p$ time, and $2p - 1$ parallel local range-join operations, each requiring $T_{ssmrj}(|R|/p, |S|/p)$. Assume each processor has enough memory to the subsets of S at any time, and hence there is no I/O operation required in Steps 2, 4 and 6. (The more detailed analysis for different cases of available memory can be found in [2].) We have the running time $T_{lap}(|R|, |S|, p)$ of procedure LAP as follows:

$$T_{comm} \cdot (p - 1)\frac{2B_S}{p} + (2p - 1) \cdot T_{ssmrj}(\frac{|R|}{p}, \frac{|S|}{p}).$$

The algorithm for linear arrays can be simply extended for meshes. In particular, the processors in the i-th row (for all $1 \le i \le n$) permute all subsets of S stored in that row by applying procedure LAP, so that these processors join their local subsets of R with every subset of S in the i-th row exactly once. Then all subsets of S in one row will be transferred in the *downward-shift* and *upward-shift* phases in turn, each having $n - 1$ iterations. Before downward-shift $P_{i,j}$ stores $S_{i,j}$ in $S_{i,j}^o$ and restores it after downward-shift.

During the j-th iteration of downward-shift, all processors in the i-th row simultaneously read the subsets of S from their neighbors in the $(i - 1)$-th row, and then apply procedure LAP, where $1 \le j \le n - 1$ and $j + 1 \le i \le n$. The upward-shift is same as the downward-shift except the subsets of S are moved in the reversed direction. The shifting algorithm for meshes is given as the following procedure *MSMP* (Minimal Storage Mesh Permute).

procedure MSMP (R, S)

{Permute relation S on an $n \times m$ mesh to compute $\bigcup_{k=1}^{n} \bigcup_{l=1}^{m} (S_{k,l} \bowtie_{e_1}^{e_2} R_{i,j})$
in $P_{i,j}$ for $1 \le i \le n$ and $1 \le j \le m$.}

begin

1: **for** $i := 1$ **to** n **do in parallel**
    LAP $(S_{i,1}, \ldots, S_{i,m})$; {Permute subsets of S in row i}

2: **for** $i := 1$ **to** n **do in parallel**
    for $j := 1$ **to** m **do in parallel**
        $S_{i,j}^{o} := S_{i,j}$; {Store $S_{i,j}$ in $S_{i,j}^{o}$}

3: **for** $j := 1$ **to** $n - 1$ **do**
    for $i := j + 1$ **to** n **do in parallel**
        3.1: **for** $k := 1$ **to** m **do in parallel**
            $S_{i,k} := S_{i-1,k}$; {Move the subsets of S 1-step down}
        3.2: LAP $(S_{i,1}, \ldots, S_{i,m})$; {Permute the subsets of S in row i}

4: **for** $i := 1$ **to** n **do in parallel**
    for $j := 1$ **to** m **do in parallel**
        $S_{i,j} := S_{i,j}^{o}$; {Restore $S_{i,j}^{o}$ to $S_{i,j}$}

5: **for** $j := n - 1$ **downto** 1 **do**
    for $i := j$ **downto** 1 **do in parallel**
        5.1: **for** $k := 1$ **to** m **do in parallel**
            $S_{i,k} := S_{i+1,k}$; {Move the subsets of S 1-step up}
        5.2: LAP $(S_{i,1}, \ldots, S_{i,m})$ {Permute the subsets of S in row i}

end

This procedure has $2n - 2$ parallel movements, each requiring $T_{comm} \cdot B_S / mn$
time, and $2m - 1$ procedure calls of LAP, each requiring $T_{lap}(|R|/n, |S|/n, m)$
time. Thus, the running time $T_{mp1}(|R|, |S|, m, n)$ of the above procedure is

$$(2m - 1)(2n - 1) \cdot T_{ssmrj}\left(\frac{|R|}{mn}, \frac{|S|}{mn}\right) + T_{comm} \cdot (2mn - 1n - 1m)\frac{2B_S}{mn}.$$

It is clear from the above algorithms that each processor in the mesh needs
to store three subsets of S during the permutation: the original subset and its
two copies before rightward- and downward-shift phases respectively.

5 Min-Movement-Shifting Parallel Join

From the preceding analysis, we know that the parallelism of the previous shifting algorithm is not very attractive. In particular, during the j-th iteration
of downward-shift, all processors on rows $1, \ldots, j$ are idle because they don't
receive any (new) subsets from their neighbors in other rows and hence they
cannot perform any local join operation at all. Similarly, during the j-th iteration of upward-shift, the processors on rows $j + 1, \ldots, n$ are idle. Moreover, the

more time each iteration requires, the longer idle period these processors have. In fact, the time for each iteration of both downward-shift and upward-shift is dominated by the time for the procedure call of LAP.

To obtain better parallelism performance, we develop a modified shifting algorithm in which every processor needs to store m subsets of S, where m is number of columns of the mesh. This algorithm consists of two phases. In the first phase, the algorithm permutes the subsets of S within each row as the previous shifting algorithm, but allows the processors to store every arriving subset. Thus, when this phase terminates, each processor $P_{i,j}$ stores all m subsets of S in row i. When receiving a new subset, $P_{i,j}$ stores it into a set $Q_{i,j}$ whose t-th element, denoted by $Q_{i,j}[t]$, is the t-th subset appended. Initially, $Q_{i,j}$ has only one element $S_{i,j}$.

Then in the second phase, the shifting algorithm then starts a loop with m steps. During the t-th step for $1 \leq t \leq m$, the t-th subset in every $Q_{i,j}$ in row i is transferred in the downward-shift and upward-shift phases in turn as in the previous shifting algorithm, but in each iteration, the procedure call of LAP in the previous algorithm is replaced by a local range-join for the arriving subset of S.

The first phase is realized by a procedure of a modified shifting algorithm for linear arrays, defined as the following procedure $MLAP$ (Modified Linear Array Permute).

procedure MLAP $(S_1, \ldots, S_p)$
{ Permute S on a linear array with p processors to compute the range-join
$\bigcup_{j=1}^{p}(S_j \bowtie_{e_1}^{e_2} R_i)$ in processor P_i for $1 \leq i \leq p$. Each processor stores all subsets of S in the linear array.}
begin
  1: **for** $i := 1$ **to** p **do in parallel**
     {Join S_i with R_i, and store into Q_i}
     1.1: SSMRJ (R_i, S_i, e_1, e_2);
     1.2: $Q_i[1] := S_i$;
  2: **for** $j := 1$ **to** $p-1$ **do**
     for $i := j+1$ **to** p **do in parallel**
     {Move S_{i-1} 1-step right, join with R_i and append to Q_i}
     2.1: $S_i := S_{i-1}$;
     2.2: SSMRJ (R_i, S_i, e_1, e_2);
     2.3: $Q_i := Q_i \cup S_i$;
  3: **for** $i := 1$ **to** p **do in parallel**
     $S_i := Q_i[1]$; {Restore S_i from $Q_i[1]$}
  4: **for** $j := p-1$ **downto** 1 **do**
     for $i := j$ **downto** 1 **do in parallel**
     {Move S_{i+1} 1-step left, join with R_i and append to Q_i}
     4.1: $S_i := S_{i+1}$;
     4.2: SSMRJ (R_i, S_i, e_1, e_2);
     4.3: $Q_i := Q_i \cup S_i$;
end

By calling the above procedure in the first phase, the modified shifting algorithm for meshes is defined as the following procedure *MMMP* (Minimal Movement Mesh Permute).

procedure MMMP (R, S)
{ Permute relation S on an $n \times m$ mesh to compute $\bigcup_{k=1}^{n} \bigcup_{l=1}^{m} (S_{k,l} \bowtie_{e_1}^{e_2} R_{i,j})$ in processor $P_{i,j}$ for $1 \le i \le n$ and $1 \le j \le m$.}
begin
  1: **for** $i := 1$ **to** n **do in parallel**
      MLAP $(S_{i,1}, \ldots, S_{i,m})$; {Permute every subset of S within its local raw}
  2: **for** $t := 1$ **to** m **do**
    2.1: **for** $i := 1$ **to** n **do in parallel**
       for $j := 1$ **to** m **do in parallel**
         $S_{i,j} := Q_{i,j}[t]$; {Restore $S_{i,j}$ from $Q_{i,j}[t]$}
    2.2: **for** $j := 1$ **to** $n-1$ **do**
       for $i := j+1$ **to** n **do in parallel**
         {Move every subset of S 1-step down & join with the subset of R}
         for $k := 1$ **to** m **do in parallel**
           2.2.1: $S_{i,k} := S_{i-1,k}$;
           2.2.2: SSMRJ $(R_{i,k}, S_{i,k}, e_1, e_2)$;
    2.3: **for** $i := 1$ **to** n **do**
       for $j := 1$ **to** m **do**
         $S_{i,j} := Q_{i,j}[t]$; {Restore $S_{i,j}$ from $Q_{i,j}[t]$}
    2.4: **for** $j := n-1$ **downto** 1 **do**
       for $i := j$ **downto** 1 **do**
         {Move every subset of S 1-step up & join with the subset of R}
         for $k := 1$ **to** m **do in parallel**
           2.4.1: $S_{i,k} := S_{i+1,k}$;
           2.4.2: SSMRJ $(R_{i,k}, S_{i,k}, e_1, e_2)$
end

Using the similar analysis in the previous section, we have the running time $T_{mlap}(|R|, |S|, p)$ of procedure MLAP

$$T_{comm} \cdot (p-1) \frac{2B_S}{p} + (2p-1) \cdot T_{ssmrj}(\frac{|R|}{p}, \frac{|S|}{p}),$$

and the running time $T_{mp2}(|R|, |S|, m, n)$ of procedure MMMP is

$$T_{comm} \cdot (mn-1) \frac{2B_S}{mn} + (2mn-1) \cdot T_{ssmrj}(\frac{|R|}{mn}, \frac{|S|}{mn}).$$

6 Hamiltonian-Cycle Parallel Join

There is a problem in the above two shifting permutation algorithms: When some processors perform the local range-join operations, the other processors are idle because no new subset arrives. This problem degrades the parallelism performance of these shifting algorithms, especially for the large local range-join operations. We hence develop another data permutation method *Hamiltonian-cycle permutation* which permutes the subsets of S along a Hamiltonian cycle of an $n \times m$ mesh for $n, m \geq 2$. In this method, a processor repeatedly reads the subset of S from its predecessor in a Hamiltonian cycle and performs a local join on the new arriving subset, until all subsets of S have visited each processor exactly once. The major and interesting problem is how to construct such a Hamiltonian cycle on a mesh.

We call an $n \times m$ mesh *even-sized* if either n or m is even. W.l.o.g., we assume that in an even-sized mesh the number of rows n is even. For an even-sized mesh, we can always construct a Hamiltonian cycle which is shown in Figure 1(a), where the vertices represent the processors and the arrows indicate the directions of data movements whose orders during the permutation are indicated by the numbers associated with them. Correspondingly, we have the following procedure *HCP* (Hamiltonian Cycle Permute):

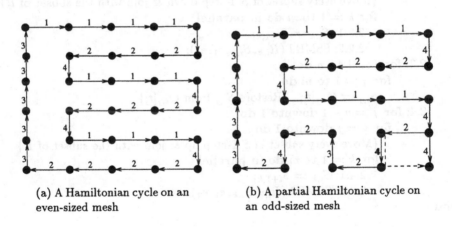

(a) A Hamiltonian cycle on an even-sized mesh

(b) A partial Hamiltonian cycle on an odd-sized mesh

Fig. 1. Data permutation patterns on meshes

procedure HCP (R, S)
{Permute S along the Hamiltonian cycle of an even-sized mesh and in $P_{i,j}$ for
  $1 \leq i \leq n$ and $1 \leq j \leq m$, compute $\bigcup_{k=1}^{n} \bigcup_{l=1}^{m} (S_{k,l} \bowtie_{e_1}^{e_2} R_{i,j})$}
begin
  1: **for** $i := 1$ **to** n **do in parallel**
      for $j := 1$ **to** m **do in parallel**
        SSMRJ $(R_{i,j}, S_{i,j}, \theta_1, e_2)$; {Compute $R_{i,j} \bowtie_{e_1}^{e_2} S_{i,j}$ in $P_{i,j}$}
  2: **for** $k := 1$ **to** $mn - 1$ **do**
    2.1: **for** $i := 1, 3, \ldots, n - 1$ **do in parallel**

for $j := 2 - \lfloor 1/i \rfloor$ to $m - 1$ do in parallel
$\quad S^p_{i,j+1} := S_{i,j};$ {Move $S_{i,j}$ rightward}
2.2: for $i := 2, 4, \ldots, n$ do in parallel
$\quad$ for $j := m$ downto $3 - \lfloor i/n \rfloor$ do in parallel
$\quad\quad S^p_{i,j-1} := S_{i,j};$ {Move $S_{i,j}$ leftward}
2.3: for $i := n$ downto 2 do in parallel
$\quad S^p_{i-1,1} := S_{i,1}$ {Move $S_{i,1}$ upward}
2.4: for $i := 1$ to n do in parallel
$\quad$ {Move $S_{i,m}$ or $S_{i,2}$ downward}
$\quad$ if $i \bmod 2 = 0$ then
$\quad\quad S^p_{i,m} := S_{i-1,m}$
$\quad$ else $S^p_{i,2} := S_{i-1,2};$
2.5: for $i := 1$ to n do in parallel
$\quad$ for $j := 1$ to m do in parallel
$\quad\quad$ {Move $S^p_{i,j}$ to $S_{i,j}$ and join with $R_{i,j}$}
$\quad\quad$ 2.5.1: $S_{i,j} := S^p_{i,j};$
$\quad\quad$ 2.5.2: SSMRJ $(R_{i,j}, S_{i,j}, e_1, e_2)$
end

This algorithm requires $(mn - 1)$ iterations to transfer all subsets of S to all processors, and each iteration requires 4 parallel data movements because parallel data movements can be carried out only in one direction at each step in an SIMD computer. Similarly, some processors (such as $P_{n,m}$) need to store two subsets of S in each iteration when they read subsets from their predecessors before transferring their subsets to their successors. The running time $T_{hcp}(|R|, |S|, m, n)$ of procedure HCP is

$$T_{comm} \cdot (mn - 1)\frac{4B_S}{mn} + mn \cdot T_{ssmrj}(\frac{|R|}{mn}, \frac{|S|}{mn}).$$

A mesh is said to be *odd-sized* if both its n and m are odd. We prove that an odd-sized mesh doesn't contain any Hamiltonian cycle by contradiction as follows. We color the mesh like a chess-board, that is, all the neighbor processors are in different colors. Suppose that such a Hamiltonian cycle exists. Starting from any processor P, this Hamiltonian cycle meets one processor in the different color from P. Similarly, the next processor which the Hamiltonian cycle meets is in the same color P, and so on. Since the total number of processors in this mesh is *odd*, the last processor P' which Hamiltonian cycle meets must in the same color as P and hence P' cannot be the neighbor of P. By contradiction, we know that there is no such a Hamiltonian cycle in the odd-sized mesh.

For an odd-side mesh, we can construct a partial Hamiltonian cycle connecting all processors except the right-bottom corner processor $P_{n,m}$. For example, Figure 1(b) shows such a partial Hamiltonian cycle for a 7×7 mesh. The subset of S stored in $P_{n,m}$ is evenly redistributed to other $mn - 1$ processors in the mesh, each processor receiving one fragment with $|S|/mn(mn - 1)$ tuples, but the subset of R is still kept in $P_{n,m}$'s memory. The fragment from $P_{n,m}$ is merged into the initial subset of S in each processor, so that the new combined subset of S is also in the sorted order, which is required by procedure SSMRJ.

In the algorithm for the odd-sized mesh, as in the algorithm for the even-sized mesh, all processors in the partial Hamiltonian cycle simultaneously perform a local range-join on their initial subsets of R and the (combined) subsets S, and then every processor repeatedly reads the subset of S from its predecessor along the cycle followed by a local range-join on the new arriving subset of S, until all subsets of S have visited each processor in the cycle exactly once. We also assume that two combined subsets of S can fit in the memory of every processor at any time in the algorithm for the odd-sized mesh.

In order to use the right-bottom processor $P_{n,m}$ which is not on the partial Hamiltonian cycle, the algorithm for the odd-sized mesh allows $P_{n,m}$ to read the subset of S from processor $P_{n-1,m}$ during the permutation. Thus, processor $P_{n,m}$ can join its local subset of R with all subsets of S in the partial Hamiltonian cycle except the one $S_{n-1,m-1}$ initially stored in processor $P_{n-1,m-1}$ because $S_{n-1,m-1}$ will stop at processor $P_{n-1,m}$ as soon as it traverses the cycle once. To solve this problem, $P_{n,m}$ reads $S_{n-1,m-1}$ and joins it with the local subset of R before the permutation (see the dashed arrow in Figure 1(b)).

7 Concluding Remarks

We have presented three new parallel permutation-based algorithms on an $n \times m$ mesh to efficiently compute the range-join of two relations. After initially sorting all subsets of both relations, all three proposed algorithms permute all sorted subsets of one relation to each processor in meshes, where they are joined with the subset of the other relation at that processor by using a sequential sort-merge range-join algorithm SSMRJ.

Each of the permutation algorithms has its own features: If the communication time T_{comm} for transferring one block data between two neighboring processors is greater than the time T_{ssmrj} for the local range join operations of two sorted subsets, the Hamiltonian-Cycle algorithm is the most efficient algorithm and requires the least storage. Otherwise, if the processors in the mesh can store m subsets of S, the Min-Movement-Shifting algorithm becomes the best approach because it takes the least communication time. If it is not the case, then the Min-Storage-Shifting algorithm is preferred although it takes more communication time and local join operations than the Min-Step-Shifting algorithm does. This suggests that, in order to achieve the most efficient, we should apply different algorithms for different configurations of meshes.

It is worthwhile to note that, as the range-join operation is the generalization of the conventional equi-join and band-join operations, all three proposed range-join algorithms can be used to compute equi-join and band-join operations without any loss of efficiency. Moreover, these permutation algorithms are general methods for data permutation on a mesh and can be applied for solving other problems whose main communication pattern is data permutation.

Future research tasks are to implement the proposed algorithms on a suitable parallel machine for performance evaluation, and to extend the algorithms for higher dimension meshes.

References

1. S. Chakravarthy and I. V. Ramakrishnan. Use of mesh connected processors for realizing fault tolerant relational database operations. In *PARBASE-90 International Conference on Databases, Parallel Architectures and Their Applications*, pages 568–70, Miami Beach, FL, USA, Mar. 1990.

2. S. D. Chen, H. Shen, and R. W. Topor. Efficient parallel permutation-based range-join algorithms on mesh-connected computers. Technical Report CIT-94-19, CIT, Griffith University, Australia, Aug. 1994.

3. S. D. Chen, H. Shen, and R. W. Topor. An improved hash-based join algorithm in the presence of double skew on a hypercube computer. In *Proceedings of the Seventeenth Australia Computer Science Conference*, Christchurch, New Zealand, Jan. 1994.

4. D. J. DeWitt and J. Gray. Parallel database systems: The future of high performance database systems. *CACM*, 35(6):85–98, 1992.

5. D. J. DeWitt, J. F. Naughton, and D. A. Schneider. An evaluation of Non-Equijoin algorithms. In *Proceedings of the Seventeenth International Conference on VLDB*, Barcelona, Spain, Sept. 1991.

6. M. Hamdi and R. W. Hall. Image processing on augmented mesh connected parallel computers. *Journal of Computer and Software Engineering*, 2(3):329–48, 1994.

7. Intel Corporation. Intel Corporation literature, Nov. 1991.

8. H. Jhang. Performance comparison of join on hypercube and mesh. In *1992 ACM Computer Science Conference*, pages 243–50, Kansas City, MO, USA, 1992.

9. F. T. Leighton. *Introduction to Parallel Algorithms and Architectures: Arrays Trees Hypercubes*. Morgan Kaufmann Publishers, San Mateo, California, 1992.

10. H. Shen. An improved selection-based parallel range-join algorithm in hypercubes. In *Proceedings of the 20th EUROMICRO Conference*, pages 65–72, Liverpool, UK, Sept. 1994.

11. M. Stonebraker. The case for shared nothing. *Database Eng.*, 9(1), 1986.

12. J. D. Ullman. *Principles of Database and Knowledge Base Systems*, volume 2. Computer Science Press, 1989.

Pipelined Band Join in Shared-Nothing Systems

Hongjun Lu   Kian-Lee Tan

Department of Information Systems & Computer Science
National University of Singapore

Abstract. A non-equijoin of relations R and S is a band join if the join predicate requires values in the join attribute of R to fall within a specified band about the values in the join attribute of S. Traditionally, R and S are split into partitions that are assigned to processors for the join to be executed concurrently and independently. Since the join is a non-equijoin, some records of R (or S) must appear in more than one partition, i.e. some records are replicated across two or more partitions. This may lead to poor performance especially when the number of records to be replicated is large. This paper presents a new algorithm, called the pipelined band join. The algorithm avoids data replication in secondary storage by dynamically creating partitions during join computation through pipelining. A preliminary study indicates that the proposed algorithm outperforms the conventional method.

1 Introduction

Among the three generic parallel database architectures [15] – *shared-memory, shared-disk* and *shared-nothing* – the shared-nothing architecture is especially attractive because of its scalability and reliability [1, 3, 4]. Such a system comprises a set of processing nodes interconnected through a communication network. Each node has its own local memory and disk drives. A processor at one node has no direct access to memory or disks of other nodes. Data sharing among processors is realized by some message-passing mechanisms. To achieve high degree of parallelism, the objects of a relation are distributed across some number of nodes. In this way, each node can process the portion of database on its disk independently. Examples of shared-nothing systems include Gamma [3], Bubba [1], NonStop SQL [6] and DBC/1012 [16].

The relational join operation [2] is one of the most important and frequently used operation that combines records from two or more relations. Records are combined when they satisfy a specified *join condition*. A *band join*[1] between two relations, R and S, on the attributes $R.A$ and $S.B$ has join condition of the form:

$$S.B - c_1 \leq R.A \leq S.B + c_2$$

---

[1] The term *band* is used because a record r in R contributes to the join result only if $r.A$ appears within a "band" of size $c_1 + c_2$ about $s.B$ [5].

where c_1 and c_2 are constants that may be equal, and either one of them, but not both, may be zero. When both c_1 and c_2 are zero, we have the *equijoin* operation.

Band joins arise in queries that require joins over continuous domains such as time or distance. For example, suppose records in R and S represent events, and the attributes $R.A$ and $S.B$ represent the times at which events occur. To answer a query for all pairs of events that occurred at nearly the same time requires a band join. Band values are not restricted to only numerical values, but can also be defined for strings or any other data types whose values can be totally ordered.

As pointed out in [5], a critical parameter of a band join is the number of records within one band. In [5, 13], it was assumed that the bands are small enough so that each record of a relation joins with no more than a few records of the other relation. However, this may not be true in general, especially when the join attribute values are highly duplicated. Even for the constants c_1 and c_2 to take on small values, the number of records within the band may still be large. For example, consider a relation of 1M records with 10K distinct join attribute values. Even when the records are uniformly distributed, and both c_1 and c_2 are equal to 1, there are 300 records within the band!

While a large number of join algorithms have been proposed for processing equijoins ([11] provides a good survey on existing join algorithms), only few papers on processing band joins have appeared in the literature [5, 13]. In multiprocessor systems, R and S are, traditionally, split into partitions that are assigned to processors for the join to be executed concurrently and independently. Since the join is a non-equijoin, some records of R (or S) must appear in more than one partition, i.e. some records are replicated across two or more partitions. This may lead to poor performance especially when the number of records to be replicated is large.

This paper presents a new partition-based algorithm for band joins, called the pipelined band join, in the context of shared-nothing multiprocessor systems. The algorithm is inspired by the temporal join algorithm proposed in [14]. The novel feature of our algorithm is that each partition of R will join with its corresponding partition of S without replicating records in the secondary storage. This is achieved by dynamically creating partitions during join computation through pipelining. A preliminary study indicates that the proposed algorithm outperforms the conventional method.

The remainder of this paper is organized as follows. In the next section, we state our assumptions and review some related work. Section 3 discusses the issues in partition-based band join algorithms. In particular, the hybrid range-partitioned band join algorithm proposed in [5] is discussed in greater depth since it will be used for comparison with the proposed algorithm. In Section 4, we present the proposed pipelined band join algorithm. Section 5 presents a preliminary performance study and its results, and finally, we conclude in Section 6 with directions for future research.

2 Preliminaries

The following assumptions are made in the remainder of the paper: we will use two relations R and S which do not have any auxiliary access paths such as indices; both relations are too large to fit in the total system memory; and all the records within the band fit in the memory of a processor. We have also assumed that relations are initially horizontally declustered across all the processors in order to increase the aggregate I/O bandwidth provided by the system.

Like equijoins, algorithms for band joins can be categorized into three approaches: the *nested-loops*, the *sort-merge* and the *hash-based* techniques. Each approach has a domain of applications where it performs better than the others, depending on parameters such as the size of the available buffer, and the distribution of join attribute values.

Nested-loops algorithms are the simplest but least efficient unless one of the relations fits in the total system memory. It picks one relation as the *outer relation* and designates the other as the *inner relation*. For each record of the outer relation, all records of the inner relation are read and compared with it. The main disadvantage of the nested-loops algorithms is that the inner relation may be scanned several times. The sort-merge algorithm first sorts both relations on the join attribute. The two sorted relations are then scanned simultaneously to produce the join result. Sort-merge algorithms perform best when the relations are already sorted. Otherwise, the cost of performing the sort operations must be included as part of the join cost, which makes the algorithm less efficient. Recently, several hash-based algorithms have been proposed for band joins [5, 13]. The basic idea is to split the two relations into partitions so that only corresponding partitions from the relations need to be joined. These algorithms perform efficiently when enough memory is available and when the join attribute values are distinct. In this paper, we focus on partition-based band join algorithms.

3 Partition-based Band Join Algorithms

Partition-based algorithms comprise two phases. In the first phase, relation R is range-partitioned into partitions R_1, R_2, ..., R_k. Relation S is also range-partitioned into the same number of partitions. In phase two, each partition of R, R_i, is joined with the corresponding partition of S, S_i, to produce resultant records. The two basic issues to be addressed are

1. How to ensure that each partition of R, R_i, fits in the memory of a processor?
2. How to ensure that, for every record r in R_i, all records of S that are joinable with r appear in S_i? To ensure this, the range of records in S_i must overlap the range of records in R_{i-1}, R_i and R_{i+1}. The range of the overlap is at most $c_1 + c_2$. There must also be an overlap between S_i and S_{i+1} of size $r_1 + r_2$ as well. Figure 1 illustrates the ranges for the partitions.

Let the join condition be $S.B - c_1 \leq R.A \leq S.B + c_2$. In [5], partitioned-based algorithms were proposed to handle the two issues as follows:

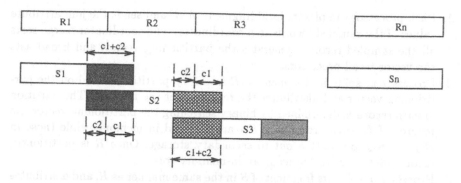

Fig. 1. Partitions for the band join $S.B - c_1 \leq R.A \leq S.B + c_2$.

1. To ensure that each partition of R fits in the memory of a processor, sampling techniques are employed. For uniprocessor systems, to guarantee that with 99% probability all partitions fit in the memory, the number of samples, s, required is given by:

$$\frac{1.628 \cdot |R|}{\sqrt{n}} \leq |R| \cdot (F - 1) \tag{1}$$

where F is the ratio of the buffer pool size to the size of a R partition. $|R| \cdot (F - 1)$ is the number of buffer pages available to handle any overflow due to errors in the estimation of the partitioning values. However, in multiprocessor systems, to ensure random sampling, collecting samples for R in parallel must be performed as if it were stored on a single processor. In [5], each processor samples s records from its local fragment of R as follows: as each processor generates a random record, it checks the local catalog information to determine if the record is stored on its local disk; if so, the record is retrieved from the disk and its join attribute value is sampled; otherwise the sample is ignored.

2. To ensure that all records of S that join with R_i must appear in S_i, some records of S are replicated across two partitions. If h_i is the greatest value appearing in $R.A$ in some record of R_i, and l_i is the least value appearing in $R.A$ in some record of R_i, then S_i must contain all records s such that $l_i - c_2 \leq s.B \leq h_i + c_1$.

In this paper, we consider the hybrid range-partitioned band join algorithm, which was shown to perform best in [5]. Suppose there are p processors, and p_i denotes the ith processor ($1 \leq i \leq p$). The algorithm partitions R into $k \cdot p$ partitions (for some integer k), and each processor is assigned k partitions. We denote the jth partitions of R at processor p_i as R_{ij}. The algorithm works as follows:[2]

---

[2] The original algorithm in [5] assumes that R fits in the total memory of the system, and so $k = 1$.

1. Each processor samples its local fragment of R, and sends the join attribute values of the sampled records to a coordinator. The coordinator merge-sorts all the sampled records, generates the partitioning vector, and broadcasts the vector to all processors.

2. Processor p_i splits its fragment of R into $k \cdot p$ partitions based on the partitioning vector and distributes the records over the network. The partition of each record is determined by binary searching the partitioning vector. As records of R arrive, records in R_{i1} are retained in memory; while those in $R_{i2}, \ldots, R_{ik}$ are written out to secondary storage. Once R is partitioned, records of R_{i1} are sorted using an in-memory sort.

3. Processor p_i splits its fragment of S in the same manner as R, and distributes the records over the network. As records of R arrive, records in S_{i1} are immediately used to join with records in R_{i1}; while the other partitions are written out to secondary storage. Since each record of S may join with the neighboring partitions, some records of S are replicated across more than one partitions.

4. For each of the remaining partitions of R at processor p_i, R_{ij}, $2 \leq j \leq k$, the following is performed: Read R_{ij} into the memory and sort the records using an in-memory sort. Then S_{ij} is read; for each record of S_{ij}, a binary search is performed on the R_{ij} records to find the first joining record of R_{ij}. Other joining records can be found by scanning R_{ij} beginning at the first joining record.

4 Pipelined Partition-based Band Join

The hybrid range-partitioned band join algorithm has a major disadvantage: some records of S have to be replicated to at least two partitions. If the band size is large, the number of records replicated may be large. This will lead to high I/O, CPU as well as communication cost. In this section, we present a new partition-based algorithm, called the pipelined band join, which is inspired by the algorithm proposed in [14]. For a join condition of $S.B - c_1 \leq R.A \leq S.B + c_2$, our algorithm ensures that each partition of R will join with the corresponding partition of S without replicating records in secondary storage. This is achieved by creating the partitions of S that join with partitions of R dynamically. In other words, only when S_i is to be joined with R_i do we have the partition S_i. Using the same notations as in the previous section, the algorithm works as follows:

1. Each processor samples its fragment of R to determine the partitioning vector as in the hybrid range-partitioned algorithm.

2. Each processor generates partitions for R in the same manner as the hybrid range-partitioned algorithm.

3. For S, we have two scenarios:

   (a) Each processor generates partitions for S_{i1} for $1 \leq i \leq p$ in the same manner as the hybrid range-partitioned algorithm. In other words, records of S_{i1} contains duplicates, and are immediately joined with R_{i1} without storing in the disks.

(b) For S_{ij}, $1 \leq i \leq p$, $2 \leq j \leq k$, instead of generating partitions, *buckets* which are subsets of partitions are generated. Let l_{ij} and h_{ij} be the least and highest value in R_{ij}. There are two types of buckets:

i) A record $s \in S$ belongs to B_{ij} for $1 < i \leq p$, $1 < j \leq k$ if

$$l_{ij} + c_1 \leq s.B \leq h_{ij} + c_1$$

ii) A record $s \in S$ belongs to B_{1j} for $1 < j \leq k$ if

$$l_{ij} - c_2 \leq s.B \leq h_{ij} + c_1$$

Thus B_{1j} overlaps buckets $B_{p(j-1)}$ for $1 < j < k$, while the other buckets do not contain any duplicates though some records may participate in more than one partitions. Figure 2(a) illustrates the jth partitions and buckets at each processor. Note that $B_{ij} \subset S_{ij}$ for $1 < i \leq p$, and $B_{1j} = S_{1j}$.

4. For each partition S_{ij}, $2 \leq j \leq k$ at processor p_i, the joining process proceeds as follows.

(a) Read R_{ij} and sort the records as in hybrid range-partitioned algorithm.

(b) Read B_{ij}, and use the records to join with R_{ij}. However, since some records of B_{ij} will join with $R_{(i+1)j}$, these records are sent to processor $i+1$ $(i < p)$. Processor p_i $(1 < i \leq p)$ receives records from processor p_{i-1}, and immediately joins these records with R_{ij}. In this way, partition S_{ij} is created dynamically and joined with R_{ij}. Figure 2(b) illustrates the join computation for bucket j.

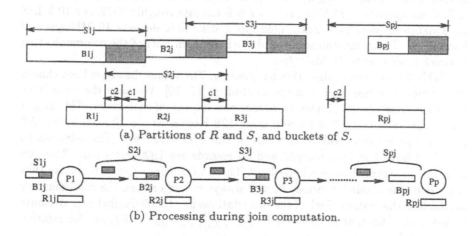

(a) Partitions of R and S, and buckets of S.

(b) Processing during join computation.

Fig. 2. Pipelined hash-based band join.

We further introduced two optimizations:

1. Since B_{1j} overlaps buckets $B_{p(j-1)}$ for $1 < j < k$, partitions R_{1j} and $R_{p(j-1)}$ are assigned to the same processor (so are B_{1j} and $B_{p(j-1)}$). In this way, only one copy of the overlapped records need to be stored.

2. If the records are evenly distributed across the partitions, processors 1 and p are likely to become the bottleneck because of the overlapped records. To overcome this, partitions R_{1j} and $R_{p(j-1)}$ are smaller than the rest (so will B_{1j} and $B_{p(j-1)}$).

5 Analytical Comparison

In this section, we present an analytical comparison of the hybrid range-partitioned and the pipelined band join algorithms. The I/O, CPU cost and communication cost at each processor are derived. As in [8, 9], we assume that there is total overlap between the I/O, CPU and communication operations within each phase, and there is no overlap between phases of an algorithm. We have not included the cost to write out the results since this cost will be the same for both algorithms.

5.1 Parameters used in cost model

The system parameters of the cost model are shown in Table 1. In choosing the parameters, we sought to follow the Amdahl/Case Rule of Thumb [7], as well as representing machines which are available today or will be available in the near future. Our settings are also similar to those used in [8, 9]. Towards this end, we have modeled a 25 Mhz processor. On database workloads, a good rule of thumb is that it takes roughly 2.5 clock ticks per instruction on RISC processors [17]. Consequently, a 25 Mhz processor will execute roughly 25/2.5 or 10 MIPS on a database workload. Each node has a disk that delivers 10 Mbits/sec of bandwidth. The communication bandwidth for each port of the communication network is also set to 10 Mbits/sec.

Table 2 lists various algorithm parameters. The values that have been chosen are similar to those used in previous studies [12, 10]. We have chosen a large I/O block size of 256 Kbytes to reduce the impact of disk seeks. This is not unreasonable since DB2 is already using 128 Kbytes as the I/O block size. All page-size parameters will be in terms of this I/O block size. The relations to be joined have 1 million records, and all records are 1000 bytes long. The join attribute is assumed to be 8 bytes long. These values are selected to ensure that the size of the smaller relation, R, will always be larger than the total memory available in the system. Each of the two relations has 10000 distinct join attribute values. Note also that for relation R, $\sum_{i=1}^{p} \sum_{j=1}^{k} \|R_{ij}\| = \|R\|$, but for relation S, $\sum_{i=1}^{p} \sum_{j=1}^{k} \|S_{ij}\| \geq \|S\|$ because of duplicate records.

Derived parameters are listed in Table reftab:table3. Most of the equations should be self-explanatory. Note that, in all the equations, CPU operations are implicitly divided by the processor MIPS rate. Thus, CPU costs are in terms of time rather than instruction counts. For example, the time to move a record

Parameter	Description	Default
mhz	clock rate of an individual processor	25 Mhz
cpi	average number of clock cycles per instruction	2.5
p	number of nodes in the system	32
d	number of disks per node	1
m	memory per processor available for join processing	10 Mbytes
io_{init}	CPU instructions to initiate an I/O	5000
io_{setup}	device time to setup an I/O	1 msec
io_{seek}	seek time of an individual disk	10 msec
$io_{latency}$	rotational latency of an individual disk	5 msec
$io_{bandwidth}$	I/O bandwidth of a disk	10 Mbits/sec
$comm_{bandwidth}$	communication channel bandwidth per node	10 Mbits/sec
$comm_{size}$	communication block size	8 Kbytes

Table 1. System parameters.

Parameter	Description	Default
io_{size}	I/O block size	256 Kbytes
$\|R\|(\|S\|)$	cardinality of relation R (S)	1000000
D	number of distinct join attribute values	10000
r	record size for all relations	1000 bytes
ja	size of the join attribute	8 bytes
$comp$	instructions to compare join attributes	100
$keyswap$	time to exchange two keys	100
$move$	instructions to move a record in memory	200
$send$	instructions to initiate sending a packet	5000
$recv$	instructions to initiate receiving a packet	5000
k	number of partitions assigned to each processor	variable
$\|R_{ij}\|(\|S_{ij}\|)$	cardinality of jth partition of R (S) at node i	variable
$bandsize_{ij}$	number of records within the band for partition R_{ij}	variable

Table 2. Algorithm parameters.

in memory is denoted as t_{move} and is equal to $move/MIPS$ sec. The only exceptions are t_{send} and t_{recv} (and $\hat{t}_{send}$ and $\hat{t}_{recv}$) which represent the amortized time to send and receive a record (join attribute) through and from the communication network respectively, that is, $t_{send} = send/mips \cdot r/comm_{size}$ and $t_{recv} = recv/mips \cdot r/comm_{size}$ (instead of r, ja is used for join attributes).

Parameter	Description
$mips$	effective MIPS rate of a single processor $mips = mhz/cpi$
$\lvert R \rvert$	size of an arbitrary relation R in blocks $\lvert R \rvert = \left\lceil \frac{\lVert R \rVert \cdot r}{io_{size}} \right\rceil$
$io_{sequential}$	time to perform a sequential block I/O $io_{sequential} = io_{setup} + io_{latency} + io_{size}/io_{bandwidth}$
io_{random}	time to perform a random block I/O $io_{random} = io_{seek} + io_{sequential}$
t_{comm}	time to send a record through the network $t_{comm} = r/comm_{bandwidth}$
$\hat{t}_{comm}$	time to send a join attribute through the network $\hat{t}_{comm} = ja/comm_{bandwidth}$
$find\_partition$	time to find the partition from the partitioning vector $find\_partition = log_2(k \cdot p) \cdot comp$
$sort(A)$	time to sort the records in memory $sort(A) = log_2(A) \cdot (keyswap + comp) + move$
$find\_firstjoin(A)$	time to find the first joining records $find\_firstjoin(A) = log_2(A) \cdot comp$

Table 3. Derived parameters.

5.2 Cost Equations

Hybrid range-partitioned band join

Cost to generate partitioning vector
Let $s \cdot p$ be the total number of samples to be taken, and is determined by Equation 1. For simplicity, we assume that each processor will take s samples. The cost to determine the partitioning vector for R includes the cost to 1) read the samples, 2) sort the local samples, 3) send the samples to the coordinator, 4) receive the partitioning vector from the coordinator. The coordinator must also 1) merge the samples and 2) broadcast the partitioning vector to all the processors. Consequently, at an arbitrary processor p_i which is not a coordinator,

$$io_i = s \cdot io_{random}$$

$$cpu_i = s \cdot io_{init} + s \cdot log_2(s) \cdot (t_{keyswap} + t_{comp}) + s \cdot \hat{t}_{send} + (k \cdot p - 1) \cdot \hat{t}_{recv}$$

$$comm_i = (s + k \cdot p - 1) \cdot \hat{t}_{comm}$$

At the coordinator, p_{coord}, the CPU and communication cost become

$$cpu_{coord} = s \cdot io_{init} + s \cdot log_2(s) \cdot (t_{keyswap} + t_{comp}) + (p-1) \cdot s \cdot \hat{t}_{recv} +$$
$$p \cdot s \cdot (t_{comp} + t_{keyswap}) + (k \cdot p - 1) \cdot \hat{t}_{send}$$

$$comm_{coord} = ((p-1) \cdot s + k \cdot p - 1) \cdot \hat{t}_{comm}$$

Cost to generate partitions of R.

The cost to partition R includes the cost to 1) read R, 2) find the partitions of records, 3) move records of partitions assigned to other nodes to their respective communication buffers and send the records to their respective destination nodes ($send\_remote_i$), 4) received records of partitions assigned to the node ($recv\_remote_i$), 5) retain the first partition in memory and sort the records, and 6) move records of remaining partitions to output buffer to be written out to disk. Thus, the I/O, CPU and communication cost at processor p_i are given respectively as:

$$io_i = (\frac{|R|}{p} + \sum_{j=2}^{k} |R_{ij}|) \cdot io_{sequential}$$

$$cpu_i = (\frac{|R|}{p} + \sum_{j=2}^{k} |R_{ij}|) \cdot io_{init} + \frac{\|R\|}{p} \cdot t_{find\_partition} + \|R_{i1}\| \cdot t_{sort}(\|R_{i1}\|) +$$

$$send\_remote_i \cdot (t_{move} + t_{send}) + recv\_remote_i \cdot t_{recv} + \sum_{j=2}^{k} \|R_{ij}\| \cdot t_{move}$$

$$comm_i = (send\_remote_i + recv\_remote_i) \cdot t_{comm}$$

Cost to generate partitions of S and perform the join of the first partition

The cost to partition S and to perform the join of the first partition at each node includes the cost to 1) read S, 2) find the partitions of records, 3) move records of partitions assigned to other nodes to their respective communication buffers and send the records to their respective destination nodes ($send\_remote_i$), 4) received records of partitions assigned to the node ($recv\_remote_i$), 5) find the joining R records for the first partition, and 6) move records of remaining partitions to output buffer to be written out to disk. Thus, the I/O, CPU and communication cost are given respectively as:

$$io_i = (\frac{|S|}{p} + \sum_{j=2}^{k} |S_{ij}|) \cdot io_{sequential}$$

$$cpu_i = (\frac{|S|}{p} + \sum_{j=2}^{k} |S_{ij}|) \cdot io_{init} + \frac{\|S\|}{p} \cdot t_{find\_partition} +$$

$$send\_remote_i \cdot (t_{move} + t_{send}) + recv\_remote_i \cdot t_{recv} +$$

$$\|S_{i1}\| \cdot (t_{find\_firstjoin}(\|S_{i1}\|) + bandsize_{i1} \cdot t_{comp}) + \sum_{j=2}^{k} \|S_{ij}\| \cdot t_{move}$$

$$comm_i = (send\_remote_i + recv\_remote_i) \cdot t_{comm}$$

Cost to perform the join of the remaining partitions
The cost to join the remaining partitions include the cost to 1) read partitions of R, 2) sort the records in memory, 3) read the corresponding partitions of S, and 4) find the joining records. Consequently, we have (there is no communication involved):

$$io_i = \sum_{j=2}^{k}(|R_{ij}| + |S_{ij}|) \cdot io_{sequential}$$

$$cpu_i = \sum_{j=2}^{k}(|R_{ij}| + |S_{ij}|) \cdot io_{init} + \sum_{j=2}^{k} \|R_{ij}\| \cdot t_{sort}(\|R_{ij}\|) +$$

$$\sum_{j=2}^{k} \|S_{ij}\| \cdot (t_{find\_firstjoin}(\|S_{ij}\|) + bandsize_{ij} \cdot t_{comp})$$

Pipelined band join

The cost for sampling, generating partitions of R, and generating buckets of S, denoted B_{ij}, and perform the join of the first partition have the same cost formulas as those of the hybrid range-partitioned algorithm. However, the values of the variables are different since most of the buckets of S that are written out do not contain duplicates. So, we will only present the cost for the join of the remaining partitions.

Cost to perform the join of the remaining partitions
The cost to join the remaining partitions include the cost to 1) read partitions R_{ij}, 2) sort the records of the partitions, 3) read the corresponding bucket of S, denoted B_{ij}, and joins with the R_{ij} in memory, 4) check each record to see if they also join with partitions in neighboring processor, 5) send out records that join with partitions in neighboring processor, 6) receive records from neighboring processor that join with R_{ij} and perform the join, 7) Consequently, we have

$$io_i = \sum_{j=2}^{k}(|R_{ij}| + |B_{ij}|) \cdot io_{sequential}$$

$$cpu_i = \sum_{j=2}^{k}(|R_{ij}| + |B_{ij}|) \cdot io_{init} + \sum_{j=2}^{k} \|R_{ij}\| \cdot t_{sort}(\|R_{ij}\|) +$$

$$\sum_{j=2}^{k} \|S_{ij}\| \cdot (t_{find\_firstjoin}(\|S_{ij}\|) + bandsize_{ij} \cdot t_{comp}) +$$

$$\sum_{j=2}^{k} \|S_{ij}\| \cdot t_{comp} + send\_remote_i \cdot (t_{move} + t_{send}) + recv\_remote_i \cdot t_{recv}$$

$$comm_i = (send\_remote_i + recv\_remote_i) \cdot t_{comm}$$

5.3 Preliminary Results

In our sensitivity analysis study, we varied the relation size, band size, and memory size. Due to the limited space, we present here results that are representative of the rest. Figures 3 and 4 summarize our findings.

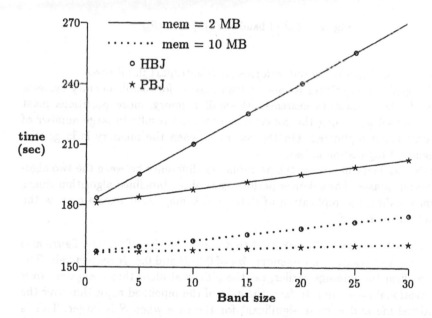

Fig. 3. Effect of band size ($|R| = |S|$).

Figure 3 shows two sets of results, one when the memory size is $0.2 \cdot R$ (corresponding to small memory scenario), while the other has memory size of $0.8 \cdot R$ (representative of large memory scenarios). We denote the hybrid range-partitioned and the pipelined band join algorithms as HBJ and PBJ respectively. ¿From the results, we see that

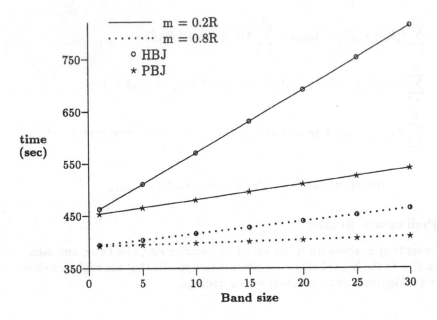

Fig. 4. Effect of band size ($|S| = 4 \cdot |R|$).

1. The pipelined algorithm outperforms its counterpart in all cases.
2. The pipelined algorithm is more advantageous for small memory systems than for large memory systems. At small memory, more partitions must be produced and using the conventional method results in large number of records being replicated. On the contrary, when the memory is large, the amount of replication is less.
3. As the band size increases, the performance difference between the two algorithms increases. The superior performance of the pipelined algorithm comes from avoiding the replication of data, which may incur excess cost as the band size increases.

In Figure 4, relation S is increased to 4 times the size of R. The figure also shows two sets of results – for memory size of $0.2 \cdot R$ and $0.8 \cdot R$ respectively. The results confirm the findings earlier, i.e. the pipelined algorithm is superior over the conventional algorithm. In fact, the gain of the pipelined algorithm over the conventional method is more significant for the case when S is larger. This is because, for larger S, the amount of replication increases, leading to higher I/O and CPU cost. On the other hand, the pipelined algorithm avoids replication.

6 Conclusion

In this paper, we have proposed a new hash-based algorithm for band joins in the context of shared-nothing multiprocessor systems. The proposed algorithm avoids the replication of records that overlap through exploiting pipelined parallelism. A preliminary study showed that the proposed algorithm outperformed the conventional hybrid range-partitioned algorithm. We plan to perform empirical study of the algorithms, and to compare the performance of the proposed algorithm with the truncating hash band join [13] and sort-merge band join [5].

References

1. H. Boral, W. Alexander, L. Clay, G. Copeland, S. Danforth, M. Franklin, B. Hart, M. Smith, and P. Valduriez. Prototyping bubba, a highly parallel database system. *IEEE Transactions on Knowledge and Data Engineering*, 2(1):4–24, March 1990.

2. E.F. Codd. A relational model of data for large shared data bank. *Communications of the ACM*, 13(6):377–387, June 1970.

3. D.J. DeWitt, S. Ghandeharizadeh, D.A. Scheneider, A. Bricker, H-I Hsiao, and R. Rasmussen. The gamma database machine project. *IEEE Trans. Knowledge and Data Engineering*, 2(1):44–62, March 1990.

4. D.J. DeWitt and J. Gray. Parallel database systems: The future of high performance database systems. *Communications of the ACM*, 35(6):85–98, June 1992.

5. D.J. DeWitt, J.F. Naughton, and D.A. Schneider. An evaluation of non-equijoin algorithms. In *Proceedings of the 17th Intl. Conf. on Very Large Data Bases*, pages 443–452, Barcelona, Spain, September 1991.

6. S. Englert, J. Gray, T. Kocher, and P. Shah. A benchmark of nonstop sql release 2 demonstrating near-linear speedup and scaleup on large databases. Technical Report Technical Report 89.4, Tandom Computer Inc., 1989.

7. J.L. Hennessy and D.A. Patterson. *Computer Architecture A Quantitative Approach (page 14)*. Morgan Kaufman Publishers Inc., 1990.

8. K.A. Hua and C. Lee. Handling data skew in multiprocessor database computers using partition tuning. In *Proceedings of the 17th International Conference on Very Large Data Bases*, pages 525–535, Barcelona, Spain, September 1991.

9. K.A. Hua, Y.L. Lo, and H.C. Young. Including the load balancing issue in the optimization of multi-way join queries for shared-nothing database computers. In *Proceedings of the 2nd International Conference on Parallel and Distributed Information Systems*, pages 74–83, San Diego, California, January 1993.

10. H. Lu, K.L. Tan, and M.C. Shan. Hash-based join algorithms for multiprocessor computers with shared memory. In *Proceedings of the 16th International Conference on Very Large Data Bases*, pages 198–209, Brisbane, Australia, August 1990.

11. P. Mishra and M.H. Eich. Join processing in relational databases. *ACM Computing Surveys*, 24(1):63–113, March 1992.

12. L. Shapiro. Join processing in database systems with large main memories. *ACM Transactions on Database Systems*, 11(3):239–264, September 1986.

13. V. Soloviev. A truncating hash algorithm for processing band-join queries. In *Proceedings of the 9th Intl. Conf. on Data Engineering*, pages 419–427, Vienna, Austria, February 1993.

14. M. Soo, R. Snodgrass, and C. Jenson. Efficient evaluation of the valid-time natural join. In *Proceedings of the 10th Intl. Conf. on Data Engineering*, pages 282–292, February 1994.

15. M. Stonebraker. The case for shared nothing. *Database Engineering*, 9(1):4–9, 1986.

16. Teradata Corporation. Dbc/1012 database computer concepts and facilities, rel. 3.1 edition, teradata document c02-0001-05. Los Angeles, CA, 1988.

17. J. Torrellas, A. Gupta, and J. Hennessy. Characterizing the cache performance and synchronization behavior of a multiprocessor operating system. Technical Report CSL-TR 92-512, Computer Systems Laboratory, Stanford University, January 1992.

Inductive Logic Programming Based on Genetic Algorithm

Kimihiro Yamamoto, Shozo Naito and Masaki Itoh

NTT Software Laboratories,
9-11, Midori-Cho 3-Chome Musashino-Shi, Tokyo 180 Japan
E-mail:{kimihiro,naito,itoh}@slab.ntt.jp

Abstract. We discuss the computability of induction in Logic Programming. It is impossible to select a hypothesis, a set of horn clauses, with fewer than several tens of examples. In order to overcome this problem, we try to computerize induction with an optimization method on the assumption that hypotheses are relative. We discuss and clarify the criteria used in an optimization method for induction. Additionally, we propose an induction system (GA-CIGOL) based on Genetic Algorithm and Inverse Resolution that induces a hypothesis from a finite set of positive or negative examples. Furthermore, we evaluate the learning ability of GA-CIGOL and discuss the problems of computerized induction with an optimization method.

1 Introduction

Previous Inductive Logic Programming methods have some restrictions: 1) An infinite number of positive or negative examples must be given one after another and 2) The target domain must be what can be constructed with the predicates that background knowledge provides. On the other hand, in this paper, we try to induce a hypothesis from a finite set of positive or negative examples without background knowledge. In this induction, hypothesis selection becomes a difficult problem.

A large number of hypotheses can be induced from a finite example set, but it has not been known which hypothesis should be chosen from among them. Therefore, we assume that hypotheses are relative and try to choose a hypothesis by an optimization method. This paper discusses only the case where the criterion used in the optimization method is scalar.

In this paper, we propose an induction system (GA-CIGOL) based on Genetic Algorithm and Inverse Resolution that induces a hypothesis from a finite set of positive or negative examples, and discuss the problems of computerized induction with an optimization method.

Sect. 2 defines the framework of induction in this paper. Sect. 3 discusses the criteria of hypotheses used in an optimization method. Sect. 4 introduces an Inductive Logic Programming method, Inverse Resolution. Sect. 5 categorizes optimization methods and reviews the previous induction system CIGOL, which is based on Hill Climbing and Inverse Resolution. Sect. 6 proposes the

GA-CIGOL system, which chooses a hypothesis by Genetic Algorithm. Sect. 7 evaluates the learning ability of the proposed method by some computer experiments. Sect. 8 discusses problems of computerized induction by the optimization method using a scalar objective function.

2 Hypothesis Selection

2.1 Objective

$\mathcal{L}$ denotes the language of a hypothesis, a horn clause set. $\mathcal{L}_0$ denotes the language of an example, a ground atom. $\mathcal{L}$ and $\mathcal{L}_0$ must be $\square \in \mathcal{L}_0 \subset \mathcal{L}$. Within these languages, the general induction problem that induces a hypothesis from an example set is defined as:

Find a finite horn clause set $T \subset \mathcal{L}$ such that $T \vdash \varepsilon^+$ and $T \not\vdash \varepsilon^-$,

where $\varepsilon^+ \subset \mathcal{L}_0$ (or $\varepsilon^- \subset \mathcal{L}_0$) denotes the ground atom set that is true (or false).

A horn clause set will be fixed iff the truth values of all the ground atoms in language $\mathcal{L}$ are given. However, there are so many ground atoms in language $\mathcal{L}$ that the oracle (a human as usual) cannot give the truth value (true or false) to all of them. Moreover, it is impossible to infer the truth value of an unknown ground atom from other things. This is why it is impossible to fix a horn clause set with fewer than several tens of positive or negative examples. This problem, called the limitation of induction[8], is difficult to overcome. A large number of horn clause sets can be induced from a finite set of examples.

Previous Inductive Logic Programming methods have some restrictions on fixing a horn clause set. *Induction in the Limit* is a type of induction framework, defined by Shapiro[10], where an infinite number of positive or negative examples must be given one after another. In the other type of induction framework, which requires the use of background knowledge in which the truth values of all the ground atoms are given, the target domain must be what can be constructed with the predicates that background knowledge provides.

In contrast, we do not use background knowledge, but try to fix a horn clause set with a finite example set. We will not determine but will predict the truth value of an unknown ground atom. This means that the induction in this paper seems to overcome, but actual does not, the limitation of induction.

In this paper, the benchmarks of induction are the Prolog programs *MEMBER, REVERSE* or *SORT*[12], which have been used by many people for a long time. We discuss the Inductive Logic Programming method, which induces the benchmark from a finite example set.

2.2 Assumption

Is there any aspect that makes it possible to select one hypothesis from among many?

There are two kinds of aspects:

1. One whose judgement criterion is absolute, and
2. One whose judgement criterion is relative.

Redundancy is an absolute aspect. None of the benchmarks are redundant. However, redundancy is not enough for selecting a hypothesis.

By the way, one previous Inductive Logic Programming method uses a human to select a hypothesis[5]. However, in that method, it is impossible for the human to select the hypothesis according to absolute aspects.

Therefore, we assume that hypotheses are relative and that comparison among hypotheses is an important process in selection. We try to computerize induction with an optimization method. In this paper, we especially discuss the case where the criterion used in an optimization method is scalar.

3 Criteria

We have discussed the criteria that should be used in an optimization method, taking induction's own meaning in account. In general, there are two conditions, both of which should be satisfied by the induced hypotheses:

1 Hypotheses should be able to perform within the finite physical resources of the computer.
2 Hypotheses should not make a mistake.

In this paper, the objective of induction is to predict the truth value of an unknown ground atom. Therefore, the second condition can be rephrased as

2' Hypotheses should not predict the wrong truth value.

We argue that all the criteria for judging the first condition fall into two kinds: one is the description length of a hypothesis and the other is the calculation time for inferring examples from a hypothesis. On the other hand, to judge the second condition, the truth values of unknown ground atoms need to be given by the oracle. However, this is opposite to the objective of induction in this paper. Therefore, the second condition judgement should or must use the truth values of examples, instead of those of unknown ground atoms. We argue that all such criteria for judging the second condition fall into two kinds: cue validity[4] and category validity[4].

We define cue validity as the frequency that a hypothesis is used for deducing an (either positive or negative) example set. We define category validity as the ratio of positive to negative cue validity. Neither cue validity nor category validity guarantees that an unknown ground atom's truth values inferred by a hypothesis are valid.

The four criteria shown above are primitive criteria for induction. In the rest of this paper, we try to computerize induction by an optimization method using these criteria.

4 Inverse Resolution

This paper focuses on Inverse Resolution(IR), which is an Inductive Logic Programming method[5].

IR has three kinds of symbolic operators: Truncation, Absorption and Intra-Construction, which backtrack the Logic Programming's deduction step called Resolution. Each IR operator receives some horn clauses as input and generates other horn clauses as output.

Truncation substitutes variables for some terms in a horn clause with the least general generalization method proposed by Plotkin [7]. Absorption introduces causal relations in a horn clause. Intra-Construction invents a new predicate.

An IR operator can receive horn clauses, each of which is the output generated by another IR operator. A horn clause set (a hypothesis) can be constructed from a positive example set, applying IR operators one after another. Fig. 1 illustrates the construction of *REVERSE* from positive examples.

The way of applying IR operators is non-deterministic. Accordingly, a large number of hypotheses can be derived from a finite set of examples.

Truncation
reverse([1,2,3],[3,2,1]).
reverse([2,3,4],[4,3,2]). ➡ reverse([A,B,C],[C,B,A]).

Absorption
reverse([1,2,3,4],[4,3,2,1]).
reverse([2,3,4],[4,3,2]). ➡ reverse([1|A],[B,C,D,1]):-reverse(A,[B,C,D]).

Intra-Construction
reverse([1|A],[B,C,D,1]):-reverse(A,[B,C,D]).
reverse([2|A],[B,C,2]):-reverse(A,[B,C]).
⟶ reverse([A|B],C):-reverse(B,D),new(A,C,D).
new(1,[A,B,C,1],[A,B,C]).
new(2,[A,B,2],[B,C]).

Fig. 1. Inverse Resolution

5 Optimization Methods

5.1 Neighborhood vs. Subgoal

It is impossible to search all the hypotheses that can be derived from a finite set of examples. The best we can do is to search for the hypothesis that is approximately the best solution in the search space, using trial and error information arising during the searching process. Such searching methods are called meta-heuristics. Two kinds of meta-heuristics have been proposed to date.

One includes famous searching methods such as Hill Climbing and Simulated Annealing. A function machine, which is fed one solution of an optimization problem and produces other new solutions each with its own probability, is called a generating function. Moreover, the set of new solutions, which a generating function produces from one solution, is called a neighborhood. If a solution of the optimization problem is described by a bit string, the neighborhood will usually be a solution set where the Hamming distances between solutions are short. This meta-heuristic uses local gradient information about the objective function in the neighborhood to get approximately the best solution in the search space.

The other meta-heuristic includes famous searching methods such as Genetic Algorithm[3]. This meta-heuristic divides the optimization problem into subgoals, called building blocks, and calculates them in parallel to get approximately the best solution in the search space.

Each meta-heuristic has its own suitable problem domain, and they differ from each other. The first type of meta-heuristic is efficient for optimization problems where the gradient of the objective function is almost monotonic. The second type is efficient for optimization problems that can be divided into subgoals. For example, consider the following deception problem[2]. The problem consists of 40 5-bit strings. Each 5-bit string scores 2.0 point for five zeros, 0.0 points if it has a single one, and 0.25 for each additional one, for a suboptimum score of 1.0 for five ones. The total score is the sum of all the 5-bit string scores. According to our empirical test, Genetic Algorithm can approximately solve this problem, while Hill Climbing cannot.

5.2 Hill Climbing Approach

CIGOL[5], which is a previous induction system based on IR, uses Hill Climbing for searching.

The generating function within CIGOL applies an IR operator to a hypothesis (a horn clause set) and constructs a new hypothesis. The objective function evaluates the description length of a hypothesis. The description length is defined[5] as

$$\text{hypothesis size } P = 1 + \sum_{i=1}^{l} H_i$$
$$\text{horn size } H_i = 1 + \sum_{j=1}^{m} F_j \tag{1}$$
$$\text{literal or term size } F_j(t_1, \ldots, t_n) = 2 + \sum_{k=1}^{n} t_k$$
$$\text{variable size } V_k = 1$$

The size of a hypothesis consisting of horn clauses is defined as 1 plus the sum of the horn clause sizes. The size of a horn clause consisting of literals is defined as 1 plus the sum of the literal sizes. The size of a literal (or term) consisting of terms is defined as 2 plus the sum of the term sizes. The size of a variable, which is a term, is defined as 1.

Whereas standard Hill Climbing defines the next search point as the best solution in the neighborhood, CIGOL defines the next search point using an acceptance function that uses a threshold and human judgement. The threshold checks for solutions with better objective function values.

Because the acceptance function is highly intelligent, CIGOL may have higher search performance than standard Hill Climbing. However, CIGOL cannot learn the benchmark of *REVERSE*, which can be constructed with IR operators. This is because the objective function values of hypotheses in the neighborhood around the benchmark are low, and because the threshold eliminates all the search paths to the benchmark.

In contrast, this paper tries to computerize induction with a Genetic Algorithm.

6 GA-CIGOL

6.1 Algorithm

GA-CIGOL learns from the provided facts—a finite set of positive or negative examples, which are given as a batch. We will not deal with an example (called noise) that has an error in its truth value.

The system constructs hypotheses from the positive example set using IR operators. There are many way of applying an IR operator to a horn clause set, and a large number of hypotheses can be derived from a positive example set. The system chooses a hypothesis among them with a Genetic Algorithm. The system uses the Genetic Algorithm known as the simple Genetic Algorithm, especially the elitist model variation.

The plan of applying IR operators corresponds to a chromosome which should be divided into sub-goals, and the system recombines this plan using two kinds of genetic operators: crossover and mutation. The system constructs a hypothesis from the positive example set according to this recombined plan.

A hypothesis constructed with IR operators often has redundancy. The system reduces this redundancy by using the reduction algorithm proposed by Buntine [1]. Furthermore, the system checks the consistency of the hypothesis with the negative example set. In general, it is impossible to decide whether or not there is a proof of example (positive or negative) using the hypothesis. In order to avoid this problem, the system assumes negation as failure and uses the depth-bounded theorem prover to decide the provability.

The system uses an objective function that returns a scalar. The system will only evaluate hypotheses that are consistent with the negative example set. The objective function values of all the other hypotheses that are inconsistent with the negative example set are 0.

As a result of a certain limited repetition of reproduction, the system learns the best hypothesis. Fig. 2 shows the GA-CIGOL learning algorithm.

```
begin
    generation t = 1;    population size M;    chromosome length L;

    read positive examples Posi and negative examples Nega;
    generate operational plans of Inverse Resolution Chromo(1 · · · M) at random;

    while     t  is less than the upper limit
    begin
        for     i = 1  to  M
        begin
            construct a hypothesis H from Posi according to Chromo(i);
            reduce the redundancy of H;
            if H is consistent with Nega
                    evaluate H with objective function and make Fitness(i)
            else  Fitness(i) = 0
        end
        for     j = 1  to  M/2
        begin
            select C₁ and C₂ from Chromo(1 · · · M) according to Fitness(1 · · · M);
            recombine C₁, C₂ forming C₁', C₂';
            if C₁' is longer than L or includes an irrecoverable gene
                    Chromo'(j * 2) = C₁'
            else  Chromo'(j * 2) = C₁
            do the same substitution C₂ for Chromo'(j * 2 + 1);
        end

        replace Chromo(1 · · · M) with Chromo'(1 · · · M);
        t = t + 1;
    end
end
```

Fig. 2. The GA-CIGOL learning algorithm

6.2 Coding

An IR operator receives some horn clauses as input and generates other horn clauses as output. We make a chromosome of genes, each of which represents the combination of an IR operator and horn clauses. Fig. 3 shows a chromosome. The system executes each gene and generates a hypothesis in accordance with a chromosome. The chromosome can be any length up to the upper limit.

An IR operator can receive horn clauses, each of which is the output generated by another operator. The relation of giving and receiving a horn clause between IR operators in Fig. 3 can be described by the directed graph, as indicated in Fig. 3. A black node denotes a virtual operator which generates positive examples. A white node denotes an IR operator. A directed arc denotes the relation of giving and receiving a horn clause. We use this directed graph to explain genetic operators.

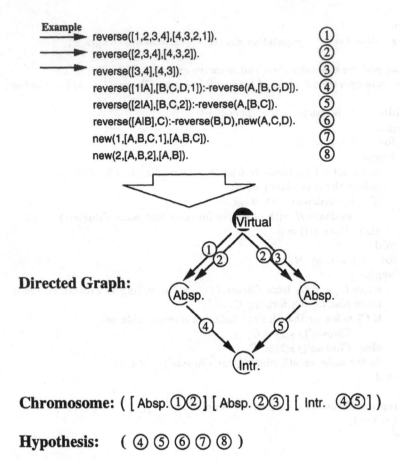

Directed Graph:

Chromosome: ([Absp. ①②] [Absp. ②③] [Intr. ④⑤])

Hypothesis: (④ ⑤ ⑥ ⑦ ⑧)

Fig. 3. Operational plan of IR described in the chromosome

6.3 Genetic Operators

The system uses two kinds of genetic operators: crossover and mutation. Crossover swaps some genes between two chromosomes with a random choice. Mutation either alters existing gene conditions or appends a new gene to the chromosome with a specific probability.

Crossover and mutation may yield a gene having at least one input arc that is not connected with another gene's output. This gene corresponds to an irrecoverable gene in biology. In order to remove irrecoverable genes, crossover and mutation check the giving or receiving relation in the directed graph.

Moreover, crossover and mutation may yield a chromosome that is longer than the upper limit. In that case, crossover and mutation replace the yielded chromosome by the original one.

6.4 Objective Functions

We provide three primitive objective functions. The system uses them separately. These evaluate description length, cue validity, and category validity.

Objective function f_1 returns the description length (size) of a hypothesis, which is defined by equation (1). The hypothesis of minimum size is desirable. The system makes the hypothesis fitness, which is the probability of propagation in Genetic Algorithm, be in the same proportion as the reciprocal value of objective function f_1.

Objective function f_2 returns the cue validity of a hypothesis. We define the cue validity by

$$\text{cue validity} = \sum_{i=1}^{n} C_i^2 / (\sum_{i=1}^{n} C_i)^2 \tag{2}$$

where C_i denotes the frequency of use of a horn clause in the proofs of positive examples. The hypothesis with the largest value of C_i^2 is desirable. The system makes the hypothesis fitness be in the same proportion as the value of objective function f_2.

Objective function f_3 returns the category validity of a hypothesis. We define the category validity by

$$\text{category validity} = \log \frac{Np}{Pp + Np} \tag{3}$$

where Pp denotes the number of positive examples that the hypothesis can prove. Np denotes the number of negative examples that the hypothesis can prove under the condition that the system changes the truth value (true or false) of all the examples to alternative ones. The hypothesis with large Pp and small Np is desirable. The system makes the hypothesis fitness be in the same proportion as the value of objective function f_3.

7 Experiments

7.1 First Set of Experiments

The first set of experiments examined the effect of chromosome length and population size on the induction. We tested GA-CIGOL's learning ability in the *REVERSE* problem with objective function f_1. Fig. 4 shows the examples we provided. The GA-CIGOL system was implemented in Quintus Prolog on a Sun SPARC Station 10.

To examine the effect of chromosome length on the induction, we used various upper limits (10, 20, 50, and 100) on chromosome length. We obtained a mutation rate (the probability of mutation) with $1/N$ =0.1, 0.05, 0.02 or 0.01 where N is the upper limit on chromosome length. The crossover rate (the probability of crossover) was 0.7, population size 100, and upper limit on the number of generations 500. A selection pressure, with a period of 25 generations, varied from a lower limit of 0.1 to an upper limit of 1.0. Fig. 5 shows performance curves of the best-of-generation fitness for various chromosome lengths. Fig. 6 shows on-line performance of the average fitness for various chromosome lengths.

The fitness on these figures was standardized so that the value of the initial positive example set was 0 and so that the value of the benchmark was 100.

To examine the effect of population size on the induction, we used various population sizes: 10, 50, 100, and 500. The upper limit on chromosome length was 25, crossover rate 0.7, mutation rate $1/N = 0.04$, and upper limit on the number of generation 500. The selection pressure was the same as above. Fig. 7 shows performance curves of the best-of-generation fitness for various population sizes. Fig. 8 shows on-line performance of the average fitness for various population sizes.

Furthermore, to find out whether the induction problem can be divided into sub-goals, we compared the best hypothesis acquired by GA-CIGOL above with the hypotheses obtained by random searching. Fig. 9 shows the distribution of the hypotheses generated by random searching. The best hypotheses are also plotted in Fig. 9. Fig. 10 shows the best hypothesis (a horn clause set) acquired by the system.

Positive	rev([],[]),rev([1],[1]),rev([2],[2]),rev([3],[3]),rev([cc],[cc]),rev([dd],[dd]),rev([1,2], [2,1]),rev([2,3],[3,2]),rev([3,4],[4,3]),rev([4,5],[5,4]),rev([5,6],[6,5]),rev([2,cc],[cc, 2]),rev([cc,dd],[dd,cc]),rev([dd,5],[5,dd]),rev([1,2,3],[3,2,1]),rev([2,3,4],[4,3,2]), rev([3,4,5],[5,4,3]),rev([4,5,6],[6,5,4]),rev([1,2,cc],[cc,2,1]),rev([2,cc,dd],[dd,cc, 2]),rev([cc,dd,5],[5,dd,cc]),rev([dd,5,6],[6,5,dd]),rev([1,2,3,4],[4,3,2,1]),rev([2,3, 4,5],[5,4,3,2]),rev([3,4,5,6],[6,5,4,3]),rev([1,2,cc,dd .....37 examples
Negative	rev([1,2],[6,5]),rev([2,3],[5,4]),rev([3,4],[3,2]),rev([4,5],[4,3]),rev([5,6],[2,1]), rev([2,1],[2,1]),rev([1,2,3],[6,5,4]),rev([2,3,4],[5,4,3]),rev([3,4,5],[4,3,2]),rev([4,5, 6],[3,2,1]),rev([2,3,4,5,6],[5,4,3,2,1]),rev([2,3,4,5,6],[6,7,4,3,2]),rev([1,2,cc,dd, 5],[1,2,cc,dd,5]),rev([1,2,3,4,5,6],[6,5,3,4,2,1]),rev([1,2,3,4,5,6,7],[6,5,4,3,2,1]), rev([1,2,cc,dd,5,6],[6,ee,dd,cc,2,1]),rev([1,2,cc,dd,5,6],[5,dd,cc,2,1]),rev([a,b,c, d,e,f,g,h,i,j,k,l,m,n],[n,m,l,k,j,i,h,g,f,e,d,c,b,a]), ...21 examples

Fig. 4. A finite set of examples

7.2 Second Set of Experiments

The second set of experiments examined the effect of objective functions on induction. We tested using three Prolog programs: *MEMBER*, *ARCH*, and *RE-VERSE*.

We chose 25 as the upper limit on chromosome length, 0.7 for the crossover rate, $1/25 = 0.04$ for the mutation rate, 100 for the population size, and 1000 for the upper limit on the number of generations. The selection pressure was the same as in the first experiments.

The second experiments separately used three objective functions, defined in Sect. 6.4, in each of three problems.

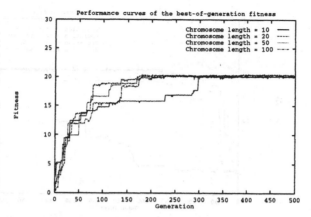

Fig. 5. Performance curves of the best-of-generation fitness for various chromosome lengths

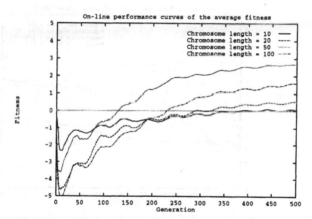

Fig. 6. On-line performance of the average fitness for various chromosome lengths

Table 1 shows convergent behavior, the number of generations in which the best hypothesis was learned by the system. Table 1 also shows the fitness of the best hypothesis.

8 Discussion

In the second set of experiments, objective functions f_1 and f_2 made it possible for the GA-CIGOL system to learn the same benchmark in the *MEMBER* and *ARCH* problems. This suggests that there is nothing to choose between description length and cue validity and that these two criteria must have equal importance in induction. On the other hand, objective function f_3 did not make

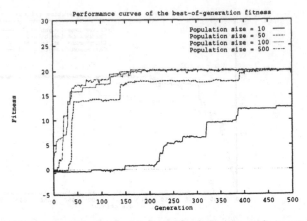

Fig. 7. Performance curves of the best-of-generation fitness for various population sizes

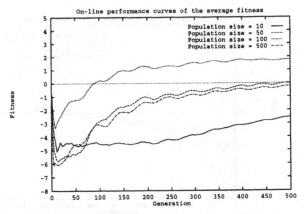

Fig. 8. On-line performance of the average fitness for various population sizes

it possible for the system to learn the benchmark in the *MEMBER* and *ARCH* problems. Category validity cannot distinguish the benchmark from the positive example set, and calculation time did not either. However, objective functions f_1 and f_2 make the system generate a hypothesis that has low category validity or take a long calculation time to prove positive examples. Category validity and calculation time can remove that hypothesis. This suggests that category validity and calculation time are auxiliary criteria for induction.

In the second set of experiments, we found the problem that none of the primitive objective functions made it possible for the system to learn the benchmark in the *REVERSE* problem. The best hypothesis that the system learned with one objective function was different from that learned with another objective function.

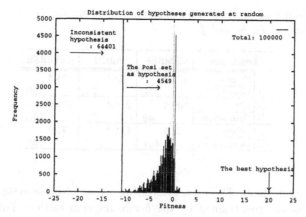

Fig. 9. Distribution of hypothesis generated at random

rev([s,ss,sss,ssss,sssss,ssssss,sssssss],[sssssss,ssssss,sssss,ssss,sss,ss,s]).
rev([a1,b1,c1,d1,e1,f1,g1,h1,i1,j1,k1],[k1,j1,i1,h1,g1,f1,e1,d1,c1,b1,a1]).
rev([a,b,c,d,e,f,g,h,i,j,k,l,m,n],[n,m,l,k,j,i,h,g,f,e,d,c,b,a]).
rev([],[]).
rev([A],[A]).
rev([A,B],[B,A]).
rev([A,B,C],[C,B,A]).
rev([A,B,C,D],[D,C,B,A]).
rev([A,B,C,D,E],[E,D,C,B,A]).
rev([1|A],[B,C,D,E,F,1]):-rev(A,[B,C,D,E,F]).

Fig. 10. The best hypothesis acquired by the GA-CIGOL system

In almost all of the first experiments in the *REVERSE* problem, the system learned the same best hypothesis, which random searching could not learn as indicated in Fig. 9, although the number of generations taken for learning differed. The convergent behavior did not depend on the upper limit on chromosome length as indicated in Fig. 5. On the other hand, a larger population size led to better convergent behavior as indicated in Fig. 7. However, the system could not learn the benchmark. On account of the architecture of the best hypothesis acquired by the system as indicated in Fig. 10, we find that the system is suitable for learning a hypothesis that has a parallel architecture and that a complicated hypothesis construction process will not be divided into sub-goals, using scalar objective functions for hypothesis optimization.

9 Related Works

We compared the performance of GA-CIGOL with FOIL[9] and Progol[6] from the viewpoints of calculation time and predictive accuracy. The refinement operators of these systems generate hypotheses and guarantee the θ-subsumption

Table 1. Results of function optimizing simulation by the GA-CIGOL system for objective functions f_1, f_2, and f_3

Benchmark		MEMBER	ARCH	REVERSE
f_1	Fitness	100.0	62.7	21.4
	Generations	132	79	139
f_2	Fitness	100.0	214.4	108.5
	Generations	48	95	266
f_3	Fitness	22.8	141.4	193.2
	Generations	451	657	743

relation between them. The most interesting aspect of these system is that their search spaces are constrained by the θ-subsumption lattice. This search technique based on the θ-subsumption has some problems.

Generally speaking, a powerful hypothesis generating operator leads to a large search space and a long calculation time. The refinement operators of FOIL and Progol guarantee the θ-subsumption relation, but are not powerful. Moreover, performance of the refinement operators depends on the background knowledge provided by human. FOIL and Progol which do not have the background knowledge about the *APPEND* predicate cannot generate the benchmark indicated in [12] or the hypothesis indicated in Fig. 10. It is usual for FOIL and Progol to be provided with the minimum background knowledge necessary to learn the target hypothesis. Decreasing the background knowledge makes the search space small. The calculation times of FOIL and Progol are short, because their search spaces are small and have the θ-subsumption lattice. In other words, augmenting the background knowledge makes the calculation time of Progol long. On the other hand, an IR operator of GA-CIGOL does not guarantee the θ-subsumption relation, but is powerful. IR operators can generate the benchmark indicated in [12] or the hypothesis indicated in Fig. 10, but GA-CIGOL could not acquire the benchmark indicated in [12] in our experiments. Unfortunately, GA-CIGOL takes a long time for calculation, because its search space is large and it does not have the θ-subsumption lattice.

The search technique based on the θ-subsumption lattice can be applied for learning the hypothesis consisting of a single horn clause, but cannot be extended to one consisting of several horn clauses. This is why Progol compresses a single horn clause, whose head is the target predicate, in order to achieve high prediction accuracy. However, FOIL and Progol achieve the same predictive accuracy[11], because their accuracy depends on their sophisticated background knowledge. On the other hand, GA-CIGOL with objective function f_1 compresses all the horn clauses which define not only the target predicate but also theoretical terms. We believe that total systemization of horn clauses makes prediction accuracy high, although GA-CIGOL proposed in this paper cannot perform the *REVERSE* problem. These results are not enough yet and it is too early to choose FOIL, Progol or GA-CIGOL from the viewpoint of prediction accuracy.

10 Conclusions

This paper dealt with the hypothesis selection problem in induction.

We tried to computerize induction with an optimization method and discussed the criteria used in it. We found that there are four primitive criteria: description length, calculation time, cue validity, and category validity. Moreover, we found that description length and cue validity are more important than calculation time and category validity.

We proposed an induction system GA-CIGOL, which induces a horn clause set from a finite set of positive or negative examples, and evaluated the learning ability of the proposed method by computer simulation. As a result, we found computerized induction's problem that a complicated hypothesis construction process will not be divided into sub-goals, using scalar objective functions for hypothesis optimization.

Acknowledgement

We would like to thank Shigeki Goto for his encouragement in this research.

References

1. Buntine, W.: Generalized subsumption and its application to induction and redundancy, *Artificial Intelligence*, 36(2), pp. 149-176 (1988).
2. Eshelman, L. J. and Schaffer, J. D.: Crossover's Niche, *Proc. of the 5th Int. Conference on Genetic Algorithms*, pp. 9-14 (1993).
3. Goldberg, D. E.: *Genetic Algorithms in Search, Optimization, and Machine Learning*, Addison Wesley Publishing (1989).
4. Medin, D. L., Wattenmaker, W. S. and Michalski, R. S.: Constraints in Inductive Learning: An Experimental Study Comparing Human and Machine Performance, *Cognitive Science*, Vol. 11, pp. 299-339 (1987).
5. Muggleton, S. and Buntine, W.: Machine Invention of First-order Predicates by Inverting Resolution, *Proc. of the 5th Int. Workshop on Machine Learning*, pp. 339-352 (1988).
6. Muggleton, S.: Inverse Entailment and Progol, *New Generation Computing*, to appear (1995).
7. Plotkin, G. D.: A Note on Inductive Generalization, *Machine Intelligence 5*, Elsevier North-Holland, New York, pp. 153-163 (1970).
8. Popper, K. R.: *The Logic of Scientific Discovery*, Basic Book, New York (1959).
9. Quinlan, J.R.: Learning logical definitions from relations, *Machine Learning*, Vol. 5, pp.239-266(1990).
10. Shapiro, E. Y.: *Algorithmic Program Debugging*, The MIT Press, Cambridge (1983).
11. Srinivasan, A., Muggleton, S. and King, R.D.: Comparing the use of background knowledge by inductive logic programming systems, *Technical report PRG-TR-9-95*, Oxford University Computing Laboratory, Oxford(1995).
12. Sterling, L. and Shapiro, E. Y.: *The Art of Prolog* The MIT Press, Cambridge (1986).

The Equivalence of the Subsumption Theorem and the Refutation-Completeness for Unconstrained Resolution

Shan-Hwei Nienhuys-Cheng   Ronald de Wolf
cheng@cs.few.eur.nl   bidewolf@cs.few.eur.nl

Department of Computer Science, H4-19

Erasmus University of Rotterdam

P.O. Box 1738, 3000 DR Rotterdam, the Netherlands

Subfield: Automated Reasoning, (Inductive) Logic Programming.

Abstract

The subsumption theorem is an important theorem concerning resolution. Essentially, it says that a set of clauses Σ logically implies a clause C, iff C is a tautology, or a clause D which subsumes C can be derived from Σ with resolution. It was originally proved in 1967 by Lee in [Lee67]. In Inductive Logic Programming, interest in this theorem is increasing since its independent rediscovery by Bain and Muggleton [BM92]. It provides a quite natural "bridge" between subsumption and logical implication. Unfortunately, a correct formulation and proof of the subsumption theorem are not available. It is not clear which forms of resolution are allowed. In fact, at least one of the current forms of this theorem is false. This causes a lot of confusion.

In this paper, we give a careful proof of the subsumption theorem for unconstrained resolution, and show that the well-known refutation-completeness of resolution is an immediate consequence of this theorem. On the other hand, we also show here that the subsumption theorem can be proved starting from the refutation-completeness. This establishes that these two results have equal strength.

Furthermore, we show that the subsumption theorem does not hold when only input resolution is used, not even in case Σ contains only one clause. Since [Mug92, Ide93a] assume the contrary, some results (for instance results on nth roots and nth powers) in these articles should perhaps be reconsidered.

1   Introduction

Inductive Logic Programming (ILP) investigates methods to learn theories from examples, within the framework of first-order logic. In ILP, the proof-method that is most often used is resolution. A very important theorem concerning resolution is the *Subsumption Theorem*, which essentially states the following. Let Σ be a set of clauses and C a clause. Then $\Sigma \models C$, iff C is a tautology or there exists a clause D which subsumes C and which can be derived from Σ by resolution.

This theorem was first stated and proved by Lee in 1967 in [Lee67], his PhD-thesis. However, we have not been able to find a copy of his thesis. So it is unclear what precisely Lee stated, and how he proved his result. Surprisingly, nowhere in the standard literature concerning resolution (not even in Lee's own book [CL73]) the theorem is mentioned.[1]

One thing is clear, though: the subsumption theorem states that logical implication between clauses can be divided in two separate steps—a derivation by resolution, and then a subsumption. Hence the theorem provides a natural "bridge" between logical implication and subsumption. Subsumption is very popular in Inductive Logic Programming, since it is decidable and machine-implementable. However, subsumption is not "enough": if D subsumes C then $D \models C$, but not always the other way around. So it is desirable to make the step from subsumption to implication, and the subsumption theorem provides an excellent tool for those who want to make this step. It is used for instance in [Mug92, Ide93a][2] for inverse resolution. In [LN94b], the theorem is used to extend the result of [LN94a] that there does not exist an ideal refinement operator[3] in the set of clauses ordered by subsumption, to the result that there is no ideal refinement operator in the ordering induced by logical implication. In [NLT93], the theorem is related to several generality orderings.

The subsumption theorem is more natural than the better-known *refutation-completeness* of resolution, which states that an unsatisfiable set of clauses has a refutation (a derivation by resolution of the empty clause $\square$). For example, if one wants to prove $\Sigma \models C$ using the refutation-completeness, one must first normalize the set $\Sigma \cup \{\neg C\}$ to a set of clauses. Usually $\Sigma \cup \{\neg C\}$ is not a set of clauses, since negating the (universally quantified) clause C yields a formula which involves existential quantifiers. So if we want to prove $\Sigma \models C$ by refuting $\Sigma \cup \{\neg C\}$, we must first apply Skolemization to C. Deriving from Σ a clause D which subsumes C, is a much more "direct" way of proving $\Sigma \models C$.

Hence we—and perhaps many others—feel that the subsumption theorem deserves at least as much attention as the refutation-completeness. We can in fact prove that the latter is a direct consequence of the former, as given in Section 3. It is surprising that the subsumption theorem was so little known. Only after Bain and Muggleton rediscovered the theorem in [BM92], people have started paying attention to it.[4]

---

[1] Recently we received a copy of [Kow70] and a reference to [SCL69] from Stephen Muggleton. [Kow70] gives a proof of the subsumption theorem for unconstrained resolution, using semantic trees, which is very different from the proof we give here. [SCL69] proves a version of the subsumption theorem for semantic resolution.

[2] [Ide93a] is a PhD-thesis based upon articles such as [Ide93b, Ide93c, Ide93d].

[3] A refinement operator is a device to specialize clauses.

[4] From recent personal communication with Stephen Muggleton, we know Bain and Mug-

A proof of the subsumption theorem, based on the refutation-completeness, is given in the appendix of [BM92]. However, this proof seems unsatisfactory. For example, it does not take *factors* into account, whereas factors are necessary for completeness. Without factors one cannot derive the empty clause $\Box$ from the unsatisfiable set $\{(P(x) \vee P(y)), (\neg P(u) \vee \neg P(v))\}$ (see [GN87]). In fact, our counterexample in Section 5 also depends on factors. Furthermore, it is not always clear how the concepts that are used in the proof are defined, and how the skolemization works. Their proof is based on transforming a refutation-tree into a derivation-tree, but this transformation is not clearly defined and thus insufficient to prove that the transformation can always be performed.

Even though the proof in [BM92] is not quite satisfactory, it is often quoted— sometimes even incorrectly. The two main formulations we have found are the following:

S Let Σ be a set of clauses and C a clause which is not a tautology. Define $\mathcal{R}^0(\Sigma) = \Sigma$ and $\mathcal{R}^n(\Sigma) = \mathcal{R}^{n-1}(\Sigma) \cup \{C : C$ is a resolvent of $C_1, C_2 \in \mathcal{R}^{n-1}(\Sigma)\}$. Also define $\mathcal{R}^*(\Sigma) = \mathcal{R}^0(\Sigma) \cup \mathcal{R}^1(\Sigma) \cup \dots$. Then the subsumption theorem is stated as follows (we assume the authors of [BM92] used '$\vdash$' for what we mean by '$\models$', i.e. logical implication):

$\Sigma \vdash C$ iff there exists a clause $D \in \mathcal{R}^*(\Sigma)$ such that D subsumes C.

S' Let Σ be a set of clauses and C a clause which is not a tautology. Define $\mathcal{L}^1(\Sigma) = \Sigma$ and $\mathcal{L}^n(\Sigma) = \{C : C$ is a resolvent of $C_1 \in \mathcal{L}^{n-1}(\Sigma)$ and $C_2 \in \Sigma\}$. Also define $\mathcal{L}^*(\Sigma) = \mathcal{L}^1(\Sigma) \cup \mathcal{L}^2(\Sigma) \cup \dots$. Then the subsumption theorem is stated as follows:

$\Sigma \models C$ iff there exists a clause $D \in \mathcal{L}^*(\Sigma)$ such that D subsumes C.

S is given in [BM92], **S'** is given in [Mug92]. In [Mug92], Muggleton does not prove **S'**, but refers instead to [BM92]. In other articles such as [Ide93a, LN94b, NLT93], the theorem is also given in the form of **S'**. These articles do not give a proof of **S'**, but refer instead to [BM92] or [Mug92]. That is, they refer to a proof of **S** assuming that this is also a proof of **S'**. But clearly that is not the case, because **S'** demands that at least one of the parent clauses of a clause in $\mathcal{L}^*(\Sigma)$ is a member of Σ, so **S'** is stronger than **S**. In fact, whereas **S** is true, **S'** *is actually false!* If **S'** were true, then input resolution would be refutation-complete (as we will show in Section 5), which it is not. An easy propositional counterexample for the refutation-completeness of input resolution is given on p. 99 of [GN87].

The confusion about **S'** is perhaps a consequence of the subtle distinction between linear resolution and input resolution. **S'** employs a form of *input* resolution, which is a special case of linear resolution. Linear resolution is complete[5], but input resolution is *not* complete. See [CL73] or [GN87].

However, the articles we mentioned do not use **S'** itself. [LN94b, NLT93] are restricted to Horn clauses. It can be shown that for Horn clauses there is

---

gleton discovered the theorem themselves, independently of [Lee67]. Only afterwards did they found out from references in other literature that their theorem was probably the same as the theorem in Lee's thesis.

[5] It is possible to prove that the subsumption theorem holds in case of linear resolution, but we will not do that here.

no problem. Due to a lack of space we will not prove that here, but in another article [NW95b]. If we examine [Mug92, Ide93a] carefully, then we see that the results of these articles only depend on a special case of S', namely the case where Σ consists of a single clause. Muggleton and others have used the definition of $\mathcal{L}^n(\{C\})$ to define *nth powers* and *nth roots*. Unfortunately, S' does not even hold in this special case. We give a counterexample in Section 5. This means that the results of [Mug92, Ide93a] which are consequences of this special case of S' need to be reconsidered.[6]

The confusion around the subsumption theorem made us investigate this theorem ourselves, which led to the discovery of the mixture of true and false results that we mentioned above. We investigated the subsumption theorem both in the case of unconstrained resolution, and in the case of SLD-resolution for Horn clauses. For the latter case we generalized the definition of SLD-resolution given in [Llo87], following an idea of [MP94]. The main results of both parts of our research can be summarized in the following sequence (where $a \Rightarrow b \Rightarrow c \Rightarrow d$).

   a. The subsumption theorem for unconstrained resolution.
   b. The refutation-completeness of unconstrained resolution.
   c. The refutation-completeness of SLD-resolution for Horn clauses.
   d. The subsumption theorem for SLD-resolution for Horn clauses.
   e. S' is false, even when Σ (the set of premises) contains only one clause.

We defer **c** and **d** to the second part of our research [NW95b]. **c** is similar to Theorem 8.4 of [Llo87], but our proof of **c** is interesting in that it avoids partial orders and fixpoints, using only the basic definitions of unconstrained resolution and SLD-resolution.

In this paper we focus on **a**, **b** and **e**. In Section 2, we prove **a**. Our proof does not presuppose the refutation-completeness, contrary to the inadequate proof in [BM92]. **b** is well-known, but it is not well-known that **b** is a direct consequence of **a**, as we will show in Section 3 (this fact can also be used to establish the falsity of S'). Thus **b** follows immediately from **a**. On the other hand, **a** can also be proved starting from **b**, as we show in Section 4. This establishes the equivalence of the subsumption theorem and the refutation-completeness: these results have equal power. Finally, in Section 5 we prove **e**, by presenting our counterexample to the special case of S' that we mentioned.

2   The Subsumption Theorem

In this section, we give a proof of the subsumption theorem. Before starting with our proof, we will first briefly define the main concepts we use. We treat a clause as a *disjunction* of literals, so we consider $P(a)$ and $P(a) \lor P(a)$ as different clauses. However, the results of our paper remain valid also for other notations, for instance if one treats a clause as a *set* of literals instead of a disjunction. For

---

[6] From recent personal communication with Peter Idestam-Almquist, we know he has adjusted his work from [Ide93a], based on our findings.

convenience, we use $C \subseteq D$ to denote that the set of literals appearing in the disjunction C is a subset of the set of literals in D.

Definition 1 Let C_1 and C_2 be clauses. If C_1 and C_2 have no variables in common, then they are said to be *standardized apart*.

Given C_1 and C_2, let $C_1' = L_1 \vee \ldots \vee L_i \vee \ldots \vee L_m$ and $C_2' = M_1 \vee \ldots \vee M_j \vee \ldots \vee M_n$ be variants of C_1 and C_2 respectively, which are standardized apart $(1 \leq i \leq m$ and $1 \leq j \leq n)$. If the substitution θ is a most general unifier (mgu) of the set $\{L_i, \neg M_j\}$, then the clause

$$(L_1 \vee \ldots \vee L_{i-1} \vee L_{i+1} \vee \ldots \vee L_m \vee M_1 \vee \ldots \vee M_{j-1} \vee M_{j+1} \vee \ldots \vee M_n)\theta$$

is called a *binary resolvent* of C_1 and C_2. The literals L_i and M_j are said to be the literals *resolved upon*. ◇

Definition 2 Let C be a clause, $L_1, \ldots, L_n$ $(n \geq 1)$ unifiable literals from C, and θ an mgu of $\{L_1, \ldots, L_n\}$. Then the clause obtained by deleting $L_2\theta, \ldots, L_n\theta$ from $C\theta$ is called a *factor* of C.

A *resolvent* C of clauses C_1 and C_2 is a binary resolvent of a factor of C_1 and a factor of C_2, where the literals resolved upon are the literals unified by the respective factors. C_1 and C_2 are called the *parent clauses* of C. ◇

Note that any non-empty clause C is a factor of itself, using the empty substitution ε as an mgu of a single literal in C.

Definition 3 Let Σ be a set of clauses and C a clause. A *derivation* of C from Σ is a finite sequence of clauses $R_1, \ldots, R_k = C$, such that each R_i is either in Σ, or a resolvent of two clauses in $\{R_1, \ldots, R_{i-1}\}$. If such a derivation exists, we write $\Sigma \vdash_r C$. A derivation of the empty clause $\square$ from Σ is called a *refutation* of Σ. ◇

Definition 4 Let C and D be clauses. We say D *subsumes* (or θ-*subsumes*) C if there exists a substitution θ such that $D\theta \subseteq C$.

Let Σ be a set of clauses and C a clause. We say there exists a *deduction* of C from Σ, written as $\Sigma \vdash_d C$, if C is a tautology, or if there exists a clause D such that $\Sigma \vdash_r D$ and D subsumes C. ◇

To illustrate these definitions, we will give an example of a deduction of the clause $C = R(a) \vee S(a)$ from the set $\Sigma = \{(P(x) \vee Q(x) \vee R(x)), (\neg P(x) \vee Q(a)), (\neg P(x) \vee \neg Q(x)), (P(x) \vee \neg Q(x))\}$. Figure 1 shows a derivation of the clause $D = R(a) \vee R(a)$ from Σ. Note that we use the factor $Q(a) \vee R(a)$ of the parent clause $C_6 = Q(x) \vee R(x) \vee Q(a)$ in the last step of the derivation, and also the factor $P(y) \vee R(y)$ of $C_5 = P(y) \vee P(y) \vee R(y)$ in the step leading to C_7. Since D subsumes C, we have $\Sigma \vdash_d C$.

It is not very difficult to see the equivalence between our definition of a derivation, and the definition of $\mathcal{R}^n(\Sigma)$ we gave in Section 1. For instance, in figure 1, C_1, C_2, C_3, C_4, C_1' are variants of clauses in $\mathcal{R}^0(\Sigma)$ (C_1 and C_1' are

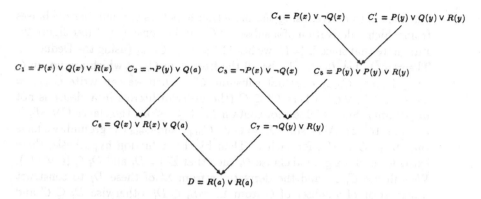

Figure 1: The tree for the derivation of D from Σ

variants of the same clause). C_5, C_6 are in $\mathcal{R}^1(\Sigma)$, C_7 is in $\mathcal{R}^2(\Sigma)$, and D is in $\mathcal{R}^3(\Sigma)$.

The subsumption theorem states that $\Sigma \models C$ iff $\Sigma \vdash_d C$. The 'if'-part of this result follows immediately from the soundness of resolution. We prove the 'only-if' part in a number of successive steps in the following subsections. First we prove the theorem in case both Σ and C are ground, then we prove it in case Σ consists of arbitrary clauses but C is ground, and finally we prove the theorem when neither Σ nor C need to be ground.

2.1 The Subsumption Theorem for Ground Σ and C

First we prove our result for the case when both Σ and C are restricted to ground clauses.

Theorem 1 *Let Σ be a set of ground clauses, and C be a ground clause. If $\Sigma \models C$, then $\Sigma \vdash_d C$.*

Proof If C is a tautology, the theorem is obvious. Assume C is not a tautology. Then we need to find a clause D, such that $\Sigma \vdash_r D$ and $D \subseteq C$ (note that for ground clauses D and C, D subsumes C iff $D \subseteq C$). The proof is by induction on the number of clauses in Σ.

1. Suppose $\Sigma = \{C_1\}$. We will show that $C_1 \subseteq C$. Suppose $C_1 \not\subseteq C$. Then there exists a literal L, such that $L \in C_1$ but $L \notin C$. Let I be an interpretation which makes L true, and all literals in C false (such an I exists, since C is not a tautology). Then I is a model of C_1, but not of C. But that contradicts $\Sigma \models C$. So $C_1 \subseteq C$, and $\Sigma \vdash_d C$.

2. Suppose the theorem holds if $|\Sigma| \leq m$. We will prove that this implies that the theorem also holds if $|\Sigma| = m + 1$. Let $\Sigma = \{C_1, \ldots, C_{m+1}\}$, and $\Sigma' = \{C_1, \ldots, C_m\}$. If C_{m+1} subsumes C or $\Sigma' \models C$, then the theorem holds. So assume C_{m+1} does not subsume C and $\Sigma' \not\models C$.

The idea is to derive, using the induction hypothesis, a number of clauses from which a derivation of a subset of C can be constructed (see figure 2). First note that since $\Sigma \models C$, we have $\Sigma' \models C \vee \neg C_{m+1}$ (using the Deduction Theorem[7]). Let $L_1, \ldots, L_k$ be all the literals in C_{m+1} which are not in C ($k \geq 1$ since C_{m+1} does not subsume C). Then we can write $C_{m+1} = L_1 \vee \ldots \vee L_k \vee C'$, where $C' \subseteq C$ (the order of literals in a clause is not important). Since C does not contain L_i ($1 \leq i \leq k$), the clause $C \vee \neg L_i$ is not a tautology. Also, since $\Sigma' \models C \vee \neg C_{m+1}$ and C_{m+1} is ground, we have that $\Sigma' \models C \vee \neg L_i$, for each i. Then by the induction hypothesis, there exists for each i a ground clause D_i such that $\Sigma' \vdash_r D_i$ and $D_i \subseteq (C \vee \neg L_i)$. We will use C_{m+1} and the derivations from Σ' of these D_i to construct a derivation of a subset of C from Σ. $\neg L_i \in D_i$, otherwise $D_i \subseteq C$ and $\Sigma' \models C$. So we can write each D_i as $\neg L_i \vee D'_i$, and $D'_i \subseteq C$. The case where some D_i contains $\neg L_i$ more than once can be solved by taking a factor of D_i.

Now we can construct a derivation of the ground clause defined as $D = C' \vee D'_1 \vee \ldots \vee D'_k$ from Σ, using C_{m+1} and the derivations of $D_1, \ldots, D_k$ from Σ'. See figure 2. In this tree, the derivations of $D_1, \ldots, D_k$ are indicated by the vertical dots. So we have that $\Sigma \vdash_r D$. Since $C' \subseteq C$, and $D'_i \subseteq C$ for each i, we have that $D \subseteq C$. Hence $\Sigma \vdash_d C$.

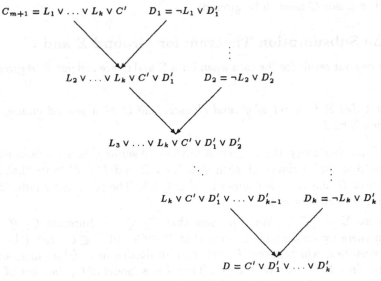

Figure 2: The tree for the derivation of D from Σ

□

---

[7] $\Sigma \cup \{C\} \models D$ iff $\Sigma \models (C \to D)$.

2.2 The Subsumption Theorem when C is Ground

In this section, we will prove the theorem in case C is ground and Σ is a set of arbitrary clauses. The idea is to "translate" $\Sigma \models C$ to $\Sigma_g \models C$, where Σ_g is a set of ground instances of clauses of Σ. Then by Theorem 1, there is a clause D such that $\Sigma_g \vdash_r D$, and D subsumes C. Afterwards, we can "lift" this to a deduction of C from Σ.

Theorem 2 (Herbrand, [CL73]) *A set Σ of clauses is unsatisfiable iff there is a finite unsatisfiable set Σ' of ground instances of clauses of Σ.*

Lemma 1 *Let Σ be a set of clauses, and C be a ground clause. If $\Sigma \models C$, then there exists a finite set of clauses Σ_g, where each clause in Σ_g is a ground instance of a clause in Σ, such that $\Sigma_g \models C$.*

Proof Let $C = L_1 \vee \ldots \vee L_k$ ($k \geq 0$). If Σ is unsatisfiable then the lemma follows immediately from Theorem 2, so suppose Σ is satisfiable. Note that since C is ground, $\neg C$ is equivalent to $\neg L_1 \wedge \ldots \wedge \neg L_k$. Then:

$\Sigma \models C$ iff (by the Deduction Theorem)
$\Sigma \cup \{\neg C\}$ is unsatisfiable iff
$\Sigma \cup \{\neg L_1, \ldots, \neg L_k\}$ is unsatisfiable iff (by Theorem 2)
there exists a finite unsatisfiable set Σ', consisting of ground instances
of clauses from $\Sigma \cup \{\neg L_1, \ldots, \neg L_k\}$.

Since Σ is satisfiable, the unsatisfiable set Σ' must contain one or more members of the set $\{\neg L_1, \ldots, \neg L_k\}$, i.e. $\Sigma' = \Sigma_g \cup \{\neg L_{i_1}, \ldots, \neg L_{i_j}\}$, where Σ_g is a finite non-empty set of ground instances of clauses in Σ. So:

Σ' is unsatisfiable iff
$\Sigma_g \cup \{\neg L_{i_1}, \ldots, \neg L_{i_j}\}$ is unsatisfiable iff
$\Sigma_g \cup \{\neg(L_{i_1} \vee \ldots \vee L_{i_j})\}$ is unsatisfiable iff (by the Deduction Theorem)
$\Sigma_g \models (L_{i_1} \vee \ldots \vee L_{i_j})$.

Since $\{L_{i_1}, \ldots, L_{i_j}\} \subseteq C$, it follows that $\Sigma_g \models C$. □

The next lemma shows that if a set Σ' consists of instances of clauses in Σ, then a derivation from Σ' can be "lifted" to a derivation from Σ. Similar lifting-lemmas are proved in [CL73, GN87]. We prove our own lifting-lemma, because our definition of resolution slightly differs from the definitions used in those books (we treat a clause as a disjunction, rather than as a set of literals). Because of its rather technical nature, we have deferred the proof to Appendix A.

Lemma 2 (Derivation Lifting) *Let Σ be a set of clauses, and Σ' be a set of instances of clauses in Σ. Suppose $R'_1, \ldots, R'_k$ is a derivation of the clause R'_k from Σ'. Then there exists a derivation $R_1, \ldots, R_k$ of the clause R_k from Σ, such that R'_i is an instance of R_i, for each i.*

Theorem 3 *Let Σ be a set of clauses, and C be a ground clause. If $\Sigma \models C$, then $\Sigma \vdash_d C$.*

Proof If C is a tautology, the theorem is obvious. Assume C is not a tautology. We want to find a clause D such that $\Sigma \vdash_r D$ and D subsumes C. From $\Sigma \models C$ and Lemma 1, there exists a finite set Σ_g such that each clause in Σ_g is a ground instance of a clause in Σ, and $\Sigma_g \models C$. Then by Theorem 1, there exists a ground clause D' such that $\Sigma_g \vdash_r D'$, and $D' \subseteq C$. Let $R'_1, \ldots, R'_k = D'$ be a derivation of D' from Σ_g. From Lemma 2, we can "lift" this to a derivation $R_1, \ldots, R_k$ of R_k from Σ, where $R_k\theta = D'$ for some θ. Let $D = R_k$. Then $D\theta = D' \subseteq C$. Hence D subsumes C. □

2.3 The Subsumption Theorem (General Case)

In this subsection, we will prove the subsumption theorem for arbitrary Σ and C. In the proof, we will use a *Skolemizing substitution*.

Definition 5 Let Σ be a set of clauses, and C a clause. Let $x_1, \ldots, x_n$ be all the variables appearing in C and $a_1, \ldots, a_n$ be distinct constants not appearing in Σ or C. Then $\{x_1/a_1, \ldots, x_n/a_n\}$ is called a *Skolemizing substitution* for C w.r.t. Σ. ◇

Lemma 3 *Let C and D be clauses. Let $\theta = \{x_1/a_1, \ldots, x_n/a_n\}$ be a Skolemizing substitution for C w.r.t. D. If D subsumes $C\theta$, then D also subsumes C.*

Proof Since D subsumes $C\theta$, there exists a substitution σ such that $D\sigma \subseteq C\theta$. Let σ be the substitution $\{y_1/t_1, \ldots, y_m/t_m\}$. Let σ' be the substitution obtained from σ by replacing each a_i by x_i in every t_j. Note that $\sigma = \sigma'\theta$. Since θ only replaces each x_i by a_i ($1 \leq i \leq n$), it follows that $D\sigma' \subseteq C$, so D subsumes C. □

Theorem 4 (Subsumption Theorem) *Let Σ be a set of clauses, and C be a clause. Then $\Sigma \models C$ iff $\Sigma \vdash_d C$.*

Proof
$\Leftarrow$: Follows immediately from the soundness of resolution, and the fact that if D subsumes C, then $D \models C$.
$\Rightarrow$: If C is a tautology, the theorem is obvious. Assume C is not a tautology. Let θ be a Skolemizing substitution for C w.r.t. Σ. Then $C\theta$ is a ground clause which is not a tautology, and $\Sigma \models C\theta$. So by Theorem 3, there is a clause D such that $\Sigma \vdash_r D$ and D subsumes $C\theta$. Since θ is a Skolemizing substitution for C w.r.t. Σ, and D can only contain constants appearing in Σ, θ is also a Skolemizing substitution for C w.r.t. D. Then by Lemma 3, D also subsumes C. Thus we have $\Sigma \vdash_d C$. □

3 The Refutation-Completeness of Resolution

The subsumption theorem actually tells us that resolution and subsumption form a complete set of proof-rules for clauses. A form of completeness that is usually stated in the literature on resolution is the refutation-completeness. This is an easy consequence of the subsumption theorem.

Theorem 5 (Refutation-Completeness of Resolution) *Let Σ be a set of clauses. Then Σ is unsatisfiable iff $\Sigma \vdash_r \Box$.*

Proof

$\Leftarrow$: Follows immediately from the soundness of resolution.

$\Rightarrow$: Suppose Σ is unsatisfiable. Then $\Sigma \models \Box$. So by Theorem 4, there exists a clause D, such that $\Sigma \vdash_r D$ and D subsumes the empty clause $\Box$. But $\Box$ is the only clause which subsumes $\Box$, so $D = \Box$. $\qquad\qquad\Box$

4 The Other Way Around

In Section 3, we showed that the refutation-completeness is a direct consequence of the subsumption theorem. In this section, we will show the converse: that we can obtain the subsumption theorem from the refutation-completeness. This establishes the equivalence of the subsumption theorem and the refutation-completeness (i.e., the one can be proved from the other).

To prove the subsumption theorem from the refutation-completeness, we will show how to turn a refutation of $\Sigma \cup \{\neg L_1, \ldots, \neg L_k\}$ into a deduction of $L_1 \vee \ldots \vee L_k$. Thus our proof, which has some similarities with the unsatisfactory proof of the subsumption theorem in [BM92], is constructive. We start with an example. Suppose $\Sigma = \{(P(x) \vee \neg R(f(f(b)))), (R(f(x)) \vee \neg R(x))\}$, and $C = P(x) \vee Q(x) \vee \neg R(b)$. It is not difficult to see that $\Sigma \models C$. We would like to produce a deduction of C from Σ. First we note that $\theta = \{x/a\}$ is a Skolemizing substitution for C w.r.t. Σ. Since $\Sigma \models C\theta$, we know that $\Sigma \cup \{\neg P(a), \neg Q(a), R(b)\}$ is unsatisfiable, and hence (by the refutation-completeness) has a refutation. Figure 3 shows such a refutation.

Now by omitting the leaves of the refutation-tree which come from $C\theta$ (the framed literals) and by making appropriate changes in the tree, we get a derivation of the clause $D = P(x) \vee \neg R(b)$. See figure 4. D subsumes C, so we have turned the refutation of figure 3 into a deduction of C from Σ.

This approach also works in the general case. The following lemma does most of the work.

Lemma 4 *Let Σ be a set of clauses, and $C = L_1 \vee \ldots \vee L_k$ be a non-tautologous ground clause. If $\Sigma \cup \{\neg L_1, \ldots, \neg L_k\} \vdash_r \Box$, then $\Sigma \vdash_d C$.*

Proof Suppose $\Sigma \cup \{\neg L_1, \ldots, \neg L_k\} \vdash_r \Box$. Then there exists a refutation $R_1, \ldots, R_n = \Box$ of $\Sigma \cup \{\neg L_1, \ldots, \neg L_k\}$. Let r be the number of resolvents in this sequence ($r = n-$the number of members of $\Sigma \cup \{\neg L_1, \ldots, \neg L_k\}$ in $R_1, \ldots, R_n$). We prove the lemma by induction on r.

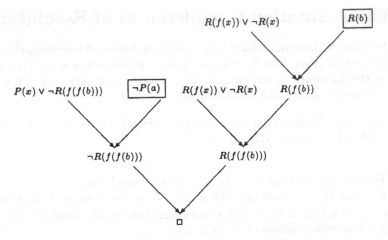

Figure 3: A refutation of $\Sigma \cup \{\neg P(a), \neg Q(a), R(b)\}$

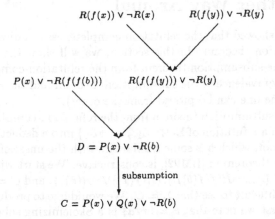

Figure 4: A deduction of C from Σ, obtained by transforming the previous figure

1. Suppose $r = 0$. Then we must have $R_n = \square \in \Sigma$, so obviously the lemma holds.
2. Suppose the lemma holds for $r \leq m$. We will prove that this implies that the lemma also holds for $r = m + 1$. Let $R_1, \ldots, R_n = \square$ be a refutation of $\Sigma \cup \{\neg L_1, \ldots, \neg L_k\}$ containing $m + 1$ resolvents. Let R_i be the first resolvent. Then $R_1, \ldots, R_n = \square$ is a refutation of $\Sigma \cup \{R_i\} \cup \{\neg L_1, \ldots, \neg L_k\}$ containing only m resolvents, since R_i is now one of the original premises. Hence by the induction hypothesis, there is a clause D, such that $\Sigma \cup \{R_i\} \vdash_r D$ and D subsumes C.

   Suppose R_i is itself a resolvent of two members of Σ. Then we also have $\Sigma \vdash_r D$, so the lemma holds in this case. Note that R_i cannot be a resolvent of two members of $\{\neg L_1, \ldots, \neg L_k\}$ because this set does not contain a complementary pair, due to the fact that C is not a tautology. The only remaining case we have to check, is where R_i is a resolvent of

$C' \in \Sigma$ and some $\neg L_s$ $(1 \leq s \leq k)$. Let $C' = M_1 \vee \ldots \vee M_j \vee \ldots \vee M_h$. Suppose R_i is a binary resolvent of $(M_1 \vee \ldots \vee M_j)\sigma$ (a factor of C', using σ as an mgu of $\{M_j, \ldots, M_h\}$) and $\neg L_s$, with θ as mgu of $M_j\sigma$ and L_s. Then $R_i = (M_1 \vee \ldots \vee M_{j-1})\sigma\theta$ and $C'\sigma\theta = R_i \vee L_s \vee \ldots \vee L_s$ $(h - j + 1$ copies of $L_s)$, since $M_j, \ldots, M_h$ are all unified to L_s by $\sigma\theta$. Now replace each time R_i appears as leaf in the derivation-tree of D, by $C'\sigma\theta = R_i \vee L_s \vee \ldots \vee L_s$, and add $L_s \vee \ldots \vee L_s$ to all descendants of such an R_i-leaf. Then we obtain a derivation of $D \vee L_s \vee \ldots \vee L_s$ from $\Sigma \cup \{C'\sigma\theta\}$. Since $C'\sigma\theta$ is an instance of a clause from Σ, we can lift (by Lemma 2) this derivation to a derivation from Σ of a clause D', which has $D \vee L_s \vee \ldots \vee L_s$ as an instance. Since D subsumes C, D' also subsumes C. Hence $\Sigma \vdash_d C$.

□

Now we can prove the subsumption theorem (Theorem 4) once more, this time starting from Theorem 5.

Theorem 4 (Subsumption Theorem) Let Σ be a set of clauses, and C be a clause. Then $\Sigma \models C$ iff $\Sigma \vdash_d C$.

Proof

$\Leftarrow$: By the soundness of resolution, and the fact that if D subsumes C, then $D \models C$.

$\Rightarrow$: If C is a tautology, the theorem is obvious. Assume C is not a tautology. Let θ be a Skolemizing substitution for C w.r.t. Σ. Let $C\theta$ be the clause $L_1 \vee \ldots \vee L_k$. Since C is not a tautology, $C\theta$ is not a tautology. $C\theta$ is ground and $\Sigma \models C\theta$, so the set of clauses $\Sigma \cup \{\neg L_1, \ldots, \neg L_k\}$ is unsatisfiable. Then it follows from Theorem 5 that $\Sigma \cup \{\neg L_1, \ldots, \neg L_k\} \vdash_r \square$. Therefore by Lemma 4, there exists a clause D such that $\Sigma \vdash_r D$, and D subsumes $C\theta$. From Lemma 3, D also subsumes C itself. Hence $\Sigma \vdash_d C$.

□

Now that we have shown that the subsumption theorem can be proved from the refutation-completeness, and vice versa, we also have the following:

Theorem 6 *For unconstrained resolution, the subsumption theorem and the refutation-completeness are equivalent.*

5   The Incompleteness of Input Resolution

Note that if S' (the subsumption theorem for input resolution) that we mentioned in Section 1 were true, then it would follow along the same lines as Theorem 5 that input resolution is refutation-complete. However, since it is well-known that input resolution is *not* refutation-complete [CL73, GN87], this again shows that S' cannot be true. Since [Mug92, Ide93a] only use the special case of S' where Σ contains only one clause, we investigate this here. We will show that S' is not even true in this special case. Hence the counterexample we give here is relevant for [Mug92, Ide93a], and also for other results based on $\mathbf{S}'$. In our counterexample we let $\Sigma = \{C\}$, with C:

$$C = P(x_1, x_2) \vee Q(x_2, x_3) \vee \neg Q(x_3, x_4) \vee \neg P(x_4, x_1).$$

Figure 5 shows that clause D (see below) can be derived from C by unconstrained resolution. This also shows that $C \models D$. Figure 5 makes use of the clauses listed below. C_1, C_2, C_3, C_4 are variants of C. D_1 is a binary resolvent of C_1 and C_2, D_2 is a binary resolvent of C_3 and C_4 (the underlined literals are the literals resolved upon). D_1' is a factor of D_1, using the subtitution $\{x_5/x_1, x_6/x_2\}$. D_2' is a factor of D_2, using $\{x_{11}/x_{12}, x_{13}/x_9\}$. Finally, D is a binary resolvent of D_1' and D_2'.

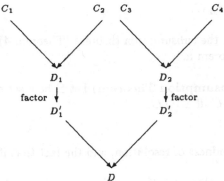

Figure 5: The derivation of D from C by unconstrained resolution

$$
\begin{aligned}
C_1 &= P(x_1, x_2) \vee \underline{Q(x_2, x_3)} \vee \neg Q(x_3, x_4) \vee \neg P(x_4, x_1) \\
C_2 &= P(x_5, x_6) \vee \overline{Q(x_6, x_7)} \vee \underline{\neg Q(x_7, x_8)} \vee \neg P(x_8, x_5) \\
C_3 &= P(x_9, x_{10}) \vee Q(x_{10}, x_{11}) \vee \underline{\neg Q(x_{11}, x_{12})} \vee \neg P(x_{12}, x_9) \\
C_4 &= P(x_{13}, x_{14}) \vee \underline{Q(x_{14}, x_{15})} \vee \neg Q(x_{15}, x_{16}) \vee \neg P(x_{16}, x_{13}) \\
D_1 &= P(x_1, x_2) \vee \neg Q(x_3, x_4) \vee \neg\overline{P(x_4, x_1)} \vee P(x_5, x_6) \vee Q(x_6, x_2) \vee \\
&\quad \neg P(x_3, x_5) \\
D_2 &= P(x_9, x_{10}) \vee \neg Q(x_{11}, x_{12}) \vee \neg P(x_{12}, x_9) \vee P(x_{13}, x_{14}) \vee \\
&\quad Q(x_{14}, x_{10}) \vee \neg P(x_{11}, x_{13}) \\
D_1' &= \underline{P(x_1, x_2)} \vee \neg Q(x_3, x_4) \vee \neg P(x_4, x_1) \vee Q(x_2, x_2) \vee \neg P(x_3, x_1) \\
D_2' &= \overline{P(x_9, x_{10})} \vee \neg Q(x_{12}, x_{12}) \vee \neg P(x_{12}, x_9) \vee P(x_9, x_{14}) \vee Q(x_{14}, x_{10}) \\
D &= \neg Q(x_3, x_4) \vee \neg P(x_4, x_1) \vee Q(x_2, x_2) \vee \neg P(x_3, x_1) \vee P(x_2, x_{10}) \vee \\
&\quad \neg Q(x_1, x_1) \vee P(x_2, x_{14}) \vee Q(x_{14}, x_{10})
\end{aligned}
$$

So D can be derived from C using unconstrained resolution. However, neither D nor a clause which subsumes D can be derived from C using only *input* resolution. We prove this in Proposition 1 (see the Introduction of this paper for the definition of $\mathcal{L}^n(\Sigma)$ and $\mathcal{L}^*(\Sigma)$). This shows that the subsumption theorem does not hold for input resolution, not even if Σ contains only one clause.

Lemma 5 *Let C be as defined above. Then for each $n \geq 1$: if $E \in \mathcal{L}^n(\{C\})$, then E contains an instance of $P(x_1, x_2) \vee \neg P(x_4, x_1)$ or an instance of $Q(x_2, x_3) \vee \neg Q(x_3, x_4)$.*

Proof By induction on n:

1. $\mathcal{L}^1(\{C\}) = \{C\}$, so the lemma is obvious for $n = 1$.
2. Suppose the lemma holds for $n \leq m$. Let $E \in \mathcal{L}^{m+1}(\{C\})$. Note that the only factor of C is C itself. Therefore E is a binary resolvent of C and a factor of a clause in $\mathcal{L}^m(\{C\})$. Let θ be the mgu used in obtaining this binary resolvent. If $P(x_1, x_2)$ or $\neg P(x_4, x_1)$ is the literal resolved upon in C, then E must contain $(Q(x_2, x_3) \vee \neg Q(x_3, x_4))\theta$. Otherwise $Q(x_2, x_3)$ or $\neg Q(x_3, x_4)$ is the literal resolved upon in C, so then E contains $(P(x_1, x_2) \vee \neg P(x_4, x_1))\theta$.

$\square$

Proposition 1 *Let C and D be as defined above. Then $\mathcal{L}^*(\{C\})$ does not contain a clause which subsumes D.*

Proof Suppose $E \in \mathcal{L}^*(\{C\})$. From Lemma 5 and the definition of $\mathcal{L}^*(\{C\})$, we know that E contains an instance of $P(x_1, x_2) \vee \neg P(x_4, x_1)$ or an instance of $Q(x_2, x_3) \vee \neg Q(x_3, x_4)$. It is easy to see that neither $P(x_1, x_2) \vee \neg P(x_4, x_1)$ nor $Q(x_2, x_3) \vee \neg Q(x_3, x_4)$ subsumes D. Then E does not subsume D. $\square$

6 Conclusion

This paper forms the first part of our research concerning the subsumption theorem. This part pertains to unconstrained resolution. The second part of our research is concerned with SLD-resolution and Horn clauses, and is described in [NW95b]. There we show that the subsumption theorem for SLD-resolution is equivalent with the refutation-completeness of SLD-resolution.

In this paper, we discussed the importance of the subsumption theorem in ILP. No really rigorous proof of this theorem for unconstrained resolution was until now available, and applications of the theorem in the literature often use the incorrect version **S'**. A proof of the subsumption theorem for unconstrained resolution was given by us. The refutation-completeness of unconstrained resolution was then shown to be an easy corollary of this theorem. Since the subsumption theorem in turn also follows from the refutation-completeness (as proved in Section 4), we have in fact proved that the subsumption theorem and the refutation-completeness are equivalent.

Finally we showed that **S'** is not even true when the set of premises consists of only one clause. This means that results based on **S'** or its special case, among which are results on nth powers and nth roots, need to be reconsidered.

References

[BM92] Bain, M., and Muggleton, S., 'Non-monotonic Learning', in: Muggleton, S. (ed.), *Inductive Logic Programming*, APIC series, no. 38, Academic Press, 1992, pp. 145–153.

[CL73] Chang, C. L., and Lee, R. C. T., *Symbolic Logic and Mechanical Theorem Proving*, Academic Press, San Diego, 1973.

[GN87]   Genesereth, M. R., and Nilsson, N. J., *Logical Foundations of Artificial Intelligence*, Morgan Kaufmann, Palo Alto, 1987.

[Ide93a]   Idestam-Almquist, P., *Generalization of Clauses*, PhD Thesis, Stockholm University, 1993.

[Ide93b]   Idestam-Almquist, P., 'Generalization under Implication by Recursive Anti-Unification', in: *Proceedings of the Tenth International Conference on Machine Learning*, Morgan Kaufmann, 1993.

[Ide93c]   Idestam-Almquist, P., 'Generalization under Implication by Using Or-Introduction', in: *Proceedings of the European Conference on Machine Learning-93*, Springer Verlag, 1993.

[Ide93d]   Idestam-Almquist, P., 'Generalization under Implication: Expansion of Clauses for Indirect Roots', in: *Scandinavian Conference on Artificial Intelligence-93*, IOS Press, Amsterdam, Netherlands, 1993.

[Kow70]   Kowalski, R., 'The Case for Using Equality Axioms in Automatic Demonstration', in: *Proc. of the Symposium on Automatic Demonstration*, Lecture Notes in Mathematics 125, Springer Verlag, 1970, pp. 112–127.

[LN94a]   van der Laag, P., and Nienhuys-Cheng, S.-H., 'Existence and Nonexistence of Complete Refinement Operators', in: *Proc. the European Conference on Machine Learning (ECML-94)*, Lecture Notes in Artificial Intelligence 784, Springer-Verlag, pp. 307–322.

[LN94b]   van der Laag, P., and Nienhuys-Cheng, S.-H., 'A Note on Ideal Refinement Operators in Inductive Logic Programming', in: Wrobel, S. (ed.), *Proc. of the Fourth Int. Workshop on Inductive Logic Programming (ILP-94)*, Bad Honnef, Germany, 1994, pp. 247–262.

[Lee67]   Lee, R. C. T., *A Completeness Theorem and a Computer Program for Finding Theorems Derivable from Given Axioms*, PhD Thesis, University of California, Berkeley, 1967.

[Llo87]   Lloyd, J. W., *Foundations of Logic Programming*, Second edition, Springer-Verlag, Berlin, 1987.

[Mug92]   Muggleton, S., 'Inverting Implication', in: Muggleton, S. H., and Furukawa, K. (eds.), *Proc. of the Second Int. Workshop on Inductive Logic Programming (ILP-92)*, ICOT Technical Memorandum TM-1182, 1992.

[MP94]   Muggleton, S., and Page, C. D., 'Self-Saturation of Definite Clauses', in: Wrobel, S. (ed.), *Proc. of the Fourth Int. Workshop on Inductive Logic Programming (ILP-94)*, Bad Honnef, Germany, 1994, pp. 101–174.

[NLT93] Nienhuys-Cheng, S.-H., van der Laag, P., and van der Torre, L., 'Constructing Refinement Operators by Deconstructing Logical Implication', in: *Proc. of the Third Congress of the Italian Association for Artificial Intelligence (AI*IA93)*, Lecture Notes in Artificial Intelligence 728, Springer-Verlag, pp. 178–189.

[NW95a] Nienhuys-Cheng, S.-H., and de Wolf, R., 'The Subsumption Theorem in Inductive Logic Programming: Facts and Fallacies', to appear in: *Proc. of the Fifth Workshop on Inductive Logic Programming (ILP-95, workreport)*, Leuven, September 1995.

[NW95b] Nienhuys-Cheng, S.-H., and de Wolf, R., 'The Subsumption Theorem Revisited: Restricted to SLD-resolution', to appear in: *Proc. of Computing Science in the Netherlands (CSN-95)*, Utrecht, November 1995.

[SCL69] Slagle, J. R., Chang, C. L., and Lee, R. C. T., 'Completeness Theorems for Semantic Resolution in Consequence-finding', in: *Proc. of the International Joint Conference on Artificial Intelligence (IJCAI-69)*, 1969, pp. 281–285.

A A Proof of the Lifting Lemma

In this appendix we give the rather technical proof of the lifting lemma.

Lemma 6 *If C_1' and C_2' are instances of C_1 and C_2, respectively, and if C' is a resolvent of C_1' and C_2', then there is a resolvent C of C_1 and C_2, such that C' is an instance of C.*

Proof We assume without loss of generality that C_1 and C_2, and C_1' and C_2' are standardized apart. Let $C_1 = L_1 \vee \ldots \vee L_m$, $C_2 = M_1 \vee \ldots \vee M_n$, $C_1' = C_1\sigma_1$, and $C_2' = C_2\sigma_2$ (here we can assume σ_k only acts on variables in C_k, $k = 1, 2$). Suppose C' is a resolvent of C_1' and C_2'. Then C' is a binary resolvent of a factor of C_1' and a factor of C_2'.

For notational convenience, we assume without loss of generality that the factor of C_1' is $(L_1 \vee \ldots \vee L_i)\sigma_1\theta_1$, where θ_1 is an mgu of $\{L_i\sigma_1, \ldots, L_m\sigma_1\}$. Similarly, the factor of C_2' that is used, is $(M_1 \vee \ldots \vee M_j)\sigma_2\theta_2$, where θ_2 is an mgu of $\{M_j\sigma_2, \ldots, M_n\sigma_2\}$. $L_i\sigma_1\theta_1$ and $M_j\sigma_2\theta_2$ are the literals resolved upon, say with mgu μ. Abbreviate $L_1 \vee \ldots \vee L_{i-1}$ to D_1, and $M_1 \vee \ldots \vee M_{j-1}$ to D_2. Then $C' = (D_1\sigma_1\theta_1 \vee D_2\sigma_2\theta_2)\mu$. By our assumption of standardizing apart, this can be written as $C' = (D_1 \vee D_2)\sigma_1\theta_1\sigma_2\theta_2\mu$.

Let γ_1 be an mgu of $\{L_i, \ldots, L_m\}$. Then $(L_1 \vee \ldots \vee L_i)\gamma_1$ is a factor of C_1. Note that $\sigma_1\theta_1$ is a unifier of $L_i, \ldots, L_m$. Since γ_1 is an mgu of $\{L_i, \ldots, L_m\}$, there exists a substitution δ_1 such that $\sigma_1\theta_1 = \gamma_1\delta_1$. Similarly, $(M_1 \vee \ldots \vee M_j)\gamma_2$ is a factor of C_2, with γ_2 as mgu of $\{M_j, \ldots, M_n\}$, and there is a δ_2 such that $\sigma_2\theta_2 = \gamma_2\delta_2$.

Since $L_i\sigma_1\theta_1$ and $\neg M_j\sigma_2\theta_2$ can be unified (they have μ as mgu) and γ_k is more general than $\sigma_k\theta_k$ $(k = 1, 2)$, $L_i\gamma_1$ and $\neg M_j\gamma_2$ can be unified. Let θ be an mgu of $L_i\gamma_1$ and $\neg M_j\gamma_2$. Define $C = (D_1\gamma_1 \vee D_2\gamma_2)\theta$, which can be written as $C = (D_1 \vee D_2)\gamma_1\gamma_2\theta$. Since C is a binary resolvent of the above-mentioned factors of C_1 and C_2, it is a resolvent of C_1 and C_2 (see figure 6 for illustration).

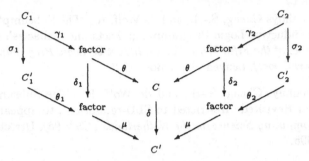

Figure 6: Lifting a resolvent

It remains to show that C' is an instance of C. Since $L_i\gamma_1\delta_1\delta_2\mu = L_i\sigma_1\theta_1\delta_2\mu = L_i\sigma_1\theta_1\mu = \neg M_j\sigma_2\theta_2\mu = \neg M_j\gamma_2\delta_2\mu = \neg M_j\gamma_2\delta_1\delta_2\mu$, the substitution $\delta_1\delta_2\mu$ is a unifier of $L_i\gamma_1$ and $\neg M_j\gamma_2$. θ is an mgu of $L_i\gamma_1$ and $\neg M_j\gamma_2$, so there exists a substitution δ such that $\delta_1\delta_2\mu = \theta\delta$. Therefore $C' = (D_1 \vee D_2)\sigma_1\theta_1\sigma_2\theta_2\mu = (D_1 \vee D_2)\gamma_1\delta_1\gamma_2\delta_2\mu = (D_1 \vee D_2)\gamma_1\gamma_2\delta_1\delta_2\mu = (D_1 \vee D_2)\gamma_1\gamma_2\theta\delta = C\delta$. Hence C' is an instance of C. $\quad\square$

Lemma 2 (Derivation Lifting) Let Σ be a set of clauses, and Σ' be a set of instances of clauses in Σ. Suppose $R'_1, \ldots, R'_k$ is a derivation of the clause R'_k from Σ'. Then there exists a derivation $R_1, \ldots, R_k$ of the clause R_k from Σ, such that R'_i is an instance of R_i, for each i.

Proof The proof is by induction on k.

1. If $k = 1$, then $R'_1 \in \Sigma'$, so there is a clause $R_1 \in \Sigma$ of which R'_1 is an instance.

2. Suppose the lemma holds if $k \leq m$. Let $R'_1, \ldots, R'_m, R'_{m+1}$ be a derivation of R'_{m+1} from Σ'. By the induction hypothesis, there exists a derivation $R_1, \ldots, R_m$ of R_m from Σ, such that R'_i is an instance of R_i, for all i $1 \leq i \leq m$. If $R'_{m+1} \in \Sigma'$, the lemma is obvious. Otherwise, R'_{m+1} is a resolvent of clauses $R'_i, R'_j \in \{R'_1, \ldots, R'_m\}$. It follows from Lemma 6 that there exists a resolvent R_{m+1} of R_i and R_j such that R'_{m+1} is an instance of R_{m+1}. $\quad\square$

Probabilistic Logic Programming and Bayesian Networks *

Liem Ngo and Peter Haddawy

Department of Electrical Engineering and Computer Science
University of Wisconsin-Milwaukee
Milwaukee, WI 53201, USA
{*liem, haddawy*} @*cs.uwm.edu*

Abstract. We present a probabilistic logic programming framework
that allows the representation of conditional probabilities. While conditional probabilities are the most commonly used method for representing
uncertainty in probabilistic expert systems, they have been largely ne-
glected by work in quantitative logic programming. We define a fixpoint
theory, declarative semantics, and proof procedure for the new class of
probabilistic logic programs. Compared to other approaches to quantitative logic programming, we provide a true probabilistic framework with
potential applications in probabilistic expert systems and decision support systems. We also discuss the relationship between such programs
and Bayesian networks, thus moving toward a unification of two major
approaches to automated reasoning.

1 Introduction

Reasoning under uncertainty is a topic of great importance to many areas of
Computer Science. Of all approaches to reasoning under uncertainty, probability
theory has the strongest theoretical foundations. In the quest to extend the fram-
work of logic programming to represent and reason with uncertain knowledge,
there have been several attempts to add numeric representations of uncertainty
to logic programming languages [19, 5, 2, 10, 13, 14, 12]. Of these attempts,
the only one to use probability is the work of Ng and Subrahmanian [14]. In
their framework, a probabilistic logic program is an annotated Horn program.
A typical example clause in a probabilistic logic program, taken from [14], is
$path(X,Y) : [0.85, 0.95] \leftarrow a(X,Y) : [1, 1]$, which says that if the probability
that a type A connection is used lies in the interval [1,1] then the reliability
of the path is between 0.85 and 0.95. As this example illustrates, their framework does not employ conditional probability, which is the most common way to
quantify degrees of influence in probabilistic reasoning and probabilistic expert
systems [16]. In [12] the authors allow clauses to be interpreted as conditional
probability statements, but they consider only the consistency of such programs,
and do not provide a query answering procedure.

---

* This work was partially supported by NSF grant IRI-9509165.

Bayesian networks [16] have become the most popular method for representing and reasoning with probabilistic information [9]. An extended form of Bayesian networks, influence diagrams, are widely used in decision analysis [16]. The strengths of causal relationships in Bayesian networks and influence diagrams are specified with conditional probabilities. A prominent feature of Bayesian networks is that they allow computation of posterior probabilities and performance of systematic sensitivity analysis, which is important when the exact probability values are hard to obtain. Bayesian networks are used as the main representation and reasoning device in probabilistic diagnostic systems and expert systems.

Bayesian networks were originally presented as static graphical models: for a problem domain the relevant random variables are identified, a Bayesian network representing the relationships between the random variables is sketched, and probability values are assessed. Inference is then performed using the entire domain model even if only a portion is relevant to a given inference problem. Recently the approach known as knowledge-based model construction [20] has attempted to address this limitation by representing probabilistic information in a knowledge base using schematic variables and indexing schemes and constructing a network model tailored to each specific problem.

The purpose of this paper is two-fold. First, we propose an extension of logic programming which allows the representation of conditional probabilities and hence can be used to write probabilistic expert systems. Second, we investigate the relationship between probabilistic logic programs and Bayesian networks. While Poole [17] shows how to represent a discrete Bayesian network in his Probabilistic Horn Abduction framework, in this paper we address both sides of this relationship. First, we show how Bayesian networks can be represented easily and intuitively by our probabilistic logic programs. Second, we present a method for answering queries on the probabilistic logic programs by constructing Bayesian networks and then propogating probabilities on the networks. We provide a declarative semantics for probabilistic logic programs and prove that the constructed Bayesian networks faithfully reflect the declarative semantics.

2 Syntax

Throughout this paper, we use Pr and sometimes Pr_P, Pr_P^C to denote a probability distribution; $A, B, \ldots$ with possible subscripts to denote atoms; names with leading capital characters to denote domain variables; names with leading small characters to denote constants and $p, q, \ldots$ with possible subscripts to denote predicates. We use a first order language containing infinitely many variable symbols and finitely many constant, function and predicate symbols. We use HB to denote the Herbrand base of the language, which can be infinite. For convenience, we use comma instead of logical AND and semicolons to seperate the sentences in a list of sentences.

Each predicate represents a class of similar random variables. In the probability models we consider, each random variable can take values from a finite set and in each possible realization of the world, that variable can have one and only one value. For example, the variable *neighborhood* of a person X can have value *bad, average, good* and, in each possible realization of the world, one and only one of these three values can be true; the others must be false. We capture this property by requiring that each predicate have at least one attribute representing the *value* of the corresponding random variable. By convention we take this to be the last attribute. For example, the variable *neighborhood* of a person X can be represented by a two-position predicate $neighborhood(X, V)$—the first position indicates the person and the second indicates the type of that person's neighborhood (bad, average or good). We associate with each predicate a *value integrity constraint* statement.

Definition 1 *The* **value integrity constraint** *statement associated with an m-ary predicate p consists of the following first order sentences (1)* $p(X_1, \ldots, X_{m-1}, V) \rightarrow V = v_1 \vee \ldots \vee V = v_n$; *(2)* $\leftarrow p(X_1, \ldots, X_{m-1}, v_i), p(X_1, \ldots, X_{m-1}, v_j)$, $\forall i, j : 1 \leq i \neq j \leq n$; *where* $n > 1, m \geq 1$ *are two integers,* $v_1, \ldots, v_n$ *are different constants, called the value constants, denoting the possible values of the random variables corresponding to p,* $X_1, \ldots, X_{m-1}$ *are different variable names and each sentence is universally quantified over the entire sentence. For convenience, we use* $EXCLUSIVE(p, v_1, \ldots, v_n)$ *to denote the above set of sentences.*

We use $=$ as the identity relation on HB and always assume our theories include Clark's Equality Theory [11]. We denote by $VAL(p)$ the set $\{v_1, \ldots, v_n\}$. If A is an atom of predicate p, we also use $VAL(A)$ as equivalent to $VAL(p)$. If A is the ground atom $p(t_1, \ldots, t_{m-1}, v)$ then $val(A)$ denotes the value v and $obj(A)$ denotes the random variable corresponding to $(p, t_1, \ldots, t_{m-1})$.

Example 1 *The value integrity constraint for the predicate neighborhood is*
$EXCLUSIVE(neighborhood, bad, average, good) =$
$\{\leftarrow neighborhood(X, bad), neighborhood(X, average)$;
$\leftarrow neighborhood(X, bad), neighborhood(X, good)$;
$\leftarrow neighborhood(X, average), neighborhood(X, good)$;
$neighborhood(X, V) \rightarrow V = bad \vee V = average \vee V = good\}$.
For a person, say named John, neighborhood(john, good) means the random variable neighborhood of John, indicated in the language by obj(neighborhood (john, good)), is good, indicated in the language by val(neighborhood(john, good)) $= good$. *In any possible world, one and only one of the following atoms is true: neighborhood(john, bad), neighborhood(john, average), or neighborhood(john, good). VAL(neighborhood), or VAL(neighborhood(john, bad)), is the set* $\{bad, average, good\}$.

We have two kinds of constants. The value constants are declared by EXCLUSIVE clauses and used as the last arguments of predicates. The non-value constants are used for the other predicate arguments.

Definition 2 *Let A be the ground atom* $p(t_1, \ldots, t_m)$. *We define Ext(A), the* **extension** *of A, to be the set* $\{p(t_1, \ldots, t_{m-1}, v) | v \in VAL(p)\}$.

Example 2 *In the burglary example, $Ext(neighborhood(john, bad)) = \{neighborhood(john, bad), neighborhood(john, average), neighborhood(john, good)\}$.*

Let A be an atom. We define $ground(A)$ to be the set of all ground instances of A. A set of ground atoms $\{A_i | 1 \leq i \leq n\}$ is called *coherent* if there do not exist any A_j and $A_{j'}$ such that $j \neq j'$ and $obj(A_j) = obj(A_{j'})$ (and $val(A_j) \neq val(A_{j'})$).

Definition 3 *A probabilistic sentence has the form $Pr(A_0 | A_1, \ldots, A_n) = \alpha$ where $n \geq 0, 0 \leq \alpha \leq 1$, and A_i are atoms. The sentence can have free variables and each free variable is universally quantified over its entire scope. The meaning of such a sentence is: If $Pr(B_0 | B_1, \ldots, B_n) = \alpha$ is a ground instance of it then the conditional probability of $obj(B_0)$ achieving the value $val(B_0)$ given $obj(B_i)$ having value $val(B_i), \forall i : 1 \leq i \leq n$, is α.*

Let S be the sentence $Pr(A_0 | A_1, \ldots, A_n) = \alpha$. We use $ante(S)$, the antecedent of S, to denote the conjunction $A_1 \wedge \ldots \wedge A_n$ and $cons(S)$, the consequent of S, to denote A_0. Sometimes, we use $ante(S)$ as the set of conjuncts. Notice that by using predicates with value attribute and integrity constraints, we can explicitly represent 'negative facts'.

2.1 Basic Probabilistic Logic Programs

Definition 4 *A basic (probabilistic logic) program consists of two parts: the probabilistic base PB is a finite set of probabilistic sentences and the set IC of value integrity constraints for the predicates in the language.*

Consider the following motivating example, which will be referred to throughout the remainder of the paper. A burglary alarm could be triggered by a burglary or a tornado. The likelihood of a burglary is influenced by the type of neighborhood one resides in. Figure 1 shows a possible basic probabilistic logic program for representing this example. We have the following predicates: *neighborhood, burglary, alarm,* and *tornado*. The interpretation of statements in *IC* is similar to that of $EXCLUSIVE(neighborhood, bad, average, good)$ shown in a previous example.

2.2 Acyclic Probabilistic Bases

In this paper, major results are achieved for a class of programs characterized by acyclicity. A probabilistic base PB is called *acyclic* if there is a mapping $ord_{PB}()$ from the set of ground instances of atoms into the set of natural numbers such that (1) For any ground instance $Pr(A_0 | A_1, \ldots, A_n) = \alpha$ of some sentence in PB, $ord_{PB}(A_0) > ord_{PB}(A_i), \forall i : 1 \leq i \leq n$. (2) If A and A' are two ground atoms such that $A' \in Ext(A)$ then $ord_{PB}(A) = ord_{PB}(A')$.

The expressiveness of acyclic logic programs is demonstrated in [1]. We expect that probabilistic logic programs with acyclic probabilistic bases will prove

$$IC = EXCLUSIVE(neighborhood, bad, average, good) \cup$$
$$EXCLUSIVE(burglary, yes, no) \cup EXCLUSIVE(alarm, yes, no) \cup$$
$$EXCLUSIVE(tornado, yes, no)$$
$$PB = \{ Pr(neighborhood(john, average)) = .4;$$
$$Pr(neighborhood(john, bad)) = .2; Pr(neighborhood(john, good)) = .4;$$
$$Pr(burglary(X, yes)|neighborhood(X, average)) = .4;$$
$$Pr(burglary(X, yes)|neighborhood(X, good)) = .2;$$
$$Pr(burglary(X, yes)|neighborhood(X, bad)) = .4;$$
$$Pr(alarm(X, yes)|burglary(X, yes)) = .98;$$
$$Pr(alarm(X, yes)|burglary(X, no)) = .05;$$
$$Pr(alarm(X, yes)|tornado(X, yes)) = .99;$$
$$Pr(alarm(X, yes)|tornado(X, no)) = .15\}$$

Fig. 1. A Basic Probabilistic Logic Program.

to have equal importance. To the best of our knowledge, knowledge bases of conditional probabilisties containing loops are considered problematic and all those considered in the literature are acyclic.

3 Fixpoint Semantics

3.1 The Relevant Atom Set

In this section, we consider the implications of the structure of basic probabilistic logic programs, ignoring the probability values associated with the sentences. We view the probabilistic sentence $Pr(A_0|A_1, \ldots, A_n) = \alpha$ as the Horn clause $A_0 \leftarrow A_1, \ldots, A_n$. Our purpose is to determine the set of *relevant atoms* implied by a program. For normal logic programs, fixpoint theory characterizes the semantics of a program by a *'minimal'* set of literals which is the fixpoint of a transformation constructed from its syntactic structure. That set consists of ground atoms that are considered true (and their negations false), and ground atoms that are considered false (and their negations true). Usually, there are other atoms whose truth values are undefined [6]. Similarly, from a basic probabilistic logic program, we can obtain (sometimes partial) probabilistic information about some ground atoms.

Example 3 *Consider the following basic program:*

$$IC = EXCLUSIVE(p, true, false) \cup EXCLUSIVE(q, bad, average, good) \cup$$
$$EXCLUSIVE(r, true, false) \cup EXCLUSIVE(s, true, false)$$
$$PB = \{ Pr(p(true)) = .4;$$
$$Pr(q(good)|p(true)) = .3; Pr(q(good)|p(false)) = .5;$$
$$Pr(r(true)|s(true)) = .6; Pr(r(true)|r(true)) = 1\}$$

Using Bayes' rule, we can derive $Pr(q(good)) = Pr(q(good) \land p(true)) + Pr(q(good) \land p(false)) = Pr(q(good)|p(true)) * Pr(p(true)) + Pr(q(good)|p(false)) *$

$Pr(p(false)) = .3 * .4 + .5 * .6 = .42$. *We know partial information about* $Pr(q(bad))$ *and* $Pr(q(average))$ *because* $Pr(q(bad)) + Pr(q(average)) = 1 - Pr(q(good)) = .58$. *But we do not know any probabilistic information about* $r(true), r(false), s(true)$ *and* $s(false)$ *(independently).*

Definition 5 *Given a basic program P. The* **fixpoint operator** $\mathbf{T_P}$ *is defined as a mapping from* 2^{HB} *into* 2^{HB} *such that for all* $I \in 2^{HB}$, $T_P(I)$ *is the smallest set in* 2^{HB} *satisfying the following properties: (1) if S is a ground instance of a sentence in P such that* $ante(S)$ *is a subset of I then* $cons(S) \in T_P(I)$; *(2) if* $A \in T_P(I)$ *then* $Ext(A) \subseteq T_P(I)$.

The transformation T_P produces only *reflexive* subsets of HB. Such subsets are important to us because when we know (partial) probabilistic information about an atom A, we also know (partial) probabilistic information about each other atom in $Ext(A)$. A subset I of HB is a **reflexive subset** if $\forall A \in I, Ext(A) \subseteq I$. We consider the *space of reflexive subsets* of HB, denoted by RHB.

Proposition 1 *(1)* RHB *is a complete lattice w.r.t. the normal* $\subseteq$ *relation. (2)* T_P *is monotonic on* RHB, *i.e.* $\forall I, I' \in RHB$: *whenever* $I \subseteq I', T_P(I) \subseteq T_P(I')$.

We define a simple iterative process for applying T_P.

Definition 6 *Let* ι *range over the set of all countable ordinals. The upward sequences* $\{I_\iota\}$ *and* I_* *are defined recursively by: (1)* $I_0 = \{\}$. *(2) If* τ *is a limit ordinal,* $I_\tau = \cup_{\iota < \tau} I_\iota$. *(3) If* $\tau = \iota + 1, I_\tau = T_P(I_\iota)$. *(4) Finally,* $I_* = \cup_\iota T_P(I_\iota)$.

The upward sequence $\{I_\iota\}$ is a monotonic sequence of elements in RHB. It follows by classical results of Tarski that the upward sequence converges to the least fixpoint.

Theorem 1 *The upward sequence* $\{I_\iota\}$ *converges to* $lfp(T_P) = I_*$, *the least fixpoint in* RHB. *Furthermore, if there are no function symbols in the language then the convergence occurs after a finite number of steps.*

We call $lfp(T_P)$ the *relevant set of atoms (RAS)*. RAS plays a similar role to well-founded partial models [6]. We use RAS to formalize the concept of possible worlds implied by a program. Let ι be a countable ordinal. An ι-**macro-world** of the logic program P is a maximal coherent subset of I_ι. A **possible world** is a maximal coherent subset of RAS. We use PW to denote the set of possible worlds. We can see that there always exist possible worlds for a program P.

Example 4 *Continuing the previous example, there are two 1-macro-worlds:* $w_{11} = \{p(true)\}$ *and* $w_{12} = \{p(false)\}$. *The possible worlds and also 2-macro-worlds are* $w_{21} = \{p(true), q(good)\}$; $w_{22} = \{p(true), q(average)\}$; $w_{23} = \{p(true), q(bad)\}$; $w_{24} = \{p(false), q(good)\}$; $w_{25} = \{p(false), q(average)\}$; $w_{26} = \{p(false), q(bad)\}$.

Let W be a possible world and $A \in W$. Then $W \cup IC$ derives $\neg A', \forall A' \in Ext(A)$ and $A' \neq A$. So, $W \cup IC$ represent a coherent assignment of values to the relevant random variables.

4 Combining Rules and Probabilistic Logic Programs

A basic probabilistic logic program will typically not be a complete specification of a probability distribution over the random variables represented by the atoms. One type of information which may be lacking is the specification of the probability of a variable given combinations of values of two or more variables which influence it. For real-world applications, this type of information can be difficult to obtain. For example, for two diseases D_1 and D_2 and a symptom S we may know $Pr(S|D_1)$ and $Pr(S|D_2)$ but not $Pr(S|D_1, D_2)$. Combining rules such as generalized noisy-OR [4, 18] are commonly used to construct such combined influences.

We define *a combining rule* as any algorithm that takes as input a (possibly infinite) set of ground probabilistic sentences with the same consequent $\{Pr(A_0|A_{i1}, \ldots, A_{in_i}) = \alpha_i | 1 \leq i \leq m(\text{m may be infinite})\}$ such that $\cup_{i=1}^{m} \{A_{i1}, \ldots, A_{in_i}\}$ is coherent and produces as output $Pr(A_0|A_1, \ldots, A_n) = \alpha$, where $A_1, \ldots,$ and A_n are all different and n is a finite integer. In addition to the standard purpose of combining rules, we also use them as one kind of default rule to augment missing causes (a cause is an atom in the antecedent). In this case, the antecedents of the output contain atoms not in the input sentences. The set of output causes can be a proper subset of the set of input causes, in which case the combining rule is performing a filtering and summarizing task.

Example 5 *Assume two diseases D_1, D_2 and one symptom S, which are represented by predicates d_1, d_2, and s, respectively. Also assume D_1, D_2 and S have values normal and abnormal. A program might contain only the following sentences: $Pr(s(abnormal)|d1(abnormal)) = .9$, $Pr(s(abnormal)|d1(normal)) = .15$,*
and $Pr(s(abnormal)|d2(normal)) = .2$. We can provide combining rules to construct from the first and third sentences a new sentence of the form $Pr(s(abnormal)|d1(abnormal), d2(normal)) = \alpha$ and from the second and third another new sentence of the form $Pr(s(abnormal)|d1(normal), d2(normal)) = \beta$, where α and β are two numbers determined by the combining rule. The combining rules may also act as default rules in augmenting the first and second sentences to achieve $Pr(s(abnormal)|d1(abnormal), d2(abnormal)) = \alpha'$ and $Pr(s(abnormal)|d1(normal), d2(abnormal)) = \beta'$, for some values α' and β'.

Definition 7 *A (probabilistic logic) program is a triple $\langle IC, PB, CR \rangle$, where $\langle IC, PB \rangle$ is a basic probabilisitic logic program and CR is a set of combining rules. We assume that for each predicate, there exists one corresponding combining rule in CR.*

5 The Combined Relevant Probabilistic Base

With the addition of combining rules, the real structure of a program changes. In this section, we consider the effect of combining rules on the relationships prescribed by the program.

Definition 8 *Given a program P, let ι be a countable ordinal. The* **set of ι-relevant probabilistic sentences** *(ι-RPB) is defined as the set of all ground instances S of some probabilistic sentence in PB, such that all atoms in S are in $I_ι$.*

The ι-RPB contains the basic relationships between atoms in $I_ι$. In the case of multiple influences represented by multiple sentences, we need combining rules to construct the combined probabilistic influence.

Definition 9 *Given a program P. Let ι be a countable ordinal. The* **combined ι-RPB** *(ι-CRPB) is constructed by applying the appropriate combining rules to each maximal set of sentences $\{S_i | i \in I\}$ (I maybe an infinite index set) in ι-RPB which have the same consequent and such that $\cup_{i \in I} ante(S_i)$ is coherent.*

Combined ι-RPB's play a similar role to completed logic programs. We assume that each sentence in ι-CRPB describes all random variables which directly influence the random variable in the consequent. We define a syntactic property of ι-CRPB which characterizes the completeness of probability specification.

Definition 10 *An ι-CRPB is* **completely quantified** *if*
(1) for all ground atoms A in $I_ι$, there exists at least one sentence in ι-CRPB with A in the consequent; and
(2) for all ground sentences S in ι-CRPB we have the following property: Let S have the form $Pr(A_0 | A_1, \ldots, A_n) = \alpha$, then for all $i = 0, .., n$, if $val(A_i) = v$ and $v' \in VAL(A_i), v \neq v'$, there exists another ground sentence S' in ι-CRPB such that S' can be constructed from S by replacing $val(A_i)$ by v' and α by some α'.

Definition 10 says that for each ground atom A we have a complete specification of the probability of all possible values $val(A)$ given all possible combinations of values of the atoms that directly influence A. If we think of each $obj(A)$ as representing a random variable in a Bayesian network model then the definition implies that we can construct a link matrix for each random variable in the model.

We call *-RPB the Relevant Probabilistic Base (RPB) and we call *-CRPB the Combined Relevant Probabilistic Base (CRPB).

Example 6 *Consider our burglary example and assume that the language contains only one non-value constant john. RAS={ neighborhood(john,bad), neighborhood(john,average), neighborhood(john,good), burglary(john,yes), burglary(john,no), alarm(john,true), alarm(john,false), tornado(john,yes), tornado(john,no)}, and RPB = {Pr(neighborhood(john,average))=.4; Pr(neighborhood(john,bad))=.2; Pr(neighborhood(john,good))=.4; Pr(burglary(john,yes)| neighborhood(john,average))=.4; Pr(burglary(john,yes)|neighborhood(john,good)) =.2; Pr(burglary(john,yes)|neighborhood(john,bad))=.4; Pr(alarm(john,yes)| tornado(john,yes))=.99; Pr(alarm(john,yes) | burglary(john,yes))=.98; Pr(alarm(john,yes)|burglary(john,no))=.05;*

$Pr(alarm(john,yes)|tornado(john,no))=.1\}$.

In the CRPB, the sentences in RPB with alarm as the consequent are transformed into sentences specifying the probability of alarm conditioned on both burglary and tornado. The other sentences in RPB remain the same in CRPB.

In conjunction with acyclicity property of probabilistic bases, we are interested in a class of combining rules which is capable of transferring the acyclicity property of a PB to the correspoding CRPB. Given a program P, we say a combining rule in CR is *self-contained* if the generated sentence $Pr(A|A_1,\ldots,A_n) = \alpha$ from the input set $\{Pr(A|A_{i1},\ldots,A_{in_i}) = \alpha_i | 1 \leq i \leq m(\text{m may be infinite})\}$ satisfies one additional property:

$\{A_1,\ldots,A_n\} \subseteq \cup_{A' \in Ext(A)}\{\{B_{i1},\ldots,B_{n_i}\} | Pr(A'|B_{i1},\ldots,B_{in_i}) = \alpha_i$ is in RPB$\}$.

Self-containedness seems to be a reasonable assumption on a combining rule: it does not allow the generation of new atoms in the antecedent which are not 'related' to any atom in the extension of the consequent. In order to generate a sentence with consequent A, a self-contained combining rule may need to collect all the sentences which have an atom in $Ext(A)$ as consequent.

Example 7 *The combining rule in the example 5 is not self-contained because the sentence $Pr(s(abnormal)|d1(abnormal), d2(abnormal)) = \alpha'$ is constructed from a set of sentences which do not contain the atom d2(abnormal). For this kind of diagnosis problem, generalized noisy-OR rule [18] always assume that if a disease is in the abnormal state then there is a probability 1 that the symptom is abnormal, that means $Pr(s(abnormal)|d2(abnormal)) = 1$. In order to use self-contained combining rules, we need to write explicitly those sentences.*

6 Model Theory

The semantics of a probabilistic program is characterized by the probability weights assigned the ground atoms. Because of space limitation, we only show how to assign weights to ground atoms.

6.1 Probabilistic Independence Assumption

In addition to the probabilitistic quantities given in the program, we assume some probabilistic independence relationships specified by the structure of probabilistic sentences. Probabilistic independence assumptions are used in all probability model construction work [20, 3, 7, 17, 8] as the main device to construct a probability distribution from local conditional probabilities. Unlike Poole [17] who assumes independence on the set of consistent *"assumable"* atoms, we formulate the independence assumption in our framework by using the structure of the sentences in ι-CRPB. We find this approach more natural since the structure of the ι-CRPB tends to reflect the causal structure of the domain and independencies are naturally thought of causally.

Definition 11 *Given a set P of ground probabilistic sentences, let A and B be two ground atoms. We say A is **influenced** by B in P if (1) there exists a sentence S, an atom A' in $Ext(A)$ and an atom B' in $Ext(B)$ such that $A' = cons(S)$ and $B' \in ante(S)$ or (2) there exists another ground p-atom C such that A is influenced by C in P and C is influenced by B in P.*

Assumption *We assume that if $Pr(A|A_1,\ldots,A_n) = \alpha$ is in ι-CRPB then for all ground atoms B which are not in $Ext(A)$ and not influenced by A in ι-CRPB, A and B are probabilistically independent given $A_1,\ldots,A_n$.*

Example 8 *Continuing the burglary example, $alarm(john, yes)$ is probabilistically independent of $neighborhood(john, good)$ and $neighborhood(john, bad)$ given $burglary(john, yes)$ and $tornado(john, no)$.*

Definition 12 *A completely quantified ι-CRPB is consistent if (1) there is no atom in I_ι which is influenced by itself in ι-CRPB and (2) for all $Pr(A_0|A_1,\ldots,A_n) = \alpha$ in ι-CRPB, $\sum \{\alpha_i | Pr(A_0'|A_1,\ldots,A_n) = \alpha_i \in \iota$-CRPB and $obj(A_0') = obj(A_0)\} = 1$.*

6.2 Possible World Semantics

In this section, we allow the language to contain function symbols. There are, in general, infinitely many possible worlds, infinitely many ι-macro -worlds. We use an approach similar to that of Poole [17] by assigning weights to only certain subsets of worlds.

Definition 13 (Rank of an atom) *Let A be a ground atom in RAS. We define $rank(A)$, the rank of A, recursively by: (1) If A is not influenced (in CRPB) by any atom then $rank(A) = 0$, otherwise (2) $rank(A) = sup\{rank(B)|Pr(A|\ldots,B,\ldots)$ is in CRPB$\} + 1$.*

Example 9 *In the burglary example, $rank(tornado(.,.)) = rank(neighborhood(.,.)) = 0, rank(burglary(.,.)) = 1$, and $rank(alarm(.,.)) = 2$. The program with the following CRPB has an atom which cannot be assigned a finite rank: $CRPB = \{Pr(q(true)|p(X,true)) = 1; Pr(p(X+1,true)|p(X,true)) = 1\}$. We cannot assign finite rank to $q(true)$ because $rank(q(true)) > rank(p(X,true)), \forall X$.*

We can see that if CRPB has no cycles then *rank* is a well-defined mapping. The following lemma will be useful in working with acyclic probabilistic bases.

Lemma 1 *Given a program P with an acyclic probabilistic base. If the combining rules are self-contained then the rank() function is well-defined.*

In defining the sample space, we will not consider individual possible world but sets of possible worlds characterized by formulae of specific forms.

Definition 14 *Given a program P, we can determine the set of all possible worlds PW. Assume that the rank function is well-defined. Let A be a ground atom in RAS. We denote the set of all possible worlds containing A by $W(A)$. We define the* **sample space** ω_P *to be the smallest set consisting of (1) $PW \in \omega_P$; (2) $\forall A \in RAS$ such that $rank(A)$ is finite, $W(A) \in \omega_P$; (3) if $W \in \omega_P$ then $PW - W \in \omega_P$; (4) if W_1, W_2 are in ω_P, then $W_1 \cap W_2$ is in ω_P.*

We consider the probability functions on the sample space ω_P. Let Pr be a probability function on the sample space, we define $Pr(A_1, \ldots, A_n)$, where $A_1, \ldots, A_n$ are atoms in RAS with finite ranks, as $Pr(\cap_{i=1}^{n} W(A_i))$. We take a sentence of the form $Pr(A_0|A_1, \ldots, A_n) = \alpha$ as shorthand for $Pr(A_0, A_1, \ldots, A_n) = \alpha \times Pr(A_1, \ldots, A_n)$. We say Pr() satisfies a sentence $Pr(A_0|A_1, \ldots, A_n) = \alpha$ if $Pr(A_0, A_1, \ldots, A_n) = \alpha \times Pr(A_1, \ldots, A_n)$ and Pr() satisfies $CRPB$ if it satisfies every sentence in $CRPB$.

Definition 15 *A* **probability distribution induced by a program P** *is a probability distribution on ω_P satisfying CRPB and the independence assumption implied by CRPB.*

Example 10 *Consider the following program:*

$IC = EXCLUSIVE(p, true, false) \cup EXCLUSIVE(q, bad, average, good)$
$PB = \{ Pr(p(0, true)) = .4; Pr(p(0, false)) = .6;$
$\quad Pr(q(good)|p(T, true)) = .3; Pr(q(good)|p(T, false)) = .5;$
$\quad Pr(p(T+1, true)|p(T, true)) = .999; Pr(p(T+1, false)|p(T, true)) = .001$
$\quad Pr(p(T+1, true)|p(T, false)) = .002; Pr(p(T+1, false)|p(T, false)) = .998\}$
$CR = \{ Generalized - Noisy - OR\}$

We can imagine that p is a timed predicate with the first attribute indicating time. The last four sentences represent persistence rules. We have
$Pr(W(p(0, true))) = .4, Pr(W(p(0, false))) = .6, Pr(W(p(1, true))) = (.999 \times .4 + .002 \times .6) = .4008, \ldots$

Theorem 2 *Given a program P, if the CRPB is completely quantified and consistent then there exists one and only one induced probability distribution.*

The following theorem allows us to handle probability of conjunctions and disjunctions in our framework.

Theorem 3 *Given a program P. Any probability function on ω_P satisfying CRPB assigns a weight to any formula of the form $\vee_{i=1}^{n} \wedge_{j=1}^{m} A_{ij}$, where n and m are finite integers and $rank(A_{ij})$ is finite, $\forall i, j$.*

7 Fixpoint Theory Revisited

We now extend the fixpoint theory to include the quantatitive information given in a program. We have constructed in a previous section the transformation T_P and the upward sequence $\{I_\iota\}$. We associate with each I_ι a sample space and a probability distribution.

Definition 16 *Given a program P, we can determine the set of possible worlds PW. Assume that the rank function is well-defined and ι is a finite ordinal. We define the sample space ω_P^ι to be the smallest set consisting of (1) $PW \in \omega_P$; (2) $\forall A \in I_\iota$ such that $rank(A) \leq \iota$, $W(A) \in \omega_P^\iota$; (3) if $W \in \omega_P^\iota$ then $PW - W \in \omega_P^\iota$; (4) if W_1, W_2 are in ω_P^ι then $W_1 \cap W_2$ is in ω_P^ι.*

Proposition 2 *If $\iota < \tau$ are two finite ordinals then $\omega_P^\iota \subseteq \omega_P^\tau \subseteq \omega_P$.*

We define the probability functions on the sample space ω_P^ι induced by a program P by replacing RAS by I_ι and CRPB by ι-CRPB in the definitions of the previous section. We call the corresponding induced probability function Pr_ι.

Theorem 4 *If $\iota < \tau$ are two finite ordinals and $W \in \omega_P^\iota$ then $Pr_\iota(W) = Pr_\tau(W) = Pr_P(W)$, where $Pr_P()$ is the probability distribution induced by P and RAS.*

So, as the upward sequence $\{I_\iota\}$ "converges" to $lfp(T_P)$, $\{\omega_P^\iota\}$ converges to ω_P and $Pr_\iota()$ "converges" to $Pr_P()$. Here, we use a "loose" definition of convergence: for any finite first order formula F of ground finite rank atoms, there exists an integer n such that for all $\iota > n$, the set $W(F)$ of possible worlds satisfying F is an element of ω_P^ι and $Pr_\iota(W(F)) = Pr_P(W(F))$.

8 Proof Theory

In the full paper, we describe the proof theory for probabilistic logic programs. We use a process similar to the SLD proof procedure with the only real difference being in the handling of combining rules. We call this proof procedure *probabilistic SLD* (p-SLD).

The procedure receives as input a query. A query is a sentence of the form $Pr(G_1, \ldots, G_n) =?$, where G_i are atoms. The query is a request to find all ground instances $G_1' \wedge \ldots \wedge G_n'$ of $G_1 \wedge \ldots \wedge G_n$ such that $Pr(G_1' \wedge \ldots \wedge G_n')$ can be determined from the program P and to return those probability values. The followings are our main results.

Theorem 5 *Given a program P with a well-defined rank() and a ground atom G. If $rank(G)$ is finite and CRPB is completely quantified and consistent then (1) the probability of G computed from the program P, $Pr_P^C(G)$, is equal to $Pr_P(G)$, where $Pr_P()$ is the probability function induced by the logic program P. (2) the p-SLD procedure will return the value $Pr_P^C(G)$ which is equal to $Pr_P(G)$.*

The condition that $rank(G)$ be finite can be assured by the acyclicity property of probabilistic logic programs. We have soundness and completeness of p-SLD for acyclic programs.

Theorem 6 *Given a program P with an acyclic probabilistic base and self-contained combining rules. If CRPB is completely quantified and consistent then p-SLD procedure is sound and complete wrt finite rank ground atoms.*

As can be seen in the recursive definition of $Pr_P^C()$, p-SLD can be easily extended to evaluate the probability of a finite conjunction of atoms. In fact, we can evaluate any finite formula of the form $\vee_i \wedge_j A_{ij}$ or $\wedge_i \vee_j A_{ij}$, where the A_{ij} are atoms of finite rank by a simple extension of p-SLD.

Negation-as-failure is used as a default rule in the SLDNF proof procedure. It allows us to conclude that a ground atom A has the truth value false if all attempts to prove A fail. In probabilistic logic programs, such default rules are desirable both to shorten the programs and to facilitate reasoning on incompletely specified programs. In the full paper we define a probabilistic analogue of negation-as-failure, called *local maximum entropy*.

9 Bayesian Network Construction

9.1 Baysian networks

Bayesian networks [16] are finite directed acyclic graphs. Each node in a Bayesian network represents a random variable, which can be assigned values from a fixed finite set. A link represents the relationship, either causal or relevance, between random variables at both ends. Usually, a link from random variable A to a random variable B indicates that A causes B. Associated with each node A is a link matrix that contains the conditional probability of each value of A given each possible combination of values of its parents. The Bayesian network formalism is an efficient approach to representing probabilistic structures and calculating posterior probabilities of random variables given a set of evidence.

In our query procedure, we will not only find the probability value of, say, a random variable but its posterior probability after observing a set of evidence.

Definition 17 *A set of* **evidence** E *is a set of atoms s.t. ground(E) is coherent.*

We compute the posterior probability by first constructing from the program the portion of the Bayesian network related to the query. We use available propagation algorithms on the constructed network to compute the posterior probability conditioned on the set of evidence.

Notice that in our framework an atom A represents the fact that the random variable denoted by $obj(A)$ receives the value $val(A)$ and $VAL(A)$ is the set of all possible values of that random variable.

Definition 18 *Given a program P and a set of evidence E, a* **complete ground query** *is a query of the form $Pr(G) =?$, where G is an atom, the last argument of G is a variable and it is the only variable in G. The meaning of such a query is: find the posterior probability distribution of $obj(G)$.*

A **complete query** *is a query of the form $Pr(G) =?$, where the last argument of G is a variable and the other arguments may also contain variables. The meaning of such a query is: find all ground instances G' of G such that the complete ground query $Pr(G') =?$ has an answer and return those answers.*

Definition 19 *Let A be a node in a Bayesian network N. The* **Bayesian network supporting** *A is the smallest subnetwork of N containing A and satisfying the following properties: (1) if B is a node in it then all parents of B are in it; and (2) the links and link matrices are exactly inherited from N.*

The Baysian network supporting a set of nodes V is the union of all supporting networks of nodes in V.

9.2 Bayesian Network Construction Procedure

Due to space limitations we omit the details of the algorithm, which can be found in the full paper. The query answering procedure works roughly as follows. Assume that we are given a program P, a set of evidence E and a complete query $Pr(G) =?$. Q^*-procedure has two main steps: build the supporting Bayesian network for $\{G\} \cup (ground(E) \cap RAS)$ by a backward chaining process similar to a Prolog engine and calculate the posterior probability conditioned on the set of evidence E using any available procedure [16]. Q^*-procedure is more complex than SLDNF because it needs to collect all relevant sentences before combining rules can be used.

We do not address the problem of the termination of Q^*-procedure. We expect that the techniques for assuring termination of Prolog programs could be applied.

Theorem 7 (Soundness) *Given a program P. If CRPB is completely quantified then Q^*-procedure is sound wrt complete queries.*

Theorem 8 (Soundness and Completeness) *Given a program P with an allowed and acyclic PB. If CRPB is completely quantified then Q^*-procedure is sound and complete wrt complete ground queries and ground finite set of evidence.*

10 Related Work

In a related paper [15] we present a temporal variant of our logic. We describe the application of this framework to representing probabilistic temporal processes and projecting probabilistic plans.

Poole [17] expresses an intention similar to ours: "there has not been a mapping between logical specifications of knowledge and Bayesian network representations ..". He provides such a mapping using probabilistic Horn abduction theory, in which knowledge is represented by Horn clauses and the independence assumption of Bayesian networks is explicitly stated. His work is developed along a different track than ours, however, by concentrating on using the theory for abduction. Our approach has several advantages over Poole's. We do not impose as many constraints on our representation language as he does. Probabilistic dependencies are directly represented in our language, while in Poole's language they are indirectly specified through the use of special predicates in the rules. Our probabilistic independence assumption is more intuitively appealing since it reflects the causality of the domain.

References

1. K. R. Apt and M. Bezem. Acyclic programs. *New Generation Computing*, pages 335–363, Sept 1991.
2. H. A. Blair and V. S. Subrahmanian. Paraconsistent logic programming. *Theoretical Computer Science*, pages 35–54, 1987. 68.
3. J.S. Breese. Construction of belief and decision networks. *Computational Intelligence*, 8(4):624–647, 1992.
4. F. J. Diez. Parameter adjustment in bayes networks: The generalized noisy or-gate. In *Proceedings of the Ninth Conference on Uncertainty in AI*, pages 99–104, July 1993.
5. M. C. Fitting. Bilattices and the semantics of logic programming. *Journal of Logic Programming*, (11):91–116, 1988.
6. A. V. Gelder, K. A. Ross, and J. S. Schlipf. The well-founded semantics for general logic programs. *JACM*, pages 620–650, July 1991.
7. R.P. Goldman and E. Charniak. A language for construction of belief networks. *IEEE Transactions on Pattern Analysis and Machine Intelligence*, 15(3):196–208, March 1993.
8. P. Haddawy. Generating Bayesian networks from probability logic knowledge bases. In *Proceedings of the Tenth Conference on Uncertainty in Artificial Intelligence*, pages 262–269, Seattle, July 1994.
9. D.E. Heckerman. Special issue on bayesian networks. *Communications of ACM*, 38(3), March 1995.
10. M. Kifer and V. S. Subramahnian. Theory of generalized annotated logic programs and its applications. *Journal of Logic Programming*, pages 335–367, 12 1992.
11. J. W. Lloyd. *Foundation of Logic Programming. Second edition.* Springer-Verlag, 1987.
12. Raymond Ng. Semantics and consistency of empirical databases. In *Proceedings of the 1993 International Conference on Logic Programming*, pages 812–826, 1993.
13. Raymond Ng and V. S. Subrahmanian. A semantical framework for supporting subjective and conditional probability in deductive databases. In *Proceedings of the 1991 International Conference on Logic Programming*, pages 565–580, 1991.
14. Raymond Ng and V. S. Subrahmanian. Probabilistic logic programming. *Information and Computation*, (2):150–201, 1992.
15. L. Ngo, P. Haddawy, and J. Helwig. A theoretical framework for context-sensitive temporal probability model construction with application to plan projection. In *Proceedings of the Eleventh Conference on Uncertainty in Artificial Intelligence*, pages 419–426, August 1995.
16. J. Pearl. *Probabilistic Reasoning in Intelligent Systems: Networks of Plausible Inference.* Morgan Kaufmann, San Mateo, CA, 1988.
17. D. Poole. Probabilistic horn abduction and bayesian networks. *Artificial Intelligence*, 64(1):81–129, November 1993.
18. S. Srinivas. A generalization of the noisy-or model. In *Proceedings of the Ninth Conference on Uncertainty in AI*, pages 208–217, July 1993.
19. van Emden M. H. Quantitative deduction and its fixpoint theory. *Journal of Logic Programming*, pages 37–53, 4 1986.
20. M.P. Wellman, J.S. Breese, and R.P. Goldman. From knowledge bases to decision models. *The Knowledge Engineering Review*, 7(1):35–53, 1992.

Deriving and Applying Logic Program Transformers*

Penny Anderson and David Basin
Max-Planck-Institut für Informatik,
Im Stadtwald, D-66123 Saarbrücken, Germany
{anderson,basin}@mpi-sb.mpg.de
phone: +49 681 302-5435 (fax: 302-5401)

Abstract

We present a methodology for logic program development based on the use of verified transformation templates. We use the Isabelle Logical Framework to formalize transformation templates as inference rules. We derive these rules in higher-order logic and afterwards use higher-order unification to apply them to develop programs in a deductive synthesis style. Our work addresses the pragmatics of template formalization and application as well as which theories and semantics of programs and data we require to derive templates.

Key words: program transformation, logic programs, higher-order unification, logical frameworks.

1 Introduction

We investigate the transformation of logic programs based on the use of *transformation templates* which formalize equivalences between schemata representing logic programs. Our focus and contributions center on three problems:

1. How may we acquire and formalize useful templates?

2. What foundations are appropriate for formally demonstrating the correctness of templates?

3. How should we organize transformation proofs so that logic programs can be developed alongside their proofs of correctness in a 'deductive synthesis' development style.

Our motivation is to provide a foundation in which templates may be derived and then applied to program development. We seek a uniform approach in which the developments of both templates and programs themselves are formal, machine supported activities which take place in a given mathematical theory.

We explore these problems within the context of the Isabelle Logical Framework [19], a theorem proving system which provides a *metalogic* and support for specifying and using *object logics*. Within a particular object logic, higher-order logic (HOL), we specify

---

*The authors were funded by the German Ministry for Research and Technology (BMFT) under grant ITS 9102. Responsibility for the content lies with the authors. The authors thank Alan Smaill for pointing them to some of the literature on logic programs as inductive definitions.

$$\text{Functional Definition for } F$$

$$\neg B(x) \quad \Rightarrow \quad F(x) = T(x) \tag{1}$$

$$B(x) \quad \Rightarrow \quad F(x) = R(F(H(x)), K(x)) \tag{2}$$

$$\text{Functional Definition for } G$$

$$\neg B(x) \quad \Rightarrow \quad G(x, y) = R(T(x), y) \tag{3}$$

$$B(x) \quad \Rightarrow \quad G(x, y) = G(H(x), R(K(x), y)) \tag{4}$$

$$\text{Applicability Conditions:}$$

$$R(x, N) = x \tag{5}$$

$$R(R(x, y), z) = R(x, R(y, z)) \tag{6}$$

$$\text{Correctness:}$$

$$F(x) = G(x, N) \tag{7}$$

Figure 1: Template for Tail Recursion Introduction, Functional Form

and reason about templates, which are formalized as proof rules expressing the equivalence of two logic program schemata. These rules are not taken as axioms, but rather derived within a conservative extension of higher-order logic. After derivation, the rules are applied, using higher-order unification, to transform logic programs during proofs of their correctness. Below we discuss these points in more detail, providing an overview to the technical development in following sections.

The first problem concerns acquiring and formalizing templates. For acquisition, we show that 'technology transfer' is possible by reformulating templates developed for functional program transformation. Although logic programs have a different operational semantics than functional programs, many of the large catalog of transformations developed for functional programs (e.g., [15, 12, 17]), when suitably reformulated, are also useful for optimizing logic programs. Figure 1 presents an example that we will consider in detail in this paper: a template for transforming functions to a tail-recursive form taken from [12] (see also [4]). This template defines, as conditional equations, functions F (Equations 1–2) and G (Equations 3–4) and states an equality between them (Equation 7) whenever two conditions hold. These applicability conditions state that the function R has a right identity N and is associative. In the context of functional program transformation, such templates have been applied using second-order matching to transform particular instances of F to G [15]; the above template, for example, may be applied to transform a naive implementation of list reversal or factorial to a more efficient tail recursive version.

We transform functional templates by *flattening* the functional schemata they contain to obtain relational templates suitable for transforming logic programs; that is, we iteratively replace n-ary functions with $n+1$-ary predicates which represent their graphs. The flattened template corresponding to the above is given in Figure 2. In the logic program context, the transformation performs *last call optimization*, which is the logic programming equivalent of tail recursion removal (e.g., see [16]).

In our work, transformation templates are formalized in the metalogic as rules, and formally verified by deriving them in an appropriate formal metatheory. However, to derive

Relational Definition for F

$$\neg B(x) \;\Rightarrow\; (F(x,y) \Leftrightarrow T(x,y)) \tag{8}$$

$$B(x) \;\Rightarrow\; (F(x,y) \Leftrightarrow \exists x_1, x_2, x_3. H(x,x_1) \wedge K(x,x_2) \wedge F(x_1,x_3) \wedge R(x_3,x_2,y)) \tag{9}$$

Relational Definition for G

$$\neg B(x) \;\Rightarrow\; (G(x,y,z) \Leftrightarrow \exists x_1. T(x,x_1) \wedge R(x_1,y,z)) \tag{10}$$

$$B(x) \;\Rightarrow\; (G(x,y,z)$$

$$\Leftrightarrow \exists x_1, x_2, x_3. H(x,x_1) \wedge K(x,x_2) \wedge R(x_2,y,x_3) \wedge G(x_1,x_3,z)) \tag{11}$$

Applicability Conditions:

$$R(x,N,y) \Leftrightarrow (x=y) \tag{12}$$

$$(\exists y_1. R(x,y,y_1) \wedge R(y_1,z,r)) \Leftrightarrow (\exists z_1. R(y,z,z_1) \wedge R(x,z_1,r)) \tag{13}$$

Correctness:

$$F(x,y) \Leftrightarrow G(x,N,y)$$

Figure 2: Template for Tail Recursion Introduction, Relational Form

relational templates there is a problem to overcome: the correctness of functional templates are typically established using proof techniques such as fixedpoint induction that are not available for logic programs, which have different semantics.

We present two solutions to this problem: template derivations based on induction over inductively defined datatypes, and derivations based on induction over inductively defined relations. In the first approach, we specialize the datatypes of some of the arguments, specialize some predicate variables, and prove the specialized rule by induction over datatypes. For example, we take the template of Figure 2, specialize the type of x to lists, instantiate some of the schematic variables to concrete predicates over lists, and prove the equivalence by structural induction on x. This is possible because, in Figure 2, we have left types implicit and interpret them polymorphically. We may specialize the template by proving it for a specialized type instance where we interpret some of the schematic variables as functions over these types. Isabelle supports this view of type polymorphism through type variables and type instantiation.

The second approach we examine yields more general templates, but it requires a more specialized semantics for logic programs; namely we take the view of logic programs put forth by Hagiya and others [20, 2, 10] where programs are considered not as sets of formulae constituting a Horn-clause theory, but rather as rules constituting an inductive definition. Under this view we may derive the equivalence of two relational schemata F and G by induction over the definitions of F and G. This approach is analogous to proofs of equivalence for functional schemata based on fixedpoint induction.

With respect to the third problem, organizing transformation proofs, we show how it is possible to generate transformed programs in the course of proving the correctness of the transformation itself. Our approach is based on applying proof rules which formalize transformation templates, using second-order unification (not matching, as is traditional) in the course of higher-order resolution. In our example, $F(x,y)$ is transformed to $G(x,N,y)$ by proving a theorem $\forall x, y. F(x,y) \Leftrightarrow? G(x,N,y)$. Here F is the name of the source program to be transformed; the question mark in $?G$ indicates that $?G$ is a second-order metavariable that is instantiated into the new transformed program during the correctness proof. Application of a transformation rule yields subgoals corresponding to the program definitions and applicability conditions which are further instantiated and simplified during later resolution steps. At the end of the proof, we are left with a definition for the transformed program G and a proof of its equivalence to F.

The remainder of the paper is organized around the problems discussed above and a running example of tail-recursion introduction is used to illustrate our proposed methodology. We begin with background, in particular in §2 we provide necessary details on Isabelle, which is the basis for our implementation of this work and will be used to illustrate our development. In §3 we show how transformation templates are formalized as inference rules. In §4 and §5 we present our approaches based on datatype and relational induction for demonstrating the correctness of these rules. In §6 we show how transformation rules may be applied and transformation proofs organized in a deductive synthesis style. Finally, in §7 we discuss experience, provide historical background, and compare our work to related approaches.

2 Background

All the work presented here has been implemented in Isabelle, and some Isabelle-specific background is necessary for the examples that follow. Note that Isabelle is not the only possible platform for this work. Any implementation of higher-order logic supporting inductively defined datatypes and relations would be sufficient; however the use of a logical framework has advantages in that we can use the metalogic to directly formalize and derive *rules* of higher-order logic as opposed to just *formulae* (this distinction will be illustrated shortly). The overview to Isabelle given here is necessarily limited, [19] provides a full account.

Isabelle is an interactive theorem prover which serves as a logical framework; this means that its logic is a metalogic in which object logics (e.g., first-order logic, set theory, etc.) are encoded. Isabelle's metalogic is a minimal higher-order logic supporting polymorphic typing. Object logics are encoded in the metalogic by declaring a signature and proof rules. Afterwards, proofs are interactively constructed by applying rules using higher-order resolution. Proof construction may be automated using *tactics* which are ML programs in the tradition of LCF that construct proofs.

Rules of object logics encoded in Isabelle are formulae in Isabelle's metalogic. For example, if we have declared a type *Form* of formulae, we might then formalize the natural deduction proof rule

$$\frac{A \land B}{A}$$

as

$$A \land B \implies A$$

where $\implies$ is implication in Isabelle's metalogic. Note that Isabelle supports type-reconstruction, and that free variables are implicitly universally quantified; hence the above is shorthand for

$$\forall A, B : Form. \, A \land B \implies B \, ,$$

where $\forall$ is universal quantification in Isabelle's metalogic. Quantification and implication in the metalogic should not be confused with declared syntax for the object logic (such as $\wedge$). In general, a rule has the form

$$[\phi_1; \ldots; \phi_n] \Longrightarrow \phi \qquad (14)$$

where the notation $[\phi_1; \ldots; \phi_n] \Longrightarrow \phi$ is shorthand for the iterated implication $\phi_1 \Longrightarrow \ldots \Longrightarrow (\phi_n \Longrightarrow \phi)$.

A rule can also be viewed as a proof-state, for the purposes of top-down proof construction, where ϕ is the goal to be established and the ϕ_i represent the subgoals to be proven. Under this view an initial proof state has the form $\phi \Longrightarrow \phi$, i.e., it has one subgoal, namely ϕ. The final proof state *is itself* the desired theorem ϕ.

Isabelle supports proof construction through higher-order resolution, which is roughly analogous to resolution in Prolog. That is, given a proof state with subgoal ψ and a rule like (14), then we higher-order unify ϕ with ψ. If this succeeds, then the unification yields a substitution σ and the proof state is updated by applying σ to it, replacing ψ with the subgoals $\sigma(\phi_1), \ldots, \sigma(\phi_n)$. This resolution step can be justified by a sequence of proof steps in the metalogic. Note that resolution provides a way to combine proof-rules, that is, we can derive new proof rules formally in the logic. For example, given our rule above for conjunction elimination, we could derive a rule like

$$(A \wedge B) \wedge C \Longrightarrow A.$$

Note too, that since unification is used to apply rules, the proof state itself may contain metavariables. We will show that this supports program transformation and synthesis during development. Finally, although rules are formalized in a natural deduction style, (14) can be read as an intuitionistic sequent where the ϕ_i are the hypotheses. Isabelle's resolution tactics apply rules in a way that maintains this illusion of working with sequents.

3 Transformation Templates as Inference Rules

We proceed in two parts. First we discuss how transformation templates for functional programs can be recast as templates for logic programs. Then we show how templates are formalized as proof rules.

3.1 From Functional to Logic Templates

A transformation template is a four-tuple consisting of:

1. a program schema (i.e., a program given in a typed higher-order language) representing the source program,

2. a program schema representing the transformed program,

3. applicability conditions, which specify requirements on relations or functions in the schemata, and

4. a correctness relation, which is the relation that holds between the original and transformed schemata.

Examples of functional and relational templates have been given in Figure 1 and Figure 2. Note that this formalization is identical to that of Huet and Lang in [15], except that they omit the correctness relation since they only consider functional programs transformation where the relation is always equality.

Functional transformation templates have been well studied and there is a large body of published examples (e.g., see [15, 17, 12]). Our interest is in transforming logic programs, so we employ relational reformulations of such functional templates. We translate functional templates by *flattening* the functional schemata to relational schemata.

Consider a functional schema of the form

$$L(x_1, \ldots x_n) = R(x_1, \ldots x_n) \tag{15}$$

where L and R represent terms built from function symbols and the x_i. We flatten such an equation to a logical equivalence by flattening each side with respect to some new variable y that represents the computed output. The term on each side of the equality corresponds to a formula involving relation symbols (including the special equality symbol =) on each side of the equivalence. If L or R is a variable, say x_i, then the flattened result is the equation $x_i = y$. Otherwise the term consists of m functions applied to variables and these are flattened to a conjunction of m relations: each n-ary function becomes an $n + 1$-ary relation, representing the function's graph. Values passed between nested functions are now passed between relations by using existentially quantified variables to represent the intermediate values. This is best illustrated with an example. Consider (2) given in Figure 1. The conditional equation

$$B(x) \Rightarrow F(x) = R(F(H(x)), K(x))$$

is flattened by forming the following conditional equivalence (we retain the condition which is already a relation)

$$B(x) \Rightarrow (F(x, y) \Leftrightarrow \exists x_1, x_2, x_3. H(x, x_1) \wedge K(x, x_2) \wedge F(x_1, x_3) \wedge R(x_3, x_2, y))$$

which is given in (9). Flattening all the equations of Figure 1 yields the translated template in Figure 2.

3.2 From Templates to Rules

A template can be recast as a rule of inference stating that the correctness condition holds under the hypotheses given by the definitions and applicability conditions. That is, if our template contains definitions $D_1, \ldots, D_m$, and applicability conditions $C_1, \ldots, C_n$, and the correctness relation G, we can express it as the rule

$$[D_1; \ldots; D_m; C_1 \ldots C_n] \Longrightarrow G$$

In the case of both functions and relations, these templates can be formalized as rules of first-order or higher-order logic. We have chosen to work with HOL because, as we will see shortly, we will want to view logic programs as inductive definitions.

Figure 3 gives the formal rule of inference corresponding to the relational template of Figure 2, expressed in Isabelle's concrete syntax. Some explanation follows. First, the object logic we use is an encoding of HOL based on Church's that comes distributed with

```
[| ALL x y. ~B(x) --> (F(x,y) = T(x,y));
   All x y. B(x) --> (F(x,y) =  EX x1 x2 x3.  H(x,x1) & K(x,x2) & F(x1,x3) &  R(x3,x2,y));
   ALL x y z. ~B(x) --> (G(x,y,z) = Ex x1. T(x,x1) &  R(x1,y,z));
   ALL x y z. B(x) --> (G(x,y,z) =  Ex x1 x2 x3. H(x,x1) &  K(x,x2) & R(x2,y,x3) & G(x1,x3,z))
   All x y. R(x,N,y) = (x = y);
   All x y z r. (Ex y1. R(x,y,y1) & R(y1,z,r)) = (Ex z1. R(y,z,z1) &  R(x,z1,r))
|] ==> All x y. F(x,y) = G(x,N,y)
```

Figure 3: Rule for Tail Recursion Introduction, Relational Form

the Isabelle system and is documented in [19]. Second, quantification for first-order variables in each equivalence is made explicit; recall that all remaining free variables are outermost universally quantified in the metalogic. Finally, note that in HOL logical equivalence is written as equality, which is defined as a relation at all types; hence we use the same symbol both for logical equivalence of propositions and equality.

We now have a proof rule that represents the relational transformation template given in Figure 2. It is a sentence of the metalogic but unfortunately it is not derivable; in the following two sections we show how variants of it can be formally derived.

4 Datatype Induction

In the functional setting we can reason about the equivalence of programs or program schemata by reasoning about their meaning relative to a given semantics. For example, if recursive functions are implemented as fixedpoints of functionals, then we can reason about a function by reasoning about the limit of its approximating functions in the semantics. This semantically justifies proof rules like Scott's fixedpoint induction. We could use such an induction rule to prove the equivalence of F and G in Figure 1.

This approach is not available for reasoning about rules corresponding to our relational templates. The rule just given is not derivable in first or higher-order logic: there are counter-models. Hence we must either specialize the schemata, the semantics, or both.

4.1 Template Specialization

We consider first datatype specialization, as it is the simpler of the two kinds of specialization that we shall address. The idea is that a relational template can be specialized in two steps: first we specialize the types of schematic variables to relations over given datatypes. Second, we partially instantiate schematic variables and simplify the resulting expression. The result of this translation is a new template which can be formulated as a rule and derived by structural induction over datatypes.

Let us work through an example, specializing the template given in Figure 2 to the one in Figure 4. To begin with, we add type declarations. In this case, we consider F and G as relations (in HOL, objects of type *bool*) over polymorphic lists. We augment our template with these type declarations, leaving types of other relations implicit (when this is translated to a rule in Isabelle, Isabelle can reconstruct the types of remaining predicates and constants).

We now instantiate some of the schematic variables and simplify the resulting schemata. In particular, we specialize the schema so that F and G compute by structural recursion

Type Declarations

$$F \quad : \quad \alpha \ list \times \beta \ list \to bool \tag{16}$$

$$G \quad : \quad \alpha \ list \times \beta \ list \times \beta \ list \to bool \tag{17}$$

Defining Relation for F

$$F([],y) \quad \Leftrightarrow \quad T(y) \tag{18}$$

$$F(h\#t,y) \quad \Leftrightarrow \quad \exists x_1, x_2.K(h,t,x_1) \wedge F(t,x_2) \wedge R(x_2,x_1,y) \tag{19}$$

Defining Equations for G

$$G([],y,z) \quad \Leftrightarrow \quad \exists x_1.T(x_1) \wedge R(x_1,y,z) \tag{20}$$

$$G(h\#t,y,z) \quad \Leftrightarrow \quad \exists x_1, x_2.K(h,t,x_1) \wedge R(x_1,y,x_2) \wedge G(t,x_2,z) \tag{21}$$

Applicability Conditions:

$$R(x,N,y) \Leftrightarrow (x=y) \tag{22}$$

$$(\exists y_1.R(x,y,y_1) \wedge R(y_1,z,r)) \Leftrightarrow (\exists z_1.R(y,z,z_1) \wedge R(x,z_1,r)) \tag{23}$$

Correctness:

$$F(x,y) \Leftrightarrow G(x,N,y)$$

Figure 4: Transformation Rule for Tail Recursion Introduction, Specialized to Lists

over lists; hence, we let $B(x)$ be the predicate $x \neq nil$. Now, in a theory of lists where lists are either the empty list, $[]$, or built from (infix) $\#$ denoting *cons*, we can eliminate the conditions $B(x)$ by substituting in the two possible cases. For example, the first defining equation

$$\neg B(x) \Rightarrow (F(x,y) \Leftrightarrow T(x,y))$$

becomes

$$\neg(x \neq []) \Rightarrow (F(x,y) \Leftrightarrow T(x,y))$$

which in turn is equivalent to

$$F([],y) \Leftrightarrow T([],y).$$

Furthermore, schematic variables like T need only be functions of variables (since any instance may contain constants like $[]$); hence we can further simplify to

$$F([],y) \Leftrightarrow T(y),$$

which is the first defining equivalence in Figure 4.

Continuing, the second defining equivalence for F in Figure 2 is

$$B(x) \Rightarrow (F(x,y) \Leftrightarrow \exists x_1, x_2, x_3.H(x,x_1) \wedge K(x,x_2) \wedge F(x_1,x_3) \wedge R(x_3,x_2,y)).$$

Substituting a cons $h\#t$ for x and simplifying away B gives us

$$F(h\#t,y) \Leftrightarrow \exists x_1, x_2, x_3.H(h\#t,x_1) \wedge K(h\#t,x_2) \wedge F(x_1,x_3) \wedge R(x_3,x_2,y).$$

Now, if F is to compute by recursion on its first argument, then $H(h\#t,x_1)$ should be the tail relation, i.e., $x_1 = t$. Making this specialization we simplify the above again to

$$F(h\#t,y) \Leftrightarrow \exists x_2, x_3.K(h\#t,x_2) \wedge F(t,x_3) \wedge R(x_3,x_2,y).$$

Finally, as above where we eliminated [] from T, we can eliminate the cons constructor in K by replacing it with a ternary relation over h, t, and x_2. Making this replacement, and renaming bound variables yields

$$F(h\#t, y) \Leftrightarrow \exists x_1, x_2. K(h, t, x_1) \wedge F(t, x_2) \wedge R(x_2, x_1, y),$$

which is the second defining relation in Figure 4. Continuing the specialization in this fashion results in the new template given there.

4.2 Formalization and Derivation in Isabelle

The formalization of the above template as a rule in HOL is straightforward. We extend HOL with an inductively defined list datatype.[1] Then we form a rule from the template, as described in §3.2.

```
1) [| ALL y. F([],y) = T(y);
2)    ALL h t y. F(h#t,y) = (EX x1 x2. K(h,t,x1) & F(t,x2) & R(x2,x1,y));
3)    ALL y z. G([],y::('a list),z) = (EX x1. T(x1) & R(x1,y,z));
4)    ALL h t y z. G(h#t,y,z) = (EX x1 x2. K(h,t,x1) & R(x1,y,x2) & G(t,x2,z));
5)    ALL x y. R(x,N::('a list),y) = (x = y);
6)    ALL x y z r. (EX y1. R(x,y,y1) & R(y1,z,r)) = (EX z1. R(y,z,z1) & R(x,z1,r))
   |] ==> ALL x y. F(x,y) = G(x,N,y)
```

Note in the above that the second argument to both G and R in hypotheses numbered[2] 3 and 5 are annotated with their type; the notation '$X :: ty$' annotates X with the type ty. Remaining types are inferred automatically, and these two in-line type declarations, plus the fact that list operators have fixed types, suffice for Isabelle to reconstruct the types given in Figure 4.

This rule may now be derived in Isabelle/HOL by a simple list induction which we briefly sketch here. We prove the conclusion $F(x, y) = G(x, N, y)$ by proving instead the generalization

$$\forall y, z. (\exists v. F(x, v) \wedge R(v, y, z)) \Leftrightarrow G(x, y, z) \tag{24}$$

This generalization implies the conclusion by instantiation of y with N and simplification using hypothesis 5.

We proceed to prove the generalization by induction over x using structural induction for the list datatype.

$$\frac{x \in \tau\ list \quad \phi([]) \quad \phi(a\#x)}{\phi(x)} \quad \begin{array}{c} [a \in \tau, \phi(x)] \\ \vdots \end{array}$$

In the base case we must show

$$\forall y, z. (\exists v. F([], v) \wedge R(v, y, z)) \Leftrightarrow G([], y, z)$$

---

[1] We omit the definition of this type here; it is defined in a standard way using Isabelle's inductive datatype package, documented in [18].

[2] We have numbered the assumptions for further reference in the text; these do not appear in the actual Isabelle declaration. Other than the omission of line continuation characters, the rest of the text is taken verbatim from an Isabelle session.

Both sides simplify to $(\exists v.T(v) \land R(v, y, z))$ using hypothesis 1 and 3 on the left and right hand sides respectively. In the step case we must show

$$\forall y, z.(\exists v.F(a\#x, v) \land R(v, y, z)) \Leftrightarrow G(a\#x, y, z).$$

Expanding the definitions of F and G and rearranging terms gives

$$\forall y, z. \quad (\exists v, x_1, x_2.R(x_2, x_1, v) \land R(v, y, z) \land K(a, x, x_1) \land F(x, x_2))$$
$$\Leftrightarrow (\exists x_1, x_2.K(a, x, x_1) \land R(x_1, y, x_2) \land G(x, x_2, z)).$$

Using associativity (hypothesis 6) and again rearranging terms gives

$$\exists x_1, z'.(\exists x_2.F(x, x_2) \land R(x_2, z', z)) \land R(x_1, y, z') \land K(a, x, x_1))$$

on the left. We then use the induction hypothesis to replace $F(x, x_2) \land R(x_2, z', z)$ by $G(x, z', z)$. Elimination of unused quantifiers and variable renaming then yields syntactically identical right and left-hand sides.

The Isabelle proof of this theorem, constructed interactively, required eight steps and directly follows the above outline.[3]

5 Relational Induction

We now present our second approach to proving templates correct, which can be seen as specializing the theory to reflect the intended semantics. Logic programs are definite clauses (clauses with exactly one positive literal) and have a standard semantics given by the least Herbrand model [21]. This model corresponds to viewing a program as constituting an inductive definition of a set of predicates: the Herbrand model is the fixedpoint of this inductive definition. First-order logic cannot characterize this model, but it can be directly expressed in higher-order logic by an inductive definition. The view of logic programs as inductive definitions has been explored (primarily in the context of negation-as-failure) by a number of authors including [10, 2, 20]. Here we adopt this view and use it to establish the correctness of the kind of templates we are considering.

5.1 Inductive Definitions

To make the paper self-contained we will give a very brief review to the kind of inductive definitions we use; the general theory can be found, for example, in [1]. We view a program as consisting of rules that define a relation (i.e., a set). A trivial example is the program

$$Num(0)$$
$$Num(s(x)) \leftarrow Num(x)$$

which defines a relation Num containing all 'numbers' viewed as objects built from 0 and the successor function s. The first clause constitutes the base case of the relation and the second explains how given a term in the relation we can add a new term to the relation. Iterating the second clause (perhaps transfinitely) we will reach a fixedpoint which corresponds to the minimal Herbrand model.

---

[3] We omit the actual proof due to length limitations. Proof scripts for all theorems appearing in this paper are available, on request, from the authors.

An inductively defined set justifies an elimination (or induction) principle corresponding to the introduction (formation) rules. In particular, an induction principle for the above would be the following familiar structural induction principle.

$$\frac{Num(x) \quad \phi(0) \quad \phi(s(x))}{\phi(x)}$$

$$[\phi(x)]$$
$$\vdots$$

We may view templates like that of Figure 2 as defining a set of rules, one corresponding to each relational definition. In particular, we can orient each equivalence from right-to-left, bring the condition into the body of the definition. For example, the first two equivalences correspond to the clauses[4]

$$F(x,y) \Leftarrow \neg B(x) \wedge T(x,y) \tag{25}$$

and

$$F(x,y) \Leftarrow B(x) \wedge H(x,x_1) \wedge K(x,x_2) \wedge R(x_3,x_2,y) \wedge F(x_1,x_3) . \tag{26}$$

Now, we can view F as being defined by the inductive definition constituted by these clauses. In this case, the corresponding induction principle is as follows.

$$\frac{F(x,y) \qquad \phi(x,y) \qquad\qquad\qquad \phi(x,y)}{\phi(x,y)}$$

$$[\neg B(x), T(x,y)] \qquad [B(x), H(x,x_1), K(x,x_2), R(x_3,x_2,y), \phi(x_1,x_3)]$$
$$\vdots \qquad\qquad\qquad\qquad\qquad\qquad \vdots$$

Similarly, the inductive schema corresponding to the definition of $G(x,y,z)$ is the following.

$$[\neg B(x), T(x,x_1), R(x_1,y,z)] \qquad [B(x), H(x,x_1), K(x,x_2), R(x_2,y,x_3), \phi(x_1,x_3,z)]$$
$$\vdots \qquad\qquad\qquad\qquad\qquad\qquad \vdots$$

$$\frac{G(x,y,z) \qquad \phi(x,y,z) \qquad\qquad\qquad \phi(x,y,z)}{\phi(x,y,z)}$$

5.2 Proving Templates by Relational Induction

To formalize the template given in Figure 2 we begin by representing F and G as inductively defined relations rather than sets of formulae. Given a relatively straightforward encoding of these inductive definition, Isabelle's support for inductive/co-inductive definitions supplies the induction principles needed for the proof (see [18] for full details). However, inductive definitions in Isabelle define *constants*, and we want to prove the rule for any F and G. Thus the problem is to somehow represent a transformation rule using such inductively-defined constants instead of metavariables. The solution is to define each inductive set in terms of parameters and to supply metavariables for these parameters when formulating the transformation rule.

In our tail-recursion example, we proceed by giving Isabelle the following parameterized inductive definitions of F and G:[5]

---

[4]These are not, strictly speaking, definite clauses as some atoms such as B occur negatively. However, they constitute parameterized inductive definitions where the relation being defined, e.g., F, only occurs positively in the defining body.

[5]We have omitted some type annotations from the Isabelle source for the sake of readability.

```
consts
  F :: "['a  => bool, ['a, 'b] => bool, ['a, 'a] => bool, ['a, 'b] => bool,
        ['b, 'b, 'b] => bool, 'b]
        => ('a * 'b)set"

  G :: "['a => bool, ['a, 'b] => bool, ['a, 'a] => bool, ['a, 'b] => bool,
        ['b, 'b, 'b] => bool, 'b]
        => ('a * 'b * 'b)set"

inductive "F(B,T,H,K,R,N)"
  intrs
  fBase  "[| ~ B(x); T(x,y) |] ==> <x,y>:F(B,T,H,K,R,N)"
  fStep  "[| B(x); H(x,x1); K(x,x2); R(x3,x2,y); <x1,x3>:F(B,T,H,K,R,N)
          |] ==> <x,y>:F(B,T,H,K,R,N)"

inductive "G(B,T,H,K,R,N)"
  intrs
  gBase  "[| ~ B(x); T(x,x1); R(x1,y,z) |]  ==> <x,y,z>:G(B,T,H,K,R,N)"
  gStep  "[| B(x); H(x,x1); K(x,x2); R(x2,y,x3); <x1,x3,z>:G(B,T,H,K,R,N)
          |] ==> <x,y,z>:G(B,T,H,K,R,N)"
end
```

The definition consists of type declarations followed by the introduction rules for the relations. Except for notational differences, the introduction rules directly formalize the clausal definitions of F and G as formulas in Isabelle's metalogic. For example, the clause fBase corresponds to (25); $F(x, y)$ is rendered as <x,y>:F(B,T,H,K,R,N) because F is a parameterized inductively defined set, not a predicate; : represents set membership and <> is pairing. (Although sets and predicates are equal in HOL, they are not identical in the metalogic.)

From this definition, Isabelle automatically constructs and derives a number of proof rules, including induction principles for F and G corresponding to those of the previous section. These allow us to prove the following goal, which, together with the inductive definitions of F and G, represents the transformation rule of Figure 2.

```
[| ALL x. R(x,N,y) = (x = y);
   ALL x y z r . (EX y1. R(y1,z,r) & R(x,y,y1)) = (EX z1. R(x,z1,r) & R(y,z,z1))
|] ==> ALL x y. (<x,y>:F(B,T,H,K,R,N)) = (<x,N,y>:G(B,T,H,K,R,N))
```

Note that this representation has the advantage of avoiding confusion between logic programs, represented as inductively defined relations, and purely logical applicability conditions, represented as logical formulae.

We have used the above induction principles to justify this rule in a theory that extends HOL with the inductive definitions of F and G given above. The proof of this rule was harder than the previous one and required 20 steps in Isabelle. Rather than bore the reader with details we just give the main proof ideas. First, we require the same generalization as in the previous section in (24). Then we split the equivalence into separate proofs for each direction. To show the RHS implies the LHS; we have the assumption $G(x, y, z)$, so using the induction rule for G we prove the induction formula ϕ given by

$$\phi(x, y, z) \equiv \exists v. F(x, v) \land R(v, y, z).$$

This follows by suitable definition expansion and simplification with the applicability conditions. In the converse direction we have $F(x, v)$ and using the induction rule for F we prove the induction formula

$$\phi(x, v) \equiv \forall y, z. R(v, y, z) \to G(x, y, z).$$

6 Application of Transformation Schemata

We use Isabelle both to derive templates as rules and to apply rules to transform programs: both activities become theorem proving. Template application exploits metavariables in schemata and goals to synthesize the transformed program by means of higher-order unification in the course of theorem-proving.

In this section we describe template application by continuing our running example: we show how the rule for tail-recursion developed in §4.2 can be applied for program optimization. After verification of the tail-recursion rule, Isabelle returns the following proof rule in which all undeclared constants become metavariables (denoted by names beginning with '?'):

```
[| ALL y. ?F([], y) = ?T(y);
   ALL h t y. ?F(h # t, y) = (EX x1 x2. ?K(h, t, x1) & ?F(t, x2) & ?R(x2, x1, y));
   ALL y z. ?G([], y, z) = (EX x1. ?T(x1) & ?R(x1, y, z));
   ALL h t y z. ?G(h # t, y, z) = (EX x1 x2. ?K(h, t, x1) & ?R(x1, y, x2) & ?G(t, x2, z));
   ALL x y. ?R(x, ?N, y) = (x = y);
   ALL x y z r.
     (EX y1. ?R(x, y, y1) & ?R(y1, z, r)) = (EX z1. ?R(y, z, z1) & ?R(x, z1, r)) |] ==>
 ALL x y. ?F(x, y) = ?G(x, ?N, y)
```

We will use this rule to optimize the naive reversal program *rev* given by the Prolog program:

```
rev([],[]).
rev([H|T],Y) :- rev(T,I1), append(I1,[H],Y)
```

This program is 'naive' because its use of *append* to place the constant H at the end of I_1 results in quadratic running time.

We begin by stating a theorem to be proved: the equivalence of the above logic program and an unknown one *?Q*. We formalize the above by translating it to list theory (which includes a definition of the append relation) and turning Horn clauses into equivalences.[6]

```
> val assums = goal thy
"[| ALL y. rev([],y) = (y = []);
    ALL h t y. rev(h#t,y) = (EX i2 i1.i2 = [h] & rev(t,i1) & append(i1,i2,y)) |]
 ==> ALL x y. rev(x,y) = ?Q(x,y)";
ALL x y. rev(x, y) = ?Q(x, y)
 1. ALL x y. rev(x, y) = ?Q(x, y)
```

Our proof steps are taken, except for slight pretty-printing, directly from an Isabelle session. The first 4 lines are typed by the user. The first states that we are beginning a new theorem and that the assumptions will be bound to the variable *assums*. The next two lines contain the assumptions, which axiomatize the above naive reverse program. This is followed by the conclusion to be proved; the metavariable *?Q* will be instantiated during proof with the transformed program. That is, metavariables in goals are interpreted existentially and the goal is satisfied if proven for some instance of *?Q*. The final two lines of transcript are Isabelle's response: the current proof state, consisting of the ultimate goal to be proved and a list of current subgoals (in this case, one subgoal identical to the ultimate goal).

---

[6]The use of an equivalence is necessary if we are to prove that the transformed program is equivalent to the original program (*sound* and *complete* in the terminology of logic programming), instead of merely implied by it. Moreover, we have developed our templates with this application in mind.

Our first step is to resolve with the transformation rule, which we have named *tail_opt*, at the same time specifying the name *qrev* for the new function represented by *?G* in the rule. This is the first line and Isabelle responds with six subgoals.

```
> by (res_inst_tac [("G","qrev")] tail_opt 1);
ALL x y. rev(x, y) = qrev(x, ?N1, y)
 1. ALL y. rev([], y) = ?T1(y)
 2. ALL h t y. rev(h # t, y) = (EX x1 x2. ?K1(h, t, x1) & rev(t, x2) & ?R1(x2, x1, y))
 3. ALL y z. qrev([], y, z) = (EX x1. ?T1(x1) & ?R1(x1, y, z))
 4. ALL h t y z. qrev(h # t, y, z) = (EX x1 x2. ?K1(h, t, x1) & ?R1(x1, y, x2) & qrev(t, x2, z))
 5. ALL x y. ?R1(x, ?N1, y) = (x = y)
 6. ALL x y z r. (EX y1. ?R1(x, y, y1) & ?R1(y1, z, r)) = (EX z1. ?R1(y, z, z1) & ?R1(x, z1, r))
```

The subgoals correspond to the six premises of *tail_opt* where resolution has instantiated *?F* in the rule to *rev*. Our plan is to solve subgoals 1, 2, 5, and 6, causing Isabelle to instantiate remaining metavariables, and to discharge subgoals 3 and 4 as assumptions, which will constitute the definition of the new function *qrev*.

The first two subgoals state the definition of the program to be transformed; we can trivially solve them by resolving with the the assumptions (bound to *assums*).

```
> by (REPEAT (resolve_tac assums 1));
ALL x y. rev(x, y) = qrev(x, ?N1, y)
 1. ALL y z. qrev([], y, z) = (EX x1. x1 = [] & append(x1, y, z))
 2. ALL h t y z. qrev(h # t, y, z) = (EX x1 x2. x1 = [h] & append(x1, y, x2) & qrev(t, x2, z))
 3. ALL x y. append(x, ?N1, y) = (x = y)
 4. ALL x y z r. (EX y1. append(x, y, y1) & append(y1, z, r)) =
        (EX z1. append(y, z, z1) & append(x, z1, r))
```

This step instantiates the metavariables *?T1*, *?K1*, and *?R1*, giving a definition for the new function *qrev* (now subgoals 1 and 2).

Goals 3 and 4 follow from simple properties of the *append* relation which we have proved and named *Append_neutral* and *Append_assoc_3*. We apply them in two resolution steps combined as follows:

```
> by (REPEAT (resolve_tac [Append_neutral, Append_assoc_3] 3));
ALL x y. rev(x, y) = qrev(x, [], y)
 1. ALL y z. qrev([], y, z) = (EX x1. x1 = [] & append(x1, y, z))
 2. ALL h t y z.
       qrev(h # t, y, z) = (EX x1 x2. x1 = [h] & append(x1, y, x2) & qrev(t, x2, z))
```

Now all the metavariables are instantiated: resolution with *Append_neutral*, which states that $append(x, [], y) = (x = y)$, provides the substitution [] for *?N1*, and we have a complete implementation of *rev* in terms of *qrev*, represented by subgoals 1 and 2. Discharging these remaining subgoals as assumptions via Isabelle's *uresult* function, we obtain the theorem:

```
[| ALL y. ?rev([], y) = (y = []);
   ALL h t y. ?rev(h # t, y) = (EX i2 i1. i2 = [h] & ?rev(t, i1) & append(i1, i2, y));
   ALL y z. ?qrev([], y, z) = (EX x1. x1 = [] & append(x1, y, z));
   ALL h t y z.
       ?qrev(h # t, y, z) = (EX x1 x2. x1 = [h] & append(x1, y, x2) & ?qrev(t, x2, z)) |] ==>
ALL x y. ?rev(x, y) = ?qrev(x, [], y)
```

We are done! This theorem states the equivalence of *rev* and *qrev* where *qrev* is defined by the third and fourth assumption. These definitions represent a reverse algorithm that can be run directly in programming languages such as Gödel [11], or translated to the following Prolog program:

```
qrev([],Y,Z) :- (X1 = []), append(X1,Y,Z).
qrev([H|T],Y,Z) :- (X1 = [H]), append(X1,Y,X2), qrev(T,X2,Z).
rev(X,Y) :- qrev(X,[],Y).
```

This program is indeed an improvement on the original. Each call to append will execute in constant time since the first argument is either bound to an empty list or a singleton list; hence, the entire program executes in linear time, and in both directions (e.g., reversing input X into output Y or vice versa).

Although the transformed program now has optimal asymptotic running time, we can perform further 'constant factor' improvements by additional theorem proving, which essentially amounts to partial evaluation. In particular, the equalities in the definition of $qrev$ are unnecessary, and can be removed using simplification/tautology checking tactics that come with the Isabelle system. Continuing from the previous proof state (prior to $uresult$), we can perform perform further simplifications and Isabelle returns the following simplified proof state.

```
ALL x y. rev(x, y) = qrev(x, [], y)
 1. ALL y z. qrev([], y, z) = (z = y)
 2. ALL h t y z. qrev(h # t, y, z) = (EX v. append([h], y, v) & qrev(t, v, z))
```

We might like to further simplify, for example, by reducing the base case of $qrev$ simply to ALL y. qrev([],y,y), however, this is not logically equivalent to (1) above. Further simplification is possible, however, if we commit to the Horn clause of $qrev$ by orienting each equivalence from right to left. In that case, we can further simplify our definition to the following familiar Prolog program.

```
qrev([],Y,Y).
qrev([H|T],Y,Z) :- qrev(T,[H|Y],Z).
rev(X,Y) :- qrev(X,[],Y).
```

The above example shows how applying rules corresponding to templates can transform programs during their correctness proofs. We have also performed the same optimization using the rule derived by relational induction in §5.2. The proof is similar to the one just given and the only differences are in representation (the use of sets instead of relations) and that there were technical difficulties in using resolution to generate instances for parameters in the inductive definitions of F and G.[7]

7 Experience and Related Work

Experience and Future Work

The methodology we described here appears to be viable for formalizing and using transformation templates and adapting functional templates to logic programs. We have translated and formally derived a number of templates taken from sources such as [15, 12]; these include templates for tail-recursion introduction, finite differencing, and tupling. These templates

---

[7] F and G are constants defined by parameterized inductive definitions and are not given as hypotheses in the transformation rule; therefore instances of the parameters cannot be generated by resolution as in the first step of the proof above. There are ways to trick Isabelle into generating these instances by unification, but such Isabelle specific details lie outside the scope of this paper.

can be easily recast as rules in higher-order logic; indeed, the recasting is sometimes simpler then the original presentation since the use of a typed metalogic and so-called higher-order abstract syntax often allow us to naturally capture side conditions on types and variable occurrences that must otherwise be explicitly stored with the transformation template (e.g., the *where* constraints of [12]). Derivation of relational rules is more difficult than in the functional case but not overwhelmingly so. The additional difficulties seem to be twofold. First, two inductions (on F and on G) must be done instead of one over an equivalence. The second difference, perhaps more serious, is a pragmatic one: there is better support in Isabelle for using rewriting to simplify functions than relations. However, in deriving both relational and functional templates, the main difficulty is the same and concerns the creative step of finding the proper generalizations.

In many respects, our work has just begun and there are a number of directions to pursue next. It is a bit unsatisfying that, through datatype specialization, we lose data polymorphism. A more general solution is to leave the schemata polymorphic, but to use Isabelle's type classes to restrict them to types with associated well-founded relations. We could then add an additional applicability condition to the template that states that the 'descent relation', which yields a value for the recursive call (e.g., in §4 this was H, which we specialized to the tail relation), is well-founded. Such rules are provable and have more general applicability; however their drawback is that application results in new (well-foundedness) proof obligations.

Another direction to pursue is formalizing and using wider classes of templates. Our work here was limited to templates drawn from functional programming; we would like to explore other kinds of templates, in particular those better suited for multi-mode logic programming, such as given by O'Keefe in [16].

Finally, our work has raised an interesting question concerning the existence of sufficient conditions for relational templates to be provable by relational induction when the corresponding functional templates are provable by fixedpoint induction. We are currently investigating this question.

Related Work

Work on template based program transformation began in the 1970s, propelled by two independent lines of research. The first was denotational semantics as carried out by Scott and others, which laid a foundation for understanding and reasoning about programs, including the equivalence of program schemata. The second was the development of higher-order unification by Huet [14], originally developed for resolution proofs in higher-order logic, but shortly thereafter applied to program transformation. For example, Huet and Lang in [15] combine these two strands: they use Scott-style domain theory (e.g., LCF) to reason about the equivalence of program schemata formulated in transformation templates and then use second-order matching to apply the templates to transform functional programs. Since then, this idea has been further developed in other projects and systems, e.g., [3, 12, 5].

In the logic programming community, transformation has for the most part centered around approaches based on deductive transformation. This loose classification includes techniques like unfold-fold [7], LOPS [6], the work of Hogger [13], Clark [9, 8], among others. In these approaches a program is represented in first-order logic and manipulated by rules (e.g., allowing partial evaluation, folding, replacement of a formula by an equivalent or stronger formula, etc.) and the result is a program with identical meaning, relative to some semantics, but with hopefully improved runtime performance.

Template based transformation can, of course, also be seen as a kind of deductive transformation. In our work, templates are deduced and then applied as rules. The above mentioned work on logic programs centers on the explicit derivation and manipulation of concrete programs; perhaps, in the appropriate logic or metalogic, the derived equivalences could be subsequently generalized and used as transformation templates. Perhaps the research closest to ours is that of Waldau [22] who suggests an intuitionistic logic for reasoning about properties of logic programs. Like us, he is concerned with appropriate logical foundations for verifying the equivalence of transformation schemata and is motivated by their subsequent use in transformation. Our work differs in the logics we use (he uses a specialized intuitionistic logic, while we use standard higher-order logic), and in the kinds of schemata we reason about (he uses primarily schemata specialized over datatypes and reasons about them by induction over the datatype). Waldau does not discuss machine implementation or how schemata would be applied, but our approaches are compatible in the sense that his approach could be implemented in the manner we suggest here.

References

[1] P. Aczel. An introduction to inductive definitions. In J. Barwise, editor, *Handbook of Mathematical Logic*, pages 739–82. North-Holland, Amsterdam, 1977.

[2] Martin Aronsson, Lars-Henrik Eriksson, Lars Hallnäs, and Per Kreuger. A survey of GLCA: A definitional approach to logic programming. In *Extensions of Logic Programming*, LNCS-475, pages 49–100. Springer-Verlag, 1991.

[3] CIP System Group: F. L. Bauer et al. *The Munich Project CIP, Volume II: The Program Transformation System CIP-S*, volume 292 of *Lecture Notes in Computer Science*. Springer-Verlag, 1987.

[4] F.L Bauer and H. Wössner. *Algorithmic Language and Program Development*. Springer-Verlag, 1982.

[5] Yves Bertot and Ranan Fraer. Reasoning with executable specifications. In *International Joint Conference of Theory and Practice of Software Development (TAPSOFT/FASE)*, volume 915. Springer-Verlag LNCS, May 1995.

[6] W. Bibel. Syntax-directed, semantics-supported program synthesis. *Artificial Intelligence*, 14:243–261, 1980.

[7] R.M. Burstall and J. Darlington. A transformation system for developing recursive programs. *Journal of the Association for Computing Machinery*, 24(1):44–67, 1977.

[8] K. L. Clark and S-Å. Tärnlund. A first order theory of data and programs. In B. Gilchrist, editor, *Information Processing*, pages 939–944. IFIP, 1977.

[9] K.L. Clark. Predicate logic as a computational formalism. Technical Report TOC 79/59, Imperial College, 1979.

[10] Masami Hagiya and Takafumi Sakurai. Foundation of logic programming based on inductive definition. *New Generation Computing*, 2:59–77, 1984.

[11] P. Hill and J. Lloyd. The Gödel Report. Technical Report TR-91-02, Department of Computer Science, University of Bristol, March 1991. Revised in September 1991.

[12] Berthold Hoffmann and Bernd Krieg-Brückner (Eds.). *Program Development by Specification and Transformation*. Springer LNCS 680, 1993.

[13] C.J. Hogger. Derivation of logic programs. *JACM*, 28(2):372–392, April 1981.

[14] Gérard Huet. A unification algorithm for typed lambda-calculus. *Theoretical Computer Science*, pages 27–57, 1975.

[15] Gérard Huet and Bernard Lang. Proving and applying program transformations expressed with second-order patterns. *Acta Informatica*, pages 31–55, 1978.

[16] Richard O'Keefe. *The Craft of Prolog*. MIT Press, Cambridge, Massachusetts, 1990.

[17] Helmut A. Partsch. *Specification and Transformation of Programs*. Springer-Verlag, 1990.

[18] Lawrence C. Paulson. A fixedpoint approach to implementing (co)inductive definitions. In *Proc. of 12th International Conference On Automated Deduction (CADE-12)*, Nancy, France, June 1994. Springer-Verlag.

[19] Lawrence C. Paulson. *Isabelle : a generic theorem prover; with contributions by Tobias Nipkow*. LNCS-828. Springer, Berlin, 1994.

[20] Lawrence C. Paulson and Andrew W. Smith. Logic programming, functional programming, and inductive definitions. In *Extensions of Logic Programming*, LNCS-475, pages 283–310. Springer-Verlag, 1991.

[21] M.H. van Emden and R.A. Kowalski. The semantics of predicate logic as a programming language. *Journal of the ACM*, 23:733–42, 1976.

[22] Mattias Waldau. Formal validation of transformation schemata. In T. Clement and K.-K. Lau, editors, *Logic Program Synthesis and Transformation*, pages 97–110. Springer-Verlag, 1991.

Performance of a Data-Parallel Concurrent Constraint Programming System

Bo-Ming Tong* and Ho-Fung Leung

Department of Computer Science and Engineering
The Chinese University of Hong Kong
Shatin, New Territories, Hong Kong
email: bmtong@cs.cuhk.hk, lhf@cs.cuhk.hk

Abstract. Finite domain constraints [27] are very effective in solving a class of integer problems which find its applications in various areas like scheduling and operations research. The advantage over conventional approaches is that the problem is specified declaratively. The actual computation is carried out by *logic inference* and *constraint satisfaction* [24]. Solving a set of finite domain constraints is an intractable problem and we propose to use massively parallel computers to obtain satisfactory performance. In our previous papers, we have shown that finite domain constraint languages can be implemented on massively parallel SIMD machines. The resulting system, Firebird, has been implemented on a DECmpp 12000 Sx-100 massively parallel computer with 8,192 processor elements. In this paper, some preliminary performance results are given. A speedup of 2 orders of magnitude is possible when we compare the performance using 8,192 processor elements and the performance using a single processor element of the same machine. On the other hand, we measure the effects of several control strategies and optimizations on execution time and memory consumption in a data-parallel context.

1 Introduction

Finite domain constraint logic programming [27] is very effective in solving a class of integer problems which find its applications in various areas like scheduling and operations research. Examples include the *car sequencing problem* [5] and time-table scheduling [30]. The advantage over conventional approaches is that the problem is specified declaratively. The actual computation is carried out by *logic inference* and *constraint satisfaction* [24]. Solving a set of finite domain constraints is an intractable problem and we propose to use massively parallel computers to obtain satisfactory performance.

We have shown that finite domain constraint programming languages can be implemented efficiently on massively parallel SIMD computer systems. The result is Firebird [22, 23], which, to the best of our knowledge, is the first data-parallel concurrent constraint programming system.

In this paper, we present some preliminary performance results of our implementation. we also measure the effects of several control strategies and optimizations on execution

---

* Present address: Department of Computer Science, University of Arizona, Tucson, AZ 85721, U.S.A. email: bmtong@cs.arizona.edu

time and memory consumption in a data-parallel context. The reader is referred to Van Hentenryck [27] for an introduction to finite domain constraints, and to Maher [13] and Saraswat *et al.* [16, 17] for concurrent constraint programming, but we give brief reviews in the rest of this section. In the next section, we give a brief review of our previous papers [22, 23]. Section 3 is the performance data and Section 4 is a comparison between SIMD MultiLog [18] and Firebird. We conclude with Section 5.

1.1 Concurrent Constraint Programming

ALPS [13] is a scheme to integrate constraint logic programming and concurrent logic programming. Saraswat [16, 17] develop the ideas further by introducing the concurrent constraint programming framework. Computation is modeled as the interaction of concurrent, cooperating *agents*[2] exchanging information via a global *store*, which is a conjunction of *constraints*. An agent may assert *(tell)* new constraints to the store, as well as inquire *(ask)* whether a constraint is implied *(entailed)* by the store. The constraints in the store must be consistent *(satisfiable)*, or the computation *aborts*.

Since each tell constraint is conjoined to the current store, the store is *monotonically refined*. As a result, a successful ask operation will remain successful throughout the rest of the computation. Thus, synchronization can be achieved by *blocking ask*—an agent blocks until the store is refined enough to entail or reject the constraint it wants to ask. It remains blocked until some other concurrently executing agents have added enough information to the store so that it is strong enough to entail the ask constraint.

1.2 Finite Domain Constraints

Recent treatment of finite domain constraints in the concurrent constraint programming framework, as in *cc(FD)* [28] and *clp(FD)* [4], represents a domain variable X with domain d as a constraint $X \in d$. As constraints are added to the store, the domain of each related variable shrinks, until it becomes a *singleton* or becomes empty. For example, X may take any value from 1 to 10 initially. A constraint $X > 4$ will rule out some of the values $(\{1 \ldots 4\})$ in d. Now X can only range from 5 to 10. When a constraint $X < 6$ is added, the domain of X becomes a *singleton*, and we can deduce that $X = 5$.

The reader is referred to Van Hentenryck [27] for a full treatment of finite domain constraints in the traditional logic programming framework [12]. It is summarized as follows. Ordinary variables are termed *h*-variables (*h* stands for *Herbrand*). A *d*-variable X with domain d is denoted by X^d. The unification algorithm must be modified to support *d*-variables. The modified algorithm is termed d-*unification*. When an *h*-variable is unified with a *d*-variable, the former is bound to the latter. When a constant c is unified with a *d*-variable X^d, X is bound to c if c is in d. Otherwise the unification fails. When two *d*-variables, X^d and Y^e, are unified, both of them are bound to the *d*-variable Z^f where $f = d \cap e$. If f is a singleton $\{c\}$, both variables are bound to the constant c. If f is empty, the unification fails. SLD-resolution extended with *d*-unification is termed *SLDD-resolution*. However, the introduction of *d*-unification alone is insufficient to solve finite domain constraints efficiently. Disequality, inequality, (arithmetic) equality constraints,

---

[2] An agent corresponds to an atom in traditional logic programming.

and even user-defined constraints, must also be handled. The *forward checking* and *looking ahead* inference rules [27] are introduced as both a theoretical basis and an implementation scheme for such constraints.

2 Firebird: A Review

2.1 The Firebird Computation Model

In Firebird, a program consists of a number of clauses and every clause is divided into a *guard* part and a *body* part by a commit operator in the same way as the concurrent logic programming language *flat GHC* [26]. Execution consists of two alternating derivation steps, *indeterministic derivation* and *nondeterministic derivation*. In an *indeterministic derivation step*, execution consists of guard tests, commitment, output unification and spawning in the same manner as committed-choice logic programming languages. In a *nondeterministic derivation step*, a choice point based on one of the domain variables in the system is set up and all possible values in its domain are attempted in an or-parallel manner. The domain variable used in a nondeterministic derivation step is said to be *labeled*[3] [27] and each or-parallel branch is called a *partition*.

2.2 Exploitation of Data-Parallelism in Firebird

In a nondeterministic derivation step (*i.e.* a *labeling* operation), the labeled domain variable becomes a vector of all possible values of its domain. Goals and constraints take these argument vectors arising from the labeling operation for the exploitation of data-parallelism.

An Illustrative Example. To illustrate how Firebird exploits data-parallelism, it is helpful to trace the execution of 4-queens and the query queen(4,[X1,X2,X3,X4]). We assume that all atoms have been reduced by indeterministic derivation. Only constraints remain in the system and they are shown in Fig. 1. At this point, all domain variables have the same domain {1,2,3,4}.

$$
\begin{array}{lll}
X1 \neq X2 & X1 \neq X2 + 1 & X1 \neq X2 - 1 \\
X1 \neq X3 & X1 \neq X3 + 2 & X1 \neq X3 - 2 \\
X1 \neq X4 & X1 \neq X4 + 3 & X1 \neq X4 - 3 \\
X2 \neq X3 & X2 \neq X3 + 1 & X2 \neq X3 - 1 \\
X2 \neq X4 & X2 \neq X4 + 2 & X2 \neq X4 - 2 \\
X3 \neq X4 & X3 \neq X4 + 1 & X3 \neq X4 - 1
\end{array}
$$

Fig. 1. Constraints remaining after the first nondeterministic derivation

If we label X1 using nondeterministic derivation, form a vector with the 4 possible values of X1 and try the 4 possible values in a data-parallel fashion, we can evaluate the

---

[3] *Labeling* a domain-variable means instantiating a domain-variable by attempting each value in its domain one by one or in parallel.

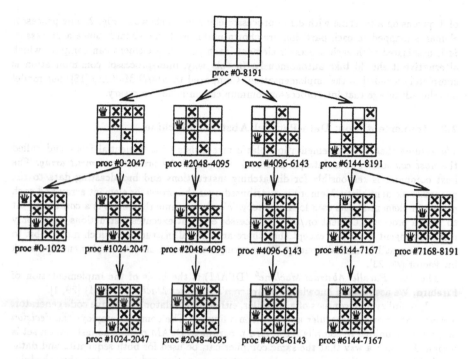

Fig. 2. Example: execution of 4-queens

first 9 constraints with an ideal 4 times speedup[4] on a SIMD machine. Because the value of X1 is now known, the domains of other variables can be deduced using the constraints in Fig. 1. Then, a second nondeterministic derivation will occur. If every branch chooses to create a choice point on X2, there will be $2 + 1 + 1 + 2 = 6$ branches (see Fig. 2). Thus the next 9 constraints can be solved with an ideal speedup of 6. Thousands of processor elements can be fully utilized easily in this way because many problems are combinatorial in nature.

Mapping Partitions to Processor Elements. In order to avoid data movement among the processor elements, a single *logical partition*, or simply a *partition*, is mapped to a number of identical *physical partitions*. Each physical partition corresponds to a single processor element of a data-parallel computer, and we use the two terms interchangeably. Initially, all processor elements execute exactly the same initial logical partition. If the data-parallel computer has N processor elements and a choice point with 4 alternatives is created, $\frac{N}{4}$ processor elements will be allocated to each alternative. A trace of the execution

---

[4] This is just a rough approximation. Amdahl's Law dictates that such an "ideal" speedup cannot be obtained in practice.

of 4-queens on a machine with 8,192 processor elements is shown in Fig. 2. The processor elements mapped to each partition are shown under each chessboard. Since a *processor-id* is associated with each processor element, each processor element can compute which alternative it should take autonomously. In this way, inter-processor communication is completely avoided in the implementation. Compared to *SIMD MultiLog* [18], our model has the advantage that interprocessor communication is not necessary.

2.3 Implementation: Data-Parallel Abstract Machine

We assume that the implementation platform consists of a sequential front end called the *host computer* and a data-parallel back end called the *processor element array*. The host computer is responsible for dispatching instructions and broadcasting data to the processor element array. Memory is distributed over the processor element array and each processor element has its own local memory. We also assume that there is a *contingent* bit to turn a processor element on/off. A processor element executes instructions if and only if its contingent bit is set, except that there are special instructions which move a bit to the contingent bit unconditionally. The contingent bits are used to implement the mask bit vector [22, 23].

The *Data-Parallel Abstract Machine*[5] (DPAM) is the basis of the implementation of Firebird. We assume the knowledge of *Warren's Abstract Machine* (WAM) [29, 1].

A Firebird system consists of a compiler, either an emulator or a native code generator, a *concurrent process scheduler* and a runtime library. The compiler employs the *decision graph* [11] technique to compile a Firebird program to DPAM code. The instruction set is designed in such a way that the same compiler can be used for both sequential and data-parallel implementations. However, the emulator or native code generator, the scheduler and the runtime library must be modified or rewritten for the sequential implementation.

The processor element array is responsible for the execution of atoms and the evaluation of constraints. Vector memory areas include the *argument stack*, the *trail stack* and the *heap*. The host computer is responsible for process scheduling and choice point management. Scalar memory areas include the *choice point stack* and the *process stack*. The reader is referred to our previous paper [23] for the details of our *parallel backtracking* scheme.

3 Experimental Results

In all the following benchmarks, execution time t_1, t_2, etc for all solutions are given in seconds, neglecting any time spent on input/output. #*proc* is the number of processor elements, *ND* the number of nondeterministic derivations, *BT* the number of backtrackings and P the number of logical partitions. P may change in the course of execution, but it can never exceed the number of processor elements. Only the value of P taken at the end of execution is given. A dash indicates that a benchmark is not available because memory is not enough for its execution. Since many parameters are studied, only one parameter is varied in each benchmark. The other parameters are listed below each table. The benchmark set is shown in Table 1. These benchmark programs are selected because

---

[5] Also known in our previous paper [22] as the *Firebird Abstract Machine*.

send	SEND + MORE = MONEY
eq10	10 simultaneous linear equations over 7 variables
eq20	20 simultaneous linear equations over 7 variables
queen	n-queens problem
magic	magic series problem
magich	magic series problem with redundant constraint $\sum_{i=0}^{n} s_i = n$.

Table 1. Benchmark set

we want to test different kinds of constraints and their combinations. For example, queen is a program with disequality constraints only. send, eq10 and eq20 have an assortment of equality and disequality constraints. magic is also included here because entailment constraints are used.

3.1 Bit Vectors of Domain Variables

Traditionally, the domain of a domain variable is represented by the minimum and maximum values of its domain and a bit vector. Many newer finite domain constraint programming systems, like *clp(FD)* [4] and *cc(FD)* [28], do not have bit vectors for contiguous domains. Only the minimum and maximum values of a domain are stored. A bit vector is created on-demand only when the domain is no longer contiguous because one or more of the invalid values are removed. For example, if $X \in \{1\ldots5\}$, $X \neq 1$, then $X \in \{2\ldots5\}$ and a bit vector is unnecessary. However, if $X \in \{1\ldots5\}$, $X \neq 3$, then $X \in \{1,2,4,5\}$ and a bit vector representing the domain is created. We test the effect of this optimization in a data-parallel context.

The optimization leads to a very slight reduction of both heap consumption and execution time, except for the n-queens problem, where both execution time and memory consumption are made worse. We find that several bit vectors may be created for a single domain variable. For example, suppose $X \in \{1\ldots5\}$ and $X \neq Y$, where Y is 1 in partition a, 3 in partition b and 5 in partition c. As a result, a bit vector is created for the X in partition b only. If there is another constraint $X \neq Z$, where Z is 3 in partition a, 4 in partition b and 5 in partition c, a bit vector will be created for partition a. Two bit vectors have been created, leading to slower execution. Under the heap frame scheme [22] both bit vectors consume heap memory.

We devise an *eager creation* scheme to get around this problem. Note that a bit vector can be created only when a disequality constraint is encountered. In processing a disequality constraint, if any of the physical partitions need a bit vector, bit vectors are created for all physical partitions. *Lazy creation* refers to the scheme in which bit vectors are created only for partitions in need. The three schemes are compared in Table 2. The heap and trail usages are given in bytes.

We conclude that the three schemes show little difference in overall execution time and memory consumption, although the eager creation scheme consumes slightly less memory

benchmark	eager creation			lazy creation			unoptimized		
	t_1	heap	trail	t_2	heap	trail	t_3	heap	trail
send	.019	460	0	.019	460	0	.019	472	0
eq10	.334	1728	162	.334	1728	162	.345	1756	162
eq20	.519	3636	0	.519	3636	0	.528	3664	0
queen(4)	.014	440	0	.014	452	0	.013	444	0
queen(6)	.042	964	0	.042	996	0	.042	968	0
queen(8)	.101	1656	0	.101	1708	0	.101	1660	0
queen(10)	1.400	3208	780	1.400	3276	780	1.397	3212	780
queen(12)	92.183	5404	1764	92.177	5484	1764	92.062	5408	1764
magic(3)	.074	2044	0	.074	2044	0	.077	2252	0
magic(6)	.791	13512	0	.791	13512	0	.822	14100	0
magic(9)	2.909	41476	0	2.908	41480	0	3.006	42644	0
magich(3)	.086	2324	0	.086	2324	0	.090	2512	0
magich(6)	.411	9276	0	.411	9276	0	.429	9800	0
magich(9)	1.210	24280	0	1.210	24280	0	1.260	25368	0
magich(12)	2.544	47596	0	2.543	47596	0	2.644	49432	0

Test conditions: $\#proc$=8,192, eager nondeterministic derivation, no solitary memory access, no priority scheduling.

Table 2. Benchmark: on-demand creation of bit vectors

than the other two schemes on every test program. The eager creation scheme is preferred because sometimes very large contiguous domains may appear in users' programs.

3.2 Lazy Nondeterministic Derivation vs Eager Nondeterministic Derivation

For implementation convenience, a constraint is treated as a process, like an atom. A constraint may suspend, resume or perform ask/tell operations on the store. In DPAM, the *ready queue* consists of processes which are ready for immediate execution. A *labeling process* is associated with each domain variable in the system. A labeling process is taken from the *labeling queue* and moved to the ready queue when a nondeterministic derivation step is needed. Please refer to our previous paper [23] for a detailed description of DPAM's scheduling subsystem.

Sometimes it is not necessary or even desirable to wait for a deadlock[6] before a nondeterministic derivation step is applied. With *eager nondeterministic derivation*, a labeling process is moved to the ready queue whenever deadlock of any physical partition is detected. *Lazy nondeterministic derivation* refers to the control strategy in which a labeling process is moved to the ready queue only after the deadlock of all physical partitions is detected. *Eager nondeterministic derivation* is chosen over *lazy nondeterministic derivation* for DPAM and we justify this choice using empirical results (Table 3).

---

[6] In concurrent constraint programming, when all agents (*i.e.* atoms) block (*i.e.* suspend), a *deadlock* is said to occur. Firebird resolves a deadlock by applying nondeterministic derivation.

From the results, we find that lazy/eager nondeterministic derivation is basically an processor utilization/execution time tradeoff. Eager nondeterministic derivation creates partitions more aggressively. As a result more parallelism can be exploited, leading to better performance. It is worth noting that although lazy nondeterministic derivation reduces the number of backtrackings, it does not lead to any performance gain because of a lower degree of parallelism.

3.3 Priority Scheduling

One way to increase the degree of parallelism is to schedule those processes resumed by a labeling process ahead of all the others. We have implemented a prototype of this *priority scheduling* scheme on top of our system and its effect on performance is measured (Table 4).

Priority scheduling is faster on average, with the best performance on the n-queens problem. A possible explanation is as follows. A suspended process p is resumed whenever resumption is needed in one or more of the partitions (let the set of such partitions be S). By the time p gets scheduled, p is executed in the other partitions $\overline{S}$ (where $\overline{S}$ denotes the set of active partitions *not* in S) as well as S. On a data-parallel computer, efficiency is independent on the number of active partitions. Therefore, it doesn't matter whether p is executed in S only or in both S and $\overline{S}$. In the best case, $\overline{S}$ entails enough information for the unblocked execution of p by the time p get scheduled. Otherwise, p must suspend again.

After a labeling operation, for each process p resumed by the instantiation of the domain variable, usually *all* partitions entail enough information for the unblocked execution of p. p does not need to suspend again and executing p results in higher processor utilization than executing other resumed processes. It is advantageous to schedule p ahead of all other resumed processes because p may enrich the constraint stores of all partitions in such a way that other resumed processes may execute unblocked, too. The reverse is not true because other resumed processes may enrich the constraint stores of only some of the partitions.

3.4 Execution Profile

We measure the time spent in nondeterministic derivation (ND), constraint solving (C), backtracking (BT) and everything else (*others*), which includes program execution, scheduling, *etc.* The backtracking time includes the time to update the choice point, unwind the trail and restore the process queues. The percentage time is shown in Table 5. The columns C, ND, BT and *others* should add up to 100%. *FND*, the execution time up to the first nondeterministic derivation step, is also shown in the same table, but it is not related to any other column.

It is evident that constraint solving dominates execution time for large problems. This implies that compiler optimizations may not be as useful as an efficient constraint solver. In large problems, very little time is spent before the first nondeterministic derivation step, which is sequential. Hence most of the time is spent on parallel execution. Nondeterministic derivation and backtracking overhead is almost negligible.

benchmark	lazy nondet. derivation				eager nondet. derivation				t_2/t_1
	t_1	ND	P	BT	t_2	ND	P	BT	
send	.019	2	4	0	.019	2	4	0	1.00
eq10	.537	4	164	0	.334	4	181	8	.62
eq20	.791	3	116	0	.519	3	140	0	.66
queen(4)	.016	2	6	0	.014	2	6	0	.88
queen(6)	.054	4	40	0	.042	4	40	0	.78
queen(8)	.201	7	416	0	.101	7	548	0	.50
queen(10)	3.542	27	2397	11	1.400	27	2399	17	.40
queen(12)	209.056	952	4171	1027	92.183	971	4165	1191	.44
magic(3)	.082	2	8	0	.074	2	11	0	.90
magic(6)	.814	2	32	0	.791	2	38	0	.97
magic(9)	3.379	2	74	0	2.909	2	83	0	.86
magich(3)	.086	2	7	0	.086	2	7	0	1.00
magich(6)	.425	2	20	0	.411	2	21	0	.97
magich(9)	1.284	2	42	0	1.210	2	45	0	.94
magich(12)	2.721	2	74	0	2.544	2	78	0	.93

Test conditions: #$proc$=8,192, eager bit vector creation, no solitary memory access, no priority scheduling.

Table 3. Benchmark: lazy nondeterministic derivation vs eager nondeterministic derivation

benchmark	priority scheduling				w/o priority scheduling				t_2/t_1
	t_1	ND	P	BT	t_2	ND	P	BT	
send	.019	2	4	0	.019	2	4	0	1.00
eq10	.299	4	226	0	.334	4	181	8	1.12
eq20	.429	3	138	0	.519	3	140	0	1.21
queen(4)	.013	2	6	0	.014	2	6	0	1.08
queen(6)	.034	4	46	0	.042	4	40	0	1.24
queen(8)	.075	7	564	0	.101	7	548	0	1.35
queen(10)	.827	27	2530	15	1.400	27	2399	17	1.69
queen(12)	57.264	952	4178	1027	92.183	971	4165	1191	1.61
magic(3)	.076	2	8	0	.074	2	11	0	.97
magic(6)	.698	2	38	0	.791	2	38	0	1.13
magic(9)	3.204	2	83	0	2.909	2	83	0	.91
magich(3)	.090	2	7	0	.086	2	7	0	.96
magich(6)	.463	2	22	0	.411	2	21	0	.89
magich(9)	1.315	2	45	0	1.210	2	45	0	.92
magich(12)	2.729	2	78	0	2.544	2	78	0	.93

Test conditions: #$proc$=8,192, eager bit vector creation, eager nondeterministic derivation, no solitary memory access.

Table 4. Benchmark: priority scheduling

benchmark	FND	C	ND	BT	others
send	75.0	78.0	2.5	0	19.5
eq10	7.0	95.8	.7	1.9	1.6
eq20	16.2	98.1	.9	0	1.0
queen(4)	52.3	59.7	.06	0	40.24
queen(6)	35.8	72.7	.06	0	27.24
queen(8)	25.8	80.6	.05	0	19.35
queen(10)	2.9	91.3	3.4	2.7	2.6
queen(12)	.08	90.9	2.8	3.7	2.6
magic(3)	40.6	57.1	.9	0	42.0
magic(6)	11.0	63.2	.1	0	36.7
magic(9)	6.0	60.4	.04	0	39.56
magich(3)	36.5	61.2	.9	0	37.9
magich(6)	19.7	66.6	.3	0	33.1
magich(9)	14.5	68.3	.1	0	31.6
magich(12)	11.3	68.5	.06	0	31.44

Test conditions: #proc=8,192, eager bit vector creation, eager nondeterministic derivation, no solitary memory access, no priority scheduling.

Table 5. Benchmark: execution profile (in %)

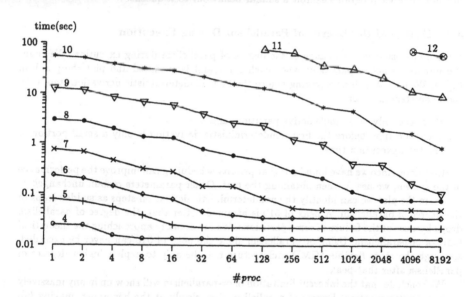

Test conditions: eager bit vector creation, eager nondeterministic derivation, no solitary memory access, priority scheduling.

Fig. 3. Benchmark: run time of n-queens

3.5 Effect of the Number of Processor Elements on Performance

Figure 3 shows the execution time of n-queens, for $4 \leq n \leq 12$, with 1 to 8,192 processor elements. We use priority scheduling because it is particularly suitable for the n-queens problem. We do not have enough memory (each processor element has only 64K bytes) to run 13-queens. Some data points are missing from Figure 3 for the same reason. This is only the limitation of the particular implementation platform we are using, but not a limitation of Firebird or DPAM.

The speed up of 7-queens levels at about 15, but 512 processor elements are required to obtain this speed up. The reason for this is that the processor elements are divided evenly in a nondeterministic derivation step, which may not be the optimal processor allocation strategy. Furthermore, a processor element will remain idle after failure until the system backtracks.

We obtain a maximum speed up of 121 for 9-queens. This may seem disappointing given that 8,192 processor elements are used, but to the best of our knowledge, no other parallel implementation of a concurrent constraint programming language has ever attained a speedup of 2 orders of magnitude. Furthermore, the shared-memory multiprocessor architecture, which is employed by most of the other parallel implementations of concurrent constraint languages, is simply incapable of scaling to that level.

Due to space limitations, we have only analyzed the performance of n-queens in detail, but not all other programs exhibit a similar behaviour to n-queens.

3.6 Change of the Degree of Parallelism During Execution

We are interested in the change of the degree of parallelism during execution. We count the number of active partitions when each constraint is executed and plot the graph in Fig. 4. We do not include anything before the first nondeterministic derivation step, with the understanding that

1. there can only be a single active partition, and
2. execution time before the first nondeterministic derivation is only a small portion of the total execution time.

Furthermore, since we have found out that priority scheduling can improve the performance of the system, we use it when obtaining the plot. Other parameters remain unchanged.

From the plot we can identify the nondeterministic derivation steps as sudden leaps in the degree of parallelism. A peak of 510 is attained. After that, the degree of parallelism drops because of the failure of some partitions. We are actually approaching the theoretical limit of or-parallelism. Using or-parallelism alone the peak of 510 can never be exceeded, although the more flexible MIMD architecture may be able to exploit higher degrees of parallelism after that peak.

We conclude that the inherent limitation of or-parallelism will show up in any massively parallel implementation. Degree of parallelism rises slowly at the beginning, making full utilization of processor elements impossible. After the peak is reached, some or-branches fail, again limiting the degree of parallelism and hence processor element utilization.

Next, we show that when the number of processor elements is very small when compared to the number of or-branches, reasonably high processor element utilization can be

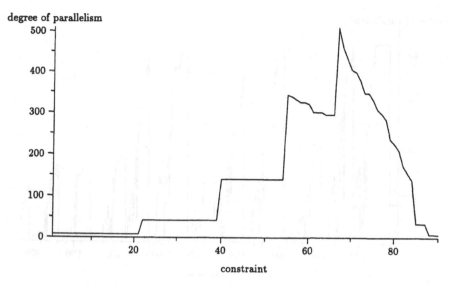

degree of parallelism

constraint

Test conditions: #proc=8,192, eager bit vector creation, eager nondeterministic derivation, no solitary memory access, priority scheduling.

Fig. 4. Execution trace of 8-queens, #proc=8,192

maintained. For the 8-queens problem, 64 processor elements are just enough for the first two nondeterministic derivation steps. The plot is shown in Fig. 5.

4 A Comparison with SIMD MultiLog

SIMD MultiLog [18] is another or-parallel system implemented on MasPar MP-1 (equivalent to the DECmpp we are using). A new *disj* operator is introduced. Solutions to a disjunctive goal *disj G* are collected. The solutions form a disjunctive set of environments and goals appearing after *G* can be executed in these environments in parallel. On the other hand, no special language constructs are needed in Firebird.

The work of Kanada *et al.* [10], SIMD MultiLog and Firebird all execute goals over a disjunctive set of environments[7], exploiting or-parallelism. The work of Kanada *et al.* [10] relies on a vectorizing compiler, MultiLog uses solution aggregation and in Firebird the environments fall out of the labeling operation on domain variables naturally.

Like our approach, MultiLog has the advantage that traditional compilation techniques are applicable. Furthermore, in MultiLog, *engine* variables which reside on the host computer are distinguished manually from *multi* variables which reside on the processor elements. This leads to higher time and space efficiency. See Smith's paper [20] for a

---

[7] An *environment* in MultiLog is analogous to a *partition* in Firebird

degree of parallelism

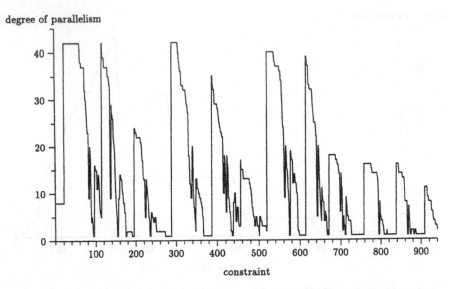

Test conditions: #*proc*=64, eager bit vector creation, eager nondeterministic derivation, no solitary memory access, priority scheduling.

Fig. 5. Execution trace of 8-queens, #*proc*=64

theoretical analysis of the resulting performance gain. Automatic compilation of the engine/multi distinction is possible and there is no inherent technical difficulty to add it to Firebird.

The current MasPar implementation of SIMD MultiLog has the overhead of environment copying which is not necessary in our Firebird implementation. Smith points out that environment copying is a performance bottleneck [18]. However, there is no technical difficulty to incorporate our processor element mapping technique to SIMD MultiLog, and we would expect a significant performance gain. Another drawback of the current SIMD MultiLog implementation is that processor element utilization may be limited when backtracking is used. Furthermore, the user has to specify how many environments should be allocated or how much memory should be used. This is not necessary in our Firebird implementation. Again, we expect a performance gain if our backtracking scheme is incorporated into SIMD MultiLog.

It may be inappropiate to compare the performance of SIMD MultiLog with that of Firebird because the former is a logic programming system but the latter is a concurrent constraint programming system. However, there is no better system for comparison because as far as we know there are no other data-parallel concurrent constraint programming systems beside Firebird, and SIMD MultiLog is implemented on the same platform as Firebird.

When the execution time of SIMD MultiLog using 8,192 processor elements and that of using a workstation are compared, 10 out of the 16 programs in a benchmark suite [19] (*Path, Sat, Tri, WIM, 12-queens, Knight, Waltz, 11-Bratko, Cube, 11-queens*) have a speedup of 3.5 or less. The remaining 6 are *WIM-dyn* (8.1), *Costas* (9.6), *Costas-dyn* (30.7), *20 bits-pal* (295.2), *20 bits-pal-n* (1872.7), *24 bits-pal-n* (2089.9). *n bits-pal* is a program which gives all n-bit strings which are palindromic (by generate and test, not unification) and *n bits-pal-n* is the same program except that naïve reverse is used.

We conclude that SIMD MultiLog attains excellent speedup in some special cases. This is because, for example, the *n bits-pal-n* benchmark forks 8,192 branches very quickly using simple generate-and-test and naïve reverse applied in parallel gives rise to a very high speedup. If we omit such generate-and-test programs from the benchmark set, the maximum speedup of SIMD MultiLog is 30.7 (*Costas-dyn*). Firebird, on the other hand, is up to 20.3 times faster than a workstation implementation of CHIP (9-queens). Therefore, the performance of the two systems are roughly equal. Many implementation techniques of one system can be applied to the other and the combination of both SIMD MultiLog and Firebird is probably more powerful than either alone.

Beside SIMD MultiLog, there are many other implementation schemes of logic programming systems (without constraints) on data-parallel computers, including [2, 3, 8, 9, 14, 15, 25, 7], but we lack the space to compare each of them to Firebird. Some of the comparisons can be found in Tong's thesis [21]. There is an implementation of *ATMS* on SIMD computers [6] but it is not in the logic programming or concurrent constraint programming frameworks.

5   Conclusion

In this paper, we present some preliminary performance results of our massively parallel implementation of Firebird. We conclude that

1. Our figures indicate that a speedup of 2 orders of magnitude is possible when we compare the performance using 8,192 processor elements and the performance using a single processor element of the same machine. It seems at first glance that a speedup of 121 is disappointing given the 8,192 processor elements used to obtain it, but we argue that the shared-memory architecture is simply incapable of scaling to that level. In fact, the design of our Data-Parallel Abstract Machine [23] is optimized for a maximum degree of parallelism, and is most suitable in situations where resources are repleted and top performance is sought after.

2. Although a massively parallel computer has thousands of processor elements, each individual processor element is very slow (An individual processor element of DECmpp is estimated to be 50 times slower than the average workstation by Smith [18]). A factor of 50 in the degree of parallelism is always lost. Our Firebird implementation on a single processor element of DECmpp is only about 4–7 times slower than a CHIP implementation on a DEC 3100 workstation, which is very good compared to the expected slow down of 50. This is achieved by a native code compiler and various small optimizations.

3. Data-parallel implementations need specific optimizations like the *on-demand creation of bit vectors, eager nondeterministic derivation* and *priority scheduling.* We measured

their effects on performance in Section 3. Very little research has been done on optimizations specific to data-parallel implementations and it is an important direction of future work.

4. Our results indicate that most of the execution time is spent on constraint solving. The overhead of nondeterministic derivation and parallel backtracking is negligible.

5. In Figure 4 and Figure 5 we observe the characteristics of or-parallelism when the number of processor elements is large. More investigation is needed and a thorough understanding of large-scale or-parallelism is crucial to massively parallel implementations.

Acknowledgement

We would like to express our thanks to Donald A. Smith, Saumya Debray, Edward Tsang, Albert Lai and Jimmy Lee for their invaluable comments and suggestions.

This research is partially supported by RGC Earmarked Grant CUHK 70/93E.

References

1. H. Aït-Kaci. *Warren's Abstract Machine: A Tutorial Reconstruction.* MIT Press, 1991.
2. A. K. Bansal and J. L. Potter. An associative model to minimize matching and backtracking overhead in logic programs with large knowledge bases. *Engineering Applications of Artificial Intelligence*, 5(3):247–262, 1992.
3. J. Barklund and H. Millroth. Providing iteration and concurrency in logic programs through bounded quantifications. In *Proceedings of the International Conference on Fifth Generation Computer Systems*, pages 817–824, ICOT, Japan, 1992.
4. D. Diaz and P. Codognet. A minimal extension of the WAM for clp(FD). In D. S. Warren, editor, *Logic Programming: Proceedings of the Tenth International Conference*, pages 774–790, Budapest, Hungary, 1993. The MIT Press.
5. M. Dincbas, P. Van Hentenryck, and H. Simonis. Solving the car sequencing problem in constraint logic programming. In *Proceedings of the European Conference on Artificial Intelligence*, Munich, Germany, August 1988.
6. M. Dixon and J. de Kleer. Massively parallel assumption-based truth maintainance. In *Proceedings of the National Conference on Artificial Intelligence*, St. Paul, Minnesota, August 1988.
7. A. González and J. Tubella. The Multipath Parallel Execution Model for Prolog. In *Proceedings of the First Int'l Conf. on Parallel Symbolic Computation PASCO'94*. World Scientific Pub., 1994.
8. S. Ivanets, N. Ilinsky, and M. Krylov. WAM specification for parallel execution on SIMD computer. In *First Russian Conference on Logic Programming*, pages 232–239, St. Petersburg, Russia, September 1990. Springer-Verlag.
9. P. Kacsuk and A. Bale. DAP Prolog: A set-oriented approach to Prolog. *The Computer Journal*, 30(5):393–403, 1987.
10. Y. Kanada, K. Kojima, and M. Sugaya. Vectorization techniques for Prolog. In *Proceedings of the ACM International Conference on Supercomputing*, pages 539–549, St. Malo, 1988.
11. S. Kliger and E. Shapiro. From decision trees to decision graphs. In S. Debray and M. Hermenegildo, editors, *Proceedings of the 1990 North American Conference on Logic Programming*, pages 97–116, Austin, 1990. ALP, The MIT Press.

12. J. W. Lloyd. *Foundations of Logic Programming, Second, Extended Edition*. Springer-Verlag, 1987.
13. M. J. Maher. Logic semantics for a class of committed-choice programs. In J.-L. Lassez, editor, *Logic Programming: Proceedings of the Fourth International Conference*, pages 858–876, Melbourne, 1987. The MIT Press.
14. M. Nilsson and H. Tanaka. A flat GHC implementation for supercomputers. In R. A. Kowalski and K. A. Bowen, editors, *Logic Programming: Proceedings of the Fifth International Conference and Symposium*, pages 1337–1350, Seatle, 1988. ALP, IEEE, The MIT Press.
15. M. Nilsson and H. Tanaka. Massively parallel implementation of flat GHC on the Connection Machine. In *Proceedings of the International Conference on Fifth Generation Computer Systems*, pages 1031–1040, Japan, 1988. ICOT.
16. V. A. Saraswat. A somewhat logical formulation of CLP synchronisation primitives. In R. A. Kowalski and K. A. Bowen, editors, *Logic Programming: Proceedings of the Fifth International Conference and Symposium*, pages 1298–1314, Seatle, 1988. ALP, IEEE, The MIT Press.
17. V. A. Saraswat and M. Rinard. Concurrent constraint programming. In *Proceedings of the 17th Symposium on Principles of Programming Languages*, pages 232–244, San Fransisco, 1990.
18. D. A. Smith. MultiLog: Data or-parallel logic programming. In D. S. Warren, editor, *Logic Programming: Proceedings of the Tenth International Conference*, pages 314–331, Budapest, Hungary, 1993. The MIT Press.
19. D. A. Smith, 1994. Personal communication.
20. D. A. Smith. Why multi-SLD beats SLD (even on a uniprocessor). In *Proceedings of the Sixth International Symposium on Programming Language Implementation and Logic Programming*, Madrid, Spain, 1994. Springer-Verlag.
21. B. M. Tong. Data-parallel concurrent constraint programming. M. Phil. thesis, Department of Computer Science, The Chinese University of Hong Kong, Hong Kong, 1994.
22. B. M. Tong and H. F. Leung. Concurrent constraint logic programming on massively parallel SIMD computers. In D. Miller, editor, *Logic Programming: Proceedings of the 1993 International Symposium*, pages 388–402, Vancouver, Canada, October 1993. The MIT Press.
23. B. M. Tong and H. F. Leung. Implementation of a data-parallel concurrent constraint programming system. In *Proceedings of the First International Symposium on Parallel Symbolic Computation*, pages 382–393, Linz, Austria, September 1994. World Scientific.
24. E. Tsang. *Foundations of Constraint Satisfaction*. Academic Press, 1993.
25. J. Tubella and A. González. A Partial Breadth-First Execution Model for Prolog. In *Proceedings of the 6th Int'l Conf. on Tools with Artificial Intelligence TAI'94*, pages 129–137, 1994.
26. K. Ueda. Guarded horn clauses. In E. Wada, editor, *Logic Programming '85 — Proceedings of the 4th Conference*, Lecture Notes in Computer Science 221, pages 168–179, Tokyo, July 1985. Springer-Verlag.
27. P. Van Hentenryck. *Constraint Satisfaction in Logic Programming*. MIT Press, 1989.
28. P. Van Hentenryck, V. A. Saraswat, and Y. Deville. Design, implementation and evaluation of the constraint language cc(FD). Technical Report CS-93-02, Department of Computer Science, Brown University, Providence, 1993.
29. D. H. D. Warren. An abstract Prolog instruction set. Technical Note 309, SRI International, Menlo Park, CA, U.S.A., 1983.
30. C. M. Yeung, S. M. Leung, and H. F. Leung. Applying constraint satisfaction technique in university timetable scheduling. In A. Roth, editor, *Proceedings of the Third International Conference on the Practical Application of Prolog*, Paris, France, April 1995. Practical Applications of Prolog.

Formalizing Inductive Proofs of
Network Algorithms

Ramesh Bharadwaj[1], Amy Felty[2], Frank Stomp[2]

[1] CRL, McMaster University, 1280 Main St. West, Hamilton, ON, Canada L8S4K1
[2] AT&T Bell Laboratories, 600 Mountain Avenue, Murray Hill, NJ 07974, USA

Abstract. Theorem proving and model checking are combined to fully formalize a correctness proof of a broadcasting protocol. The protocol is executed in a network of processors which constitutes a binary tree of arbitrary size. We use the theorem prover CoQ and the model checker SPIN to verify the broadcasting protocol.

Our goals in this work are twofold. The *first* one is to provide a strategy for carrying out formal, mechanical correctness proofs of distributed network algorithms. Even though logical specifications of programs implementing such algorithms are often defined precisely enough to allow a human verifier to prove the program's correctness, the definition of the network is often only informal or implicit. Our example illustrates how an underlying network can be formally defined by means of *induction*, and how to reason about network algorithms by structural induction. Our *second* goal is to integrate theorem proving and model checking to increase the class of algorithms for which mechanical verification is practical. Theorem provers are expressive and powerful, but require sophisticated insight and guidance by the user. Model checkers are fully automatic and effective for verifying finite state automata, but limited to finite spaces of a certain size. We provide a proof strategy which draws on the strengths of both techniques.

1 Introduction

In general, distributed network algorithms are designed to function properly for a specific class of networks, such as rings or complete networks. In most cases the size of the network is unknown and the algorithms are described in a generic way. The (topology of the) underlying network is crucial for the correctness of an algorithm. However, the definition of the network is often left out of the logical specification of the program implementing the algorithm; it is often informal and only implicitly defined. As a consequence, it is not directly possible to *mechanically* check whether a correctness proof (constructed manually) itself is correct. The current paper addresses this problem, and shows how a combination of model checking and theorem proving can be used to reason about programs executed in a specific class of networks when the size and exact shape of the network are unknown.

Model checking has been used to verify a number of distributed network algorithms and protocols. It is a powerful verification technique that provides full automation. However, model checkers cannot handle networks of arbitrary size. Theorem provers, on the other hand, generally implement very expressive logics which can handle infinite or arbitrary parameters, such as the number of processes. But they require sophisticated insight and guidance by the user. In this paper, we present an integration of theorem proving and model checking such that structural induction over the network is done within a theorem prover, whereas the base case and many of the subcases of the induction step are verified using a model checker.

In our combined approach, we use the COQ Proof Development System [6] and the SPIN Verification System [15]. COQ is an interactive tactic-style theorem prover which implements the Calculus of Inductive Constructions (CIC), a higher-order type theory that supports inductive types. When a type is defined inductively in COQ, a principle of structural induction and an operator for defining functions recursively over that type are automatically generated. SPIN is a model checker for establishing temporal properties of systems modeled in a guarded commands-like language called PROMELA.

The example we consider to demonstrate our techniques is the PIF-protocol, a broadcasting algorithm developed by Segall [26], executed in a network that constitutes a binary tree. ("PIF" stands for Propagation of Information with Feedback.) The size of the tree is left unspecified. The PIF-protocol is important because it can be identified in many distributed network algorithms, such as the spanning tree algorithm in [8] and the minimum path algorithms in [26]. Intuitively, the PIF-protocol achieves the following: A value, initially recorded by the root of the tree, has to be broadcast and eventually every node in the tree should record this value. Also, the root should eventually be notified that every node has recorded the value.

We specify the PIF-protocol in Manna and Pnueli's Linear Time Temporal Logic (LTL) [19]. The program implementing the PIF-protocol is a pair consisting of a state formula and a finite set of actions formulated as in UNITY [3]. (A state formula is an LTL formula without temporal operators.) The formula characterizes the states in which the program may start its execution. Our correctness proof of the PIF-protocol can be decomposed into three parts: (a) a proof that some state formula continuously holds; (b) a proof that some state formula is stable (once the formula holds, it continues to hold); and (c) a proof of a liveness property.

For part (a) we have applied (a variant of) the S_Inv rule of Manna and Pnueli [19]. This rule states that state formula I is always true if there exists a state formula Inv such that Inv holds initially; it is preserved under every action of the program; and it is stronger than I. The technical formulation of this rule is as follows, where $\Box$ denotes the always-operator from LTL.

$$\frac{\Theta \to Inv, \quad \{Inv\}\tau_i\{Inv\}, i = 1, \ldots, n, \quad Inv \to I}{Prog \vdash \Box I} \quad \text{for } Prog = \langle \Theta, \{\tau_1, \ldots, \tau_n\} \rangle$$

Here Θ is the initial condition and $\tau_1, \ldots, \tau_n$ are the actions of program $Prog$. The formula $\{p\}\tau\{q\}$ denotes a Hoare triple interpreted as usual: if state formula p holds before action τ is executed, then state formula q holds after. Using COQ and SPIN, we prove the premises of the S_Inv rule for an arbitrary binary tree. Formula I expresses that whenever the root has been notified that all nodes have recorded the value broadcast, all nodes have indeed recorded that value. There are four parts to the proof:

1. Definitions are given in COQ to specify programs as well as the syntax and inference rules for the fragment of LTL needed for our example.
2. The structure of the network is formally specified by defining binary trees of arbitrary size using the built-in inductive types of COQ.
3. The definition of trees is used to define two functions, one which maps a binary tree to a set of actions expressing the program for that tree, and one which maps a binary tree to an LTL formula which expresses the invariant Inv for that tree.
4. The premises of the S_Inv rule are established by structural induction on binary trees.

As mentioned, correctness of the PIF-protocol also involves proving a stable property and a liveness property. The stable property has been established in the same way as the formula in (a) above by application of a proof rule similar to rule S_Inv. We have not done the proof of the liveness property. This proof will be similar to the other two because it again involves reasoning about the program's actions.

The premises of the S_Inv rule are proved by three inductive arguments, one each for the first and last premises, and one for all of the remaining premises. The first two do not involve reasoning about actions. SPIN is used to handle some tedious but straightforward propositional reasoning. For the third inductive argument, the base case (for the one-node tree) involves reasoning about a program containing two actions. SPIN easily verifies that the invariant holds for each action. In the induction step, we assume that the invariant holds for the program of a tree t, and we must show that a slightly larger invariant holds for a slightly larger program obtained from tree t with two new nodes attached at some leaf. We decompose the inductive case into many cases, of which twenty-six are verified by SPIN. These cases are generally obtained from subgoals of the form $\{p \wedge q\}\tau\{p \wedge q\}$, for state formulas p, q and action τ. These cases can be split into two subgoals $\{p\}\tau\{p\}$ and $\{q\}\tau\{q\}$ such that the former can be proved easily using the theorem prover, and the latter can be mapped directly to a PROMELA program and verified using SPIN. The formula q in these cases is quite large and a direct proof in COQ involves a lot of detailed repetitive reasoning, which we avoid because of our use of the model checker.

In related work, COQ is used in [1, 14] to verify the Alternating Bit Protocol and a data link protocol without the aid of a model checker. In both these proofs the network is fixed. Chou [4] verifies the PIF-protocol for arbitrary connected graphs in the HOL theorem prover [11] again without the aid of a model checker. His proof uses abstraction to reduce the concrete version of the problem to an abstract one. In particular, he defines an abstract version of the concrete program, shows that the property holds for the abstract program, and shows that any property that holds for the abstract program also holds for the concrete one. In contrast to his proof, our proof does not use abstraction; ours is direct and, in addition, supported by a model checker. It is straightforward to extend our proof to cope with arbitrary connected graphs.

As mentioned, mechanical assistance in proofs is also offered by model checkers [5, 15, 21, 16]. They establish validity of formulae in a model, are fully automated, and are extremely fast for reasonably sized models. All model checkers suffer from the state explosion problem, which has been attacked in [10, 20, 24, 28]. Model checkers have been used to verify a number of complex systems, see for example [21]. Several methods for inductive reasoning about systems consisting of an arbitrary number of (identical or similar) processes have been proposed in the literature. German and Sistla [9] present a fully automatic method. Their algorithm is doubly exponential in the size of the system, and therefore inefficient. Induction principles based on equivalences between systems have been proposed by Browne, Clarke, and Grumberg [2] and by Shtadler and Grumberg [27]. Pre-orders, rather than equivalences, between systems are used in the methods of Kurshan and McMillan [18] and of Wolper and Lovinfosse [29]. In contrast to our use of CoQ's built-in structural induction, each of the above mentioned induction principles is tailored to a specific application.

Kurshan and Lamport [17] and others have investigated how to integrate theorem proving and model checking to verify programs when pure model checking fails. In [17] a 64-bit multiplier is proved correct. Rajan, Shankar, and Srivas [25] and Müller and Nipkow [22] combine theorem proving and model checking to verify infinite state systems. In these two papers, the underlying idea is to reduce an infinite state system to a finite one using abstraction techniques as in [4]. Unlike [4], in [25] and [22] the finite state system is verified by a model checker, whereas the reduction is verified using the theorem prover. In our example presented here, instead of abstraction, we handle the arbitrary parameter (in our case the number of nodes) by a direct inductive argument and use model checking whenever applicable on the subcases.

The rest of this paper is organized as follows: The PIF-protocol is described in Sect. 2. In Sect. 3, we briefly present CoQ and SPIN. In Sect. 4, we outline how our correctness proof has been carried out using a combination of these two systems. Finally, Sect. 5 draws some conclusions.

2 The PIF-Protocol

In this section we specify and implement the PIF-protocol as analyzed in the rest of this paper.

2.1 Specification

Consider a fixed, but arbitrary network constituting a non-empty, finite, binary tree. Nodes in the tree are identified with processes; edges with communication channels. One node R is identified with the tree's root. Assume that R has recorded some value V. The informal specification of the PIF-protocol is:

(1) Eventually every process in the network records V.

(2) Eventually R is notified that all processes have recorded value V; and once this notification has taken place, all processes continue to record that value.

For a given graph (N, E), where N is a set of nodes and E is a set of edges, let $Tree(N, E)$ denote that this graph is a non-empty, finite, binary tree. Let $R \in N$ denote the tree's root. Every process $n \in N$ has its own variable v_n for recording the broadcast value V. Initially $v_R = V$ holds, *i.e.*, process R has recorded value V, whereas the initial values of variables v_n, for processes n different from R, are irrelevant. The root also has its own variable $done_R$ used to record whether all processes in the network have recorded value V. Initially, $done_R = 0$ holds. (Actually, for nodes n different from R, we have introduced $done_n$ to allow generic descriptions of the processes, but they are never used.)

Using the always-operator $\square$ and the eventual-operator $\Diamond$ from LTL, it is required that the following holds: If $R \in N \wedge v_R = V \wedge done_R = 0$ holds initially, then

$$Tree(N, E) \rightarrow \quad \square(done_R = 1 \rightarrow \forall n \in N.v_n = V)$$
$$\wedge \ \square(done_R = 1 \rightarrow \square done_R = 1)$$
$$\wedge \ \Diamond done_R = 1$$

is true. That is, it is always the case that all processes in the network have recorded value V if $done_R = 1$ holds; once $done_R = 1$ holds, it continues to hold ($done_R = 1$ is stable); and eventually $done_R = 1$ holds. These three conjuncts correspond to properties (a), (b), and (c) mentioned in the previous section. The proof described in the current paper is that of the first conjunct, property (a).

2.2 Implementation

A program consists of two parts (*cf.* [3]): a state formula and a (finite) collection of guarded actions. The formula characterizes the initial states in which the program may start its execution. A guarded action is of the form $g \rightarrow x_1 := e_1, \ldots, x_m := e_m$ for some natural number $m > 0$, consisting of *guard* g and *body* $x_1 := e_1, \ldots, x_m := e_m$. Here, x_i are distinct variables (to avoid name-clashes) and e_i are expressions ($i = 1, \ldots, m$). Guard g is a boolean expression without quantifiers. An action is *enabled* in a state if its guard evaluates to true in that state. If in some state during execution no action of the program is enabled, then the program is considered terminated as in [19]. Otherwise, an enabled action $g \rightarrow x_1 := e_1, \ldots, x_m := e_m$ is nondeterministically chosen for execution. Execution of this action means that the assignments $x_1 := e_1, \ldots, x_m := e_m$ are executed atomically and simultaneously.

The actions of the program implementing the PIF-protocol are given in Fig. 1. There n ranges over the nodes in the tree; par denotes the parent of n, provided that n has a parent; and l and r denote the left and right child of n, respectively. As described above, each node n maintains variables v_n and $done_n$. In addition, every node maintains a variable pc_n, which can be thought of as n's program counter. Initially, $pc_R=1$ holds, whereas $pc_n=0$ holds for all nodes n different from R. We have also used variables cc_n for nodes n in the

$a0 :: cc_n = 0 \wedge pc_n = 1 \rightarrow pc_n := 4, done_n := 1$

$a2\_down :: cc_n = 2 \wedge pc_n = 1 \wedge pc_l = 0 \wedge pc_r = 0 \rightarrow pc_l := 1, v_l := v_n, pc_r := 1, v_r := v_n$

$a3\_down :: cc_n = 3 \wedge pc_n = 1 \wedge pc_l = 0 \wedge pc_r = 0 \rightarrow pc_l := 1, v_l := v_n, pc_r := 1, v_r := v_n$

$a1\_up :: cc_n = 1 \wedge pc_n = 1 \rightarrow pc_{par} := pc_{par} + 1, pc_n := 4$

$a3\_up :: cc_n = 3 \wedge pc_n = 3 \rightarrow pc_{par} := pc_{par} + 1, pc_n := 4$

$a2\_term :: cc_n = 2 \wedge pc_n = 3 \rightarrow pc_n := 4, done_n := 1$

Fig. 1. Actions executed by every node in the tree. The collection of these actions, for all nodes in the tree, constitutes the PIF-protocol.

tree. Variables cc_n cannot be changed by any action and represents the number of n's neighbors in the tree. Thus, for the root of the tree either $cc_R=0$ or $cc_R=2$ holds. In the first case, R is the only node in the tree; in the second case, the tree consists of more than one node. There exists exactly one node n in the tree satisfying $cc_n=0$ or $cc_n=2$. We identify this node with the root R. For other nodes n in the tree, we have that either $cc_n=1$ (n is a leaf) or $cc_n=3$ (n is an internal node) holds. The initial values of the cc variables, the pc variables, $done_R = 0$, $v_R = V$, and $R \in N$ characterize the states in which the execution of the program may start. Action $a0$ in Fig. 1 can be executed only if the tree consists of one node. In this case, the node sets its variable pc_R to 4 and its variable $done_R$ to 1 and the program terminates. If the tree consists of more than one node, the root initiates the program by passing on value V to its neighbors (action $a2\_down$). After an internal node has received value V, it passes V on to its children (action $a3\_down$). When a leaf has received value V, it informs its parent about this (action $a1\_up$). After an internal node has been informed that both its children have received the value, the node itself informs its parent (action $a3\_up$). Eventually, when the root gets the information that its children (hence, all other nodes in the tree) have received value V, it sets its variable $done_R$ to 1 and the program terminates (action $a2\_term$).

3 COQ and SPIN

We briefly introduce the COQ Proof Development System and the SPIN Verification System.

3.1 The COQ Proof Development System

As stated, COQ is an implementation of the Calculus of Inductive Constructions (CIC). Familiarity with CIC is not required for understanding the proofs in the next section. We simply introduce the syntax used there. Let x represent variables and M, N represent terms of CIC. The syntax of terms is as follows.

$$Prop \mid Set \mid Type \mid x \mid M\,N \mid \lambda x : M.N \mid \forall x : M.N \mid M \rightarrow N \mid$$
$$M \wedge N \mid M \vee N \mid \exists x : M.N \mid \neg M \mid M = N \mid Ind\, x : M\, \{N_1 \mid \cdots \mid N_n\} \mid$$
$$Rec\, M\, N \mid Case\, x : M\, of\, M_1 \Rightarrow N_1, \ldots, M_n \Rightarrow N_n$$

Prop is the type of logical propositions, whereas *Set* is the type of data types. *Type* is the type of both *Prop* and *Set*. In CIC, variables and constants are not distinguished. In COQ, a new constant can be introduced and given with its type using the Parameter keyword. It is also possible to introduce new constants via definitions. The Definition keyword is used for this purpose.

Application is represented as juxtaposition of terms. Abstraction is represented as usual where the bound variable is typed. The logical operators $\forall, \rightarrow, \wedge, \vee, \exists, \neg, =$ are the familiar ones from higher-order logic.

The *Ind* constant is used to build inductive definitions where M is the type of the class of terms being defined and $N_1, \ldots, N_n$ where $n \geq 0$ are the types of the constructors. In COQ, inductive definitions are introduced with an Inductive declaration where each constructor is named and given with its type separated by vertical bars. *Rec* and *Case* are the operators for defining recursive and inductive functions, respectively, over inductive types.

3.2 The SPIN Verification System

As stated, SPIN [15] is a tool for establishing temporal properties of systems modeled in a guarded commands-like language called PROMELA. SPIN has been used to prove properties of communication protocols and asynchronous hardware. It can also be used to prove termination of systems. As we have noted, model checking provides complete automation. The algorithms underlying a model checker such as SPIN suffer from scalability: They are PSPACE hard. Consequently, one quickly runs out space as the size of the model increases.

A PROMELA program consists of a section in which variables are declared and statements. In essence, statements are built up from assignments, the empty statement *skip*, sequential composition, assert statements, conditional statements, and loops. (We will not use loops in this paper.) The conditional statements we use in this paper are of the form $if :: g_1 \rightarrow S_1 :: \cdots :: g_n \rightarrow S_n\ fi$, where symbol "::" separates the *guarded actions* $g_i \rightarrow S_i$ where g_i is a guard and S_i is a statement $(i = 1, \ldots, n)$. (Conditional statements in PROMELA are more general.) If a guard is the constant *true* then it may be omitted. These conditional statements have the same interpretation as, for example, Dijkstra's conditional statements with the exception that in PROMELA the process blocks (and does not abort) when none of its guards is enabled. An assert statement is of the form $assert\{g\}$, for a guard g. This statement acts like *skip* when executed in a state satisfying g; otherwise the execution is aborted.

For a finite set of states, one can generate an arbitrary state by means of a conditional statement. For example, $if :: x := 0 :: x := 1\ fi; if :: y := 1 :: y := 2\ fi$ generates some state in the set characterized by predicate $(x = 0 \vee x = 1) \wedge (y = 1 \vee y = 2)$.

Partial correctness $\{p\}\ T\ \{q\}$ of program T w.r.t. precondition p and postcondition q is interpreted as usual (*cf.* Sect. 1). We have that $\{p\}\ g \rightarrow a\ \{q\}$ holds iff $\{p \wedge g\}\ a\ \{q\}$ holds. In our proof, we often need to prove such a partial correctness formula, where a always terminates. Consider the finite set of states corresponding to the possible combinations of values that the variables may take.

Let S be the PROMELA program that generates an arbitrary state from this set in the manner described above. The partial correctness formula $\{p \wedge g\}\ a\ \{q\}$ can be shown to be equivalent to termination of the PROMELA program

$S;\ if :: p \wedge g \to a;\ assert\{q\} :: \neg(p \wedge g) \to skip\ fi$.

Similarly, validity of the implication $p \to q$ can be translated into the question of whether or not the PROMELA program

$S;\ if :: p \to assert\{q\} :: \neg p \to skip\ fi$

always terminates. Validation of such implications and of partial correctness formulas of single actions are the only two ways in which we use SPIN. (In our example p and q are generally very large.)

4 Correctness Proof of the PIF-Protocol

In this section we outline our correctness proof of the PIF-protocol executed in an arbitrary binary tree.

4.1 Specification of State Formulas and Actions

First, we give definitions in COQ specifying the syntax of state formulas and actions. State formulas are formed from atomic formulas expressing equality between terms and the logical connectives $\wedge, \vee, \to, \neg$. Terms are formed from variables, the constant zero, and the successor function. These are the only expressions needed for our example. Variables, terms, and state formulas are specified as inductive types in COQ. Processes or nodes in the tree are uniquely identified with a natural number using nat, the predefined type of natural numbers in COQ. Variables will take an argument of type nat indicating the process to which it belongs. There are four variables for each process defined as follows.

$\mathsf{Inductive}\ var := pc:nat \to var \mid v:nat \to var \mid cc:nat \to var \mid done:nat \to var$.

The logical operators $\to, \wedge, \vee, \neg, =$ appear both in CIC expressions and in state formulas which we want to encode in CIC. To avoid confusion, we superscript many of the symbols in the COQ definitions of state formulas with a "$*$". Terms and formulas are defined as follows.

$\mathsf{Inductive}\ tm := 0^* : tm \mid s^* : tm \to tm \mid x : var \to tm$.
$\mathsf{Inductive}\ form := \ False : form \mid \neg^* : form \to form$
$\mid\ \wedge^* : form \to form \to form \mid \vee^* : form \to form \to form$
$\mid\ \to^* : form \to form \to form \mid =^* : tm \to tm \to form$.

We adopt the usual convention that the constructor $\to$ associates to the right. For readability, we abbreviate both the variable $(pc\ n)$ and the term $(x\ (pc\ n))$ as pc_n, and similarly for the other three kinds of variables. It will always be clear from context which is meant. In addition we use infix notation for the binary connectives $\wedge^*, \vee^*, \to^*, =^*$. For example, the state formula $pc_n = 0$ is represented by the term $(=^*\ (x\ (pc\ n))\ 0^*)$ of type $form$, which we write as $(pc_n =^* 0^*)$. We introduce a parameter V for the value passed through the network. By making it a parameter, our theorems will hold for any instantiation of V. We also define 1^* for convenience later. The terms $2^*, 3^*, 4^*$ are defined similarly.

Parameter $V : tm$.

Definition $1^* := (s^* \; 0^*)$.

We do not include any temporal operators here since they are not needed to prove the premises of the S_Inv rule, which contain only state formulas. We express provability of state formulas via an inductive definition of a predicate *prov* of type *form* $\rightarrow$ *Prop*. We do not give its definition here. It specifies a natural deduction inference system for the fraction of first-order classical logic that we need and is similar to specifications given in [23, 13, 7]. From this definition, we can prove for example:

Lemma *provable_and_i* : $\forall A, B : form.((prov\; A) \wedge (prov\; B)) \rightarrow (prov\; (A \wedge^* B))$.

Actions consist of a guard and a list of assignment statements. The formulas that can occur in guards are the same as state formulas defined by the type *form*. Assignment statements and actions are defined below. The latter uses the built-in *list* type of CoQ.

Inductive *Assign* : *Set* := *assign* : *var* $\rightarrow$ *tm* $\rightarrow$ *Assign*.

Inductive *Action* : *Set* := *action* : *form* $\rightarrow$ (*list Assign*) $\rightarrow$ *Action*.

We specify substitution on terms as a set of equations at the object-level. The CoQ term (*subst A y t*) encodes $[t/y]A$, *i.e.*, the formula obtained from A by replacing every free occurrence of y in A by t. Using the definition of *subst*, we define a function *ht* of type *form* $\rightarrow$ *Action* $\rightarrow$ *form* $\rightarrow$ *form* which maps a Hoare triple $\{p\}g \rightarrow x_1 := t_1, \ldots, x_n := t_n\{q\}$ to the equivalent state formula $(p \wedge g) \rightarrow [\bar{t}/\bar{x}]q$. Here, $[\bar{t}/\bar{x}]q$ denotes the simultaneous replacement of all free occurrences of x_i in q by t_i, $1 \le i \le n$. (We omit the details.)

4.2 CoQ Specification of the Network

Binary trees of processors are defined by the following inductive definition.

Inductive *BinTree* := *root* : *nat* $\rightarrow$ *BinTree*

       | *children* : *BinTree* $\rightarrow$ *nat* $\rightarrow$ *nat* $\rightarrow$ *nat* $\rightarrow$ *BinTree*.

Here, (*root n*) is a tree containing only processor n, and (*children t* n_1 n_2 n) is the tree obtained by adding two new children n_1 and n_2 to leaf n in t. We choose this definition of binary trees over the more standard one in which a tree is either a leaf or a node with two subtrees, because it simplifies our proofs by structural induction over trees. Of course, for our definition, we need additional predicates to ensure that a tree is well-formed. For example, in (*children t* n_1 n_2 n), n must occur as a leaf in t, and n_1 and n_2 must be distinct and not already occur in t. For this purpose, we define the sets and predicates below. Instead of giving their formal definitions, we give a short explanation. They are all defined recursively over the type *BinTree*. The set theory library of CoQ is used in these definitions.

- (*troot t*) evaluates to the root of tree t.
- (*pids t*) gives the set of natural numbers (processes) in t.
- (*parents t*) evaluates to the set of nodes in t that occur as parents.
- (*distinct_nodes t*) holds if all of the process identifiers that occur at the nodes in t are distinct from one another. For a one-node tree, this predicate always

holds. The proposition $(distinct\_nodes\ (children\ t\ n_1\ n_2\ n))$ is equivalent to
$\neg(n_1 \in (pids\ t)) \land \neg(n_2 \in (pids\ t)) \land \neg(n_1 = n_2) \land (distinct\_nodes\ t)$.

- $(correct\_parents\ t)$ holds if every time two children are added at a node n, n
occurs in t and does not already have children. This predicate always holds
for one-node trees, and $(correct\_parents\ (children\ t\ n_1\ n_2\ n))$ is equivalent to
$(n \in (pids\ t)) \land \neg(n \in (parents\ t)) \land (correct\_parents\ t)$.

The predicate *tree* which holds only for well-formed trees is defined as follows.

Definition $tree := \lambda t : BinTree.(distinct\_nodes\ t) \land (correct\_parents\ t)$.

In COQ, each time an inductive definition is given, a structural induction
principle is automatically generated and proved. The induction principle for
trees, which plays an essential role in the proofs here, is the following.

$\forall P : BinTree \to Prop.$
$(\forall n : nat.(P\ (root\ n))) \to$
$(\forall t : BinTree.(P\ t) \to \forall n_1, n_2, n : nat.(P\ (children\ t\ n_1\ n_2\ n))) \to$
$\forall t : BinTree.(P\ t).$

Using this principle, the following theorem, for example, can be proved easily.

Lemma $tree\_subtree : \forall t : BinTree.\forall n_1, n_2, n : nat.$
$(tree\ (children\ t\ n_1\ n_2\ n)) \to (tree\ t)$.

4.3 Basic Definitions for the PIF-Protocol

As stated, we define a function which maps a tree to a set of actions implementing
the PIF-protocol and another function which maps a tree to an invariant used
in proving properties of this implementation. To define the former, we encode
each action as a function from natural numbers (nodes) to actions. For example
the $a1\_up$ action is encoded as follows (where brackets are used to denote lists
in COQ and commas are used to separate list items).

Definition $a1\_up := \lambda n, par : nat.$
$(action\ ((cc_n =^* 1^*) \land^* (pc_n =^* 1^*))\ [(assign\ pc_{par}\ (s^*\ pc_{par})), (assign\ pc_n\ 4^*)])$.

We then define a function *actions* of type $BinTree \to (set\ Action)$ that takes a
tree and returns a set containing $a0$, $a2\_down$, and $a2\_term$ for the root, $a3\_down$
and $a3\_up$ for each internal node, and $a1\_up$ for each leaf.

The invariant used in our proofs is defined as a conjunction of state formulas
where each conjunct is one of the formulas below instantiated for a particular
node. In these formulas, n refers to an arbitrary node, l refers to n's left child,
r refers to n's right child, and par refers to n's parent.

(I1) $cc_n = 0 \to (v_n = V \land ((pc_n = 1 \land done_n = 0) \lor (pc_n = 4 \land done_n = 1)))$

(I2) $cc_n = 1 \to ((pc_n = 0 \lor pc_n = 1 \lor pc_n = 4) \land (\neg pc_n = 0 \to v_n = V))$

(I3) $cc_n = 2 \to (v_n = V \land (((pc_n = 1 \lor pc_n = 2 \lor pc_n = 3) \land done_n = 0)$
$\lor(pc_n = 4 \land done_n = 1)))$

(I4) $cc_n = 3 \to ((pc_n = 0 \lor pc_n = 1 \lor pc_n = 2 \lor pc_n = 3 \lor pc_n = 4)$
$\land (\neg pc_n = 0 \to v_n = V))$

(I5) $(cc_n = 3 \land pc_n = 0) \to (pc_l = 0 \land pc_r = 0)$

(I6) $((cc_n = 1 \lor cc_n = 3) \land pc_n = 0) \to (pc_{par} = 0 \lor pc_{par} = 1)$

(I7) $((cc_n = 2 \lor cc_n = 3) \land pc_n = 1) \to ((pc_l = 0 \land pc_r = 0)$
$$\lor ((pc_l = 1 \lor pc_l = 2 \lor pc_l = 3)$$
$$\land (pc_r = 1 \lor pc_r = 2 \lor pc_r = 3)))$$

(I8) $((cc_n = 1 \lor cc_n = 3) \land pc_n = 1) \to (pc_{par} = 1 \lor pc_{par} = 2)$

(I9) $((cc_n = 2 \lor cc_n = 3) \land pc_n = 2) \to ((pc_l = 4 \land (pc_r = 1 \lor pc_r = 2 \lor pc_r = 3))$
$$\lor (pc_r = 4 \land (pc_l = 1 \lor pc_l = 2 \lor pc_l = 3)))$$

(I10) $(cc_n = 3 \land pc_n = 2) \to (pc_{par} = 1 \lor pc_{par} = 2)$

(I11) $((cc_n = 2 \lor cc_n = 3) \land pc_n = 3) \to (pc_l = 4 \land pc_r = 4)$

(I12) $(cc_n = 3 \land pc_n = 3) \to (pc_{par} = 1 \lor pc_{par} = 2)$

(I13) $((cc_n = 2 \lor cc_n = 3) \land pc_n = 4) \to (pc_l = 4 \land pc_r = 4)$

(I14) $((cc_n = 1 \lor cc_n = 3) \land pc_n = 4) \to (pc_{par} = 2 \lor pc_{par} = 3 \lor pc_{par} = 4)$

Each of these formulas is easy to understand. For example, conjunct (I9) states that for an internal node or root n of a tree consisting of more than one node, the following is true: If $pc_n = 2$ then the pc variable of one of n's children equals 4, and the pc variable of the other child is in the range from 1 to 3. Each of these formulas is encoded in COQ as a function from natural numbers (nodes) to type *form* in the obvious way. For example, the encoding of (I9) is:

Definition $I9 := \lambda n, l, r : nat.((cc_n =^* 2^* \lor^* cc_n =^* 3^*) \land^* pc_n =^* 2^*) \to^*$
$((pc_l =^* 4^* \land^* (pc_r =^* 1^* \lor^* pc_r =^* 2^* \lor^* pc_r =^* 3^*)) \lor^*$
$(pc_r =^* 4^* \land^* (pc_l =^* 1^* \lor^* pc_l =^* 2^* \lor^* pc_l =^* 3^*)))$.

Using these definitions, we define a function Inv of type $BinTree \to form$ that takes a tree as its argument, and returns a formula that is a large conjunction of each of the fourteen formulas of the invariant included for each internal node in the tree, each of the formulas except those that relate a node to its children for each leaf of the tree, and each of the conjuncts except those that relate a node to its parent for the root. We omit the precise definition here. It uses an auxiliary definition inv_triple, where $(inv\_triple\ n\ n_1\ n_2)$ characterizes that part of the invariant that relates the variables of nodes n, n_1, n_2 to each other. Using this definition, the formula $(Inv\ (children\ t\ n_1\ n_2\ n))$ is equivalent to $(Inv\ t) \land (inv\_triple\ n\ n_1\ n_2)$.

The initial condition and the safety property of the PIF-protocol that we want to prove are defined in COQ as follows.

Definition $Init := \lambda t : BinTree.\forall n : nat.(n \in (pids\ t)) \to$
$(prov\ (((cc_n =^* 0^*) \lor^* (cc_n =^* 2^*)) \to^*$
$((pc_n =^* 1^*) \land^* (v_n =^* V) \land^* (done_n =^* 0^*))) \land^*$
$(((cc_n =^* 1^*) \lor^* (cc_n =^* 3^*)) \to^* (pc_n =^* 0^*)))$.
Definition $I := \lambda t : BinTree.(prov\ (done_{(troot\ t)} =^* 1^*)) \to$
$\forall n : nat.(n \in (pids\ t)) \to (prov\ (v_n =^* V))$.

4.4 Discussion of our Correctness Proof

We next discuss our correctness proof of the PIF protocol. We concentrate on application of the S_Inv rule to establish the invariance of property $(I\ t)$ for arbitrary tree t.

As preparation we derive the values that each variable may take. For example, the values of every *pc* variable are 0, 1, 2, 3, or 4. (Of course, we derive these properties by means of theorem proving.) We need these properties, because model checkers can deal only with variables whose values are in a certain (finite) range.

The following theorems correspond to the first and last premises of the S_Inv rule. They are proved by induction, using SPIN for some propositional reasoning.

Theorem *init_imp_inv* : $\forall t : BinTree.(tree\ t) \rightarrow (Init\ t) \rightarrow (prov\ (Inv\ t))$.

Theorem *inv_imp_I* : $\forall t : BinTree.(tree\ t) \rightarrow (prov\ (Inv\ t)) \rightarrow (I\ t)$.

The next theorem is the most complex, establishing the premises of the S_Inv rule that deal with the actions of the program.

Theorem *invariant_actions* : $\forall t : BinTree.(tree\ t) \rightarrow \forall a : Action.$
$(a \in (actions\ t)) \rightarrow (provable\ (ht\ (Inv\ t)\ a\ (Inv\ t)))$.

The proof is by induction on t. For the basis of induction we have two cases, one for action $a0$ and one for action $a2\_term$. Each of this cases is easily model checked. For the induction step, when tree t is of the form $(children\ t'\ n_1\ n_2\ n)$, we have to show that $(Inv\ (children\ t'\ n_1\ n_2\ n))$ is preserved by every action that can be executed by nodes in t. By theorem proving we deduce that this holds if (1) and (2) below both hold.

(1) $(Inv\ (children\ t'\ n_1\ n_2\ n))$ is preserved by each of the six "new" actions whose execution involves one of the nodes n_1, n_2 (and n).
(2) $(Inv\ (children\ t'\ n_1\ n_2\ n))$ is preserved by "old" actions whose execution involves only nodes in t'.

For both (1) and (2), we decompose the reasoning by some simple Hoare rules, which we have proved using COQ. For ease of exposition, we consider one kind of subcase that arises when proving (1) in which t is of the form shown in Fig. 2. This kind of subcase results from another inductive argument. (We omit the details of this subinduction.) Thus, node n and at least one of

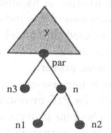

Fig. 2. Binary tree to illustrate our proof strategy.

the nodes $n1, n2$ are involved in the execution of action a. Let t' be the sub-tree of t consisting of tree y, as in Fig. 2, and the nodes $n, n3$. We then use COQ to show that $(Inv\ (children\ t'\ n_1\ n_2\ n))$ is equivalent to the conjunction of $(inv\_triple\ n\ n_1\ n_2)$, $(inv\_triple\ par\ n_3\ n)$, and some formula J, where J does not refer to variables of the nodes n, n_1, n_2. Using the theorem prover we show that J is preserved by action a, because J does not refer to variables that can be modified by a. Then we prove property $\{P\}a\{P\}$, for P defined as the conjunction of $(inv\_triple\ n\ n_1\ n_2)$ and $(inv\_triple\ par\ n_3\ n)$. This is done by showing that for action $a \equiv g \to bd$ the PROMELA program

$$S;\ if :: P \wedge g \to bd;\ assert\{P\} :: \neg(P \wedge g) \to skip\ fi$$

always terminates (cf. Sect. 2.2). As before, S is a program that generates possible values of the variables. Application of Hoare rules then completes this subcase.

In total, (1) and (2) consist of about fifteen problems. Intuitively, we have used CoQ to decompose –without much effort, because theorem provers do this well– each of the problems into subproblems so that each of these subproblems is solved by a model checker. We have identified twenty-six cases which could be model checked. The amount of time taken by SPIN to validate the subproblems ranges from a few seconds to about one hour; the amount of states enumerated needed to do so ranged from about 200 to 200,000,000. We could only apply model checking to problems in which the predicates and actions were "concrete".

We have also verified the PIF-protocol by theorem proving techniques only, and found that the use of a model checker significantly simplifies the size of the proof as well as the effort that we, as human verifiers, have to invest. Even though some of the problems required about an hour to be model checked, constructing a proof requires a lot more effort.

5 Conclusion

Model checking and theorem proving have been combined to show that inductive reasoning about network algorithms can be carried out to mechanically verify network algorithms. As an example we proved correctness of the PIF-protocol when the underlying network constitutes a binary tree. The proof is by structural induction on the binary tree. Induction is handled by the theorem prover, and the base case as well as many subcases in the induction step are handled by the model checker. Although we have used the model checker SPIN and the theorem prover CoQ, our results would not be affected by another choice of model checker or higher-order tactic-style theorem prover.

Model checkers are attractive because they provide complete automation. On their own, they cannot verify the PIF-protocol, because the state space is of arbitrary, although finite size. Theorem provers are attractive because of their generality, and can be used to prove correctness of the PIF-protocol. Yet such proofs require sophisticated insight and guidance by the user. Combining both techniques as we have offers the advantages of each of them, while overcoming their drawbacks. We have identified those subproblems where model checking applies. The theorem prover has been used only to tackle those subproblems that are out of reach of model checkers, or to bring a subproblem into a form that is within the reach of a model checker.

We plan to formulate more general induction principles and to show that our approach scales up by proving correctness of larger algorithms. We also plan to analyze algorithms whose correctness proofs can be structured so that model checking is not only applied to single-step programs, as in the current paper, but to more complicated ones in order to take fuller advantage of model checking techniques. An example of a proof rule that allows such structuring is the rule in [12] for proving strongly-fair termination of programs, because the rule must be applied recursively to smaller programs. One of the premises of the rule requires proving strongly-fair termination of a smaller program, which can be model checked if feasible. Otherwise, the theorem prover must be used to repeatedly apply the rule to decompose the problem into subproblems until a program is obtained that is small enough to be model checked.

References

1. Marc Bezem and Jan Friso Groote. A formal verification of the alternating bit protocol in the calculus of constructions. Technical Report Logic Group Reprint Series No. 88, Utrecht University, 1993.
2. M. C. Browne, E. M. Clarke, and O. Grumberg. Reasoning about networks with many identical processes. In *Proceedings of the 5th Symposium on Principles of Distributed Computing*, 1986.
3. K. M. Chandy and J. Misra. *Parallel Program Design—A Foundation*. Addison-Wesley, 1988.
4. Ching-Tsun Chou. Mechanical verification of distributed algorithms in higher-order logic. *The Computer Journal*, 1995. To appear.
5. E. M. Clarke, E. A. Emerson, and A. P. Sistla. Automatic verification of finite-state concurrent systems using temporal logic specifications. *ACM Transactions on Programming Languages and Systems*, 8(2):244–263, 1986.
6. Cristina Cornes, Judicaël Courant, Jean-Christophe Filliâtre, Gérard Huet, Pascal Manoury, Christine Paulin-Mohring, César Muñoz, Chetan Murthy, Catherine Parent, Amokrane Saïbi, and Benjamin Werner. The Coq Proof Assistant reference manual. Technical report, INRIA, 1995.
7. Amy Felty. Implementing tactics and tacticals in a higher-order logic programming language. *Journal of Automated Reasoning*, 11(1):43–81, August 1993.
8. R. T. Gallager, P. A. Humblet, and P. M. Spira. A distributed algorithm for minimum-weight spanning trees. *ACM Transactions on Programming Languages and Systems*, 5(1):66–77, 1983.
9. S. M. German and A. P. Sistla. Reasoning about systems with many processes. *Journal of the Association for Computing Machinery*, 39(3):675–735, 1992.
10. Patrice Godefroid. Using partial orders to improve automatic verification methods (extended abstract). In *Proceedings of the 2nd International Workshop on Computer-Aided Verification*, pages 176–185. Springer Verlag Lecture Notes in Computer Science 513, 1990.
11. M. J. C. Gordon and T. F. Melham. *Introduction to HOL—A Theorem Proving Environment for Higher Order Logic*. Cambridge University Press, 1993.
12. O. Grumberg, N. Francez, J. A. Makowsky, and W. P. de Roever. A proof rule for fair termination of guarded commands. *Information and Control*, 66(1/2):83–102, July/August 1985.

13. Robert Harper, Furio Honsell, and Gordon Plotkin. A framework for defining logics. *Journal of the ACM*, 40(1):143–184, January 1993.
14. L. Helmink, M. P. A. Sellink, and F. W. Vaandrager. Proof-checking a data link protocol. In *Proceedings of the ESPRIT BRA Workshop on Types for Proofs and Programs*, 1994.
15. Gerard J. Holzmann. *Design and Validation of Computer Protocols*. Prentice-Hall Software Series, 1991.
16. R. P. Kurshan. Analysis of discrete event coordination. In *Stepwise Refinement of Distributed Systems: Models, Formalisms, Correctness (REX Workshop)*, pages 414–453. Springer Verlag Lecture Notes in Computer Science 430, 1989.
17. R. P. Kurshan and Leslie Lamport. Verification of a multiplier: 64 bits and beyond. In *Proceedings of the 5th International Workshop on Computer-Aided Verification*, pages 166–179. Springer Verlag Lecture Notes in Computer Science 697, 1993.
18. R. P. Kurshan and K. L. McMillan. A structural induction theorem for processes. *Information and Computation*, 117:1–11, 1995.
19. Z. Manna and A. Pnueli. *The Temporal Logic of Reactive and Concurrent Systems*. Springer Verlag, 1991.
20. K. L. McMillan. Using unfoldings to avoid the state explosion problem in the verification of asynchronous circuits. In *Proceedings of the 4th International Workshop on Computer-Aided Verification*, pages 164–177. Springer Verlag Lecture Notes in Computer Science 663, 1992.
21. K. L. McMillan. *Symbolic Model Checking*. Kluwer Academic Publishers, 1993.
22. Olaf Müller and Tobias Nipkow. Combining model checking and deduction for I/O-automata. In *Proceedings of the First Workshop on Tools and Algorithms for the Construction and Analysis of Systems*, pages 1–12. Technical Report NS-95-2,BRICS Notes Series, Aarhus, 1995.
23. Lawrence C. Paulson. The foundation of a generic theorem prover. *Journal of Automated Reasoning*, 5(3):363–397, 1989.
24. Doron Peled. Combining partial order reductions with on-the-fly model-checking. In *Proceedings of the 6th International Workshop on Computer-Aided Verification*. Springer Verlag Lecture Notes in Computer Science 801, 1994.
25. S. Rajan, N. Shankar, and M. K. Srivas. An integration of model-checking with automated proof checking. In *Proceedings of the 7th International Workshop on Computer-Aided Verification*. Springer Verlag Lecture Notes in Computer Science, 1995.
26. A. Segall. Distributed network protocols. *IEEE Trans. on Inf. Theory*, IT29(1), 1983.
27. Z. Shtadler and O. Grumberg. Network grammars, communication behavior, and automatic verification. In *Proceedings of the Workshop on Automatic Verification Methods for Finite State Systems*, pages 151–165. Springer Verlag Lecture Notes in Computer Science, 1989.
28. Antti Valmari. A stubborn attack on state explosion (abridged version). In *Proceedings of the 2nd International Workshop on Computer-Aided Verification*, pages 156–165. Springer Verlag Lecture Notes in Computer Science 513, 1990.
29. P. Wolper and V. Lovinfosse. Verifying properties of large sets of processes with network invariants. In *Proceedings of the Workshop on Automatic Verification Methods for Finite State Systems*, pages 68–80. Springer Verlag Lecture Notes in Computer Science, 1989.

TROM - An Object Model for Reactive System Development[*]

R. Achuthan, V. S. Alagar and T. Radhakrishnan

Department of Computer Science
Concordia University
Montreal, PQ, Canada - H3G 1M8
{ramesh,alagar,krishnan}@cs.concordia.ca

Abstract. *This paper introduces and illustrates the use of* TROM *based methodology for formally specifying and reasoning about complex real-time reactive systems. The methodology provides a means to structure system specifications into independent, modular, and reusable components, thereby making the specification to be beneficial for system design and maintenance. The underlying formal semantics of* TROM *facilitates validation and formal verification of system requirements.*

1 Introduction

Recently, the study on reactive systems[13] has attracted a great deal of attention. In [13] there is an exhaustive description of a temporal logical formalism for specifying reactive systems. In [5] a functional model for describing reactive systems was proposed and the expressive power of the formalism was brought out by an example from robotics. Specifications based on logical and functional paradigms are inadequate for describing the system design of reactive systems. This paper introduces a formal object-oriented (OO) approach for the development of reactive systems.

Some of the important factors that contribute to the complexity of a reactive system are the largeness, criticality, concurrency, and the time-dependent behavior of the real-world processes they control. Large reactive systems are generally difficult to comprehend, maintain, and modify. A formal approach that can adequately model the real-world entities of reactive systems in a way that appears natural to system designers could help to alleviate these difficulties [7]. Towards this end, we propose a methodology incorporating the following concepts:

Object-orientation: Among all the OO features, the instantiation relationship for partitioning the universe of objects into classes, inheritance and subtype relationships among classes for incremental development, and aggregation mechanisms for building large systems by reusing modules are most important.

Abstraction: Our object model supports abstract specification of system components by means of hierarchical state machines, abstract data models, assertional

---

[*] This work is supported by grants from NSERC, Canada and FCAR, Quebec.

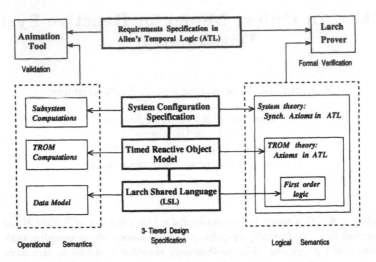

Fig. 1. An overview of our methodology

specification of computations by Hoare logic, conceptual specialization by inheritance, and non-determinism.

Modularity: The model supports modularity by encapsulating timing constraints, data model, and the computational functionality of each component.

Separation of concerns: By separating the architectural details of a system from the internal details of the components, the methodology brings out separation of concerns and hence division of effort. Furthermore, the mathematical abstractions of data models used in specifying a component are separated from the stimulus-response behavior of the component.

The goal of this paper is to describe briefly the TROM formal model and illustrate the expressive power of the model using a case study on mobile telephone system. Due to lack of space we omit the formal verification part and refer the reader to [2, 3] for details.

This paper is organized as follows: In the next section we present an overview of our approach. In Sect. 3, we introduce the reactive-object model and in Sect. 4 we illustrate the model with an abstracted case study of a mobile telephone system. This is followed in Sect. 5 by a discussion on modeling subsystems and systems. Sect. 6 discusses inheritance as an incremental development mechanism. In Sect. 7, we conclude the paper with a brief assessment of our methodology, in the context of modeling complex systems.

2 Three-tiered Approach

Our methodology (see Fig.1) supports a *dual language* approach to reactive system development, with Allen's temporal logic (ATL)[6] as the language for requirements specification and a newly proposed three-tiered framework as the language for design specification. Safety properties and other requirements are specified in ATL, while the system level architectural details and the component level behavioral details are specified in the three-tiered framework.

In the three-tiered design framework, the details of the configuration of objects, the stimulus-response behavior of objects, and the data abstractions encapsulated in objects are presented in separate tiers. The top most tier constitutes *System Configuration Specification* (SCS), which describes the system architecture by succinctly specifying the interaction relationship that can exist between the objects in a system. The middle tier gives the detailed specification of the objects used in the upper tier by means of class definitions in *Timed-Reactive Object model* (TROM) [1]. The lowest tier specifies the data abstractions used in the class definitions of the middle tier by means of the *Larch Shared Language* (LSL), one of the languages of Larch [11]. Due to this approach, the design specification framework not only provides an architectural specification of the system but also forms a means for formally specifying detailed design of the system components.

The three-tiered design language has an *operational* semantics as well as a *logical* semantics. An animation tool based on operational semantics can facilitate the behavioral execution of the specification and hence the validation of system requirements. In contrast, the logical semantics encompassing the first order logical axiomatization of TROM and the axioms of LSL traits, facilitates formal verification of requirements properties such as safety and time critical properties with respect to system designs. A partial mechanization of the verification process is achieved using Larch Prover [11].

3 Modeling Reactive Objects

TROM is a hierarchical finite state machine augmented with ports, attributes, logical assertions on the attributes, and time constraints. A reactive object modeled in TROM is assumed to have a single thread of control. A TROM communicates with its environment by *synchronous message passing* which is assumed to occur at a *port* associated with the TROM. Message passing involves an *event* and underscores an activity which takes an atomic interval of time.

A port is an abstraction of an access point for a bidirectional communication channel between a TROM and its environment. Each port has a unique *port-type* that dictates the set of events and the possible event sequences that are allowed at the port. A TROM can have multiple port-types associated with it and can also have multiple ports of the same type associated with it.

Fig.2 illustrates the elements of a TROM. The filled arrows indicate flow of events. An input-event results due to an incoming interaction defined by the external stimulus, the TROM's state, and the port constrained by the port-condition. As shown, every event causes a computation which updates the state and the attributes. The attributes which can be updated by a computation are determined by the attribute function, shown by the arrow labeled with 'Att. Func'. The role of the port-condition is to constrain the ports at which an interaction, based on the values of the attributes, can happen. The dotted arrow

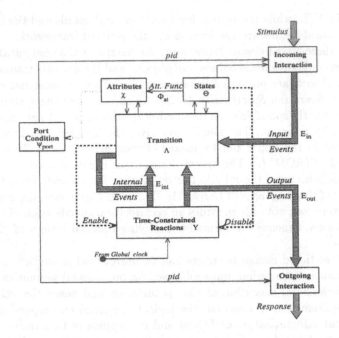

Fig. 2. The elements of a TROM

connecting the box of transition to that of the time-constrained reaction signifies the enabling of a reaction due to a computation. Similarly, a change of state may result in the disabling of an outstanding reaction. Based on the input from a global clock, an outstanding reaction may be fired (in the form of a transition), thereby generating an internal event or an output event. All generated output events will result as a response at the port specified by the port-condition. Below, we give a formal definition of the various components of a TROM and informally explain TROM's features.

Definition 1 *A TROM defining a reactive object is an 8-tuple ($\mathcal{P}$, $\mathcal{E}$, Θ, $\mathcal{X}$, $\mathcal{L}$, Φ, Λ, Υ) such that:*

- Ports *($\mathcal{P}$) is a finite set of port-types with a finite set of ports associated with each port-type.*
- Events *($\mathcal{E}$) is a finite set of events and includes the silent-event tick. The set $\mathcal{E} - \{tick\}$ is partitioned into three disjoint subsets: $\mathcal{E}_{in}$ is the set of input events, $\mathcal{E}_{out}$ is the set of output events, and $\mathcal{E}_{int}$ is the set of internal events. Each $e \in (\mathcal{E}_{in} \cup \mathcal{E}_{out})$, is associated with a unique port-type $P \in \mathcal{P}$. Also, such events may involve argument passing denoted by e(arg : type,...).*
- States *(Θ) is a finite set of states. $\theta_0 \in \Theta$, is the initial state.*
- Attributes *($\mathcal{X}$) is a finite set of typed attributes. The attributes can be of one of the following two types: i) an abstract data type signifying a data model; ii) a port reference type.*

- Traits $(\mathcal{L})$ *is a finite set of LSL traits introducing the abstract data types used in* $\mathcal{X}$.
- Φ *is a function-vector* (Φ_s, Φ_{at}) *where,*
  - Hierarchy-Function (Φ_s) : $\Theta \to 2^\Theta$ *associates with each state* θ *a set of states, possibly empty, called substates. A state* θ *is called atomic, if* $\Phi_s(\theta) = \emptyset$. *By definition, the initial state* θ_0 *is atomic.*
  - Attribute-Function (Φ_{at}) : $\Theta \to 2^{\mathcal{X}}$ *associates with each state* θ *a set of attributes, possibly empty, called active attribute set.*
- Transition-Specifications (Λ) *is a finite set of transition specifications including* λ_{init}. *A transition specification* $\lambda \in \Lambda$ *is represented as* λ : $\langle \theta, \theta' \rangle$; $e(arg_1, \ldots)(\varphi_{port}); \varphi_{en} \implies \varphi_{post}$; *where:*
  - $\langle \theta, \theta' \rangle$, *where* $\theta, \theta' \in \Theta$ *are the source and destination states of the transition, respectively.*
  - $e(arg_1, \ldots)(\varphi_{port})$ *where event* $e \in \mathcal{E}$ *labels the transition;$arg_1, \ldots$ are arguments associated with the event.* φ_{port} *is an assertion on the attributes in* $\mathcal{X}$ *and a reserved variable* pid. pid *signifies the identifier of the port at which an interaction associated with the transition can occur. If* $e \in \mathcal{E}_{int} \cup \{\text{tick}\}$, *then the assertion* φ_{port} *is absent.*
  - $\varphi_{en} \implies \varphi_{post}$, *where* φ_{en} *is the enabling condition and* φ_{post} *is post-conditions of the transition.* φ_{en} *is an assertion on the attributes in* $\mathcal{X}$ *specifying the condition under which the transition is enabled.* φ_{post} *is an assertion on the attributes in* $\mathcal{X}$, *primed attributes in* $\Phi_{at}(\theta')$ *and the variable* pid *specifying the data computation associated with the transition.*

  For each $\theta \in \Theta$, *the silent-transition* $\lambda_{s\theta} \in \Lambda$ *is such that,*
  $$\lambda_{s\theta} : \langle \theta, \theta \rangle; \text{tick}; true \implies \forall x \in \Phi_s(\theta) : x = x';$$
- Time-Constraints (Υ) *is a finite set of time-constraints. A time constraint* $v_i \in \Upsilon$ *is a tuple* $(\lambda_i, e'_i, [l, u], \Theta_i)$ *where,*
  - $\lambda_i \neq \lambda_s$ *is a transition specification.*
  - $e'_i \in (\mathcal{E}_{out} \cup \mathcal{E}_{int})$ *is the constrained event.*
  - $[l, u]$ *defines the minimum and maximum response times.*
  - $\Theta_i \subseteq \Theta$ *is the set of states wherein the time constraint* v_i *will not be respected.*

$\square$

In a TROM, the vocabulary for the assertions in the transition-specifications are provided by the LSL traits included in $\mathcal{L}$. The assertion φ_{port} essentially defines the values (i.e., port identifiers) that can be bound to pid. In particular, if φ_{port} is true then pid could be bound to any port belonging to the port-type of the event associated with the transition. The assertion φ_{en} specifies the *necessary* condition for the transition to take place. The post-condition φ_{post} represents a relation between the values of attributes before and after the transition as in Hoare logic. An unprimed variable in φ_{post} refers to the value before the transition and a primed variable refers to the value after the transition. Arguments are used by output event to send data values, while they are used by input event to receive data values.

The interpretation of a time constraint $v_i = (\lambda_i, e_i', [l, u], \Theta_i) \in \Upsilon$ is as follows: whenever the event e associated with λ_i is signaled at time t, then the event e_i' should be fired at time t', such that t' is within the minimal and maximal delay of l and u units of time from t, respectively; provided that the TROM does not enter any of the states in Θ_i in between t and t'. The constrained event e' signifies the *response* corresponding to the *stimulus* represented by the event labeling λ_i. Once triggered, a time constraint becomes and remains active until satisfied or disabled. A time constraint is satisfied by the firing of the constrained event within the imposed time bounds; it is disabled if the TROM enters into one of the disabling states in Θ_i before the constraint is satisfied. The interval $[l, u]$ specifies lower and upper bounds on the delay between the triggering and satisfaction (or disabling) of the time constraint.

At any instant, a TROM will exhibit a *signal* which signifies one of the following: a message passing, an internal activity, the activity of remaining idle. A signal exhibited by a TROM $\mathcal{A}$, is represented by a tuple $\langle e, p_i, t \rangle$ and underscores the occurrence of an event e, at a specific instant in time t, at the port p_i of $\mathcal{A}$. The *status* of a TROM $\mathcal{A}$ at any instant t is a triple $(\theta, \mathbf{a}, \mathcal{R})$, where θ is the state at t, $\mathbf{a}$ is a vector signifying values of attributes of $\mathcal{A}$ at t, and $\mathcal{R}$ is the set of outstanding reactions of $\mathcal{A}$ at t due to previously triggered time-constraints. A *computation* of a TROM $\mathcal{A}$, is an alternating sequence of status and signals, starting from an initial-status.

By associating attributes to states in a TROM, an attribute has to have a defined value only in those states where it is active. This resolves the frame problem. The hierarchical state descriptions provide the flexibility in selecting the level of detail that can be specified. In addition, hierarchical states help to control the complexity of specification by structuring the behavior into sets of simpler units which could be comprehended individually. The port-condition together with the temporal ordering of events asserted by the state machine provides a means for specifying the patterns of interaction between objects in the system. The model allows the specification of several typical real-time features such as minimal and maximal delays, exact occurrences, and periodicity of event occurrences, in combination with temporal relations such as stimulus-response, response-response, stimulus-stimulus and response-stimulus. The model also provides encapsulation of timing constraints by precluding an input event from being a constrained event.

4 A Case Study

A mobile telecommunication system [9, 8] consists of a collection of mobiles, cells and mobile telecommunication switching offices(MTSO). The mobiles are serviced by cells which transmit signals to, and receive signals from, the mobiles. A cell is associated with exactly one MTSO and is controlled by the MTSO. The communication between a cell and a mobile is through radio channels while that between a cell and an MTSO is through the land-line network. A cell can interact with one or more mobiles and an MTSO can control one or more cells. All interaction between mobiles and MTSO are only through cells. Similarly, all interactions between a cell and the rest of the communication network is only through its associated MTSO.

A call to a mobile (known as a mobile-completed call) typically involves a sequence of activities: paging (from cells to mobiles), cell site selection (by mobiles), page reply (mobile to cell), voice channel frequency allocation (cell to mobile), alerting (cell to mobile), and talking. The MTSO controlling a cell prompts that cell to do paging and allocates the voice channel frequency for the call.

When a mobile wishes to make a call (known as a mobile-originated call) the sequence of activities that occurs are: dialing (in mobile), cell site selection (in mobile), call origination (mobile to cell), voice channel frequency allocation (cell to mobile), digit outpulsing (in MTSO) for call completion, and talking. In such situations also the MTSO allocates the voice channel frequency for the call.

In order to build the formal specification of the system, we first model the components mobile, cell, and MTSO using TROM. Later (in Sect. 6.1), we use inheritance to enhance the behavior of each of the components in the system, so as to model the activity of handing-over of a mobile from one cell to another cell.

Mobile. Fig. 3 shows the TROM model of a mobile. A mobile has two types of ports $@C$ and $@U$, to interact with cell and user, respectively. Each mobile has a unique identifier mid, which is assigned at the time of instantiation.. A mobile remains in the $idle$ state scanning for a paging signal, until it is paged by a cell or dialed by a user. In the state $selectCell$ a mobile selects nearest cell for communication using some strategy that is intentionally left unspecified at this stage. A collision occurs when more than one mobile attempts to access a cell at the same time. If there is a collision, the mobile waits for a certain period of time (here 4 units of time) and tries to access the cell again. Once the mobile accesses the cell, it informs the cell by the event $PageRpy$ in case of mobile-completed call and by the event $Call$ in case of a mobile-originated call. As soon as the mobile receives the input event $TuneTo$, it will set its communication frequency to the received value and enter into a talking state or ringing state depending upon the type of the call. The port-condition of the transition R_7 asserts that the event $TuneTo$ can be received only at the port from which the mobile has accessed the cell. Thus, it is ensured that the mobile waits until the event $TuneTo$ from the cell to which the mobile is dynamically associated for that particular call is received. While in the state $talking$ an $OnHook$ event puts the mobile into the state $idle$. The time-constraints triggered by the transition R_3 asserts that after the mobile selects a cell, it should access the cell within 5 units of time unless there is a collision which puts the mobile in state $s1$.

Cell. The TROM describing a cell is shown in Fig. 4. A cell's interaction with a mobile happens at a port of type $@M$ and a cell's interaction with an MTSO happens at a port of $@S$, respectively. A cell will initially be in the $ready$ state.

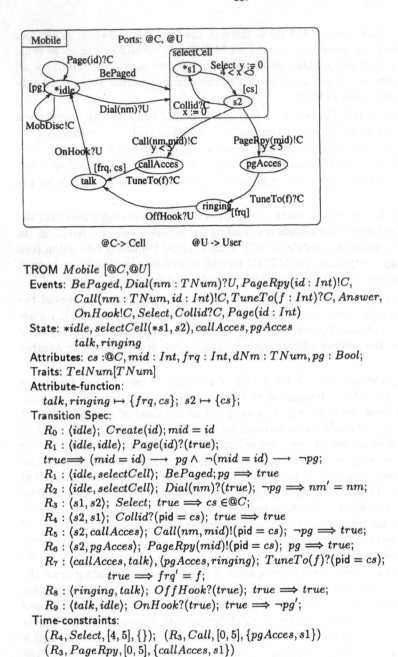

@C-> Cell   @U -> User

TROM *Mobile* [@C,@U]
  Events: *BePaged, Dial(nm : TNum)?U, PageRpy(id : Int)!C,*
           Call(nm : TNum, id : Int)!C, TuneTo(f : Int)?C, Answer,
           OnHook!C, Select, Collid?C, Page(id : Int)
  State: **idle, selectCell(*s1, s2), callAcces, pgAcces*
        talk, ringing
  Attributes: *cs :@C, mid : Int, frq : Int, dNm : TNum, pg : Bool*;
  Traits: *TelNum*[*TNum*]
  Attribute-function:
    talk, ringing $\mapsto$ {*frq, cs*}; *s2* $\mapsto$ {*cs*};
  Transition Spec:
    R_0 : $\langle idle\rangle$; *Create(id)*; *mid = id*
    R_1 : $\langle idle, idle\rangle$; *Page(id)?(true)*;
    true $\Longrightarrow$ (*mid = id*) $\longrightarrow$ *pg* $\wedge$ $\neg$(*mid = id*) $\longrightarrow$ $\neg pg$;
    R_1 : $\langle idle, selectCell\rangle$; *BePaged*; *pg* $\Longrightarrow$ *true*
    R_2 : $\langle idle, selectCell\rangle$; *Dial(nm)?(true)*; $\neg pg$ $\Longrightarrow$ *nm' = nm*;
    R_3 : $\langle s1, s2\rangle$; *Select*; *true* $\Longrightarrow$ *cs* $\in$@C;
    R_4 : $\langle s2, s1\rangle$; *Collid?(pid = cs)*; *true* $\Longrightarrow$ *true*
    R_5 : $\langle s2, callAcces\rangle$; *Call(nm, mid)!(pid = cs)*; $\neg pg$ $\Longrightarrow$ *true*;
    R_6 : $\langle s2, pgAcces\rangle$; *PageRpy(mid)!(pid = cs)*; *pg* $\Longrightarrow$ *true*;
    R_7 : $\langle callAcces, talk\rangle, \langle pgAcces, ringing\rangle$; *TuneTo(f)?(pid = cs)*;
           true $\Longrightarrow$ *frq' = f*;
    R_8 : $\langle ringing, talk\rangle$; *OffHook?(true)*; *true* $\Longrightarrow$ *true*;
    R_9 : $\langle talk, idle\rangle$; *OnHook?(true)*; *true* $\Longrightarrow$ $\neg pg'$;
  Time-constraints:
    (R_4, *Select*, [4, 5], {});   (R_3, *Call*, [0, 5], {*pgAcces, s1*})
    (R_3, *PageRpy*, [0, 5], {*callAcces, s1*})
end

Fig. 3. Class specification of a mobile

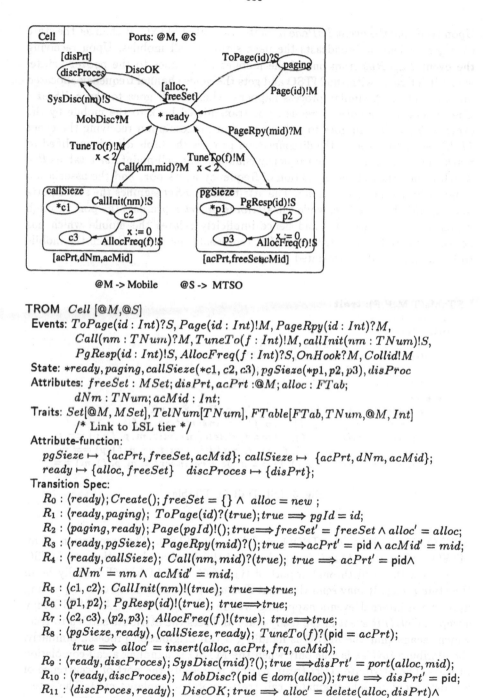

@M -> Mobile   @S -> MTSO

TROM *Cell* [@*M*,@*S*]

  Events: $ToPage(id : Int)?S, Page(id : Int)!M, PageRpy(id : Int)?M,$
        $Call(nm : TNum)?M, TuneTo(f : Int)!M, callInit(nm : TNum)!S,$
        $PgResp(id : Int)!S, AllocFreq(f : Int)?S, OnHook?M, Collid!M$

  State: $*ready, paging, callSieze(*c1, c2, c3), pgSieze(*p1, p2, p3), disProc$

  Attributes: $freeSet : MSet; disPrt, acPrt :@M; alloc : FTab;$
        $dNm : TNum; acMid : Int;$

  Traits: $Set[@M, MSet], TelNum[TNum], FTable[FTab, TNum, @M, Int]$
        /* Link to LSL tier */

  Attribute-function:
    $pgSieze \mapsto \{acPrt, freeSet, acMid\}; callSieze \mapsto \{acPrt, dNm, acMid\};$
    $ready \mapsto \{alloc, freeSet\} \quad discProces \mapsto \{disPrt\};$

  Transition Spec:
    $R_0 : \langle ready\rangle; Create(); freeSet = \{\} \wedge alloc = new ;$
    $R_1 : \langle ready, paging\rangle; ToPage(id)?(true); true \Longrightarrow pgId = id;$
    $R_2 : \langle paging, ready\rangle; Page(pgId)!(); true \Longrightarrow freeSet' = freeSet \wedge alloc' = alloc;$
    $R_3 : \langle ready, pgSieze\rangle; PageRpy(mid)?(); true \Longrightarrow acPrt' = pid \wedge acMid' = mid;$
    $R_4 : \langle ready, callSieze\rangle; Call(nm, mid)?(true); true \Longrightarrow acPrt' = pid \wedge$
        $dNm' = nm \wedge acMid' = mid;$
    $R_5 : \langle c1, c2\rangle; CallInit(nm)!(true); true \Longrightarrow true;$
    $R_6 : \langle p1, p2\rangle; PgResp(id)!(true); true \Longrightarrow true;$
    $R_7 : \langle c2, c3\rangle, \langle p2, p3\rangle; AllocFreq(f)!(true); true \Longrightarrow true;$
    $R_8 : \langle pgSieze, ready\rangle, \langle callSieze, ready\rangle; TuneTo(f)?(pid = acPrt);$
        $true \Longrightarrow alloc' = insert(alloc, acPrt, frq, acMid);$
    $R_9 : \langle ready, discProces\rangle; SysDisc(mid)?(); true \Longrightarrow disPrt' = port(alloc, mid);$
    $R_{10} : \langle ready, discProces\rangle; MobDisc?(pid \in dom(alloc)); true \Longrightarrow disPrt' = pid;$
    $R_{11} : \langle discProces, ready\rangle; DiscOK; true \Longrightarrow alloc' = delete(alloc, disPrt) \wedge$
        $freeSet' = freeSet \cup \{pid\};$

  Time-constraints: $(R_7, TuneTo, [0, 2], \{\});$
end

Fig. 4. Class specification of a cell

Upon receiving the event *ToPage* from its associated MTSO, it changes the state to *paging* where it broadcasts the page signal to all mobiles. Upon receiving the event *PageRpy* from one of the mobiles a cell goes to the *pgSieze* state, where it interacts with the MTSO and gets the voice channel frequency allocated for the mobile. A similar process happens when a cell goes to the *callSieze*. The allocated value of the frequency is transmitted back to the mobile by the event *ToTune*. A cell goes to a disconnection process upon receiving the event *MobDisc* or *SysDis*. In the disconnection process the table *alloc* is modified to mark the deallocation of the frequency channel. The cell maintains a table *alloc* which keeps track of the allocation of frequency at its port and the association of ports to the mobile-identifier. The attribute *freeSet* signifies the set of ports of type @M that are free, while the attribute *acPrt* represents the port through which the cell is accessed and hence implicitly relates the mobile which has accessed the cell. The attribute *disPrt* represents the port at which the mobile to be disconnected is associated.

FTable(T,M,P,F): **trait**
  includes Integer
  introduces
    $new: \rightarrow T$; *insert*: T,M,P,F $\rightarrow$ T;
    delete: T,F $\rightarrow$ T; *delete*: T,M $\rightarrow$ T;
    delete: T,P $\rightarrow$ T; *getId*: T,P $\rightarrow$ M;
    getPrt: T,F $\rightarrow$ P; *getFrq*: T,M $\rightarrow$ F;
  asserts
    S **generated by** {}, *insert*; $\forall$ m: M, p: P, f: F, t : T;
      $insert(insert(t, m, p, f), m, p, f) == insert(t, m, p, f)$;
      $delete(insert(t, m, p, f), m) == t$; $delete(insert(t, m, p, f), p) == t$;
      $delete(insert(t, m, p, f), f) == t$; $getId(insert(t, m, p, f), p) == m$;
      $getPrt(insert(t, m, p, f), f) == p$; $getFrq(insert(t, m, p, f), m) == f$;

Fig. 5. LSL Trait for FTable

MTSO. Fig.6 shows the TROM modeling an MTSO. The interaction of an MTSO with another MTSO is not shown at this level of abstraction. An MTSO interacts with a cell through a port of type @C. An MTSO will initially be in the state *ready*. It may send the event *ToPage* to its associated cells depending upon some internal events happening within the state *ready*. An MTSO may accept a *CallInit* event in the ready state and sets the attribute *calOrg* to true, which means that the MTSO is handling a call origination process.. Similarly, the attribute *calDes* is true only when the MTSO is handling a call-completion process. The attribute *clPrt* (resp. *pgPrt*) represents the port of occurrence of a most recent mobile-originated call (resp. mobile-completed call). The internal event *Check* is triggered whenever the attributes *calOrg* or *calDes* is true, thereby changing the state to *validate*. In the state *validate*, an MTSO validates the telephone number of the destination. If it is valid, the MTSO switches to the state *allocFreq* if the type of call is mobile-originated; otherwise, it switches to the state *ready* and waits for the event *PgResp* from one of its associated cells. In the state *allocFreq*, the MTSO allocates an available voice channel frequency for the cell-mobile communication. The algorithm for allocating the frequency is not discussed at this level of abstraction. From the state *validate* if the destination number is invalid then the MTSO goes to the state *erHandle*. Similarly after sending the event *ToPage* if the event *PgResp* does not occur within a certain time then the internal event *NoPageResp* occurs and the MTSO goes to error handling.

5 Modeling Subsystems and Systems

A *system configuration specification* (SCS) is defined to specify a system or a subsystem by composing objects modeled in TROM or by composing smaller subsystems. The SCS defining a mobile telecommunication system obtained by composing the instantiated objects of TROMs is shown in Fig. 7. The Include clause is optional and is useful for importing system/subsystem definitions from other SCS. A reactive object is defined in the Instantiate clause of an SCS by parameterizing a TROM with the cardinality of ports and the value of the active attributes (if any) in the initial state of the TROM. For instance, $B_1 :: Cell[@M : 2, @S : 1]$ defines the object B_1 to be the TROM *Cell*, having the ports m_1 and m_2 of type M and the port s_1 of type S. The port m_1 of B_1 is syntactically represented as $B_1.@m_1$.

The Configure clause defines a system/subsystem obtained by composing objects specified in the Instantiate clause and subsystem specifications imported through the Include clause. The composition operator $\leftrightarrow$ is used in the Configure clause to link the ports of various interacting objects/subsystems. For instance, a link $A_i.@c_j \leftrightarrow B_k.@p_l$ in the Configure clause signifies that the port c_j of the object A_i is linked with the port p_l of the object B_k. In a composition, only those ports that are *compatible* for linking can be linked. The notion of compatibility of ports for linking are discussed in [2]. Informally, two ports are compatible if an event sent at one port is acceptable as an input at the other port at the same time, focusing synchronous message passing. Relationships such as *one-one, one-many*, and *many-many* can be specified in the Configure clause. For instance, a many-many relationship between objects of the TROMs Cell and Mobile and one-many relationship between the objects of TROMs MTSO and Cell, exist. Thus, there can be multiple cells associated with an MTSO. Also, a mobile can select any one of the Cells depending upon its cell site selection strategy.

The Constraints clause specifies the constraints among the attribute initialization of a collection of interacting objects. For instance, one of the constraints in the system can be that each mobile has a unique identifier. Another possible constraint can be that the sets of frequencies allocated for cells are disjoint.

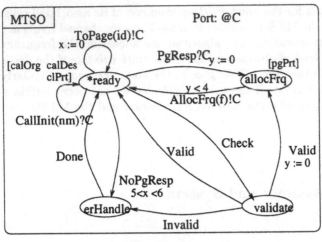

@C --> Cell

TROM *MTSO* [@C]
Events: $ToPage(id : Int)!C, PgResp(id : Int)?C, AllocFrq(f : Int)!C,$
   $CallInit(nm : TNum)?C, Valid, Invalid, Check, NoPgResp$
State: $*ready, allocFrq, validate, erHandle$
Attributes: $calOrg, calDes : Bool; pgPrt, clPrt : @C;$
Traits: $TelNum[TNum]$ /* Link to LSL tier */
Attribute-function:
   $ready \mapsto \{calOrg, calDes, clPrt\}$
   $allocFreq \mapsto \{pgPrt\}; validate, erHandle \mapsto \{\};$
Transition Spec:
   $R_0 : \langle ready \rangle; Create(); calOrg = false \wedge calDes = false \wedge clPrt = c1$;
   $R_1 : \langle ready, ready \rangle; ToPage(id)!(true); true \Longrightarrow true$
   $R_2 : \langle ready, ready \rangle; CallInit(nm)?(true); true \Longrightarrow clPrt' = pid \wedge$
      $clNm' = nm \wedge calOrg = true$
   $R_3 : \langle ready, allocFrq \rangle; PgResp(mid)?(true); true \Longrightarrow pgPrt' = pid;$
   $R_4 : \langle ready, validate \rangle; Check(nm); calOrg \vee calDes \Longrightarrow true;$
   $R_5 : \langle validate, ready \rangle; Valid(nm); calDes \Longrightarrow calDes' = true \wedge$
      $calOrg' = false;$
   $R_6 : \langle ready, erHandleRg; NoPgResp(nm); calDes \Longrightarrow true;$
   $R_7 : \langle erHandle, ready \rangle; Done; true \Longrightarrow calDes' = false \wedge calOrg' = false;$
   $R_8 : \langle allocFrq, ready \rangle; AllocFrq(f)!C; true \Longrightarrow calDes' = false \wedge$
      $calOrg' = false;;$
   $R_9 : \langle validate, allocFrq \rangle; Valid(nm); calOrg \Longrightarrow true;$
Time-constraints:
   $(R_3, AllocFrq, [0, 4], \{\}); (R_9, AllocFrq, [0, 4], \{\})$
   $(R_1, NoPgResp, [5, 6], \{allocFrq\})$
end

Fig. 6. Class specification of an MTSO

```
SCS MobileTelecomSystem
  Include:
  Instantiate:
      A₁,...,Aₙ :: Mobile[@C : l,@U : 1].Create(midᵢ)
      B₁,...,Bₗ :: Cell[@M : n,@S : 1].Create(FSetᵢ)
      C₁ :: MTSO[@C : l].Create()
  Configure:
      ∀i ∈ 1...n,  j ∈ 1...l
      Aᵢⱼ.@cⱼ ↔ Bⱼ.@mᵢ
      Bⱼ.@s₁ ↔ C₁.@cⱼ
  Constraints:
      ∀i,j • midᵢ = midⱼ ⟶ Aᵢ = Aⱼ
      ∀i,j • isEmpty(FSetᵢ ∩ FSetⱼ);
end
```

Fig. 7. System Configuration Specification - Mobile telecommunication system

6 Inheritance for Incremental Development

In this section, we informally present the concept of inheritance and subtyping in our framework; a comprehensive formal treatment is presented in [2]. Class definitions may inherit merely as a convenience of construction; but it leads to more readable and maintainable system if every subclass relationship is associated with a behavioral relationship. Class relationships which embody subtyping through inheritance are of special interest during system designs since they facilitate system enhancements and adaptability. Towards this end, we classify the concept of subtype-inheritance in our framework into the following three distinct, orthogonal concepts: *Behavioral inheritance* in which the post-condition and the enabling-condition of transition specifications are strengthened. They deal with a constrained range of prior states, or produce more strongly determined results. It may also strengthen a time-constraint by increasing the minimum delay or decreasing the maximum delay for firing the constrained event. *Extensional inheritance* that provides more detail for state-space, differentiating individual states into substates and possibly provides more events enriching the signature and behavior of ports. Intuitively, this form of inheritance corresponds to model refinement where abstract concepts are described at a greater detail. *Polymorphic inheritance* where a superclass is used to characterize the common aspects of several subclasses. New ports and new events signifying interactions with new components in the environment may be added as a part of the inheritance. Intuitively, this form of inheritance corresponds to adding more features to an existing model.

6.1 Case Study: Enhancing the system

We illustrate the use of the notion of extensional inheritance and polymorphic inheritance for enhancing the system design presented in Sect. 5.

Enhancement. As a mobile wanders throughout a designated region, the cell responsible for transmitting and receiving signals to and from the mobile may need to change. The process of changing cells when a mobile is already tuned to a cell is known as *handoff*. The current cell releases the associated frequency, while the new cell allocates a new frequency and instructs the mobile to tune to this new frequency. The state diagram of the enhanced components are shown in Fig.8. It can be shown by using the results in [2] that the TROMs *NewMobile*, *NewCell*, and *NewMTSO* preserve the behavior of their respective superclasses. Thus, all the properties verified to remain true in the original system will be true for the enhanced system.

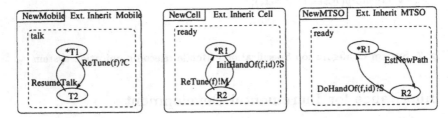

Fig. 8. Enhanced state diagrams of Mobile, Cell and MTSO

7 Conclusion

A complete and rigorous treatment of TROM theory, different forms of subtypes and their relationship to inheritance with formal proofs are given in [2]. The goal of this paper is to show that our approach is sufficiently powerful to structure system specifications into modular, independent, and reusable components, at various levels of abstraction. The case study taken in our paper is a simple instance of a complex real-time reactive system – mobile telephone system. We have illustrated how inheritance can provide enhancements to system design. The proposed methodology has been applied on several case studies such as robotic assembly system[4], a distributed arbiter and a user-interface system. A comparison of this approach with other related methods such as Object-Z[8], Disco[12], and ObjChart[10] indicates that our methodology is more appropriate for the development and maintenance of large and complex reactive systems due to the following reasons:

Comprehensibility. The modularity achieved due to the three-tiered approach helps to understand each specification unit independently. Moreover, the state machine formalism, its hierarchical structure and the graphical notation make the system specification easy to understand.

Testability. Due to the operational semantics of the model, animation tools are easy to build.

Adaptability. Inheritance supports incremental specification, while aggregation in SCS supports reconfiguration of system models.

Reusability. Our three-tiered framework supports: 1) reuse of LSL traits; 2) reuse of class definitions by inheritance or by inclusion in one or more subsystem specifications; 3) reuse of subsystem specifications in building system models. **Scalability.** The instantiation, the aggregation, and the inheritance relationships, together with the separation of concerns achieved through the three-tiered approach help to modularize a large specification, into manageable units. In addition, the Includes clause in SCS helps to build specifications of large systems by importing specifications at subsystem level. Although we have conducted formal verification of time-dependent properties on several case studies, the scalability of the verification methods that we have devised, is not completely assessed. **Expressiveness.** The use of attributes in TROM helps to mitigate the state explosion problem. The type of an attribute in TROM could be complex such as a Btree, or an assembly part, and these can be precisely specified using LSL traits.

References

1. R. Achuthan, V.S. Alagar, and T. Radhakrishnan. A formal methodology for object-oriented development of real-time reactive systems. In *Workshop on Object-Oriented Real-Time Systems (OOPSLA '94), Portland, OR,* October 1994.
2. R. Achuthan, V.S. Alagar, and T. Radhakrishnan. A formal model for object-oriented development of real-time reactive systems. Technical report, Concorida University, Montreal, Canada, March 1995.
3. R. Achuthan, V.S. Alagar, and T. Radhakrishnan. A formal model for specification and verification of real-time reactive systems. In *Workshop on Models snd Proofs for Concurrent and Real-Time Systems, Bordeaux, France.* June 1995.
4. R. Achuthan, V.S. Alagar, and T. Radhakrishnan. An object-oriented modeling of real-time robotic assembly system. In *IEEE International Conference on Engineering Complex Computer Systems, Florida.* Nov. 1995.
5. V.S. Alagar and G. Ramanathan. Functional specification and proof of correctness for time dependent behavior of reactive systems. *Formal Aspects of Computing,* (3):253–283, 1991.
6. J. F. Allen. Towards a general theory of action and time. *Artificial Inteligence (23),* 1984.
7. T. E. Bihari and P. Gopinath. Object-oriented real-time systems: Concepts and examples. *IEEE Computer,* 25(12):25–32, December 1992.
8. R. Duke, G. Rose, and A. Lee. Object-oriented protocol specification. In *Protocol Testing and Verification,* pages 323–339. 1990.
9. Z. Fluhr and P. Porter. Control architecture. *Bell Sys. Tech. Journal,* 1(58):43–69, 1979.
10. D. Gangopadhyay and S. Mitra. Objchart: Tangible specification of reactive object behavior. In *European Conference on Object Oriented Programming - 93,* 1993.
11. J.V. Guttag and J.J. Horning. *Larch: Languages and Tools for Formal Specifications.* Springer-Verlag, 1993.
12. H. Jarvinen, R. Kurki-Suonio, M. Sakkinen, and K. Systa. Object-oriented specification of reactive systems. In *Proc. 12th IEEE Conference Software Engineering,* 1990.
13. Z. Manna and A. Pnueli. *The temporal logic of reactive and concurrent systems: Specification.* Springer-Verlag, 1992.

Duration Calculus Specification of Scheduling for Tasks with Shared Resources

Philip Chan and Dang Van Hung

United Nations University
International Institute for Software Technology, Macau
pc,dvh@iist.unu.edu

Abstract. This paper presents a formalization in the duration calculus (DC) of scheduling policies for tasks with shared resources. Two frameworks are presented for specifying classes of schedulers. With these specifications, some properties of these schedulers were proved using the formal deduction of DC. This paper aims to encourage other researchers to formally treat real-time aspects of operating systems which in the past were conventionally a piece of ad hoc territory in computer science.

1 Introduction

Operating systems have been a subject of design and implementation for many years. Despite their widespread use in almost every computing environment, formal techniques have been applied only on relatively simple aspects of their dynamic behavior. This is mainly due to the fact that operating systems are complex and it is not a trivial task to formally describe properties of real-time operating systems and their components unless these are simplified.

Formally specifying and reasoning about properties of real-time systems requires the use of a notation with formal deduction capabilities. In this paper, we make use of the duration calculus (DC) because of its many desirable features that provide explicit support for modelling real-time behavior. DC has been applied in the context of operating systems, such as in [6, 14] and more recently, the work on proving formally the correctness of the *Deadline Driven Scheduler* [10]. This paper aims to be another step in this direction by focusing on more elaborate real-time scheduling systems, specifically scheduling of tasks with shared resources.

We assume that resources are allocated on a mutually exclusive fashion, i.e. a resource can be held by at most one task at a time, and resource allocation is non-preemptive. Therefore, aside from satisfying the deadline requirements of tasks, scheduling policies have to deal with the potential for deadlocks and priority inversion.

Let T_i, T_j denote arbitrary tasks and let r_k denote any resource. A priority inversion occurs when a lower-priority task T_i is blocking the execution of a higher-priority task T_j. This occurs when T_i is holding a resource r_k that T_j needs and is preempted by the arrival of T_j. If T_j requests for r_k, T_j will be blocked since r_k is not available and cannot be preempted from T_i. Existing policies either ensure that the priority inversion is bounded or prevents it from happening at all [2, 3] by restricting the schedules.

Our intention of using DC is threefold: (a) to show the expressive ability of DC in formally specifying more complex schedulers; (b) to present a framework for uniformly specifying schedulers within the same class; and (c) to use the specifications from these frameworks to reason about properties of these schedulers.

A comprehensive review of techniques for controlling access to shared resources is presented in [1]. In this paper, we are specifically interested in two kinds of protocols: (a) those that allow priority inversions to occur; and (b) those that schedule the use of resources in such a way so that no priority inversions occur.

The rest of the paper is organized as follows: Section 2 presents a review of the duration calculus. Section 3 presents the formalization of the schedulers grouped under two classes. Proofs of certain properties of these schedulers are presented in section 4. Finally, we present some conclusions and discussion in section 5.

2 Duration Calculus

The duration calculus (DC) [11], an extension of interval temporal logic, is a notation to specify and reason about properties of real-time systems and is a logic to verify theorems about specifications of such systems. Since its introduction in 1991, the original duration calculus has been extended into several calculi to increase its versatility in modelling various kinds of systems.

In the extended duration calculus (EDC) [15], piecewise continuous/ differentiable functions were introduced, providing the capability to capture properties of continuous states. This calculus is especially useful for modelling and reasoning about hybrid systems. Another extension of DC is the mean-value duration calculus (MVDC) [12]. In MVDC, integrals of Boolean functions are replaced by their mean values, and as a result, δ-functions are used to represent instantaneous actions such as events. This calculus is suitable to model systems with state and events. DC has also been extended with probabilities, namely: the probabilistic duration calculus for discrete time [7] and for continuous time [5]. With these two probabilistic calculi, it is possible to reason about and calculate the dependability of a system with respect to its components. More recently, infinite intervals were introduced into the duration calculus (DC^i) [13]. By introducing limits, DC^i can deal with unbounded liveness and fairness and can also measure live states by duration limits.

A state in DC is a Boolean function over time. When a state P has a value of 1 at time t, P is said to be present, otherwise, it is absent. States can be combined by the usual Boolean connectives $\neg, \wedge, \vee, \cdots$ to form composite states.

One of the most significant features of DC is its ability to express *integrals* of time durations of states. Given an arbitrary state P and an arbitrary observation interval $[b, e]$ ($b, e \in \mathbf{R}$ and $e \geq b$), the duration of P is defined as:

$$\int P \stackrel{\text{def}}{=} \int_b^e P(t)dt$$

Let ℓ denote the length of the observation interval, that is,

$$\ell[b,e] \stackrel{\text{def}}{=} e - b$$

then the duration of the trivial state 1 is defined as follows:

$$\int 1 \stackrel{\frown}{=} \ell$$

In DC, $\int P$ and ℓ are terms and can be combined into formulae using arithmetic predicates and the interval modality *chop* ($\frown$) operator. The formula $B \frown C$ is satisfied by a non-point interval if it can be chopped into two subintervals such that the first subinterval satisfies B and the second satisfies C.

$$(B \frown C)[b,e] \stackrel{\text{def}}{=} \exists m \bullet (b \le m \le e)B[b,m] \wedge C[m,e]$$

Using the chop ($\frown$) operator, the conventional modalities can then be defined as follows:

$\diamond A \stackrel{\frown}{=} true \frown A \frown true$ reads "for some subinterval A holds"

$\square A \stackrel{\frown}{=} \neg\diamond\neg A$ reads "for all subintervals A holds"

The formula $\lceil P \rceil$ is true if state P holds everywhere (almost) in this non-point interval and $\lceil \; \rceil$ is true for point intervals only.

$\lceil P \rceil \stackrel{\frown}{=} (\int P = \ell) \wedge (\ell > 0)$

$\lceil \; \rceil \stackrel{\frown}{=} \ell = 0$

$\lceil P \rceil^* \stackrel{\frown}{=} \lceil \; \rceil \vee \lceil P \rceil$

And it follows that:

$\lceil 1 \rceil \Leftrightarrow (\ell > 0)$

$\lceil 0 \rceil \Leftrightarrow false$

We also use $\diamond A$ to mean that formula A holds for some initial subintervals of an interval.

$\diamond A \stackrel{\frown}{=} A \frown true$

$\square A \stackrel{\frown}{=} \neg\diamond\neg A$

Proof System of DC:

By being an extension of *Interval Temporal Logic* (ITL), DC inherited the powerful proof system in ITL. Some of the theorems adopted by DC from ITL are as follows:

(2.1) $A \Rightarrow B \vdash (A \frown C \Rightarrow B \frown C) \wedge (C \frown A \Rightarrow C \frown B)$(Monotonicity)

(2.2) $(A \frown B) \frown C \Leftrightarrow A \frown (B \frown C)$ (Associativity)

(2.3) $(A \frown \lceil \; \rceil) \Leftrightarrow (\lceil \; \rceil \frown A) \Leftrightarrow A$ (Unit)

(2.4) $(A \frown false) \Leftrightarrow (false \frown A) \Leftrightarrow false$ (Zero)

(2.5) $(A \vee B) \frown C \Leftrightarrow (A \frown C) \vee (B \frown C)$ ($\vee$-

       $C \frown (A \vee B) \Leftrightarrow (C \frown A) \vee (C \frown B)$ distributivity)

(2.6) $\square A \wedge (B \frown C) \Rightarrow (\square A \wedge B) \frown (\square A \wedge C)$ ($\square$-

                                              distributivity)

(2.7) $\square A \wedge (B \frown C) \Rightarrow (\square A \wedge B) \frown C$ ($\square$-distributivity)

Note that although $\frown$ is associative (2.2), has the point interval ($\lceil \; \rceil$) as unit (2.3), it only distributes through disjunction ($\vee$) (2.5), but not through conjunction ($\wedge$). The following, however, is a theorem:

(2.8) $(A \wedge B) \frown C \Rightarrow (A \frown C) \wedge (B \frown C)$

        $C \frown (A \wedge B) \Rightarrow (C \frown A) \wedge (C \frown B)$

The following are the axioms of DC:

(2.9) $\int 0 = 0$

(2.10) $\int P \geq 0$

(2.11) $\int P + \int Q = (\int P \vee \int Q) + (\int P \wedge \int Q)$

(2.12) $\int P = r + s \Leftrightarrow \int P = r \frown \int P = s$

¿From these axioms, it is not difficult to show that the following are also theorems in DC:

(2.13) $\lceil P \rceil \frown \lceil P \rceil \Leftrightarrow \lceil P \rceil$

(2.14) $\lceil P \rceil \Rightarrow \Box(\lceil P \rceil^*)$

(2.15) $\lceil P \rceil \wedge \lceil Q \rceil \Leftrightarrow \lceil P \wedge Q \rceil$

(2.16) $\lceil P \rceil \wedge \lceil A \rceil \frown \lceil B \rceil \Leftrightarrow (\lceil P \rceil \wedge \lceil A \rceil) \frown (\lceil P \rceil \wedge \lceil B \rceil)$

States in the duration calculus must satisfy the finite variability property. Informally, this property means that for every state expression P, any interval $[b, e]$ where $b < e$, can be divided or partitioned into finitely many subintervals such that P is constant on each open subinterval.

First, let $\Gamma_1, \Gamma_2, ..., \Gamma_n \vdash \Gamma$ mean that we can make a formal deduction of the formula Γ from $\Gamma_1, \Gamma_2, ..., \Gamma_n$ (called assumption formulas) using the proof system of DC. A formal deduction of the formula Γ from $\Gamma_1, \Gamma_2, ..., \Gamma_n$ is a finite sequence of one or more formulas, such that each formula in the sequence is either one of the $\Gamma_1, \Gamma_2, ..., \Gamma_n$ or an axiom, or an immediate consequence of the preceding formulas of the sequence. The formula Γ is the last formula in the sequence and is called the conclusion.

This finite variability property is formalized as the following two induction rules:

Forward Induction: Let $\mathcal{H}(\mathcal{X})$ be a DC formula schema containing the formula letter $\mathcal{X}$, and let P be any state expression.

If $\quad \mathcal{H}(\lceil \ \rceil)$ and $\mathcal{H}(\mathcal{X}) \vdash \mathcal{H}(\mathcal{X} \vee (\mathcal{X} \frown \lceil P \rceil) \vee (\mathcal{X} \frown \lceil \neg P \rceil))$
then $\quad \mathcal{H}(true)$

Backward Induction: Let $\mathcal{H}(\mathcal{X})$ be a DC formula schema containing the formula letter $\mathcal{X}$, and let P be any state expression.

If $\quad \mathcal{H}(\lceil \ \rceil)$ and $\mathcal{H}(\mathcal{X}) \vdash \mathcal{H}(\mathcal{X} \vee (\lceil P \rceil \frown \mathcal{X}) \vee (\lceil \neg P \rceil \frown \mathcal{X}))$
then $\quad \mathcal{H}(true)$

3 Formalization of Scheduling

The system is modelled as having a set $\mathcal{T}$ of n tasks, $T_i, 1 \leq i \leq n$. Tasks are released at arbitrary predetermined times λ_i and are non-recurrent. Each task T_i has computation time C_i, relative deadline d_i and priority p_i. We assume that the priority of a task depends on its deadline and is fixed.

The system also maintains a set $\mathcal{R}$ of m non-preemptive resources, $r_k, 1 \leq k \leq m$. Associated with each task T_i is a set $R_i \subseteq \mathcal{R}$ of resources it will require during execution. For simplicity, we assume each resource $r_k \in R_i$ is requested and released by T_i once during its execution. Tasks may have only one outstanding request at a time. This means that tasks requests for resources in a sequential manner. Each resource $r_k \in R_i$ will be needed by T_i after having accumulated a runtime of $\chi_i(r_k)$. If a task T_i locks resource r_k, it will voluntarily release r_k

only after accumulating a runtime of $v_i(r_k)$. For the priority inheritance protocol (PIP) and the priority ceiling protocol (PCP), resource access is assumed to be properly nested, that is, while a task is acquiring resources, it cannot release any. But once it has started to release a resource, it cannot acquire resources anymore.

For the first class of protocols, we assume a uniprocessor model. For the second class of protocols, we assume that the number of processors is equal to n, the number of tasks.

The following state variables are introduced for task T_i:

$T_i.arrived$	- task T_i is in the system
$T_i.rdy$	- task T_i is ready to be allocated a processor
$T_i.run$	- task T_i is running on a processor
$T_i.requests(r_k)$	- task T_i is accessing resource r_k
$T_i.blocked(r_k)$	- task T_i is blocked on resource r_k
$T_i.holds(r_k)$	- resource r_k is currently held by task T_i
$T_i.done$	- task T_i is done and has left the system

The relationship between these states are expressed by the following state expressions:

- For all tasks T_i, either $T_i.arrived$ or $T_i.done$
$$T_i.arrived \lor T_i.done \qquad\qquad TS_1$$
These two states are mutually exclusive:
$$T_i.arrived \Rightarrow \neg T_i.done \qquad\qquad TS_2$$
- A task that is present in the system is either ready or blocked
$$T_i.arrived \Leftrightarrow T_i.rdy \lor T_i.blocked \qquad\qquad TS_3$$
where $T_i.blocked \triangleq \bigvee_{r_k \in \mathcal{R}} T_i.blocked(r_k)$
States $T_i.rdy$ and $T_i.blocked$ are mutually exclusive:
$$T_i.rdy \Rightarrow \neg T_i.blocked \qquad\qquad TS_4$$
- A task T_i runs only if it is ready
$$T_i.run \Rightarrow T_i.rdy \qquad\qquad TS_5$$
- When a task T_i is requesting for a resource r_k, it is either holding it or blocked on it
$$\bigwedge_{r_k \in \mathcal{R}} (T_i.requests(r_k) \Leftrightarrow T_i.holds(r_k) \lor T_i.blocked(r_k)) \qquad TS_6$$

A task T_i can request resources if it is present in the system:
$$\bigwedge_{r_k \in \mathcal{R}} (T_i.requests(r_k) \Rightarrow T_i.arrived) \qquad\qquad TS_7$$
States $T_i.holds(r_k)$ and $T_i.blocked(r_k)$ are mutually exclusive:
$$\bigwedge_{r_k \in \mathcal{R}} (T_i.holds(r_k) \Rightarrow \neg T_i.blocked(r_k)) \qquad\qquad TS_8$$

Let us denote all these predicates as:
$$TSREL \triangleq \bigwedge_{i=1}^{8} TS_i$$

With these states, the behavior of tasks in any interval $[0, t]$ is specified as follows:

Arrival Time: A task T_i arrives after λ_i time units (assuming that $\lambda_i > 0$):

$$ARR \ \hat{=}\ \bigwedge_{T_i \in T} \Box \left(\begin{aligned} &\ell > \lambda_i \\ &\Rightarrow (\ell = \lambda_i \wedge \lceil \neg T_i.arrived \rceil) ^\frown \lceil T_i.arrived \rceil ^\frown true \end{aligned} \right)$$

Completion Time: A task T_i stays in the system until it has accumulated C_i time units of processor time:

$$CPLT \ \hat{=}\ \bigwedge_{T_i \in T} \Box \left(\begin{aligned} &\int T_i.run = C_i ^\frown \ell > 0 \\ &\Leftrightarrow \int T_i.run = C_i ^\frown \lceil T_i.done \rceil ^\frown true \end{aligned} \right)$$

Resources

Resources are allocated in a mutually exclusive manner, i.e. a resource can be held by at most one task at any time:

$$MUTX \ \hat{=}\ \bigwedge_{T_i \in T} \left(\bigwedge_{r_k \in \mathcal{R}} (T_i.holds(r_k) \Rightarrow \bigwedge_{T_j \neq T_i \in T} \neg T_j.holds(r_k)) \right)$$

Resource allocation is nonpreemptive:

$$NPRV \ \hat{=}\ \bigwedge_{T_i \in T} \bigwedge_{r_k \in R_i} \Box \left(\begin{aligned} &\lceil T_i.holds(r_k) \rceil ^\frown \lceil T_i.requests(r_k) \rceil \\ &\Rightarrow \lceil T_i.holds(r_k) \rceil \end{aligned} \right)$$

Conjoining the predicates above, we have:

$$RES \ \hat{=}\ MUTX \wedge NPRV$$

Behavior of Tasks and Resources

Now we model the behavior of tasks with respect to resources. The first thing is representing precisely when a task will request for a particular resource it needs:

Acquisition Time A task T_i will need the resource $r_k \in R_i$ only after having accumulated processor time of exactly $\chi_i(r_k)$ time units.

Let $T_i.NOT\text{-}REQ(r_k) \ \hat{=}\ (\int T_i.run - \chi_i(r_k) \wedge \lceil \neg T_i.requests(r_k) \rceil^*)$ then

$$ACQ \ \hat{=}\ \bigwedge_{T_i \in T} \bigwedge_{r_k \in R_i} \Box \left(\begin{aligned} &\lceil \neg T_i.requests(r_k) \rceil^* ^\frown \lceil T_i.requests(r_k) \rceil \\ &\Rightarrow T_i.NOT\text{-}REQ(r_k) ^\frown \lceil T_i.requests(r_k) \rceil \end{aligned} \right)$$

The following formula specifies how long a task will hold onto a resource once it has been allocated it.

Hold Time A task T_i releases a resource r_k after it has received accumulated processor time of $\upsilon_i(r_k)$ time units while holding r_k.

$$HOLD \ \hat{=}\ \bigwedge_{T_i \in T} \bigwedge_{r_k \in R_i} \Box \left(\begin{aligned} &INUSE(T_i, r_k) \\ &\Rightarrow \int (T_i.run \wedge T_i.holds(r_k)) = \upsilon_i(r_k) \end{aligned} \right)$$

where $INUSE(T_i, r_k) \hat{=} \lceil \neg T_i.requests(r_k) \rceil^* ^\frown \lceil T_i.requests(r_k) \rceil ^\frown \lceil \neg T_i.requests(r_k) \rceil$

It is natural to assume that a task needs to be allocated processor time in order to request access to any resource. This is expressed as:

$$REQ \ \hat{=}\ \bigwedge_{T_i \in T} \bigwedge_{r_k \in R_i} \Box (\lceil \neg T_i.requests(r_k) \rceil ^\frown \lceil T_i.requests(r_k) \rceil \Rightarrow \Diamond \lceil T_i.run \rceil)$$

For PIP and PCP, accesses to resources are properly nested. For each task T_i, there is a total order among resources R_i, denoted by $<_i$, such that:

$$NEST \ \hat{=}\ \bigwedge_{T_i \in T} \bigwedge_{r_k \neq r_l \in R_i} \Box \left(\begin{aligned} &r_k <_i r_l \wedge \lceil T_i.requests(r_k) \rceil \\ &\Rightarrow \lceil T_i.requests(r_l) \rceil \end{aligned} \right)$$

This formula means that given any two resources, r_k and r_l, if the request for r_k is nested within the request for r_l, then $r_k <_i r_l$.

It is also obviously reasonable for all tasks to release all resources they are holding on or before termination.

$$REL \; \cong \; \bigwedge_{T_i \in \mathcal{T}} \bigwedge_{r_k \in R_i} (\chi_i(r_k) + v_i(r_k) \leq C_i)$$

The conjunction of the preceding formulas constitute our model for the tasks for the PIP and PCP.

$$TASK \; \cong \; ARR \; \wedge \; CPLT \; \wedge \; ACQ \; \wedge \; HOLD \; \wedge \; REQ \; \wedge \; NEST \; \wedge$$
$$REL \; \wedge \; TSREL \; \wedge \; RES$$

However, for the second class of protocols, TPB and RP, this nested access assumption is relaxed. Hence we have:

$$TASK2 \; \cong \; ARR \; \wedge \; CPLT \; \wedge \; ACQ \; \wedge \; HOLD \; \wedge \; REQ \; \wedge \; REL \; \wedge$$
$$TSREL \; \wedge \; RES$$

Environment

Priority assignment is a total order:

$$PRIO \; \cong \; \bigwedge_{T_i \neq T_j \in \mathcal{T}} (p_i < p_j \vee p_i > p_j)$$

Since uniprocessor and multiprocessor schedulers are considered here, we will present DC formulae to express these:

Under a uniprocessor model, we have:

$$ONEPROC \; \cong \; \bigwedge_{T_i \neq T_j \in \mathcal{T}} \Box \lceil T_i.run \Rightarrow \neg T_j.run \rceil^*$$

Under our multiprocessor model (where there is one processor for each task), we have:

$$MULPROC \; \cong \; \bigwedge_{T_i \in \mathcal{T}} \Box \lceil T_i.rdy \Rightarrow T_i.run \rceil^*$$

This means that there is no need to separately specify the scheduler for the processor, since a task can run as soon as it is ready.

There is no overhead for the scheduler:

$$NOHD \; \cong \; \bigwedge_{T_i \in \mathcal{T}} \Box \lceil T_i.rdy \Rightarrow \bigvee_{T_j \in \mathcal{T}} T_j.run \rceil^*$$

Hence for the uniprocessor model, we have:

$$ENV1 \; \cong \; PRIO \wedge ONEPROC \wedge NOHD$$

For the multiprocessor model, the environment is:

$$ENV2 \; \cong \; PRIO \wedge MULPROC$$

Scheduler

The scheduler for tasks with shared resources can be expressed as having two components:

Processor Scheduling: policy concerned with the selection of tasks to run on the processor; and

Resource Control: policy concerning the selection of which task will be allocated a resource it is requesting.

There are three rules for resource control:

Granting Rule: used to decide if the resource requested is granted or not.

Blocking Rule: used to decide when a task is blocked on its request for a resource or not; and

Unblocking Rule: used for deciding which among the blocked tasks is to be granted the resource.

With this general framework, the protocols identified earlier can now be precisely specified. There are two classes of protocols: (a) protocols that allow priority inversions to occur; and (b) protocols that explicitly prevent priority inversions from occurring.

3.1 Protocols that Permit Priority Inversion

Using the framework presented above, we present duration calculus formula schemas for specification of schedulers within this class of protocols. The schemas serve as templates for formulas in the sense that to specify a scheduler or protocol, the only thing to do is to define certain functions to be used with the formula schemas.

First, the formula schema for the preemptive priority scheduler is presented as follows:

Preemptive Priority Scheduler

Let $HiPri(T_i, T_j)$ be a Boolean-valued relation for denoting which task between T_i and T_j is to be executed by the processor. The preemptive priority scheduler can be expressed in terms of $HiPri$ as:

$$PPS(HiPri) \; \hat{=} \; \bigwedge_{T_i \neq T_j \in \mathcal{T}} \Box(\lceil T_i.run \rceil \wedge \lceil T_j.rdy \rceil \; \Rightarrow \; \lceil HiPri(T_i, T_j) \rceil)$$

Resource control can be specified by defining the three rules mentioned earlier. The granting rule for this class of protocols is expressed as:

Granting Rule

$$PTCL1(Right) \; \hat{=} \; \bigwedge_{T_i \in \mathcal{T}} \bigwedge_{r_k \in \mathcal{R}} \Box \left(\begin{array}{c} \lceil \neg T_i.holds(r_k) \rceil ^\frown \lceil T_i.holds(r_k) \rceil \\ \Rightarrow \Diamond \lceil Right(T_i, r_k) \rceil \end{array} \right)$$

where $Right(T_i, r_k)$ is a relation that holds if task T_i is granted access to resource r_k.

The blocking rule for this class of protocols can be expressed as:

Blocking Rule

$$PTCL2(Right) \; \hat{=} \; \bigwedge_{T_i \in \mathcal{T}} \bigwedge_{r_k \in \mathcal{R}} \Box(\lceil T_i.blocked(r_k) \rceil \Rightarrow \lceil \neg Right(T_i, r_k) \rceil)$$

Finally, the unblocking rule can be specified as:

Unblocking Rule

$$PTCL3(HiPri) \; \hat{=} \; \bigwedge_{T_i \neq T_j \in \mathcal{T}} \bigwedge_{r_k \in \mathcal{R}} \Box \left(\begin{array}{c} UNBLOCK(T_i, T_j, r_k) \\ \Rightarrow true ^\frown \lceil HiPri(T_i, T_j) \rceil \end{array} \right)$$

where $UNBLOCK(T_i, T_j, r_k) \hat{=} \lceil T_i.blocked(r_k) \wedge T_j.blocked(r_k) \rceil ^\frown \lceil \neg T_i.blocked(r_k) \rceil$

By combining these formula schemas together, the scheduler, $\mathcal{SCH}$, is obtained:

$$\mathcal{SCH}(HiPri, Right) \; \hat{=} \; \left(\begin{array}{c} PPS(HiPri) \wedge PTCL1(Right) \\ \wedge PTCL2(Right) \wedge PTCL3(HiPri) \end{array} \right)$$

First, let us consider protocols are permit priority inversions to occur. In [1], these protocols are also classified as *preemptive blocking protocols*, since a task T_i holding a resource r can be preempted (from the processor) by higher priority tasks and T_i can block other tasks that requests for the resource r.

Trivial Protocol A

This protocol works as follows: If a task T_i requests for a resource r_k, it is granted if r_k is available. Otherwise, T_i is blocked on r_k. When r_k becomes available, the protocol selects the highest priority task among the tasks that are blocked on r_k to lock and use the r_k.

First, the relation $HiPri_{TPA}$ is defined using the original priority assigned to tasks:

$$HiPri_{TPA}(T_i, T_j) \; \hat{=} \; (p_i > p_j)$$

and the relation $Right_{TPA}$ is defined as:

$$Right_{TPA}(T_i, r_k) \; \hat{=} \; \bigwedge_{T_j \neq T_i \in T} \neg T_j.holds(r_k)$$

¿From these, the TPA scheduler can be instantiated from the formula schema $\mathcal{SCH}$ as:

$$TPA \; \hat{=} \; \mathcal{SCH}(HiPri_{TPA}, Right_{TPA})$$

Priority Inheritance Protocol

The difference between the priority inheritance protocol and the trivial protocol A above is in the assignment of priorities to tasks.

The protocol works as follows: A task T_i that wants to acquire a resource r_k must obey the following rule:

(a)   if r_k is available, it is granted to T_i;

(b)   otherwise (i.e. there is a task, say T_j, that is currently holding r_k), T_i is blocked on r_k and if $p_i > p_j$ then task T_j inherits p_i.

The priority inheritance protocol bounds the length of priority inversions by temporarily assigning a higher priority to tasks while they are blocking other tasks [9]. First we define the following abbreviation:

$$T_i.blockedby(T_j) \; \hat{=} \; \bigvee_{r_k \in \mathcal{R}} (T_j.holds(r_k) \wedge T_i.blocked(r_k))$$

¿From this, the state function $HiPri$ for PIP, $HiPri_{PIP}$, satisfies the following inheritance properties:

(a) $HiPri_{PIP}$ is a total order:

$$\bigwedge_{T_i \neq T_j \in T} (HiPri_{PIP}(T_i, T_j) \; \Rightarrow \; \neg HiPri_{PIP}(T_j, T_i))$$

$$\bigwedge_{T_i \neq T_j \neq T_k \in T} \left(\begin{array}{l} HiPri_{PIP}(T_i, T_k) \; \wedge \; HiPri_{PIP}(T_k, T_j) \\ \Rightarrow \; HiPri_{PIP}(T_i, T_j) \end{array} \right)$$

(b) $HiPri_{PIP}$ depends on the priority inherited by tasks:

$$\bigwedge_{T_i \neq T_j \neq T_k \in T} \left(\begin{array}{l} T_k.blockedby(T_i) \\ \Rightarrow \; (HiPri_{PIP}(T_k, T_j) \; \Rightarrow \; HiPri_{PIP}(T_i, T_j)) \end{array} \right)$$

$$\bigwedge_{T_i \neq T_j \in T} \left(\begin{array}{l} \bigwedge_{T_k \in T}(\neg T_k.blockedby(T_i)) \\ \Rightarrow \; (HiPri_{PIP}(T_i, T_j) \; \Rightarrow \; p_i > p_j) \end{array} \right)$$

The first formula in (b) states when a task T_i inherits the priority of another task T_k, if $HiPri_{PIP}(T_k, T_j)$ then $HiPri_{PIP}(T_i, T_j)$. The second formula states that if a task T_i does not inherit any priority, then the relation $HiPri_{PIP}$ is consistent with the original assigned priorities.

Hence, the formula for PIP is:

$$PIP \;\hat{=}\; SCH(HiPri_{PIP}, Right_{TPA})$$

It should be noted that the granting and blocking rules for PIP is the same as the one used in TPA, so the $Right$ function defined for TPA is used here for PIP.

Priority Ceiling Protocol

The priority ceiling protocol [8, 9] was designed to address the deadlock and chaining problems of the priority inheritance protocol. This protocol, which also employs priority inheritance mechanism, works as follows:

(a)   each resource r_k is assigned a priority ceiling, $c(r_k)$, which is equal to the highest priority of all tasks that can lock it; and

(b)   if a task T_i requests for a resource r_k, it is granted if $p_i > c(r_l)$, for all resources r_l currently held by tasks T_j other than T_i.

First, the priority ceiling of resources is formalized. Since the number of tasks in the system and the priorities of the tasks are constant, therefore, the priority ceiling of resource r_k, $c(r_k)$ is also constant. Hence,

$$c(r_k) \;\hat{=}\; \max_i \{ p_i \mid r_k \in R_i \}$$

The $blockedby$ state function for PCP is:

$$T_i.blockedby'(T_j) \;\hat{=}\; \bigvee_{r_k \in \mathcal{R}} (T_j.holds(r_k) \wedge T_i.blocked \wedge c(r_k) \geq p_i)$$

PCP is a form of priority inheritance protocol, so the relation $HiPri_{PCP}$ also satisfies the inheritance properties for $HiPri_{PIP}$ except that we use $T_i.blockedby'$ instead of $T_i.blockedby$.

The $Right$ function for PCP is:

$$Right_{PCP}(T_i) \;\hat{=}\; \bigwedge_{r_k \in \mathcal{R}} (\bigwedge_{T_j \neq T_i \in \mathcal{T}} T_j.holds(r_k) \Rightarrow p_i > c(r_k))$$

Hence, for PCP we have:

$$PCP \;\hat{=}\; SCH(HiPri_{PCP}, Right_{PCP})$$

3.2 Protocols that Prevent Priority Inversions

Protocols in this class prevent priority inversions by delaying lower priority tasks sufficiently long to prevent them from blocking higher priority tasks. The environment here is a multiprocessor environment, $ENV2$. To model these protocols, the state function $Right$ will be replaced with a DC formula which serves the same purpose but can deal with conditions pertaining to a time interval and not just the current state of the system at a specific time point.

$DRight(T_i, r_k)$ is defined to be the DC formula that holds if task T_i is granted resource r_k based on the conditions in the observation interval.

The blocking and unblocking rule are specified in terms of $DRight$ as follows:

$$PTCL'(DRight) \triangleq \bigwedge_{T_i \in \mathcal{T}} \bigwedge_{r_k \in \mathcal{R}} \Box(true^\frown \lceil \neg T_i.blocked(r_k) \rceil) \Leftrightarrow DRight(T_i, r_k))$$

¿From this, the scheduler SCH' for the second class of protocols is expressed as the following:

$$SCH'(DRight) \triangleq PTCL'(DRight)$$

Trivial Protocol B

This protocol works as follows: a task T_i that requests a resource r_k is granted if all other higher priority tasks have finished using r_k.

The DC formula to denote when a task is granted a resource is defined as:

$$DRight_{TPB}(T_i, r_k) \triangleq \left(\begin{matrix} true^\frown \lceil T_i.requests(r_k) \rceil \Rightarrow \\ \bigwedge_{T_j \neq T_i \in \mathcal{T}} (p_j > p_i \wedge r_k \in R_j \Rightarrow Finished(T_j, r_k)) \end{matrix} \right)$$

where $Finished(T_j, r_k) \triangleq \int T_j.run \geq \chi_j(r_k) + v_j(r_k)$.

Hence for TPB, the scheduler is defined as:

$$TPB \triangleq SCH'(DRight_{TPB})$$

Reservation Protocol

Informally, this protocol works as follows [2, 3]: a task T_i that requests a resource r_k is granted if either it will release r_k before the any higher priority task request r_k or all higher priority tasks have finished using r_k.

The expression $DRight_{RP}$ is defined as:

$$DRight_{RP}(T_i, r_k) \triangleq \left(\begin{matrix} true^\frown \lceil T_i.requests(r_k) \rceil \Rightarrow \\ \bigwedge_{T_j \neq T_i \in \mathcal{T}} \left(\begin{matrix} p_j > p_i \wedge r_k \in R_j \Rightarrow \\ NotReq(T_i, T_j, r_k) \vee Finished(T_j, r_k) \end{matrix} \right) \end{matrix} \right)$$

where

$$NotReq(T_i, T_j, r_k) \triangleq \ell - \int (T_i.holds(r_k) \wedge T_i.run) + v_i(r_k) \leq$$
$$\lambda_j + \chi_j(r_k) + v_j(r_k)$$
$$Finished(T_j, r_k) \triangleq \int T_j.run \geq \chi_j(r_k) + v_j(r_k)$$

The formula $NotReq(T_i, T_j, r_k)$ holds on an observation interval if T_i will release resource r_k before task T_j requests for it.

Finally, we have

$$RP \triangleq SCH'(DRight_{RP})$$

3.3 Requirements

The requirement that deadlines of all tasks are to be met can be expressed as:

$$RQT \triangleq \bigwedge_{T_i \in \mathcal{T}} \Box \left(\begin{matrix} true^\frown (\lceil T_i.arrived \rceil \wedge \ell = d_i) \\ \Rightarrow \int T_i.run = C_i \end{matrix} \right)$$

Other requirements for schedulers are: deadlock freedom and no priority inversion.

One way to express deadlock freedom in DC is:

$$NODLCK \triangleq \Box \neg (\lceil \bigwedge_{T_i \in \mathcal{T}} (T_i.done \vee T_i.blocked) \wedge \bigvee_{i \in \mathcal{T}} T_i.blocked \rceil)$$

and no priority inversion can be expressed as:

$$NOINV \triangleq \bigwedge_{T_i \neq T_j \in \mathcal{T}} \bigwedge_{r_k \in \mathcal{R}} \square \left(\begin{array}{l} \lceil T_i.holds(r_k) \wedge T_j.blocked(r_k) \rceil \\ \Rightarrow HiPri(T_i, T_j) \end{array} \right)$$

In the next section, we present formal proofs that some schedulers satisfy some of these requirements.

4 Proving Properties

The advantages of using a formal specification language like the duration calculus is in the ability to prove properties from the specifications. In this section, we will show how we can use some of these specifications in the previous section to prove properties of these protocols like blocked at most once, deadlock freedom and no priority inversion.

4.1 Blocked At Most Once Property of PCP

In order to prove this property, we need to make a distinction between a task being in the prempted (from processor) state and blocked state. We make the assumption that while a task is preempted by a higher priority task, it is not blocked.

$$A1 \triangleq \bigwedge_{T_i \neq T_j \in \mathcal{T}} \square \left(\begin{array}{l} \lceil T_i.run \rceil^\frown \lceil \bigvee_{T_j \neq T_i \in \mathcal{T}} (T_j.run \wedge p_j > p_i) \rceil \\ \Rightarrow \lceil T_i.run \rceil^\frown \lceil \neg T_i.blocked \rceil \end{array} \right)$$

First, we define the notion of *critical region* for a task. Since resources are accessed in a properly nested manner, the critical region for a task T_i is defined as the time interval beginning at the acquisition of its first resource and ending at the release of the last resource it is holding.

Formally,

Definition 1. $\quad T_i.in\text{-}cr \triangleq \bigvee_{r_k \in \mathcal{R}} T_i.holds(r_k)$

First we have the following 2 lemmas:

$$A1 \wedge PCP \wedge TASK \wedge ENV \vdash$$

Lemma 2.
$$\bigwedge_{T_i \in \mathcal{T}} \square \left(\begin{array}{l} \lceil T_i.in\text{-}cr \rceil \Rightarrow \\ \left\lceil \bigwedge_{T_j \neq T_i \in \mathcal{T}} \bigwedge_{r_l \in \mathcal{R}} \left(\begin{array}{l} T_j.holds(r_l) \wedge HiPri_{PCP}(T_i, T_j) \\ \Rightarrow p_i > c(r_l) \end{array} \right) \right\rceil \end{array} \right)$$

PROOF. See [4].

$$A1 \wedge PCP \wedge TASK \wedge ENV \vdash$$

Lemma 3.
$$\bigwedge_{T_i \in \mathcal{T}} \square \left(\begin{array}{l} \lceil \neg Right_{PCP}(T_i) \wedge T_i.in\text{-}cr \rceil \\ \Rightarrow \lceil \bigvee_{T_j \neq T_i \in \mathcal{T}} (T_j.run \wedge HiPri_{PCP}(T_j, T_i)) \rceil \end{array} \right)$$

PROOF. See [4].

The property of PCP where a task is blocked at most once before entering its critical region can be expressed as follows:

Theorem 4. $\quad A1 \wedge PCP \wedge TASK \wedge ENV \vdash$
$$\bigwedge_{T_i \in \mathcal{T}} \Box(\lceil T_i.in\text{-}cr \rceil \Rightarrow \lceil \neg T_i.blocked \rceil)$$

PROOF.

We prove this by induction: First, assume:
$$\mathcal{H}(\mathcal{X}) \triangleq \mathcal{X} \wedge \lceil T_i.in\text{-}cr \rceil \Rightarrow \lceil \neg T_i.blocked \rceil$$
$$\Gamma \quad \triangleq A1 \wedge PCP \wedge TASK \wedge ENV$$

Base case: $\Gamma \vdash \mathcal{H}(\lceil\ \rceil)$

$\lceil\ \rceil \wedge \lceil T_i.in\text{-}cr \rceil \Rightarrow \lceil \neg T_i.blocked \rceil$

$\quad \Rightarrow false \Rightarrow \lceil \neg T_i.blocked \rceil \qquad\qquad\qquad\qquad\qquad$ ITL

$\quad \Rightarrow true \qquad\qquad\qquad\qquad\qquad\qquad\qquad\qquad\qquad$ ITL

For the inductive step, we must establish:
$$\Gamma, \mathcal{H}(\mathcal{X}) \vdash \mathcal{H}(\mathcal{X} \vee (\mathcal{X}^\frown \lceil Right_{PCP}(T_i) \rceil) \vee (\mathcal{X}^\frown \lceil \neg Right_{PCP}(T_i) \rceil))$$

We now consider two cases:

1. $\Gamma, \mathcal{H}(\mathcal{X}) \vdash \mathcal{H}(\mathcal{X}^\frown \lceil Right_{PCP}(T_i) \rceil)$
2. $\Gamma, \mathcal{H}(\mathcal{X}) \vdash \mathcal{H}(\mathcal{X}^\frown \lceil \neg Right_{PCP}(T_i) \rceil)$

Case 1: $\Gamma, \mathcal{H}(\mathcal{X}) \vdash \mathcal{H}(\mathcal{X}^\frown \lceil Right_{PCP}(T_i) \rceil)$

$\mathcal{X}^\frown \lceil Right_{PCP}(T_i) \rceil \wedge \lceil T_i.in\text{-}cr \rceil$

$\quad \Rightarrow (\mathcal{X} \wedge \lceil T_i.in\text{-}cr \rceil)^\frown(\lceil Right_{PCP}(T_i) \rceil \wedge \lceil T_i.in\text{-}cr \rceil) \qquad$ Theorem 2.16

$\quad \Rightarrow \lceil \neg T_i.blocked \rceil^\frown(\lceil Right_{PCP}(T_i) \rceil \wedge \lceil T_i.in\text{-}cr \rceil) \qquad\quad$ $\mathcal{H}(\mathcal{X})$

$\quad \Rightarrow \lceil \neg T_i.blocked \rceil^\frown \lceil \neg T_i.blocked \rceil \qquad\qquad\qquad\qquad$ PCP

$\quad \Rightarrow \lceil \neg T_i.blocked \rceil \qquad\qquad\qquad\qquad\qquad\qquad$ Theorem 2.13

Case 2: $\Gamma, \mathcal{H}(\mathcal{X}) \vdash \mathcal{H}(\mathcal{X}^\frown \lceil \neg Right_{PCP}(T_i) \rceil)$

$\mathcal{X}^\frown \lceil \neg Right_{PCP}(T_i) \rceil \wedge \lceil T_i.in\text{-}cr \rceil$

$\quad \Rightarrow (\mathcal{X} \wedge \lceil T_i.in\text{-}cr \rceil)^\frown(\lceil \neg Right_{PCP}(T_i) \rceil \wedge \lceil T_i.in\text{-}cr \rceil) \qquad$ Theorem 2.16

$\quad \Rightarrow \lceil \neg T_i.blocked \rceil^\frown(\lceil \neg Right_{PCP}(T_i) \rceil \wedge \lceil T_i.in\text{-}cr \rceil) \qquad\quad$ $\mathcal{H}(\mathcal{X})$

$\quad \Rightarrow \lceil \neg T_i.blocked \rceil^\frown(\lceil \neg Right_{PCP}(T_i) \wedge T_i.in\text{-}cr \rceil) \qquad\quad$ Theorem 2.15

$\quad \Rightarrow \lceil \neg T_i.blocked \rceil^\frown \lceil \bigvee_{T_j \in \mathcal{T}} (T_j.run \wedge HiPri_{PCP}(T_j, T_i)) \rceil \qquad$ LEMMA 3

$\quad \Rightarrow \lceil \neg T_i.blocked \rceil^\frown \lceil \neg T_i.blocked \rceil \qquad\qquad\qquad\qquad$ A1

$\quad \Rightarrow \lceil \neg T_i.blocked \rceil \qquad\qquad\qquad\qquad\qquad\qquad$ Theorem 2.13

This completes the proof of the theorem. $\qquad\qquad\qquad\qquad\qquad$ $\Box$

4.2 PCP is Deadlock Free

We prove this property by contradiction.

Theorem 5. $\quad A1 \wedge PCP \wedge TASK \wedge ENV \vdash NODLCK$

PROOF.

$\quad$ (1) $\neg \Box \neg (\lceil \bigwedge_{T_i \in \mathcal{T}} (T_i.done \vee T_i.blocked) \wedge \bigvee_{i \in \mathcal{T}} T_i.blocked \rceil) \qquad$ Assume

(2) $\Diamond(\bigwedge_{T_i \in \mathcal{T}} \lceil (T_i.done \lor T_i.blocked) \rceil \land \bigvee_{T_i \in \mathcal{T}} \lceil T_i.blocked \rceil)$ ITL

(3) $\Box(\bigwedge_{T_i \in \mathcal{T}} (\lceil T_i.blocked \rceil \Rightarrow \lceil \bigvee_{T_j \in \mathcal{T}} T_j.in\text{-}cr \rceil))$ PCP - $PTCL2$ $(Right_{PCP})$, Def. of $Right_{PCP}$, Def. 1

(4) $\Box(\lceil \bigvee_{T_i \in \mathcal{T}} T_i.in\text{-}cr \rceil \Rightarrow \lceil \bigvee_{T_i \in \mathcal{T}} (\neg T_i.blocked \land T_i.in\text{-}cr) \rceil)$ (3), THEOREM 4, ITL

(5) $\Box(\bigwedge_{T_i \in \mathcal{T}} (\lceil T_i.blocked \rceil \Rightarrow \lceil \bigvee_{T_j \in \mathcal{T}} (\neg T_j.blocked \land T_j.in\text{-}cr) \rceil))$ (3), (4), Prop. Logic

(6) $\Diamond(\bigwedge_{T_i \in \mathcal{T}} \lceil (T_i.done \lor T_i.blocked) \rceil \land \bigvee_{T_i \in \mathcal{T}} \lceil \neg T_i.blocked \land T_i.in\text{-}cr \rceil)$ (2), (5), Prop. Logic

(7) $\Diamond(\bigvee_{T_i \in \mathcal{T}} \lceil \neg T_i.blocked \land T_i.in\text{-}cr \land (T_i.done \lor T_i.blocked) \rceil)$ (6), Prop. Logic

(8) $false$ (7), TASK, Prop. Logic

(9) $NODLCK$ (1), (8), Prop. Logic

$\Box$

4.3 No Priority Inversion

Now, we will prove that the Reservation Protocol does not permit priority inversions to occur. First, we consider a lemma:

$$RP \land TASK2 \land ENV2 \vdash$$

Lemma 6. $\bigwedge_{T_i \in \mathcal{T}} \bigwedge_{r_k \in \mathcal{R}} \Box \left(\begin{array}{c} \lceil \neg T_i.holds(r_k) \rceil \frown \lceil T_i.holds(r_k) \rceil \Rightarrow \\ \bigwedge_{T_j \neq T_i \in \mathcal{T}} \left(\begin{array}{c} p_j > p_i \land r_k \in R_j \Rightarrow \\ \lceil \neg T_i.holds(r_k) \rceil \frown \lceil \neg T_j.blocked(r_k) \rceil \end{array} \right) \end{array} \right)$

PROOF.

$true \frown \lceil T_i.holds(r_k) \rceil$

$\Rightarrow \quad true \frown \lceil \neg T_i.blocked(r_k) \rceil$ Def. of $holds$

$\Rightarrow \quad DRight_{RP}(T_i, r_k)$ RP

$\Rightarrow \quad \left(\begin{array}{c} true \frown \lceil T_i.requests(r_k) \rceil \\ \Rightarrow \bigwedge_{T_j \neq T_i \in \mathcal{T}} \left(\begin{array}{c} p_j > p_i \land r_k \in R_j \\ \Rightarrow NotReq(T_i, T_j, r_k) \lor Finished(T_j, r_k) \end{array} \right) \end{array} \right)$ Def. of $DRight_{RP}$

$\Rightarrow \quad \bigwedge_{T_j \neq T_i \in \mathcal{T}} \left(\begin{array}{c} p_j > p_i \land r_k \in R_j \\ \Rightarrow NotReq(T_i, T_j, r_k) \lor Finished(T_j, r_k) \end{array} \right)$ $TASK2$ - TS_6, Prop. Logic

$\Rightarrow \quad \bigwedge_{T_j \neq T_i \in \mathcal{T}} \left(\begin{array}{c} p_j > p_i \land r_k \in R_j \\ \Rightarrow true \frown \lceil \neg T_j.requests(r_k) \rceil \end{array} \right)$ $ENV2$, $TASK2$ - ACQ, $HOLD$

$$\Rightarrow \bigwedge_{T_j \neq T_i \in \mathcal{T}} \left(\begin{matrix} p_j > p_i \wedge r_k \in R_j \\ \Rightarrow true^\frown \lceil \neg T_j.blocked(r_k) \rceil \end{matrix} \right) \qquad TASK2 - TS_6$$

□

The Reservation Protocol ensures no priority inversions.

Theorem 7. $\qquad RP \wedge TASK2 \wedge ENV2 \vdash NOINV$

PROOF.

The proof follows directly from LEMMA 6. □

5 Conclusions

In this paper, we presented formal specifications of 5 schedulers for tasks with shared resources. With these specifications, we were able to prove properties like deadlock freedom, blocked at most once, and no priority inversion.

More importantly, we presented two frameworks by which the specifications where based on. The first framework is applicable to schedulers which makes decisions based on the current state of the system, e.g. state of the resources, etc. The second framework concerns schedulers which makes decisions based on events that happened already or future events that will take place shortly. These frameworks can be used in the future for specifying a variety of other protocols [1] such as the Ceiling Semaphore Protocol, Semaphore Control Protocol, etc.

References

1. Neil C.Audsley, "Resource Control for Hard Real-Time Systems: A Review" Technical Report YCS 159, Department of Computer Science, University of York, U.K., August 1991.
2. Ozalp Babaoglu, Keith Marzullo and Fred B.Schneider, "Priority Inversion and its Prevention in Real-Time Systems", TR-90-1088, Department of Computer Science, Cornell University, March 1990.
3. Ozalp Babaoglu, Keith Marzullo and Fred B.Schneider, "A Formalization of Priority Inversion", *Real-Time Systems*, 5(4), pp. 285-303, October 1993.
4. Philip Chan and Dang Van Hung, "Duration Calculus Specification of Scheduling for Tasks with Shared Resources", UNU/IIST Report No. 44, June 1995.
5. Dang Van Hung and Zhou Chao Chen, "Probabilistic Duration Calculus for Continuous Time", UNU/IIST Report No. 25, May 1994. Submitted to *Formal Aspects of Computing*.
6. He Jifeng and Jonathan Bowen, "Time Interval Semantics and Implementation of a Real-Time Programming Language" *Proc. 4th Euromicro Workshop on Real-Time Systems*, IEEE Press, June 1992.
7. Liu Zhimming, Anders P.Ravn, Erling V.Sørensen and Zhou Chao Chen, "A Probabilistic Duration Calculus," In *Dependable Computing and Fault-Tolerant Systems, Vol. 7: Responsive Computer Systems, Edited by H.Kopetz and Y.Kakuda*, pp. 30-52, Springer-Verlag, 1993.
8. L.Sha, R.Rajkumar and J.P.Lehoczky, "Priority Inheritance Protocols: An Approach to Real-Time Synchronization", CMU-CS-87-181, Computer Science Department, Carnegie-Mellon University, December 1987.

9. L.Sha, R.Rajkumar and J.P.Lehoczky, "Priority Inheritance Protocols: An Approach to Real-Time Synchronization", *IEEE Transactions on Computers*, **39**(9), pp. 1175-1185, September 1990.

10. Zheng Yuhua and Zhou Chao Chen, "A Formal Proof of the Deadline Driven Scheduler" UNU/IIST Research Report No. 16, February 1994. In: *Formal Techniques in Real-Time and Fault-Tolerant Systems, LNCS 863. Edited by H.Langmaack, W.-P.de Roever and J.Vytopil*, pp. 756-775, Springer-Verlag, 1994.

11. Zhou Chao Chen, C.A.R.Hoare and Ander P.Ravn, "A Calculus of Durations" *Information Processing Letters*, **40**(5), pp 269-276, 1991.

12. Zhou Chao Chen and Li Xiao Shan, "A Mean Value Calculus of Durations" In *A Classical Mind (Essays in Honour of C.A.R. Hoare), Edited by A.W.Roscoe*, Prentice-Hall, pp. 431-451, 1994.

13. Zhou Chao Chen, Dang Van Hung and Li Xiao Shan, "A Duration Calculus with Infinite Intervals, " UNU/IIST Report No. 40, February 1995.

14. Zhou Chao Chen, Michael R.Hansen, Ander P.Ravn and Hans Rischel, "Duration Specifications for Shared Processors" In *Proc. of the Symposium on Formal Techniques in Real-Time and Fault Tolerant Systems*, Nijmegen, January 1992. LNCS 571, pp 21-32, 1992.

15. Zhou Chao Chen, Ander P.Ravn and Michael R.Hansen, "An Extended Duration Calculus for Hybrid Real-Time Systems" In *Hybrid Sytems*, LNCS 736, Springer-Verlag, pp 36-59, 1993.

Trace Specifications of Non-Deterministic Multi-Object Modules

Michal Iglewski (e-mail: iglewski@uqah.uquebec.ca)
Département d'informatique, Université du Québec à Hull, Hull, Québec, Canada J8X 3X7

Marcin Kubica (e-mail: kubica@mimuw.edu.pl)
Jan Madey (e-mail: madey@mimuw.edu.pl)
Institute of Informatics, Warsaw University, Banacha 2, 02-097 Warsaw, Poland

ABSTRACT

The *Trace Assertion Method* (in short: TAM) is a formal method for abstract specification of interfaces of software modules being designed according to the "information hiding" principle. A trace specification is a "black-box" specification, i.e., it describes only those features of a module that are *externally observable*. The method was introduced by W. Bartusek and D.L. Parnas some 15 years ago and since then has undergone many modifications. In recent years there has been an increased interest in TAM. Software tools supporting practical usage of TAM for software engineering projects are under development, the method is being tested on different applications, its foundations are being studied.

Recent experiments with TAM have showed the need for further study in the case of non-deterministic multi-object modules. In this paper we investigate the expressiveness of the method for such modules. We present a formal model of a module and its TAM specification, show that the method requires some extensions and propose solutions. Our considerations are illustrated on TAM but could also be generally applied to modules with hidden non-determinism.

The full version of our investigations, including all definitions, lemmas, proofs and examples, is presented in university technical reports.

1 Introduction

The *Trace Assertion Method* (in short: TAM) is a formal method for abstract specification of interfaces of software *modules* being designed according to the "information hiding" principle [12]. A module implements one or more *objects*. A trace specification is a "black-box" specification, i.e., it describes only those features of an object that are *externally observable* and hides details of its internal structure. The method was first formulated in [1], and since then has undergone many modifications [3, 4, 7, 9, 11, 14, 15]. In recent years, there has been an increased interest in TAM, especially within the framework of the "functional approach" [13]. Software tools supporting practical usage of TAM are under development (e.g. [6, 15]), the method is being tested on different applications (e.g. [2, 9]), and its foundations are being studied (e.g. [8, 9, 15]).

Let us now justify our decision to study non-deterministic multi-object version of TAM. Firstly, a given module may be designed in TAM to implement either a single object or a number of objects. There is a distinct difference in the complexity of TAM in these two cases. While introducing TAM we often limit our considerations to its single-object version, thus omitting certain problems (both syntactic and semantic) which arise in a more general case. In practical applications, however, a module is usually understood as an abstract data type, and a single-object module is treated as its special case, where there can be only one variable of that type. The present paper is a continuation and extension of [8] where TAM restricted to single-object modules was investigated and specifications were modelled as Mealy machines.

Secondly, non-determinism can be understood not only as a possible requirement (one may like to have a non-deterministic behavior of the program under development) but also as a certain philosophy in system design. A higher level of abstraction should leave as much freedom as possible to a specifier of a lower level which could be expressed in TAM by allowing non-deterministic modules. We think it is very important.

The structure of this paper is as follows. In Section 2 we present a formal model for multi-object modules. In Section 3 trace specifications for such modules are described. In Section 4 we show an example of a multi-object module that cannot be specified in the current version of TAM. A modified simple model of trace specifications which covers a wider class of non-determinism in multi-object modules is proposed in Section 5. Related changes in TAM and the expressiveness of a proposed version of TAM are discussed in Section 6. Final conclusions and future plans are briefly presented in Section 7.

2 A Formal Model for Multi-Object Modules

2.1 Introduction

We assume that time is discrete, linear, with an "initial" instant, and without a "final" one. Instants of time are represented by natural numbers.

The notion of an *object* can be characterized as follows. An object is any entity which has *states*, can be affected by *events*, and satisfies the following properties:

- at every instant of time the object is in one of its states; initially, the object is in the *initial* state,
- the object may change its state only as a result of an event; if the event occurs at the instant t, the object is in a new state at the instant $t + 1$.

Objects are grouped in modules: we say that a *module* implements a number of homogeneous and independent objects. If a module implements one object it is called a *single-object* module. A *multi-object* module can implement a given (including infinite) number of objects. In this paper we deal with multi-object modules.

Objects implemented by a given module are called *domestic*, while those implemented by other modules are called *foreign*. For each module there is a specific set of events that can affect its domestic objects.

There are two kinds of events that can affect an object:

- *access-program invocations* (calls of programs exported by the module),
- *input variable events* (changes of values of the module's input variables).

We assume that at most one event can occur at a given instant of time and that objects in the module can be affected only by a finite sequence of events.

In this paper we deal only with the first kind of events. However, we do not lose the generality of discussion since an input variable event can be expressed in terms of an access-program invocation. Input variables are described in detail in [2, 3, 14].

For each module there is a finite number of access-programs. Each access-program operates on at least one domestic object and possibly on foreign objects. As a result of an access-program invocation the arguments can change their states, possibly non-deterministically. For the sake of simplicity, we will treat values returned by functions as arguments which can change their states but with irrelevant initial values. For each access-program invocation, the next state of each argument depends only on the previous states of the arguments of this invocation. We assume that all arguments of access-programs are different objects. In practice, however, one object can be passed through several arguments of an access-program. This does not cause any loss of generality because we can model an access-program whose arguments might possibly represent the same objects by several access-programs whose arguments are always different objects. For example, an access-program P with two domestic arguments, which can represent the same object, can be modeled by two access programs:

- one with two domestic arguments (representing different objects passed as arguments of P), and
- one with only one domestic argument (representing one object passed through both arguments of P).

2.2 Modules

Def. 1 A *module* is the following tuple: (Q, q_0, O, F, I, E), where:
- Q is a non-empty set; its elements are called *states of domestic objects*,
- $q_0 \in Q$ and it is called the *initial state of domestic objects*,
- O is a non-empty set (possibly infinite); its elements are called *names of domestic objects*,
- F is a non-empty set; its elements are called *states of foreign objects*,
- I is a non-empty finite set; its elements are called *names of access-programs*,
- $E = (E_i)_{i \in I}$ is a sequence of relations $E_i \subseteq Q^{k_i} \times F^{l_i} \times Q^{k_i} \times F^{l_i}$ such that $k_i \in N$ (natural numbers), $1 \leq k_i \leq |O|$, and

$$\forall q \in Q^{k_i}, r \in F^{l_i} \exists q' \in Q^{k_i}, r' \in F^{l_i} [E_i(q, r, q', r')]$$

For each $i \in I$, E_i is a relation specifying changes of states of arguments of the access-program i. $E_i(q, r, q', r')$ means that if an invocation of the access-program i operates on certain domestic objects being in states q, and certain foreign objects being in states r, then the states of these objects after the invocation can be q', and r' respectively.

A tuple described in this definition can be treated as an extension of a Mealy machine — instead of a single state of an automaton we have many states of many objects.

Def. 2   A *state of a module* is a function $s:O \to Q$. It represents the states of all objects implemented by this module.

Def. 3   A *history of a module* is a function $H:N \to \wp\,(O \to Q)\setminus\{\varnothing\}$ (by $\wp\,(X)$ we denote the power set of X) such that $H(0) = \{s\}$, where $s(o) = q_0$ for all $o \in O$. It represents sets of possible states of this module at all instants of time. At the initial instant, all objects are in the initial state.

Def. 4   An *event* (i.e., an access-program invocation) is a tuple $e = (i, o, r)$, where:

- $i \in I$,
- $o \in O^{k_i}$ is a vector of different names of domestic objects; its elements identify domestic arguments of the event,
- $r \in F^{l_i}$ is a vector; its elements represent states of foreign arguments of the event.

Def. 5   An *output* of an event (i, o, r) is a vector $r' \in F^{l_i}$; its elements represent new states of foreign arguments of the event.

Def. 6   A *step of computation* is a pair $c = (e, r')$, where e is an event and r' is an output of e.

A step of computation represents externally (i.e. from outside of the module) observable aspects of an access-program invocation:

- which access-program is invoked,
- on which domestic objects the access-program operates,
- what are the states of passed foreign arguments, and
- what are the states of foreign arguments after the invocation.

Def. 7   A state s' of a module is *reachable* from a state s of the module in a step of computation $c = ((i, o, r), r')$ iff:

$$E_i\left(\left(s(o_1), ..., s\left(o_{k_i}\right)\right), r, \left(s'(o_1), ..., s'\left(o_{k_i}\right)\right), r'\right) \wedge$$

$$\forall j \in O\setminus\{o_1, ..., o_{k_i}\} \; [s(j) = s'(j)]$$

We denote it by $s \xrightarrow{c} s'$.

For a given $c = (e, r')$, $s \xrightarrow{c} s'$ means that if a module is in a state s, an event e takes place and new states of its foreign arguments are equal to r', then a new state of the module can be s'.

Def. 8   A *computation* is a finite sequence of steps of computation, $\left((e_j, r'_j)\right)_{j=0}^{m}$, where $m \geq -1$, $e_j = (i_j, o_j, r_j)$ is an event, and $r'_j \in F^{l_{i_j}}$ is an output of e_j.

A computation denotes externally observable aspects of a sequence of invocations of access-programs. For $m = -1$ this definition denotes an empty sequence of invocations.

Def. 9   We say that a history H *satisfies a computation* $C = (c_j)_{j=0}^{m}$ iff for all $t \in N$:

$$\left(t \le m \;\Rightarrow\; H(t+1) = \{ s' : O \to Q \mid \exists s \in H(t) \left[\, s \overset{c_t}{\to} s' \, \right] \} \right) \wedge$$
$$(t > m \;\Rightarrow\; H(t+1) = H(t)).$$

A history represents possible states of domestic objects during the computation. Notice that if there exists a history satisfying a given computation then there is only one such history.

Def. 10 We say that a computation is *feasible* if there exists a history satisfying this computation.

One should recall that the value of a history at a given instant of time is a non-empty set of possible states of the module. Hence, there can be (and usually are) computations that are not feasible.

The set of feasible computations fully characterizes an externally observable behavior of a module. According to the information-hiding principle, we often deal only with externally observable aspects of a module, i.e., we are not interested in the concrete states of domestic objects — we observe only the identity of domestic arguments and the values of foreign arguments of events. Hence, there can be several modules that cannot be externally distinguished.

Def. 11 We say that two modules are *observationally equivalent* iff they have the same sets of feasible computations.

Sometimes we are interested in reducing a module to a simpler, observationally equivalent module. A simple reduction can be done by removing states which can never appear.

Def. 12 The set A of *reachable states of objects* of a module $M = (Q, q_0, O, F, I, E)$ is the subset of Q of all states appearing in histories satisfying feasible computations:

$$A = \{ q \in Q \mid \exists C\text{-feasible}, H\text{-satisfying}\, C, t \in N, s \in H(t), o \in O \, [q = s(o)] \}$$

Notice that always $q_0 \in A$. Non-reachable states of a module do not appear in any history satisfying any feasible computation. Hence, they are irrelevant to the behavior of the module.

3 Trace Specifications of Multi-Object Modules

3.1 Trace-Modules

Def. 13 A *trace-module* is a module (Q, q_0, O, F, I, E) such that for each $i \in I$ there exist:

- a relation $R_i \subseteq Q^{k_i} \times F^{l_i} \times F^{l_i}$,
- a function $X_i : R_i \to Q^{k_i}$,

such that:
$$\forall q, q' \in Q^{k_i}, r, r' \in F^{l_i} \, [F_i(q, r, q', r') \Leftrightarrow R_i(q, r, r') \wedge X_i(q, r, r') = q'] \,.$$

R_i is called a *return relation* (between values of arguments of an access-program invocation and its output); X_i is called an *extension function* and describes the values of domestic arguments after this invocation, depending on the values of arguments and the output of the invocation.

Intuitively, a module (Q, q_0, O, F, I, E) is a trace-module iff for each $i \in I$ the relation E_i can be viewed as a composition of a relation (R_i) denoting new states of foreign arguments and a function (X_i) denoting new states of domestic arguments. Generally, states of trace-modules have simpler forms than states of modules — for each feasible computation and an instant of time, there is only one possible state of a trace-module.

Lemma 1: If M is a trace-module, C is a computation, H is a history satisfying C, and $t \in N$, then $H(t)$ is a singleton.

A proof of this lemma can be found in [5].

One should note that if the given module is deterministic, then it is also a trace-module, since for each $i \in I$, E_i is a function.

3.2 Traces

One of the basic notions in TAM is the notion of traces. Intuitively, a *trace* is a term describing a fragment of a computation of a trace-module, containing all steps of that computation that can influence the current state of a given object.

Def. 14 The set of *syntactically correct* traces of a trace-module $M = (Q, q_0, O, F, I, E)$ is the smallest set such that:

1. the empty trace, denoted by "_", is a syntactically correct trace, and

2. if $l \in I$, $r, r' \in F^l$, $T_1, ..., T_k$ are syntactically correct traces, then for each $1 \leq j \leq k_i$ the following term:

$$T_j . i\left(T_1, ..., T_{j-1}, *, T_{j+1}, ..., T_{k_i}, r, r' \right) \text{ if } T_j \neq \_, \text{ or}$$

$$i\left(T_1, ..., T_{j-1}, *, T_{j+1}, ..., T_{k_i}, r, r' \right) \text{ if } T_j = \_$$

is a syntactically correct trace.

This definition of syntactically correct traces is simplified, according to our model of modules (cf. Section 2.1). Detailed descriptions of traces can be found in [7, 14].

We use a dot (".") as an operator of concatenation of syntactically correct traces with the empty trace being neutral element (for each syntactically correct trace T, $T._{\_} = \_.T = T$).

Not all syntactically correct traces denote fragments of feasible computations of a trace-module.

Def. 15 Let $C = (c_i)_{i=0}^{m}$ be a feasible computation of a trace-module $M = (Q, q_0, O, F, I, E)$, H be a history satisfying C, $t \in N$ be an instant of time and $o \in O$ be an object. A *syntactically correct trace T representing the state of object o at instant t in computation C* (from lemma 1 we know that $H(t)$ is a singleton, and hence, there is only one such state) is defined as follows:

1. if $t = 0$ then $T =$ _ , and

2. if $0 < t \le m + 1$ then let $c_{t-1} = \left(\left(i, \left(o_1, ..., o_{k_i} \right), r \right), r' \right)$:

- if $o \notin \{ o_1, ..., o_{k_i} \}$, then T is equal to the trace representing the state of object o at instant $t - 1$,

- if $o = o_j$, $1 \le j \le k_i$, $T_1, ..., T_{k_i}$ are traces representing the states of objects $o_1, ..., o_{k_i}$ at instant $t - 1$, then:

$$T = T_j.i \left(T_1, ..., T_{j-1}, *, T_{j+1}, ..., T_{k_i}, r, r' \right), \text{ and}$$

3. if $t > m + 1$, then T is equal to the trace representing the state of object o at instant $m + 1$.

We also say that a syntactically correct trace T *represents a state* q if a feasible computation C, a history H satisfying C, an object $o \in O$ and an instant of time $t \in N$ exist such that $H(t) = \{s\}$ and $q = s(o)$.

Note that there can be many traces representing one state, but one syntactically correct trace can represent at most one state. One should also note that a state is represented by one or more traces iff it is a reachable state.

Def. 16 A syntactically correct trace of a trace-module is *feasible* iff it represents a state.

For each module, the empty trace ("_") is always feasible and represents the initial state of every object.

Further on in this section by "traces" we mean always "feasible traces". In TAM, states of domestic objects are represented by traces. However, a state is often represented by many traces.

Def. 17 Two traces T_1 and T_2 are *equivalent* $(T_1 \equiv T_2)$ iff they represent the same state.

Notice that "$\equiv$" is an equivalence relation. Thus we can represent states of domestic objects by the equivalence classes of "$\equiv$". In TAM we do not use the equivalence classes as such but we represent states of objects by the fixed representatives of the equivalence classes. These representatives are called *canonical traces*.

3.3 Trace Specifications

The goal of this paper is to study specifications of non-deterministic, multi-object modules. Without sacrificing generality, we will limit our considerations to non-parameterized specifications only. (Since the semantics of a parameterized specification for the given actual parameters is a non-parameterized specification, all our observations apply to parameterized specifications also).

A trace specification (i.e., a specification in TAM) of a module is a document consisting of the following five parts: Characteristics Section, Syntax Section, Canonical Section, Equivalence Section, Return Values Section. Precise descriptions of trace specifications can be found e.g. in [7, 14] Here, we only briefly summarize the contents of those sections. Example specifications can be found in [7, 9].

The Characteristics Section contains information about:

- the name of the module specified by the given specification,
- foreign modules used by this module; they implicitly define the set of states of foreign objects,
- the set of names of objects implemented by the module, and
- features of the module (e.g, whether it is single-object or multi-object).

The Syntax Section defines the set of access-programs and the types of their arguments. In particular, for each access-program, the Syntax Section defines the number of domestic and foreign arguments. The Syntax Section provides some information that is not expressed in our model, e.g., the order of domestic and foreign arguments for each access-program. In our model this order is fixed. Nor does our model distinguish types of foreign arguments. One should note that the Syntax Section implicitly defines the set of names of access-programs and the set of syntactically correct traces.

The Canonical Section defines the characteristic predicate (*canonical*) of the set of canonical traces. If the empty trace is not canonical, then this section explicitly defines a canonical trace representing the initial state. The set of canonical traces depends on the particular specification. In the rest of the specification, states of domestic objects are represented by canonical traces, i.e., the set of states of domestic objects is the set of canonical traces. This section of the specification can also define some auxiliary functions and/or relations used in the rest of the specification.

For each access-program, the Equivalence Section contains a definition of the *extension function*. The domain of this function contains states of all arguments of the access-program before the invocation and new states of all of its foreign arguments after the invocation. The range of this function contains new states of all domestic arguments of the access-program, and a sort of a marker (called *a token*) describing the correctness of the invocation. This marker is not expressed in our model. The correctness of the invocation has no effect on the behavior of the module. In the rest of this paper we will skip this aspect of extension functions. One can assume that every invocation is specified as a correct one.

The Return Values Section for each access-program defines a relation called the *return relation*. This is a relation between states of all arguments of the access-program before the invocation, and new states of all of its foreign arguments. This relation determines possible new states of foreign arguments of the access-program.

A trace specification can be modelled by a trace-module as follows:

- Q is the set of canonical traces,
- $q_0 \in Q$ is the canonical trace representing the initial state,
- O is the set of names of objects implemented by the module,
- F is the union of sets of canonical traces of foreign modules,
- I is the set of names of access-programs,
- E_i is such that:

$$\forall q, q' \in Q^{k_i}, r, r' \in F^{l_i} [E_i(q, r, q', r') \Leftrightarrow R_i(q, r, r') \wedge X_i(q, r, r') = q']$$

where R_i is a return relation and X_i is an extension function for an access-program i.

A trace-module thus defined is called the *trace-module obtained from a trace specification*.

Def. 18 We say that a *module satisfies a trace specification* iff it is observationally equivalent to the trace-module obtained from the trace specification. In this case we also say that the *specification specifies the module*.

We are not only able to represent trace specifications by trace-modules but we can specify every trace-module, which is more interesting.

Theorem: For each trace-module there exists a trace specification satisfied by this module.

A proof of this theorem can be found in [5].

This theorem proves that the class of modules that can be specified in TAM is equal to the class of modules observationally equivalent to certain trace-modules. One should also note that since every deterministic module is a trace-module, every deterministic module can be specified in TAM.

4 Non-Determinism Non-Expressible in the Trace Assertion Method

In this section we prove (by providing a counter-example) that not every non-deterministic multi-object module can be specified in TAM.

Theorem: There exists a module that does not satisfy any trace specification.

Proof: Let $M = (Q, q_0, O, F, I, E)$ be a module, where:

- $Q = \wp(\{0, 1\})$,
- $q_0 = \varnothing$,
- $O = \{a, b\}$,
- $F = \{0, 1, true, false\}$,
- $I = \{Ins, In, Cross\}$,
- $E_{Ins} \subseteq Q \times F \times Q \times F$,
  $E_{Ins}(q, r, q', r') \equiv r' = r \wedge q' = q \cup (\{r\} \cap \{0, 1\})$,
- $E_{In} \subseteq Q \times F \times Q \times F$, $E_{In}(q, r, q', r') \equiv q = q' \wedge r' = (r \in q)$,
- $E_{Cross} \subseteq Q^2 \times Q^2$,
  $E_{Cross}(q_1, q_2, q'_1, q'_2) \equiv q_1 \cup q_2 = q'_1 \cup q'_2 \wedge q'_1 \cap q'_2 = \varnothing$.

The module M implements two sets that both can contain two elements, 0 and 1, with the following operations:

- *Ins* inserts an element into a set,
- *In* checks if an element is in a set,
- *Cross* takes two sets and divides non-deterministically their union into two disjoint sets.

We will show that there does not exist a trace specification satisfied by M.

The proof is by contradiction. Let us assume that such a trace specification X exists. Let $\bar{M} = \left(Q, \bar{q}_0, O, F, I, E \right)$ be a trace-module obtained from X.

Let us consider the following computations:

$$C_1 = (((Ins, a, 1), 1), ((Cross, a, b)), ((In, a, 1), true), ((In, b, 1), false)),$$

$$C_2 = (((Ins, a, 1), 1), ((Cross, a, b)), ((In, b, 1), true), ((In, a, 1), false)),$$

$$C_3 = (((Ins, a, 1), 1), ((Cross, a, b)), ((In, a, 1), true), ((In, b, 1), true)).$$

C_1 and C_2 are feasible computations for M and hence also for $\bar{M}$ but C_3 is not feasible for M. This means that when we insert 1 into set a, and then apply the access-program $Cross$ to sets a and b, 1 is in one of these sets but not in both.

We will obtain the contradiction by proving that the computation C_3 is feasible for module $\bar{M}$.

Let H_1, H_2 be two histories of a trace-module $\bar{M}$ satisfying, respectively, computations C_1 and C_2. H_1 and H_2 have the same first two elements and hence, $H_1(2) = H_2(2)$. From lemma 1, $H_1(t)$ and $H_2(t)$ are singletons (for each $t \in N$). Let $H_1(2) = H_2(2) = \{s_1\}$, $H_1(3) = \{s_2\}$, and $H_2(3) = \{s_3\}$.

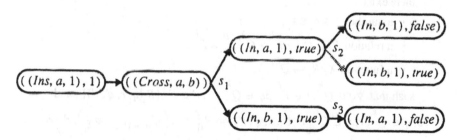

Notice that $s_1(b) = s_2(b)$ because $C_{1,2} = C_{3,2} = ((In, a, 1), true)$ cannot change the state of object b, and $s_1(a) = s_3(a)$ because $C_{2,2} = ((In, b, 1), true)$ cannot change the state of object a.

To prove that C_3 is feasible for $\bar{M}$ we show that for $C_{3,3} = ((In, b, 1), true)$ there exists a state s_4 of a trace-module $\bar{M}$ such that $s_2 \overset{C_{3,3}}{\longrightarrow} s_4$. Notice that $C_{3,3}$ cannot change the value of object a, so $s_4(a) = s_2(a)$. On the other hand, $s_4(b) = s_3(b)$ because $s_2(b) = s_1(b)$ and $C_{3,3} = C_{2,2} = ((In, b, 1), true)$. Hence, state s_4 can be defined as follows:

$$s_4(j) = \begin{cases} s_2(a) & \text{if } j = a \\ s_3(b) & \text{if } j = b \end{cases}$$

Notice that for $z = ((In, a, 1), true)$ also $s_3 \overset{z}{\rightarrow} s_4$.

A history H_3 satisfying computation C_3 is defined as follows:

$$H_3(t) = \begin{cases} H_1(t) & \text{if } t \leq 3 \\ \{s_4\} & \text{if } t > 3 \end{cases}$$

Thus, computation C_3 is feasible for $\overline{M}$ but not feasible for M. Module $\overline{M}$ is not observationally equivalent to M, and M does not satisfy X. ∎

5 "New" Trace-Modules

We will now redefine the notion of trace-modules in such a way, that for every module there exists an observationally equivalent "new trace-module". This reduces the problem of specification of multi-object modules in TAM to that of specification of new trace-modules.

Def. 19 A *new trace-module* is such a module (Q, q_0, O, F, I, E) that for each E_i there exist:

- a number $1 \leq p_i \leq k_i$,
- a relation $R_i \subseteq Q^{k_i} \times F^{l_i} \times Q^{k_i - p_i} \times F^{l_i}$,
- a function $X_i : R_i \to Q^{p_i}$,

such that $\forall q \in Q^{k_i}, r \in F^{l_i} \exists q' \in Q^{k_i - p_i}, r' \in F^{l_i} [R_i(q, r, q', r')]$, and

$$\forall q, q' \in Q^{k_i}, r, r' \in Q^{l_i} \Big[E_i(q, r, q', r') \Leftrightarrow R_i \Big(q, r, \Big(q'_{p_i + 1}, ..., q'_{k_i} \Big), r' \Big) \wedge$$
$$X_i \Big(q, r, \Big(q'_{p_i + 1}, ..., q'_{k_i} \Big), r' \Big) = \Big(q'_1, ..., q'_{p_i} \Big) \Big]$$

R_i is called a *return relation*, X_i is called an *extension function* and p_i is called a *number of primary domestic arguments* of access-program i. The largest p_i is called the *maximum number of primary domestic arguments* of access-program i.

Intuitively, in new trace-modules we allow new states of some domestic arguments to be specified by the return relation. One should note that for a given new trace-module and the numbers of primary domestic arguments, for each access-program there exist exactly one return relation and one extension function.

Each trace-module is also a new trace-module (for $p_i = k_i$); however, the class of new trace-modules is wider than the class of trace-modules.

Theorem: For each module M, there exists a new trace-module $\overline{M}$ observationally equivalent to M.

A proof of this theorem can be found in [5].

6 "New" Trace Specifications

The basic difference between new trace-modules and trace-modules is in the definition of the extension function:

- in trace-modules, an extension function determines new states of all domestic arguments of an access-program,
- in new trace-modules, an extension function defines only new values of some (at least one) domestic arguments, called *the primary (domestic) arguments*; possible new values of the rest of domestic arguments, called *the secondary (domestic) arguments*, are defined by the return relation.

This difference is reflected by including within a new-trace, new-traces that denote new states of the secondary domestic arguments. It also changes the interpretation of traces. A trace represents a new value of one of the primary domestic arguments of its last invocation.

Def. 20 Let $M = (Q, q_0, O, F, I, E)$ be a new trace-module and $(p_i)_{i \in I}$ be the maximum numbers of primary domestic arguments of access-programs. The set of *syntactically correct new-traces of M* is the smallest set such that:

1. the empty trace, denoted by "_", is a syntactically correct new-trace, and

2. if $i \in I$, $1 \leq j \leq u \leq p_i$, $r, r' \in F^i$, $T_1, ..., T_{k_i}$ and $U_{u+1}, ..., U_{k_i}$ are syntactically correct new-traces, then the following term:

$$T_j . i \left(T_1, ..., T_{j-1}, *, T_{j+1}, ..., T_{k_i}, r, U_{u+1}, ..., U_{k_i}, r' \right) \text{ if } T_j \neq \_, \text{ or}$$

$$i \left(T_1, ..., T_{j-1}, *, T_{j+1}, ..., T_{k_i}, r, U_{u+1}, ..., U_{k_i}, r' \right) \text{ if } T_j = \_$$

is a syntactically correct new-trace.

Numbers of primary arguments influence the form of new-traces in such a way that a new-trace includes sub-new-traces describing new states of all secondary arguments of access-program invocations. This definition allows all possible numbers of primary arguments, i.e., from 1 to the maximum number of primary arguments $(1 \leq u \leq p_i)$. However, the simplest, not redundant form is for the maximum number of primary arguments $(u = p_i)$.

The definition of feasibility of new-traces and the definition of feasible new-traces representing states are more complex and can be found in [5].

We allow new-traces with different numbers of primary arguments, however the most expressible are new-traces with the maximum number of primary arguments. They contain the fewest sub-new-traces representing new states of secondary domestic arguments, and they can represent new states of the largest number of domestic arguments. Each new-trace with the number of primary arguments less than the maximum can be easily transformed to one with the maximum number of primary arguments by removing some of sub-new-traces denoting new states of secondary domestic arguments.

The equivalence relation on feasible new-traces ("$\equiv$") and the set of canonical new-traces can be defined the same way as for traces. However, it can happen that some of reachable states cannot be represented by any feasible new-trace. We discuss the consequences of this fact later on.

Def. 21 We say that a state $q \in Q$ of an object implemented by a new trace-module $M = (Q, q_0, O, F, I, E)$ is *trace-expressible* if there exists a feasible new-trace representing q.

The form of a new trace specification is similar to the form of a trace specification. The form of the Characteristics Section is the same. The Syntax Section defines also numbers of primary arguments of access-programs. It defines implicitly the subset of new-traces used in the specification. The Canonical Section defines a set of canonical new-traces and a canonical new-trace representing the initial state. The Equivalence Section defines an extension function for each access program. The range of this function contains only canonical new-traces, representing new states of the primary arguments. The Return Values Section defines a return relation for each access program. However, this relation is defined on states of all arguments passed to the access-program, and new states of all secondary domestic arguments and all foreign arguments of the access-program.

A new trace specification can be modelled as a new trace-module (Q, q_0, O, F, I, E) in the following way:

- Q is the set of canonical new-traces,
- q_0 is the canonical new-trace representing the initial state,
- O is the set of names of objects implemented by the module,
- F is the union of sets of canonical traces of all foreign modules,
- I is the set of names of access programs,
- for each $i \in I$, E_i is a relation defined as follows:

$$\forall q, q' \in Q^{k_i}, r, r' \in F^{l_i} \Big[E_i(q, r, q', r') \Leftrightarrow R_i\Big(q, r, r', \Big(q'_{p_i + 1}, ..., q'_{k_i} \Big) \Big) \wedge$$
$$X_i\Big(q, r, r', \Big(q'_{p_i + 1}, ..., q'_{k_i} \Big) \Big) = \Big(q'_1, ..., q'_{p_i} \Big) \Big]$$

An example specification of the module with the "Cross" access-program (cf. Section 4) can be found in [5].

It turns out that not all new trace-modules can be specified in the proposed version of TAM. It can happen that some of the reachable states are not trace-expressible. In such a case we are simply unable to represent these states in the specification. But if all reachable states of a new trace-module are trace-expressible then we can specify such a module in the proposed version of TAM.

Theorem: Let $M = (Q, q_0, O, F, I, E)$ be a new trace-module. If all reachable states of M are trace-expressible, then there exists a new trace specification satisfied by M.

A proof of this theorem can be found in [5].

A class of modules which can be specified in the proposed version of TAM is the class of modules observationally equivalent to some new trace-modules having all (reachable) states trace-expressible.

7 Conclusions

The main goal of this paper was to investigate the expressiveness of TAM. As it was proved in [8], every single-object module can be specified in TAM. Also every deterministic multi-object module can be specified in TAM. However, there exists a non-deterministic multi-object module which cannot be specified in TAM.

We have defined a sub-class of modules (called trace-modules) which effectively characterizes the expressiveness of TAM. Each trace-module can be specified in TAM and each specification can be modelled by a trace-module. Hence, the class of multi-object modules which can be specified in TAM is the class of modules observationally equivalent to some trace-modules. This situation can be illustrated by the following diagram:

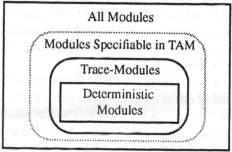

We have also proposed some modifications in TAM and we have defined an appropriate sub-class of modules (called new trace-modules) to model specifications in the proposed version of TAM. It is a property of this class that each module is observationally equivalent to some new trace-module. We have extended the expressiveness of TAM, although we have not covered the whole class of non-deterministic multi-object modules. Not all new trace-modules can be specified in the proposed version of TAM because it can happen that some (reachable) states of objects implemented by the module cannot be expressed by traces.

If we could express by traces all (reachable) states of objects implemented by new trace-modules then we would be able to specify all modules in TAM. This problem still limits the usefulness of TAM in specification of some non-deterministic multi-object modules. Extension of the expressiveness of traces, to cover all reachable states of new trace-modules, will be one of our goals in future research.

Acknowledgements

This paper emerged from many discussions on TAM we have had in Hamilton (with D.L. Parnas and his group), in Hull, and in Warsaw. We are very grateful to all our colleagues for their contribution, and especially to J. Mincer-Daszkiewicz and K. Stencel.

This work was partly supported by the Natural Sciences and Engineering Research Council of Canada (NSERC), by the State Committee for Scientific Research in Poland (KBN, grant 8 S503 040 04), by Digital Equipment's European External Research Programme (EERP PL-002), and by NATO Linkage grant (HTECH.LG.941314).

References

1. Bartussek, W., Parnas, D.L., "Using Traces to Write Abstract Specifications for Software Modules", in Gehani, N., McGettrick, A.D. (Eds.), *Software Specification Techniques*, AT&T Bell Telephone Laboratories, 1985, pp. 111-130.

2. Bojanowski, J., Iglewski, M., Madey, J., Obaid, A., "Functional Approach to Protocol Specification", in *Protocol Specification, Testing and Verification XIV*, Vuong, S.T., Chanson, S.T. (Eds.), Chapman & Hall, 1995, pp. 395-402.

3. Erskine, N., "The Usefulness of the Trace Assertion Method for Specifying Device Module Interfaces", *CRL Report* No. 258, McMaster Univ., CRL, Telecommun. Res. Inst. of Ontario (TRIO), Hamilton, Ont., Canada, 1992.

4. Hoffman, D.M., "The Trace Specification of Communications Protocols", *IEEE Trans. on Computers*, Vol. C-34, No. 12, Dec.r 1985, pp. 1102-1113.

5. Iglewski, M., Kubica, M, Madey, J., "Trace Specifications of Non-deterministic Multi-object Modules", *Technical Report* TR 95-05 (205), Warsaw Univ., Inst. of Informatics, Warsaw, Poland, 1995.

6. Iglewski, M., Kubica, M, Madey, J.,"Editor for the Trace Assertion Method", in: *Proc. 10th Int. Conf. of CAD/CAM, Robotics and Factories of the Future: CARs & FOF'94*, Zaremba, M. (Ed.), OCRI, Ottawa, Ont., Canada, 1994, pp. 876-881.

7. Iglewski, M., Madey, J., Parnas, D.L., Kelly, P.C., "Documentation Paradigms", *CRL Report* No. 270, McMaster Univ., CRL, Telecommun. Res. Inst. of Ontario (TRIO), Hamilton, Ont., Canada, 1993.

8. Iglewski, M., Madey, J., Stencel, K., "On Fundamentals of the Trace Assertion Method", *Technical Report* TR 94-09 (198), Warsaw Univ., Inst. of Informatics, Warsaw, Poland, 1994.

9. Iglewski, M., Mincer-Daszkiewicz., J., Stencel, K., "Some Experiences with Specification of Non-deterministic Modules", *Technical Report* RR 94/09-7, Université du Québec à Hull, Département d'Informatique, Hull, Québec, Canada, 1994.

10. Iglewski, M., Kubica, M., Madey, J., Mincer-Daszkiewicz, J., Stencel, K., "Report of the Trace Assertion Method 95", *in preparation*.

11. McLean, J.D., "A Formal Foundation for the Abstract Specification of Software", *Journal of the ACM*, Vol. 31, No. 3, July 1984, pp. 600-627.

12. Parnas, D.L., "On the Criteria to be used in Decomposing Systems into Modules", *Commun. ACM*, Vol. 15, No. 12, Dec. 1972, pp. 1053-1058.

13. Parnas, D.L., Madey, J., "Functional Documents for Computer Systems", *Science of Computer Programming*, to appear in 1995.

14. Parnas, D.L., Wang, Y., "The Trace Assertion Method of Module Interface Specification", *Technical Report* 89-261, Queen's Univ., C&IS, Telecommun. Res. Inst. of Ontario (TRIO), Kingston, Ont., Canada, 1989.

15. Wang, Y., "Specifying and Simulating the Externally Observable Behavior of Modules", (Ph.D. Thesis), *CRL Report* No. 292, McMaster Univ., CRL, Telecommun. Res. Inst. of Ontario (TRIO), Hamilton, Ont., Canada, 1994.

ESP-MC: An Experiment in the Use of Verification Tools*

Xiaojun Chen[1], Paola Inverardi[2], Carlo Montangero[3]

[1] Dip. di Scienze dell'Informazione, Università di Roma "La Sapienza"
[2] Dip. di Matematica Pura ed Applicata, Università di L'Aquila
[3] Dip. di Scienze dell'Informazione, Università di Pisa

Abstract. We present an experiment of applying existing verification tools for process algebra, namely ACTL model checker and AUTO, to a system based on parallel logic programming: Extended Shared Prolog (ESP). The constructed tool ESP-MC (a semi-automatic model checker for ESP) models value passing by suitably expanding all the data that influence the control part of the specification. The same expansion of data is performed both in the generated model and in the logic formulae. In this way symbolic formulae can be proved on a finite model of the ESP program, which provides the base for the analysis of the properties in the infinite ESP models.

1 Introduction

This paper describes an approach to support the analysis and the verification of properties of systems specified in Extended Shared Prolog (ESP) [1], a logic programming language based on the blackboard paradigm. The ESP-MC (Model Checker for ESP) is obtained as the result of applying existing verification tools for process algebra [3, 11, 14], namely AUTO [8] and ACTL Model Checker [15].

ESP is a coordination language used to describe software processes in Oikos [1], a software process environment. In order to characterize software process systems, ESP extends the integration of the blackboard and logic programming, by introducing a hierarchy of blackboards. In ESP, agents work in parallel, and the communication and interaction among agents are allowed only via blackboards, which may contain any facts (prolog atoms). ESP has been given an operational semantics [5] based on labelled transition systems (lts for short) by using partial specifications with predicates [2]. A notion of *observation* is defined on the input/output sequences of facts from/to the external world. The goal of the present work is to provide a semi-automatic support for the analysis of ESP systems properties.

The idea of using already existing verification tools for process algebras is based on the fact that both ESP and process algebras have an lts operational semantics [17] and that the considered tools use lts as internal representation of processes. Then it is necessary to see how ESP system properties can be verified

---

* Research partially supported by HCM Express

in terms of the properties of the corresponding lts in the process algebras tool considered.

AUTO is a verification system for process calculi with the facility of bisimulation equivalence proving. The main functionality of AUTO is the construction and manipulation of *automata*. There are many functions for constructing automata because most of them apply reductions at intermediate levels with respect to a variety of user parameterized semantics (strong and weak bisimulation, trace equivalence, elimination of τ-loops and single τ-transitions, transitive closure of τ transition). These reductions enable the size of the automata to be smaller. Functions to explore and display automata are provided as well. Moreover, there are functions which allow the user to check two automata for equivalence according to strong, weak and branching bisimulation.

The propositional branching time temporal logic CTL [4, 9, 10] is a subset of the full-branching time logic CTL*. It shows its usefulness mainly due to two facts: (i) its expressibility is good enough for many applications; (ii) there exists efficient model checker to verify the truth of its formulas in a given model [7]. ACTL [15] is an action-based version of CTL. It is interpreted on labelled transition systems instead of on Kripke Structure as in CTL, and the verification of formulas can also be done in linear time.

AUTO has been integrated with ACTL in order to obtain a general verification environment which enables the user to verify both bisimulation equivalences and ACTL properties.

Taking this approach, we simply have to transform an ESP system into its corresponding lts. In this way, the notion of observation mentioned above can be straightforwardly obtained by using the *equivalences* functionalities in AUTO on the ESP automata. Furthermore, thanks to the model checking capabilities, we can either prove logical properties on a single ESP system, or obtain examples which cause an ESP system to fail to satisfy a property.

The main problem here is that these tools can only be applied to finite state structures while ESP models are infinite ones: (i) an ESP system may contain evolving structures; (ii) an ESP system may exhibit arbitrary complex sequences of ESP facts in the actions. Here we do not consider ESP systems with evolving structures. For point (ii), there are basically two approaches: In [14], value passing CCS is considered as notational shorthand of basic CCS. But the basic CCS expansion might be too large for automatic verification. The other approach is to introduce parameterized transition systems to represent infinite structures, e.g. [12]. Data are separated into two classes: the one that influences the control part (i.e. data that are tested by *if* or changed by a function), and the one that has nothing to do with the control part. The idea is then to expand the former set of data, leaving the latter one unexpanded, and to concentrate on the cases in which the former set is finite.

Our experiment follows this second approach. However, in ESP system, data that influence the control part are still infinite, and it is not straightforward to classify the infinite states into finite ones. At this point, the verification of ESP programs is supposed to be done by top-level induction based on the properties of the finite parts of the systems: We discuss finite interactions between a system and its environment, and conditions are assumed to guarantee that, in the case of finite interactions, the generated model is a finite state transition system.

So far the verifications is given on the finite parts of the system. In the following, when there is no confusion, we will also call such finite parts of the systems/models as ESP systems/models. These models can then be considered as an automata generated by AUTO. Since automata in AUTO are represented in a standard format FC2 [13], the lts of ESP is written in FC2 as well. In this way, we can use all the AUTO functionalities on automata: minimization, bisimulation, graphical display, etc. The minimized automata obtained from AUTO for a given ESP system can be given to the ACTL Model Checker to verify logic properties. Due to the fact that the actions contain complex ESP facts, the properties we want to check are first order logic formulas. This implies that they cannot directly be expressed as ACTL propositional formulae. Our solution to this problem is to give an integrated expansion of data both in the generated model and in the logic formulae: the same information used for the expansion of data when generating the lts is used to instantiate first order logic formulas into propositional ones. In this way the symbolic formulae can be proven on a model of the ESP program.

The internal structure of our ESP-MC tool is illustrated in Figure 1. The

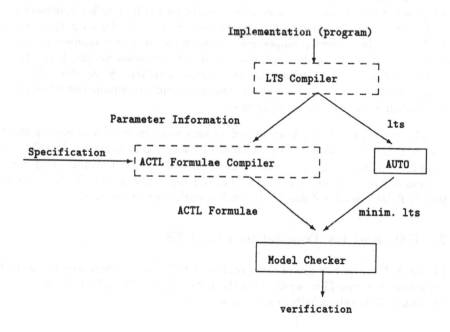

Fig. 1. internal structure of tool ESP-MC

LTS Compiler receives the ESP implementation (ESP program + initial state) and produces the lts; the produced lts is given to AUTO, and the minimized lts resulting from AUTO is given to the ACTL Model Checker. The ACTL Formula Compiler receives the specification of the properties as first order formulae (i.e. with variables), and creates the proper ACTL propositional formulae. The action variables which appear in the property are unified with the facts (prolog atoms) in the initial state of the system. In doing so, the ACTL model checker makes use of the information (from the LTS Compiler) related to the lts representing the ESP system under verification.

In the following, we give an informal presentation of a small system, called Client-and-Server, which is taken from the Oikos project. Some of the tipical properties we are interested in for verification are also listed. In this paper, we will describe a simplified version of this system in ESP language, and show how these properties are expressed and verified in our tool ESP-MC.

Example 1. The Client-and-Server system contains a database of documents. Users (*clients*) can modify this database by applying a *transaction* for editing a document in it. Such an application might be refused by the system if the document is in use. Once a user owns a transaction, he can repeatedly edit the acquired document before applying to terminate this transaction. Clients cannot access the database directly: modifications are done through *servers*, which filter commands from users, create and keep the transactions on the documents, while refusing requests to access a document already owned by another transaction.

Properties to be satisfied by this system include: (i) for each transaction application, the system prompts one and only one of two responses: accepted or refused; (ii) if the application is accepted, a transaction number is returned, which must not conflict with other transaction numbers in use; (iii) after the application to terminate a transaction, the command to continue this transaction (to edit the same document) is ignored.

The rest of the paper is organized in this way: In section 2, after a short review of ESP and its formalism in labelled transition systems, we describe our compiler which constructs a finite transition system under certain conditions; Section 3 gives a short review of ACTL and describes the ACTL Compiler in tool ESP-MC. Section 4 deals with final remarks and future work.

2   ESP and Its Translation into LTS

In this section, we first give a short review of ESP and its formalism in labelled transition systems. Then we describe the LTS Compiler for ESP and discuss the conditions to obtain a finite transition system.

2.1   A Short Review of ESP and Its Formalism

ESP is based on the blackboard model of problem solving. This model is oriented to partition the knowledge into distinct subsets, in order to keep domain knowledge separated from control knowledge and to organize communications via a centralized data structure, namely, the blackboard.

ESP extends the blackboard paradigm by introducing a hierarchy of blackboards. A blackboard system in ESP is a tree whose nodes are blackboards. A blackboard may contain any prolog atoms, also called *facts*, which do not need to be ground, and may contain *agents*. The blackboard an agent belongs to is the source of messages for it, and each agent has a list of target blackboards where it can send its outputs.

Agents work in parallel, and communication and interaction among agents are allowed via blackboards only. Read and write on the same blackboard are mutually exclusive. The behaviour of an agent is defined by means of a theory. A theory has a name, a set of activation patterns, and a prolog program. The theory's name may contain parameters. The instantiation of the parameters is propagated to all the patterns in the theory.

For each agent, at one time, only one pattern may be (nondeterministically) activated. A pattern has the form

{In-guard} Read-guard | Body {Out-set}

which specifies: (i) a set of atoms to be consumed before the pattern can be activated (In-guard); (ii) some conditions to be verified on the blackboard before the pattern can be activated (Read-guard); (iii) the initial goal of the logic program of the pattern (Body); (iv) sets of atoms that will be written on the blackboards at the end of the activation (Out-set).

The verification of guards adopts unification and the obtained substitution is propagated to the rest of the pattern.

Example 2. The Client_and_Server system sketched in the Introduction, is described in ESP in the following way: there are two blackboards named *client* and *server* respectively. Blackboard *client* contains facts *edit(u1,d)*, *continue(0)*, etc. representing the requests from the users, and several agents each of them serving a client. Blackboard *server* contains facts like *doc(d,c)* representing the documents managed by the server. It also holds a fact *trans(0)* that allows to start transactions identifying them uniquely. Besides, the *server* holds multiple copies of the agent *manager*, to create and keep the transactions on the documents, and to refuse access requests to a document already owned by another transaction.

Figure 2 gives a graphic view of an initial state: the blackboards are represented by boxes with their names in the up-left corners. Agents are denoted by a circle with arrows (from the agent to the blackboard or outside) for its targets. In this figure, there are two agents in *client*, and only one in *server*.

In Table 1, we give the two theories for the agents in the example, respectively. The agents in the blackboard *client* execute according to the first theory (*user*) and the agents in *server* according to the second one (*transaction_manager*).

In the first theory, we have two parameters (separated from name *user* by symbol ":-"): the user identifier U and the coordinate blackboard named *Server*.

theory *user(U, Server)* :-
      {*edit(U, D)*}
      |
      {*apply(U, D)*}@*Server*
      #
      {*applied(U, D, K)*}
      |
      {*applied(U, D, K)*}@*Out*
      #
      {*busy(U, D)*}
      |
      {*busy(U, D)*}@*Out*
      #
      {*continue(K)*} *trans(U, K)*
      |
      {*continue(K)*}@*Server*
      #
      {*terminate(K)*, *trans(U, K)*} not *continue(K)*
      |
      {*terminate(K)*}@*Server*
      #
      {*terminated(K)*}
      |
      {*terminated(K)*}@*Out*

theory *transaction_manager(Client)* :-
      {*apply(U, D)*, *trans(K)*, *doc(D, C)*} $K1$ is $K + 1$
      | *change(C, C1)*
      {*in_use(D, C1, K)*, *trans(K1)*}
      {*trans(U, K)*, *applied(U, D, K)*}@*Client*
      #
      {*apply(U, D)*} not *doc(D, _)*
      |
      {*busy(U, D)*}@*Client*
      #
      {*continue(K)*, *in_use(D, C, K)*}
      | *change(C, C1)*
      {*in_use(D, C1, K)*}
      #
      {*terminate(K)*, *in_use(D, C, K)*} not *continue(K)*
      |
      {*doc(D, C)*}
      {*terminate(K)*}@*Client*
  with *change(C, C1)* :- ......

Table 1. theories *user* and *transaction_manager*

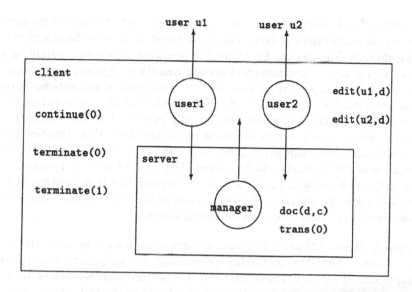

Fig. 2. initial state of Client_and_Server

Server is instantiated to *server* while *U* should be instantiated to *u1*, *u2* for user *user1*, *user2* respectively. The first pattern (patterns are separated by "#") of the theory *user* consumes the fact *edit(U,D)* from the blackboard *client*. This is a request of the user *U* from outside to start a transaction, and sends the fact *apply(U,D)* to the target blackboard *Server* which is instantiated to *server* (target blackboard is denoted by symbol "@" while the agent's own blackboard may be omitted as target).

This request can be accepted by the *transaction_manager* on *server* provided that *doc(D,C)* exists on this blackboard, i.e. that document *D* is free to use. This is expressed by the first pattern of the *transaction_manager*, which consumes facts *apply(U,D)*, *doc(U,D)*, augments the current transaction number *K* (consuming *trans(K)* and putting back *trans(K1)*), and gives response *applied(U,D,K)* to the client: user *U* owns transaction *K*. After the execution of this pattern, fact *doc(D,C)* is consumed while *in_use(D,C1,K)* appears. Here *C1* is introduced by the particular *change(C,C1)* in the body (the clauses following the keyword *with*), which represents the editing of a document and the change of its contents from *C* to *C1*.

A complete description of ESP as an lts is given in [5] using partial specifications with predicates in abstract data type. We recall that *labelled transition system* is a triple $(S, A, \rightarrow)$ where S is the set of states, A the set of labells, and $\rightarrow \subseteq S \times A \times S$ is the transition relationship. A *state* is described as a data type containing global information, a set of agents and a set of states of its subsystems, where a subsystem is defined again as a system since we have a hierarchy of blackboards. The axioms for transition predicates are given mainly in two levels, namely agent transitions and system transitions. System transitions are built up using the agent transitions and the transitions of subsystems, according to the SMoLCS methodology [2]. The procedure of the computation of the pattern bodies is left unspecified: we are only interested in the verification of communications among agents by means of the guards in their theories and of the blackboards hierarchically organized. See appendix for more details on the translation of ESP systems into lts, examplified by the Client_and_Server.

A notion of observation is defined on the sequences of input/output of facts from/to outside: the exchange of messages among blackboards inside the system is considered as invisible, denoted by special action τ.

Example 3. In our Client_and_Server, an action sequence can be a stream of users' requests (starting/continuing/terminating a transaction) and system's prompts indicating for example that the request has been refused or that the transaction is terminated. The activation of patterns of the *transaction_manager* is invisible because all facts on the blackboard *server* are assumed to be produced by agents on the blackboard *client*. Fact *edit(u1,d)* on *client* however is considered as input from user, and thus the activation of the first pattern of theory *user* is visible.

The invisible actions, on the other hand, include the requirements sending to blackboard *server* by agents in blackboard *client* and the responses sending to blackboard *client* from agent *transition_manager*. For the theory *user*, the output of the first pattern in order to apply a transaction from *server* is invisible, while the output *applied(U,D,K)* of the second pattern is visible. This output models a prompt answer to the user that the request of starting a transaction is applied with transaction number K.

Figure 3 shows the autograph [18] of the minimized lts for the Client_and_Server example with initial state in Figure 2. Note that usually, the outputs contain two parts: the targets and the facts. In our example, since "users" is always the only target, we omit it for simplicity.

2.2 LTS Compiler for ESP

The LTS Compiler for ESP is the main part of the tool ESP-MC: creating the lts from a given ESP program. It considers a simplified version of the previously defined labelled transition system for ESP: (i) we ignore the data types and the state correctness check for sake of simplicity; (ii) in order to be able to generate an LTS from an ESP system, we require a technical condition, i.e. the guards in the theory of an agent should be more general than the facts on the blackboard where the agent belongs ("more general" in the sense of unification); (iii) we assume that the ESP system has a finite number of input facts. (iv) For the moment, in order to obtain a finite lts, we adopt the following sufficient

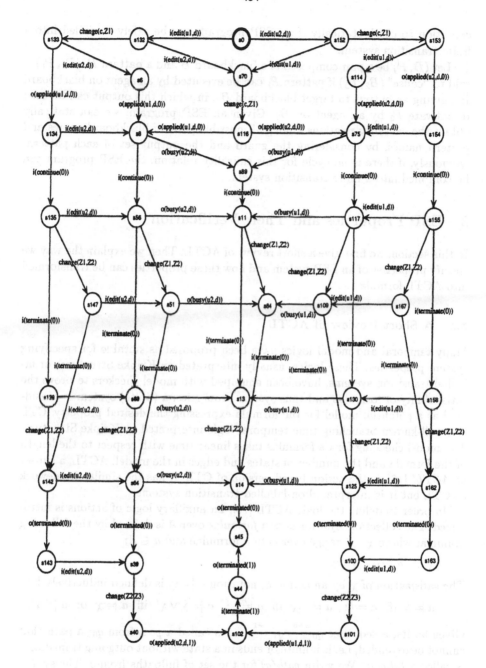

Fig. 3. autograph of the minimized lts for Client_and_Server

condition to check statically if an ESP program can be safely compiled into a finite transition system.

Let (B, P) be a pair composed of a blackboard B and a pattern P. (B_1, P_1) is said to "cause" (B_2, P_2) if pattern P_1 can be executed by an agent on blackboard B_1, giving an output to target blackboard B_2, in which this output can be used to activate P_2 by an agent on B_2. Given an ESP program, we can statically obtain the causality relations among all possible pairs of blackboard names and pattern names, by considering the guard and the output set of each pattern. Obviously, if there is no cycle for this causality relation, the ESP program can be compiled into a finite transition system.

3 ESP Properties and Their Verification

In this section, we first give a short review of ACTL. Then we explain the way we specify properties of an ESP system and how these properties can be transformed into ACTL formula.

3.1 A Short Review of ACTL

Many temporal and modal logics have been proposed as suitable for specifying system properties. These logics, usually interpreted on Kripke Structures or labelled transition systems, have been equipped with model checkers to prove the satisfiability of formulae and thus system properties: a (finite) system is considered as a potential model for the formula expressing the desired property. CTL is a well-known branching time temporal logic interpreted on Kripke Structure. The model checking for its formulas takes linear time with respect to the length of the formula and the number of states and edges in the model. ACTL, a subset of $ACTL^*$ [16], is the action-based version of CTL: it has the similar framework as CTL but it is interpreted on labelled transition systems.

In order to define the logic ACTL [16], an auxiliary logic of actions is introduced. The collection $Afor$ for *action formulae* over A is defined by the following grammar where χ, χ' range over action formulae and $a \in A$:

$$\chi ::= a \mid \neg\chi \mid \chi \vee \chi'$$

The satisfaction of χ by an action a, notation $a \models \chi$, is defined inductively by

$$a \models b \text{ iff } a = b; \quad a \models \neg\chi \text{ iff } a \not\models \chi; \quad a \models \chi \vee \chi' \text{ iff } a \models \chi \text{ or } a \models \chi'.$$

Given an lts, a sequence $q_0 \xrightarrow{a_0} q_1 \xrightarrow{a_1} \ldots$ is called a *path* from q_0; a path that cannot be extended, i.e. is infinite or ends in a state without outgoing transitions, is called a *fullpath*. We write $path(q)$ for the set of fullpaths from q. The syntax of ACTL is given in terms of path formulae that are interpreted over paths and state formulae that are true or false of a state. It is defined by the state formulae generated by the following grammar, where ϕ, $\phi', \ldots$ range over state formulae, γ over path formulae and χ and χ' are action formulae.

$$\phi ::= true \mid \neg\phi \mid \phi \wedge \phi' \mid \exists\gamma \mid \forall\gamma$$

$$\gamma ::= X_\chi \phi \mid X_\tau \phi \mid \phi_\chi U_{\chi'} \phi' \mid \phi_\chi U \phi'$$

Let A be the set of actions and A_τ denotes $A \cup \{\tau\}$. Let $(S, A, \rightarrow, s_0)$ be an lts where s_0 is the initial state. The *satisfaction* of a state formula φ (path formula γ) by a state q (path ρ), notation $q \models \phi$ ($\rho \models \gamma$), is given inductively by:

$q \models true$	always	
$q \models \neg\phi$	iff	$q \not\models \phi$
$q \models \phi_1 \wedge \phi_2$	iff	$q \models \phi_1$ and $q \models \phi_2$
$q \models \exists\gamma$	iff	there exists a path $\theta \in path(q)$ such that $\theta \models \gamma$
$q \models \forall\gamma$	iff	for all path $\theta \in path(q)$, $\theta \models \gamma$
$\rho \models \phi_\chi U_{\chi'} \phi'$	iff	there exists a suffix θ of ρ, $\theta = (q, a, q')\theta'$, s.t. $q' \models \phi'$, $a \models \chi'$, $q \models \phi$, and for all $\eta = (r, \beta, r')\eta'$ suffixes of ρ with θ as proper suffix, then $r \models \phi$ and $(\beta \models \chi$ or $\beta = \tau)$
$\rho \models \phi_\chi U \phi'$	iff	there exists a suffix θ of ρ, s.t. $first(\theta) \models \phi'$, and for all $\eta = (r, \beta, r')\eta'$, of which θ is a proper suffix, we have $r \models \phi$ and $(\beta \models \chi$ or $\beta = \tau)$
$\rho \models X_\chi \phi$	iff	$\rho = (q, a, q')\theta$, $q' \models \phi$ and $a \models \chi$
$\rho \models X_\tau \phi$	iff	$\rho = (q, \tau, q')\theta$ and $q' \models \phi$

The indexed *next* modalities X_χ, X_τ say that in the next state of the path, reached respectively by an action in χ or by a τ, the formula ϕ holds. The indexed *until* modality $\phi_\chi U_{\chi'} \phi'$ says that along the path, all states will satisfy ϕ and reached by actions in χ, until a state that satisfies ϕ' and reached by an action in χ'.

Example 4. $\neg \exists true_{\neg a} U_b true$ expresses that there is no path beginning by actions all different from a until b, i.e. b can only happen when a has happened.

3.2 ACTL Formulae Compiler

In ESP, since the actions contain complex ESP facts, it is natural that the properties we want to check are first order logic formulas. This implies that they cannot directly be expressed as ACTL propositional formulae: they include variables, which are intended to be universally quantified.

Example 5.

> $o(busy(U,D))$ can happen provided that $i(edit(U,D))$ has happened.

for $U \in \{u1, u2\}$, $D \in \{d\}$, means that

> $o(busy(u1,d))$ can happen provided that $i(edit(u1,d))$ has happened, and

> $o(busy(u2,d))$ can happen provided that $i(edit(u2,d))$ has happened.

Note we talk about these properties with respect to *Server*; $i(edit(U, D))$ means $edit(U, D)$ is input; $o(busy(U, D))$ means that $busy(U, D)$ is sent out. Its unique target *Client* is omitted for simplicity. □

So far in order to carry on the verification, we need an ACTL Formula Compiler to transform an ESP property into a suitable ACTL formula. Given an ESP property, i.e. a formula in ACTL style but containing variables, the ACTL Formula Compiler generates the proper ACTL formula, by instantiating the free variables according to the information recorded when generating the lts.

Example 6. $\neg\exists true_{\neg i(edit(U,D))} U_{o(busy(U,D))} true$ says that $o(busy(U,D))$ can happen provided that $i(edit(U,D))$ has happened. From the information of LTS Compiler, we know that $U \in \{u1, u2\}$, $D \in \{d\}$, so the instantiation gives

$$\neg\exists true_{\neg i(edit(u1,d))} U_{o(busy(u1,d))} true \wedge \neg\exists true_{\neg i(edit(u2,d))} U_{o(busy(u2,d))} true$$

The LTS Compiler may pass two kinds of instantiation information to the ACTL Formula Compiler: (i) the instantiation of variables to the ones in the initial state, as the above example shows; (ii) the new instances generated by the LTS Compiler. For example, in the compilation of the lts of the Client_and_Server, we know that K has been assigned twice a value, 0 and 1 respectively. So "after $o(busy(U,D))$, $o(applied(U,D,K))$ can no more happen", expressed by

$$\neg\exists true_{true} U_{o(busy(U,D))} (\exists true_{true} U_{o(applied(U,D,K))} true)$$

is compiled into

$$\neg\exists true_{true} U_{o(busy(u1,d))} (\exists true_{true} U_{o(applied(u1,d,0))} true) \wedge$$
$$\neg\exists true_{true} U_{o(busy(u2,d))} (\exists true_{true} U_{o(applied(u2,d,0))} true) \wedge$$
$$\neg\exists true_{true} U_{o(busy(u1,d))} (\exists true_{true} U_{o(applied(u1,d,1))} true) \wedge$$
$$\neg\exists true_{true} U_{o(busy(u2,d))} (\exists true_{true} U_{o(applied(u2,d,1))} true)$$

Putting together this property, the property in Example 6, and the property that "$o(applied(U,D))$ can happen provided that $i(edit(U,D))$ has happened" which is expressed similarly as the one in Example 6, we have

both *busy(U,D)* and *applied(U,D,K)* are responses for an application request, while after each request, only one of these two kinds of responses can be given.

which is an essential property that we mentioned in the Introduction.

As an important fact, notice that once we have known the behaviour of a system with fixed inputs, we could also know the system's behaviour with inputs less general than the considered ones. In other words, let $P(X_1 \ldots X_n)$ be the program with X_i in the initial state, and suppose that it satisfies the property $\varphi(X_1 \ldots X_n)$. Then it is true that $P(a_1 \ldots a_n)$ satisfies property $\varphi(a_1 \ldots a_n)$ provided that the transition relations are preserved under substitution. In [6], a sufficient condition is provided so that the transition relations are preserved under substitution.

As we have mentioned at the beginning, the analysis of the total ESP system is supposed to be done by induction. This means that we need to predict the further behaviour of the system based on the fixed inputs: if the system terminates with a state which can be considered as an instantiation of the initial state (ignoring inputs), then we can deduce the behaviours of the system for the whole class of instantiation inputs. In order to check if one state is a suitable instance of another state, we can only rely on semi-automatic techniques.

4   Final Remarks and Future Work

In this work we have described the ESP-MC verification tool. ESP-MC has been obtained by interfacing and integrating already developed verification tools for process algebras, namely AUTO and ACTL model checker. We have shown that it is possible to *reuse* rather specific tools in a completely different application domain by modelling a sort of *value passing*. So far we have mainly exploited the model checking facilities to prove properties of ESP systems. For AUTO, we have only used its minimization functionality: other automatic supports from AUTO are expected to be exploited for the analysis of ESP systems, especially for the refinement relation mentioned in [6].

The experiment is currently rather restricted: better technique is expected to check statically if a given program with fixed inputs can be safely translated into a finite transition system.

References

1. V. Ambriola, P. Ciancarini, and C. Montangero. Software process enactment in Oikos. In R. N. Taylor, editor, *Proc. of ACM SIGSOFT '90, ACM Soft. Eng. Notes 15(6)*, Dec. 1990.
2. E. Astesiano and G. Reggio. SMoLCS-Driven concurrent calculi. *Lecture Notes in Computer Science*, 249:169–201, 1987.
3. J.A. Bergstra and J.W. Klop. Process algebra for synchronous communication. *Information and Control*, 60(1/3):109–137, 1984.
4. M.C. Browne, E.M. Clarke, and O. Grumberg. Characterizing finite Kripke structure in propositional temporal logic. *Theoretical Computer Science*, 59:115–131, 1988.
5. X. J. Chen and C. Montangero. Compositional refinements of multiple blackboard systems. *Lecture Notes in Computer Science*, 582:93–109, 1992.
6. X. J. Chen and C. Montangero. Compositional refinements of multiple blackboard systems. *Acta Informatica*, 32:5, 1995.
7. E.M. Clarke, E.A. Emerson, and A.P. Sistla. Automatic verification of finite state concurrent systems using temporal logic specification. *ACM TOPLAS*, 8(2):244 – 263, 1986.
8. R. de Simone and D. Vergamini. Aboard AUTO. Technical Report 111, INRIA, 1989.
9. E.A. Emerson and J.Y. Halpern. "Sometimes" and "Not Never" revisited: on branching time versus linear time temporal logic. *Journal of ACM*, 33(1):151–178, 1986.
10. E.A. Emerson and J. Srinivasan. Branching time temporal logic. *Linear Time, Branching Time and Partial Order in Logics and Models for Concurrency, LNCS*, 354:123–172, 1989.

11. C.A.R. Hoare. *Communicating Sequential Processes*. Prentice Hall Int., London, 1985.

12. B. Jonsson and J. Parrow. Deciding bisimulation equivalences for a class of non-finte-state programs. In *Proc. 6th Symposium on Theoretical Aspects of Computer Science, LNCS 349*, pages 421–433. Springer-Verlag, 1989.

13. E. Madelaine. Verification tools for the concur project. *Bull. EATCS*, 47:110–120, 1992.

14. R. Milner. *Communication and Concurrency*. Prentice Hall, London, 1989.

15. R. De Nicola, A. Fantechi, S. Gnesi, and G. Ristori. An action based framework for verifying logical and behavioural properties of concurrent systems. *Computer Networks and ISDN Systems*, 25(7):761–778, Feb. 1993.

16. R. De Nicola and F. Vaandrager. Action versus state based logics for transition systems. *Proceedings Ecole de Printemps on Semantics of Concurrency, LNCS*, 469, 1990.

17. G. Plotkin. A structural approach to operational semantics. Technical Report DAIMI FN-19, Aarhus University, 1981.

18. V. Roy and R. de Simone. An AUTOGRAPH primer. Technical Report 112, I.N.R.I.A., 1989.

Appendix 1 The Formalism of ESP in LTS: A Short Review

In CONESP, each state of the blackboard system is expressed as $< I, Ac >$ where I represents the global information and Ac the active components, namely, the agents and the subsystems. I carries three pieces of information: the blackboard tree, the set of names of its current subsystems and the condition to terminate the system (final condition). The blackboard tree is introduced to represent the evolving state of the system, its nodes being multisets of facts. We use $R(B, F)$ to denote a tree with only a root B containing facts F. (T, B_1, B_2, F) is a tree generated from tree T by adding a new blackboard B_2 under blackboard B_1, with the initial set of facts F. ϕ is the empty multiset of facts.

Example 1   The global information for the initial state of Client-and-Server can be expressed as (T, ϕ, F) where ϕ denotes the empty set of names of its current subsystems, F the final condition, and

$$T=(R(client, \{edit(u1,d), edit(u2,d), continue(0), terminate(0), terminate(1)\}),$$
$$client, server, \{doc(d,c), trans(0)\}).$$ □

An agent $((B, Th, Ins), Astate)$ is constructed from the information (B, Th, Ins) it carries and its execution state $Astate$. The former part, which does not change once the agent is created, consists of three parts: (i) a coordinate blackboard B, denoting the source to get facts; (ii) a theory Th defining the task it executes; (iii) the instantiation Ins of the parameters of theory Th when the agent is created.

Example 2   At the beginning, the agent *user1* in the intial state of Client-and-Server is described as

$$< (client, user, [u1, server]), Initial>$$ (A1)

which specifies an agent in blackboard *client*, executing theory *user*, whose parameters are instantiated to *u1* and *server*. *Initial* is an execution state in which the agent is ready to choose and activcated one of its patterns. □

The transition relations have two parts: agent transitions and system transitions. Agent transitions describe how the agents work on their theories.

The specification for ESP systems is a schema. Its main parameter is the transition axioms for agent transitions which define the pattern activations for theories in actual ESP programs, as shown in the following example.

Example 3   The agent *user1* in state *A1* (*Example 2*) may transit into *A1'*:

$$A1 \xRightarrow{Rec(B,\{edit(U,D)\},\phi,[U/u1,D/d])} A1'$$

where *A1'* is *<(client, user, [u1, server]), Astate1>* and *Astate1* contains the information for the computation when its first pattern is activated with instantiation of the variables *[U/u1, D/d]*. □

Here, *Rec(B,Ig,Rg,θ)* is an action for agent transition, with blackboard *B* where the agent stays, the In_Guard *Ig*, Read_Guard *Rg* of its pattern being activated, and the instantiation *θ* of the guards with the facts on blackboard *P*

The information carried on the action is used to construct the system transitions, illustrated by

Example 4   Similar as the agent transition in *Example 3*, we have that agent *user2* may also transit from state

$$<(client, user, [u2, server]), Initial> \tag{A2}$$

to state *A2'* which is similar as *A1'* in *Example 3*, with action

$$Rec(B, \{edit(U,D)\}, \phi, [U/u2, D/d]).$$

Now, based on this transition and the one in *Example 3*, we have the system transition for the initial state of Client_and_Server:

$$< I, A1 \mid A2 \mid A3 > \xrightarrow{\tau} < I', A1' \mid A2' \mid A3 >$$

Here, *A3* denotes the agent state of *manager*, and the global information *I* (*Example 1*) is changed into *I'*:

$$((R(client, \{continue(0), terminate(0), terminate(1)\}),$$

$$client, server, \{doc(d,c), trans(0)\}), \phi, F)$$

where facts *edit(u1,d), edit(u2,d)* are disappeared from blackboard *client*. The transformation is invisible from outside.

Springer-Verlag
and the Environment

We at Springer-Verlag firmly believe that an international science publisher has a special obligation to the environment, and our corporate policies consistently reflect this conviction.

We also expect our business partners – paper mills, printers, packaging manufacturers, etc. – to commit themselves to using environmentally friendly materials and production processes.

The paper in this book is made from low- or no-chlorine pulp and is acid free, in conformance with international standards for paper permanency.

Lecture Notes in Computer Science

For information about Vols. 1–945

please contact your bookseller or Springer-Verlag